Introduction to Entrepreneurship

Eighth Edition

Dr. Donald F. Kuratko

The Jack M. Gill Chair of Entrepreneurship
Professor of Entrepreneurship and Executive Director
Johnson Center for Entrepreneurship & Innovation
The Kelley School of Business
Indiana University–Bloomington

SOUTH-WESTERN
CENGAGE Learning

Australia • Brazil • Japan • Korea • Mexico • Singapore • Spain • United Kingdom • United States

SOUTH-WESTERN
CENGAGE Learning·

Introduction to Entrepreneurship
Eighth Edition
Donald F. Kuratko

Vice President of Editorial, Business: Jack
W. Calhoun

Vice President/Editor-in-Chief: Melissa
S. Acuña

Sr. Acquisitions Editor: Michele Rhoades

Developmental Editor: Erin Curtis, Ohlinger
Publishing Services

Editorial Assistant: Ruth Belanger

Executive Marketing Manager: Kimberly
Kanakes

Marketing Manager: Clint Kernen

Sr. Marketing Coordinator: Sarah Rose

Sr. Marketing Communications Manager:
Jim Overly

Sr. Content Project Manager: Martha Conway

Media Editor: Rob Ellington

Sr. Frontlist Buyer, Manufacturing: Doug Wilke

Production Service: ICC Macmillan Inc.

Sr. Art Director: Tippy McIntosh

Interior Designer: c miller design

Text Permissions Manager: Timothy Sisler

Cover Image: © Brand X Pictures, Inc.

For product information and technology assistance, contact us at
Cengage Learning Customer & Sales Support, 1-800-354-9706

For permission to use material from this text or product,
submit all requests online at **www.cengage.com/permissions**
Further permissions questions can be emailed to
permissionrequest@cengage.com

Library of Congress Control Number: 2008932634

International Student Edition ISBN 13: 978-0-324-59086-9 International Student Edition ISBN 10: 0-324-59086-5

Cengage Learning International Offices

Asia
cengageasia.com
tel: (65) 6410 1200

Australia/New Zealand
cengage.com.au
tel: (61) 3 9685 4111

Brazil
cengage.com.br
tel: (011) 3665 9900

India
cengage.co.in
tel: (91) 11 30484837/38

Latin America
cengage.com.mx
tel: +52 (55) 1500 6000

UK/Europe/Middle East/Africa
cengage.co.uk
tel: (44) 207 067 2500

Represented in Canada by Nelson Education, Ltd.
nelson.com
tel: (416) 752 9100/(800) 668 0671

For product information: **international.cengage.com**
Visit your local office: **international.cengage.com/regions**
Visit our corporate website: **cengage.com**

Printed in Canada
1 2 3 4 5 6 7 12 11 10 09 08

Brief Contents

Contents

Preface

Entrepreneurship is the most powerful economic force known to humankind. The Entrepreneurial Revolution that captured our imagination during the 1990s has now permeated every aspect of business thinking and planning. As exemplified by the "dynasty builders" of the previous decades, such as Sam Walton of Wal-Mart, Fred Smith of FedEx, Bill Gates of Microsoft, Michael Dell of Dell Computers, Herb Kelleher of Southwest Airlines, and Steve Jobs of Apple, the applications of creativity, risk taking, innovation, and passion lead the way to economic development far greater than anyone could imagine. Today we witness the immense impact of entrepreneurial companies such as Google, Yahoo, Facebook, MySpace, and BlackBerry, which have produced technological breakthroughs and become a part of our everyday lives. The twenty-first century has presented us with newer and sometimes more complex challenges than ever before conceived in the form of green technologies, social entrepreneurship, and technological advancements. The entrepreneurial drive and determination of our yet-to-be-discovered dynasty builders will be our greatest solution to all of these challenges.

The process of transforming creative ideas into commercially viable businesses continues to be a major force in today's world economy. Successful entrepreneurship requires more than merely luck and money. It is a cohesive process of creativity, risk taking, and planning. Students today need courses and programs that set forth a basic framework for understanding the process of entrepreneurship. I wrote this textbook to structure and illustrate the discipline of entrepreneurship in a manner that is as unique and creative as entrepreneurship itself. Text, cases, and exercises appear in *Introduction to Entrepreneurship*, 8th edition, to bring together in one place the most significant resources for exploring the development of new and emerging ventures and to present them in an exciting, organized, and challenging manner.

Organization

The new chapter sequence in *Introduction to Entrepreneurship*, 8th edition, is systematically organized around the initiation, planning, growth, and development of new and emerging ventures. The text has been streamlined from 18 to 15 chapters and now includes more in-depth coverage of the topics in each chapter. New chapters include Chapter 4: The Social and Ethical Perspectives of Entrepreneurship; Chapter 5: Creativity and Innovation; Chapter 6: Methods to Initiate Ventures; and Chapter 13: Strategic Growth in Entrepreneurship. Each major part of the text contains chapters that specifically address these pertinent concepts of entrepreneurship.

Part 1 (Chapters 1–4) introduces the entrepreneurial mind-set that permeates our twenty-first century. Examining the Entrepreneurial Revolution throughout the world, this part reveals the evolving nature of entrepreneurship and its importance to the entire global economy. We address the entrepreneurial mind-set that resides within individuals by exploring individual characteristics as well as the "dark side" of entrepreneurship. From an organizational perspective, we introduce the concept of corporate entrepreneurship as an emerging corporate strategy to foster entrepreneurial innovations within the larger domain. Finally, and perhaps most importantly, we focus on social entrepreneurship and the ethical perspective that entrepreneurs need to take in developing a morally conscious approach to business.

Part 2 (Chapters 5–8) examines the initiation of entrepreneurial ventures. We begin with the pursuit of ideas and opportunity recognition by examining creativity for individuals and the concept of innovation. The pathways to enter into a new venture are then explored, whether one is starting a brand new venture, acquiring an existing firm, or purchasing a franchise. The legal perspective is discussed through structures of organizations (sole proprietorships, partnerships, and corporations). We also present certain critical legal issues, such as proprietary protections (patents, copyrights, and trademarks), and bankruptcy laws are examined. This part concludes with a thorough examination of the sources of capital formation available to entrepreneurs.

Part 3 (Chapters 9–12) focuses on the development of an entrepreneurial plan. This part includes the methods of assessing new ventures and business opportunities, as well as a discussion of the issues in marketing that affect the preparing, planning, and operating of entrepreneurial start-ups. The financial tools that entrepreneurs need also are discussed. Finally, the development of a clear and comprehensive business plan is examined. A complete sample business plan appears in the Appendix following Chapter 12.

Part 4 (Chapters 13–15) focuses on the growth, valuation, and harvest of entrepreneurial ventures. The need for strategic planning, the challenge of managing entrepreneurial growth, and the global opportunities available to entrepreneurs are all discussed in this part. We then present the valuation process for an entrepreneurial venture, as well as the effective methods for valuation that need to be considered. Finally, we look at the harvest strategies available to the entrepreneurial firm.

Distinguishing Features

Introduction to Entrepreneurship, 8th edition, presents an organized, systematic study of entrepreneurship. Certain distinguishing features enhance its usefulness for both students and professors. Each chapter contains the following specific learning items.

Opening Quotations for Each Chapter

Thought-provoking quotes capture the students' interest about the basic idea for the chapter.

Chapter Objectives

A clear set of learning objectives provides a preview of the chapter material and can be used by students to check whether they have understood and retained important points.

Figures and Tables

Numerous charts and tables illustrate specific text material, expand chapter ideas, or refer to outside source material.

Chapter Summary and Discussion Questions

Each chapter closes with a summary of key points to be retained. The discussion questions are a complementary learning tool that will enable students to check their understanding of key issues, to think beyond basic concepts, and to determine areas that require further study. The summary and discussion questions help students discriminate between main and supporting points and provide mechanisms for self-teaching.

Key Terms

The most important terms that appear in each chapter are shown in boldface where they first appear. A list of the key terms appears at the end of each chapter, and a complete glossary is included at the end of the book.

Experiential Exercises

A short exercise at the end of each chapter applies principles presented in the chapter, giving students practice on such topics as developing a business plan, analyzing funding sources, and taking self-tests to determine whether they are high achievers.

Challenging and Innovative Learning Tools

Entrepreneurship in Practice

Boxed items throughout the text illustrate one or more innovative ideas related to entrepreneurship. The topics range from finding an entrepreneurial niche to revealing the secrets of the entrepreneurial spirit. Each one is unique in its application to entrepreneurial activity.

The Entrepreneurial Process

Short vignettes about the entrepreneurial process are included throughout the text to show how practicing entrepreneurs handle specific challenges and opportunities that are considered the leading edge today.

The Global Perspective

New to this edition, these short illustrations present interesting entrepreneurial issues around the world to demonstrate how practicing entrepreneurs handle specific challenges from the global environment that are prevalent today.

Entrepreneurial Case Analyses

Comprehensive case studies that illustrate venture creations or managerial ideas confronted by actual firms are located in an appendix at the end of the book. The companies are real, so students can appreciate the value of analyzing the situations and data presented and can compare their conclusions with the actual outcomes of the cases provided in the *Instructor's Resource Manual.*

Comprehensive Exercises

Comprehensive exercises that encourage students to go beyond the text material to apply the concepts and experience activities related to the entrepreneur are provided at the end of each part.

New for the 8th Edition

New Models and Process Diagrams

This edition contains the most recent models and process diagrams developed by scholars in the entrepreneurship field. Some examples include new illustrations in corporate entrepreneurship (Chapter 3), entrepreneurial ethics (Chapter 4), legal concepts (Chapter7), venture capital (Chapter 8), strategic entrepreneurship (Chapter 13), and harvesting (Chapter 15).

New Business Plan

Appendix 12A (following Chapter 12) presents a complete business plan developed for national competitions by Andrew F. Vincent as he completed his MBA degree at Indiana

University's Kelley School of Business. Not only was this plan successful in the competitions, it also served as the foundation for an actual start-up venture, DropToMe.com.

New Entrepreneurial Case Analyses

Located in an appendix at the end of the book, three new Entrepreneurial Case Analyses have been added that feature issues in social entrepreneurship (Homeboy Industries) wholesale distribution (DTG) and global energy (Energy for a Clean Planet). These cases were all based on actual instances and were published in *Entrepreneurship Theory and Practice* journal. Each of the case authors was intimately involved with his or her respective case.

New Global Entrepreneurship Boxes

To demonstrate the global nature of entrepreneurship, we have developed special boxed features in which specific international issues are illustrated within the context of the entrepreneurial environment. They range from the NAFTA Agreement (Chapter 1) to the perils of marketing the 2008 Olympics in China (Chapter 10) to currency losing its value in the global market (Chapter 11). These boxes, entitled "The Global Perspective," appear in each chapter in order to highlight certain interesting aspects that relate to the chapter from the international realm.

New Entrepreneurial Process Boxes

Newer and updated issues have been developed for the "Entrepreneurial Process" boxes found in each chapter. These stories reflect some of the more interesting issues surrounding the material presented in the chapter. Some examples include: "Entrepreneurial Fear 101" in Chapter 2, "Corporate Entrepreneurship at IBM" in Chapter 3, "Shaping an Ethical Strategy" in Chapter 4, "The Uniform Franchise Offering Circular" in Chapter 6, "Going Public: The Acid Test" in Chapter 8, and "What Is This Venture Worth?" in Chapter 14.

New Entrepreneurship in Practice Boxes

Newer and updated stories have been added to illustrate one or more of the ideas presented in each chapter. The focus of these stories is the application of entrepreneurship theory in today's marketplace, such as "Patent Protection—A Practical Perspective" and "Fighting Back Legally Against the IRS" in Chapter 7, "eBay Entrepreneurship" in Chapter 9, and "Buy/Sell Agreements" in Chapter 15.

New References and Citations

In an effort to make *Introduction to Entrepreneurship,* 8th edition, the most comprehensive text available, every chapter contains a wealth of endnotes located at the end of each chapter. These references have been carefully selected to provide professors and students with a thorough background of the latest research that relates to the entrepreneurship material being presented. The focus here is on the "theoretical" component of entrepreneurship.

Acknowledgments

Many individuals played an important role in helping to write, develop, and refine the text, and they deserve special recognition. First, my wife, Debbie, and my two daughters, Christina and Kellie (all of whom I am very proud), from whom I took so much time, deserve my deepest love and appreciation. Appreciation is extended to the staff at Cengage Learning, in particular Michele Rhoades, Martha Conway, Tippy McIntosh, Clint Kernen, and Rob Ellington. In addition, I would like to thank Erin Curtis of Ohlinger Publishing Services. The professionals who reviewed the manuscript and offered copious suggestions for improvement played a decisive role in the final result. I would first like to acknowledge the reviewers for the earlier editions, including: Mary Allender, University of Portland; James Almeida, Fairleigh Dickinson University; Jeffrey Alves, Wilkes University; Joseph S. Anderson, Northern Arizona University; Lawrence Aronhime, Johns Hopkins University; Kenneth M. Becker, University of Vermont; Ted Berzinski, Mars Hill College; Thomas M. Box, Pittsburg State University; Stephen Braun, Concordia University; Martin Bressler, Houston Baptist University; Debbi Brock, Berea College; John Callister, Cornell University; Don Cassidy, Inver Hills Community College; A. A. Farhad Chowdhury, Mississippi Valley State University; James J. Chrisman, Mississippi State University; John E. Clarkin, College of Charleston; Teresa A. Daniel, Marshall University; Judy Dietert, Texas State University–San Marcos; Barbara Frazier, Western Michigan University; Barry Gilmore, University of Memphis; Judith Grenkowicz, Kirtland Community College; Stephanie Haaland, Linfield College; Peter Hackbert, Sierra Nevada College; David M. Hall, Saginaw Valley State University; Barton Hamilton, Olin School of Business, Washington University; Brenda Harper, Athens State University; Tim Hatten, Mesa State College; Daniel R. Hogan, Jr., Loyola University; Kathie K. Holland, University of Central Florida; Frank Hoy, University of Texas–El Paso; Rusty Juban, Southeastern Louisiana University; Ronald Kath, Life University; James T. Kilinski, Purdue University Calumet; Michael Krajsa, DeSales University; Stewart D. Langdon, Spring Hill College; Karl LaPan, Indiana University–Purdue University Fort Wayne; Hector Lopez, Hostos Community College/CUNY; Louis Marino, University of Alabama; Charles H. Matthews, University of Cincinnati; Todd Mick, Missouri Western State College; Angela Mitchell, Wilmington College; David Mosby, University of Texas at Arlington; Lynn Neeley, Northern Illinois University; Charles Nichols, Sullivan University; Terry W. Noel, Illinois State University; John H. Nugent, Montana Tech of the University of Montana; Don Okhomina, Alabama State University; Joseph C. Picken, University of Texas at Dallas; Paul Preston, University of Montevallo; J. Harold Ranck, Jr., Duquesne University; Christina Roeder, James Madison University; William J. Rossi, University of Florida; Jonathan Silberman, Arizona State University West; Cynthia Simerly, Lakeland Community College; Ladd W. Simms, Mississippi Valley State University; Marsha O. Smith, Middle Tennessee State University; Richard L. Smith, Iowa State University; Marcene Sonneborn, Syracuse University; Timothy Stearns, California State University–Fresno; Charles Stowe, Sam Houston State University; Michael Stull, California State University San Bernardino; Thomas C. Taveggia, University of Arizona; Jill Thomas-Jorgenson, Lewis-Clark State College; Judy Thompson, Briar Cliff University; Charles N. Toftoy, George Washington University; Monica Zimmerman Treichel, Temple University; Henry T. Ulrich, Central Connecticut State University; Michael Wasserman, Clarkson University; Joan Winn, University of Denver; Amy Wojciechowski, West Shore Community College; Nicholas Young, University of St. Thomas; Raymond Zagorski, Kenai Peninsula College/University of Alaska; and Anatoly Zhuplev, Loyola Marymount University.

I would like to acknowledge the additional reviewers for this edition: Solochidi Ahiarah, SUNY College at Buffalo (Buffalo State College); Michael Giuliano, University of Maryland University, College Asia; James V. Green, University of Maryland, College Park; Jeffrey S. Sugheir, Boise State University; and Randall Wade, Rogue Community College.

I would also like to thank Andrew F. Vincent, creator of the "DropToMe.com" business plan that appears as the Appendix following Chapter 12. In addition, thanks to Jason B. Correll, author of "Rockwood Lodge & Canoe Outfitters," the acquisition business plan located on the text Web site. Both individuals prepared excellent and comprehensive examples of business plans from which students are sure to benefit.

I would also like to express my deepest appreciation of my colleagues at the Kelley School of Business at Indiana University–Bloomington for their tremendous support. In particular, I thank the staff at the Johnson Center for Entrepreneurship & Innovation at the Kelley School of Business, Indiana University–Bloomington, including Travis J. Brown, for assistance in preparing many of the inserted stories that appear as "Entrepreneurship in Practice," "Entrepreneurial Process," or "Global Perspectives." A special thanks to Patricia P. McDougall, the Haeberle Professor of Entrepreneurship and Associate Dean at the Kelley School of Business,

Indiana University, and Jeffrey G. Covin, the Glaubinger Professor of Entrepreneurship at the Kelley School of Business, Indiana University, both of whom have always provided incredible support for my efforts. Finally, my immense respect and appreciation to Daniel C. Smith, dean of the Kelley School of Business, Indiana University, for his outstanding leadership and enthusiastic support.

Dr. Donald F. Kuratko (Dr. K)
The Kelley School of Business
Indiana University–Bloomington

About the Author

DR. DONALD F. KURATKO

Dr. Kuratko (known as "Dr. K") is the Jack M. Gill Chair of Entrepreneurship; Professor of Entrepreneurship and Executive Director, The Johnson Center for Entrepreneurship & Innovation, The Kelley School of Business, Indiana University–Bloomington. Dr. Kuratko is considered a prominent scholar and national leader in the field of entrepreneurship. He has published more than 160 articles on aspects of entrepreneurship, new venture development, and corporate entrepreneurship. His work has been published in journals such as *Strategic Management Journal, Academy of Management Executive, Journal of Business Venturing, Entrepreneurship Theory and Practice, Journal of Operations Management, Journal of Small Business Management, Family Business Review,* and the *Journal of Business Ethics.* Professor Kuratko has authored 24 books, including the leading entrepreneurship book in American universities today, *Entrepreneurship: Theory, Process, Practice,* 8th ed. (South-Western/Cengage Learning, 2009), as well as *Corporate Entrepreneurship & Innovation,* 2nd ed. (South-Western/Cengage Learning, 2008), *New Venture Management* (Pearson/Prentice Hall, 2009), and *Strategic Entrepreneurial Growth,* 2nd ed. (South-Western/Cengage Learning, 2004). In addition, Dr. Kuratko has been consultant on corporate innovation and entrepreneurial strategies to a number of major corporations, such as Anthem Blue Cross/Blue Shield, AT&T, United Technologies, Ameritech, Walgreens, McKesson, Union Carbide Corporation, ServiceMaster, and TruServ. Dr. Kuratko also serves as the executive director of the Global Consortium of Entrepreneurship Centers (GCEC), an organization that comprises more than 250 top university entrepreneurship centers throughout the world.

Under Professor Kuratko's leadership and with one of the most prolific entrepreneurship faculties in the world, Indiana University's Entrepreneurship Program has recently been ranked the #1 Graduate Business School (Public Institutions) for Entrepreneurship by *U.S. News & World Report* and the #1 Undergraduate Business School for Entrepreneurship (Public Institutions) by *U.S. News & World Report.* In 2007, Indiana University was awarded the National Model MBA Program in Entrepreneurship for the MBA Program in entrepreneurship and innovation developed by Dr. Kuratko. Before coming to Indiana University, he was the Stoops Distinguished Professor of Entrepreneurship and founding director of the Entrepreneurship Program at Ball State University. In addition, he was the executive director of the Midwest Entrepreneurial Education Center.

Dr. Kuratko was the first professor ever to be named a Distinguished Professor for the College of Business at Ball State University and held that position for 15 years. The entrepreneurship program that Dr. Kuratko developed at Ball State University continually earned national rankings, including: Top 20 in *Business Week* and *Success* magazines; Top 10 business schools for entrepreneurship research (*Journal of Management*); Top 4 in *U.S. News & World Report* (including the #1 Public University for Entrepreneurship); and the #1 Regional Entrepreneurship Program in *Entrepreneur* magazine.

Professor Kuratko's honors include being named the *Entrepreneur of the Year* for the state of Indiana (sponsored by Ernst & Young, *Inc.* magazine, and Merrill Lynch) and being inducted into the Institute of American Entrepreneurs Hall of Fame. He has been honored with the George Washington Medal of Honor, the Leavey Foundation Award for Excellence in Private Enterprise, the NFIB Entrepreneurship Excellence Award, and the National Model Innovative Pedagogy Award for Entrepreneurship. In addition, Dr. Kuratko was named the National Outstanding Entrepreneurship Educator by the U.S. Association for Small Business and Entrepreneurship, and he was selected one of the Top Three Entrepreneurship Professors in the United States by the Kauffman Foundation, Ernst & Young, *Inc.* magazine, and Merrill Lynch. He received the Thomas W. Binford Memorial Award for Outstanding Contribution to Entrepreneurial Development by the Indiana Health Industry Forum, and he was named a 21st Century Entrepreneurship Research Fellow by the Global Consortium of Entrepreneurship Centers. In his years at Ball State University, he earned the College of Business Teaching Award for 15 consecutive years and was the only professor in the history of Ball State University to receive all four of the university's major lifetime awards, which included the Outstanding Young Faculty Award, Outstanding Teaching Award, Outstanding Faculty Award, and Outstanding Researcher Award. Dr. Kuratko was honored by his peers in *Entrepreneur* magazine as one of the Top Two Entrepreneurship Program Directors in the nation for three consecutive years, including the #1 Entrepreneurship Program Director in the nation in 2003. In 2007, the U.S. Association for Small Business & Entrepreneurship honored him with the prestigious John E. Hughes Entrepreneurial Advocacy Award for his career achievements in entrepreneurship and corporate innovation. Also in 2007, the National Academy of Management honored Professor Kuratko with the highest award bestowed in entrepreneurship—the prestigious Entrepreneurship Advocate Award—for his contributions to the development and advancement of the discipline of entrepreneurship.

In Remembrance

Dr. Richard M. Hodgetts (1942–2001)

On November 17, 2001, Dr. Richard M. Hodgetts passed away after a three-and-a-half-year battle with bone marrow cancer. The field of management lost one of its most significant contributors.

Dr. Hodgetts was a prolific author. He authored or coauthored more than 45 college texts in numerous languages and published more than 125 articles in some of the world's most highly regarded research journals. He was also the founding editor of the *Journal of Leadership Studies* and served on a number of editorial boards.

Dr. Hodgetts was an active Academy of Management member throughout his career; he served as program chair in 1991, chair of the Management History Division, editor of the New Time special issue of *Academy of Management Executive,* and on the Board of Governors from 1993–1996. For all of his dedicated service, he was inducted into the Academy Fellows. In 1999, Dr. Hodgetts received the prestigious Distinguished Educator Award from the Academy of Management.

Besides his tremendous contributions to the knowledge base of management, Dr. Hodgetts was a truly outstanding teacher. He won every Distinguished Teaching Award offered at both his first job of ten years at the University of Nebraska and his home school for 25 years at Florida International University, including Faculty Member of the Year by the executive MBA students in the year of his passing. He literally developed thousands of students at all levels—undergraduate, MBA, executive development, and doctoral—and millions across the world were influenced by his texts and innovative distance education materials and courses. Simply put, he was the ultimate educator.

Dr. Hodgett's distinguished career as a scholar and educator was exemplified in his humor, his dedication to research, his genuine interest in his students, his compassion, and his true courage. Millions of students and practicing leaders have been and will continue to be influenced by his teaching and publications. His legacy will live forever!

Introduction

The Theory of Entrepreneurship

Not too long ago, the field of entrepreneurship was considered little more than an applied trade as opposed to an academic area of study. There was no "research" to be accomplished, because it was thought that those who could not attend college would simply "practice" the concept of new business start-up. Yet our economy was actually based upon entrepreneurship, and history has proven that with each downturn in the economy, it is entrepreneurial drive and persistence that bring us back. Thus, individual scholars began to examine entrepreneurship from a research perspective, and in doing so they initiated an academic field of scholarly pursuit. So we look back at some of the "believers" among the academic community, such as Arnold C. Cooper (Purdue University), Karl A. Vesper (University of Washington), Donald L. Sexton (Ohio State University), Robert C. Ronstadt (Babson College), and Howard H. Stevenson (Harvard University), all of whom are examples of the pioneering researchers in the embryonic days of entrepreneurship. Their wisdom, scholarship, and persistence guided the field of entrepreneurship from what was once considered a disrespected academic area to a field that has gained unimaginable respect and admiration among business schools in the twenty-first century. Their willingness to delve into the research issues important to this developing discipline provided motivation for the next generation of scholars to pursue the entrepreneurship field with greater vigor.

Today we celebrate the immense growth in entrepreneurship research as evidenced by the number of academic journals devoted to entrepreneurship (44), the number of endowed professorships and chairs in entrepreneurship (more than 300), the development of the 21st Century Entrepreneurship Research Fellows by the Global Consortium of Entrepreneurship Centers, and the increasing number of top scholars who devote much of their valuable research time and efforts to publishing on aspects of entrepreneurship in the top academic journals. It is indeed gratifying to see *Academy of Management Journal, Academy of Management Review, Strategic Management Journal, Journal of Operations Management,* and *Journal of Management* publishing more entrepreneurship research; this increase is in direct proportion to the change in the journals' editorial review boards to include more scholars from the entrepreneurship field. Finally, many universities now include certain entrepreneurship journals in their lists of the top journals in which faculty should publish. Many of the top business schools in the United States have accepted the two academic journals in the field of entrepreneurship in their prestigious lists of top tier journals:, the *Journal of Business Venturing and Entrepreneurship Theory and Practice.* Additionally, a number of major academic institutions have developed programs in entrepreneurial research, and every year Babson College conducts a symposium entitled "Frontiers in Entrepreneurship Research." Since 1981, the conference has provided an outlet for the latest developments in entrepreneurship.

In 1998, the National Consortium of Entrepreneurship Centers (NCEC) was founded for the purpose of continued collaboration among the established entrepreneurship centers, as well as the newer emerging centers, to work together to share information, develop special projects, and assist one another in advancing and improving their centers' impact. Today that organization has changed its name to the Global

Consortium of Entrepreneurship Centers (GCEC) to better reflect the international growth of entrepreneurship centers. As mentioned earlier, this consortium also established the 21st Century Entrepreneurship Research Fellows, a growing collection of scholars in the field of entrepreneurship who have created a mission to identify leading-edge research issues and domains and to develop high-profile research initiatives that demonstrate the highest level of scholarship to entrepreneurship centers and the academic community at large. Research drives business schools. Today we see research in entrepreneurship as an accepted and respected part of this drive.

The Process of Entrepreneurship

Beginning with the "early adopters" of the discipline of entrepreneurship, such as the University of Southern California (USC), Babson College, Harvard University, and Indiana University, the number of schools teaching and researching entrepreneurship has exploded to more than 600 schools that offer majors in entrepreneurship, an additional 400 with concentrations in entrepreneurship, and at least one course in entrepreneurship now taught at more than 1,600 universities worldwide! Some of the more prestigious research universities in the United States, such as Indiana University, University of Colorado, Syracuse University, University of South Carolina, and University of Pittsburgh, have developed PhD programs in entrepreneurship in order to prepare the next generation of scholars and researchers. The academic field of entrepreneurship has evolved dramatically over the last 35 years. In the midst of this huge expansion of courses remains the challenge of teaching entrepreneurship more effectively.

It has become clear that entrepreneurship, or certain facets of it, *can* be taught. Business educators and professionals have evolved beyond the myth that entrepreneurs are born, not made. Peter Drucker, recognized as one of the leading management thinkers of our time, has said, "The entrepreneurial mystique? It's not magic, it's not mysterious, and it has nothing to do with the genes. It's a discipline. And, like any discipline, it can be learned."[1] Additional support for this view comes from a ten-year literature review of enterprise, entrepreneurship, and small-business management education that reported, "Most of the empirical studies surveyed indicated that entrepreneurship can be taught, or at least encouraged, by entrepreneurship education."[2]

Given the widely accepted notion that entrepreneurial ventures are the key to innovation, productivity, and effective competition, the question of whether entrepreneurship can be taught is obsolete. Robert C. Ronstadt posed the more relevant question regarding entrepreneurial education: What should be taught, and how should it be taught? He proposed that entrepreneurial programs should be designed so that potential entrepreneurs are aware of barriers to initiating their entrepreneurial careers and can devise ways to overcome them. He contended that an effective program must show students "how" to behave entrepreneurially and should also introduce them to people who might be able to facilitate their success.[3]

Four years later, researchers Robinson and Hayes conducted a survey of universities with enrollments of at least 10,000 students to determine the extent of the growth in entrepreneurship education.[4] Although significant growth was cited, two specific challenges were pointed out: developing existing programs and personnel, thus improving the quality of the field. Several obstacles need to be overcome to facilitate the development of quality in the field. At the heart may be the lack of solid theoretical bases upon which to build pedagogical models and methods, as well as the lack of formal academic programs, representing an absence of commitment on the part of institutions. Professors Robinson and Hayes believed that entrepreneurship education had come a long way in 20 years, yet there were several weak points in the field that were identified through their research. Of primary concern was the lack of depth in most of the programs that already had been started. Further growth would depend on how new programs were integrated with and nurtured by the established entrepreneurship education system. In the years that followed, we experienced greater depth in the academic programs as well as newer initiatives to integrate entrepreneurship throughout the campuses.

In more recent times, researchers Solomon, Duffy, and Tarabishy conducted one of the most comprehensive empirical analyses on entrepreneurship education. In their review of entrepreneurship pedagogy, they stated, "A core objective of entrepreneurship education is that it differentiates from typical business education. Business entry is fundamentally a different activity than managing a business."[5] They concluded that pedagogy is changing based on a broadening market interest in entrepreneurial education. New interdisciplinary programs use faculty teams to develop programs for the nonbusiness student, and there is a growing trend in courses specifically designed for art, engineering, and science students. In addition to courses focused on preparing the future entrepreneur, instructional methodologies are being developed for those who manage entrepreneurs in organizations, potential resource people (accountants, lawyers, consultants) used by entrepreneurs, and top managers who provide vision and leadership for corporations, which must innovate to survive. Today's entrepreneurship educators are challenged with designing effective learning opportunities for entrepreneurship students.

The current trend in most universities is to develop or expand entrepreneurship programs and to design unique and challenging curricula specifically for entrepreneurship students. More significantly, national recognition is now being given to the top entrepreneurial schools through awards, such as the United States Association for Small Business and Entrepreneurship (USASBE) National Model Programs, and national rankings, such as those done by *U.S. News & World Report* and *Fortune Small Business* magazine. This kind of experience is offered to students in innovative entrepreneurship programs recognized by the USASBE. Highlights of these programs can be found at www.usasbe.org. These awarded model programs include undergraduate majors and concentrations, graduate-level programs, innovative pedagogy, and specialized programs. All of these universities have produced entrepreneurship education that has had a real impact on students and a lasting impact on the entrepreneurship field.

The Practice of Entrepreneurship

The final aspect of entrepreneurship is its application in practice. We have seen this exhibited in the thousands of successful entrepreneurs throughout the last 30 years. They and their new ventures have changed our world forever. However, it is important to understand the differences between mere opportunistic moneymaking and the real practice of entrepreneurship. For example, in the late 1990s we experienced the dot-com frenzy, during which everyone thought he was an entrepreneur simply because he put a business title on the Internet. As I have pointed out many times, in the 1940s it cost $20 billion to invent the atomic bomb. It took another $20 billion to put man on the moon 20 years later. In 1999, the dot-coms burned right through $20 billion to achieve . . . well, nothing really. The dot-com bust hurt more than the cash-burning Internet start-ups and the venture capitalists that funded them. This plague spread like wildfire, collapsing the true entrepreneurial spirit of building one's dream into an enduring entity. Our classrooms became infatuated with the drive for investment and liquidity, fast cash, quick exits, and no real commitment. We pursued an "investment mentality" rather than facilitating the search for an "enduring enterprise." We have survived that time, but it did leave us a legacy to *learn* from. We must again focus on the real goals of entrepreneurs and the motivation that permeates from them. We must educate our next generation of entrepreneurs to learn from the dot-com evaporation and return to the roots of business formation and development. Exit strategies are fine, but they should not dominate the pursuit of entrepreneurial opportunity. One author referred to the dot-com individuals as "opportuneurs" rather than entrepreneurs, because they uncoupled wealth from contribution, replaced risk taking with risk faking, and exploited external opportunity rather than pursuing inner vision.[6]

It should be the mission of all entrepreneurship educators to teach the students of today about the *true* entrepreneur. It is the mission of this book to integrate entrepreneurs and their pursuits into the text material. I want to be sure that today's practicing entrepreneurs and their interesting stories are presented to illustrate the real problems and issues involved with their ventures. Students need exposure to those entrepreneurs who have paid the price, faced the challenges, and endured the failures. I want the lessons learned from our experienced entrepreneurs to make a difference. Only by reading about and studying their practices can we truly learn the real application of the entrepreneurial theories and processes.

Final Thoughts Before Venturing into the Text

After reviewing the major facets of theory, process, and practice that are so integral to the study of entrepreneurship, the question remains: How do I approach this subject? The answer is neither complex nor profound. The answer is really an appreciation of your abilities and the recognition that each one of us can make a difference if we try. Remember, the journey of 10,000 miles always starts with the first step! Let this book and your entrepreneurial course be your first step.

Entrepreneurship is the new revolution, and it's about continual innovation and creativity. It is the future of our world economy. Today, the words used to describe the new innovation regime of the twenty-first century are: dream, create, explore, invent, pioneer, and imagine. I believe that we are at a point in time when the gap between what can be imagined and what can be accomplished has never been smaller. This is the challenge for all of today's entrepreneurship students. To paraphrase the late Robert F. Kennedy in a speech made more than 40 years ago: You are living in one of the rarest moments in education history—a time when all around us the old order of things is crumbling, and a new world society is painfully struggling to take shape. If you shrink from this struggle and the many difficulties it entails, you will betray the trust that your own position forces upon you. You possess one of the most privileged positions; for you have been given the opportunity to educate and to lead. You can use your enormous privilege and opportunity to seek purely your tenure and security. But entrepreneurial history will judge you, and, as the years pass, you will ultimately judge yourself on the extent to which you have used your abilities to pioneer and lead into new horizons. In your hands . . . is the future of your entrepreneurial world and the fulfillment of the best qualities of your own spirit.[7]

Notes

1. Peter F. Drucker, *Innovation and Entrepreneurship* (New York: Harper and Row, 1985).

2. G. Gorman, D. Hanlon, and W. King, "Some Research Perspectives on Entrepreneurship Education, Enterprise Education, and Education for Small Business Management: A Ten-Year Literature Review," *International Small Business Journal* 15 (1997): 56–77.

3. Robert C. Ronstadt, "The Educated Entrepreneurs: A New Era of Entrepreneurial Education is Beginning," *American Journal of Small Business* 11, no. 4 (1987): 37–53.

4. Peter Robinson and Michael Hayes, "Entrepreneurship Education in America's Major Universities," *Entrepreneurship Theory & Practice* 15, no. 3 (1991): 41–52.

5. George T. Solomon, Susan Duffy, and Ayman Tarabishy, "The State of Entrepreneurship Education in the United States: A Nationwide Survey and Analysis," *International Journal of Entrepreneurship Education* 1, no. 1 (2002): 65–86.

6. Jerry Useem, "The Risktaker Returns," *FSB* (May 2001): 70–71.

7. Donald F. Kuratko, "The Emergence of Entrepreneurship Education: Development, Trends and Challenges," *Entrepreneurship Theory & Practice* 29, no. 5 (2005): 577–97.

Understanding the Entrepreneurial Mind-Set

part 1

The Revolutionary Impact of Entrepreneurship

Entrepreneurial Thought

Most of what you hear about entrepreneurship, says America's leading management thinker, is all wrong. It's not magic; it's not mysterious; and it has nothing to do with genes. It's a discipline and, like any discipline, it can be learned.

— **PETER F. DRUCKER,** *Innovation and Entrepreneurship*

Chapter Objectives

1 To examine the historical development of entrepreneurship

2 To explore and debunk the myths of entrepreneurship

3 To define and explore the major schools of entrepreneurial thought

4 To explain the process approaches to the study of entrepreneurship

5 To set forth a comprehensive definition of entrepreneurship

6 To examine the Entrepreneurial Revolution taking place today

7 To illustrate today's entrepreneurial environment

Entrepreneurs—Challenging the Unknown

Entrepreneurs are individuals who recognize opportunities where others see chaos or confusion. They are aggressive catalysts for change within the marketplace. They have been compared to Olympic athletes challenging themselves to break new barriers, to long-distance runners dealing with the agony of the miles, to symphony orchestra conductors who balance the different skills and sounds into a cohesive whole, and to top-gun pilots who continually push the envelope of speed and daring. Whatever the passion—because they all fit in some way—entrepreneurs are the heroes of today's marketplace. They start companies and create jobs at a breathtaking pace. The U.S. economy has been revitalized because of the efforts of entrepreneurs, and the world has turned now to free enterprise as a model for economic development. The passion and drive of entrepreneurs move the world of business forward. They challenge the unknown and continuously create the future.

One anonymous quote sums up the realities for entrepreneurs. "Anyone [can be an entrepreneur] who wants to experience the deep, dark canyons of uncertainty and ambiguity; and who wants to walk the breathtaking highlands of success. But I caution, do not plan to walk the latter, until you have experienced the former."[1]

Entrepreneurs/Small-Business Owners: A Distinction

The terms *entrepreneur* and *small-business owner* sometimes are used interchangeably. Although some situations encompass both terms, it is important to note the differences in the titles. Small businesses are independently owned and operated, are not dominant in their fields, and usually do not engage in many new or innovative practices. They may never grow large and the owners may prefer a more stable and less aggressive approach to running these businesses; in other words, they manage their businesses by expecting stable sales, profits, and growth. Because small firms include those purchased as already established businesses as well as franchises, small-business owners can be viewed as *managers* of small businesses.

On the other hand, entrepreneurial ventures are those for which the entrepreneur's principal objectives are innovation, profitability, and growth. Thus, the business is characterized by innovative strategic practices and sustainable growth. Entrepreneurs and their financial backers are usually seeking rapid growth and immediate profits. They may even seek the sale of their businesses if there is potential for large capital gains. Thus, entrepreneurs may be viewed as having a different perspective from small-business owners on the development of their firms.

In this book, we concentrate on entrepreneurs and the effective development of entrepreneurship, including the entrepreneurial mind-set in established organizations. Some of the particular points in this book may apply to both small-business owners and entrepreneurs; however, keep in mind that our focus is on the aspects of innovation and growth associated with entrepreneurs.

Entrepreneurship: A Mind-Set

Entrepreneurship is more than the mere creation of business. Although that is certainly an important facet, it's not the complete picture. The characteristics of seeking opportunities, taking risks beyond security, and having the tenacity to push an idea through to reality combine into a special perspective that permeates entrepreneurs. As we will illustrate in Chapter 2, an entrepreneurial mind-set can be developed in individuals. This mind-set can be exhibited inside or outside an organization, in profit or not-for-profit enterprises, and in business or nonbusiness activities for the purpose of bringing forth creative ideas. Thus, entrepreneurship is an integrated concept that permeates an individual's business in an innovative manner. It is this mind-set that has revolutionized the way business is conducted at every level and in every country. *Inc.* magazine reported some time ago that, "America is once again becoming a nation of risk takers and the way we do business will never be the same." So it is. The revolution has begun in an economic sense, and the entrepreneurial mindset is the dominant force.

The Evolution of Entrepreneurship

The word entrepreneur is derived from the French *entreprendre,* meaning "to undertake." The entrepreneur is one who undertakes to organize, manage, and assume the risks of a business. In recent years, entrepreneurs have been doing so many things that it is now necessary to broaden this definition. Today, an entrepreneur is an innovator or developer who recognizes and seizes opportunities; converts those opportunities into workable/marketable ideas; adds value through time, effort, money, or skills; assumes the risks of the competitive marketplace to implement these ideas; and realizes the rewards from these efforts.[2]

The entrepreneur is the aggressive catalyst for change in the world of business. He or she is an independent thinker who dares to be different amid a background of common events. The literature of entrepreneurial research reveals some similarities, as well as a great many differences, in the characteristics of entrepreneurs. Chief among these characteristics are personal initiative, the ability to consolidate resources, management skills, a desire for autonomy, and risk taking. Other characteristics include aggressiveness, competitiveness, goal-oriented behavior, confidence, opportunistic behavior, intuitiveness, reality-based actions, the ability to learn from mistakes, and the ability to employ human relations skills.[3]

Although no single definition of *entrepreneur* exists and no one profile can represent today's entrepreneur, research is beginning to provide an increasingly sharper focus on the subject. A brief review of the history of entrepreneurship illustrates this.

America currently is in the midst of a new wave of business and economic development, and entrepreneurship is its catalyst. Yet the social and economic forces of entrepreneurial activity existed long before the new millennium. In fact, the entrepreneurial spirit has driven many of humanity's achievements.

Humanity's progress—from caves to campuses—has been explained in numerous ways. But central to virtually all of these theories has been the role of the "agent of change," the force that initiates and implements material progress. Today we recognize that the agent of change in human history has been, and most likely will continue to be, the entrepreneur.[4]

The recognition of entrepreneurs dates back to eighteenth-century France, when economist Richard Cantillon associated the "risk-bearing" activity in the economy with the entrepreneur. The Industrial Revolution was evolving in England during the same period, with the entrepreneur playing a visible role in risk taking and the transformation of resources.[5]

The association of entrepreneurship and economics has long been the accepted norm. In fact, until the 1950s the majority of definitions and references to entrepreneurship had come from economists. For example, the aforementioned Cantillon (1725), the French economist Jean Baptiste Say (1803), and twentieth-century economist Joseph Schumpeter (1934) all wrote about entrepreneurship and its impact on economic development.[6] Since that time, researchers have continued to try to describe or define what entrepreneurship is all about. Following are some examples:

> Entrepreneurship . . . consists in doing things that are not generally done in the ordinary course of business routine; it is essentially a phenomenon that comes under the wider aspect of leadership.[7]
>
> Entrepreneurship, at least in all nonauthoritarian societies, constitutes a bridge between society as a whole, especially the noneconomic aspects of that society, and the profit-oriented institutions established to take advantage of its economic endowments and to satisfy, as best they can, its economic desires.[8]
>
> In . . . entrepreneurship, there is agreement that we are talking about a kind of behavior that includes: (1) initiative taking, (2) the organizing or reorganizing of social economic mechanisms to turn resources and situations to practical account, and (3) the acceptance of risk of failure.[9]

After reviewing the evolution of entrepreneurship and examining its varying definitions, Robert C. Ronstadt put together a summary description:

> Entrepreneurship is the dynamic process of creating incremental wealth. This wealth is created by individuals who assume the major risks in terms of equity, time, and/or career commitment of providing value for some product or service. The product or service itself may or may not be new or unique but value must somehow be infused by the entrepreneur by securing and allocating the necessary skills and resources.[10]

Entrepreneurship as a topic for discussion and analysis was introduced by the economists of the eighteenth century, and it continued to attract the interest of economists in the nineteenth century. In the twentieth century, the word *entrepreneurship* became synonymous—or at least closely linked—with free enterprise and capitalism. Also, it was generally recognized that entrepreneurs serve as agents of change; they provide creative, innovative ideas for business enterprises; and they help businesses grow and become profitable.

Whatever the specific activity they engage in, entrepreneurs in the twenty-first century are considered the heroes of free enterprise. Many of them have used innovation and creativity to build multimillion-dollar enterprises from fledgling businesses—some in less than a decade! These individuals have created new products and services, and have assumed the risks associated with these ventures. Many people now regard entrepreneurship as "pioneership" on the frontier of business.

In recognizing the importance of the evolution of entrepreneurship into the twenty-first century, we have developed an integrated definition that acknowledges the critical factors needed for this phenomenon.

> *Entrepreneurship* is a dynamic process of vision, change, and creation. It requires an application of energy and passion toward the creation and implementation of new ideas and creative solutions. Essential ingredients include the willingness to take calculated risks—in terms of time, equity, or career; the ability to formulate an effective venture team; the creative skill to marshal needed resources; the fundamental skill of building a solid business plan; and, finally, the vision to recognize opportunity where others see chaos, contradiction, and confusion.

Avoiding Folklore: The Myths of Entrepreneurship

Throughout the years, many myths have arisen about entrepreneurship—primarily because of a lack of research on the subject. As many researchers in the field have noted, the study of entrepreneurship is still emerging, and thus "folklore" tends to prevail until it is dispelled with contemporary research findings. Ten of the most notable myths (and an explanation to dispel each myth) are as follows.

Myth 1: Entrepreneurs Are Doers, Not Thinkers

Although it is true that entrepreneurs tend toward action, they are also thinkers. Indeed, they are often very methodical people who plan their moves carefully. The emphasis today on the creation of clear and complete business plans (see Chapter 12) is an indication that "thinking" entrepreneurs are as important as "doing" entrepreneurs.

Myth 2: Entrepreneurs Are Born, Not Made

The idea that the characteristics of entrepreneurs cannot be taught or learned—that they are innate traits one must be born with—has long been prevalent. These traits include aggressiveness, initiative, drive, a willingness to take risks, analytical ability, and skill in human relations. Today, however, the recognition of entrepreneurship as a discipline is helping to dispel this myth. Like all disciplines, entrepreneurship has models, processes, and case studies that allow the topic to be studied and the knowledge to be acquired.

Myth 3: Entrepreneurs Are Always Inventors

The idea that entrepreneurs are inventors is a result of misunderstanding and tunnel vision. Although many inventors are also entrepreneurs, numerous entrepreneurs encompass all sorts of innovative activity.[11] For example, Ray Kroc did not invent the fast-food franchise, but his innovative ideas made McDonald's the largest fast-food enterprise in the world. A contemporary understanding of entrepreneurship covers more than just invention; it requires a complete understanding of innovative behavior in all its forms.

Myth 4: Entrepreneurs Are Academic and Social Misfits

The belief that entrepreneurs are academically and socially ineffective is a result of some business owners having started successful enterprises after dropping out of school or quitting a job. In many cases, such an event has been blown out of proportion in an attempt to "profile" the typical entrepreneur. Historically, in fact, educational and social organizations did not recognize the entrepreneur. They abandoned him or her as a misfit in a world of corporate giants. Business education, for example, was aimed primarily at the study of corporate activity. Today the entrepreneur is considered a hero—socially, economically, and academically. No longer a misfit, the entrepreneur is now viewed as a professional role model.

Myth 5: Entrepreneurs Must Fit the Profile

Many books and articles have presented checklists of characteristics of the successful entrepreneur. These lists were neither validated nor complete; they were based on case studies and on research findings among achievement-oriented people. Today we realize that a standard entrepreneurial profile is hard to compile. The environment, the venture, and the entrepreneur have interactive effects, which result in many different types of profiles. Contemporary studies conducted at universities across the United States will, in the future, provide more accurate insights into the various profiles of successful entrepreneurs. As we will show in Chapter 2, an "entrepreneurial mind-set" within individuals is more understandable than a particular profile.

Myth 6: All Entrepreneurs Need Is Money

It is true that a venture needs capital to survive; it is also true that a large number of business failures occur because of a lack of adequate financing. However, money is not the only bulwark against failure. Failure due to a lack of proper financing is often an indicator of other problems: managerial incompetence, lack of financial understanding, poor investments, poor planning, and the like. Many successful entrepreneurs have overcome a lack of money while establishing their ventures. To those entrepreneurs, money is a resource but never an end in itself.

Myth 7: All Entrepreneurs Need Is Luck

Being in "the right place at the right time" is always an advantage—but "luck happens when preparation meets opportunity" is an equally appropriate adage. Prepared entrepreneurs who seize the opportunity when it arises often seem "lucky." They are, in fact, simply better prepared to deal with situations and turn them into successes. What appears to be luck is actually preparation, determination, desire, knowledge, and innovativeness.

Myth 8: Entrepreneurship Is Unstructured and Chaotic

There is a tendency to think of entrepreneurs as gunslingers—people who shoot from the hip and ask questions later. They are assumed by some to be disorganized and unstructured, leaving it to others to keep things on track. The reality is that entrepreneurs are heavily involved in all facets of their ventures and they usually have a number of balls in the air at the same time. As a result, they are typically well-organized individuals. They tend to have a system—perhaps elaborate, perhaps not—that is personally designed to keep things straight and maintain priorities. In fact, their system may seem strange to the casual observer, but it works.

entrepreneurship in practice

The E-Myth

Michael E. Gerber has written a book titled *The E-Myth: Why Most Businesses Don't Work and What to Do About It*, in which he clearly delineates the differences among the types of people involved with contemporary small businesses:

- The *entrepreneur* invents a business that works without him or her. This person is a visionary who makes a business unique by imbuing it with a special and exciting sense of purpose and direction. The entrepreneur's far-reaching perspective enables him or her to anticipate changes and needs in the marketplace and to initiate activities to capitalize on them.

- The *manager* produces results through employees by developing and implementing effective systems and, by interacting with employees, enhances their self-esteem and ability to produce good results. The manager can actualize the entrepreneur's vision through planning, implementation, and analysis.

- The *technician* performs specific tasks according to systems and standards management developed. The technician, in the best of businesses, not only gets the work done but also provides input to supervisors for improvement of those systems and standards.

Understanding these definitions is important, because Gerber contends that most small businesses *don't work*—their owners do. In other words, he believes that today's small-business owner works too hard at a job that he or she has created for himself or herself rather than working to create a business. Thus, most small businesses fail because the owner is more of a technician than an entrepreneur. Working only as a technician, the small-business owner realizes too little reward for so much effort, and eventually, according to Gerber, the business fails.

The e-myth is that today's business owners are not true entrepreneurs who create businesses but merely technicians who have created a job for themselves. The solution to this myth lies in the owner's willingness to begin thinking and acting like a true entrepreneur: to imagine how the business would work without him or her. In other words, the owner must begin working *on* the business, in addition to working *in* it. He or she must leverage the company's capacity through systems development and implementation. The key is for a person to develop an "entrepreneurial perspective."

Source: Adapted from Michael E. Gerber, *The E-Myth Revisited: Why Most Businesses Don't Work and What to Do About It* (New York: Harper Business, 1995) and personal interview.

Myth 9: Most Entrepreneurial Initiatives Fail

Many entrepreneurs do suffer a number of failures before they are successful. They follow the adage "If at first you don't succeed, try, try, again." In fact, failure can teach many lessons to those willing to learn, and often it leads to future successes. This is clearly shown by the **corridor principle**, which states that, with every venture launched, new and unintended opportunities often arise. The 3M Corporation invented Post-it Notes using a glue that had not been strong enough for its intended use. Rather than throwing away the glue, the company focused on finding another use for it and, in the process, developed a multimillion-dollar product.

However, the statistics of entrepreneurial failure rates have been misleading over the years. In fact, one researcher, Bruce A. Kirchoff, has reported that the "high failure rate" most commonly accepted might be misleading. In 1993, Kirchoff traced 814,000 businesses started in 1977 and found that more than 50 percent were still surviving under their original owners or new owners. Additionally, 28 percent voluntarily closed down, and only 18 percent actually "failed" in the sense of leaving behind outstanding liabilities.[12]

Myth 10: Entrepreneurs Are Extreme Risk Takers . . . the Gamblers!

As we will show in Chapter 2, the concept of risk is a major element in the entrepreneurial process. However, the public's perception of the risk most entrepreneurs assume is distorted. Although it may appear that an entrepreneur is "gambling" on a wild chance, the entrepreneur is usually working on a moderate or "calculated" risk. Most successful entrepreneurs work hard—through planning and preparation—to minimize the risk involved and better control the destiny of their vision.

These ten myths have been presented to provide a background for today's current thinking on entrepreneurship. By sidestepping the folklore, we can build a foundation for critically researching the contemporary theories and processes of entrepreneurship.

Approaches to Entrepreneurship

To understand the nature of entrepreneurship and better recognize its emerging importance, it is important to consider some of its theory development. The research on entrepreneurship has grown dramatically over the years. As the field has developed, research methodology has progressed from empirical surveys of entrepreneurs to more contextual and process-oriented research. Theory development is what drives a field of study. Entrepreneurship theory has been developing for the last 35 years, and it is apparent that the field is growing. We need to understand some of that development to better appreciate the discipline of entrepreneurship. The study of the basic theories in entrepreneurship also helps to form a foundation upon which a student can build an understanding of the process and practice of entrepreneurship.

A *theory of entrepreneurship* is a verifiable and logically coherent formulation of relationships, or underlying principles, that either explain entrepreneurship, predict entrepreneurial activity (for example, by characterizing conditions that are likely to lead to new profit opportunities or to the formation of new enterprises), or provide normative guidance (that is, prescribe the right action in particular circumstances).[13] It has become increasingly apparent in the new millennium that we need to have some cohesive theories or classifications to better understand this emerging field.

In the study of contemporary entrepreneurship, one concept recurs: Entrepreneurship is interdisciplinary. It contains various approaches that can increase one's understanding of the field.[14] Thus, we need to recognize the diversity of theories as an emergence of entrepreneurial understanding. One way to examine these theories is with a "schools of thought" approach that divides entrepreneurship into specific activities. These activities may be within a "macro" view or a "micro" view, but all address the conceptual nature of entrepreneurship.

The Schools of Entrepreneurial Thought

In this section, we highlight the ideas emanating from the macro and micro views of entrepreneurial thought, and we further break down these two major views into six distinct schools of thought—three within each entrepreneurial view (see Figure 1.1). Although this presentation does not purport to be all-inclusive, neither does it claim to limit the schools to these six, for a movement may develop for unification or expansion. Whatever the future holds, however, it is important to become familiar with these conceptual ideas on entrepreneurship to avoid the semantic warfare that has plagued general management thought for so many years.[15]

The Macro View

The **macro view of entrepreneurship** presents a broad array of factors that relate to success or failure in contemporary entrepreneurial ventures. This array includes external processes that are sometimes beyond the control of the individual entrepreneur, for they exhibit a strong **external locus of control** point of view.

Figure	1.1	Entrepreneurial Schools-of-Thought Approach

Macro View
- Environmental School of Thought
- Financial/Capital School of Thought
- Displacement School of Thought

Micro View
- Entrepreneurial Trait School of Thought (People School)
- Venture Opportunity School of Thought
- Strategic Formulation School of Thought

Three schools of entrepreneurial thought represent a breakdown of the macro view: (1) the environmental school of thought, (2) the financial/capital school of thought, and (3) the displacement school of thought. The first of these is the broadest and most pervasive school.

THE ENVIRONMENTAL SCHOOL OF THOUGHT

The environmental school of thought deals with the external factors that affect a potential entrepreneur's lifestyle. These can be either positive or negative forces in the molding of entrepreneurial desires. The focus is on institutions, values, and mores that—grouped together—form a sociopolitical environmental framework that strongly influences the development of entrepreneurs.[16] For example, if a middle manager experiences the freedom and support to develop ideas, initiate contracts, or create and institute new methods, the work environment will serve to promote that person's desire to pursue an entrepreneurial career. Another environmental factor that often affects the potential development of entrepreneurs is their social group. The atmosphere of friends and relatives can influence the desire to become an entrepreneur.

THE FINANCIAL/CAPITAL SCHOOL OF THOUGHT

The financial/capital school of thought is based on the capital-seeking process—the search for seed and growth capital is the entire focus of this entrepreneurial emphasis. Certain literature is devoted specifically to this process, whereas other sources tend to treat it as but one segment of the entrepreneurial venture.[17] In any case, the venture capital process is vital to an entrepreneur's development. Business-planning guides and texts for entrepreneurs emphasize this phase, and development seminars that focus on the funds application process are offered throughout the country on a continuous basis. This school of thought views the entire entrepreneurial venture from a financial management standpoint. As is apparent from Table 1.1, decisions involving finances occur at every major point in the venture process.

THE DISPLACEMENT SCHOOL OF THOUGHT

The displacement school of thought focuses on the negative side of group phenomena, in which someone feels out of place—or is literally "displaced"—from the group. It holds that the group hinders a person from advancing or eliminates certain critical factors needed for that person to advance. As a result, the frustrated individual will be projected into an entrepreneurial pursuit out of his or her own motivations to succeed. As Ronstadt

Table **1.1**	**Financial Analysis Emphasis**

Venture Stage	Financial Consideration	Decision
Start-up or acquisition	Seed capital Venture capital sources	Proceed or abandon
Ongoing	Cash management Investments Financial analysis and evaluation	Maintain, increase, or reduce size
Decline or succession	Profit question Corporate buyout Succession question	Sell, retire, or dissolve operations

has noted, individuals will not pursue a venture unless they are prevented or displaced from doing other activities.[18] Three major types of displacement illustrate this school of thought:

1. *Political displacement.* Caused by factors ranging from an entire political regime that rejects free enterprise (international environment) to governmental regulations and policies that limit or redirect certain industries.

2. *Cultural displacement.* Deals with social groups precluded from professional fields. Ethnic background, religion, race, and sex are examples of factors that figure in the minority experience. Increasingly, this experience turns various individuals away from standard business professions and toward entrepreneurial ventures. According to the U.S. government, the number of minority businesses grew by nearly half a million during the last ten years and represents one-tenth of all the nation's businesses.[19]

3. *Economic displacement.* Concerned with the economic variations of recession and depression. Job loss, capital shrinkage, or simply "bad times" can create the foundation for entrepreneurial pursuits, just as it can affect venture development and reduction.

These examples of displacement illustrate the external forces that can influence the development of entrepreneurship. Cultural awareness, knowledge of political and public policy, and economic indoctrination will aid and improve entrepreneurial understanding under the displacement school of thought. The broader the educational base in economics and political science, the stronger the entrepreneurial understanding.

The Micro View

The micro view of entrepreneurship examines the factors that are specific to entrepreneurship and are part of the internal locus of control. The potential entrepreneur has the ability, or control, to direct or adjust the outcome of each major influence in this view. Although some researchers have developed this approach into various definitions and segments—as shown in Table 1.2—our approach presents the *entrepreneurial trait* theory (sometimes referred to as the "people school of thought"), the *venture opportunity* theory, and the *strategic formulation* theory. Unlike the macro approach, which focuses on events from the outside looking in, the micro approach concentrates on specifics from the inside looking out. The first of these schools of thought is the most widely recognized.

THE ENTREPRENEURIAL TRAIT SCHOOL OF THOUGHT

Many researchers and writers have been interested in identifying traits common to successful entrepreneurs.[20] This approach of the entrepreneurial trait school of thought is grounded in

Table	1.2	Definitions and Criteria of One Approach to the Micro View

Entrepreneurial Model	Definition	Measures	Questions
"Great person"	"Extraordinary achievers"	Personal principles Personal histories Experiences	What principles do you have? What are your achievements?
Psychological characteristics	Founder Control over the means of production	Locus of control Tolerance of ambiguity Need for achievement	What are your values?
Classical	People who make innovations bearing risk and uncertainty "Creative destruction"	Decision making Ability to see opportunities Creativity	What are the opportunities? What is your vision? How do you respond?
Management	Creating value through the recognition of business opportunity, the management of risk taking, the communicative and management skills to mobilize, etc.	Expertise Technical knowledge Technical plans	What are your plans? What are your capabilities? What are your credentials?
Leadership	"Social architect" Promotion and protection of values	Attitudes, styles Management of people	How do you manage people?
Intrapreneurship	Those who pull together to promote innovation	Decision making	How do you change and adapt?

Source: Adapted from J. Barton Cunningham and Joe Lischeron, "Defining Entrepreneurship," *Journal of Small Business Management* (January 1991): 56.

the study of successful people who tend to exhibit similar characteristics that, if copied, would increase success opportunities for the emulators. For example, achievement, creativity, determination, and technical knowledge are four factors that *usually* are exhibited by successful entrepreneurs. Family development and educational incubation are also examined. Certain researchers have argued against educational development of entrepreneurs because they believe it inhibits the creative and challenging nature of entrepreneurship.[21] Other authors, however, contend that new programs and educational developments are on the increase because they have been found to aid in entrepreneurial development.[22] The family development idea focuses on the nurturing and support that exist within the home atmosphere of an entrepreneurial family. This reasoning promotes the belief that certain traits established and supported early in life will lead eventually to entrepreneurial success.

THE VENTURE OPPORTUNITY SCHOOL OF THOUGHT

The **venture opportunity school of thought** focuses on the opportunity aspect of venture development. The search for idea sources, the development of concepts, and the implementation of venture opportunities are the important interest areas for this school. Creativity and market awareness are viewed as essential. Additionally, according to this school of thought, developing the right idea at the right time for the right market niche is the key to entrepreneurial success.

Another development from this school of thought is the previously described corridor principle: New pathways or opportunities will arise that lead entrepreneurs in different directions. The ability to recognize these opportunities when they arise and to implement the necessary steps for action are key factors. The maxim that preparation meeting opportunity equals "luck" underlies this corridor principle. Proponents of this school of thought believe that proper preparation in the interdisciplinary business segments will enhance an entrepreneur's ability to recognize venture opportunities.

THE STRATEGIC FORMULATION SCHOOL OF THOUGHT

George Steiner once stated that "strategic planning is inextricably interwoven into the entire fabric of management; it is not something separate and distinct from the process of management."[23] The strategic formulation school of thought approach to entrepreneurial theory emphasizes the planning process in successful venture development.[24]

One way to view strategic formulation is as a leveraging of unique elements.[25] Unique markets, unique people, unique products, or unique resources are identified, used, or constructed into effective venture formations. The interdisciplinary aspects of strategic adaptation are apparent in the following characteristic elements (and their corresponding strategies):

- **Unique markets.** Mountain versus **mountain gap strategies,** which refers to identifying major market segments as well as interstice (in-between) markets that arise from larger markets.
- **Unique people.** **Great chef strategies,** which refers to the skills or special talents of one or more individuals around whom the venture is built.
- **Unique products.** **Better widget strategies,** which refers to innovations that encompass new or existing markets.
- **Unique resources.** **Water well strategies,** which refers to the ability to gather or harness special resources (land, labor, capital, raw materials) over the long term.

Without question, the strategic formulation school encompasses a breadth of managerial capability that requires an interdisciplinary approach.[26]

Schools of Entrepreneurial Thought: A Summary

Although the knowledge and research available in entrepreneurship are in an emerging stage, it is still possible to piece together and describe current schools of thought in the field. We can begin to develop an appreciation for the schools and view them as a foundation for entrepreneurial theory. However, just as the field of management has used a "jungle" of theories as a basis for understanding the field and its capabilities, so too must the field of entrepreneurship use a number of theories in its growth and development.

Process Approaches

Another way to examine the activities involved in entrepreneurship is through a *process approach*. Although numerous methods and models attempt to structure the entrepreneurial process and its various factors, we shall examine two of the more traditional process approaches here.[27]

First, we discuss the *integrative* approach, as described by Michael H. Morris, P. Lewis, and Donald L. Sexton.[28] Their model incorporates theoretical and practical concepts as they affect entrepreneurship activity. Then we explore the *assessment* approach based on an entrepreneurial perspective developed by Robert C. Ronstadt. Both of these methods attempt to describe the entrepreneurial process as a consolidation of diverse factors, which is the thrust of this book.

the entrepreneurial process

The Hot Trends to Watch

The following categories are ones in which business opportunities promise to be strong in the coming years. Although these segments are consistently popular, the trends within each are in constant flux.

Food and Beverages

Spirits, Wine, and Beer—Consumers historically are drinking less alcohol, but they are drinking better-quality beverages, which suggests big opportunities for high-end spirits, wines, and craft beers.

Enhanced Beverages—Consumers under the age of 30 are now looking to beverages to give them not only the nutrients they need but their energy as well. An important item to note in this area is customers' preference for all-natural products.

Special-Needs Food—Organic foods are old news. Customers are now looking to buy foods that are allergen free, gluten free, and low glycemic.

On the horizon are two concepts that might be worth considering: gastropubs (bars that serve high-quality cuisine) and upscale frozen desserts (premium ice creams, gelato, and frozen yogurt).

Health

Biotech and Health Tech—This area requires extensive scientific expertise, capital, and—in turn—risk tolerance. The opportunities for (and the impact of) businesses in this sector are significant, but the commitment of time and money is important to consider.

Health Care Staffing—Because of the expected shortfall of health care workers, entrepreneurs capable of recruiting and, more importantly, understanding the medical community are well positioned. The trick is to be comfortable speaking in both medical and business circles.

Senior Services and Products—As the baby boomers continue to age, the demand for services and products to address their growing health needs shows no signs of slowing down. Caregivers understand what is currently available in the market as well as what is needed, so working with them is a clear path to developing a winning solution.

Two ideas that have been popular and will continue to be are in-home nonmedical care (providers capable of caring for seniors in their homes) and gyms targeting seniors (providers of both facilities and fitness education).

Kids

Kids and Teens—With purchasing power of more than $40 billion annually, tweens—children ages 8 to 14—are to be taken seriously. Their large budgets and short attention spans ensure that there is ample opportunity for entrepreneurs who can define the new "must-have" products.

College Planning Consultants—College-bound students and their parents look for help when applying to schools; once they have been accepted, they need just as much help with finding ways to pay for the education.

High School Athletes—High school athletics is becoming a big market, given its more than 7 million participants. From products to recruiting to transportation services, the opportunities are hard to ignore.

An area that continues to be popular is tech training and enrichment courses (educational offerings made available online).

Green

Green Apparel—Demand continues to grow for any clothing that is manufactured using environmentally friendly methods and/or materials. Organic cotton is still popular, but alternatives such as bamboo and soy are gaining traction.

Green Business Services—Entrepreneurs are now seeing the benefit of pursuing sustainable products and services for their businesses. From recycling to eco-friendly suppliers, companies are looking for ways to become as socially minded as possible.

Solar Energy Products—As a result of the burgeoning market for solar power, opportunities abound for products and services that will help both businesses and consumers take advantage of this alternative form of energy.

Continued

Tech

Tech Consulting—The need for technology consulting services has been around for a while, but it is still going strong. Technology spending is increasing within small to mid-size businesses, and business owners need assistance to make sense of all of their options.

Web Applications—The low cost of doing business online guarantees that entrepreneurs will continue to discover new opportunities on the Web. One current development to track is the transition of applications from being installed on computers to being made available online.

Apparel

High-End Accessories—Accessories have become status symbols—especially sunglasses and handbags. Customers are looking for high-end fashion for every element of their wardrobe, so define your target market and emphasize your product's quality.

Specialty Shoes—Consumers are now demanding stylish footwear that is also comfortable to wear, making this the fastest-growing segment in the fashion industry. The key to serving this market is to find your market niche and provide a design that specifically caters to that group.

Miscellaneous

Household Management for the Rich—The more possessions a person has, the more time it takes him or her to maintain those assets, which is especially true for real estate. Wealthy customers expect that employees will be trained beforehand, so entrepreneurs should expect to hire sophisticated and experienced staff to meet their clients' expectations.

Executive Recruiting—Finding and hiring top talent has always been a challenge for organizations. Companies that provide assistance with this process will find plenty of customers, especially when they cater to a specific industry.

Crafts and Handmade Goods—Customers like the idea of their products being one-of-a-kind, which explains the demand for handmade items. If your product does well, you have to be prepared to outsource manufacturing to make your business scalable.

Source: Adapted from Lindsay Holloway, Amanda Kooser, James Park, Laura Tiffany, and Nichole Torres, "2008 Hot List," *Entrepreneur* (December 2007): 80–95.

An Integrative Approach

An integrative picture of the entrepreneurial process is provided by Morris, Lewis, and Sexton.[29] Presented in Figure 1.2, this model is built around the concepts of input to the entrepreneurial process and outcomes from the entrepreneurial process. The input component of Figure 1.2 focuses on the entrepreneurial process itself and identifies five key elements that contribute to the process. The first element is environmental opportunities, such as a demographic change, the development of a new technology, or a modification to current regulations. Next is the individual entrepreneur, the person who assumes personal responsibility for conceptualizing and implementing a new venture. The entrepreneur develops some type of business concept to capitalize on the opportunity (for example, a creative approach to solving a particular customer need). Implementing this business concept typically requires some type of organizational context, which could range from a sole proprietorship run out of the entrepreneur's home or a franchise of some national chain to an autonomous business unit within a large corporation. Finally, a wide variety of financial and nonfinancial resources are required on an ongoing basis. These key elements then are combined throughout the stages of the entrepreneurial process. Stated differently, the process provides a logical framework for organizing entrepreneurial inputs.

The outcome component of Figure 1.2 first includes the level of entrepreneurship being achieved. As we shall discuss in more detail in the next chapter, entrepreneurship is a variable. Thus, the process can result in any number of entrepreneurial events and can produce events that vary considerably in terms of how entrepreneurial they are. Based on this level of "entrepreneurial intensity," final outcomes can include one or more going ventures, value creation, new products and processes, new technologies, profit, jobs, and economic growth. Moreover, the outcome can certainly be failure and thereby include the corresponding economic, psychic, and social costs.

Figure	1.2	An Integrative Model of Entrepreneurial Inputs and Outcomes

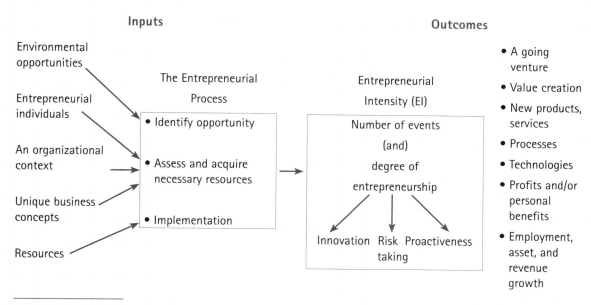

Source: Michael H. Morris, P. Lewis, and Donald L. Sexton, "Reconceptualizing Entrepreneurship: An Input-Output Perspective," SAM *Advanced Management Journal* 59, no.1 (Winter 1994): 21–31.

This model not only provides a fairly comprehensive picture regarding the nature of entrepreneurship, it also can be applied at different levels. For example, the model describes the phenomenon of entrepreneurship in both the independent start-up company and within a department, division, or strategic business unit of a large corporation.

Entrepreneurial Assessment Approach

The entrepreneurial assessment approach, developed by Robert C. Ronstadt, stresses making assessments qualitatively, quantitatively, strategically, and ethically in regard to the entrepreneur, the venture, and the environment (see Figure 1.3).[30] To examine entrepreneurship, the results of these assessments must be compared to the stage of the entrepreneurial career—early, mid-career, or late. Ronstadt termed this process "the entrepreneurial perspective." We focus on this idea in Chapter 2 when we examine the individual characteristics of entrepreneurship.

Our Entrepreneurial Economy—The Environment for Entrepreneurship

Entrepreneurship is the symbol of business tenacity and achievement. Entrepreneurs were the pioneers of today's business successes. Their sense of opportunity, their drive to innovate, and their capacity for accomplishment have become the standard by which free enterprise is now measured. This standard has taken hold throughout the entire world.

We have experienced an **Entrepreneurial Revolution** in the United States. This revolution will continue to be as important (if not more!) to the twenty-first century as the Industrial Revolution was to the twentieth century.

Entrepreneurs will continue to be critical contributors to economic growth through their leadership, management, innovation, research and development effectiveness, job creation, competitiveness, productivity, and formation of new industry.

| Figure | 1.3 | **Entrepreneurial Assessment Approach** |

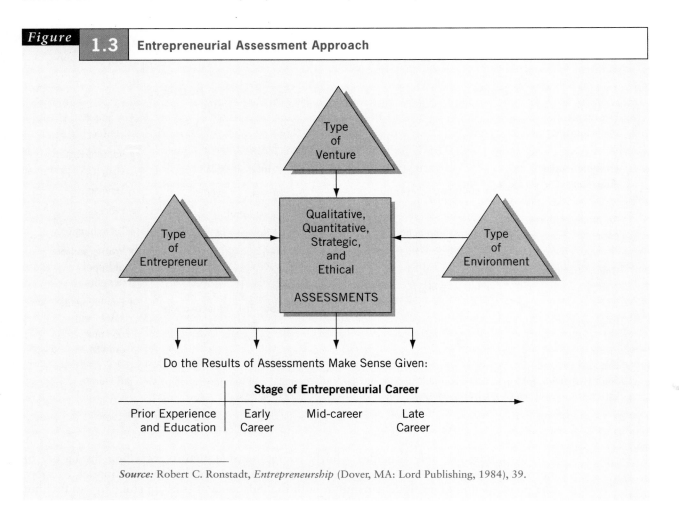

Do the Results of Assessments Make Sense Given:

Stage of Entrepreneurial Career

| Prior Experience and Education | Early Career | Mid-career | Late Career |

Source: Robert C. Ronstadt, *Entrepreneurship* (Dover, MA: Lord Publishing, 1984), 39.

To understand the nature of entrepreneurship, it is important to consider from two perspectives the environment in which entrepreneurial firms operate. The first perspective is statistical, providing actual aggregate numbers to emphasize the importance of small firms in our economy. The second perspective examines some of the trends in entrepreneurial research and education to reflect the emerging importance of entrepreneurship in academic developments.

Predominance of New Ventures in the Economy

The past 15 years have witnessed the powerful emergence of entrepreneurial activity in the United States. Many statistics illustrate this fact. For example, the U.S. Small Business Administration reported that, during the past ten years, new business start-ups numbered nearly 600,000 *per year*. Although many of these incorporations may have previously been sole proprietorships or partnerships, the trend still demonstrates the popularity of venture activity, whether through start-ups, expansions, or development. More specifically, in the new millennium we have witnessed the number of businesses in the United States soar to more than 25 million, and that number is still growing at a rate of 2 percent annually. Let us examine some of the historical numbers supporting this phenomenon.

It would seem safe to assume that new firms with employees may number more than 600,000 in a given year, and that another couple million new business entities—in the form of self-employment—may also come into being each year. Approximately one new firm with employees is established every year for every 300 adults in the United States. Because the typical new firm has at least two owners/managers, 1 of every 150 adults participates in the founding of a new firm each year. Substantially more—1 in 12—are involved in trying to launch a new firm.

The net result, then, is that the United States has a very robust level of firm creation. Among the 6 million establishments (single- and multisite firms) with employees, approximately 600,000 to 800,000 are added each year. That translates into an annual birthrate of 14 to 16 per 100 existing establishments.[31]

The Global Entrepreneurship Monitor (GEM) is a unique, large-scale, long-term project initiated in 1999 and developed jointly by Babson College, London Business School, and the Kauffman Foundation. Now reaching 42 countries worldwide, GEM provides an annual assessment of the entrepreneurial environment of each country. According to the latest GEM study, North America outranks the rest of the world in high expectations of entrepreneurial ability, particularly with regard to enterprises expected to generate 50 or more jobs within five years. The entrepreneurial sector is poised to be an even more important factor in North America's future economic growth due to its adaptability to changing conditions and continued significant job creation.

Entrepreneurs lead to economic growth in several different ways. Entrepreneurs enter and expand existing markets, thereby increasing competition and economic efficiency. Entrepreneurs also create entirely new markets by offering innovative products. These new markets present profit opportunities to others, further spurring economic growth. Additionally, a full 14 percent of entrepreneurs who started a business claimed their product had no direct competitor—a clear indication of new markets being created by entrepreneurs.

Some of the reasons cited for the exceptional entrepreneurial activity in the United States include:

- The United States is a culture that supports risk taking and seeking opportunities.
- Americans are relatively alert to unexploited economic opportunity and have a relatively low fear of failure.
- The United States is a leader in entrepreneurship education at both the undergraduate and graduate levels.
- The United States is home to a high percentage of individuals with professional, technological, or business degrees, a group that registers at the highest entrepreneurial activity rate.

Overall, every study continues to demonstrate that entrepreneurs' ability to expand existing markets and create new markets makes entrepreneurship important for individuals, firms, and entire nations.[32]

the global perspective

The Costs of Free Trade

The North American Free Trade Agreement (NAFTA)—which links the United States, Canada, and Mexico as the largest trading bloc in the world and was once touted as an opportunity for Americans to outsource manufacturing to cheaper labor in Mexico to create higher-paying jobs in the United States—is now being blamed for the loss of countless American jobs. The larger concern is now less about manufacturing jobs and instead focuses on the possibility that service industry jobs will be the next target, largely due to the ease in which business can be conducted across international borders with modern technology.

The new movement in U.S. politics is toward *fair* rather than *free* trade. As antitrade sentiment continues to grow, a sense of nationalism has taken hold not only in

Continued

the United States but in other developed countries. The question that remains is whether the costs associated with free trade are worth it. The answer—although it concerns a sensitive, highly politicized topic—would suggest that economies are better off with free trade; however, the fact remains that factories shutting down in small American towns are a symbol of the problems inherent with opening American borders to facilitate business with neighboring countries. The other question, which few politicians want to address, is whether anything can be done to stop global commerce, even if the country would benefit from such a stoppage.

The answer to the question of halting free trade is that the days of isolated pockets of commerce protected by national borders are over. Some analysts argue that the decades of economic prosperity enjoyed by the United States have led to this sense of dread. The reality is that, when problems arise—such as increased unemployment—entrepreneurs rise to the occasion with solutions that allow for a changed, yet sustainable, way of life. Agriculture has led to industry, which has led to technology; each has resulted in change but also in the creation of greater wealth. The global market is here to stay, so the only question worth asking is how to seize the opportunities that it presents.

Source: Adapted from Nina Easton, "North America Sours on Free Trade," *Fortune*, January 18, 2008, http://money.cnn .com/2008/01/18/news/economy/worldgoaway.fortune/index .htm (accessed March 26, 2008).

The Age of the Gazelles

New and smaller firms create the most jobs in the U.S. economy. The facts speak for themselves: The vast majority of these job-creating companies are fast-growing businesses. David Birch of Cognetics, Inc., has named these firms *gazelles*.[33] A gazelle, by Birch's definition, is a business establishment with at least 20 percent sales growth every year (for five years), starting with a base of at least $100,000.

Despite the continual downsizing in major corporations during the 1990s, the gazelles produced 5 million jobs and brought the net employment growth to 4.2 million jobs. More recently, gazelles (which currently number about 358,000, or 4 percent of all ongoing companies) generated practically as many jobs (10.7 million) as the entire U.S. economy (11.1 million) during the same period. Their extraordinary performance and contribution warrants recognition.[34] (See Table 1.3 for myths associated with gazelles.)

Innovation

Gazelles are leaders in innovation, as shown by the following:

- New and smaller firms have been responsible for 55 percent of the innovations in 362 different industries and 95 percent of all radical innovations.
- Gazelles produce twice as many product innovations per employee as do larger firms.
- New and smaller firms obtain more patents per sales dollar than do larger firms.

Growth

Note how these growth data indicate the current "Age of the Gazelles":

- During the past ten years, business start-ups have approached nearly 600,000 per year, according to the U.S. Small Business Administration.
- Of approximately 25 million businesses in the United States (based on IRS tax returns), only 17,000 qualify as "large" businesses.
- The compound growth rate in the number of businesses over a 12-year span is 3.9 percent.

Table	1.3	**Mythology Associated with Gazelles**

Gazelles are the goal of all entrepreneurs. Creating a gazelle can be rewarding not only financially but professionally; however, not all entrepreneurs are suited for the high-stress environment that running a gazelle provides. The more successful a firm becomes, the more society scrutinizes the actions of the management. Once the world is watching, keeping a gazelle growing takes not only tenacity but composure under extreme pressure.

Gazelles receive venture capital. Although venture capital (VC) firms prefer to invest in gazelles, many gazelles have never received VC funding. With gazelles numbering close to 400,000, less than 2% of these companies have received funding, even in boom times.

Gazelles were never mice. By definition, gazelles are companies created with the intent of high growth and wealth creation, whereas *mice* are companies created with the goal of merely generating income and no intention of growth. Companies can be gazelles at birth; however, many businesses become gazelles later in life. As many as 20% of gazelles have been in operation for more than 30 years.

Gazelles are high tech. To be classified as a gazelle, a company must have grown sales by 20% for at least a five-year period—which can include firms in any industry. This myth most likely stems from the high margins enjoyed by most technology-based companies; however, gazelles are commonly found in low-tech sectors. Two prevalent examples are Best Buy and Starbucks.

Gazelles are global. The scope of a business has no role in its distinction as a gazelle, so even though some gazelles are operating on a global scale, it is not a necessary characteristic. Making the decision to expand overseas prematurely can just as quickly lead to the death of a business as it can lead to its success. Beyond the risks, international trade accounts for more than $800 billion annually in economic activity—but without careful planning, going global could lead to going out of business.

- Each year, about 14 percent of firms with employees drop from the unemployment insurance rolls while about 16 percent new and successor firms—firms with management changes—are added. This represents the disappearance or reorganization of half of all listed firms every five years!
- In 2010, demographers estimate that 30 million firms will exist in the United States, up significantly from the 22.5 million firms that existed in 2000.

Survival

How many gazelles survive? The simple answer is "none." Sooner or later, all companies wither and die. The more relevant question, therefore, is: Over any particular interval, how many firms die, and to what degree is it a function of their age at the beginning of the period?

The common myth that 85 percent of all firms fail in the first year (or the first two years, according to some versions of the myth) is obviously not true. The origins of this myth have been traced by David Birch, formerly with the Massachusetts Institute of Technology (MIT) and later his own firm, Cognetics, to a perfectly accurate piece of research stating that 85 percent of all firms fail. This finding may have been extended to become "85 percent of all small start-up firms fail in the first year."

Whatever the origin of this myth, the more accurate statement is that about half of all start-ups last between five and seven years, depending on economic conditions following the start.

Entrepreneurial Firms' Impact

The United States has achieved its highest economic performance during the last ten years by fostering and promoting entrepreneurial activity; its success has at least three entrepreneurial components.

First, large firms that existed in mature industries adapted, downsized, restructured, and reinvented themselves in early 2000 and are now thriving. These large businesses have learned to become more entrepreneurial. As large firms have become leaner, their sales and profits have increased sharply. For example, General Electric cut its workforce by 40 percent and its sales increased fourfold, from less than $20 billion to nearly $80 billion, over the same period. This goal was accomplished in many cases by returning to the firm's "core competencies" and by contracting out functions formerly done in-house to small firms.

Second, while these large companies have been transforming themselves, new entrepreneurial companies have been blossoming. Twenty years ago, Nucor Steel was a small steel manufacturer with a few hundred employees. It embraced a new technology called thin slab casting, which allowed it to thrive while other steel companies were stumbling. Nucor grew to 59,000 employees, with sales of $3.4 billion and a net income of $274 million. Newer entrepreneurial companies—some of which did not exist 25 years ago—have collectively created 1.4 million new jobs during the past decade.

Third, thousands of smaller firms have been founded, including many established by women, minorities, and immigrants. These new companies have come from every sector of the economy and every part of the country. Together these small firms make a formidable contribution to the economy, as many firms have hired one or two employees to create more than one million net new jobs in the last few years.

In summary, entrepreneurial firms make two indispensable contributions to the U.S. economy. First, they are an integral part of the renewal process that pervades and defines market economies. Entrepreneurial firms play a crucial role in the innovations that lead to technological change and productivity growth. In short, they are about change and competition because they change market structure. The U.S. economy is a dynamic, organic entity that is always in the process of "becoming," rather than an established one that has already arrived. It is about prospects for the future, not the inheritance of the past.

Second, entrepreneurial firms are the essential mechanism by which millions enter the economic and social mainstream of American society. Small businesses enable millions of people—including women, minorities, and immigrants—to access the American Dream. The greatest source of U.S. strength has always been the American Dream of economic growth, equal opportunity, and upward mobility. In this evolutionary process, entrepreneurship plays the crucial and indispensable role of providing the "social glue" that binds together both high-tech and "Main Street" activities.[35]

New-business formations are the critical foundations for any net increase in global employment. All of our detailed information provides insight into why the global economic future may well lie in the development of our entrepreneurial abilities.

Twenty-First-Century Trends in Entrepreneurship Research

As we continue our study of entrepreneurship, it is important to note the research and educational developments that have occurred in this century. The major themes that characterize recent research about entrepreneurs and new-venture creation can be summarized as follows:

1. *Venture financing*, including both venture capital and angel capital financing as well as other innovative financing techniques, emerged in the 1990s with unprecedented strength, fueling entrepreneurship in the twenty-first century.[36]

2. *Corporate entrepreneurship* (entrepreneurial actions within large organizations) and the need for entrepreneurial cultures have gained much attention during the past few years.[37]

3. *Social entrepreneurship* has emerged with unprecedented strength among the new generation of entrepreneurs.[38]

4. *Entrepreneurial cognition* (examining the great variety among types of entrepreneurs and the methods they have used to achieve success) is a wave of research on the psychological aspects of the entrepreneurial process.[39]

5. *Women and minority entrepreneurs* have emerged in unprecedented numbers. They appear to face obstacles and difficulties different from those that other entrepreneurs face.[40]

6. The *global entrepreneurial movement* is increasing, judging by the enormous growth of interest in entrepreneurship around the world in the past few years.[41]

the entrepreneurial process

The Best Business Schools for Entrepreneurship

The Best Graduate Programs in Entrepreneurship

- Babson College
- Indiana University–Bloomington
- Stanford University
- Harvard University
- Massachusetts Institute of Technology
- University of California–Berkeley
- University of Arizona**
- Syracuse University
- University of Pennsylvania

The Best Undergraduate Programs in Entrepreneurship

- Babson College
- Indiana University–Bloomington
- University of Pennsylvania
- University of Southern California
- University of Arizona**
- Syracuse University

** denotes public university

Source: Adapted from "Best Business School Rankings for the Year 2008," *U.S. News & World Report* (April 2008) and "Best Colleges for Aspiring Entrepreneurs," *Fortune Small Business* (September 2008).

7. *Family businesses* have become a stronger focus of research. The economic and social contributions of entrepreneurs with family businesses have been shown to make immensely disproportionate contributions to job creation, innovation, and economic renewal. [42]

8. *Entrepreneurial education* has become one of the hottest topics in business and engineering schools throughout the world. The number of schools teaching an entrepreneurship or similar course has grown from as few as two dozen 20 years ago to more than 1600 at this time.[43]

Key Concepts

Before concluding our discussion of the nature of entrepreneurship, we need to put into perspective three key concepts: entrepreneurship, entrepreneur, and entrepreneurial management.

Entrepreneurship

Entrepreneurship is a dynamic process of vision, change, and creation that requires an application of energy and passion toward the creation and implementation of new ideas and creative solutions. This process of innovation and new-venture creation is accomplished through four major dimensions—individual, organizational, environmental, and process—and is aided by collaborative networks in government, education, and institutions. All of the macro and micro positions of entrepreneurial thought must be considered while recognizing and seizing opportunities that can be converted into marketable ideas capable of competing for implementation in today's economy.

Entrepreneur

As we demonstrated earlier in the chapter, the *entrepreneur* is an innovator or developer who recognizes and seizes opportunities; converts those opportunities into workable/marketable ideas; adds value through time, effort, money, or skills; and assumes the risks of the competitive marketplace to implement these ideas. The entrepreneur is a catalyst for economic change who uses purposeful searching, careful planning, and sound judgment when carrying out the entrepreneurial process. The entrepreneur—uniquely optimistic and committed—works creatively to establish new resources or endow old ones with a new capacity, all for the purpose of creating wealth.

Entrepreneurial Management

The underlying theme of this book is the discipline of **entrepreneurial management**, a concept that has been delineated as follows:

> Entrepreneurship is based upon the same principles, whether the entrepreneur is an existing large institution or an individual starting his or her new venture single-handed. It makes little or no difference whether the entrepreneur is a business or a nonbusiness public-service organization, nor even whether the entrepreneur is a governmental or nongovernmental institution. The rules are pretty much the same, the things that work and those that don't are pretty much the same, and so are the kinds of innovation and where to look for them. In every case there is a discipline we might call *entrepreneurial management*.[44] The techniques and principles of this emerging discipline will drive the entrepreneurial economy in the twenty-first century.

Summary

This chapter examined the evolution of entrepreneurship, providing a foundation for further study of this dynamic and developing discipline. By exploring the early economic definitions as well as select contemporary ones, the chapter presented a historical picture of how entrepreneurship has been viewed. In addition, the ten major myths of entrepreneurship were discussed to permit a better understanding of the folklore that surrounds this newly developing field of study. Contemporary research is broadening the horizon for studying entrepreneurship and is providing a better focus on the what, how, and why behind this discipline.

The approaches to entrepreneurship were examined from two different perspectives: schools of thought and process. Six selected schools of thought were presented, and three approaches for understanding contemporary entrepreneurship as a process were discussed.

This chapter then attempted to provide a broad perspective on the Entrepreneurial Revolution that is occurring throughout the United States and the world. The chapter discussed important statistics that support our entrepreneurial economy. A description of gazelles and their impact on the economy was presented: Gazelles are business establishments with at least 20 percent sales growth every year, starting from a base of $100,000.

The chapter concluded with definitions of three key concepts: entrepreneurship, entrepreneur, and entrepreneurial management.

Key Terms and Concepts

better widget strategy	entrepreneurial assessment approach	entrepreneurial trait school of thought
corridor principle		
displacement school of thought	entrepreneurial management	entrepreneurship
entrepreneur	Entrepreneurial Revolution	environmental school of thought

external locus of control

financial/capital school of thought

gazelle

great chef strategies

internal locus of control

macro view of entrepreneurship

micro view of entrepreneurship

mountain gap strategies

strategic formulation school of thought

venture opportunity school of thought

water well strategies

Review and Discussion Questions

1. Briefly describe the evolution of the term *entrepreneurship*.
2. What are the ten myths associated with entrepreneurship? Debunk each.
3. What is the macro view of entrepreneurship?
4. What are the schools of thought that use the macro view of entrepreneurship?
5. What is the micro view of entrepreneurship?
6. What are the schools of thought that use the micro view of entrepreneurship?
7. What are the three specific types of displacement?

8. In the strategic formulation school of thought, what are the four types of strategies involved with unique elements? Give an illustration of each.
9. What is the process approach to entrepreneurship? In your answer, describe the entrepreneurial assessment approach.
10. Describe the predominance of new ventures in the economy.
11. How have most *net* new jobs been created in the economy?
12. Define a *gazelle* and discuss its importance.

Experiential Exercise

UNDERSTANDING YOUR BELIEFS ABOUT SUCCESSFUL ENTREPRENEURS

Read each of the following ten statements, and to the left of each indicate your agreement or disagreement. If you fully agree with the statement, put a *10* on the line at the left. If you totally disagree, put a *1*. If you tend to agree more than you disagree, give a response between *6* and *9*, depending on how much you agree. If you tend to disagree, give a response between *2* and *5*.

1. Successful entrepreneurs are often methodical and analytical individuals who carefully plan out what they are going to do and then do it.
2. The most successful entrepreneurs are born with special characteristics such as high achievement drive and a winning personality, and these traits serve them well in their entrepreneurial endeavors.
3. Many of the characteristics needed for successful entrepreneurship can be learned through study and experience.
4. The most successful entrepreneurs are those who invent a unique product or service.
5. Highly successful entrepreneurs tend to have very little formal schooling.
6. Most successful entrepreneurs admit that dropping out of school was the best thing they ever did.
7. Because they are unique and individualistic in their approach to business, most successful entrepreneurs find it hard to socialize with others; they just do not fit in.
8. Research shows that, although it is important to have adequate financing before beginning an entrepreneurial venture, it is often more important to have managerial competence and proper planning.

9. Successful entrepreneurship is more a matter of preparation and desire than it is of luck.

10. Most successful entrepreneurs do well in their first venture, which encourages them to continue; failures tend to come later, as the enterprise grows.

Enter your responses on the following list in this way: *(a)* Enter your numerical responses to numbers 1, 3, 8, and 9 just as they appear, and then *(b)* subtract the answers to 2, 4, 5, 6, 7, and 10 from 11 before entering them here. Thus, if you gave an answer of *8* to number 1, put an *8* before number 1 here. However, if you gave an answer of *7* to number 2 here, place a *4* before number 2 here. Then add both columns of answers and enter your total on the appropriate line.

_____1	_____6*	
_____2*	_____7*	
_____3	_____8	
_____4*	_____9	
_____5*	_____10*	_____Total

Interpretation: This exercise measures how much you believe the myths of entrepreneurship. The lower your total, the stronger your beliefs; the higher your total, the less strong your beliefs. Numbers 1, 3, 8, and 9 are accurate statements; numbers 2, 4, 5, 6, 7, and 10 are inaccurate statements. The scoring key is as follows:

80–100   Excellent. You know the facts about entrepreneurs.

61–79   Good, but you still believe in a couple of myths.

41–60   Fair. You need to review the chapter material on the myths of entrepreneurship.

0–40   Poor. You need to reread the chapter material on the myths of entrepreneurship and study these findings.

Case 1.1

GAZELLE . . . OR TURTLE?

Summit Software, Inc., recently celebrated its fifth year of business. Jim Mueller, the proprietor, started the software manufacturing and distribution company when he was still working as a professor at the local college, but now he enjoys being in the fast-paced technology industry. Growth and expansion were easy for Jim, thanks to his knowledge, his contacts, and the pool of readily available workers from which to choose. The company that originated in his den now occupies a nice space close to downtown.

Going into the sixth year, Jim continues to serve the same target market with customer support and lengthy projects. He acknowledges that technological advancements and new clientele are in the immediate future. All of the current and forecasted work leaves Jim and his three employees with little time to spend on administrative duties—let alone new accounts. Jim also realizes that the company needs its own upgrades to continue its rate of success and to stay competitive. Looking at Summit's financials and the amount of work necessary to maintain the business, he's not sure where to go from here. Following is a snapshot of Jim's annual sales since inception:

Year 1	$112,000
Year 2	195,000
Year 3	250,000
Year 4	335,000
Year 5	487,000

QUESTIONS

1. Is Summit Software a gazelle? Support your answer.

2. What problems may Jim face by owning such a fast-growing business?

3. Are gazelles more important to the economy than traditional growth businesses? Why or why not?

Notes

1. Jeffry A. Timmons and Stephen Spinelli, *New Venture Creation*, 7th ed. (New York: McGraw-Hill/Irwin, 2007), 3.

2. For a compilation of definitions, see Robert C. Ronstadt, *Entrepreneurship* (Dover, MA: Lord Publishing, 1984), 28; Howard H. Stevenson and David E. Gumpert, "The Heart of Entrepreneurship," *Harvard Business Review* (March/April 1985): 85–94; and J. Barton Cunningham and Joe Lischeron, "Defining Entrepreneurship," *Journal of Small Business Management* (January 1991): 45–61.

3. See Calvin A. Kent, Donald L. Sexton, and Karl H. Vesper, *Encyclopedia of Entrepreneurship* (Englewood Cliffs, NJ: Prentice Hall, 1982); Ray V. Montagno and Donald F. Kuratko, "Perception of Entrepreneurial Success Characteristics," *American Journal of Small Business* (Winter 1986): 25–32; Thomas M. Begley and David P. Boyd, "Psychological Characteristics Associated with Performance in Entrepreneurial Firms and Smaller Businesses," *Journal of Business Venturing* (Winter 1987): 79–91; and Donald F. Kuratko, "Entrepreneurship," *International Encyclopedia of Business and Management*, 2nd ed. (London: Routledge Publishers, 2002), 168–76.

4. Kent, Sexton, and Vesper, *Encyclopedia of Entrepreneurship*, xxix.

5. Israel M. Kirzner, *Perception, Opportunity, and Profit: Studies in the Theory of Entrepreneurship* (Chicago: University of Chicago Press, 1979), 38–39.

6. See Ronstadt, *Entrepreneurship*, 9–12.

7. Joseph Schumpeter, "Change and the Entrepreneur," in *Essays of J. A. Schumpeter,* ed. Richard V. Clemence (Reading, MA: Addison-Wesley, 1951), 255.

8. Arthur Cole, *Business Enterprise in Its Social Setting* (Cambridge, MA: Harvard University Press, 1959), 27–28.

9. Albert Shapero, *Entrepreneurship and Economic Development,* Project ISEED, Ltd. (Milwaukee, WI: Center for Venture Management, 1975), 187.

10. Ronstadt, *Entrepreneurship*, 28.

11. John B. Miner, Norman R. Smith, and Jeffrey S. Bracker, "Defining the Inventor-Entrepreneur in the Context of Established Typologies," *Journal of Business Venturing* (March 1992): 103–13.

12. "A Surprising Finding on New-Business Mortality Rates," *Business Week* (June 14, 1993): 22.

13. Ivan Bull and Gary E. Willard, "Towards a Theory of Entrepreneurship," *Journal of Business Venturing* (May 1993): 183–95; Ian C. MacMillan and Jerome A. Katz, "Idiosyncratic Milieus of Entrepreneurship Research: The Need for Comprehensive Theories," *Journal of Business Venturing* (January 1992): 1–8; Scott Shane and S. Venkataraman, "The Promise of Entrepreneurship as a Field of Research," *Academy of Management Review* (January 2000): 217–26; and Phillip H. Phan, "Entrepreneurship Theory: Possibilities and Future Directions," *Journal of Business Venturing* 19, no. 5 (September 2004): 617–20.

14. William B. Gartner, "What Are We Talking About When We Talk About Entrepreneurship?" *Journal of Business Venturing* (January 1990): 15–28; see also Lanny Herron, Harry J. Sapienza, and Deborah Smith Cook, "Entrepreneurship Theory from an Interdisciplinary Perspective," *Entrepreneurship Theory and Practice* (Spring 1992): 5–12; Saras D. Sarasvathy, "The Questions We Ask and the Questions We Care About: Reformulating Some Problems in Entrepreneurship Research," *Journal of Business Venturing* 19, no. 5 (September 2004): 707–17; and Benyamin B. Lichtenstein, Nancy M. Carter, Kevin J. Dooley, and William B. Gartner, "Complexity Dynamics of Nascent Entrepreneurship," *Journal of Business Venturing,* 22, no. 2 (2007): 236–61.

15. See Harold Koontz, "The Management Theory Jungle Revisited," *Academy of Management Review* (April 1980): 175–87; Richard M. Hodgetts and Donald F. Kuratko, "The Management Theory Jungle—Quo Vadis?" *Southern Management Association Proceedings* (November 1983): 280–83; J. Barton Cunningham and Joe Lischeron, "Defining Entrepreneurship," *Journal of Small Business Management* (January 1991): 45–61; Ian C. MacMillan and Jerome A. Katz, "Idiosyncratic Milieus of Entrepreneurship Research: The Need for Comprehensive Theories," *Journal of Business Venturing* (January 1992): 1–8; d Murray B. Low, "The Adolescence of Entrepreneurship Research: Specification of Purpose," *Entrepreneurship Theory and Practice* 25, no. 4 (2001): 17–25.

16. See Andrew H. Van de Ven, "The Development of an Infrastructure for Entrepreneurship," *Journal of Business Venturing* (May 1993): 211–30.

17. See David J. Brophy and Joel M. Shulman, "A Finance Perspective on Entrepreneurship Research," *Entrepreneurship Theory and Practice* (Spring 1992): 61–71; and Truls Erikson, "Entrepreneurial Capital: The Emerging Venture's Most Important Asset and Competitive Advantage," *Journal of Business Venturing* 17, no. 3 (2002): 275–90.

18. Ronstadt, *Entrepreneurship.*

19. Small Business Administration, *The State of Small Business: 1997: A Report of the President* (Washington, DC: Government Printing Office, 1997); and Matthew C. Sonfield, "Re-Defining Minority Businesses: Challenges and Opportunities," *Journal of Developmental Entrepreneurship* 6, no. 3 (2001): 269–76.

20. Kelly G. Shaver and Linda R. Scott, "Person, Process, Choice: The Psychology of New Venture Creation," *Entrepreneurship Theory and Practice* (Winter 1991): 23–45; and Ronald K. Mitchell, Lowell Busenitz, Theresa Lant, Patricia P. McDougall, Eric A. Morse, and J. Brock Smith, "The Distinctive and Inclusive Domain of Entrepreneurial Cognition Research," *Entrepreneurship Theory and Practice* 28, no. 6 (Winter 2004): 505–18.

21. See Magnus Aronsson, "Education Matters—But Does Entrepreneurship Education? An Interview with David Birch," *Academy of Management Learning & Education* 3, no. 3 (2004): 289–92.

22. See Jerry A. Katz, "The Chronology and Intellectual Trajectory of American Entrepreneurship Education," *Journal of Business Venturing* 18, no. 2 (2003): 283–300; Donald F. Kuratko, "The Emergence of Entrepreneurship Education: Development, Trends, and Challenges," *Entrepreneurship Theory and Practice* 29, no. 5 (2005): 577–98; and Dean A. Shepherd, "Educating Entrepreneurship Students About Emotion and Learning from Failure," *Academy of Management Learning & Education* 3, no. 3 (2004): 274–87.

23. George A. Steiner, *Strategic Planning* (New York: Free Press, 1979), 3.

24. See Marjorie A. Lyles, Inga S. Baird, J. Burdeane Orris, and Donald F. Kuratko, "Formalized Planning in Small Business: Increasing Strategic Choices," *Journal of Small Business Management* (April 1993): 38–50; and R. Duane Ireland, Michael A. Hitt, S. Michael Camp, and Donald L. Sexton, "Integrating Entrepreneurship and Strategic Management Actions to Create Firm Wealth," *Academy of Management Executive* 15, no. 1 (2001): 49–63.

25. Ronstadt, *Entrepreneurship,* 112–15.

26. Michael A. Hitt, R. Duane Ireland, S. Michael Camp, and Donald L. Sexton, "Strategic Entrepreneurship: Entrepreneurial Strategies for Wealth Creation," special issue, *Strategic Management Journal* 22, no. 6 (2001): 479–92.

27. See the special issue, dealing with models, of *Entrepreneurship: Theory and Practice* 17, no. 2 (1993); see also James J. Chrisman, Alan Bauerschmidt, and Charles W. Hofer, "The Determinants of New Venture Performance: An Extended Model," *Entrepreneurship Theory and Practice* (Fall 1998): 5–30.

28. Michael H. Morris, P. Lewis, and Donald L. Sexton, "Reconceptualizing Entrepreneurship: An Input-Output Perspective," *Advanced Management Journal* 59, no. 1 (Winter 1994): 21–31.

29. Morris, Lewis, and Sexton, "Reconceptualizing Entrepreneurship."

30. Ronstadt, *Entrepreneurship,* 39.

31. Paul D. Reynolds, Michael Hay, and S. Michael Camp, *Global Entrepreneurship Monitor* (Kansas City, MO: Kauffman Center for Entrepreneurial Leadership, 1999).

32. Maria Minniti and William D. Bygrave, *Global Entrepreneurship Monitor* (Kansas City, MO: Kauffman Center for Entrepreneurial Leadership, 2004); and Erkko Autio, *Global Report on High Growth Entrepreneurship,* (Wellesley, MA: Babson College, 2007).

33. David Birch's research firm, Cognetics, Inc., traces the employment and sales records of some 14 million companies with a Dun & Bradstreet file.

34. David Birch, Jan Gundersen, Anne Haggerty, and William Parsons, *Corporate Demographics* (Cambridge, MA: Cognetics, Inc., 1999).

35. "The New American Revolution: The Role and Impact of Small Firms" (Washington, DC: U.S. Small Business Administration, Office of Economic Research, 1998); and William J. Dennis, Jr., and Lloyd W. Fernald, Jr., "The Chances of Financial Success (and Loss) from Small Business Ownership," *Entrepreneurship Theory and Practice* 26, no. 1 (2000): 75–83.

36. Dean A. Shepherd and Andrew Zacharakis, "Speed to Initial Public Offering of VC-Backed Companies," *Entrepreneurship Theory and Practice* 25, no. 3 (2001): 59–69; Dean A. Shepherd and Andrew Zacharakis, "Venture Capitalists' Expertise: A Call for Research into Decision Aids and Cognitive Feedback," *Journal of Business Venturing* 17, no. 1 (2002): 1–20; Lowell W. Busenitz, James O. Fiet, and Douglas D. Moesel, "Reconsidering the Venture Capitalists' 'Value Added' Proposition: An Interorganizational Learning Perspective," *Journal of Business Venturing* 19, no. 6 (2004): 787–807; and Dimo Dimov, Dean A. Shepherd, and Kathleen M. Sutcliffe, "Requisite Expertise, Firm Reputation, and Status in Venture Capital Investment Allocation Decisions," *Journal of Business Venturing,* 22, no. 4 (2007): 481–502.

37. Donald F. Kuratko, R. Duane Ireland, and Jeffrey S. Hornsby, "Improving Firm Performance Through Entrepreneurial Actions: Acordia's Corporate Entrepreneurship Strategy," *Academy of Management Executive* 15, no. 4 (2001): 60–71; Donald F. Kuratko, Jeffrey S. Hornsby, and Michael G. Goldsby, "Sustaining Corporate Entrepreneurship: A Proposed Model of Perceived Implementation/Outcome Comparisons at the Organizational and Individual Levels," *International Journal of Entrepreneurship and Innovation,* 5, no. 2 (2004): 77–89; Michael H. Morris, Donald F. Kuratko, and Jeffrey G. Covin, *Corporate Entrepreneurship and Innovation* (Mason, OH: South-Western/Cengage Learning, 2008); and R. Duane Ireland, Jeffrey G. Covin, and Donald F. Kuratko, "Conceptualizing Corporate Entrepreneurship Strategy," *Entrepreneurship Theory and Practice* 33, no. 1 (forthcoming).

38. Johanna Mair and Ignasi Marti, "Social Entrepreneurship Research: A Source of Explanation, Prediction, and Delight," *Journal of World Business* 41 (2006): 36–44; Ana Maria Peredo and Murdith McLean, "Social Entrepreneurship: A Critical Review

of the Concept," *Journal of World Business* 41 (2006): 56–65; James Austin, Howard Stevenson, and Jane Wei-Skillern, "Social and Commercial Entrepreneurship: Same, Different, or Both?" *Entrepreneurship Theory and Practice* 30, no. 1 (2006): 1–22; and Thomas J. Dean and Jeffery S. McMullen, "Toward a Theory of Sustainable Entrepreneurship: Reducing Environmental Degradation Through Entrepreneurial Action," *Journal of Business Venturing* 22, no. 1 (2007): 50–76.

39. Jill Kickul and Lisa K. Gundry, "Prospecting for Strategic Advantage: The Proactive Entrepreneurial Personality and Small Firm Innovation," *Journal of Small Business Management* 40, no. 2 (2002): 85–97; Robert A. Baron, "The Role of Affect in the Entrepreneurial Process," *Academy of Management Review,* 33, no. 2 (2008): 328–40.

40. Lisa K. Gundry and Harold P. Welsch, "The Ambitious Entrepreneur: High Growth Strategies of Women-Owned Enterprises," *Journal of Business Venturing* 16, no. 5 (2001): 453–70; Anne de Bruin, Candida G. Brush, and Friederike Welter, "Towards Building Cumulative Knowledge on Women's Entrepreneurship," *Entrepreneurship Theory and Practice* 30, no. 5 (2006): 585–94; and Dawn R. DeTienne and Gaylen N. Chandler, "The Role of Gender in Opportunity Identification," *Entrepreneurship Theory and Practice* 31, no. 3 (2007): 365–86.

41. Shaker A. Zahra, James Hayton, Jeremy Marcel, and Hugh O'Neill, "Fostering Entrepreneurship During International Expansion: Managing Key Challenges," *European Management Journal* 19, no. 4 (2001): 359–69; Mike W. Peng, "How Entrepreneurs Create Wealth in Transition Economies," *Academy of Management Executive* 15, no. 1 (2001): 95–110; and Paul Westhead, Mike Wright, and Deniz Ucbasaran, "The Internationalization of New and Small Firms: A Resource-Based View," *Journal of Business Venturing* 16, no. 4 (2001): 333–58.

42. Nancy Upton, Elisabeth J. Teal, and Joe T. Felan, "Strategic and Business Planning Practices of Fast-Growing Family Firms," *Journal of Small Business Management* 39, no. 4 (2001): 60–72; Zhenyu Wu, Jess H. Chua, and James J. Chrisman, "Effects of Family Ownership and Management on Small Business Equity Financing," *Journal of Business Venturing* 22, no. 6 (2007): 875–95.

43. Alberta Charney and Gary D. Libecap, "Impact of Entrepreneurship Education," *Insights: A Kauffman Research Series* (Kansas City, MO: Kauffman Center for Entrepreneurial Leadership, 2000); Donald F. Kuratko, "The Emergence of Entrepreneurship Education: Development, Trends, Challenges," *Entrepreneurship Theory and Practice* 29, no. 3 (2005): 577–98; and Jerry A. Katz "The Chronology and Intellectual Trajectory of American Entrepreneurship Education," *Journal of Business Venturing* 18, no. 2 (2003): 283–300.

44. Peter F. Drucker, *Innovation and Entrepreneurship* (New York: Harper & Row, 1985), 143; see also Howard H. Stevenson and J. Carlos Jarillo, "A Paradigm of Entrepreneurship: Entrepreneurial Management," *Strategic Management Journal* (Summer 1990): 17–27.

CHAPTER 2

The Individual Entrepreneurial Mind-Set

Entrepreneurial Thought

For all we know about balance sheets, income statements, and cash flow accounting; for all of our understanding about marketing strategies, tactics, and techniques; and for everything we have learned about management principles and practices, there remains something essential, yet mysterious, at the core of entrepreneurship. It is so mysterious that we cannot see it or touch it; yet we feel it and know it exists. It cannot be mined, manufactured, or bought; yet it can de discovered. Its source is invisible; yet its results are tangible and measurable. This mysterious core is so powerful that it can make the remarkable appear ordinary, so contagious that it can spread like wildfire from one to another and so persuasive that it can transform doubt and uncertainty into conviction. This mysterious core is PASSION!

— **RAY SMILOR, PH.D.** *Daring Visionaries*

Chapter Objectives

1   To describe the entrepreneurial mind-set

2   To present the major sources of information that are useful in profiling the entrepreneurial mind-set

3   To identify and discuss the most commonly cited characteristics found in successful entrepreneurs

4   To discuss the "dark side" of entrepreneurship

5   To identify and describe the different types of risk entrepreneurs face as well as the major causes of stress for these individuals and the ways they can handle stress

6   To examine entrepreneurial motivation

The Entrepreneurial Mind-Set

Today's younger generation is sometimes referred to as Generation X because they feel "X-ed" out of traditional opportunities. This generation of the twenty–first century eventually may be known as Generation E, however, because they are becoming the most entrepreneurial generation since the Industrial Revolution. Millions of individuals younger than age 35 are actively trying to start their own businesses today. One-third of new entrepreneurs are younger than age 30, and a huge percentage of 18- to 30-year-olds study entrepreneurship in business schools today. Major universities are devoting more resources to entrepreneurship, and the success stories of young entrepreneurs are increasing.[1]

Every person has the potential and free choice to pursue a career as an entrepreneur. Exactly what motivates individuals to make a choice for entrepreneurship has not been identified—at least not as one single event, characteristic, or trait. As we demonstrated in Chapter 1, researchers continually strive to learn more about the entire entrepreneurial process to better understand the driving forces within entrepreneurs.[2]

The chapters in this book focus on learning the discipline of entrepreneurship. This chapter, however, is devoted to a more psychological look at entrepreneurs; it describes the most common characteristics associated with successful entrepreneurs, as well as the elements associated with the "dark side" of entrepreneurship. In this manner, we can gain a more complete perspective on the entrepreneurial behavior that is involved with the entrepreneurial mind-set an individual exhibits. Although it certainly is not an exact science, examining this mind-set provides an interesting look at the entrepreneurial potential within every individual.[3]

Who Are Entrepreneurs?

Frank Carney, the founder of Pizza Hut, Inc., once described entrepreneurs as the cornerstone of the American enterprise system, the self-renewing agents for our economic environment. Entrepreneurs—normally defined as "risk takers" in new-venture creations—are uniquely optimistic, hard-driving, committed individuals who derive great satisfaction from being independent. Starting a new business requires more than just an idea; it requires a special person, an entrepreneur, who combines sound judgment and planning with risk taking to ensure the success of his or her own business.

Entrepreneurs, driven by an intense commitment and determined perseverance, work very hard. They are optimists who see the cup as half full rather than half empty. They strive for integrity. They burn with the competitive desire to excel. They use failure as a tool for learning. They have enough confidence in themselves to believe that they personally can make a major difference in the final outcome of their ventures.[4]

The substantial failure rate of new ventures attests to the difficulty of entrepreneurship. Inexperience and incompetent management are the main reasons for failure. But what are the factors for success? Do they apply to all components of entrepreneurship? These are some of the issues we shall explore in this chapter.

Sources of Research on Entrepreneurs

Three major sources of information supply data related to the entrepreneurial mind-set. The first source is publications—both research-based and popular. The following are among the more important of these publications:

1. **Technical and professional journals.** These are refereed journals that contain articles dealing with research—methodology, results, and application of results—that are well designed and tightly structured. Examples include *Entrepreneurship Theory and Practice, Journal of Business Venturing, Journal of Small Business Management, Strategic Management Journal, Journal of Small Business Strategy, Academy of Management Review, Academy of Management Journal, Family Business Review,* and *Strategic Entrepreneurship Journal.*

2. **Textbooks on entrepreneurship.** These texts typically address the operation of new ventures and entrepreneurial organizations. Sections or chapters frequently are devoted

to research on entrepreneurs. Examples include *New Venture Creation, New Venture Management, Entrepreneurship,* and *Corporate Entrepreneurship & Innovation.*[5]

3. **Books about entrepreneurship.** Most of these books are written as practitioners' "how-to" guides. Some deal with the problems that face the individual who starts a business; others deal with a specific aspect of the subject. Examples include *Startup, In the Owner's Chair, Rethinking Marketing: The Entrepreneurial Imperative, Nuts,* and *The Breakthrough Company.*[6]

4. **Biographies or autobiographies of entrepreneurs.** Examples include *Business at the Speed of Thought* and *Radicals and Visionaries.*[7]

5. **Compendiums about entrepreneurs.** These are collections that deal with several selected individuals or that present statistical information or overviews of perceived general trends. Examples include *The Entrepreneurs,*[8] which is a compendium of information about selected living entrepreneurs; *The Enterprising Americans,*[9] which provides a summary of trends; and *The Venture Café,*[10] which examines strategies and stories from high-tech start-ups.

6. **News periodicals.** Many newspapers and news periodicals run stories on entrepreneurs either regularly or periodically. Examples include *Business Week, Fortune, U.S. News and World Report, Forbes,* and the *Wall Street Journal.*

7. **Venture periodicals.** A growing number of new magazines are concerned specifically with new-business ventures. Most, if not all, of each issue's contents are related to entrepreneurship. Examples include *Black Enterprise, Entrepreneur, Fortune Small Business, Inc.,* and *Family Business.*

8. **Newsletters.** A number of newsletters are devoted exclusively to entrepreneurship. The *Liaison* newsletter, from the U.S. Association for Small Business and Entrepreneurship, is one example.

9. **Proceedings of conferences.** Publications related to annual or periodic conferences deal at least in part with entrepreneurship. Examples include *Proceedings of the Academy of Management, Proceedings of the International Council for Small Business, Proceedings of the U.S. Association for Small Business and Entrepreneurship,* and *Frontiers in Entrepreneurship Research* (proceedings of the Babson College Entrepreneurship Research Conference).

10. **The Internet.** Simply entering into a search engine the topic "successful entrepreneurial stories" produces no less than 229,000 potential sources at this time. Many states have produced stories on their successful entrepreneurs. One example is the U.S. Small Business Administration (SBA) Web site, www.sba.gov.

The second major source of information about the entrepreneurial mind-set is direct observation of practicing entrepreneurs. The experiences of individual entrepreneurs can be related through the use of interviews, surveys, and case studies. Analysis of these experiences can provide insights into the traits, characteristics, and personalities of individual entrepreneurs and leads to the discovery of commonalities that help explain the mind-set.

The final source of entrepreneurial information is speeches and presentations (including seminars) given by practicing entrepreneurs. This source may not go as far in-depth as the other two do, but it does provide an opportunity to learn about the entrepreneurial mind-set. Entrepreneur-in-residence programs at various universities illustrate the added value that oral presentations may have in educating people about entrepreneurship.

Common Characteristics Associated with Entrepreneurs

A review of the literature related to entrepreneurial characteristics reveals the existence of a large number of factors that can be consolidated into a much smaller set of profile dimensions. For example, the following is one list of common characteristics that has been compiled:

- Total commitment, determination, and perseverance
- Drive to achieve and grow
- Opportunity and goal orientation

- Taking initiative and personal responsibility
- Persistent problem-solving
- Realism and a sense of humor
- Seeking and using feedback
- Internal locus of control
- Calculated risk taking and risk seeking
- Low need for status and power
- Integrity and reliability

Howard H. Stevenson and David E. Gumpert have presented an outline of the entrepreneurial organization that reveals such characteristics as imagination, flexibility, and willingness to accept risks.[11] William B. Gartner examined the literature and found a diversity of reported characteristics.[12] John Hornaday examined various research sources and formulated a list of 42 characteristics often attributed to entrepreneurs (see Table 2.1).

In the simplest of theoretical forms for studying entrepreneurship, entrepreneurs cause entrepreneurship. That is, $E + f(e)$ states that entrepreneurship is a function of the entrepreneur.

Table **2.1**   **Characteristics Often Attributed to Entrepreneurs**

1. Confidence	22. Responsibility
2. Perseverance, determination	23. Foresight
3. Energy, diligence	24. Accuracy, thoroughness
4. Resourcefulness	25. Cooperativeness
5. Ability to take calculated risks	26. Profit orientation
6. Dynamism, leadership	27. Ability to learn from mistakes
7. Optimism	28. Sense of power
8. Need to achieve	29. Pleasant personality
9. Versatility; knowledge of product, market, machinery, technology	30. Egotism
10. Creativity	31. Courage
11. Ability to influence others	32. Imagination
12. Ability to get along well with people	33. Perceptiveness
13. Initiative	34. Toleration for ambiguity
14. Flexibility	35. Aggressiveness
15. Intelligence	36. Capacity for enjoyment
16. Orientation to clear goals	37. Efficacy
17. Positive response to challenges	38. Commitment
18. Independence	39. Ability to trust workers
19. Responsiveness to suggestions and criticism	40. Sensitivity to others
20. Time competence, efficiency	41. Honesty, integrity
21. Ability to make decisions quickly	42. Maturity, balance

Source: John A. Hornaday, "Research about Living Entrepreneurs," in *Encyclopedia of Entrepreneurship*, ed. Calvin Kent, Donald Sexton, and Karl Vesper (Englewood Cliffs, NJ: Prentice Hall, 1982), 26–27. Adapted by permission of Prentice Hall, Englewood Cliffs, NJ.

Thus, the continuous examination of entrepreneurial characteristics aids the evolving understanding of entrepreneurship. One author provides the following description:

> Would-be entrepreneurs live in a sea of dreams. Their destinations are private islands—places to build, create, and transform their particular dreams into reality. Being an entrepreneur entails envisioning your island, and even more importantly, it means getting in the boat and rowing to your island. Some leave the shore and drift aimlessly in the shallow waters close to shore, while others paddle furiously and get nowhere, because they don't know how to paddle or steer. Worst of all are those who remain on the shore of the mainland, afraid to get in the boat. Yet, all those dreamers may one day be entrepreneurs if they can marshal the resources—external and internal—needed to transform their dreams into reality.
>
> Everyone has dreams. We all dream while asleep, even if we don't remember dreaming. Entrepreneurs' dreams are different. Their dreams are not limited to dreams about fantasy islands or fast cars. Theirs are about business.[13]

Entrepreneurship also has been characterized as the interaction of the following skills: inner control, planning and goal setting, risk taking, innovation, reality perception, use of feedback, decision making, human relations, and independence. In addition, many people believe that successful entrepreneurs are individuals who are not afraid to fail.

Research continues to expand our understanding of the cognitions of entrepreneurs.[14] New characteristics are continually being added to this ever-growing list. At this point, however, let us examine some of the most often cited entrepreneurial characteristics. Although this list admittedly is incomplete, it does provide important insights into the entrepreneurial mind-set.

COMMITMENT, DETERMINATION, AND PERSEVERANCE

More than any other factor, total dedication to success as an entrepreneur can overcome obstacles and setbacks. Sheer determination and an unwavering commitment to succeed often win out against odds that many people would consider insurmountable. They also can compensate for personal shortcomings. Often, entrepreneurs with a high-potential venture and a plan that includes venture capital financing can expect investors to measure their commitment in several ways. Examples include a willingness to mortgage their house, take a cut in pay, sacrifice family time, and reduce their standard of living.

DRIVE TO ACHIEVE

Entrepreneurs are self-starters who appear to others to be internally driven by a strong desire to compete, to excel against self-imposed standards, and to pursue and attain challenging goals. This drive to achieve has been well documented in the entrepreneurial literature, beginning with David McClelland's pioneering work on motivation in the 1950s and 1960s.[15] High achievers tend to be moderate risk takers. They examine a situation, determine how to increase the odds of winning, and then push ahead. As a result, high-risk decisions for the average businessperson often are moderate risks for the well-prepared high achiever.

OPPORTUNITY ORIENTATION

One clear pattern among successful, growth-minded entrepreneurs is their focus on opportunity rather than on resources, structure, or strategy. Opportunity orientation is the constant awareness of opportunities that exist in everyday life. Successful entrepreneurs start with the opportunity and let their understanding of it guide other important issues. They are goal oriented in their pursuit of opportunities. Setting high but attainable goals enables them to focus their energies, to selectively sort out opportunities, and to know when to say "no." Their goal orientation also helps them to define priorities and provides them with measures of how well they are performing.

INITIATIVE AND RESPONSIBILITY

Historically, the entrepreneur has been viewed as an independent and highly self-reliant innovator. Most researchers agree that effective entrepreneurs actively seek and take the initiative. They willingly put themselves in situations where they are personally responsible

Taking University Entrepreneurship Global

For those students who come out of school with business experience, opportunities abound. At the top of most students' lists is the matter of compensation, but some students look for an alternative path—their career route after school becomes more about the experience than the financial gain.

MBAs Without Borders (MWB) is an organization that was established in Canada to help third world countries by pairing social projects with recent business graduates. It is one of several organizations that gives students the opportunity to do more than just read about social entrepreneurship. The students have the opportunity to apply their business know-how to initiatives that will have an immediate impact on the health and financial well-being of the local citizens, with whom they work side-by-side.

Omar Yaqub was a 28-year-old MBA graduate of the University of Alberta. Upon finishing school, he decided that he was not ready for a corporate position, so he joined MWB and was sent to Nigeria. His project was

to help market life-saving antimalaria sleeping nets. Despite the nets' proven efficacy, Nigerians viewed them as cheap and archaic. To change the perception of the nets, Yaqub conducted focus groups and, based on his results, convinced the manufacturers to develop the nets in more vibrant colors. He also worked with Nigerian film producers to strategically place the nets in movies and television shows. As a result of their efforts, Yaqub and his team were able to negotiate deals for the distribution of close to 4 million nets.

Participants in these programs certainly have chosen a far less glamorous path than their peers who have instead taken permanent jobs; however, the fact that students who have completed their first project often opt to take on a second or a third suggests that the benefits outweigh the costs for everyone involved.

Source: Adapted from Peter Viles, "The Do-Gooder's MBA," *Business 2.0*, August 22, 2007, http://money.cnn.com/2007/08/22/magazines/business2/mbas_overseas.biz2/index.htm (accessed March 26, 2008).

for the success or failure of the operation. They like to take the initiative in solving a problem or in filling a vacuum where no leadership exists. They also like situations where their personal impact on problems can be measured. This is the action-oriented nature of the entrepreneur expressing itself.

PERSISTENT PROBLEM-SOLVING

Entrepreneurs are not intimidated by difficult situations. In fact, their self-confidence and general optimism seem to translate into a view that the impossible just takes a little longer. Yet they are neither aimless nor foolhardy in their relentless attack on a problem or an obstacle that is impeding business operations. If the task is extremely easy or perceived to be unsolvable, entrepreneurs often will give up sooner than others—simple problems bore them; unsolvable ones do not warrant their time. Moreover, although entrepreneurs are extremely persistent, they are realistic in recognizing what they can and cannot do and where they can get help to solve difficult but unavoidable tasks.

SEEKING FEEDBACK

Effective entrepreneurs often are described as quick learners. Unlike many people, however, they also have a strong desire to know how well they are doing and how they might improve their performance. In attempting to make these determinations, they actively seek out and use feedback. Feedback is also central to their learning from mistakes and setbacks.

INTERNAL LOCUS OF CONTROL

Successful entrepreneurs believe in themselves. They do not believe that the success or failure of their venture will be governed by fate, luck, or similar forces. They believe that their accomplishments and setbacks are within their own control and influence, and that they can affect the outcome of their actions. This attribute is consistent with a high-achievement motivational drive, the desire to take personal responsibility, and self-confidence.

TOLERANCE FOR AMBIGUITY

Start-up entrepreneurs face uncertainty compounded by constant changes that introduce ambiguity and stress into every aspect of the enterprise. Setbacks and surprises are inevitable; lack of organization, structure, and order is a way of life. A tolerance for ambiguity exists when the entrepreneur can deal with the various setbacks and changes that constantly confront him or her. Successful entrepreneurs thrive on the fluidity and excitement of such an ambiguous existence. Job security and retirement generally are of no concern to them.

CALCULATED RISK TAKING

Successful entrepreneurs are not gamblers—they are calculated risk takers. When they decide to participate in a venture, they do so in a very calculated, carefully thought-out manner. They do everything possible to get the odds in their favor, and they often avoid taking unnecessary risks. These strategies include getting others to share inherent financial and business risks with them—for example, by persuading partners and investors to put up money, creditors to offer special terms, and suppliers to advance merchandise.

INTEGRITY AND RELIABILITY

Integrity and reliability are the glue and fiber that bind successful personal and business relationships and make them endure. Investors, partners, customers, and creditors alike value these attributes highly. Integrity and reliability help build and sustain trust and confidence. Small-business entrepreneurs, in particular, find these two characteristics crucial to success.

TOLERANCE FOR FAILURE

Entrepreneurs use failure as a learning experience; hence, they have a tolerance for failure. The iterative, trial-and-error nature of becoming a successful entrepreneur makes serious setbacks and disappointments an integral part of the learning process. The most effective entrepreneurs are realistic enough to expect such difficulties. Furthermore, they do not become disappointed, discouraged, or depressed by a setback or failure. In adverse and difficult times, they look for opportunity. Many of them believe that they learn more from their early failures than from their early successes.

HIGH ENERGY LEVEL

The extraordinary workloads and stressful demands placed on entrepreneurs put a premium on their energy. Many entrepreneurs fine-tune their energy levels by carefully monitoring what they eat and drink, establishing exercise routines, and knowing when to get away for relaxation.

CREATIVITY AND INNOVATIVENESS

Creativity was once regarded as an exclusively inherited trait. Judging by the level of creativity and innovation in the United States compared with that of equally sophisticated but less creative and innovative cultures, it appears unlikely that this trait is solely genetic. An expanding school of thought believes that creativity can be learned (Chapter 5 provides a comprehensive examination of this critical characteristic). New ventures often possess a collective creativity that emerges from the joint efforts of the founders and personnel and produces unique goods and services.

entrepreneurship in practice

Perseverance and Commitment

"If at first you don't succeed, try and try again." "If you fall off the horse, you have to get back on." "What doesn't kill you only makes you stronger." Whatever adage you choose, Richard Schulze is a living example of it. Schulze—the CEO and chairman of Best Buy Company, Inc., as well as Ernst & Young's 1999 Entrepreneur of the Year—is "tenaciousness" personified. His story, amazing enough to be a work of fiction, spans three decades and defies the odds.

Richard Schulze dropped out of college to work for his father at his electronics distribution company. After gaining experience in the business, he began to pitch improvement ideas, only to learn that his father was happy with the status quo. This ultimately drove Schulze to quit; in 1966, he opened his own retail audio store, The Sound of Music, in St. Paul, Minnesota. The economy of the late 1960s and 1970s was agreeable with the small business, and the chain grew to nine stores.

In 1981, however, Schulze's largest and most profitable store was obliterated by a tornado. The sun did shine after the storm, however—the stock in the storeroom was left unscathed. Ever optimistic, Schulze rounded up his employees and held a "Tornado Sale" in the store's parking lot. Because he hoped to liquidate the stock, Schulze used the marketing budget to promote the event. Little did he know that the natural disaster would actually be a turn for the better. When the line to get into the lot exceeded two miles, Schulze was convinced he'd found a cash cow. The customers confirmed his theory when he questioned them about "what they truly wanted when shopping for technology products." Their overall response was "a hassle-free shopping experience, broad selection of name-brand products readily available on shelves, informed sales assistance, service when needed, and a quick and easy checkout process." The overall result: Schulze utilized personal assets to reposition the company, included new product lines, and renamed the business Best Buy.

A relentless and savvy Schulze grew the chain to 251 stores by 1996. Life and business were good, and

Schulze probably had begun work on his retirement portfolio. In fact, business was so good that Schulze decided to borrow $300 million to pad his computer inventory for the 1996 Christmas season. Much to his chagrin, disaster found him again when Intel introduced its new Pentium chip soon after the inventory purchase. Best Buy's stock fell from $22 per share to $5 as the company's earnings plummeted due to its now obsolete assets. Apparently the experienced salesman was also not proficient with the financial aspect of running a large business: The company was pricing its items too low, and operations were less than desirable. Best Buy's debt, already at $271 million in 1995, encompassed 72 percent of equity.

After a second disaster, most people would throw in the towel. But shareholders and family pressure didn't deter this entrepreneur from prevailing over the malcontents and saving the company. Drastic changes were made over a 14-month period, the most important being the dismissal of the company's "no money down, no monthly payment, no interest" policy. Marketing, management, and inventory control were changed, and low-margin items were replaced with profitable ones. The textbook reconstruction yielded a 5,500 percent increase in earnings, rocketing them to $94.5 million in fiscal 1998. Schulze claims the happy ending was a result of his unwavering ethics, solid culture, and value system.

He never gave up, he got back on the horse, and his experiences certainly made him stronger. The perseverance and commitment Schulze demonstrated over the years justify his designation as Entrepreneur of the Year, but his business acumen isn't the best reason for the title. In 1994, Schulze created the Best Buy Children's Foundation to support mentorship, leadership, and educational opportunities for the youth of Best Buy communities. Furthermore, amid the 1996 upheaval, he and his wife piloted the Schulze Family Fund—appropriately created to provide crisis relief to company employees.

The story isn't over yet. New chapters will be written, as Best Buy now has 830 retail stores, 105,000 employees,

Continued

and in 2002 opened its first global sourcing office in China. E-commerce and international opportunities are also at the top of the agenda. The electronics market is on the rise, and Best Buy has a front-row seat. Richard Schulze has the necessary experience to mold the story for the better, no matter what twists are thrown into the plot.

Source: Ernst & Young, LLP, "Entrepreneur of the Year," *EOY Magazine* (1999): 13–15, and updated on www.bestbuy.com, 2005.

VISION

Entrepreneurs know where they want to go. They have a vision or concept of what their firms can be. For example, Steve Jobs of Apple Computer fame wanted his firm to provide microcomputers that could be used by everyone, from schoolchildren to businesspeople. The computer would be more than a machine. It would be an integral part of the person's life in terms of learning and communicating. This vision helped make Apple a major competitor in the microcomputer industry. Not all entrepreneurs have predetermined visions for their firms, however. In many cases, this vision develops over time as the individual begins to realize what the firm is and what it can become.

SELF-CONFIDENCE AND OPTIMISM

Although entrepreneurs often face major obstacles, their belief in their ability seldom wavers. During down periods, they maintain their confidence and let those around them know it. This helps others sustain their own optimism and creates the level of self-confidence necessary for efficient group effort.

INDEPENDENCE

The desire for independence is a driving force behind contemporary entrepreneurs. A frustration with rigid bureaucratic systems, coupled with a sincere commitment to make a difference, adds up to an independent personality trying to accomplish tasks his or her own way. This is not to say that entrepreneurs must make *all* of the decisions; however, they do want the authority to make the important ones.

TEAM BUILDING

The desire for independence and autonomy does not preclude the entrepreneur's desire to build a strong entrepreneurial team. Most successful entrepreneurs have highly qualified, well-motivated teams that help handle the venture's growth and development. In fact, although the entrepreneur may have the clearest vision of where the firm is (or should be) headed, the personnel often are more qualified to handle the day-to-day implementation challenges.[16]

The Entrepreneurial Journey

As we discussed in Chapter 1, the prevalent view in the literature is that entrepreneurs create ventures. Although that is a true statement, its narrow framing neglects the complete process of entrepreneurship and much of the reality regarding how ventures and entrepreneurs come into being. Researchers Minet Schindehutte, Michael H. Morris, and Donald F. Kuratko point out that—similar to a painting that emerges based on the individual interacting with, feeling, and agonizing over his or her creation—a venture is not simply produced by an entrepreneur. Entrepreneurs do not preexist; they emerge as a function of the novel, idiosyncratic, and experiential nature of the venture creation process. Venture creation is a lived experience that, as it unfolds, forms the entrepreneur. In fact, the creation of a sustainable enterprise involves three parallel, interactive phenomena: emergence of the opportunity, emergence of the venture, and emergence of the entrepreneur. None are predetermined or fixed—they define and are defined by one another.[17] Thus, this perspective on the entrepreneur has gained new momentum in the entrepreneurship research of the twenty-first century.

the entrepreneurial process

Exuding Passion in Your Venture

People are drawn to passion, so emphasizing the passion you have for your business is an effective method for getting people's attention. By being self-confident and articulating the value your business provides your clients, people will in turn share your enthusiasm and grow more comfortable maintaining their business relationship with you. Your customers will not believe in someone who does not believe in him- or herself, so be confident and outspoken about what you have to offer. The following steps will get you started:

1. **Be genuine in your excitement.** Do not put up a façade in an attempt to win customers. Keeping customers happy is hard enough without having to maintain a false image. People are more inclined to buy from businesses they trust, and the entrepreneurs associated with those businesses are instrumental in building their confidence. To start a business requires a tremendous amount of enthusiasm and energy; do not be afraid to let it show when you talk with potential customers. If people are excited about you, they are more willing to compromise when it comes time to do business.

2. **Redefine rejection as learning.** You can please some of the people all of the time and all of the people some of the time, but you cannot please all of the people all of the time. Remembering this truism is important when trying to win customers. Embracing rejection is a trait that all successful entrepreneurs eventually develop: You will learn much more from your failures than you will from your successes. When people are not receptive to what you have to say, tweak your message or find another group of people. Even the best ideas will have their naysayers, so listen to both positive and negative feedback, improve your message, and start again.

3. **Convey personal successes.** Do not hide your accomplishments. Starting a business is hard work—when your dedication pays off, let it be known. People like to believe that they are backing a winner, so talking about your victories is a sure way to get people to see you in that light. Also, remember that lessons learned are milestones; relaying your experiences and what you have gained from them demonstrates that you are wise enough to learn and grow so that you will not make the same mistakes twice.

4. **Empathize with others.** Empathizing with your customers lets them know that you understand their position and, more importantly that you are interested in helping them. Regardless of whether you are speaking with the CEO or her assistant, showing that you care about the other person's problems helps to build a rapport. Once your listeners grow comfortable, they will be more willing to share information that you could use to better cater to your industry's needs. Being creative and willing to customize your product to fit the needs of an organization will show the people involved how much their business means to you.

By taking these steps, you will convey not only your enthusiasm but also your ability to do what you promise. Do not be ashamed to be proud of your accomplishments and what you have to offer. If people believe in you, they will believe in your business, and if they believe in your business, they will most likely become a customer. Let that passion exude brightly!

Source: Adapted from Romanus Wolter, "Let It Shine," *Entrepreneur* (February 2008): 130-131.

This experiential view of the entrepreneur captures the emergent and temporal nature of entrepreneurship. It moves us past a more static "snapshot" approach and encourages consideration of a dynamic, socially situated process that involves numerous actors and events. It allows for the fact that the many activities addressed as a venture unfolds are experienced by different actors in different ways.[18] Moreover, it acknowledges that venture creation transcends rational thought processes to include emotions, impulses, and physiological responses as individuals react to a diverse, multifaceted, and imposing array of activities, events, and developments. This perspective is consistent with recent research interest in a situated view of entrepreneurial action.[19] However, we must be aware that this psychological aspect of entrepreneurship presents a dark side as well.

The Dark Side of Entrepreneurship

A great deal of literature is devoted to extolling the rewards, successes, and achievements of entrepreneurs. However, a dark side of entrepreneurship also exists, and its destructive source can be found within the energetic drive of successful entrepreneurs. In examining this dual-edged approach to the entrepreneurial personality, researcher Manfred Kets de Vries has acknowledged the existence of certain negative factors that may envelop entrepreneurs and dominate their behavior.[20] Although each of these factors possesses a positive aspect, it is important for entrepreneurs to understand their potential destructive side as well.

The Entrepreneur's Confrontation with Risk

Starting or buying a new business involves risk. The higher the rewards, the greater the risks entrepreneurs usually face. This is why entrepreneurs tend to evaluate risk very carefully.

In an attempt to describe the risk-taking activity of entrepreneurs, researchers developed a typology of entrepreneurial styles.[21] Figure 2.1 illustrates these classifications in terms of the financial risk endured when a new venture is undertaken. In this model, the financial risk is measured against the level of *profit motive* (the desire for monetary gain or return from the venture), coupled with the type of activity. Profit-seeking activity is associated with the strong desire to maximize profit, and activity seeking refers to other activities associated with entrepreneurship, such as independence or the work of the venture itself. The thrust of this theory argues that entrepreneurs vary with regard to the relationship between risk and

Figure 2.1   **Typology of Entrepreneurial Styles**

Level of Personal Financial Risk

		Low	High
	Low	Risk avoiding Activity seeking	Risk accepting Activity seeking
Level of Profit Motive			
	High	Risk avoiding Profit seeking	Risk accepting Profit seeking

Source: Thomas Monroy and Robert Folger, "A Typology of Entrepreneurial Styles: Beyond Economic Rationality," *Journal of Private Enterprise* IX, no. 2 (1993): 71.

financial return. This typology highlights the need to explore within economic theory the styles or entrepreneurial motivations that deviate from the styles most characteristic of the rational person.

"If different entrepreneurial styles exist, then not every person who founds a new business enterprise does so by seeking to minimize financial risk and maximize financial return. Models of organization formation would thus have to be adjusted for differences among those who form organizations."[22] Thus, not all entrepreneurs are driven solely by monetary gain, and the level of financial risk cannot be completely explained by profit opportunity. Entrepreneurial risk is a complex issue that requires far more than a simple economic risk-versus-return explanation.

It should be noted that "people who successfully innovate and start businesses come in all shapes and sizes. But they do have a few things others do not. In the deepest sense, they are willing to accept risk for what they believe in. They have the ability to cope with a professional life riddled by ambiguity, and a consistent lack of clarity. Most have a drive to put their imprint on whatever they are creating. And while unbridled ego can be a destructive thing, try to find an entrepreneur whose ego isn't wrapped up in the enterprise."[23]

Entrepreneurs face a number of different types of risk. These can be grouped into four basic areas: (1) financial risk, (2) career risk, (3) family and social risk, and (4) psychic risk. [24]

FINANCIAL RISK

In most new ventures, the individual puts a significant portion of his or her savings or other resources at stake, which creates a serious financial risk. This money or these resources will, in all likelihood, be lost if the venture fails. The entrepreneur also may be required to sign personally on company obligations that far exceed his or her personal net worth. The entrepreneur is thus exposed to personal bankruptcy. Many people are unwilling to risk their savings, house, property, and salary to start a new business.

CAREER RISK

A question frequently raised by would-be entrepreneurs is whether they will be able to find a job or go back to their old job should their venture fail. This career risk is a major concern to managers who have a secure organizational job with a high salary and a good benefit package.

FAMILY AND SOCIAL RISK

Starting a new venture requires much of the entrepreneur's energy and time, which can in turn create a family and social risk. Consequently, his or her other commitments may suffer. Entrepreneurs who are married, and especially those with children, expose their families to the risks of an incomplete family experience and the possibility of permanent emotional scars. In addition, old friends may vanish eventually because of missed get-togethers.

PSYCHIC RISK

The psychic risk may be the greatest risk to the well-being of the entrepreneur. Money can be replaced; a new house can be built; spouses, children, and friends usually can adapt. But some entrepreneurs who have suffered financial catastrophes have been unable to bounce back, at least not immediately. The psychological impact has proven to be too severe for them.

Stress and the Entrepreneur

Some of the most common entrepreneurial goals are independence, wealth, and work satisfaction. Research studies of entrepreneurs show that those who achieve these goals often pay a high price.[25] A majority of entrepreneurs surveyed had back problems, indigestion, insomnia, or headaches. To achieve their goals, however, these entrepreneurs were willing to tolerate these effects of stress. The rewards justified the costs.

What Is Entrepreneurial Stress?

In general, stress can be viewed as a function of discrepancies between a person's expectations and ability to meet demands, as well as discrepancies between the individual's expectations and personality. If a person is unable to fulfill role demands, stress occurs. When entrepreneurs' work demands and expectations exceed their abilities to perform as venture initiators, they are likely to experience stress. One researcher has pointed out how entrepreneurial roles and operating environments can lead to stress. Initiating and managing a business requires taking significant risk. As previously mentioned, these risks may be described as financial, career, family, social, or psychic. Entrepreneurs also must engage in constant communication activities—interacting with relevant external constituencies such as customers, suppliers, regulators, lawyers, and accountants—which can be stressful.

Lacking the depth of resources, entrepreneurs must bear the cost of their mistakes while playing a multitude of roles, such as salesperson, recruiter, spokesperson, and negotiator. These simultaneous demands can lead to role overload. Owning and operating a business requires a large commitment of time and energy, as noted previously, often at the expense of family and social activities. Finally, entrepreneurs often work alone or with a small number of employees and therefore lack the support from colleagues that may be available to managers in a large corporation.[26]

In addition to the roles and environment experienced by entrepreneurs, stress can result from a basic personality structure. Referred to as *type A* behavior, this personality structure describes people who are impatient, demanding, and overstrung. These individuals gravitate toward heavy workloads and find themselves completely immersed in their business demands. Some of the distinguishing characteristics associated with type A personalities are as follows:

- Chronic and severe sense of time urgency. For instance, type A people become particularly frustrated in traffic jams.
- Constant involvement in multiple projects subject to deadlines. Type A people take delight in the feeling of being swamped with work.
- Neglect of all aspects of life except work. These workaholics live to work rather than work to live.
- A tendency to take on excessive responsibility, combined with the feeling that "only I am capable of taking care of this matter."
- Explosiveness of speech and a tendency to speak faster than most people. Type A people are prone to ranting and swearing when upset. A widespread belief in the stress literature is that type A behavior is related to coronary heart disease and that stress is a contributor to heart disease.[27]

Thus, to better understand stress, entrepreneurs need to be aware of their particular personality as well as the roles and operating environments that differentiate their business pursuits.[28]

Sources of Stress

Researchers David P. Boyd and David E. Gumpert have identified four causes of entrepreneurial stress: (1) loneliness, (2) immersion in business, (3) people problems, and (4) the need to achieve.[29]

LONELINESS

Although entrepreneurs usually are surrounded by others—employees, customers, accountants, and lawyers—they often are isolated from people in whom they can confide. Long hours at work prevent them from seeking the comfort and counsel of friends and family members. Moreover, they tend not to participate in social activities unless they provide a business benefit. A sense of loneliness can set in because of the inner feelings of isolation.

IMMERSION IN BUSINESS

One of the ironies of entrepreneurship is that successful entrepreneurs make enough money to partake of a variety of leisure activities, but they often cannot take that exotic cruise, fishing trip, or skiing vacation because their business will not allow their absence. Most entrepreneurs are married to their business—immersion in business can mean they work long hours and have little time for civic organizations, recreation, or further education.

PEOPLE PROBLEMS

Entrepreneurs must depend on and work with partners, employees, customers, bankers, and professionals. Many experience frustration, disappointment, and aggravation in their experiences with these people. Successful entrepreneurs are to some extent perfectionists and know how they want things done; often they spend a lot of time trying to get lackadaisical employees to meet their strict performance standards. Frequently, because of irreconcilable conflict, partnerships are dissolved.

NEED TO ACHIEVE

Achievement brings satisfaction. During the Boyd and Gumpert study, however, it became clear that a fine line exists between attempting to achieve too much and failing to achieve enough. More often than not, the entrepreneur was trying to accomplish too much. Many are never satisfied with their work, no matter how well it is done. They seem to recognize the dangers (for example, to their health) of unbridled ambition, but they have a difficult time tempering their achievement need. They appear to believe that if they stop or slow down, some competitor is going to come from behind and destroy everything they have worked so hard to build.

Dealing with Stress

It is important to point out that not all stress is bad. Certainly, if stress becomes overbearing and unrelenting in a person's life, it wears down the body's physical abilities. However, if stress can be kept within constructive bounds, it can increase a person's efficiency and improve performance.

Researchers David P. Boyd and David E. Gumpert made a significant contribution to defining the causes of entrepreneurial stress, but what makes their study particularly noteworthy is the presentation of stress-reduction techniques—ways entrepreneurs can improve the quality of their business and personal lives.[30] Although classic stress-reduction techniques such as meditation, biofeedback, muscle relaxation, and regular exercise help reduce stress, Boyd and Gumpert suggest that another important step entrepreneurs can take is to clarify the causes of their stress. Having identified these causes, entrepreneurs then can combat excessive stress by (1) acknowledging its existence, (2) developing coping mechanisms, and (3) probing unacknowledged personal needs.

Following are six specific ways entrepreneurs can cope with stress.

NETWORKING

One way to relieve the loneliness of running a business is to share experiences by networking with other business owners. The objectivity gained from hearing about the triumphs and errors of others is itself therapeutic.

GETTING AWAY FROM IT ALL

The best antidote to immersion in business, report many entrepreneurs, is a holiday. If vacation days or weeks are limited by valid business constraints, short breaks still may be possible. Such interludes allow a measure of self-renewal.

COMMUNICATING WITH EMPLOYEES

Entrepreneurs are in close contact with employees and can readily assess the concerns of their staffs. The personal touches often unavailable in large corporations—such as company-wide outings, flexible hours, and small loans to tide workers over until payday—are possible here. In such settings, employees often are more productive than their counterparts in large organizations and may experience less stress due to the personal touches that are applied.

FINDING SATISFACTION OUTSIDE THE COMPANY

Countering the obsessive need to achieve can be difficult, because the entrepreneur's personality is inextricably woven into the company fabric. Entrepreneurs need to get away from the business occasionally and become more passionate about life itself; they need to gain some new perspectives.

DELEGATING

Implementation of coping mechanisms requires implementation time. To gain this time, the entrepreneur has to delegate tasks. Entrepreneurs often find delegation difficult, because they think they have to be at the business all of the time and be involved in every aspect of the operation. But if time is to be used for alleviation of stress, appropriate delegatees must be found and trained.

EXERCISING RIGOROUSLY

Researchers Michael G. Goldsby, Donald F. Kuratko, and James W. Bishop examined the relationship between exercise and the attainment of personal and professional goals for entrepreneurs.[31] The study addressed the issue by examining the exercise regimens of 366 entrepreneurs and the relationship of exercise frequency with both the company's sales and the entrepreneur's personal goals. Specifically, the study examined the relationship that two types of exercise—running and weightlifting—had with sales volume, extrinsic rewards, and intrinsic rewards. The results indicated that running is positively related to all three outcome variables, and weightlifting is positively related to extrinsic and intrinsic rewards. This study demonstrates the value of exercise regimens on relieving the stress associated with entrepreneurs.

The Entrepreneurial Ego

In addition to the challenges of risk and stress, the entrepreneur also may experience the negative effects of an inflated ego. In other words, certain characteristics that usually propel entrepreneurs into success also can be exhibited to their extreme. We examine four of these characteristics that may hold destructive implications for entrepreneurs.[32]

Overbearing Need for Control

Entrepreneurs are driven by a strong need to control both their venture and their destiny. This internal focus of control spills over into a preoccupation with controlling everything. An obsession with autonomy and control may cause entrepreneurs to work in structured situations *only* when they have created the structure on *their* terms. This, of course, has serious implications for networking in an entrepreneurial team, because entrepreneurs can visualize external control by others as a threat of subjection or infringement on their will. Thus, the same characteristic that entrepreneurs need for successful venture creation also contains a destructive side.

Sense of Distrust

To remain alert to competition, customers, and government regulations, entrepreneurs must continually scan the environment. They try to anticipate and act on developments that others might recognize too late. This distrustful state can result in their focusing on trivial things and cause them to lose sight of reality, distort reasoning and logic, and take destructive actions. Again, distrust is a dual-edged characteristic.

Overriding Desire for Success

The entrepreneur's ego is involved in the desire for success. Although many of today's entrepreneurs believe they are living on the edge of existence, constantly stirring within them is a strong desire to succeed in spite of the odds. Thus, the entrepreneur rises up as a defiant

the entrepreneurial process

Entrepreneurial Fear 101

The fear an entrepreneur experiences has its own taste, its own smell, and its own gut-wrenching pain—and it does not go away as long as the person remains an entrepreneur. It becomes an education: Entrepreneurial Fear 101. Although the course is very exclusive, admission is automatic; permission is neither needed nor sought, and tenure is indefinite. The fear that entrepreneurs experience cannot be anticipated, cannot be escaped, and cannot be prepared for. Because most entrepreneurs do not admit that they have experienced this entrepreneurial fear, it remains a deep, dark secret. Because it is not talked about, most entrepreneurs believe that they are the only ones who have ever experienced it.

According to Wilson Harrell, an entrepreneur from Jacksonville, Florida, entrepreneurial fear is much different from simple fear. Fear is usually accidental, unexpected, and short lived—such as the sudden rush of adrenaline experienced when you almost get hit by a bus, he explains. Entrepreneurial fear, on the other hand, is self-inflicted. It is a private world in which no sleep occurs, where nightmares filled with monsters constantly try to destroy every morsel of the entrepreneur's being.

What causes this fear? It is not the money—any entrepreneur will explain that money is simply a bonus of the accomplishment, and losing money is one of the risks taken. Fear of failure has a lot to do with it. Entrepreneurs do not want to become just another businessperson and pass into oblivion without leaving their mark. What induces this complex fear has yet to be determined.

For Harrell, the fear came when he started his own food brokerage business to sell products on military bases in Europe. Harrell was appointed a representative of Kraft Food Company and did so well increasing its sales that he sold himself out of a job. Because he had made his job look so easy, it was suggested to Kraft's management team that its own salespeople could do the work better and cheaper. So what did Harrell do? Because losing the Kraft account would put him out of business, he placed everything on the line and proposed that if Kraft kept brokering through his company and not take over the brokering in Germany, Harrell would help Kraft take over the food industry everywhere. While Harrell experienced 30 days of immeasurable terror, Kraft made the decision to trust Harrell and to continue brokering through his company. Although Harrell later sold his business, 30 years later the company still represents Kraft, Inc.—not only in Europe but also in the Far East and many other countries. The company has grown into the largest military-representative organization in the field and was sold in 1985 for more than $40 million.

What is the secret to entrepreneurship, given such fear? Reward. No matter what pain is experienced because of the fear, the elation of success surmounts it. That high, along with fear, is an emotion reserved for entrepreneurs and becomes food for the spirit. It is like a roller-coaster ride: In the beginning, imagine pulling yourself up the incline very slowly, making any tough decisions with a growing sense of excitement and foreboding. Then, when you hit the top, for a brief moment it is frightening, and the anticipation accelerates before you lose all feelings of control. As you go screaming into the unknown, fear takes over. At first, all you feel is fear; then, suddenly, the ride is over and the fear is gone, but the exhilaration remains. What is next for the entrepreneur? He or she buys another ticket.

So, what is the key ingredient for entrepreneurial success? According to Wilson Harrell, it is the ability to handle fear. He believes that the lonely entrepreneur, living with his or her personal fear, breathes life and excitement into an otherwise dull and mundane world.

Source: Adapted from Wilson Harrell, "Entrepreneurial Terror," *Inc.* (February 1987): 74–76.

person who creatively acts to deny any feelings of insignificance. The individual is driven to succeed and takes pride in demonstrating that success. Therein lie the seeds of possible destructiveness. If the entrepreneur seeks to demonstrate achievement through the erection of a monument—such as a huge office building, an imposing factory, or a plush office—the danger exists that the individual will become more important than the venture itself. A loss of perspective like this can, of course, be the destructive side of the desire to succeed.

Unrealistic Optimism

The ceaseless optimism that emanates from entrepreneurs (even through the bleak times) is a key factor in the drive toward success. Entrepreneurs maintain a high enthusiasm level that becomes an external optimism—which allows others to believe in them during rough periods. However, when taken to its extreme, this optimistic attitude can lead to a fantasy approach to the business. A self-deceptive state may arise in which entrepreneurs ignore trends, facts, and reports and delude themselves into thinking everything will turn out fine. This type of behavior can lead to an inability to handle the reality of the business world.

These examples do not imply that *all* entrepreneurs fall prey to these scenarios, nor that each of the characteristics presented always gives way to the "destructive" side. Nevertheless, all potential entrepreneurs need to know that the dark side of entrepreneurship exists.

Entrepreneurial Motivation

Examining why people start businesses and how they differ from those who do not (or from those who start unsuccessful businesses) may help explain how the motivation that entrepreneurs exhibit during start-up is linked to the sustaining behavior exhibited later. Lanny Herron and Harry J. Sapienza have stated, "Because motivation plays an important part in the creation of new organizations, theories of organization creation that fail to address this notion are incomplete."[33] One researcher—in his review of achievement motivation and the entrepreneur—said, "It remains worthwhile to carefully study the role of the individual, including his or her psychological profile. Individuals are, after all, the energizers of the entrepreneurial process."[34]

Thus, although research on the psychological characteristics of entrepreneurs has not provided an agreed-on "profile" of an entrepreneur, it is still important to recognize the contribution of psychological factors to the entrepreneurial process.[35] In fact, the quest for new-venture creation as well as the willingness to *sustain* that venture is directly related to an entrepreneur's motivation.[36] One research study examined the importance of satisfaction to an entrepreneur's willingness to remain with the venture. Particular goals, attitudes, and backgrounds were all important determinants of an entrepreneur's eventual satisfaction.[37] In that vein, one research approach examines the motivational process an entrepreneur experiences.[38] Figure 2.2 illustrates the key elements of this approach.

The decision to behave entrepreneurially is the result of the interaction of several factors. One set of factors includes the individual's personal characteristics, the individual's personal environment, the relevant business environment, the individual's personal goal set, and the existence of a viable business idea.[39] In addition, the individual compares his or her perception of the probable outcomes with the personal expectations he or she has in mind. Next, an individual looks at the relationship between the entrepreneurial behavior he or she would implement and the expected outcomes.

According to the model, the entrepreneur's expectations finally are compared with the actual or perceived firm outcomes. Future entrepreneurial behavior is based on the results of all of these comparisons. When outcomes meet or exceed expectations, the entrepreneurial behavior is positively reinforced, and the individual is motivated to continue to behave entrepreneurially—either within the current venture or possibly through the initiation of additional ventures, depending on the existing entrepreneurial goal. When outcomes fail to meet expectations, the entrepreneur's motivation will be lower and will have a corresponding impact on the decision to continue to act entrepreneurially. These perceptions also affect succeeding strategies, strategy implementation, and management of the firm.[40]

| *Figure* | **2.2** | **A Model of Entrepreneurial Motivation** |

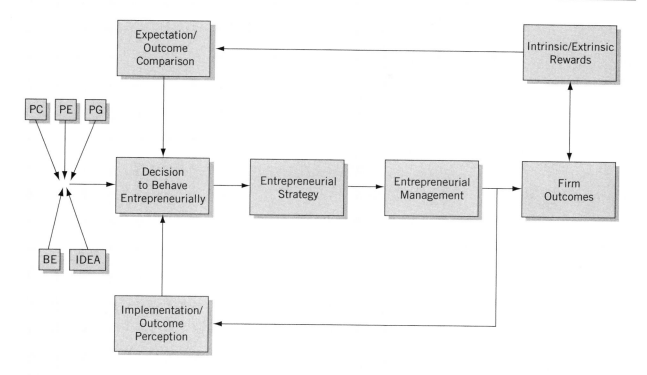

PC = **Personal Characteristics**
PE = **Personal Environment**
PG = **Personal Goals**
BE = **Business Environment**

Source: Douglas W. Naffziger, Jeffrey S. Hornsby, and Donald F. Kuratko, "A Proposed Research Model of Entrepreneurial Motivation," *Entrepreneurship Theory and Practice* (Spring 1994): 33.

Summary

In attempting to explain the entrepreneurial mind-set within individuals, this chapter presented the most common characteristics exhibited by successful entrepreneurs. Next, a review of the "dark side" of entrepreneurship revealed certain factors that possess a destructive vein for entrepreneurs. Finally, a motivational model of entrepreneurship was discussed.

First, it is important to recognize that a number of sources of information related to the entrepreneurial mind-set exist. Three major ones are publications, direct observation, and presentations by or case studies of practicing entrepreneurs.

Several studies have been conducted to determine the personal qualities and traits of successful entrepreneurs. Some of these characteristics were examined in the chapter: commitment, determination, and perseverance; drive to achieve; opportunity orientation; initiative and responsibility; persistent problem-solving; seeking feedback; internal locus of control; tolerance for ambiguity; calculated risk taking; integrity and reliability; tolerance for failure; high energy level; creativity and innovativeness; vision; self-confidence and optimism; independence; and team building.

The next part of the chapter focused on the dark side of entrepreneurship, including the confrontation with risk, the problems of stress, and the particular traits that may permeate the entrepreneurial ego.

Finally, the chapter introduced a model of entrepreneurial motivation. This model, which recognizes the contribution of psychological factors to the process of entrepreneurship, demonstrated the importance of entrepreneurs' perceived expectations and actual outcomes in their motivation to start and sustain a venture.

Key Terms and Concepts

calculated risk taker	external optimism	psychic risk
career risk	family and social risk	risk
dark side of entrepreneurship	financial risk	stress
delegating	immersion in business	tolerance for ambiguity
drive to achieve	loneliness	tolerance for failure
entrepreneurial behavior	need to control	vision
entrepreneurial mind-set	networking	
entrepreneur's motivation	opportunity orientation	

Review and Discussion Questions

1. Identify and describe the three major sources of information that supply data related to the entrepreneurial mind-set.
2. How do the following traits relate to entrepreneurs: desire to achieve, opportunity orientation, initiative, and responsibility?
3. Some of the characteristics attributed to entrepreneurs include persistent problem solving, continuous seeking of feedback, and internal locus of control. What does this statement mean? Be complete in your answer.
4. Entrepreneurs have a tolerance for ambiguity, are calculated risk takers, and have a high regard for integrity and reliability. What does this statement mean? Be complete in your answer.
5. Is it true that most successful entrepreneurs have failed at some point in their business careers? Explain.

6. In what way is "vision" important to an entrepreneur? Self-confidence? Independence?
7. Entrepreneurship has a "dark side." What is meant by this statement? Be complete in your answer.
8. What are the four specific areas of risk that entrepreneurs face? Describe each.
9. What are four causes of stress among entrepreneurs? How can an entrepreneur deal with each of them?
10. Describe the factors associated with the entrepreneurial ego.
11. What is the concept of entrepreneurial motivation?
12. How does the model depicted in the chapter illustrate an entrepreneur's motivation? Be specific.

Experiential Exercise

ARE YOU A HIGH ACHIEVER?

One of the most important characteristics of a successful entrepreneur is the desire to be a high achiever. The following ten questions are designed to help identify your achievement drive. Write the letter preceding your answer in the blank to the left of each question. Scoring information is provided at the end of the exercise.

1. _____ An instructor in one of your college classes has asked you to vote on three grading options: (*a*) Study the course material, take the exams, and receive the grade you earn; (*b*) roll a die and get an A if you roll an odd number and a D if you roll an even number; (*c*) show up for all class lectures, turn in a short term paper, and get a C. Which of these options would you choose?

2. _____ How would you describe yourself as a risk taker? (*a*) high, (*b*) moderate, (*c*) low.

3. _____ You have just been asked by your boss to take on a new project in addition to the many tasks you are already doing. What would you tell your boss? (*a*) Since I'm already snowed under, I can't handle any more. (*b*) Sure, I'm happy to help out; give it to me. (*c*) Let me look over my current workload and get back to you tomorrow about whether I can take on any more work.

4. _____ Which one of these people would you most like to be? (*a*) Steve Jobs, founder of Apple Computers, (*b*) Lee Iacocca of Chrysler fame, (*c*) Jack Welch, former CEO of General Electric.

5. _____ Which one of these games would you most like to play? (*a*) Monopoly, (*b*) bingo, (*c*) roulette.

6. _____ You have decided to become more physically active. Which one of these approaches has the greatest attraction for you? (*a*) join a neighborhood team, (*b*) work out on your own, (*c*) join a local health club.

7. _____ With which one of these groups would you most enjoy playing poker? (*a*) friends, (*b*) high-stake players, (*c*) individuals who can challenge you.

8. _____ Which one of these persons would you most like to be? (*a*) a detective solving a crime, (*b*) a politician giving a victory statement, (*c*) a millionaire sailing on his or her yacht.

9. _____ Which one of these activities would you prefer to do on an evening off? (*a*) visit a friend, (*b*) work on a hobby, (*c*) watch television.

10. _____ Which one of these occupations has the greatest career appeal for you? (*a*) computer salesperson, (*b*) corporate accountant, (*c*) criminal lawyer.

Scoring: Transfer each of your answers to the following scoring key by circling the appropriate number (for example, if your answer to question 1 is *c*, you will circle the number 2 in row 1). Then total all three columns to arrive at your final score.

	a	b	c
1.	10	0	2
2.	2	10	2
3.	6	2	10
4.	7	10	5
5.	10	0	0
6.	2	10	6
7.	4	2	10
8.	10	7	4
9.	4	10	4
10.	10	5	10
	_____ +	_____ +	_____ = _____

High achievers	76–100
Moderate achievers	50–75
Low achievers	Less than 50

Interpretation:

1. High achievers take personal responsibility for their actions. They do not like to rely on luck. The third option (*c*) assumes that the class time saved by not having to study for exams will be used to study for other classes; otherwise, the answer would be a zero.

2. High achievers are moderate risk takers in important situations.

3. High achievers like to study a situation before committing themselves to a course of action.

4. Jobs is a high-achieving individual but is more interested in design and engineering than in goal accomplishment; Iacocca is an extremely high-achieving salesperson/executive; Jack Welch is more driven by the need for power than the need to achieve.

5. Monopoly allows the high achiever to use his or her skills; bingo and roulette depend on luck.

6. The high achiever would work out on his or her own. The second-best choice is to join a health club, which allows less individual freedom but provides the chance to get feedback and guidance from individuals who understand how to work out effectively.

7. High achievers like challenges but not high risks. If you are a very good poker player and you chose (b), you can raise your score on this question from 2 to 10.

8. Because high achievers like to accomplish goals, the detective would have the greatest appeal for them. The politician is more interested in power, and the millionaire is simply enjoying him- or herself.

9. High achievers like to do constructive things that help them improve themselves, so working on a hobby would be their first choice.

10. The computer salesperson and the criminal lawyer have a much higher need to achieve than does the corporate accountant.

Case 2.1

JANE'S EVALUATION

Paul Medwick is a commercial banker. In the past month, he has received loan applications from three entrepreneurs. All three have fledgling businesses with strong potential. However, Paul believes it is important to look at more than just the business itself; the individual also needs close scrutiny.

The three entrepreneurs are (1) Robin Wood, owner of a small delicatessen located in the heart of a thriving business district; (2) Richard Trumpe, owner of a ten-minute oil-change-and-lube operation; and (3) Phil Hartack, owner of a bookstore that specializes in best sellers and cookbooks. Paul has had the bank's outside consultant, Professor Jane Jackson, interview each of the three entrepreneurs. Jane has done a lot of work with entrepreneurs and—after a couple hours of discussion—usually can evaluate a person's entrepreneurial qualities. In the past, Jane has recommended 87 people for loans, and only two of these ventures have failed. This success rate is much higher than that for commercial loans in general. Following is Jane's evaluation of the three people she interviewed.

Characteristic	Robin Wood	Richard Trumpe	Phil Hartack
Perseverance	H	M	M
Drive to achieve	M	H	M
Initiative	M	H	M
Persistent problem-solving	M	M	H
Tolerance for ambiguity	L	M	H
Integrity and reliability	H	M	H
Tolerance for failure	H	H	H
Creativity and innovativeness	M	H	M
Self-confidence	H	H	H
Independence	H	H	H

H = High;   M = Medium;   L = Low.

QUESTIONS

1. Which of the three applicants do you think comes closest to having the mind-set of an ideal entrepreneur? Why?

2. To which applicant would you recommend that the bank lend money? (Assume that each has asked for a loan of $50,000.) Defend your answer.

3. Can these three entrepreneurs do anything to improve their entrepreneurial profile and their chances for success? Be specific in your answer.

Case 2.2

TO STAY OR TO GO?

Mary Gunther has been a sales representative for a large computer firm for seven years. She took the job following her graduation from a large university, where she majored in computer science. Recently, Mary has been thinking about leaving the company and starting her own business. Her knowledge of the computer field would put her in an ideal position to be a computer consultant.

Mary understands computer hardware and software, is knowledgeable about the strong and weak points of all the latest market offerings, and has a solid understanding of how to implement a computer system throughout an organization. Mary believes that many medium-sized firms around the country would like to introduce computer technology but do not know how to do so. The large manufacturers, such as the one for which she works, are more interested in selling hardware than in helping their clients develop a fully integrated, company-wide computer system. Small consulting firms have to be brought in to do this. Mary feels that, as a consultant, she not only would be able to evaluate a computer's effectiveness, she also would know how to set up the machines to provide maximum benefit to the company.

Mary estimates that, if she were to leave the computer firm tomorrow, she could line up ten clients immediately. This would provide her with sufficient income for six months. She is sure that—during this period—she would have little difficulty getting more clients. Six of these ten firms are located on the East Coast, two of them are in the Midwest, and the remaining two are in California. Mary estimates that it would take about two weeks to install a system and have it working, and it would probably take another two days to correct any problems that occur later. These problems would be handled during a follow-up visit, usually 10 to 14 days after the initial installation and setup.

The idea of starting her own venture appeals to Mary. However, she is not sure she wants to leave her job and assume all of the responsibilities associated with running her own operation. Before going any further, she has decided to evaluate her own abilities and desires to determine whether this is the right career move for her.

QUESTIONS

1. Identify three major characteristics that Mary should have if she hopes to succeed in this new venture. Defend your choices.

2. How can Figure 2.1 help Mary decide if she is sufficiently entrepreneurial to succeed in this new venture? Which quadrant would she have to be in to succeed?

Notes

1. Bruce Tulgan, "Generation X: The Future Is Now," *Entrepreneur of the Year Magazine* (Fall 1999): 42; and Brian Dumaine and Elaine Pofeldt, "Best Colleges for Aspiring Entrepreneurs," *Fortune Small Business* (September 2007): 61–75.

2. See, for example, William D. Bygrave and Charles W. Hofer, "Theorizing about Entrepreneurship," *Entrepreneurship Theory and Practice* (Winter 1991): 12–22; Ivan Bull and Gary E. Willard, "Towards a Theory of Entrepreneurship," *Journal of Business*

Venturing 8 (May 1993): 183–96; William B. Gartner, "Is There an Elephant in Entrepreneurship? Blind Assumptions in Theory Development," *Entrepreneurship Theory and Practice* 25, no. 4 (2001): 27–39; and Jeffery S. McMullen and Dean A. Shepherd, "Entrepreneurial Action and the Role of Uncertainty in the Theory of the Entrepreneur," *Academy of Management Review* 31, no. 1 (2006): 132–52.

3. See Robert A. Baron, "Cognitive Mechanisms in Entrepreneurship: Why and When Entrepreneurs Think Differently Than Other People," *Journal of Business Venturing* (April 1998): 275–94; and Norris F. Krueger, "What Lies Beneath: The Experiential Essence of Entrepreneurial Thinking," *Entrepreneurship Theory and Practice* 31, no. 1 (2007): 123–38.

4. Melissa S. Cardon, Charlene Zietsma, Patrick Saparito, Brett P. Matherne, and Carolyn Davis, "A Tale of Passion, New Insights into Entrepreneurship from a Parenthood Metaphor," *Journal of Business Venturing* 20, no. 1 (January 2005): 23–45.

5. Jeffry A. Timmons and Stephen Spinelli, *New Venture Creation* (New York: McGraw-Hill/Irwin, 2007); Donald F. Kuratko and Jeffrey S. Hornsby, *New Venture Management* (Upper Saddle River, N. J.: Pearson/Prentice Hall, 2009); Robert D. Hisrich, Michael P. Peters, and Dean A. Shepherd, *Entrepreneurship* (New York: McGraw-Hill/Irwin, 2008); and Michael H. Morris, Donald F. Kuratko, and Jeffrey G. Covin, *Corporate Entrepreneurship and Innovation* (Mason, OH: South-Western/Cengage Learning, 2008).

6. William J. Stolze, *Startup: An Entrepreneur's Guide to Launching and Managing a New Venture* (Hawthorne, NJ: Career Press, 1992); Ronald W. Torrence, *In the Owner's Chair* (Englewood Cliffs, NJ: Prentice Hall, 1992); Minet Schindehutte and Michael H. Morris, *Rethinking Marketing: The Entrepreneurial Imperative* (Upper Saddle River, N. J.: Pearson/Prentice Hall, 2009); Kevin and Jackie Freiberg, *Nuts: Southwest Airlines' Crazy Recipe for Business and Personal Success* (New York: Broadway Books, 1997); and Keith R. McFarland, *The Breakthrough Company* (New York: Crown, 2008).

7. Bill Gates, *Business at the Speed of Thought* (New York: Time Warner, 1999); and Thaddeus Wawro, *Radicals and Visionaries: The True Life Stories Behind the Entrepreneurs Who Revolutionized the 20th Century* (Irvine, CA: Entrepreneur Media, 2000).

8. Robert L. Shook, *The Entrepreneurs* (New York: Harper & Row, 1980); see also Robert Sobel, *The Entrepreneurs: Explorations within the American Business Tradition* (New York: Weybright and Talley, 1974).

9. John Chamberlin, *The Enterprising Americans: A Business History of the United States* (New York: Harper & Row, 1963).

10. Teresa Esser, *The Venture Café* (New York: Warner Books, 2002).

11. Howard H. Stevenson and David E. Gumpert, "The Heart of Entrepreneurship," *Harvard Business Review* (March/April 1985): 85–94.

12. See William B. Gartner, "Some Suggestions for Research on Entrepreneurial Traits and Characteristics," *Entrepreneurship Theory and Practice* (Fall 1989): 27–38.

13. Lloyd E. Shefsky, *Entrepreneurs Are Made Not Born* (New York: McGraw-Hill, Inc., 1994).

14. Robert J. Sternberg, "Successful Intelligence as a Basis for Entrepreneurship," *Journal of Business Venturing* 19, no. 2 (March 2004): 189–201; Robert A. Baron, "The Cognitive Perspective: A Valuable Tool for Answering Entrepreneurship's Basic 'Why' Questions," *Journal of Business Venturing* 19, no. 2 (March 2004): 221–39; Ronald K. Mitchell, Lowell Busenitz, Theresa Lant, Patricia P. McDougall, Eric A. Morse, and J. Brock Smith, "The Distinctive and Inclusive Domain of Entrepreneurial Cognition Research," *Entrepreneurship Theory and Practice* 28, no. 6 (Winter 2004): 505–18; and Robert A. Baron and Thomas B. Ward, "Expanding Entrepreneurial Cognition's Toolbox: Potential Contributions from the Field of Cognitive Science," *Entrepreneurship Theory and Practice* 28, no. 6 (Winter 2004): 553–74.

15. David C. McClelland, *The Achieving Society* (New York: Van Nostrand, 1961); and "Business Drive and National Achievement," *Harvard Business Review* (July/August 1962): 99–112.

16. For some articles on entrepreneurial characteristics, see Rita Gunther McGrath, Ian C. MacMillan, and Sari Scheinberg, "Elitists, Risk Takers, and Rugged Individualists? An Exploratory Analysis of Cultural Differences between Entrepreneurs and Non-Entrepreneurs," *Journal of Business Venturing* (March 1992): 115–36; Jill Kickul and Lisa K. Gundry, "Prospecting for Strategic Advantage: The Proactive Entrepreneurial Personality and Small Firm Innovation," *Journal of Small Business Management* 40, no. 2 (2002): 85–97; Moren Levesque and Maria Minniti, "The Effect of Aging in the Dynamics of New Venture Creation," *Journal of Business Venturing*, 21, no. 2 (2006): 177–94; and Keith H. Brigham, Julio O. DeCastro, and Dean A. Shepherd, "A Person-Organization Fit Model of Owners-Managers' Cognitive Style and Organization Demands," *Entrepreneurship Theory and Practice* 31, no. 1 (2007): 29–51.

17. Minet Schindehutte, Michael H. Morris, and Donald F. Kuratko, "Framing Entrepreneurial Experience: The Journey as the Destination" (working manuscript, June 2008).

18. Diamanto Politis, "The Process of Entrepreneurial Learning: A Conceptual Framework," *Entrepreneurship Theory and Practice*, 29, no. 4 (2005): 399–424.

19. Per Davidsson, "A General Theory of Entrepreneurship: The Individual-Opportunity Nexus," *International Small Business Journal*, 22, no. 2 (2004): 206–19; and Henrik Berglund, "Entrepreneurship and Phenomenology: Researching Entrepreneurship as Lived Experience," in *Handbook of Qualitative Research Methods in Entrepreneurship*, ed. John Ulhoi and Helle Neergaard (London: Edward Elgar, 2007), 75–96.

20. Manfred F. R. Kets de Vries, "The Dark Side of Entrepreneurship," *Harvard Business Review* (November/December 1985): 160–67; see also Shaker A. Zahra, R. Isil Yavuz, and Deniz Ucbascaran, "How Much Do You Trust Me? The Dark Side of Relational Trust in New Business Creation in Established Companies," *Entrepreneurship Theory and Practice,* 30, no. 2 (2006): 541–59.

21. Thomas Monroy and Robert Folger, "A Typology of Entrepreneurial Styles: Beyond Economic Rationality," *Journal of Private Enterprise* IX, no. 2 (1993): 64–79.

22. Ibid., 75–76.

23. Michael O'Neal, "Just What Is an Entrepreneur?" special enterprise issue, *Business Week* (1993): 104–12.

24. Patrick R. Liles, *New Business Ventures and the Entrepreneur* (Homewood, IL: Irwin, 1974), 14–15; see also Jay J. Janney and Gregory G. Dess, "The Risk Concept for Entrepreneurs Reconsidered: New Challenges to the Conventional Wisdom," *Journal of Business Venturing,* 21, no. 3 (2006): 385–400.

25. Adebowale Akande, "Coping with Entrepreneurial Stress," *Leadership & Organization Development Journal* 13, no. 2 (1992): 27–32; and E. Holly Buttner, "Entrepreneurial Stress: Is It Hazardous to Your Health?" *Journal of Managerial Issues* (Summer 1992): 223–40.

26. Buttner, "Entrepreneurial Stress"; see also M. Afzalur Rabin, "Stress, Strain, and Their Moderators: An Empirical Comparison of Entrepreneurs and Managers," *Journal of Small Business Management* (January 1996): 46–58.

27. See K. A. Mathews and S. C. Haynes, "Type A Behavior Pattern and Coronary Disease Risk," *American Journal of Epistemology* 123 (1986): 923–60.

28. Akande, "Coping with Entrepreneurial Stress."

29. David P. Boyd and David E. Gumpert, "Coping with Entrepreneurial Stress," *Harvard Business Review* (March/April 1983): 46–56.

30. Boyd and Gumpert, "Coping with Entrepreneurial Stress."

31. Michael G. Goldsby, Donald F. Kuratko, and James W. Bishop, "Entrepreneurship and Fitness: An Examination of Rigorous Exercise and Goal Attainment among Small Business Owners," *Journal*

of Small Business Management, 43, no. 1 (January 2005): 78–92; see also Moren Levesque and Maria Minniti, "The Effect of Aging on Entrepreneurial Behavior," *Journal of Business Venturing,* 21, no. 2 (2006): 177–94.

32. Kets de Vries, "The Dark Side of Entrepreneurship."

33. Lanny Herron and Harry J. Sapienza, "The Entrepreneur and the Initiation of New Venture Launch Activities," *Entrepreneurship Theory and Practice* (Fall 1992): 49–55.

34. Bradley R. Johnson, "Toward a Multidimensional Model of Entrepreneurship: The Case of Achievement Motivation and the Entrepreneur," *Entrepreneurship Theory and Practice* (Spring 1990): 39–54; see also Wayne H. Stewart and Philip L. Roth, "A Meta-Analysis of Achievement Motivation Differences between Entrepreneurs and Managers" Journal of Small Business Management (October, 2007) 45(4): 401-421.

35. See Kelly G. Shaver and Linda R. Scott, "Person, Process, Choice: The Psychology of New Venture Creation," *Entrepreneurship Theory and Practice* (Winter 1991): 23–45.

36. Don E. Bradley and James A. Roberts, "Self-Employment and Job Satisfaction: Investigating and Role of Self-Efficacy, Depression, and Seniority," *Journal of Small Business Management* 42, no. 1 (January 2004): 37–58; see also J. Robert Baum, J. and Edwin A. Locke, "The Relationship of Entrepreneurial Traits, Skill, and Motivation to Subsequent Venture Growth," *Journal of Applied Psychology* 89, no. 4 (2004): 587–98.

37. Arnold C. Cooper and Kendall W. Artz, "Determinants of Satisfaction for Entrepreneurs," *Journal of Business Venturing* (November 1995): 439–58.

38. Douglas W. Naffziger, Jeffrey S. Hornsby, and Donald F. Kuratko, "A Proposed Research Model of Entrepreneurial Motivation," *Entrepreneurship Theory and Practice* (Spring 1994): 29–42.

39. A. Rebecca Reuber and Eileen Fischer, "Understanding the Consequences of Founders' Experience," *Journal of Small Business Management* (February 1999): 30–45.

40. Donald F. Kuratko, Jeffrey S. Hornsby, and Douglas W. Naffziger, "An Examination of Owner's Goals in Sustaining Entrepreneurship," *Journal of Small Business Management* (January 1997): 24–33.

CHAPTER 3

Corporate Entrepreneurial Mind-Set

Entrepreneurial Thought

There is nothing more difficult to take in hand, more perilous to conduct, than to take a lead in the introduction of a new order of things, because the innovation has for enemies all those who have done well under the old conditions and lukewarm defenders in those who may do well under the new.

— **MACHIAVELLI** *The Prince*

Chapter Objectives

1 To understand the entrepreneurial mind-set in organizations

2 To illustrate the need for entrepreneurial thinking in organizations

3 To define the term *corporate entrepreneurship*

4 To describe the corporate obstacles that prevent innovation within corporations

5 To highlight the considerations involved in reengineering corporate thinking

6 To describe the specific elements of a corporate entrepreneurial strategy

7 To examine the methods of developing managers for corporate entrepreneurship

8 To illustrate the interactive process of corporate entrepreneurship

The Entrepreneurial Mind-Set in Organizations

The global economy is creating profound and substantial changes for organizations and industries throughout the world. These changes make it necessary for business firms to carefully examine their purpose and to devote a great deal of attention to selecting and following strategies that have a high probability of satisfying multiple stakeholders. In response to rapid, discontinuous, and significant changes in their external and internal environments, many established companies have restructured their operations in fundamental and meaningful ways. In fact, after years of restructuring, some of these companies bear little resemblance to their ancestors in business scope, culture, or competitive approach.[1]

The new century is seeing corporate strategies that are focused heavily on innovation. This new emphasis on entrepreneurial thinking developed during the **entrepreneurial economy** of the last two decades.[2] Peter Drucker, the renowned management expert, described four major developments that explain the emergence of this economy. First, the rapid evolution of knowledge and technology promoted the use of high-tech entrepreneurial start-ups. Second, demographic trends such as two-wage-earner families, continuing education of adults, and the aging population added fuel to the proliferation of newly developing ventures. Third, the venture capital market became an effective funding mechanism for entrepreneurial ventures. Fourth, American industry began to learn how to manage entrepreneurship.[3]

The contemporary thrust of entrepreneurship as the major force in American business has led to a desire for this type of activity *inside* enterprises. Although some earlier researchers concluded that entrepreneurship and bureaucracies were mutually exclusive and could not coexist,[4] today we find many researchers examining entrepreneurial ventures within the enterprise framework.[5] Successful corporate venturing has been used in many different companies, including 3M, AT&T, General Electric, Wellpoint, and Abbott Laboratories.[6] A wealth of popular business literature describes a new "corporate revolution" taking place, thanks to the infusion of entrepreneurial thinking into large bureaucratic structures.[7] This infusion is referred to as **corporate entrepreneurship**,[8] or **intrapreneurship**.[9] Why has this concept become so popular? One reason is that it allows corporations to tap the innovative talents of their own workers and managers. Steven Brandt puts it this way:

> The challenge is relatively straightforward. The United States must upgrade its innovative prowess. To do so, U.S. companies must tap into the creative power of their members. Ideas come from people. Innovation is a capability of the many. That capability is utilized when people give commitment to the mission and life of the enterprise and have the power to do something with their capabilities. Noncommitment is the price of obsolete managing practices, not the lack of talent or desire.[10]

Continuous innovation (in terms of products, processes, and administrative routines and structures) and an ability to compete effectively in the global markets are among the skills that increasingly are expected to influence corporate performance in this twenty-first century. Today's executives agree that innovation is the most important pathway for companies to accelerate their pace of change in the global environment. Corporate entrepreneurship (CE) is envisioned as a process that can facilitate firms' efforts to innovate constantly and cope effectively with the competitive realities that companies encounter when competing in world markets. Leading strategic thinkers are moving beyond the traditional product and service innovations to pioneering innovation in processes, value chains, business models, and all functions of management. Thus, entrepreneurial attitudes and behaviors are necessary for firms of all sizes to prosper and flourish in competitive environments.[11]

Reengineering Organizational Thinking

To establish an entrepreneurial mind-set, organizations need to provide the freedom and encouragement required for employees to develop their ideas.[12] This is often a problem in enterprises, because many top managers do not believe that entrepreneurial ideas can be nurtured and developed in their environment. They also find it difficult to implement policies that encourage freedom and unstructured activity. But managers need to develop policies that will help innovative people reach their full potential. Five important steps for establishing this new thinking follow:

1. Set *explicit innovation goals.* These goals need to be mutually agreed on by the employee and management so that specific steps can be achieved.

2. Create a system of *feedback* and *positive reinforcement.* This is necessary for potential innovators or creators of ideas to realize that acceptance and reward exist.

3. Emphasize *individual responsibility.* Confidence, trust, and accountability are key features in the success of any innovative program.

4. Provide *rewards* for innovative ideas. Reward systems should enhance and encourage others to risk and to achieve.

5. *Do not punish failures.* Real learning takes place when failed projects are examined closely for what can be learned by individuals. In addition, individuals must feel free to experiment without fear of punishment.

Although each enterprise must develop a philosophy most appropriate for its own entrepreneurial process, a number of key questions can assist in establishing the type of process an organization has. Organizations can use the following questions to assess their enterprise. Applying these questions helps them feed back to the planning process for a proper approach.

- *Does your company encourage entrepreneurial thinking?* Will individuals receive the corporation's blessing for their self-appointed idea creations? Some corporations foolishly try to appoint people to carry out an innovation when, in fact, the ideas must surface on their own.

- *Does your company provide ways for innovators to stay with their ideas?* When the innovation process involves switching the people working on an idea—that is, handing off a developing business or product from a committed innovator to whoever is next in line—that person often is not as committed as the originator of the project.

- *Are people in your company permitted to do the job in their own way, or are they constantly stopping to explain their actions and ask for permission?* Some organizations push decisions up through a multilevel approval process so that the doers and the deciders never even meet.

- *Has your company evolved quick and informal ways to access the resources to try new ideas?* Innovators usually need discretionary resources to explore and develop new ideas. Some companies give employees the freedom to use a percentage of their time on projects of their own choosing and set aside funds to explore new ideas when they occur. Others control resources so tightly that nothing is available for the new and unexpected—the result is nothing new.

- *Has your company developed ways to manage many small and experimental innovations?* Today's corporate cultures favor a few well-studied, well-planned attempts to hit a home run. In fact, nobody bats 1,000; it is better to make more frequent attempts, with less careful and expensive preparation for each.

- *Is your system set up to encourage risk taking and to tolerate mistakes?* Innovation cannot be achieved without risk and mistakes. Even successful innovation generally begins with blunders and false starts.

- *Are people in your company more concerned with new ideas or with defending their turf?* Because new ideas almost always cross the boundaries of existing patterns of organization, a jealous tendency to "turf protection" blocks innovation.

- *How easy is it to form functionally complete, autonomous teams in your corporate environment?* Small teams with full responsibility for developing an innovation solve many of the basic problems, yet some companies resist their formation.[13]

Another way to create an innovative corporate atmosphere is to apply rules for innovation. The rules in Table 3.1 can provide hands-on guidelines for developing the necessary innovative philosophy.

When these rules are followed, they create an environment conducive to and supportive of potential entrepreneurial thinking. The result is a corporate philosophy that supports innovative behavior.

Table 3.1	Rules for an Innovative Environment

1. Encourage action.

2. Use informal meetings whenever possible.

3. Tolerate failure, and use it as a learning experience.

4. Persist in getting an idea to market.

5. Reward innovation for innovation's sake.

6. Plan the physical layout of the enterprise to encourage informal communication.

7. Expect clever *bootlegging* of ideas—secretly working on new ideas on company time as well as on personal time.

8. Put people on small teams for future-oriented projects.

9. Encourage personnel to circumvent rigid procedures and bureaucratic red tape.

10. Reward and promote innovative personnel.

What can a corporation do to reengineer its thinking to foster the entrepreneurial process? The organization needs to examine and revise its management philosophy. Many enterprises have obsolete ideas about cooperative cultures, management techniques, and the values of managers and employees. Unfortunately, doing old tasks more efficiently is not the answer to new challenges; a new culture with new values has to be developed.[14] Bureaucrats and controllers must learn to coexist with—or give way to—the designer and innovator. Unfortunately, this is easier said than done. Organizations can, however, use the following methods to help restructure corporate thinking and encourage an entrepreneurial environment: (1) early identification of potential innovators, (2) top management sponsorship of innovative projects, (3) creation of innovation goals in strategic activities, (4) promotion of entrepreneurial thinking through experimentation, and (5) development of collaboration between innovators and the organization at large.[15]

Developing a corporate entrepreneurial philosophy provides a number of advantages. One is that this type of atmosphere often leads to the development of new products and services, and it helps the organization expand and grow. Second, it creates a workforce that can help the enterprise maintain its competitive posture. A third advantage is that it promotes a climate conducive to high achievers and helps the enterprise motivate and keep its best people.

The Nature of Corporate Entrepreneurship

In recent years, the subject of corporate entrepreneurship/innovation has become quite popular, though very few people thoroughly understand the concept. Most researchers agree that the term refers to entrepreneurial activities that receive organizational sanction and resource commitments for the purpose of innovative results.[16] The major thrust of corporate innovation is to develop the entrepreneurial spirit within organizational boundaries, thus allowing an atmosphere of innovation to prosper.

Defining the Concept

Operational definitions of corporate entrepreneurship have evolved over the last 30 years through scholars' work. For example, one researcher noted that corporate innovation is a very broad concept that includes the generation, development, and implementation of new ideas or behaviors. An innovation can be a new product or service, an administrative system, or a new plan or program that pertains to organizational members.[17] In this context, corporate entrepreneurship centers on reenergizing and enhancing the firm's ability to acquire innovative skills and capabilities.

Researcher Shaker A. Zahra observed that "corporate entrepreneurship may be formal or informal activities aimed at creating new businesses in established companies through product and process innovations and market developments. These activities may take place at the corporate, division (business), functional, or project levels, with the unifying objective of improving a company's competitive position and financial performance."[18] William D. Guth and Ari Ginsberg have stressed that corporate entrepreneurship encompasses two major phenomena: new venture creation within existing organizations and the transformation of organizations through strategic renewal.[19]

Researchers Michael H. Morris, Donald F. Kuratko, and Jeffrey G. Covin have cited two empirical phenomena as constituting the domain of corporate entrepreneurship—namely, corporate venturing and strategic entrepreneurship. Corporate venturing approaches have as their commonality the adding of new businesses (or portions of new businesses via equity investments) to the corporation. This can be accomplished through three implementation modes: internal corporate venturing, cooperative corporate venturing, and external corporate venturing. By contrast, strategic entrepreneurship approaches have as their commonality the exhibition of large-scale or otherwise highly consequential innovations that are adopted in the firm's pursuit of competitive advantage. These innovations may or may not result in new businesses for the corporation. With strategic entrepreneurship approaches, innovation can be in any of five areas: the firm's strategy, product offerings, served markets, internal organization (i.e., structure, processes, and capabilities), or business model.[20] Each of these categories of corporate entrepreneurship is outlined in Figure 3.1.

After a thorough analysis of the entrepreneurship construct and its dimensions, recent research has defined corporate entrepreneurship as a process whereby an individual (or a group of individuals), in association with an existing organization, creates a new organization or instigates renewal or innovation within the organization. Under this definition, strategic renewal (which is concerned with organizational renewal involving major strategic and/or structural changes), innovation (which is concerned with introducing something new to the marketplace), and corporate venturing (corporate entrepreneurial efforts that lead to the creation of new business organizations within the corporate organization) are all important and legitimate parts of the corporate entrepreneurship process.[21]

As the field has further evolved, the concept of a corporate entrepreneurship strategy has developed. Researchers R. Duane Ireland, Jeffrey G. Covin, and Donald F. Kuratko define a corporate entrepreneurial strategy as "a vision-directed, organization-wide reliance on

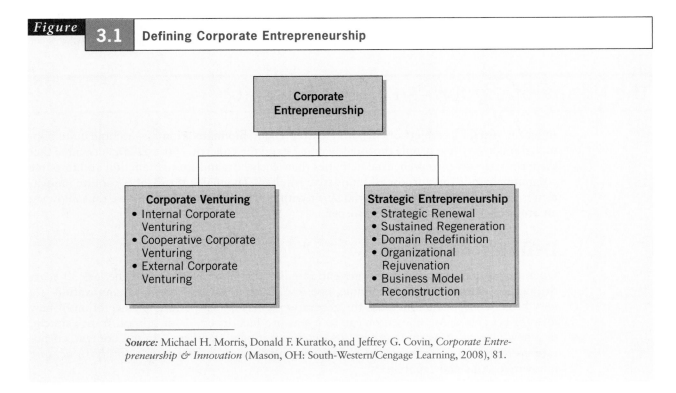

Figure 3.1 Defining Corporate Entrepreneurship

Source: Michael H. Morris, Donald F. Kuratko, and Jeffrey G. Covin, *Corporate Entrepreneurship & Innovation* (Mason, OH: South-Western/Cengage Learning, 2008), 81.

entrepreneurial behavior that purposefully and continuously rejuvenates the organization and shapes the scope of its operations through the recognition and exploitation of entrepreneurial opportunity."[22]

The Need for Corporate Entrepreneuring

Many companies today are recognizing the need for corporate entrepreneuring. Articles in popular business magazines (*Business Week, Fortune, U.S. News & World Report*) report the infusion of entrepreneurial thinking into large bureaucratic structures. In fact, in many of today's popular business books, entire sections are devoted to innovation within the corporation.[23] Quite obviously, both business firms and consultants/authors are recognizing the need for in-house entrepreneurship.

This need has arisen in response to a number of pressing problems, including rapid growth in the number of new and sophisticated competitors, a sense of distrust in the traditional methods of corporate management, an exodus of some of the best and brightest people from corporations to become small-business entrepreneurs, international competition, downsizing of major corporations, and an overall desire to improve efficiency and productivity.[24]

The first of these issues, the problem of competition, has always plagued businesses. However, today's high-tech economy supports a far greater number of competitors than ever before. In contrast to previous decades, changes, innovations, and improvements are now very common in the marketplace. Thus, corporations must either innovate or become obsolete.

Another of these problems, losing the brightest people to independent entrepreneurship, is escalating as a result of two major developments. First, entrepreneurship is on the rise in terms of status, publicity, and economic development. This enhancement of entrepreneurship has made the choice more appealing to both young and seasoned employees. Second, in recent years venture capital has grown into a large industry capable of financing more new ventures than ever before. More significantly, as we will see in greater detail in Chapter 8, "angel investors" have emerged in unprecedented strength, which has created a new opportunity for capital funding. These healthy capital funding markets have enabled new entrepreneurs to launch their ideas. As a result, people with innovative ideas are more likely to leave large corporations and strike out on their own.

The modern organization, then, is forced into seeking avenues to develop in-house entrepreneuring. To do otherwise is to wait for stagnation, loss of personnel, and decline. This new "corporate revolution" represents an appreciation for and a desire to develop innovators within the corporate structure.

Corporate Venturing Obstacles

It should be noted that many obstacles exist for the corporate entrepreneurship process. The obstacles to corporate entrepreneuring usually reflect the ineffectiveness of traditional management techniques as applied to innovation development. Although it is unintentional, the adverse impact of a particular traditional management technique can be so destructive that the individuals within an enterprise will tend to avoid corporate entrepreneurial behavior. Table 3.2 provides a list of traditional management techniques, their adverse effects (when the technique is rigidly enforced), and the recommended actions to change or adjust the practice.

Understanding these obstacles is critical to fostering corporate entrepreneurship, because they are the foundation points for all other motivational efforts. To gain support and foster excitement for innovation development, managers must remove the perceived obstacles and seek alternative management actions.[25]

After recognizing the obstacles, managers need to adapt to the principles of successful innovative companies. James Brian Quinn, an expert in the innovation field, found the following factors in large corporations who have exhibited successful innovations:

- *Atmosphere and vision.* Innovative companies have a clear-cut vision of—and the recognized support for—an innovative atmosphere.
- *Orientation to the market.* Innovative companies tie their visions to the realities of the marketplace.

Table 3.2	Sources of and Solutions to Obstacles in Corporate Venturing

Traditional Management Practices	Adverse Effects	Recommended Actions
Enforce standard procedures to avoid mistakes	Innovative solutions blocked, funds misspent	Make ground rules specific to each situation
Manage resources for efficiency and return on investment (ROI)	Competitive lead lost, low market penetration	Focus effort on critical issues (e.g., market share)
Control against plan	Facts ignored that should replace assumptions	Change plan to reflect new learning
Plan for the long term	Nonviable goals locked in, high failure costs	Envision a goal, then set interim milestones, reassess after each
Manage functionally	Entrepreneur failure and/or venture failure	Support entrepreneur with managerial and multidiscipline skills
Avoid moves that risk the base business	Missed opportunities	Take small steps, build out from strengths
Protect the base business at all costs	Venturing dumped when base business is threatened	Make venturing mainstream, take affordable risks
Judge new steps from prior experience	Wrong decisions about competition and markets	Use learning strategies, test assumptions
Compensate uniformly	Low motivation and inefficient operations	Balance risk and reward, employ special compensation
Promote compatible individuals	Loss of innovators	Accommodate "boat rockers" and "doers"

Source: Reprinted by permission of the publisher from Hollister B. Sykes and Zenas Block, "Corporate Venturing Obstacles: Sources and Solutions," *Journal of Business Venturing* (Winter 1989): 161. Copyright © 1989 by Elsevier Science Publishing Co., Inc.

- *Small, flat organizations.* Most innovative companies keep the total organization flat and project teams small.
- *Multiple approaches.* Innovative managers encourage several projects to proceed in parallel development.
- *Interactive learning.* Within an innovative environment, **interactive learning** and investigation of ideas cut across traditional functional lines in the organization.
- *Skunk Works.* **"Skunk Works"** is a nickname given to small groups that work on their ideas outside of normal organizational time and structure. Every highly innovative enterprise uses groups that function outside traditional lines of authority. This eliminates bureaucracy, permits rapid turnaround, and instills a high level of group identity and loyalty.[26]

Conceptualizing Corporate Entrepreneurship Strategy

As mentioned earlier, we define a corporate entrepreneurship strategy as a vision-directed, organization-wide reliance on entrepreneurial behavior that purposefully and continuously rejuvenates the organization and shapes the scope of its operations through the recognition

the entrepreneurial process

Innovation Inside Whirlpool

A sense of urgency set in at Whirlpool Corporation when rival company Maytag introduced the revolutionary front–loading washing machine. The retaliatory strategy? Individual employee innovation.

Chairman and CEO David R. Whitwam believed that any one of Whirlpool's 55,000 employees could come up with innovative products or services, given the proper guidance. Whitwam understands that most employees may not have the time or insight to develop an entire business or product line, but feels he must encourage all employees to at least *think* like entrepreneurs. The alternative option, according to Whitwam, is to resign the company to slow growth, diminishing margins, and faltering share prices.

The results have been a success. A KitchenAid division employee, Josh Gitlin, dreamt up a company specializing in in-home cooking classes taught by a network of branded chefs. The company, Inspired Chef, was launched and funded by Whirlpool and expanded to 33 states.

Whitwam now wants crazier ideas and more creative brainstorming. As a stimulus, he reserved 20 percent of Whirlpool's capital budget and is prepared to set away at least 35 percent toward innovation. To motivate the executive-level employees, he has linked their pay to the revenue derived from these new product and service launches.

Because venture success often necessitates a conducive environment, Whirlpool has created a network of mentors around the world to contribute to ideas and remove roadblocks. There are now 35 full-time "innovation consultants" and 177 part-time "innovation mentors" at the disposal of any employee with the next great idea. Once the idea is ready for financing, the employee and his or her innovative consultant are given 100 days and $100,000 to develop prototypes and conduct customer research.

The number of ventures continues to increase; the KitchenAid division is introducing a line of outdoor-grilling equipment, and Whirlpool is testing a mini-fridge that can be turned into an oven to cook a meal, all controlled via the Internet.

Source: "Whirlpool Taps Its Inner Entrepreneur," *Business-Week Online,* February 7, 2002, http://www.businessweek.com/smallbiz/content/feb2002/sb2002027_3066.htm (accessed March 8, 2008).

and exploitation of entrepreneurial opportunity. As is true for all strategies, a corporate entrepreneurship strategy should be thought of in continuous, rather than dichotomous, terms. Stated more directly, corporate entrepreneurship strategies vary in their degree of entrepreneurial intensity.

Developed by researchers Jeffrey G. Covin, R. Duane Ireland, and Donald F. Kuratko, Figure 3.2 presents a model that illustrates how a corporate entrepreneurship strategy is manifested through the presence of three elements: an entrepreneurial strategic vision, a pro-entrepreneurship organizational architecture, and entrepreneurial processes and behavior as exhibited across the organizational hierarchy.[27] This model has several linkages, which include: (1) individual entrepreneurial cognitions of the organization's members, (2) external environmental conditions that invite entrepreneurial activity, (3) top management's entrepreneurial strategic vision for the firm, (4) organizational architectures that encourage entrepreneurial processes and behavior, (5) the entrepreneurial processes that are reflected in entrepreneurial behavior, and (6) organizational outcomes that result from entrepreneurial actions.

The model suggests that individual entrepreneurial cognitions and external environmental conditions are the initial impetus for adopting a CE strategy, and outcomes are assessed to provide justification for the strategy's continuance, modification, or rejection. The CE strategy itself is reflected in the three elements cited previously: an entrepreneurial strategic vision, a pro-entrepreneurship organizational architecture, and entrepreneurial processes and

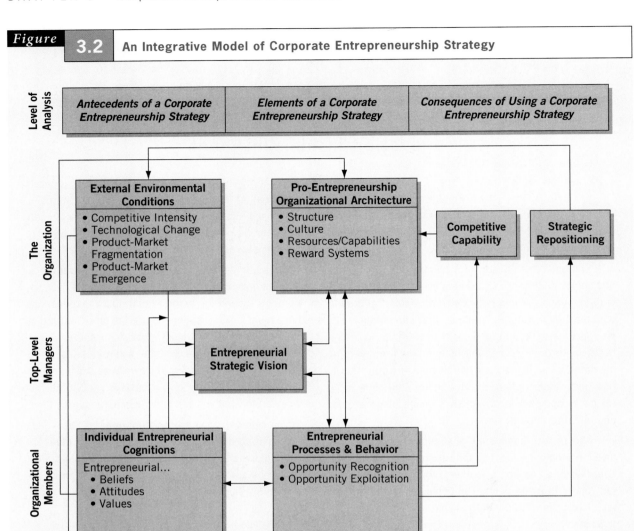

Figure **3.2**   **An Integrative Model of Corporate Entrepreneurship Strategy**

Source: Duane Ireland, Jeffery G. Covin, and Donald F. Kuratko, "Conceptualizing Corporate Entrepreneurship Strategy," *Entrepreneurship Theory and Practice* 33, no. 1 (January, 2009).

behavior as exhibited throughout the organization. A CE strategy cannot be consciously chosen and quickly enacted the way some strategies, such as acquisition, can be—it requires more than just a decision, act, or event. It requires the creation of congruence between the entrepreneurial vision of the organization's leaders and the entrepreneurial actions of those throughout the organization, as facilitated through the existence of a pro-entrepreneurship organizational architecture. CE strategy is about creating self-renewing organizations through the unleashing and focusing of the entrepreneurial potential that exists throughout those organizations. It is also about consistency in approach and regularity in behavior. Firms that engage in CE strategies must encourage entrepreneurial behavior on a relatively regular or continuous basis. Obviously, how extensively firms must engage in entrepreneurial behavior before the presence of a CE strategy can be claimed is a matter of degree. At one end of the continuum is stability, or the absence of innovation; at the other end is chaos, or overwhelming innovation. Researchers Charles Baden-Fuller and Henk Volberda rightfully assert that.

> Resolving the paradox of change and preservation means recognizing that continuous renewal inside a complex firm is misleading. Too much change will lead to chaos, loss of cultural glue, fatigue, and organizational breakdown. While in the short-term, organizations that are chaotic can survive, in the longer term they are likely to collapse.[28]

Researchers Kathleen Eisenhardt, Shona Brown, and Heidi Neck perhaps best captured where firms with CE strategies lie along the innovation continuum in their observations concerning "competing on the entrepreneurial edge." Firms with CE strategies remain close to the "edge of time," judiciously balancing the exploitation of current entrepreneurial opportunities with the search for future entrepreneurial opportunities. Such firms are always near chaos, both strategically and structurally, but they have the wisdom and discipline to recognize the possibility of (and avoid) the extreme collapse referred to earlier.[29]

Thus, for CE to operate as a strategy, it must "run deep" within organizations. Top managers are increasingly recognizing the need to respond to the entrepreneurial imperatives created by their competitive landscapes. Minimal responses to these entrepreneurial imperatives—reflecting superficial commitments to CE strategy—are bound to fail. Moreover, although top management can instigate the strategy, top management cannot dictate it. Those at the middle and lower ranks of an organization have a tremendous effect on and significant roles within entrepreneurial and strategic processes.[30] Without sustained and strong commitment from these lower levels of the organization, entrepreneurial behavior will never be a defining characteristic of the organization, as is required by CE strategy.

CE strategy will be hard to create and, perhaps, even harder to perpetuate in organizations. The presence of certain external environmental conditions may be sufficient to prompt an organization's leaders to explore the possibility of adopting a CE strategy. However, the commitment of individuals throughout the organization to making such a strategy work, and the realization of personal and organizational entrepreneurial outcomes that reinforce this commitment, will be necessary to assure that entrepreneurial behavior becomes a defining aspect of the organization. Thus, breakdowns in any of the three elements of CE strategy, or in linkages between or among these elements, would undermine the viability of such strategy. Moreover, alignments must be created in evaluation and reward systems such that congruence is achieved in the entrepreneurial behaviors induced at the individual and organizational levels. Although external conditions may be increasingly conducive to the adoption of CE strategies, managers should harbor no illusions that the effective implementation of these strategies will be easily accomplished.

Corporations that create an entrepreneurial strategy find that the ethos of the original enterprise often changes dramatically.[31] Traditions are set aside in favor of new processes and procedures. Some people, unaccustomed to operating in this environment, will leave; others will discover a new motivational system that encourages creativity, ingenuity, risk taking, teamwork, and informal networking, all designed to increase productivity and make the organization more viable. Some people thrive in an entrepreneurial environment; others dislike it intensely.

The five critical steps of a corporate entrepreneurship strategy are: (1) developing the vision, (2) encouraging innovation, (3) structuring for an entrepreneurial climate, (4) developing individual managers for corporate entrepreneurship, and (5) developing venture teams. Each of these is now discussed in greater detail.

Developing the Vision

The first step in planning a corporate entrepreneurship strategy for the enterprise is to share the vision of innovation that the corporate leaders wish to achieve.[32] The vision must be clearly articulated by the organization's leaders; however, the specific objectives are then developed by the managers and employees of the organization. Because it is suggested that corporate entrepreneuring results from the creative talents of people within the organization, employees need to know about and understand this vision. Shared vision is a critical element for a strategy that seeks high achievement (see Figure 3.3). This shared vision requires identification of specific objectives for corporate entrepreneuring strategies and of the programs needed to achieve those objectives. Author and researcher Rosabeth Moss Kanter has described three major objectives and their respective programs designed for venture development within companies. These are outlined in Table 3.3.

Figure 3.3	Shared Vision

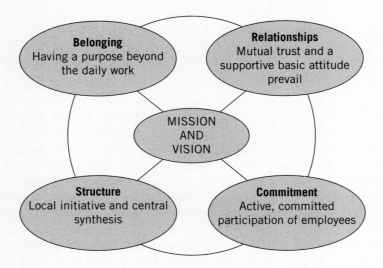

Source: Jon Arild Johannessen, "A Systematic Approach to the Problem of Rooting a Vision in the Basic Components of an Organization," *Entrepreneurship, Innovation, and Change* (March 1994): 47. Reprinted with permission from Plenum Publishing Corporation.

Table 3.3	Objectives and Programs for Venture Development

Objectives	Programs
Make sure that current systems, structures, and practices do not present insurmountable road-blocks to the flexibility and fast action needed for innovation.	Reduce unnecessary bureaucracy and encourage communication across departments and functions.
Provide the incentives and tools for intrapreneurial projects.	Use internal "venture capital" and special project budgets. (This money has been termed *intracapital* to signify a special fund for intrapreneurial projects.) Allow discretionary time for projects (bootlegging time).
Seek synergies across business areas so new opportunities are discovered in new combinations.	Encourage joint projects and ventures among divisions, departments, and companies. Allow and encourage employees to discuss and brainstorm new ideas.

Source: Adapted by permission of the publisher from Rosabeth Moss Kanter, "Supporting Innovation and Venture Development in Established Companies," *Journal of Business Venturing* (Winter 1985): 56–59. Copyright © 1985 by Elsevier Science Publishing Co., Inc.

Encouraging Innovation

As will be discussed in Chapter 5, innovation is the specific tool of the entrepreneur. Therefore, corporations must understand and develop innovation as the key element in their strategy. Numerous researchers have examined the importance of innovation within the corporate environment.[33]

Innovation is described as chaotic and unplanned by some authors,[34] while other researchers insist it is a systematic discipline.[35] Both of these positions can be true, depending on the nature of the innovation. One way to understand this concept is to focus on two different types of innovation: radical and incremental.[36]

Radical innovation is the launching of inaugural breakthroughs such as personal computers, Post-it® notes, disposable diapers, and overnight mail delivery. These innovations take experimentation and determined vision, which are not necessarily managed but *must* be recognized and nurtured.

Incremental innovation refers to the systematic evolution of a product or service into newer or larger markets. Examples include microwave popcorn, popcorn used for packaging (to replace Styrofoam®), frozen yogurt, and so forth. Many times, the incremental innovation will take over after a radical innovation introduces a breakthrough. The structure, marketing, financing, and formal systems of a corporation can help implement incremental innovation. It has been said that an organization, through its people, can do 1,000 things 1 percent better rather than waiting to do one thing 1,000 percent better.

Both types of innovation require vision and support. This support takes different steps for effective development (Table 3.4). In addition, they both need a champion—a person with a vision and the ability to share it.[37] Finally, both types of innovation require an effort by the top management of the corporation to develop and educate employees concerning innovation and intrapreneurship, a concept known as top management support.[38]

Encouraging innovation requires a willingness not only to tolerate failure but also to learn from it. For example, one of the founders of 3M, Francis G. Oakie, had an idea to

Table 3.4   Developing and Supporting Radical and Incremental Innovation

Radical	Incremental
Stimulate through challenges and puzzles.	Set systematic goals and deadlines.
Remove budgetary and deadline constraints when possible.	Stimulate through competitive pressures.
Encourage technical education and exposure to customers.	Encourage technical education and exposure to customers.
Allow technical sharing and brainstorming sessions.	Hold weekly meetings that include key management and marketing staff.
Give personal attention—develop relationships of trust.	Delegate more responsibility.
Encourage praise from outside parties.	Set clear financial rewards for meeting goals and deadlines.
Have flexible funds for opportunities that arise.	
Reward with freedom and capital for new projects and interests.	

Source: Adapted from Harry S. Dent, Jr., "Growth through New Product Development," *Small Business Reports* (November 1990): 36.

replace razor blades with sandpaper. He believed that men could rub sandpaper on their face rather than use a sharp razor. He was wrong, and the idea failed, but his ideas evolved until he developed a waterproof sandpaper for the auto industry, which was a blockbuster success!

Thus, 3M's philosophy was born. Innovation is a numbers game: The more ideas, the better the chances for a successful innovation. In other words, to master innovation, companies must have a tolerance for failure. This philosophy has paid off for 3M. Antistatic videotape, translucent dental braces, synthetic ligaments for knee surgery, heavy-duty reflective sheeting for construction signs, and, of course, Post-it notes are just some of the great innovations developed by the organization. Overall, the company has a catalog of 60,000 products.[39]

Today, 3M follows a set of innovative rules that encourages employees to foster ideas. The key rules include the following:

- *Don't kill a project.* If an idea can't find a home in one of 3M's divisions, a staffer can devote 15 percent of his or her time to prove it is workable. For those who need seed money, as many as 90 Genesis grants of $50,000 are awarded each year.

- *Tolerate failure.* Encouraging plenty of experimentation and risk taking allows more chances for a new product hit. The goal: Divisions must derive 25 percent of sales from products introduced in the past five years. The target may be boosted to 30 percent in some cases.

- *Keep divisions small.* Division managers must know each staffer's first name. When a division gets too big, perhaps reaching $250 million to $300 million in sales, it is split up.

- *Motivate the champions.* When a 3M employee has a product idea, he or she recruits an action team to develop it. Salaries and promotions are tied into the product's progress. The champion has a chance to someday run his or her own product group or division.

- *Stay close to the customer.* Researchers, marketers, and managers visit with customers and routinely invite them to help brainstorm product ideas.

- *Share the wealth.* Technology, wherever it is developed, belongs to everyone.[40]

the global perspective

Global Innovation: Changing Winds in Japan

It is not hard to remember when Japan was a bastion of technical innovation, with Sony leading the charge; however, due to companies like Apple and Google entering the scene with far more innovative company cultures, Japanese companies are trying to determine how to regain their mojo. The irony is that Japan appears to offer everything that an entrepreneur could want. In 2006, Japan's spending on R&D as a percentage of its gross domestic product (GDP) was more than that of the United States or the European Union, and it files more patents than any other country (including the United States). Yet, innovators are finding the country to be an increasingly difficult place to be creative. Companies have become mired in old management paradigms, which has opened the door for foreign countries to attract historically loyal Japanese consumers.

The most recent chapter in this saga is the fall of DoCoMo. The fact that you probably have never heard of this company is only slightly surprising. DoCoMo has conducted its business primarily in Japan; it is, however, known to be a manufacturer of highly innovative products and has over 50 million customers. So, why has the company not garnered more international attention? At the beginning of the century, the company's executives developed a strategy to attain the company's rightful place on the global landscape. DoCoMo's i-mode, a popular mobile Internet application in Japan, was positioned as the lynchpin of the new business model. The company planned to make strategic acquisitions that it could leverage to set wireless Internet standards on an international scale.

When DoCoMo's acquisitions did not bear fruit, the company forged ahead. Rather than taking the introspective approach needed to correct their course of action, executives remained faithful that the company's superior product offerings eventually would win over foreign consumers. One major oversight in this approach was the shift in consumer preferences toward simpler interfaces. Although Japanese customers seemed enamored by the complicated menus available with i-mode, and took advantage of all the functionality it offered, non-Japanese consumers were less than impressed with what they found to be a confusing system. The leading cause of the company's blind faith was the fact that its entire management team was Japanese, resulting in a lack of understanding of other cultural preferences. Once considered to have the potential to be the next Google, the company is now struggling to regain its domestic customers from its more agile foreign competitors.

At the top of the list of Japanese companies' most admired international rivals is Apple, largely due to the ability of the iPod and iPhone to overshadow Sony, the poster-child for Japanese innovation. Companies like Apple and Google have taken a holistic approach to developing new products, which includes not only new designs but also effective marketing and distribution. This novel approach has left Japanese companies wondering where they went wrong. Their model of incremental improvements on existing products is obsolete when their competitors are inventing entirely new product categories. Sony's Walkman was once the essence of cool in consumer electronics, but Apple's iPod overtook that position long ago. Outside of Japan, few young consumers even know of the once revolutionary Walkman, and Sony has not been able to develop anything to take its place, which has made Apple the reigning champ of innovative consumer electronics.

Japan's problems run deeper than just a couple of bureaucratic corporations. The whole country seemingly has lost its ability to make major innovations. Opponents to such a perspective could easily cite Nintendo's success with the Wii console, which has managed to take the spotlight from Microsoft's Xbox and Sony's Playstation; however, Nintendo's executives chose to base the company in Kyoto to avoid the lethargy that has recently plagued companies located in the capital city of Tokyo. Despite such exceptions, most large corporations are either unable or unmotivated to innovate. The emphasis on hierarchies in Japanese companies is blamed for the lack of creativity, given that employees are discouraged from straying outside of their narrowly define roles.

The game is certainly far from over for Japan, but the rules are changing and the competition is getting better. If Japanese firms want to remain competitive, they will have to learn to break down corporate barriers and encourage their employees to present their ideas. Apple and Google may have taken the lead, but other countries will not sit idly by. Japan is well positioned to compete—resting on its laurels will guarantee its precipitous decline.

Source: Adapted from Christian Caryl and Akiko Kashiwagi, "Not Made in Japan," *Newsweek,* (February 25, 2008), E10.

Structuring for a Corporate Entrepreneurial Environment

When reestablishing the drive to innovate in today's corporations, the final and possibly most critical step is to invest heavily in *entrepreneurial activities* that allow new ideas to flourish in an innovative environment. This concept, when coupled with the other elements of an innovation strategy, can enhance the potential for employees to become venture developers. To develop employees as a source of innovation for corporations, companies need to provide more nurturing and information-sharing activities.[41] In addition, they need to develop an environment that will help innovative-minded people reach their full potential. Employee perception of an innovative environment is critical for stressing the importance of management's commitment not only to the organization's people but also to the innovative projects.

The importance of an organizational environment for corporate entrepreneurship is further emphasized by researcher Deborah V. Brazeal's model for internally developed ventures.[42] Figure 3.4 illustrates the model's focus on a joint function between innovative

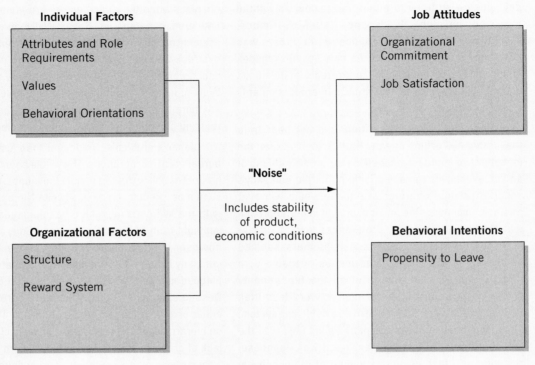

Figure 3.4 **Intrapreneurial Development: Joint Function of Individual and Organizational Factors**

Source: Deborah V. Brazeal, "Organizing for Internally Developed Corporate Ventures," *Journal of Business Venturing* (January 1993): 80.

individuals and organizational factors. Brazeal defines corporate venturing as "an internal process that embraces the ultimate goal of growth through the development of innovative products, processes, and technologies" that should be institutionalized with an emphasis on long-term prosperity. Thus, for organizations to promote innovation among their employees, they must give careful attention to the melding of an individual's attitudes, values, and behavioral orientations with the organizational factors of structure and reward. Ultimately, the key objective is to enhance a firm's innovative abilities by developing an organizational environment that is supportive of individuals.

PREPARING FOR FAILURE

There have been numerous advocates for the acceptance of failure among innovative projects in organizations. The idea of "learning from failure" has become an axiom in the corporate entrepreneurial community. However, dealing with failure on a personal level is something that only recently has been examined for managers. Researchers Dean A. Shepherd, Jeffrey G. Covin, and Donald F. Kuratko proposed the importance of managing the grief process that results from project failure. The literature seldom recognizes the importance of grief in the failure experience. Grief is a negative emotional response to the loss of something important, which triggers behavioral, psychological, and physiological symptoms. Managing grief therefore represents a particularly salient task in the context of corporate entrepreneurship practice, because the amount of commitment essential to a project's success also generates grief when the project fails.

Project failure is a common occurrence, and organizational routines and rituals are likely to influence the grief recovery of those involved in the failed project. To the extent that a social support system could be offered by the organizational environment for individuals' negative emotions, there will likely be greater learning and motivational outcomes. The inevitability of entrepreneurial project failure encourages the adoption of social support mechanisms as means to develop failure-related coping skills among corporate managers. The need in dedicated corporate innovation units for social support mechanisms that enable corporate entrepreneurs to cope with failure-related grief will likely help to build coping self-efficacy in individuals.[43]

Developing Individual Managers for Corporate Entrepreneurship

As a way for organizations to develop key environmental factors for entrepreneurial activity, a corporate entrepreneurship/innovation training program often induces the change needed in the work atmosphere. It is not our intent to elaborate completely on the content of a training program here, but a brief summary of an actual program is presented to provide a general understanding of how such a program is designed to introduce an entrepreneurial environment in a company. This award-winning training program is intended to create an awareness of entrepreneurial opportunities in organizations. The Corporate Innovation Training Program consists of six modules, each designed to train participants to support corporate innovations in their own work area.[44] The modules and a brief summary of their contents are as follows:

1. **The Entrepreneurial Experience.** An enthusiastic overview of the Entrepreneurial Experience, in which participants are introduced to the entrepreneurial revolution that has taken place throughout the world over the last three decades. Participants are challenged to think innovatively and recognize the need for breaking out of the old paradigms in today's organizations.

2. **Innovative Thinking.** The process of thinking innovatively is foreign to most traditional organizations. The misconceptions about thinking innovatively are reviewed, and a discussion of the most common inhibitors is presented. After completing an innovation inventory, managers engage in several exercises designed to facilitate their own innovative thinking.

3. **Idea Acceleration Process.** Managers generate a set of specific ideas on which they would like to work. The process includes examining a number of aspects of the corporation, including structural barriers and facilitators. Additionally, managers determine resources needed to accomplish their projects.

4. **Barriers and Facilitators to Innovative Thinking.** The most common barriers to innovative behavior are reviewed and discussed. Managers complete several exercises that will help them deal with barriers in the workplace. In addition, video case histories are shown that depict actual corporate innovators that have been successful in dealing with corporate barriers.

5. **Sustaining Innovation Teams (I–Teams).** The concept of forming I-Teams to focus on specific innovations is examined. Managers work together to form teams based on the ideas that have been circulating among the entire group. Team dynamics are reviewed for each group to understand.

6. **The Innovation Action Plan.** After managers examine several aspects of facilitators and barriers to behaving innovatively in their organization, teams are asked to begin the process of completing an action plan. The plan includes setting goals, establishing an I-Team team, assessing current conditions, developing a step-by-step timetable for project completion, and project evaluation.

To validate the training program's effectiveness, a questionnaire titled the Corporate Entrepreneurship Assessment Instrument (CEAI) was developed by researchers Donald F. Kuratko and Jeffrey S. Hornsby to provide for a psychometrically sound instrument that measured key entrepreneurial climate factors from the existing corporate entrepreneurship literature. The responses to the CEAI were statistically analyzed and resulted in five identified factors. These five factors are critical to the internal environment of an organization seeking to have its managers pursue innovative activity. It is important to understand these factors in order to assess the organization's readiness for corporate entrepreneurial activity. Each of the factors discussed next are aspects of the organization over which management has some control. Each is briefly defined and includes illustrations of specific elements of a firm's environment relative to each dimension.

MANAGEMENT SUPPORT

This is the extent to which the management structure itself encourages employees to believe that innovation is, in fact, part of the role set for all organization members. Some of the specific conditions that reflect management support include quick adoption of employee ideas, recognition of people who bring ideas forward, support for small experimental projects, and seed money to get projects off the ground.

AUTONOMY/WORK DISCRETION

Workers have discretion to the extent that they are able to make decisions about performing their own work in the way they believe is most effective. Organizations should allow employees to make decisions about their work process and should avoid criticizing them for making mistakes when innovating.

REWARDS/REINFORCEMENT

Rewards and reinforcement enhance the motivation of individuals to engage in innovative behavior. Organizations must be characterized by providing rewards contingent on performance, providing challenges, increasing responsibilities, and making the ideas of innovative people known to others in the organizational hierarchy.

TIME AVAILABILITY

The fostering of new and innovative ideas requires that individuals have time to incubate these ideas. Organizations must moderate the workload of people, avoid putting time constraints on all aspects of a person's job, and allow people to work with others on long-term problem solving.

ORGANIZATIONAL BOUNDARIES

These boundaries, real and imagined, prevent people from looking at problems outside their own jobs. People must be encouraged to look at the organization from a broad perspective. Organizations should avoid having standard operating procedures for all major parts of jobs, and should reduce dependence on narrow job descriptions and rigid performance standards.[45]

The statistical results from the CEAI demonstrated support for this underlying set of internal environmental factors that organizations need to focus on when seeking to introduce an innovative strategy. These factors, as well as the previous research mentioned, are the foundation for the critical steps involved in introducing a corporate entrepreneurial climate.

Another researcher, Vijay Sathe, has suggested a number of areas on which corporations must focus if they are going to facilitate corporate entrepreneurial behavior. The first is to encourage—not mandate—innovative activity. Managers should use financial rewards and strong company recognition rather than rules or strict procedures to encourage corporate entrepreneurship. This is actually a stronger internal control and direction method than traditional parameters.

Another area of focus is the proper control of human resource policies. Managers need to remain in positions long enough to allow them to learn an industry and a particular division. Rather than move managers around in positions, as is the case in many companies, Sathe suggests "selected rotation," in which managers are exposed to different but related territories. This helps managers gain sufficient knowledge for innovation development.

Table	3.5	The Corporate Innovator's Commandments

1. Come to work each day *willing* to give up your job for the innovation.

2. Circumvent any bureaucratic orders aimed at stopping your innovation.

3. Ignore your job description—do any job needed to make your innovation work.

4. Build a spirited innovation team that has the "fire" to make it happen.

5. Keep your innovation "underground" until it is prepared for demonstration to the corporate management.

6. Find a key upper-level manager who believes in you and your ideas and who will serve as a sponsor to your innovation.

7. Permission is rarely granted in organizations; thus, always seek forgiveness for the "ignorance" of the rules that you will display.

8. Always be realistic about the ways to achieve the innovation goals.

9. Share the glory of the accomplishments with everyone on the team.

10. Convey the innovation's vision through a strong venture plan.

A third factor is for management to sustain a commitment to innovative projects long enough for momentum to occur. Failures will inevitably occur, and learning must be the key aftermath of those failures. Thus, sustained commitment is an important element in managing corporate entrepreneurship.

A final element suggested by Sathe is to bet on people, not on analysis. Although analysis is always important to judge a project's progression, it should be done in a supportive rather than an imposed style. The supportive challenge can help innovators realize errors, test their convictions, and accomplish a self-analysis.[46]

It should be mentioned that the exact rewards for corporate entrepreneuring are not yet agreed on by most researchers.[47] Some believe that allowing the inventor to take charge of the new venture is the best reward. Others say it is allowing the corporate entrepreneur more discretionary time to work on future projects. Still others insist that special capital, called intracapital, should be set aside for the corporate entrepreneur to use whenever investment money is needed for further research ideas.

In light of these climate elements, it is clear that change in the corporate structure is inevitable if innovative activity is going to exist and prosper. The change process consists of a series of emerging constructions of people, corporate goals, and existing needs. In short, the organization can encourage innovation by relinquishing controls and changing the traditional bureaucratic structure. (See Table 3.5 for the Corporate Innovator's Commandments.)

Developing I-Teams

Innovation teams and the potential they hold for producing innovative results are recognized as a productivity breakthrough for the twenty-first century. Certainly, no one doubts that their popularity is on the rise. Companies that have committed to an innovation team approach often label the change they have undergone a "transformation" or "revolution." This modern breed of work team is a new strategy for many firms. It is referred to as self-directing, self-managing, or high performing, although in reality an (I)-team fits all of those descriptions.[48]

In examining the entrepreneurial development for corporations, Robert Reich found that entrepreneurial thinking is not the sole province of the company's founder or its top managers. Rather, it is diffused throughout the company, where experimentation and development occur all the time as the company searches for new ways to build on the knowledge already accumulated by its workers. Reich defines collective entrepreneurship as follows:

In collective entrepreneurship, individual skills are integrated into a group; this collective capacity to innovate becomes something greater than the sum of its parts. Over time, as group members work through various problems and approaches, they learn about each other's abilities. They learn how they can help one another perform better, what each can contribute to a particular project, how they can best take advantage of one another's experience. Each participant is constantly on the lookout for small adjustments that will speed and smooth the evolution of the whole. The net result of many such small-scale adaptations, effected throughout the organization, is to propel the enterprise forward.[49]

In keeping with Reich's focus on collective entrepreneurship, innovation teams offer corporations the opportunity to use the talents of individuals without losing a sense of teamwork.

An **innovation team**, or **I-team**, is composed of two or more people who formally create and share ownership of a new organization.[50] The unit is semiautonomous in the sense that it has its own budget as well as a leader with the freedom to make decisions within broad guidelines. Sometimes the leader is called an "innovation champion" or a "corporate entrepreneur." The unit often is separated from other parts of the firm—in particular, from parts involved with daily activities. This prevents the unit from engaging in procedures that can stifle innovative activities. If the innovation proves successful, however, it eventually is treated the same as other outputs the organization produces. It is then integrated into the larger organization.[51]

In many ways, an I-team is a small business operating within a large business, and its strength is its focus on design (that is, structure and process) issues for innovative activities. One organization that operated successfully with the innovation team concept was the Signode Corporation (see "Entrepreneurship in Practice").

Specific entrepreneurial strategies vary from firm to firm. However, they all follow similar patterns of seeking a proactive change of the status quo and a new, flexible approach to operations management.

Sustaining Corporate Entrepreneurship

It is well documented in the conceptual literature that managers at all structural levels have critical strategic roles to fulfill for the organization to be successful. Senior-, middle-, and first-level managers possess distinct responsibilities with respect to each subprocess. *Senior-level managers* have ratifying, recognizing, and directing roles that in turn are associated with particular managerial actions.[52] Researchers Donald F. Kuratko, R. Duane Ireland, Jeffrey G. Covin, and Jeffrey S. Hornsby contend that *middle-level managers* endorse, refine, and shepherd entrepreneurial opportunities, and identify, acquire, and deploy the resources needed to pursue those opportunities. *First-level managers* have experimenting roles that correspond to the competence definition subprocess, adjusting roles that correspond to the competence modification subprocess, and conforming roles that correspond to the competence deployment subprocess.

Thus, organizations that pursue corporate entrepreneurship strategies likely exhibit a cascading yet integrated set of entrepreneurial actions at the senior, middle, and first levels of management. At the senior level, managers act in concert with others throughout the firm to identify effective means through which new businesses can be created or existing ones reconfigured. Corporate entrepreneurship is pursued in light of environmental opportunities and threats, with the purpose of creating a more effective alignment between the company and conditions in its external environment. The entrepreneurial actions expected of middle-level managers are framed around the need for this group to propose and interpret entrepreneurial opportunities that might create new business for the firm or increase the firm's competitiveness in current business domains. First-line managers exhibit the "experimenting" role as they unearth the operational ideas for innovative improvements. An important interpretation of previous research has been the belief that managers would surface ideas for entrepreneurial actions from every level of management, particularly the first-line and middle levels. Therefore, managers across levels are jointly responsible for their organization's entrepreneurial actions.[53]

entrepreneurship **in practice**

A Timeless Lesson: Signode's I–Teams

Robert F. Hettinger, a venture manager with Signode Industries, Inc., in Glenview, Illinois, smiles as he recounts the strategy initiated by Jack Campbell, director of corporate development. "He strongly believed," Hettinger says, "that you have to kiss a lot of frogs in order to find a prince. Most ideas in raw form aren't winners—you really have to work them out before success sets in."

Signode, a $750 million-a-year manufacturer of plastic and steel strapping for packaging and materials handling, wanted to chart new directions to become a $1 billion-plus firm by 1990. In pursuit of this goal, Signode set out in 1983 to devise an aggressive strategy for growth: developing "new legs" for the company to stand on. It formed a corporate development group to pursue markets outside the company's core businesses but within the framework of its corporate strengths.

Before launching the first of its innovation teams, Signode's top management identified the firm's global business strengths and broad areas with potential for new product lines: warehousing/shipping; packaging; plastics for nonpackaging, fastening, and joining systems; and product identification and control systems. Each new business opportunity suggested by an innovation team was to have the potential to generate $50 million in business within five years. In addition, each opportunity had to build on one of Signode's strengths: industrial customer base and marketing expertise, systems sales and service capabilities, containment and reinforcement technology, steel and plastic process technology, machine and design capabilities, and productivity and distribution know-how.

The criteria were based on business-to-business selling only; Signode did not want to market directly to retailers or consumers. The basic technology to be employed in the new business had to already exist and had to have a strong likelihood of attaining a major market share within a niche. Finally, the initial investment in the new opportunity had to be $30 million or less.

Based on these criteria, Signode began to build its "V-Team" (innovation team) approach to intrapreneurship. It took three months to select the first team members. The six initial teams had three common traits: high risk-taking ability, creativity, and the ability to deal with ambiguity. All were multidisciplinary volunteers who would work full-time on developing new consumer-product packaging businesses. The team members came from such backgrounds as design engineering, marketing, sales, and product development. They set up shop in rented office space five miles from the firm's headquarters. "We put them off-campus in order to create an entrepreneurial environment," Hettinger recalls.

The first innovation team recommendation, complete with a business plan, was to produce plastic trays for frozen entrees that could be used in either regular or microwave ovens. The business potential for this product was estimated to be in excess of $50 million a year within five years.

Signode launched a total of six teams between October 1983 and April 1986. All team volunteers passed a rigorous selection process. Typically, the employees were borrowed from operating divisions; after their team's work was finished, they either returned to their old positions or took positions with the newly formed business unit and further championed the new ideas.

According to Hettinger, the I-team experience rekindled enthusiasm and affected morale overall. In every case, an I-team member became a better contributor to Signode. Most important, their V-Team approach became a strategy for members to invent the future rather than waiting for things to happen.

Source: Mark Frohman and Perry Pascarella, "Achieving Purpose-Driven Innovation," *Industry Week* (March 19, 1990): 20–26; and personal interviews, 2005.

An organization's sustained effort in corporate entrepreneurship is contingent upon individual members continuing to undertake innovative activities and upon positive perceptions of the activity by the organization's executive management, which will in turn support the further allocation of necessary organizational antecedents. Figure 3.5 illustrates the

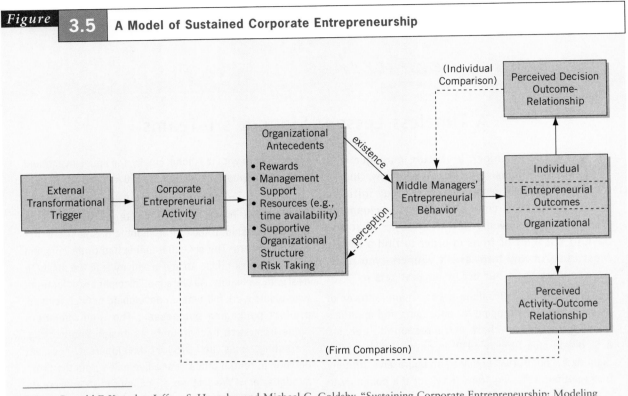

Figure **3.5**   **A Model of Sustained Corporate Entrepreneurship**

Source: Donald F. Kuratko, Jeffrey S. Hornsby, and Michael G. Goldsby, "Sustaining Corporate Entrepreneurship: Modeling Perceived Implementation and Outcome Comparisons at Organizational and Individual Levels," *International Journal of Entrepreneurship and Innovation* 5, no. 2 (May 2004): 79.

importance of perceived implementation/output relationships at the organizational and individual levels for sustaining corporate entrepreneurship.[54]

The first part of the model is based on theoretical foundations from previous strategy and entrepreneurship research. The second part of the model considers the comparisons made at the individual and organizational level on organizational outcomes, both perceived and real, that influence the continuation of the entrepreneurial activity.

The model demonstrates that a transformational trigger (something external or internal to the company that causes a change to take place) initiates the need for strategic adaptation or change. One such change that can be chosen is corporate entrepreneurial activity. Based on this choice of strategic direction, the proposed model centers around the individual's decision to behave entrepreneurially. Sustained entrepreneurial activity is the result of the perception of the existence of several organizational antecedents, such as top management support, autonomy, rewards, resources, and flexible organizational boundaries. The outcomes realized from this entrepreneurial activity are then compared at both the individual and organizational level to previous expectations. Thus, corporate entrepreneurial activities are a result of an equity perception by both the individual and the organization. Both must be satisfied with the outcomes for the entrepreneurial activities to continue from the organizational perspective as well as the individual perspective. Satisfaction with performance outcomes serves as a feedback mechanism for either sustaining the current strategy or selecting an alternative one. Individuals, as agents of the strategic change, must also be satisfied with the intrinsic and extrinsic outcomes they receive for their entrepreneurial behavior. While it may be a "chicken-and-egg" question as to whether individual behavior or organizational strategy should change first, the model suggests that—for a major strategic change—both are instrumental in making the change successful.

the entrepreneurial *process*

Corporate Entrepreneurship at IBM

The CEO of IBM, Lou Gerstner, read in one of his division's monthly reports that quarterly pressure had forced a discontinuance of a promising new technology. He summoned J. Bruce Herreld, the senior vice president for strategy, who quickly analyzed the firm and found 22 other such cases. Although IBM was known for its research labs that had obtained thousands of patents, upstarts like Oracle and Cisco built dynasties around those very same technologies. Why? The answer was old-guard thinking: rewarding short-term results in deference to any potential long-term risks. From that realization was born a company-wide corporate entrepreneurship effort four years later that aimed at finding new business opportunities. Under then CEO Samuel J. Palmisano and vice president Bruce Herreld, the Emerging Business Opportunity (EBO) Program was launched. Today the program stands as a model with a remarkable record of successes, such as the $2 billion Linux business, which charges for consulting on free software; a $1.7 billion digital media business, which helps companies manage video, audio, and images; and a $4.8 billion life sciences initiative that focuses on "info-based medicine." These successes are just the beginning, but this new journey for IBM is already effecting profound changes in its culture and its way of managing. Following are some of IBM's key rules for the EBO Program.

1. **Think big . . . really big.** Immerse into the customer sector and examine what their needs and wishes are. Opportunities that EBOs search for have the potential to become billion-dollar businesses in five to seven years.

2. **Bring in the A-team.** Search for the star performers in some of the core areas and recruit them to lead the EBO teams. They possess the experience, talent, and security necessary to launch into the risky arena of new business development. Entrepreneurial growth is far too important for novices to tackle.

3. **Start small.** Use pilot programs to gain some clarity before launching full blast. "First of a kind" engagements with key customers will help resist the temptation to ramp up too quickly.

4. **Establish unique measurement techniques.** Feedback from market trials, customer visits, partnership efforts, and the like are all areas for developing newer gauges of progress and success. Revenues and profits are the old guard, and they could easily kill an entrepreneurial effort early on. Look to set up the right parameters for judging the worthiness of the EBO effort.

Source: Adapted from Alan Deutschman, "Building a Better Skunk Works," *Fast Company* (March 2005): 68–73.

Summary

Corporate entrepreneurship is the process of profitably creating innovation within an organizational setting. Most companies are realizing the need for corporate entrepreneurship as a response to (1) the rapidly growing number of new, sophisticated competitors; (2) a sense of distrust in the traditional methods of corporate management; and (3) an exodus of some of the best and brightest people from corporations to become small-business entrepreneurs.

To create the right climate for in-house entrepreneurship, companies must develop the following four characteristics: (1) explicit goals, (2) a system of feedback and positive reinforcement, (3) an emphasis on individual responsibility, (4) rewards based on results, and

(5) no punishment for failures. Organizations create corporate entrepreneurship in a number of ways. The first step is to understand the obstacles to corporate venturing; these usually are based on the adverse impact of traditional management techniques. The next step is to adopt innovative principles that include atmosphere and vision, multiple approaches, interactive learning, and Skunk Works.

Specific strategies for corporate entrepreneurship entail the development of both vision and innovation. Two types of innovation exist: radical and incremental. To facilitate the development of innovation, corporations need to focus on the key factors of top management support, time, resources, and rewards. Thus, commitment to and support of innovative activity are critical.

Innovation teams are the semiautonomous units that have the collective capacity to develop new ideas. Sometimes referred to as self-managing or high-performance teams, innovation teams are emerging as the new breed of work teams formed to strengthen innovative developments.

At the end of this chapter, we discussed the process of corporate entrepreneurship by examining the role of middle managers in corporate entrepreneurial activity and the concept of sustained corporate entrepreneurship.

Key Terms and Concepts

bootlegging

champion

collective entrepreneurship

corporate entrepreneurship

Corporate Entrepreneurship
Assessment Instrument (CEAI)

corporate venturing

entrepreneurial economy

incremental innovation

innovation team (I-team)

interactive learning

intracapital

intrapreneurship

radical innovation

Skunk Works

strategic entrepreneurship

top management support

Review and Discussion Questions

1. In your own words, what is corporate entrepreneurship?
2. What are two reasons that such a strong desire to develop corporate entrepreneurs has arisen in recent years?
3. What are some of the corporate obstacles that must be overcome to establish a corporate entrepreneurial environment?
4. What are some of the innovative principles identified by James Brian Quinn that companies need to establish?
5. A number of corporations today are working to reengineer corporate thinking and encourage an innovative environment. What types of steps would you recommend? Offer at least three and explain each.
6. What are five useful rules for innovation?

7. What are three advantages of developing a corporate entrepreneurial philosophy?
8. Identify the four key elements on which managers should concentrate to develop a corporate entrepreneurship strategy.
9. Explain the differences between radical and incremental innovation.
10. Identify the five specific entrepreneurial climate factors that organizations need to address in structuring their environment.
11. Why are innovation teams emerging as part of a new strategy for many corporations?
12. What are the roles of middle managers in corporate entrepreneurship? Be specific.
13. Describe the elements that are involved in sustaining corporate entrepreneurship.

Experiential Exercise

DEVELOPING CORPORATE ENTREPRENEURSHIP

Many ways of developing corporate entrepreneurship exist. Some of these are presented in the following list. Write *yes* next to those that would help develop corporate entrepreneurship and *no* next to those that would not help develop corporate entrepreneurship.

1. _____ Create an innovative climate.

2. _____ Set implicit goals.

3. _____ Provide feedback on performance.

4. _____ Provide positive reinforcement.

5. _____ Encourage structured activity.

6. _____ Develop a well-defined hierarchical structure, and stick to it.

7. _____ Tolerate failure.

8. _____ Encourage a bias for action.

9. _____ Make extensive use of formal meetings.

10. _____ Allow bootlegging of ideas.

11. _____ Reward successful personnel.

12. _____ Fire those who make mistakes as a way of creating a good example for others.

13. _____ Make extensive use of informal meetings.

14. _____ Encourage communication throughout the organization.

15. _____ Discourage joint projects and ventures among different departments.

16. _____ Encourage brainstorming.

17. _____ Encourage moderate risk taking.

18. _____ Encourage networking with others in the enterprise.

19. _____ Encourage personnel not to fear failing.

20. _____ Encourage personnel to be willing to succeed even if it means doing unethical things.

Answers: 1. Y, 2. N, 3. Y, 4. Y, 5. N, 6. N, 7. Y, 8. Y, 9. N, 10. Y, 11. Y, 12. N, 13. Y, 14. Y, 15. N, 16. Y, 17. N, 18. Y, 19. Y, 20. N

Case 3.1

SOUTHWEST AIRLINES: POSITIVELY OUTRAGEOUS LEADERSHIP

When Southwest Airlines first taxied onto the runway of Dallas's Love Field in 1971, industry gurus predicted it would be a short trip to bankruptcy for the Texas-based airline. But the first short-haul, low-fare, high-frequency, point-to-point carrier took a unique idea and made it fly. Today, Southwest Airlines is the most profitable commercial airline in the world.

It took more than a wing and a prayer for Southwest to soar to such lofty altitudes—it required a maverick spirit. From the beginning, Southwest has flown against convention. Southwest's fleet of 737s—considered by many the safest in the industry—still makes only short hauls to 45 cities. The average flight distance is 394 miles. The airline does not give seat assignments, and the only food it serves passengers is a "snack pack." But what Southwest may lack in amenities, it seems to more than make up for in what could be called positively outrageous service. "Fun" is the company's mandate. Leading the way is founder and CEO, Herb Kelleher. "Herb Kelleher is definitely the zaniest CEO in the world," Libby Sartain, vice president of Southwest Airlines's People

Department, admits. "Where else would you find a CEO who dresses up as Elvis Presley, who's on a first-name basis with 20,000 employees, and who has a heart as big as the state of Texas? His style has fostered an atmosphere where people feel comfortable being themselves—where they can have a good time when they work."

Legendary for his love of laughter, Kelleher calls his unique leadership style *management by fooling around*. "An important part of leadership, I think, is enjoying what you're doing and letting it show to the people that you work with," Kelleher reveals. "And I would much rather have a company that is bound by love, rather than bound by fear." Kelleher's philosophy has been enthusiastically embraced by a workforce that is 85 percent unionized. "Southwest's culture is designed to promote high spirit and avoid complacency. We have little hierarchy here. Our employees are encouraged to be creative and innovative, to break rules when they need to in order to provide good service to our customers," Sartain explains. "If you create the type of environment that a person really feels valued and they feel they make a difference, then they're going to be motivated. That's the type of environment we create here for our employees," adds Rita Bailey, Southwest's director of training.

Beginning with its new-employee orientation, the airline nurtures intrapreneurship by grooming a workforce of leaders. "You can do whatever it takes to keep this airline on top," an orientation instructor tells his class of newly hired staffers. At Southwest Airlines's University for People, future managers and supervisors attend a course titled "Leading with Integrity." Through a series of role-playing exercises, employees learn that trust, cooperation, mutual respect, and good communication are the components of success. "An organization that has an esprit, that does things cooperatively and voluntarily rather than through coercion, is the most competitive organization you can have," Kelleher asserts. These guiding principles have earned Southwest Airlines the distinction of being named one of the ten best companies to work for in America.

Employees are valued and recognized for their achievements in many ways. Perhaps the most prestigious is Southwest's "Heroes of the Heart" award: Each year, one outstanding department has its name tattooed on a Southwest jet. Southwest also was the first airline to offer stock options to its employees. Today, employees own approximately 10 percent of the company.

In the lobby of Southwest Airlines' corporate headquarters is a prominent tribute to the men and women of Southwest. It reads: "The people of Southwest Airlines are the creators of what we have become—and what we will be. Our people transformed an idea into a legend. That legend will continue to grow only so long as it is nourished by our people's indomitable spirit, boundless energy, immense goodwill, and burning desire to excel. Our thanks and our love to the people of Southwest Airlines for creating a marvelous family and wondrous airline."

QUESTIONS

1. Describe some of the factors needed to reengineer the corporate thinking that Southwest Airlines already exhibits.

2. What specific elements of a corporate entrepreneurial strategy are apparent within Southwest Airlines?

3. How has Herb Kelleher structured a climate conducive to entrepreneurial activity?

Notes

1. Shaker A. Zahra, Donald F. Kuratko, and Daniel F. Jennings, "Entrepreneurship and the Acquisition of Dynamic Organizational Capabilities," *Entrepreneurship Theory and Practice* (Spring 1999): 5–10.

2. Peter F. Drucker, "Our Entrepreneurial Economy," *Harvard Business Review* (January/February 1984): 59–64.

3. Ibid., 60–61.

4. See, for example, C. Wesley Morse, "The Delusion of Intrapreneurship," *Long Range Planning* 19 (1986):

92–95; W. Jack Duncan et al., "Intrapreneurship and the Reinvention of the Corporation," *Business Horizons* (May/June 1988): 16–21; and Neal Thornberry, "Corporate Entrepreneurship: Antidote or Oxymoron?" *European Management Journal* 19, no. 5 (2001): 526–33.

5. Donald F. Kuratko, R. Duane Ireland, and Jeffrey S. Hornsby, "Improving Firm Performance Through Entrepreneurial Actions: Acordia's Corporate Entrepreneurship Strategy," *Academy of Management Executive* 15, no. 4 (2001): 60–71; Jeffrey G. Covin

and Morgan P. Miles, "Strategic Use of Corporate Venturing," *Entrepreneurship Theory and Practice* 31, no. 2 (2007): 183–207; and Matthew R. Marvel, Abbie Griffin, John Hebda, and Bruce Vojak, "Examining the Technical Corporate Entrepreneurs' Motivation: Voices form the Field," *Entrepreneurship Theory and Practice* 31, no. 5 (2007): 753–68.

6. For example, see Michael H. Morris and J. Don Trotter, "Institutionalizing Entrepreneurship in a Large Company: A Case Study at AT&T," *Industrial Marketing Management* 19 (1990): 131–34; Brian McWilliams, "Strength from Within–How Today's Companies Nurture Entrepreneurs," *Enterprise* (April 1993): 43–44; Donald F. Kuratko, Michael D. Houk, and Richard M. Hodgetts, "Acordia, Inc. Leadership Through the Transformation of Growing Small," *Journal of Leadership Studies* (Spring 1998): 152–64; and Michael H. Morris, Donald F. Kuratko, and Jeffrey G. Covin, *Corporate Entrepreneurship and Innovation* (Mason, OH: South-Western/Cengage Learning, 2008).

7. See, for example, Zenas Block and Ian C. MacMillan, *Corporate Venturing* (Boston: Harvard Business School Press, 1993); Thomas D. Kuczmarski, Innovation (Chicago: NTC Publishing, 1996); Gary Hamel, *Leading the Revolution* (Boston: Harvard Business School Press, 2000); and Keith McFarland, *The Breakthrough Company* (New York: Crown, 2008).

8. Shaker A. Zahra, Daniel F. Jennings, and Donald F. Kuratko, "The Antecedents and Consequences of Firm-Level Entrepreneurship: The State of the Field," *Entrepreneurship Theory and Practice* 24, no. 2 (1999): 45–65; Donald F. Kuratko, *Corporate Entrepreneurship*, Foundations and Trends in Entrepreneurship (Boston: Now Publishers, 2007); and Michael H. Morris, Donald F. Kuratko, and Jeffrey G. Covin, *Corporate Entrepreneurship and Innovation* (Mason, OH: South-Western/Cengage Learning, 2008).

9. Gifford Pinchot III, *Intrapreneuring* (New York: Harper & Row, 1985).

10. Steven C. Brandt, *Entrepreneuring in Established Companies* (Homewood, IL: Dow Jones-Irwin, 1986), 54.

11. Bruce R. Barringer and Alan C. Bluedorn, "Corporate Entrepreneurship and Strategic Management," *Strategic Management Journal* 20 (1999): 421–44; see also Jeffrey G. Covin and Morgan P. Miles, "Corporate Entrepreneurship and the Pursuit of Competitive Advantage," *Entrepreneurship Theory and Practice* (March 1999): 47–64; and Joanna Barsh, Marla M. Capozzi, and Jonathan Davidson, "Leadership & Innovation," *The McKinsey Quarterly* 1 (2008): 37–47.

12. Dennis P. Slevin and Jeffrey G. Covin, "Juggling Entrepreneurial Style and Organizational Structure: How to Get Your Act Together," Sloan Management Review (Winter 1990): 43–53; and Gregory G. Dess, G. T. Lumpkin, and Jeffrey E. McGee, "Linking Corporate Entrepreneurship to Strategy, Structure, and Process: Suggested Research Directions," *Entrepreneurship Theory and Practice* 23, no. 3 (1999): 85–102.

13. Adapted from: Pinchot III, *Intrapreneuring*, 198–99.

14. Robert Simons, "How Risky Is Your Company?" *Harvard Business Review* (May/June 1999): 85–94.

15. Deborah Dougherty, "Managing Your Core Incompetencies for Corporate Venturing," *Entrepreneurship Theory and Practice* (Spring 1995): 113–35.

16. See R. Duane Ireland, Michael A. Hitt, S. Michael Camp, and Donald L. Sexton, "Integrating Entrepreneurship and Strategic Actions to Create Firm Wealth," *Academy of Management Executive* 15, no. 1 (2001): 49–63; Robert A. Burgelman and L. Valikangas, "Managing Internal Corporate Venturing Cycles," *MIT Sloan Management Review* 45, no. 4 (2004): 47–55; and Donald F. Kuratko, *Corporate Entrepreneurship*, Foundations and Trends in Entrepreneurship (Boston: Now Publishers, 2007).

17. Fariborz Damanpour, "Organizational Innovation: A Meta-analysis of Determinant and Moderators," *Academy of Management Journal* 34 (1991): 355–90.

18. Shaker A. Zahra, "Predictors and Financial Outcomes of Corporate Entrepreneurship: An Exploratory Study," *Journal of Business Venturing* 6 (1991): 259–86.

19. William D. Guth and Ari Ginsberg, "Corporate Entrepreneurship," Special issue, *Strategic Management Journal* 11 (1990): 5–15.

20. Michael H. Morris, Donald F. Kuratko, and Jeffrey G. Covin, *Corporate Entrepreneurship and Innovation* (Mason, OH: South-Western/Cengage Learning), 2008.

21. Pramodita Sharma and James J. Chrisman, "Toward a Reconciliation of the Definitional Issues in the Field of Corporate Entrepreneurship," *Entrepreneurship Theory and Practice* (spring 1999): 11–28.

22. R. Duane Ireland, Donald F. Kuratko, and Jeffrey G. Covin, "Antecedents, Elements, and Consequences of Corporate Entrepreneurship," *Best Paper Proceedings: National Academy of Management* (August 2003), CD-ROM: L1–L6; and R. Duane Ireland, Jeffrey G. Covin, and Donald F. Kuratko, "Conceptualizing Corporate Entrepreneurship Strategy," *Entrepreneurship Theory and Practice* 33, no. 1 (forthcoming).

23. Tom Peters, *Liberation Management* (New York: Alfred A. Knopf, 1992); Tom Peters, *The Circle of Innovation* (New York: Alfred A. Knopf, 1997); and Tom Peters, *Re-Imagine! Business Excellence in a Disruptive Age*, (New York: DK Ltd., 2003).

24. Amanda Bennett, *The Death of the Organization Man* (New York: Simon & Schuster, 1990); Donald F. Kuratko, "Developing Entrepreneurship within Organizations Is Today's Challenge," *Entrepreneurship, Innovation, and Change* (June 1995): 99–104; and Morgan P. Miles and Jeffrey G. Covin, "Exploring the Practice of Corporate Venturing: Some Common Forms and Their Organizational Implications," *Entrepreneurship Theory and Practice* 26, no. 3 (2002): 21–40.

25. Hollister B. Sykes and Zenas Block, "Corporate Venturing Obstacles: Sources and Solutions," *Journal of Business Venturing* (Winter 1989): 159–67; Ian

C. MacMillan, Zenas Block, and P. M. Subba Narasimha, "Corporate Venturing: Alternatives, Obstacles Encountered, and Experience Effects," *Journal of Business Venturing* (Spring 1986): 177–91; Ari Ginsberg and Michael Hay, "Confronting the Challenges of Corporate Entrepreneurship: Guidelines for Venture Managers," *European Management Journal* 12 (1994): 382–89; and G. T. Lumpkin and Gregory G. Dess, "Linking Two Dimensions of Entrepreneurial Orientation to Firm Performance: The Moderating Role of Environment and Industry Life Cycle," *Journal of Business Venturing* 16, no. 5 (2001): 429–52.

26. James Brian Quinn, "Managing Innovation: Controlled Chaos," *Harvard Business Review* (May/June 1985): 73–84; see also James Brian Quinn, Jordan J. Baruch, and Karen Anne Zien, *Innovation Explosion* (New York: The Free Press, 1997).

27. R. Duane Ireland, Donald F. Kuratko, and Jeffrey G. Covin, "Antecedents, Elements, and Consequences of Corporate Entrepreneurship," *Best Paper Proceedings: Academy of Management* (August 2003), CD-ROM: L1–L6; and R. Duane Ireland, Jeffrey G. Covin, and Donald F. Kuratko, "Conceptualizing Corporate Entrepreneurship Strategy," *Entrepreneurship Theory and Practice* 33, no. 1 (January, 2009).

28. Charles Baden-Fuller and Henk W. Volberda, "Strategic Renewal: How Large Complex Organizations Prepare for the Future, *International Studies of Management & Organization*, 27, no. 2 (1997): 95–120.

29. Kathleen M. Eisenhardt, Shona L. Brown, and Heidi M. Neck, "Competing on the Entrepreneurial Edge," in *Entrepreneurship as Strategy*, ed. G. D. Meyer and K. A. Heppard (Thousand Oaks, CA: Sage Publications, 2000), 49–62.

30. See Donald F. Kuratko, R. Duane Ireland, Jeffrey G. Covin, and Jeffrey S. Hornsby, "A Model of Middle-Level Managers Corporate Entrepreneurial Behavior," *Entrepreneurship Theory and Practice* 29, no. 6 (2005): 699–716; Andrew C. Corbett and Keith M. Hmieleski, "The Conflicting Cognitions of Corporate Entrepreneurs," *Entrepreneurship Theory and Practice* 31, no. 1 (2007): 103–21; and Jeffrey S. Hornsby, Donald F. Kuratko, Dean A. Shepherd, and Jennifer P. Bott, "Managers' Corporate Entrepreneurial Actions: Examining Perception and Position," *Journal of Business Venturing* (forthcoming).

31. See Gregory G. Dess, G. T. Lumpkin, and Jeffrey E. McGee, "Linking Corporate Entrepreneurship to Strategy, Structure, and Process: Suggested Research Directions," *Entrepreneurship Theory and Practice* (March 1999): 85–102.

32. James C. Collins and Jerry I. Porras, "Building Your Company's Vision," *Harvard Business Review* (September/October 1996): 65–77.

33. See, for example, Dean M. Schroeder, "A Dynamic Perspective on the Impact of Process Innovation upon Competitive Strategies," *Strategic Management Journal* 2 (1990): 25–41; and C. Marlene Fiol, "Thought Worlds Colliding: The Role of

Contradiction in Corporate Innovation Processes," *Entrepreneurship Theory and Practice* (Spring 1995): 71–90.

34. Thomas J. Peters, *Thriving on Chaos* (New York: Harper & Row, 1987).

35. Peter F. Drucker, "The Discipline of Innovation," *Harvard Business Review* (May/June 1985): 67–72.

36. Harry S. Dent, Jr., "Reinventing Corporate Innovation," *Small Business Reports* (June 1990): 31–42.

37. Jane M. Howell and Christopher A. Higgins, "Champions of Change: Identifying, Understanding, and Supporting Champions of Technology Innovations," *Organizational Dynamics* (Summer 1990): 40–55; and Patricia G. Greene, Candida G. Brush, and Myra M. Hart, "The Corporate Venture Champion: A Resource-based Approach to Role and Process," *Entrepreneurship Theory and Practice* (March 1999): 103–22.

38. John A. Pearce II, Tracy Robertson Kramer, and D. Keith Robbins, "Effects of Managers' Entrepreneurial Behavior on Subordinates," *Journal of Business Venturing* 12 (1997): 147–60.

39. See Russell Mitchell, "Masters of Innovation," *Business Week* (April 1989): 58–63; *3M Annual Report*, 1995; and Rosabeth M. Kanter, John Kao, and Fred Wiersema, *Innovation: Breakthrough Ideas at 3M, DuPont, Pfizer, and Rubbermaid* (New York: HarperCollins, 1997).

40. Eric Von Hipple, Stefan Thomke, and Mary Sonnack, "Creating Breakthroughs at 3M," *Harvard Business Review* (September/October 1999): 47–57.

41. David Krackhardt, "Entrepreneurial Opportunities in an Entrepreneurial Firm: A Structural Approach," *Entrepreneurship Theory and Practice* (Spring 1995): 53–70; and Morgan P. Miles and Jeffrey G. Covin, "Exploring the Practice of Corporate Venturing: Some Common Forms and Their Organizational Implications," *Entrepreneurship Theory and Practice* 26, no. 3 (2002): 21–40.

42. Deborah V. Brazeal, "Organizing for Internally Developed Corporate Ventures," *Journal of Business Venturing* (January 1993): 75–90.

43. Dean A. Shepherd, Jeffrey G. Covin, and Donald F. Kuratko, "Project Failure form Corporate Entrepreneurship: Managing the Grief Process," *Journal of Business Venturing* (forthcoming); see also Dean A. Shepherd, "Learning from Business Failure: Propositions about the Grief Recovery Process for the Self-Employed," *Academy of Management Review* 28 (2003): 318–29.

44. Donald F. Kuratko and Jeffrey S. Hornsby, "Developing Entrepreneurial Leadership in Contemporary Organizations," *Journal of Management Systems* 8 (1997): 17–24.

45. Jeffrey S. Hornsby, Donald F. Kuratko, and Shaker A. Zahra, "Middle Managers' Perception of the

Internal Environment for Corporate Entrepreneurship: Assessing a Measurement Scale," *Journal of Business Venturing* 17, no. 3 (2002): 253–73; Jeffrey S. Hornsby, Donald F. Kuratko, Dean A. Shepherd, and Jennifer P. Bott, "Managers' Corporate Entrepreneurial Actions: Examining Perception and Position," *Journal of Business Venturing* (forthcoming); and Jeffrey S. Hornsby, Daniel T. Holt, and Donald F. Kuratko, "The Dynamic Nature of Corporate Entrepreneurship Constructs: Assessing the CEAI," *National Academy of Management Best Paper Proceedings*, August, 2008. CD ROM.

46. Vijay Sathe, "From Surface to Deep Corporate Entrepreneurship," *Human Resource Management* (Winter 1988): 389–411.

47. Rosabeth M. Kanter, *Innovative Reward Systems for the Changing Workplace* (New York: McGraw-Hill, 1994).

48. Chris Lee, "Beyond Teamwork," *Training* (June 1990): 25–32; Michael F. Wolff, "Building Teams— What Works," *Research Technology Management* (November/December 1989): 9–10; and Deborah H. Francis and William R. Sandberg, "Friendship within Entrepreneurial Teams and Its Association with Team and Venture Performance," *Entrepreneurship Theory and Practice* 25, no. 2 (2002): 5–25.

49. Robert B. Reich, "The Team as Hero," *Harvard Business Review* (May/June 1987): 81.

50. Judith B. Kamm and Aaron J. Nurick, "The Stages of Team Venture Formulation: A Decision-Making Model," *Entrepreneurship Theory and Practice* (Winter 1993): 17–27; and Michael A. Hitt, Robert D. Nixon, Robert E. Hoskisson, and Rahul Kochhar, "Corporate Entrepreneurship and Cross-functional Fertilization: Activation, Process, and Disintegration of a New Product Design Team," *Entrepreneurship Theory and Practice* 23 (1999): 145–68.

51. R. Duane Ireland, Donald F. Kuratko, and Michael H. Morris, "A Health Audit for Corporate Entrepreneurship: Innovation at All Levels," *Journal of Business Strategy*, 27, no. 1 (2006): 10–17.

52. Steven W. Floyd and P. J. Lane, "Strategizing Throughout the Organization: Managing Role Conflict in Strategic Renewal," *Academy of Management Review* 25 (2000): 154–77.

53. Donald F. Kuratko, R. Duane Ireland, Jeffrey G. Covin, and Jeffrey S. Hornsby, "A Model of Middle-Level Managers Corporate Entrepreneurial Behavior," *Entrepreneurship Theory and Practice* 29, no. 6 (2005): 699–716; see also Ethel Brundin, Holger Pazelt, and Dean A. Shepherd, "Managers' Emotional Displays and Employees' Willingness to Act Entrepreneurially," *Journal of Business Venturing* 23, no. 2 (2008): 221–43; and Stewart Thornhill and Raphael Amit, "A Dynamic Perspective of Internal Fit in Corporate Venturing," *Journal of Business Venturing* 16, no. 1 (2001): 25–50.

54. Donald F. Kuratko, Jeffrey S. Hornsby, and Michael G. Goldsby, "Sustaining Corporate Entrepreneurship: Modeling Perceived Implementation and Outcome Comparisons at Organizational and Individual Levels," *International Journal of Entrepreneurship and Innovation* 5, no. 2 (May 2004): 77–89.

The Social and Ethical Perspectives of Entrepreneurship

Entrepreneurial Thought

Ownership is hope. It's curiosity, openness, an eagerness to learn and grow. It's caring about yourself and the people around you. It's wanting to contribute, to make a difference. It's the courage and conviction to face the future. It's confidence, self-esteem, and pride. It's the ability to handle diversity. It's giving back to your community and appreciating the gifts you've received. Those are great qualities to have in a business . . . and they're the qualities we need now more than ever!!

— **JACK STACK, CEO, SRC HOLDINGS CORP.** *A Stake in the Outcome*

Chapter Objectives

1 To examine the concept of social entrepreneurship

2 To introduce the challenges of social enterprise

3 To discuss the importance of ethics for entrepreneurs

4 To define the term *ethics*

5 To study ethics in a conceptual framework for a dynamic environment

6 To review the constant dilemma of law versus ethics

7 To present strategies for establishing ethical responsibility

8 To emphasize the importance of entrepreneurial ethical leadership

The Social Entrepreneurship Movement

Social entrepreneurship is a new form of entrepreneurship that exhibits characteristics of nonprofits, governments, and businesses. It applies traditional (private-sector) entrepreneurship's focus on innovation, risk taking, and large-scale transformation to social problem solving. The social entrepreneurship process begins with a perceived social opportunity that is translated into an enterprise concept; resources are then ascertained and acquired to execute the enterprise's goals.[1] This new movement has garnered attention in a number of ways in recent years:

- In 2006, Teach For America founder Wendy Kopp and City Year cofounders Michael Brown and Alan Khazei were profiled among *U.S. News & World Report's* Top 25 Leaders.

- Muhammad Yunus and his organization, the Grameen Bank, were awarded a Nobel Peace Prize.

- Victoria Hale of the Institute for OneWorld Health and Jim Fructerman of Benetech received "genius awards" from the MacArthur Foundation. They identify themselves as social entrepreneurs.

- In 2005, the Public Broadcasting System (PBS) and the Skoll Foundation created and aired a two-part miniseries profiling "The New Heroes," who were 14 social entrepreneurs from around the globe. They followed the series with a three-year grant program encouraging film-makers, documentary filmmakers, and journalists to "produce work that promotes large-scale public awareness of social entrepreneurship."[2]

- For the past six years, the World Economic Forum, which annually brings together business, government, and national leaders who are "committed to improving the state of the world," has hosted a Social Entrepreneurs' Summit. In partnership with the Schwab Foundation, the forum convenes social entrepreneurs as one of its special-interest communities, placing social entrepreneurship on par with only nine other interest groups, including global growth companies, international media, and labor leaders.[3]

- Founded in 1980 by Bill Drayton, Ashoka is leading a profound transformation in society. Beginning with the first Ashoka Fellows elected in India in 1981, Ashoka has grown to an association of more than 1,800 Fellows in more than 60 countries on the world's five main continents. Along with the global network of Fellows, business entrepreneurs, policy makers, investors, academics, and journalists, Ashoka is now working collectively to ensure that social entrepreneurs and their innovations continue to inspire a new generation of local change makers to create positive social change.[4]

The term *social entrepreneur* has come to mean a person (or small group of individuals) who founds and/or leads an organization or initiative engaged in social entrepreneurship. Social entrepreneurs sometimes are referred to as "public entrepreneurs," "civic entrepreneurs," or "social innovators." Noted expert Arthur C. Brooks outlines the following activities that characterize the social entrepreneur:

- Adoption of a mission to create and sustain social value (beyond personal value)
- Recognition and relentless pursuit of opportunities for social value
- Engagement in continuous innovation and learning
- Action beyond the limited resources at hand
- Heightened sense of accountability[5]

Numerous publications have brought the term *social entrepreneurship* into wider recognition. For example, in recent years the *New York Times*, the *Economist*, and the *Harvard Business Review* have all printed stories that focus on social entrepreneurship.[6]

As social entrepreneurship rapidly finds its way into the vocabulary of policy makers, journalists, academics, and the general public, the world faces incredible societal challenges. The boom of the field of social entrepreneurship, and its promise as a means to address the daunting social problems across the globe, are of particular importance for every entrepreneur.

entrepreneurship in practice

Benetech: A Sustainable Social Innovation

Twenty years ago, if a blind person wanted to read printed text not available in Braille, depending on the help of someone else was just about the only choice. The best available technology for a blind person to read printed text was a machine the size of a washing machine with a five-figure price tag. This was an unrealistic and unaffordable option for accomplishing daily tasks like browsing a newspaper or looking over a piece of mail. The technology for creating an affordable, portable machine existed. However, the potential customer base—blind individuals and their employers—was too small to promise a traditional return on investment. As a result, technology investors were unwilling to take the risk to develop such a product.

Benetech was founded as a low-profit-market approach to ensuring the development of technology that promises to have a high social value despite low potential for generating a typical return on investment. As founder Jim Fructerman explains, "The last 18 years have been great years for the computer industry. Computers have gotten faster, better, cheaper, smaller, lighter, brighter. What we've done is essentially ridden the back of that industry to say: 'How can we take advantage of these high-performance, low-cost platforms and turn them into effective tools for people with disabilities?'" The company's first product, the Arkenstone Reading Machine, makes use of the optical character recognition (OCR) technology found in scanners, and can be used with a personal computer to scan and read text aloud. At a cost of less than $2,000, the Arkenstone Reading Machine quickly found a larger customer base than originally predicted. In addition to blind individuals and

their employers, people with learning disabilities and government agencies that serve the disabled—including the U.S. Department of Veterans Affairs—began purchasing the product. This unexpected, expanded customer base helped to generate millions of dollars in revenue annually, and ultimately led to the sale of the reading machine and the Arkenstone brand to a for-profit distributor of disabilities products. The machine is now in its fourth release and remains an industry-leading product.

The Arkenstone Reading Machine provides an example of how a low-profit-market approach eventually may develop a market that can be served by a traditional for-profit approach. In Benetech's case, selling the reading machine to a for-profit distributor once there was a sufficient market has enabled the organization to fund the development of other socially valuable technology solutions without being constrained to those projects with high potential for significant profitability.

Benetech was able to test and ultimately develop a self-sustaining solution to a problem caused by a market failure that government was unable to address. Its inexpensive reading machine, tested in the early stages by accepting below-average returns, ultimately created a new and profitable market in addition to serving the thousands of Americans who previously were unable to read printed text on their own.

Source: Adapted from U.S. Small Business Administration, "The Small Business Economy: A Report to the President" (Washington, DC: U.S. Government Printing Office, 2007); and Christian Seelos and Johanna Mair. "Social Entrepreneurship: Creating New Business Models to Serve the Poor." *Business Horizons* 48 (2005): 241–46.

By adapting some of the same principles that have been so effective in successful entrepreneurship, all leaders have a similar opportunity to support social entrepreneurship—and thereby generate transformative, financially sustainable solutions to social problems that face the nation. As stated in a recent article for the *Stanford Social Innovation Review,* "Social entrepreneurship, we believe, is as vital to the progress of societies as is entrepreneurship to the progress of economies, and it merits more rigorous, serious attention than it has attracted so far."[7]

Ashoka founder Bill Drayton has famously commented that "social entrepreneurs are not content just to give a fish or teach how to fish. They will not rest until they have revolutionized the fishing industry."[8] Like other entrepreneurs, social entrepreneurs are creative thinkers continuously striving for innovation, which can involve new technologies, supply sources, distribution outlets, or methods of production. Innovation may also mean starting new organizations, or offering new products or services. Innovative ideas can be completely new inventions or creative adaptations of existing ones.[9]

Social entrepreneurs are change agents; they create large-scale change using pattern-breaking ideas, they address the root causes of social problems, and they possess the ambition to create systemic change by introducing a new idea and persuading others to adopt it. These types of transformative changes can be national or global. They also can be highly localized—but no less powerful—in their impact. Most often, social entrepreneurs who create transformative changes combine innovative practices, a deep knowledge of their social issue area, and cutting-edge research to achieve their goals. For entrepreneurs working in the social realm, innovation is not a one-time event—rather, it is a lifetime pursuit.

The Social Enterprise Challenge

It is obvious from the preceding section that, in the twenty-first century, social enterprise has emerged as a major issue among entrepreneurial thinkers.[10] Although it takes various forms for different industries and companies, the basic challenge is the same for all. Generally speaking, social enterprise consists of obligations a business has to society. These obligations extend to many different areas (Table 4.1 presents some examples). The diversity of social enterprise opens the door to questions concerning the *extent* to which corporations should be involved.

An examination of the stages or levels of social enterprise behavior that corporations exhibit reveals that distinct differences exist in the way corporations respond. S. Prakesh Sethi, a researcher in social enterprise, has established a framework that classifies the social actions of corporations into three distinct categories: social obligation, social enterprise, and social responsiveness (see Table 4.2).

This framework illustrates the range of corporate intensity about social issues. Some firms simply react to social issues through obedience to the laws (social obligation); others respond more actively, accepting responsibility for various programs (social responsibility); still others are highly proactive and are even willing to be evaluated by the public for various activities (social responsiveness).

Only a few studies have examined different features of social enterprise by entrepreneurs.[11] For example, in one study the researchers used a random telephone survey to explore the general public's perceptions of social responsibility in large versus small businesses. Their findings indicated that entrepreneurs were more critical of their own performance than was the general public.[12]

Environmental Awareness

The twenty-first century is one of greater environmental concern. The reawakening of the need to preserve and protect our natural resources has motivated businesses toward a stronger environmental awareness. As illustrated in Table 4.1, the environment stands out as one of the major challenges of social enterprise. Green capitalism has emerged as a powerful new force in examining the manner in which business is conducted in relation to the environment. This term refers to a concept of *ecologically* sustainable development being transformed into *economically* sustainable development. Our recent "throwaway" culture has endangered our natural resources, from soil to water to air. Environmentalists Paul Hawken (co-author of *Natural Capitalism: Creating the Next Industrial Revolution*) and William McDonough state: "Industry is being told that if it puts its hamburgers in coated-paper wrappers, eliminates emissions, and plants two trees for every car sold, we will be on the way to an environmentally sound world. Nothing could be further from the truth. The danger lies not in the half measures but in the illusions they foster, the belief

Table **4.1**	**What Is the Nature of Social Enterprise?**

Environment	Pollution control
	Restoration or protection of environment
	Conservation of natural resources
	Recycling efforts
Energy	Conservation of energy in production and marketing operations
	Efforts to increase the energy efficiency of products
	Other energy-saving programs (for example, company-sponsored carpools)
Fair Business Practices	Employment and advancement of women and minorities
	Employment and advancement of disadvantaged individuals (disabled, Vietnam veterans, ex-offenders, former drug addicts, mentally retarded, and hard-core unemployed)
	Support for minority-owned businesses
Human Resources	Promotion of employee health and safety
	Employee training and development
	Remedial education programs for disadvantaged employees
	Alcohol and drug counseling programs
	Career counseling
	Child day-care facilities for working parents
	Employee physical fitness and stress management programs
Community Involvement	Donations of cash, products, services, or employee time
	Sponsorship of public health projects
	Support of education and the arts
	Support of community recreation programs
	Cooperation in community projects (recycling centers, disaster assistance, and urban renewal)
Products	Enhancement of product safety
	Sponsorship of product safety education programs
	Reduction of polluting potential of products
	Improvement in nutritional value of products
	Improvement in packaging and labeling

Source: Richard M. Hodgetts and Donald F. Kuratko, *Management,* 3rd ed. (San Diego, CA: Harcourt Brace Jovanovich, 1991), 670.

that subtle course corrections can guide us to a good life that will include a 'conserved' natural world and cozy shopping malls."[13]

   This quote illustrates the enormous challenges entrepreneurs confront as they attempt to build socially responsible organizations for the future. Of the 100 million enterprises world-wide, a growing number are attempting to redefine their social responsibilities because they no longer accept the notion that the business of business is business. Because of an international ability to communicate information widely and quickly, many entrepreneurs are

Table **4.2**	Classifying Social Enterprise Behavior		

Dimension of Behavior	Stage One: Social Obligation	Stage Two: Social Responsibility	Stage Three: Social Responsiveness
Response to social pressures	Maintains low public profile, but if attacked, uses PR methods to upgrade its public image; denies any deficiencies; blames public dissatisfaction on ignorance or failure to understand corporate functions; discloses information only where legally required	Accepts responsibility for solving current problems; will admit deficiencies in former practices and attempt to persuade public that its current practices meet social norms; attitude toward critics conciliatory; freer information disclosures than stage one	Willingly discusses activities with outside groups; makes information freely available to the public; accepts formal and informal inputs from outside groups in decision making; is willing to be publicly evaluated for its various activities
Philanthropy	Contributes only when direct benefit to it clearly shown; otherwise, views contributions as responsibility of individual employees	Contributes to noncontroversial and established causes; matches employee contributions	Activities of stage two, *plus* support and contributions to new, controversial groups whose needs it sees as unfulfilled and increasingly important

Source: Excerpted from S. Prakash Sethi, "A Conceptual Framework for Environmental Analysis of Social Issues and Evaluation of Business Patterns," *Academy of Management Journal* (January 1979): 68. Copyright 1979 by the Academy of Management. Reproduced with permission of the Academy of Management.

beginning to recognize their responsibility to the world around them. Entrepreneurial organizations, the dominant inspiration for change throughout the world, are beginning the arduous task of addressing social-environmental problems.

Entrepreneurs need to take the lead in designing a new approach to business in which everyday acts of work and life accumulate—as a matter of course—into a better world. One theorist has developed the term ecovision to describe a possible leadership style for innovative organizations.[14] Ecovision encourages open and flexible structures that encompass the employees, the organization, and the environment, with attention to evolving social demands.

The environmental movement consists of many initiatives connected primarily by values rather than by design. A plan to create a sustainable future should realize its objectives through a practical, clearly stated strategy. Some of the key steps recommended by Hawken and McDonough are as follows:

1. **Eliminate the concept of waste.** Seek newer methods of production and recycling.

2. **Restore accountability.** Encourage consumer involvement in making companies accountable.

3. **Make prices reflect costs.** Reconstruct the system to incorporate a "green fee" where taxes are added to energy, raw materials, and services to encourage conservation.

4. **Promote diversity.** Continue researching the needed compatibility of our ever-evolving products and inventions.

5. **Make conservation profitable.** Rather than demanding "low prices" to encourage production shortcuts, allow new costs for environmental stewardship.

6. **Insist on accountability of nations.** Develop a plan for every trading nation of sustainable development enforced by tariffs.[15]

Ecosystem Services

Ecosystem services is a corporate-environmental concept that recently has gained popularity. The underlying notion of such services is an attempt to compensate nature for the products and services that it provides, which include clean water and carbon storage. Although companies that invest in such efforts certainly reap the benefits of their efforts, the fact remains that the environment is also a beneficiary.

Coca-Cola is one company that has implemented an ecosystem services plan. Its initiatives are directed toward protecting fresh water and, in some cases, generating it. One of the company's initiatives involves working with Guatemalan farmers to implement more eco-friendly farming systems to protect watersheds. Part of this program includes providing more-efficient wood-burning stoves to the local villagers to lessen their need to cut down trees. As skeptics of Coca-Cola's intentions would surely point out, the company's core products require a ready supply of fresh water, so any efforts toward protecting those supplies can hardly be considered unselfish, philanthropic acts; yet, there is no doubt that the local inhabitants also require a reliable source of fresh water for survival.

Other companies are beginning to explore strategies for satisfying corporate goals while simultaneously maintaining the ecology that serves as the foundation for their industry. As another example, the travel industry does not appear to be dependent on the environment in any way. After all, travel agencies and hotel chains are service providers that do not have to concern themselves with sources of raw materials. The problem with this perspective is that it undermines the importance that nature's beauty plays in tourism. Marriott is currently considering a program to curb deforestation in the Amazon. This plan is not part of some radical effort by Marriott to open new locations in a remote rainforest; rather, it deals with the company's attempt to address global warming, which impacts nature across the globe.

Broad-minded initiatives such as these are based on companies' recognition that suffering ecologies are bad for business, from both a public relations perspective and an operational one. Starbucks has recently begun its own initiative with Conservation International to develop CAFÉ standards—environmental and social guidelines for Starbucks' growers—that will result in Starbucks paying higher prices when the policies are followed. The next step in Starbucks' effort to ensure that its core product is secure is to protect the land around locations where coffee is grown. The aim is to assist coffee farmers in also acting as carbon farmers in order to claim a share of the carbon finance business, which has quickly grown to $70 billion.

This particular project involves Starbucks financing Conservation International's efforts to protect the landscapes around coffee-growing areas through their work with local growers. By partnering with local governments or by undertaking the initiatives on their own, growers commit themselves to preserving forests by avoiding their destruction or by replanting them. Through this program, the participants qualify for carbon credits from companies such as Yahoo!, Google, and News Corp., which already have programs in place to offset their carbon emissions voluntarily. The thinking is that forestry projects, such as the one being pursued by Starbucks, will grow in popularity when new rules that require companies in the United States to reduce their carbon emissions are implemented as part of the Kyoto framework. Once these rules are in place—scheduled for post-2012—the carbon credits that these local parties will have to sell will be even more valuable.

Starbucks has plans to move forward with its current strategy, expanding its efforts to areas in Sumatra, Indonesia, and Chiapas, Mexico. The hope is that all will go well, resulting in further expansion to Latin America, Africa, and Asia. The initiative will both reinforce Starbucks' corporate image as a socially minded company and benefit the suppliers on which Starbucks' business model depends. Supporting the environment is no longer just about social responsibility—it is also good for the bottom line.

Source: Adapted from Marc Gunther, "Starbucks Sows Carbon Farmers," *Fortune,* March 21, 2008, http://money.cnn.com/2008/03/20/news/companies/gunther_starbucks.fortune/index.htm?postversion=2008032106 (accessed March 21, 2008).

Although the results of studies specific to ethics, social enterprise, and entrepreneurs are still emerging, a number of views are already widely accepted. The research is showing differences in the ethical environment, ethical precepts, and ethical perceptions between large firms and small firms. The reasons relate to the structure of smaller firms, which have fewer professional specialists, less formality, and a stronger influence by the owner/entrepreneur.

The Ethical Side of Entrepreneurship

Ethical issues in business are of great importance today, and with good reason. The prevalence of scandals, fraud, and various forms of executive misconduct in corporations has spurred the watchful eye of the public.[16]

Ethics is not a new topic, however. It has figured prominently in philosophical thought since the time of Socrates, Plato, and Aristotle. Derived from the Greek word *ethos,* meaning custom or mode of conduct, ethics has challenged philosophers for centuries to determine what exactly represents right or wrong conduct. For example, business executive Vernon R. Loucks, Jr., notes that "it was about 560 B.C. . . . when the Greek thinker Chilon registered the opinion that a merchant does better to take a loss than to make a dishonest profit. His reasoning was that a loss may be painful for a while, but dishonesty hurts forever—and it's still timely."[17]

Today's entrepreneurs are faced with many ethical decisions, especially during the early stages of their new ventures. And, as Sir Adrian Cadbury observed, "There is no simple universal formula for solving ethical problems. We have to choose from our own codes of conduct whichever rules are appropriate to the case in hand; the outcome of these choices makes us who we are."[18]

In the following sections, we examine some of the issues surrounding ethics and entrepreneurship. It is our hope that aspiring entrepreneurs will realize the powerful impact that integrity and ethical conduct have on creating a successful venture.

Defining Ethics

In the broadest sense, ethics provides the basic rules or parameters for conducting any activity in an "acceptable" manner. More specifically, ethics represents a set of principles prescribing a behavioral code that explains what is good and right or bad and wrong; ethics may, in addition, outline moral duty and obligations.[19] The problem with most definitions of the term is not the description itself but its implications for implementation. The definition is a static description implying that society agrees on certain universal principles. Because society operates in a dynamic and ever-changing environment, however, such a consensus does not exist.[20] In fact, continual conflict over the ethical nature of decisions is quite prevalent.

This conflict arises for a number of reasons. First, business enterprises are confronted by many interests, both inside and outside the organization—for example, stockholders, customers, managers, the community, the government, employees, private interest groups, unions, peers, and so on. Second, society is undergoing dramatic change. Values, mores, and societal norms have gone through a drastic evolution in the past few decades. A definition of ethics in such a rapidly changing environment must be based more on a process than on a static code. Figure 4.1 illustrates a conceptual framework for viewing this process. As one ethicist states, "Deciding what is good or right or bad and wrong in such a dynamic environment is necessarily 'situational.' Therefore, instead of relying on a set of fixed ethical principles, we must now develop an ethical process."[21]

The quadrants depicted in Figure 4.1 demonstrate the age-old dilemma between law and ethics. Moving from the ideal ethical and legal position (Quadrant I) to an unethical and illegal position (Quadrant IV), one can see the continuum of activities within an ethical process. Yet legality provides societal standards but not definitive answers to ethical questions.

| *Figure* | **4.1** | **Classifying Decisions Using a Conceptual Framework** |

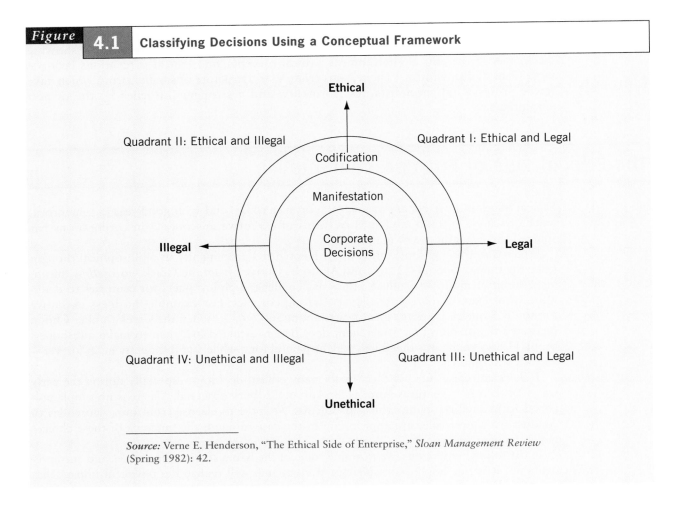

Source: Verne E. Henderson, "The Ethical Side of Enterprise," *Sloan Management Review* (Spring 1982): 42.

Ethics and Laws

For the entrepreneur, the legal versus ethical dilemma is a vital one. Just how far can an entrepreneur go to establish his or her venture? Survival of the venture is a strong motivation for entrepreneurs, and, although the law provides the boundaries for what is illegal (even though the laws are subject to constant interpretation), it does not supply answers for ethical considerations.

Managerial Rationalizations

One researcher suggests that legal behavior represents one of four **rationalizations** managers use to justify questionable conduct. The four rationalizations are believing (1) that the activity is not "really" illegal or immoral; (2) that it is in the individual's or the corporation's best interest; (3) that it will never be found out; and (4) that, because it helps the company, the company will condone it.[22]

These rationalizations appear realistic, given the behavior of many business enterprises today. However, the legal aspect can be the most dubious. This is because the business world (and society) relies heavily on the law to qualify the actions of various situations. The law interprets the situations within the prescribed framework. Unfortunately, this framework does not always include ethical or moral behavior. This is left up to the individual, which is the precise reason for the dilemma.

In any examination of the realm of managerial rationalizations, the idea of morally questionable acts becomes a major concern for understanding ethical conduct. One research

Table	4.3	Types of Morally Questionable Acts

Type	Direct Effect	Examples
Nonrole	Against the firm	Expense account cheating
		Embezzlement
		Stealing supplies
Role failure	Against the firm	Superficial performance appraisal
		Not confronting expense account cheating
		Palming off a poor performer with inflated praise
Role distortion	For the firm	Bribery
		Price fixing
		Manipulating suppliers
Role assertion	For the firm	Investing in South Africa
		Using nuclear technology for energy generation
		Not withdrawing product line in face of initial allegations of inadequate safety

Source: James A. Waters and Frederick Bird, "Attending to Ethics in Management," *Journal of Business Ethics* 5 (1989): 494.

study developed a typology of morally questionable acts (Table 4.3 summarizes the distinctions made in this typology).[23] Morally questionable acts are either "against the firm" or "on behalf of the firm." In addition, the managerial role differs for various acts. **Nonrole** acts are those the person takes outside of his or her role as manager, yet they go against the firm; examples include expense account cheating and embezzlement. **Role failure** acts also go against the firm, but they involve a person failing to perform his or her managerial role, including superficial performance appraisals (not totally honest) and not confronting someone who is cheating on expense accounts. **Role distortion** acts and **role assertion** acts are rationalized as being "for the firm." These acts involve managers/entrepreneurs who rationalize that the long-run interests of the firm are foremost. Examples include bribery, price fixing, manipulating suppliers, and failing to withdraw a potentially dangerous product from the market. Role distortion is the behavior of individuals who think they are acting in the best interests of the firm, so their roles are "distorted." Role assertion is the behavior of individuals who assert their roles beyond what they should be, thinking (falsely) that they are helping the firm.

All four of the roles involved in the morally questionable acts—whether "for" or "against" the firm—illustrate the types of rationalizations that can occur. In addition, this typology presents an interesting insight into the distinctions involved with managerial rationalization.

The Matter of Morality

Ethical conduct may reach beyond the limits of the law.[24] As one group of noted legal writers has pointed out, morals and law are not synonymous but may be viewed as two circles partially superimposed on each other (see Figure 4.2). The area covered by both the moral standards circle and the legal requirements circle represents the body of ideas that is both moral and legal. Yet the largest expanse of area is outside this overlapping

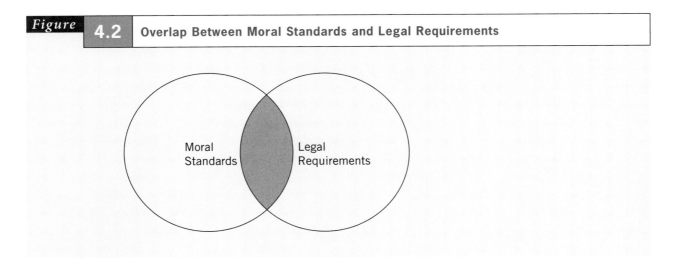

Figure **4.2   Overlap Between Moral Standards and Legal Requirements**

portion, indicating the vast difference that sometimes exists between morality (ethics) and law.[25]

Ethics researcher, LaRue T. Hosmer, has reached three conclusions regarding the relationship between legal requirements and moral judgment. First, as noted earlier, the requirements of law may overlap at times but do not duplicate the moral standards of society. Some laws have no moral content whatsoever (for example, driving on the right side of the road), some laws are morally unjust (for example, racial segregation laws before the 1960s), and some moral standards have no legal basis (for example, telling a lie). Second, legal requirements tend to be negative (forbidding acts), whereas morality tends to be positive (encouraging acts). Third, legal requirements usually lag behind the acceptable moral standards of society.[26]

In addition, even if the argument were made that laws are supposed to be the collective moral judgment of society, inherent problems arise when people believe that laws represent morality. Whether it is because of a lack of information on issues, misrepresentation of values or laws, or an imprecise judicial system, the legal environment has difficulty encompassing all ethical and moral expectations. Thus, the issue of law and ethics will continue to be a dilemma for entrepreneurs.

Economic Trade-Offs

Innovation, risk taking, and venture creation are the backbone of the free enterprise system. From this system emerge the qualities of individualism and competition. These qualities have produced an economic system that creates jobs (approximately 20 million in the past decade) and enormous growth in ventures (more than 600,000 incorporations each year). However, these same qualities also have produced complex trade-offs between economic profits and social welfare. On one hand is the generation of profits, jobs, and efficiency; on the other hand is the quest for personal and social respect, honesty, and integrity. A utilitarian ethical norm would calculate what the greatest good for the greatest number would be. This calculation also would take into account future generations.[27] Unfortunately, although the calculation sounds easy, in practice it borders on the impossible. To illustrate, one study reported that 65 percent of the public said executives would do everything they could to make a profit, even if it meant ignoring society's needs.[28] Another study reported that a Darwinian ethic was now prevailing in business that spreads a "profit-at-any-price" attitude among business owners and managers.[29]

Yet the public's perception may be based more on a misunderstanding of the free enterprise system than a condemnation of it. One ethicist, Margaret Maxey, reminds us that—in a complex world of changing technology and valuable innovations—we cannot blame single individuals for the ethical problems of free enterprise. Rather, we must understand the total, systematic impact that free enterprise has on the common good.[30]

the entrepreneurial process

Avoiding Another Enron Disaster

Enron, Tyco, Arthur Andersen, and Computer Associates: Why was the recent boom period plagued with so many unethical practices among companies? Historically, misconduct and bad judgment often have coincided with periods of great prosperity. When attitudes are characterized by "anything goes," and the market is typified by expanding profits and stocks at full throttle, the economy is at peak danger—greed and prosperity blur the line between right and wrong.

The greatest equivalent of today's ethical lapses is the Roaring Twenties and the stock market crash of 1929. This period was made notorious by, among other people, Ivar Kreuger. Kreuger founded an international conglomerate in wooden matches by lending money to foreign governments in return for nationwide match monopolies—the money from such loans came from the sale of stock. Later, an audit of his books revealed that $250 million in assets never really existed. Eventually, all this activity led to the creation of the Securities and Exchange Commission (SEC).

Today, the possibilities to create spectacular financial debacles have increased due to more complex financial vehicles that take advantage of the "gray" areas in accounting. The following list explains five ways investors are demanding more information from companies to ensure that corporate accounting is not finagling the financials.

1. *Bring hidden liabilities back onto the balance sheet.* It was the disclosure of billions of dollars in off-balance-sheet debt tucked away in special purpose entities, or SPEs (entities created to hide potential losses or debt from public view), that brought Enron's problems to the forefront. Though they are legitimate, SPEs have been controversial for nearly 30 years. Current practices allow removal of an SPE from the balance sheet if an investor is willing to contribute just 3 percent of its capital.

2. *Highlight the things that matter.* Anything less than 5 or 10 percent of earnings or assets generally was considered immaterial to overall performance and allowed to be left off the statements. Now the SEC and the Financial Accounting Standards Board are evaluating the qualitative factors in addition to the quantitative factors.

3. *List the risks and assumptions built into the numbers.* Corporate "guesstimations" can play a large role in corporate earnings; from future demand of a product line to discounted rates due to risk factors, investors are demanding to know the assumptions.

4. *Standardize operating income.* Standard & Poor's has made a proposal for what should be included and excluded from pro forma operating earnings. Currently, there is no uniformity to detail what companies add and subtract from the net income to generate their pro formas.

5. *Provide aid in figuring free-cash flow.* Analysts currently calculate free-cash flow themselves by utilizing past results. Investors are, therefore, left to guess what information should be used.

Source: Heesun Wee, "The Dirt a Bull Market Leaves Behind," *BusinessWeek Online*, June 13, 2002, http://www.businessweek.com/bwdaily/dnflash/jun2002/nf20020613_1338.htm (accessed April 10, 2008); and Nanette Byrnes, "Commentary: Five Ways to Avoid More Enrons," *BusinessWeek Online*, February 18, 2002, http://www.businessweek.com/magazine/content/02_07/b3770056.htm (accessed April 10, 2008).

Despite these misconceptions, the fact remains that unethical behavior does take place. Why? A few possible explanations include (1) greed, (2) distinctions between activities at work and activities at home, (3) a lack of a foundation in ethics, (4) survival (bottom-line thinking), and (5) a reliance on other social institutions to convey and reinforce ethics. Whatever the reasons, ethical decision-making is a challenge that confronts every businessperson involved in large or small enterprises.[31]

Establishing a Strategy for Ethical Enterprise

Because the free enterprise system in which the entrepreneur flourishes is fraught with myriad conflicts, entrepreneurs need to commit to an established strategy for ethical enterprise.

Ethical Practices and Codes of Conduct

A code of conduct is a statement of ethical practices or guidelines to which an enterprise adheres. Many such codes exist—some related to industry at large and others related directly to corporate conduct. These codes cover a multitude of subjects, ranging from misuse of corporate assets, conflict of interest, and use of inside information to equal employment practices, falsification of books or records, and antitrust violations. Based on the results of recent research, two important conclusions can be reached. First, codes of conduct are becoming more prevalent in industry. Management is not just giving lip service to ethics and moral behavior; it is putting its ideas into writing and distributing these guidelines for everyone in the organization to read and follow. Second, in contrast to earlier codes, the more recent ones are proving to be more meaningful in terms of external legal and social development, more comprehensive in terms of their coverage, and easier to implement in terms of the administrative procedures used to enforce them.[32]

Of course, the most important question remains to be answered: Will management really adhere to a high moral code? Many managers would respond to this question by answering "yes." Why? The main reason is that it is good business. One top executive put the idea this way: "Singly or in combination, unethical practices have a corrosive effect on free markets and free trade, which are fundamental to the survival of the free enterprise system. They subvert the laws of supply and demand, and they short-circuit competition based on classical ideas of product quality, service, and price. Free markets become replaced by contrived markets. The need for constant improvement in products or services is thus removed."[33]

A second, related reason is that by improving the moral climate of the enterprise, the corporation can eventually win back the public's confidence. This would mark a turnaround, because many people today question the moral and ethical integrity of companies and believe that businesspeople try to get away with everything they can. Only time will tell whether codes of conduct will improve business practices. Current trends indicate, however, that the business community is working hard to achieve this objective.[34]

Approaches to Managerial Ethics

When focusing on an ethical position, entrepreneurs should analyze various organizational characteristics. One study examined ethical norms, motives, goals, orientation toward law, and strategy and used these characteristics to define three distinct types of management: **immoral management, amoral management, and moral management.**[35] Table 4.4 provides a summary of each characteristic within each of the ethical types. These characteristics are important for gaining insight into the continuum of behaviors that can be exhibited. Before entrepreneurs set forth any strategy, it is imperative that they analyze their own reactions to these characteristics and thus their own ethical styles.

Moving from an immoral or amoral position to a moral position requires a great deal of personal effort. Whether it is a commitment to sending employees to training seminars on business ethics, establishing codes of conduct, or exhibiting tighter operational controls, the entrepreneur needs to develop particular areas around which a strategy can be formulated.

A HOLISTIC APPROACH

One author has suggested a holistic management approach that encompasses ethics in its perspective. This dual-focused approach includes "knowing how" and "knowing that." Admittedly, it is an aesthetic, philosophical perspective, but the understanding of it "reminds the administrator that there exist complementary forms of acquiring managerial knowledge."[36]

Table 4.4	Approaches to Managerial Ethics		
Organizational Characteristics	Immoral Management	Amoral Management	Moral Management
Ethical norms	Managerial decisions, actions, and behavior imply a positive and active opposition to what is moral (ethical). Decisions are discordant with accepted ethical principles. An active negation of what is moral is implied.	Management is neither moral nor immoral, but decisions lie outside the sphere to which moral judgments apply. Managerial activity is outside or beyond the moral order of a particular code. A lack of ethical perception and moral awareness may be implied.	Managerial activity conforms to a standard of ethical, or right, behavior. Managers conform to accepted professional standards of conduct. Ethical leadership is commonplace on the part of management.
Motives	Selfish: Management cares only about its or the company's gains.	Well-intentioned but selfish: The impact on others is not considered.	Good: Management wants to succeed but only within the confines of sound ethical precepts (fairness, justice, due process).
Goals	Profitability and organizational success at any price.	Profitability; other goals not considered.	Profitability within the confines of legal obedience and ethical standards.
Orientation toward law	Legal standards are barriers management must overcome to accomplish what it wants.	Law is the ethical guide, preferably the letter of the law. The central question is what managers can do legally.	Obedience is toward the letter and spirit of the law. Law is a minimal ethical behavior. Managers prefer to operate well above what the law mandates.
Strategy	Exploit opportunities for corporate gain. Cut corners when it appears useful.	Give managers free rein. Personal ethics may apply, but only if managers choose. Respond to legal mandates if caught and required to do so.	Live by sound ethical standards. Assume leadership position when ethical dilemmas arise. Enlightened self-interest prevails.

Source: Archie B. Carroll, "In Search of the Moral Manager," *Business Horizons* (March/April 1987): 12. Copyright © 1987 by the Foundation for the School of Business at Indiana University. Reprinted by permission.

In other words, managerial practices as well as the ethical implications of those practices need to be acquired.

To apply a holistic approach, entrepreneurs can develop specific principles that will assist them in taking the right external steps as their ventures develop. Following are one executive's four principles for ethical management:

- Principle 1: *Hire the right people.* Employees who are inclined to be ethical are the best insurance you can have. They may be the only insurance. Look for people with principles. Let them know that those principles are an important part of their qualifications for the job.

- Principle 2: *Set standards more than rules.* You can't write a code of conduct airtight enough to cover every eventuality. A person inclined to fraud or misconduct isn't going to blink at

the entrepreneurial process

Shaping an Ethical Strategy

The development of an organizational climate for responsible and ethically sound behavior requires continuing effort and investment of time and resources. A code of conduct, ethics officers, training programs, and annual ethics audits do not necessarily add up to a responsible, ethical organization. A formal ethics program can serve as a catalyst and a support system, but organizational integrity depends on the integration of the company's values into its driving systems.

Following are a few key elements that entrepreneurs should keep in mind when developing an ethical strategy.

- *The entrepreneur's guiding values and commitments must make sense and be clearly communicated.* They should reflect important organizational obligations and widely shared aspirations that appeal to the organization's members. Employees at all levels must take them seriously, feel comfortable discussing them, and have a concrete understanding of their practical importance.

- *Entrepreneurs must be personally committed, credible, and willing to take action on the values they espouse.* They are not mere mouthpieces. They

must be willing to scrutinize their own decisions. Consistency on the part of leadership is key. Entrepreneurs must assume responsibility for making tough calls when ethical obligations conflict.

- *The espoused values must be integrated into the normal channels of the organization's critical activities:* planning innovation, resource allocation, information communication, and personnel promotion and advancement.

- *The venture's systems and structures must support and reinforce its values.* Information systems, for example, must be designed to provide timely and accurate information. Reporting relationships must be structured to build in checks and balances to promote objective judgment.

- *Employees throughout the company must have the decision-making skills, knowledge, and competencies needed to make ethically sound decisions every day.* Ethical thinking and awareness must be part of every employee's skills.

Source: Adapted from Lynn Sharp Paine, "Managing for Organizational Integrity," *Harvard Business Review* (March/ April 1994): 106–17.

signing your code anyway. Don't waste your time on heavy regulations. Instead, be clear about standards. Let people know the level of performance you expect—and that ethics is not negotiable.

- Principle 3: *Don't let yourself get isolated.* You already know that managers can lose track of markets and competitors by moving into the ivory tower. But they also can lose sight of what's going on within their own operations. You are responsible for whatever happens in your office or department or corporation, whether or not you know about it.

- Principle 4: *The most important principle is to let your ethical example at all times be absolutely impeccable.* This isn't just a matter of how you act in matters of accounting, competition, or interpersonal relationships. Be aware also of the signals you send to those around you. Steady harping on the importance of quarterly gains in earnings, for example, rather easily leads people to believe that you don't care much about how the results are achieved.[37]

Mark Twain once said, "Always do the right thing. This will surprise some people and astonish the rest." It will also motivate them to do the right thing. Indeed, without a good example from the top, ethical problems (and all the costs that go with them) are probably inevitable within your organization.

ETHICAL RESPONSIBILITY

Establishing a strategy for ethical responsibility is not an easy task for entrepreneurs. No single, ideal approach to organizational ethics exists. Entrepreneurs need to analyze the ethical consciousness of their organization, the process and structure devised to enhance ethical activity, and, finally, their own commitment to institutionalize ethical objectives within the company.[38] Keeping these points in mind, entrepreneurs eventually can begin to establish a strategy for ethical responsibility. This strategy should encompass three major elements: ethical consciousness, ethical process and structure, and institutionalization:

- **Ethical Consciousness** The development of ethical consciousness is the responsibility of the entrepreneur, because his or her vision created the venture. The key figure to set the tone for ethical decision-making and behavior is the entrepreneur. An open exchange of issues and processes within the venture, established codes of ethics for the company, and the setting of examples by the entrepreneur are all illustrations of how this is done. For example, when the CEO of a large corporation discovered bookkeeping discrepancies in one of the departments, he directed the 20 implicated employees to make retribution by donating $8,500 to charity.[39] This action commanded positive ethical action and set the tone for ethical expectations.

- **Ethical Process and Structure** Ethical process and structure refer to the procedures, position statements (codes), and announced ethical goals designed to avoid ambiguity. Having all key personnel read the venture's specific ethical goals and sign affidavits affirming their willingness to follow those policies is a good practice for ventures.

- **Institutionalization** Institutionalization is a deliberate step to incorporate the entrepreneur's ethical objectives with the economic objectives of the venture. At times, an entrepreneur may have to modify policies or operations that become too intense and infringe on the ethics of the situation. This is where the entrepreneur's commitment to ethics and values is tested. Constant review of procedures and feedback in operations are vital to institutionalizing ethical responsibility.[40]

Ethics and Business Decisions

In addition to the normal challenges of business decisions, the entrepreneur is faced with specific ethical dilemmas. Figure 4.3 illustrates four main themes of ethical dilemmas: conflict of interests, personality traits, responsibility to stakeholders, and level of openness.[41] The conflict of interests theme deals with much of what was mentioned earlier in the chapter concerning morality and economic trade-offs. It involves the constant tension of trying to separate the person from the business decision. Personality traits relate more specifically to relationships and personal issues. In many instances, the personal issues or individual personalities cause the dilemma. The responsibility to stakeholders incorporates the pressure of managerial rationalization discussed earlier and emphasizes the importance of having a code of conduct. Finally, the level of openness suggests that entrepreneurs need to be more public about their values and expectations. Once again, the value of a code of conduct is evident with this theme.

Amid these dilemmas, entrepreneurs are challenged by the need to make business decisions each day. Many of these decisions are complex and raise ethical considerations.

Complexity of Decisions

The business decisions of entrepreneurs are highly complex for five reasons. First, ethical decisions have extended consequences. They often have a ripple effect in that the consequences are felt by others outside the venture. For example, the decision to use inexpensive but unsafe products in operations will affect both workers and consumers of the final good.

Second, business decisions that involve ethical questions have multiple alternatives—the choices are not always "do" or "don't do." Many decisions have a wide range of alternatives that may involve several less important decisions. With regard to the first example about the

Figure   **4.3**   **Four Main Themes of Ethical Dilemmas for Entrepreneurs**

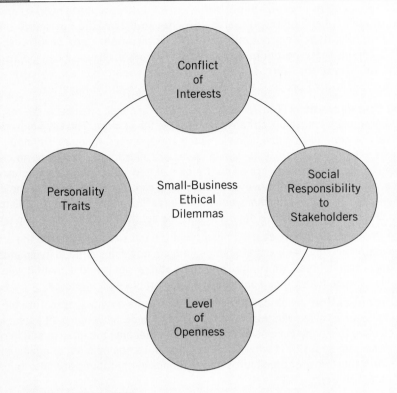

Source: Shailendra Vyakarnam, Andy Bailey, Andrew Myers, and Donna Burnett,
"Towards an Understanding of Ethical Behavior in Small Firms," *Journal of Business
Ethics* 14, no. 15 (1977): 1625–36.

use of unsafe products, the entrepreneur may have the alternative of using still less expensive but nevertheless safe products.

Third, ethical business decisions often have mixed outcomes. Social benefits as well as costs are involved with every major business decision, as are financial revenues and expenses.

Fourth, most business decisions have uncertain ethical consequences. It is never absolutely certain what actual consequence(s) a decision will have, even when it appears logical; in other words, a decision is never without ethical risk.

Finally, most ethical business decisions have personal implications. It is difficult for an entrepreneur to divorce him- or herself from a decision and its potential outcome. Venture success, financial opportunity, and new-product development are all areas that may be affected by decisions with ethical consequences. The entrepreneur often will find it impossible to make a purely impersonal decision.[42]

These five statements about business decisions need to be considered when an entrepreneur is developing a new venture. They indicate the need to grasp as much information as possible about each major decision. One ethicist, who believes that this implies understanding the characteristic features of a venture's activities (which in turn allows for a stronger sensitivity to the outcomes), has noted that "someone in business needs to know its general tendencies—the special tracks it leaves—to anticipate points of crisis, and of special concern to us, to increase the possibility of intelligent moral actions."[43]

Some pertinent questions that can be used to examine the ethics of business decisions are as follows:

1. Have you defined the problem accurately?

2. How would you define the problem if you stood on the other side of the fence?

3. How did this situation occur in the first place?

4. To whom and to what do you give your loyalty as a person and as a corporation member?

5. What is your intention in making this decision?

6. How does this intention compare with the probable results?

7. Whom could your decision or action injure?

8. Can you discuss the problem with the affected parties before you make your decision?

9. Are you confident that your position will be as valid over a long period of time as it seems now?

10. Could you disclose without qualms your decision or action to your boss, your CEO, the board of directors, your family, and society as a whole?

11. What is the symbolic potential of your action if understood? If misunderstood?

12. Under what conditions would you allow exceptions to your stand?[44]

Although this is not a conclusive list, it does provide a frame of reference for entrepreneurs wrestling with the complexity of decisions concerning their venture.

Ethics, as we have seen, is extremely difficult to define, codify, and implement because of the personal values and morality issues it surfaces. Yet the importance of ethics when initiating new enterprises must be stressed. As one writer has noted, "The singular importance of enterprises to our daily lives and our collective future demands our careful attention and finest efforts."[45]

Ethical Considerations in Corporate Entrepreneurship

Corporate entrepreneurs—described in the academic literature as those managers or employees who do not follow the status quo of their coworkers—are depicted as visionaries who dream of taking the company in new directions. As a result, in overcoming internal obstacles to reaching their professional goals, they often walk a fine line between clever resourcefulness and outright rule-breaking. Researchers Donald F. Kuratko and Michael G. Goldsby developed a framework as a guideline for managers and organizations seeking to impede unethical behaviors in the pursuit of entrepreneurial activity (Figure 4.4).[46] They examined the barriers that middle managers face in trying to be entrepreneurial in less supportive environments, the unethical consequences that can result, and a suggested assessment and training program to avert such dilemmas.

The barriers include organizational obstacles in two major categories: internal network issues and leadership issues. The specific barriers to innovative actions include systems, structures, policies and procedures, culture, strategic direction, and people. Based on these barriers and the managerial dilemmas that can be caused, the researchers advise companies that embrace corporate entrepreneurship to: (1) establish the needed flexibility, innovation, and support of employee initiative and risk taking; (2) remove the barriers that the entrepreneurial middle manager may face to more closely align personal and organizational initiatives and reduce the need to behave unethically; and (3) include an ethical component to corporate training that will provide guidelines for instituting compliance and values components into state-of-the-art corporate entrepreneurship programs. However, even if corporate entrepreneurship is supported, some managers still may pose ethical risks to the company. Rarely will everyone in an organization do the right thing. For this reason, it would be wise to include an ethical component in corporate training programs to ensure that everyone is aware of the expectations and vision of senior management. A more complete training program and approach to corporate entrepreneurship should make for a better future—for both the organization and its members—and prevent future ethical crises.

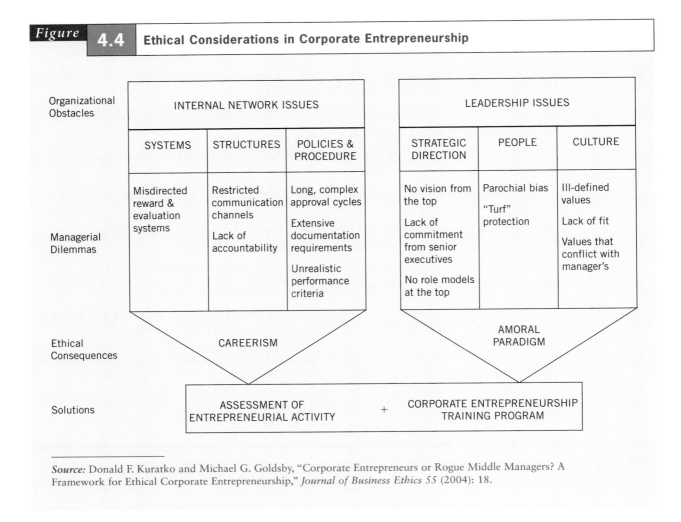

Figure 4.4   Ethical Considerations in Corporate Entrepreneurship

Source: Donald F. Kuratko and Michael G. Goldsby, "Corporate Entrepreneurs or Rogue Middle Managers? A Framework for Ethical Corporate Entrepreneurship," *Journal of Business Ethics 55* (2004): 18.

Ethical Leadership by Entrepreneurs

Although ethics and social responsibility present complex challenges for entrepreneurs, the value system of an owner/entrepreneur is the key to establishing an ethical organization.[47] An owner has the unique opportunity to display honesty, integrity, and ethics in all key decisions. The owner's actions serve as a model for all other employees to follow.

In small businesses, the ethical influence of the owner is more powerful than in larger corporations because his or her leadership is not diffused through layers of management. Owners are easily identified, and employees usually can observe them on a regular basis in a small business. Therefore, entrepreneurs possess a strong potential to establish high ethical standards in all business decisions.

To illustrate, one study examined the ethical concerns of owner/entrepreneurs regarding specific business issues.[48] Table 4.5 provides a list of the issues owners believed needed a strong ethical stance, as well as the issues the same entrepreneurs viewed with greater tolerance in regard to demanding ethics. This study verifies that ethical decision-making is a complex challenge because of the nature and personal perception of various issues.[49]

Another research study found that an owner's value system was a critical component of the ethical considerations that surround a business decision. This study also had implications for entrepreneurs who are seeking to establish an ethical environment within which employees and other constituents can work. For example, it was shown that the preparation of a specific policy statement on ethics (code of ethics) by the owner and his or her other employees may provide the clear understanding needed for administrative decision-making. Small-business owners also may need to specifically address administrative decision-making

Table **4.5**	Issues Viewed by Entrepreneurs/Owners

Demands Strong Ethical Stance	Greater Tolerance Regarding Ethical Position
Faulty investment advice	Padded expense account
Favoritism in promotion	Tax evasion
Acquiescing in dangerous design flaw	Collusion in bidding
Misleading financial reporting	Insider trading
Misleading advertising	Discrimination against women
Defending healthfulness of cigarette smoking	Copying computer software

Source: Justin G. Longenecker, Joseph A. McKinney, and Carlos W. Moore, "Ethics in Small Business," *Journal of Small Business Management* (January 1989): 30.

processes. In addition, they may need to spend some time developing benchmarks or guidelines concerning ethical behaviors of employees. Although these guidelines cannot be expected to cover every possible scenario, they nevertheless will help address the business development/profit motive dimension. Finally, if entrepreneurs can carefully establish explicit rewards and punishments based upon ethical behaviors (and enforced), the concerns of crime and theft can begin to be addressed.[50]

entrepreneurship in practice

Software Piracy

When you hear the words *business ethics*, do you think about software piracy? From Fortune 500 corporations to sole proprietorships, companies of all shapes and sizes can fall victim to the ethical seesaw that is software piracy. For many, piracy is not a goal or an intended action. A business manager or owner has enough problems to face without having to keep track of who is using what software on what computers, and whether the company paid for its use. In addition, those who are aware that they are committing an illegal act may not realize the problems they're creating for themselves and their businesses, should they get caught. Software manufacturers lose an estimated $2.3 billion in revenue annually because ethical standards are not practiced or enforced in the workplace.

The Business Software Alliance (BSA) is a collaboration of software manufacturers aimed at stopping companies from illegally using, and making money from, copyrighted software. The BSA, on average, catches and threatens with legal proceedings one company per day. Over the past six years, this alliance of companies (such as Novell and Microsoft) has recovered $37 million in lost revenues. Currently, it is striving to make the job easier by providing businesses with the tools necessary to help them stay legal. BSA offers free audit software on its Web site,

Continued

www.bsa.org, so companies can fix themselves before it's too late.

Larry Lightman, vice president of sales and marketing at Elliot Laboratories, admits that his company may have been a little naïve. "Whenever people wanted to purchase software, they were reimbursed for it, and anyone could install it. Some software was purchased, and some wasn't. There wasn't any rhyme or reason behind it."

Ad hoc installation of software is one of the main reasons piracy exists. Legally, for every computer in use, separate software packages should be bought, registered, and recorded. Although this may sound very expensive, the cost pales in comparison to the fines incurred if you get caught using illegal software. Elliot Laboratories was fined only $60,000 for its mistake. If the case had gone to court, the company may have been fined $100,000 for each copyright infringement. Furthermore, the BSA member may be granted a portion of the profits the offending company earned from use of its software.

How can this punishment be avoided? Elliot Laboratories created a FileMaker database that keeps track of all of its computers, their users, and the serial numbers and licensing information of each installed application. Having one person keep control of the computer and software use is the best way to avoid an avalanche. Purchasing personal computers without bundled software may also help curb the problem. These packages, as alluring as they are, often do not include the licenses needed for protection.

Stopping piracy at its source is the safest option. It is always better to be proactive than reactive. It's true that, if it weren't for disgruntled employees, many companies would be "home free." The no-piracy hotline is a great way for unhappy workers to get revenge when they're feeling cheated or abused. No business owner wants to see the U.S. Marshals at his or her front door, so don't give them a reason to be there.

Source: Adapted from David G. Propson, "Cease and Desist," *Small Business Computing* (December 1999): 61–66.

As a result of the growing number of female entrepreneurs, companies are now examining the ethics of caring. Caring is a feminine alternative to the more traditional and masculine ethics based on rules and regulations.[51] The focus of feminist philosophies is the fostering of positive relationships in all areas of life, or, as Milton Mayeroff states, "To care for another person, in the most significant sense, is to help him grow and actualize himself."[52] Following laws may not lead to building relationships as strong as one could. However, by considering the interests of others and maintaining healthy relationships, caring—according to feminists—can lead to more genuinely moral climates.

Overall, entrepreneurs must realize that their personal integrity and ethical example will be the key to their employees' ethical performance. Their values can permeate and characterize the organization. This unique advantage creates a position of ethical leadership for entrepreneurs.[53]

Summary

The challenge of social enterprise has emerged in this century as a major issue for entrepreneurs. Social enterprise consists of obligations that a business has to society. The social actions of corporations are classified into three categories: social obligation, social responsibility, and social responsiveness. Studies have revealed that entrepreneurs recognize social enterprise as part of their role and that the structure of smaller firms allows entrepreneurs to more personally influence the organization. This opportunity for entrepreneurs to exert ethical influence on their ventures creates a unique challenge of ethical leadership for all entrepreneurs.

Ethics is a set of principles prescribing a behavioral code that explains right and wrong; it also may outline moral duty and obligations. Because it is so difficult to define the term *ethics*, it is helpful to look at it more as a process than as a static code. Entrepreneurs face many ethical decisions, especially during the early stages of their new ventures.

Decisions may be legal without being ethical, and vice versa. As a result, entrepreneurs can make four types of decisions: legal and ethical, legal and unethical, illegal and ethical, and illegal and unethical. When entrepreneurs make decisions that border on the unethical, they commonly rationalize their choices. These rationalizations may be based on morally questionable acts committed "against the firm" or "on behalf of the firm" by the managers involved. Within this framework are four distinct types of managerial roles: nonrole, role failure, role distortion, and role assertion.

Sometimes the entrepreneur must make decisions that involve economic trade-offs. In some situations, the company will make a profit but others in society may suffer. To establish ethical strategies, some corporations create codes of conduct. A code of conduct is a statement of ethical practices or guidelines to which an enterprise adheres. Codes are becoming more prevalent in organizations today, and they are proving to be more meaningful in their implementation.

Some ethicists have attempted to provide a clearer view of morality by examining organizational behavior along a continuum that includes immoral, amoral, and moral management. However, entrepreneurs need to focus on a holistic approach that places ethics in perspective and allows personnel to understand what they can and cannot do. In this way, the blurred line between ethical and unethical behavior becomes clearer.

It is also important for entrepreneurs to realize that many decisions are complex and that it can be difficult to deal with all of a decision's ethical considerations. Some of these considerations may be overlooked, and some may be sidestepped because the economic cost is too high. In the final analysis, ethics is sometimes a judgment call, and what is unethical to one entrepreneur is viewed as ethical to another. Despite the ever-present lack of clarity and direction in ethics, however, ethics will continue to be a major issue for entrepreneurs during the new century.

Key Terms and Concepts

amoral management

code of conduct

ecovision

environmental awareness

ethics

green capitalism

immoral management

moral management

nonrole

rationalizations

role assertion

role distortion

role failure

social entrepreneurship

social obligation

social responsibility

social responsiveness

Review and Discussion Questions

1. Social enterprise can be classified into three distinct categories. Describe each category, and discuss the efforts of entrepreneurs to become more socially responsible.
2. Describe the critical threat to our environment as a major challenge of social enterprise.
3. What is *ecovision*? Outline some specific recommendations for entrepreneurs to consider that promote environmental awareness.
4. In your own words, what is meant by the term *ethics*?
5. Ethics must be based more on a process than on a static code. What does this statement mean? Do you agree? Why or why not?
6. A small pharmaceutical firm has just received permission from the Food and Drug Administration (FDA) to market its new anticholesterol drug. Although the product has been tested for five years, management believes that serious side effects may still result from its use, and a warning to this effect is being printed on the label. If the company markets this FDA-approved drug, how would you describe its actions from an ethical and legal standpoint? Use Figure 4.1 to help you.
7. Marcia White, the leading salesperson for a small manufacturer, has been giving purchasing managers a kickback from her commissions in return for their buying more of the company's goods. The manufacturer has a strict rule against this practice. Using Figure 4.1, how would you describe Marcia's behavior? What would you suggest the company do about it?

8. Explain the four distinct roles that managers may take in rationalizing morally questionable acts "against the firm" or "on behalf of the firm." Be complete in your answer.

9. What is a code of conduct, and how useful is it in promoting ethical behavior?

10. Describe carefully the differences between immoral, amoral, and moral management. Use Table 4.3 in your answer.

11. Why do complex decisions often raise ethical considerations for the entrepreneur?

12. How can entrepreneurs develop a position of ethical leadership in business today?

13. Cal Whiting believes that entrepreneurs need to address the importance of ethics in their organizations. However, he is unsure of where to begin in his own company because the entire area is unclear to him. What would you suggest? Where can he begin? What should he do? Be as practical as you can in your suggestions.

Experiential Exercise

KNOWING THE DIFFERENCE

Most entrepreneurial actions are ethical and legal. Sometimes, however, they are unethical and/or illegal. The four categories of ethical/legal actions and a list of examples of each category (*a* through *h*) follow. Place the number of the correct category next to appropriate examples from the list (two are given for each category).

1. Ethical and legal

2. Unethical and legal

3. Ethical and illegal

4. Unethical and illegal

    a. _____ Giving a gift of $50,000 to a foreign minister to secure a business contract with his country (a customary practice in his country) and then writing off the gift as a tax-deductible item

    b. _____ Knowing that 1 percent of all tires have production defects but shipping them anyway and giving mileage allowances to anyone whose tires wear out prematurely

    c. _____ Manufacturing a new fuel additive that will increase gas mileage by 10 percent

    d. _____ Offering a member of the city council $100,000 to vote to give the entrepreneur the local cable television franchise

    e. _____ Publishing a newspaper story that wrongly implies but does not openly state that the governor (a political opponent of the newspaper) is deliberately withholding state funds for education in the newspaper's effort to win nomination support for its candidate from the state teachers union

    f. _____ Obtaining inside information from another brokerage that results in the entrepreneur netting more than $2 million

    g. _____ Producing a vaccine, already approved by the Food and Drug Administration, that will retard the growth of bone cancer

    h. _____ Producing and selling a drug that will reduce heart attacks but failing to complete all of the paperwork that must be filed with the government prior to selling the product

Answers: a. 3, b. 2, c. 1, d. 4, e. 2, f. 4, g. 1, h. 3

Case 4.1

LETTING THE FAMILY IN

When Carmine Guion started his retail company three years ago, he had more than enough working capital to keep operations going. This abundance of money helped him grow rapidly, and today he has outlets in 16 states. In order to become larger, however, he is going to have to secure outside funding. Carmine has decided to issue stock. The investment house advising him has suggested that he float an issue of 1 million shares at $5 each. After all expenses, he will clear $4.50 per share. Carmine and his wife intend to hold on to 250,000 shares and sell 750,000 shares. Carmine feels that, between his shares and those that will be bought by his relatives and friends, he need have little concern about the firm's being taken over by outside investors.

Carmine talked to his father, who agreed to buy 10,000 shares at $5 each. Carmine's two uncles are each buying 5,000 shares at $5 each. A group of 20 other relatives is going to buy an additional 5,000 shares.

Earlier this week, Carmine received some good news from his accountant. His profit estimate for next year is going to be at least double what he had previously estimated. When Carmine shared this information with the investment brokers, they were delighted. "When this news gets out," one of them told him, "your stock will rise to between $13 and $15 per share. Anyone who gets in on the original offering at $5 will do very well indeed."

Carmine has told only his father and two uncles the good news. Based on this information, the three of them have decided to buy three times as much stock as previously planned. "When it rises to around $12," his father said, "I'll sell 10,000 shares and hang on to the other 20,000." His uncles intend to do the same thing. Carmine is delighted. He also intends to tell some of his other relatives about the improved profit picture prior to the time the initial stock offering is made.

QUESTIONS

1. Has Carmine been unethical in his conduct? What is your reasoning?

2. Is it ethical for Carmine to tell his other relatives the good news? Why or why not?

3. If you were advising Carmine, what would you tell him? Why?

Case 4.2

A FRIEND FOR LIFE

The Glades Company is a small manufacturer. It has produced and marketed a number of different toys and appliances that have done very well in the marketplace. Late last year, the product designer at the company, Tom Berringer, told the president, Paula Glades, that he had invented a small, cuddly, talking bear that might have a great deal of appeal. The bear is made of fluffy brown material that simulates fur, and it has a tape inside that contains 50 messages.

The Glades Company decided to find out exactly how much market appeal the bear would have. Fifty of the bears were produced and placed in kindergartens and nurseries around town. The results were better than the firm had hoped. One of the nurseries reported: "The bear was so popular that most of the children wanted to take it home for an evening." Another said the bear was the most popular toy in the school.

Based on these data, the company decided to manufacture and market 1,000 of the bears. At the same time, a catchy marketing slogan was formulated: "A Friend for Life." The bear was marketed as a product a child could play with for years and years. The first batch of 1,000 bears sold out within a week. The company then scheduled another production run, this time for 25,000 bears. Last week, in the middle of the production run, a problem was uncovered. The process of making the bear fur was much more expensive than anticipated. The company is now faced with two options: It can absorb the extra cost and have the simulated fur produced, or it can use a substitute fur that will not last as long. Specifically, the original simulated fur will last for up to seven years of normal use; the less-expensive simulated fur will last for only eight months.

Some of the managers at Glades believe that most children are not interested in playing with the same toy for more than eight months; therefore, substituting the less-expensive simulated fur for the more-expensive fur should be no problem. Others believe that the company will damage its reputation if it opts for the substitute fur. "We are going to have complaints within eight months, and we are going to rue the day we agreed to a cheaper substitute," the production manager argues. The sales manager disagrees, contending that "the market is ready for this product, and we ought to provide it." In the middle of this crisis, the accounting department issued its cost analysis of the venture. If the company goes with the more-expensive simulated fur, it will lose $2.75 per bear. If it chooses the less-expensive simulated fur, it will make a profit of $4.98 per bear.

The final decision on the matter rests with Paula Glades. People on both sides of the issue have given her their opinion. One of the last to speak was the vice president of manufacturing, who said, "If you opt for the less-expensive fur, think of what this is going to do to your marketing campaign of 'A Friend for Life.' Are you going to change this slogan to 'A Friend for Eight Months'?" But the marketing vice president urged a different course of action: "We have a fortune tied up in this bear. If you stop production now or go to the more-expensive substitute, we'll lose our shirts. We aren't doing anything illegal by substituting the fur. The bear looks the same. Who's to know?"

QUESTIONS

1. Is the recommendation of the marketing vice president legal? Is it ethical? Why or why not?

2. Would it be ethical if the firm used the less-expensive simulated fur but did not change its slogan of "A Friend for Life" and did not tell the buyer about the change in the production process? Why or why not?

3. If you were advising Paula, what would you recommend?

Notes

1. J. Gregory Dees, "Enterprising Nonprofits," *Harvard Business Review* 76, no. 1 (1998): 54–67; David Bornstein, *How to Change the World: Social Entrepreneurs and the Power of New Ideas,* (Oxford: Oxford University Press, 2004); Johanna Mair and Ignasi Marti, "Social Entrepreneurship Research: A Source of Explanation, Prediction, and Delight," *Journal of World Business* 41 (2006): 36–44; Ana Maria Peredo and Murdith McLean, "Social Entrepreneurship: A Critical Review of the Concept," *Journal of World Business* 41 (2006): 56–65; and James Austin, Howard Stevenson, and Jane Wei-Skillern, "Social and Commercial Entrepreneurship: Same, Different, or Both?" *Entrepreneurship Theory and Practice* (January 2006): 1–22.

2. Skoll Foundation, "PBS Foundation and Skoll Foundation Establish Fund to Produce Unique Programming About Social Entrepreneurship," September 19, 2006, http://www.skollfoundation.org/media/press_releases/internal/092006.asp (accessed April 21, 2008).

3. Schwab Foundation for Social Entrepreneurship, Social Entrepreneurs' Summit, Rüschlikon, Switzerland, January 20–22, 2008, http://www.schwabfound.org/the.htm?p=102 (accessed March 24, 2008).

4. "What Is a Social Entrepreneur?" Ashoka, http://ashoka.org/social_entrepreneur (accessed March 24, 2008).

5. Arthur C. Brooks, *Social Entrepreneurship: A Modern Approach to Social Value Creation* (Upper Saddle River, NJ: Pearson/Prentice Hall, 2008).

6. Alan Finder, "A Subject for Those Who Want to Make a Difference," *New York Times,* August 17, 2005,

education section; Matthew Bishop, "The Rise of the Social Entrepreneur," *Economist*, February 25, 2006, 11–13; and Dees, J. Gregory. "Enterprising Nonprofits," *Harvard Business Review* 76, no. 1 (1998): 54–67.

7. Roger L. Martin and Sally Osberg, "Social Entrepreneurship: The Case for Definition," *Stanford Social Innovation Review* (Spring 2007): 29–39; see also Christine A. Hemingway, "Personal Values as a Catalyst for Corporate Social Entrepreneurship," *Journal of Business Ethics*, 60 (2005): 233–49.

8. "What Is a Social Entrepreneur?" Ashoka, http://ashoka.org/social_entrepreneur (accessed March 24, 2008).

9. Sarah H. Alvord, David L. Brown, and Christine W. Letts, "Social Entrepreneurship and Societal Transformation: An Exploratory Study," *Journal of Applied Behavioral Science* 40, no. 3 (2004): 260–82; and U.S. Small Business Administration, *The Small Business Economy: A Report to the President* (Washington, DC: U.S. Government Printing Office, 2007), 151–211.

10. Ana Maria Peredo and James J. Chrisman, "Toward a Theory of Community-Based Enterprise," *Academy of Management Review* 31, no. 2 (2006): 309–28.

11. Judith Kenner Thompson and Howard L. Smith, "Social Responsibility and Small Business: Suggestions for Research," *Journal of Small Business Management* (January 1991): 30–44; for the latest research, see Justin G. Longenecker, Carlos W. Moore, J. William Petty, and Joseph A. McKinney, "Ethical Attitudes in Small Business: Theory and Empirical Findings from a Tracking Study Spanning Three Decades," *Journal of Small Business Management* 44, no. 2 (2006): 167–83.

12. James J. Chrisman and Fred L. Fry, "Public versus Business Expectations: Two Views on Social Responsibility for Small Business," *Journal of Small Business Management* (January 1982): 19–26.

13. Paul Hawken and William McDonough, "Seven Steps to Doing Good Business," *Inc.* (November 1993): 79–92.

14. Reginald Shareef, "Ecovision: A Leadership Theory for Innovative Organizations," *Organizational Dynamics* 20 (Summer 1991): 50–63; and Thomas J. Dean and Jeffery S. McMullen, "Toward a Theory of Sustainable Entrepreneurship: Reducing Environmental Degradation Through Entrepreneurial Action," *Journal of Business Venturing* 22, no. 1 (2007): 50–76.

15. Hawken and McDonough, "Seven Steps," 81–88.

16. Bruce Horovitz, "Scandals Shake Public Trust," *USA Today,* July 16, 2002, 1A–2A; John A. Byrne, Michael Arndt, Wendy Zellner, and Mike McNamee, "Restoring Trust in Corporate America: Business Must Lead the Way to Reform," *Business Week,* June 24, 2002, 31–39; and Amey Stone, "Putting Teeth in Corporate Ethics," *BusinessWeek Online,* February 19, 2004, http://www.businessweek.com/bwdaily/dnflash/feb2004/nf20040219_5613_db035.htm (accessed May 23, 2008).

17. Vernon R. Loucks, Jr., "A CEO Looks at Ethics," *Business Horizons* (March/April 1987): 2.

18. Sir Adrian Cadbury, "Ethical Managers Make Their Own Rules," *Harvard Business Review* (September/October 1987): 64.

19. Verne E. Henderson, "The Ethical Side of Enterprise," *Sloan Management Review* (Spring 1982): 38.

20 Richard Evans, "Business Ethics and Changes in Society," *Journal of Business Ethics* 10 (1991): 871–76; and Goran Svensson and Greg Wood, "A Model of Business Ethics," *Journal of Business Ethics,* 77 (2008): 303–23.

21. Henderson, "The Ethical Side," 40.

22. Saul W. Gellerman, "Why Good Managers Make Bad Ethical Choices," *Harvard Business Review* (July/August 1986): 85.

23. James A. Waters and Frederick Bird, "Attending to Ethics in Management," *Journal of Business Ethics* 5 (1989): 493–97.

24. Christopher D. Stone, *Where the Law Ends: The Social Control of Corporate Behavior* (New York: Harper & Row, 1975).

25. Al H. Ringlab, Roger E. Meiners, and Frances L. Edwards, *Managing in the Legal Environment,* 3rd ed. (St. Paul, MN: West, 1996), 12–14; see also Roger LeRoy Miller and Frank B. Cross, *The Legal Environment Today* (St. Paul, MN: West, 1996), 33–37.

26. LaRue T. Hosmer, *The Ethics of Management,* 2nd ed. (Homewood, IL: Richard D. Irwin, 1991), 81–83.

27. Edward L. Hennessy, "Business Ethics—Is It a Priority for Corporate America?" *Financial Executive* (October 1986): 14–15.

28. Myron Magnet, "The Decline and Fall of Business Ethics," *Fortune,* December 8, 1986, 65–72.

29. Margaret N. Maxey, "Bioethical Reflections on the Case for Private/Free Enterprise," in *The Future of Private Enterprise,* ed. Craig E. Aronoff, Randall B. Goodwin, and John L. Ward (Atlanta: Georgia State University Publications, 1986), 145–164.

30. Charles R. Stoner, "The Foundation of Business Ethics: Exploring the Relationship between Organization Culture, Moral Values, and Actions," *SAM Advanced Management Journal* (summer 1989): 38–43; James B. Lucas, "How to Avoid Enronism," *American Management Association MWorld* (spring 2002): 6–11; and Charles Haddad, Dean Foust, and Steve Rosenbush, "WorldCom's Sorry Legacy," *Business Week* (July 8, 2002): 38–41.

31. Susan J. Harrington, "What Corporate America Is Teaching about Ethics," *Academy of Management Executive* (February 1991): 21–30.

32. For more on this topic, see Donald R. Cressey and Charles A. Moore, "Managerial Values and Corporate Codes of Conduct," *California Management Review* (Summer 1983): 121–27; Steven Weller, "The Effectiveness of Corporate Codes of Ethics," *Journal of Business Ethics* (July 1988): 389–95; and Diane E. Kirrane, "Managing Values: A Systematic Approach to Business Ethics," *Training & Development Journal* (November 1990): 53–60.

33. Reported in Darrell J. Fashing, "A Case of Corporate and Management Ethics," *California Management Review* (Spring 1981): 84.

34. Amitai Etzioni, "Do Good Ethics Ensure Good Profits?" *Business and Society Review* (Summer 1989): 4–10; L. J. Brooks, "Corporate Ethical Performance: Trends, Forecasts, and Outlooks," *Journal of Business Ethics* 8 (1989): 31–38; Harrington, "What Corporate America Is Teaching about Ethics"; and Simcha B. Werner, "The Movement for Reforming American Business Ethics: A Twenty Year Perspective," *Journal of Business Ethics* 11 (1992): 61–70.

35. Archie B. Carroll, "In Search of the Moral Manager," *Business Horizons* (March/April 1987): 7–15.

36. F. Neil Brady, "Aesthetic Components of Management Ethics," *Academy of Management Review* (April 1986): 344.

37. Adapted from Vernon R. Loucks, Jr., "A CEO Looks at Ethics," *Business Horizons* (March/April 1987): 6. Copyright © 1987 by the Foundation for the School of Business at Indiana University. Reprinted by permission.

38. Patrick E. Murphy, "Creating Ethical Corporate Structures," *Sloan Management Review* (Winter 1989): 81–87.

39. Joseph A. Raelin, "The Professional as the Executive's Ethical Aide-de-Camp," *The Academy of Management Executive* (August 1987): 176.

40. Ibid., 177.

41. Shailendra Vyakarnam, Andy Bailey, Andrew Myers, and Donna Burnett, "Towards an Understanding of Ethical Behavior in Small Firms," *Journal of Business Ethics* 16, no. 15 (1997): 1625–36.

42. LaRue T. Hosmer, *The Ethics of Management* (Homewood, IL: Richard D. Irwin, 1987), 13–15.

43. Wade L. Robison, "Management and Ethical Decision-Making," *Journal of Business Ethics* (Spring 1984): 287.

44. Laura L. Nash, "Ethics without the Sermon," *Harvard Business Review* (November/December 1981). Copyright © 1981 by the President and Fellows of Harvard College; all rights reserved. For additional questions, see Diane E. Kirrane, "Managing Values: A Systematic Approach to Business Ethics," *Training & Development Journal* (November 1990): 53–60.

45. Henderson, "The Ethical Side," 46.

46. Donald F. Kuratko and Michael G. Goldsby, "Corporate Entrepreneurs or Rogue Middle Managers? A Framework for Ethical Corporate Entrepreneurship," *Journal of Business Ethics* 55 (2004): 13–30.

47. Elisabeth J. Teal and Archie B. Carroll, "Moral Reasoning Skills: Are Entrepreneurs Different?" *Journal of Business Ethics* (March 1999): 229–40; and Dinah Payne and Brenda E. Joyner, "Successful U.S. Entrepreneurs: Identifying Ethical Decision-Making and Social Responsibility Behaviors," *Journal of Business Ethics*, 65 (2006): 203–217.

48. Justin G. Longenecker, Joseph A. McKinney, and Carlos W. Moore, "Ethics in Small Business," *Journal of Small Business Management* (January 1989): 27–31.

49. Neil Humphreys, Donald P. Robin, R. Eric Reidenbach, and Donald L. Moak, "The Ethical Decision Making Process of Small Business Owner/Managers and Their Customers," *Journal of Small Business Management* (July 1993): 9–22; and Jeffrey S. Hornsby, Donald F. Kuratko, Douglas W. Naffziger, William R. LaFollette, and Richard M. Hodgetts, "The Ethical Perceptions of Small Business Owners: A Factor Analytic Study," *Journal of Small Business Management* (October 1994): 9–16.

50. Hornsby, Kuratko, Naffziger, LaFollette, and Hodgetts, "The Ethical Perceptions of Small Business Owners," 9–16.

51. Nel Noddings, *Caring: A Feminine Approach to Ethics and Moral Education* (Berkeley: University of California Press, 1984).

52. Milton Mayeroff, *On Caring* (New York: Harper & Row, 1971), 1.

53. Justin G. Longenecker, Joseph A. McKinney, and Carlos W. Moore, "Do Smaller Firms Have Higher Ethics?" *Business and Society Review* (Fall 1989): 19–21; Paul J. Serwinek, "Demographic and Related Differences in Ethical Views among Small Businesses," *Journal of Business Ethics* (July 1992): 555–66; Donald F. Kuratko, "The Ethical Challenge for Entrepreneurs," *Entrepreneurship, Innovation, and Change* (December 1995): 291–94; and Donald F. Kuratko, Michael G. Goldsby, and Jeffrey S. Hornsby, "The Ethical Perspectives of Entrepreneurs: An Examination of Stakeholder Salience," *Journal of Applied Management and Entrepreneurship* 9, no. 4 (October 2004): 19–42.

part 1 exercise

How Ethical Are You?

DIRECTIONS:

Please read the following business situations and write the number in the blank that shows the degree to which you personally feel they are ethically acceptable.

Never Acceptable			Indifferent			Always Acceptable
1	2	3	4	5	6	7

1. An executive earning $50,000 per year padded his expense account by almost $1,500 per year. _____

2. In order to increase profits, a general manager used a production process that exceeded legal limits for environmental pollution. _____

3. Because of pressure from his brokerage firm, a stockbroker recommended a type of bond that he did not consider to be a good investment. _____

4. A small business received one-fourth of its gross revenue in the form of cash. The owner reported only one-half of the cash receipts for income tax purposes. _____

5. A company paid a $350,000 "consulting" fee to an official of a foreign country. In return, the official promised assistance in obtaining a contract that should produce a $10 million profit for the contracting company. _____

6. A company president found out that a competitor had made an important scientific discovery that would sharply reduce the profits of his own company. He then hired a key employee of the competitor's in an attempt to learn the details of the discovery. _____

7. A highway building contractor deplored the chaotic bidding situation and cutthroat competition. He reached an understanding with other major contractors to permit bidding that would provide a reasonable profit. _____

8. A company president recognized that sending expensive Christmas gifts to purchasing agents might compromise their positions. However, he continued the policy because it was common practice and changing it might result in loss of business. _____

9. A corporate director learned that his company intended to announce a stock split and increase its dividend. On the basis of this information, he bought additional shares and sold them at a gain following the announcement. _____

10. A corporate executive promoted a loyal friend and competent manager to the position of divisional vice president in preference to a better-qualified manager with whom he had no close ties. _____

11. An engineer discovered what he perceived to be a product design flaw that constituted a safety hazard. His company declined to correct the flaw. The engineer decided to keep quiet rather than take his complaint outside the company. _____

12. A comptroller selected a legal method of financial reporting that concealed some embarrassing financial facts that would otherwise have become public knowledge. _____

13. An employer received applications for a supervisor's position from two equally qualified applicants but hired the male applicant because he thought some employees might resent being supervised by a female. _____

14. As part of the marketing strategy for a product, the producer changed its color and marketed it as "new and improved," even though its other characteristics were unchanged. _____

15. A cigarette manufacturer launched a publicity campaign challenging new evidence from the Surgeon General's office that cigarette smoking is harmful to the smoker's health. _____

16. An owner of a small firm obtained a free copy of a copyrighted computer software program from a business friend rather than spending $500 to obtain his own program from the software dealer. _____

Survey Results: Here is how 240 entrepreneurs responded

1. Mean response = 2.0
2. Mean response = 1.5
3. Mean response = 1.7
4. Mean response = 2.7
5. Mean response = 3.3
6. Mean response = 3.9
7. Mean response = 3.2
8. Mean response = 3.2

9. Mean response = 2.8
10. Mean response = 3.5
11. Mean response = 2.3
12. Mean response = 4.1
13. Mean response = 3.1
14. Mean response = 3.2
15. Mean response = 3.5
16. Mean response = 3.6

Launching Entrepreneurial Ventures

part
2

CHAPTER 5

Creativity and Innovation

Entrepreneurial Thought

The era of the intelligent man/woman is almost over and a new one is emerging—the era of the creative man/woman.

— PINCHAS NOY

Chapter Objectives

1 To explore the opportunity identification process

2 To define and illustrate the sources of innovative ideas for entrepreneurs

3 To examine the role of creativity and to review the major components of the creative process: knowledge accumulation, incubation process, idea experience, evaluation, and implementation

4 To present ways of developing personal creativity: recognize relationships, develop a functional perspective, use your "brains," and eliminate muddling mind-sets

5 To introduce the four major types of innovation: invention, extension, duplication, and synthesis

6 To review some of the major myths associated with innovation and to define the ten principles of innovation

Opportunity Identification: The Search for New Ideas

Opportunity identification is central to the domain of entrepreneurship. As one researcher stated, "At its core entrepreneurship revolves around the questions of why, when, and how opportunities for the creation of goods and services in the future arise in an economy. Thus, opportunity recognition is the progenitor of both personal and societal wealth."[1] It has been argued that understanding the opportunity identification process is one of the primary challenges within the domain of entrepreneurship research.[2] To give a better perspective of this entrepreneurial search, this chapter is devoted to examining the creative pursuit of ideas and the innovation process. These two major topics are keys to understanding opportunity and its development for entrepreneurs.

The first step for any entrepreneur is the identification of a "good idea." However, the search for good ideas is never easy. Thus, we examine the sources that can be used in this search and how an entrepreneur can work toward the discovery of a good idea. The most important areas to be aware of are within the grasp of our own knowledge. Let us examine some of the key sources of innovative ideas.

Sources of Innovative Ideas

Potential entrepreneurs must always be alert to the opportunities that lie in the external and internal environments in which they live. This alertness will allow an entrepreneur to create an idea from what others simply cannot recognize. The following are some of the most effective sources of entrepreneurial opportunities.

TRENDS

Trends signal shifts in the current paradigm (or thinking) of the major population. Observing trends closely will grant an entrepreneur the ability to recognize a potential opportunity. Trends need to be observed in society, technology, economy, and government. Following are some examples of such trends:

Societal Trends: aging demographics, health and fitness growth, senior living

Technology Trends: mobile (cell phone) technology, e-commerce, Internet advances

Economic Trends: higher disposable income, dual wage-earner families, performance pressures

Government Trends: increased regulations, petroleum prices, terrorism

UNEXPECTED OCCURRENCES

These are successes or failures that, because they were unanticipated or unplanned, often prove to be a major innovative surprise to everyone. The infamous 9/11 terrorist attack on the United States is a good example of an unexpected occurrence; it produced an influx of innovative solutions to the newly created challenge of homeland security. (See "Entrepreneurship in Practice: Terrorism Ignites Creativity" on page 125.)

INCONGRUITIES

Incongruities occur when a gap or difference exists between expectations and reality. For example, when Fred Smith proposed overnight mail delivery, he was told, "If it were that profitable, the U.S. Post Office would be doing it." It turned out Smith was right. An incongruity existed between what Smith felt was needed and the way business was currently conducted; thus, he created FedEx.

PROCESS NEEDS

These occur when an answer to a particular need is required. Venture capitalists often refer to these needs as "pain" that exists in the marketplace—the entrepreneur must recognize an innovative solution, or "painkiller." Examples include the creation of new medical devices, health foods, pharmaceuticals, and time-saving innovations.

INDUSTRY AND MARKET CHANGES

Continual shifts in the marketplace are caused by developments such as consumer attitudes, advancements in technology, and industry growth. Industries and markets always undergo changes in structure, design, or definition. An example can be found in the health care industry—hospital care has undergone radical changes, and home health care and preventive medicine have replaced hospitalization and surgery as primary focus areas. The entrepreneur needs to be aware of and seize these emerging opportunities.

DEMOGRAPHIC CHANGES

These arise from trend changes in population, age, education, occupations, geographic locations, and similar factors. Demographic shifts are important and often provide new entrepreneurial opportunities. For example, as the average population age in Florida and Arizona has increased (due largely to the influx of retirees), land development, recreational, and health care industries all have profited.

PERCEPTUAL CHANGES

These are changes that occur in people's interpretation of facts and concepts. Perceptual changes are intangible but meaningful. Perception can cause major shifts in ideas to take place. The current fitness craze, caused by the perceived need to be healthy and physically fit, has created a demand for both health foods and health facilities throughout the country. Another example is people's desire to better use their personal time. As a result, the travel industry has capitalized on consumers' current need to "see the world" while they are young and healthy, and time-share condominiums and travel clubs have increased.

KNOWLEDGE-BASED CONCEPTS

These are the basis for the creation or development of something brand new. Inventions are knowledge based; they are the product of new thinking, new methods, and new knowledge. Such innovations often require the longest time period between initiation and market implementation because of the need for testing and modification. For example, today's cell phone technology has advanced to include not just phone service but cameras, Internet access, and music. This has revolutionized the way we use different technologies today. These concepts were not thought possible just five years ago; some examples of these innovation sources are presented in Table 5.1.

Table 5.1	Sources of Innovative Ideas

Source	Examples
Unexpected occurrences	Unexpected success: Apple Computer (microcomputers)
	Unexpected tragedy: 9/11 terrorist attack
Incongruities	Overnight package delivery
Process needs	Sugar-free products
	Caffeine-free coffee
	Microwave ovens
Industry and market changes	Health care industry: changing to home health care
Demographic changes	Retirement communities for older people
Perceptual changes	Exercise (aerobics) and the growing concern for fitness
Knowledge-based concepts	Mobile (cell phone) technology, pharmaceutical industry, robotics

the global perspective

Africa: Opportunities or Peril

Due to civil unrest in parts of Africa, entrepreneurs and investors alike have been disinclined to do business on the continent; however, a brave few have uncovered significant opportunity by being innovative in their approach to conducting business in a relatively unstable environment. With Africa's economy growing between 5 and 6 percent annually and its inflation dropping, companies that have been willing and able to adjust are well positioned as the climate continues to improve.

Emerging Capital Partners (ECP), a private equity firm in Washington, DC, has focused on Africa since 1999 and has experienced a return of three times its initial investment on average. The firm admits that it has encountered problems, including having to exit 18 of the 48 countries in which it has made investments; however, the overall performance of its portfolio has rewarded the company's tenacity. Following are a few of the top performers for its portfolio:

- CelTel, a mobile phone company that operates in 13 countries; ECP invested $50 million, resulting in a $215 million payout when it was sold five years later.

- Ecobank, a banking group; ECP invested $12 million, leading to a $36 million return at the end of seven years.

- Societe International de Plantations D'Heveas, a rubber exporter; ECP invested $14.8 million and cashed out for $48.1 million two years later.

ECP emphasizes that its investors are experienced in working with international businesses, so the risk is somewhat mitigated by their prior knowledge; however, local entrepreneurs' drive to succeed and the lack of available capital have created an ideal environment for ECP to diversity its portfolio by investing in multiple countries while negotiating terms that have allowed the firm to effectively hedge its investments. Although this environment will most likely change as other investors enter the continent, ECP's willingness to pursue opportunities where others saw only disaster has given the firm an advantage over its competition.

Source: Adapted from Marc Gunther, "Investment in Africa Starts to Pay Off," *Fortune*, February 18, 2008, http://money.cnn.com/2008/02/13/magazines/fortune/gunther_africa.fortune/index.htm (accessed March 26, 2008).

The Process of Knowledge and Learning

Once the sources of ideas are recognized, entrepreneurs must use their existing knowledge base to identify an actual opportunity; that knowledge serves as the basis for interacting with the new experience. This knowledge base could take the form of general industry knowledge, prior market knowledge, prior customer understanding, specific interest knowledge, or any previous knowledge that helps the entrepreneur to better identify opportunities.[3] Every prospective entrepreneur needs to use his or her previous knowledge base to interpret the unusual sources of innovative ideas into a potential opportunity. Thus, each individual's experiences are uniquely valuable to the opportunity recognition process.

In addition, entrepreneurs must learn from their experiences as well. Researcher Andrew C. Corbett has identified the importance of acquiring and transforming information and knowledge through the learning process. His research lent credence to theories about the cognitive ability of individuals to transform information into recognizable opportunities.[4] How an individual entrepreneur acquires, processes, and learns from prior knowledge that he or she has gained is critical to the complete opportunity identification process. With that in mind, we examine the imagination and creativity needed to help transform and learn from prior experiences.

Entrepreneurial Imagination and Creativity

Entrepreneurs blend imaginative and creative thinking with a systematic, logical process ability. This combination is a key to successful innovation. In addition, potential entrepreneurs are always looking for unique opportunities to fill needs or wants. They sense economic potential in business problems by continually asking "What if . . . ?" or "Why not . . . ?" They develop an ability to see, recognize, and create opportunity where others find only problems. It has been said that the first rule for developing entrepreneurial vision is to recognize that problems are to solutions what demand is to supply. Applying this rule means an entrepreneur will analyze a problem from every possible angle: What is the problem? Whom does it affect? How does it affect them? What costs are involved? Can it be solved? Would the marketplace pay for a solution? This is the type of analysis that blends creative thinking with systematic analysis.[5]

The Role of Creative Thinking

It is important to recognize the role of creative thinking in the innovative process. Creativity is the generation of ideas that results in the improved efficiency or effectiveness of a system.[6]

Two important aspects of creativity exist: process and people. The process is goal oriented; it is designed to attain a solution to a problem. The people are the resources that determine the solution. The process remains the same, but the approach that the people use will vary. For example, sometimes they will adapt a solution, and other times they will formulate a highly innovative solution.[7] Table 5.2 compares these two approaches.

One study examined the validity of these two approaches for distinguishing innovative entrepreneurs from adaptive entrepreneurs and found their application very effective.[8] Thus, understanding the problem-solving orientation of individuals helps develop their creative abilities.

Table 5.2   Two Approaches to Creative Problem-Solving

Adaptor	Innovator
Employs a disciplined, precise, methodical approach	Approaches tasks from unusual angles
Is concerned with solving, rather than finding, problems	Discovers problems and avenues of solutions
Attempts to refine current practices	Questions basic assumptions related to current practices
Tends to be means oriented	Has little regard for means; is more interested in ends
Is capable of extended detail work	Has little tolerance for routine work
Is sensitive to group cohesion and cooperation	Has little or no need for consensus; often is insensitive to others

Source: Michael Kirton, "Adaptors and Innovators: A Description and Measure," *Journal of Applied Psychology* (October 1976): 623. Copyright © 1976 by The American Psychological Association.

The Nature of the Creative Process

Creativity is a process that can be developed and improved.[9] Everyone is creative to some degree. However, as is the case with many abilities and talents (athletic, artistic, etc.), some individuals have a greater aptitude for creativity than others. Also, some people have been raised and educated in an environment that encouraged them to develop their creativity. They have been taught to think and act creatively. For others, the process is more difficult because they have not been positively reinforced; if they are to be creative, they must learn how to implement the creative process.[10]

Many people incorrectly believe that only a genius can be creative.[11] Most people also assume that some people are born creative and others are not, or that only the gifted or highly intelligent person is capable of generating creative ideas and insights. Yet, the real barriers to creative thinking are sometimes the inadvertent "killer phrases" we use in our communications. Table 5.3 lists the ten key idea "killers" we use. People may not intentionally stop a creative idea, but these simple, negative phrases prohibit people from thinking any further.[12]

Creativity is not some mysterious and rare talent reserved for a select few. It is a distinct way of looking at the world that is often illogical. The creative process involves seeing relationships among things that others have not seen (for example, the use of USB flash drives, known as thumb drives, to store or transfer data among computers).[13]

The creative process has four commonly agreed-on phases or steps. Most experts agree on the general nature and relationships among these phases, although they refer to them by a variety of names.[14] Experts also agree that these phases do not always occur in the same order for every creative activity. For creativity to occur, chaos is necessary—but a structured and focused chaos. We shall examine this four-step process using the most typical structural development.

PHASE 1: BACKGROUND OR KNOWLEDGE ACCUMULATION

Successful creations are generally preceded by investigation and information gathering. This usually involves extensive reading, conversations with others working in the field, attendance at professional meetings and workshops, and a general absorption of information relative to the problem or issue under study. Additional investigation in both related and unrelated fields is sometimes involved. This exploration provides the individual with a variety of perspectives on the problem, and it is particularly important to the entrepreneur, who

Table **5.3**	**The Most Common Idea Killers**

1. "Naah."
2. "Can't" (said with a shake of the head and an air of finality).
3. "That's the dumbest thing I've ever heard."
4. "Yeah, but if you did that . . ." (poses an extreme or unlikely disaster case).
5. "We already tried that—years ago."
6. "I don't see anything wrong with the way we're doing it now."
7. "We've never done anything like that before."
8. "We've got deadlines to meet—we don't have time to consider that."
9. "It's not in the budget."
10. "Where do you get these weird ideas?"

Source: Adapted from *The Creative Process,* ed. Angelo M. Biondi (Hadley, MA: The Creative Education Foundation, 1986).

needs a basic understanding of all aspects of the development of a new product, service, or business venture.

People practice the creative search for background knowledge in a number of ways. Some of the most helpful are to: (1) read in a variety of fields; (2) join professional groups and associations; (3) attend professional meetings and seminars; (4) travel to new places; (5) talk to anyone and everyone about your subject; (6) scan magazines, newspapers, and journals for articles related to the subject; (7) develop a subject library for future reference; (8) carry a small notebook and record useful information; and (9) devote time to pursue natural curiosities.[15]

PHASE 2: THE INCUBATION PROCESS

Creative individuals allow their subconscious to mull over the tremendous amounts of information they gather during the preparation phase. This incubation process often occurs while they are engaged in activities totally unrelated to the subject or problem. It happens even when they are sleeping. This accounts for the advice frequently given to a person who is frustrated by what appears to be an unsolvable problem: "Why don't you sleep on it?"[16] Getting away from a problem and letting the subconscious mind work on it allows creativity to spring forth. Some of the most helpful steps to induce incubation are to: (1) engage in routine, "mindless" activities (cutting the grass, painting the house); (2) exercise regularly; (3) play (sports, board games, puzzles); (4) think about the project or problem before falling asleep; (5) meditate or practice self-hypnosis; and (6) sit back and relax on a regular basis.[17]

PHASE 3: THE IDEA EXPERIENCE

This phase of the creative process is often the most exciting, because it is when the idea or solution the individual is seeking is discovered. Sometimes referred to as the "eureka factor," this phase is also the one the average person incorrectly perceives as the only component of creativity.[18]

As with the incubation process, new and innovative ideas often emerge while the person is busy doing something unrelated to the enterprise, venture, or investigation (for example, taking a shower, driving on an interstate highway, or leafing through a newspaper).[19] Sometimes the idea appears as a bolt out of the blue. In most cases, however, the answer comes to the individual incrementally. Slowly but surely, the person begins to formulate the solution. Because it is often difficult to determine when the incubation process ends and the idea experience phase begins, many people are unaware of moving from Phase 2 to Phase 3.

Following are ways to speed up the idea experience: (1) daydream and fantasize about your project, (2) practice your hobbies, (3) work in a leisurely environment (for example, at home instead of at the office), (4) put the problem on the back burner, (5) keep a notebook at bedside to record late-night or early-morning ideas, and (6) take breaks while working.[20]

PHASE 4: EVALUATION AND IMPLEMENTATION

This is the most difficult step of a creative endeavor and requires a great deal of courage, self-discipline, and perseverance. Successful entrepreneurs can identify ideas that are workable and that they have the skills to implement. More importantly, they do not give up when they run into temporary obstacles.[21] Often they will fail several times before they successfully develop their best ideas. In some cases, entrepreneurs will take the idea in an entirely different direction or will discover a new and more workable idea while struggling to implement the original one.

Another important part of this phase is the reworking of ideas to put them into final form. Frequently an idea emerges from Phase 3 in rough form, so it needs to be modified or tested to achieve its final shape. Some of the most useful suggestions for carrying out this phase are to: (1) increase your energy level with proper exercise, diet, and rest; (2) educate yourself in the business-planning process and all facets of business; (3) test your ideas with knowledgeable people; (4) take notice of your intuitive hunches and feelings; (5) educate yourself in the selling process; (6) learn about organizational policies and practices; (7) seek advice from others (friends, experts, etc.); and (8) view the problems you encounter while implementing your ideas as challenges.[22]

Figure 5.1 illustrates the four phases of the creative thinking process. If a person encounters a major problem while moving through the process, it is sometimes helpful to go back to a previous phase and try again. For example, if an individual is unable to formulate an idea or solution (Phase 3), a return to Phase 1 often helps. By immersing him- or herself in the data, the individual allows the unconscious mind to begin anew processing the data, establishing cause-effect relationships, and formulating potential solutions.

Developing Your Creativity

You can do a number of things to improve your own creative talents; one of the most helpful is to become aware of some of the habits and mental blocks that stifle creativity.[23] Of course, as with most processes, your development will be more effective if you regularly practice exercises designed to increase your creative abilities. The following section is designed to improve your awareness of some of the thought habits that limit your creativity and to assist you in developing a personalized creativity improvement program.

RECOGNIZING RELATIONSHIPS

Many inventions and innovations are a result of the inventor's ability to see new and different relationships among objects, processes, materials, technologies, and people.[24] Examples range widely and include (1) adding fruit juice to soft drinks to create Izze®, (2) combining combustion engine technology with the wheel to create the automobile, and (3) using a 330-pound defensive football player as a running back and pass receiver.

If you wish to improve your creativity, it helps to look for different or unorthodox relationships among the elements and people around you. This activity involves *perceiving in a relational mode*. You can develop this talent by viewing things and people as existing in a complementary or appositional relationship with other things and people. Simply stated, things and people exist in the world in relation to other things and people. Creative people seem to be intuitively aware of this phenomenon and have developed a talent for recognizing new and different relationships. These relationships often lead to visions that result in new ideas, products,

| Figure | 5.1 | The Critical Thinking Process |

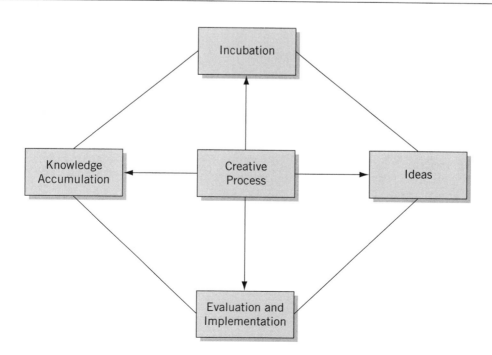

and services.[25] In order to develop the ability to recognize new relationships, you must practice perceiving in a relational mode. The following exercise helps with this development.

A Creative Exercise

Analyze and elaborate on how the following pairs relate to each other in a complementary way: nut and bolt, husband and wife, chocolate cake and vanilla ice cream, grass clippings and tomato plants, peanut butter and jelly, athlete and coach, humanity and water, winning and losing, television and overhead projectors, and managers and production workers.

DEVELOPING A FUNCTIONAL PERSPECTIVE

If expanded, the principle of perceiving in a relational mode helps develop a **functional perspective** toward things and people. A creative person tends to view things and people in terms of how they can satisfy his or her needs and help complete a project. For example, a homemaker who cannot find a screwdriver often will use a butter knife to tighten a loose screw, or a cereal manufacturer will add fruit to its product to create a new product line that appeals to a health-conscious market.

If you wish to become more innovative and creative, you need to visualize yourself in complementary relationships to the things and people of the world. You must learn to look at them in terms of how they complement attempts to satisfy your own needs and to complete your projects. You must begin to look at things and people in nonconventional ways and from a different perspective.[26] The following exercise is designed to help you develop a functional perspective.

A Creative Exercise

Think of and write down all of the functions you can imagine for the following items (spend five minutes on each item):

- An egotistical staff member
- A large pebble
- A fallen tree branch
- A chair
- A computer "whiz kid"
- An obsessively organized employee
- The office "gossip"
- An old hubcap
- A new secretary
- An empty roll of masking tape
- A yardstick
- An old coat hanger
- The office "tightwad"
- This exercise

USING YOUR BRAINS

Ever since split-brain studies were conducted in the 1950s and 1960s, experts on creativity, innovation, and self-development have emphasized the importance of developing the skills associated with both hemispheres of the brain.[27]

The **right brain** hemisphere helps an individual understand analogies, imagine things, and synthesize information. The **left brain** hemisphere helps the person analyze, verbalize,

Opportunity Trends

She doesn't use a crystal ball, but futurist Faith Popcorn can see some of the major trends that sway consumer buying decisions. Popcorn believes that those who understand the future will make fewer mistakes and become more successful. By spotting the trends that will shape marketplaces, she hopes to help entrepreneurs start and grow their businesses. She reaches those entrepreneurs through her marketing consulting firm, Brain-Reserve. How well does Popcorn predict the trends of tomorrow? According to her, she hasn't been wrong about a trend yet.

Popcorn states that, as a marketer, she finds trend knowledge invaluable. In her book *Clicking*, she identified some of the most influential trends driving the marketplace. These are not fads—they are big, sweeping consumer movements that savvy entrepreneurs see as opportunities for big profits. Since her book was published, she has provided a yearly set of predictions regarding consumer trends. The following are her predicted trends for the twenty-first century.

- **Cocooning**—The desire to shelter ourselves from the harsh realities of the outside world.

- **Fantasy Adventure**—The need for the new and unconventional. We seek out ways to escape from our problems and experiment with our desires.

- **Skin Deeper**—According to Popcorn, our material focus has left us emotionally starving. Due to increasing work hours and more emphasis on virtual relationships, we will increasingly want physical contact.

- **Brain Fitness**—According to Popcorn, a mental fitness boom is on the horizon. The focus on mental agility will parallel the need to prolong physical fitness and youthful appearance.

- **Secondhand Nostalgia**—Due to the stresses and concerns of life, we will seek out safe places that allow for a retreat. We will also trend toward activities that were popular during safe times, such as the 1950s.

- **America's Next Top Surgery**—The rage of reality surgery shows and the increased medical advancements will cause an obsession with risky surgeries. Also, playing to the Fantasy Adventure trend, people will be motivated to try new surgeries to cure illnesses and improve appearance.

- **No Olds Barred**—The enormous baby boomer market is aging into its 60s and 70s. These boomers view themselves as young and will demand products to meet their needs but not be labeled as products for the elderly. Popcorn suggests that one such outcome could be larger, easier-to-read dials in luxury automobiles (such as BMW or Infinity).

- **ExpertEASE**—Given the availability of information on the Internet, expertise takes on a new meaning. According to Popcorn, "Expertise is no longer earned through years of training; all it takes is a little research." She claims that we have lost the preferred taste for actual experience and have replaced it with virtual experiences.

- **DeBug-ReBug**—In the past, we have focused on removing bad organisms from the environment. Recently, biologists have identified that some organisms can be beneficial and improve health. Popcorn suggests that spas and health care entities will offer "designer" treatments of advantageous organisms.

- **Mood Tuning**—According to Popcorn, we now expect that the things we buy will adjust our feelings. We will seek out biologically enhanced purchases that will cause us to feel more confident, sexy, or whatever the situation dictates.

Source: Adapted from "Faith Popcorn's Predictions for 2006," *Arizona Reporter,* http://managecamp.typepad.com/brand_managecamp_weblog/files/faith_popcorn_2006_predictions.pdf (accessed October 10, 2006).

and use rational approaches to problem solving. Although these two brain hemispheres process information differently and are responsible for different brain activities and skills (Table 5.4), they are integrated through a group of connecting nerve fibers called the corpus callosum. Because of this connection and the nature of the relationship between the activities of each hemisphere, each hemisphere should be viewed as existing and functioning in a complementary relationship with the other hemisphere.[28]

The creative process involves logical and analytical thinking in the knowledge accumulation, evaluation, and implementation stages. In addition, it calls for imagination, intuition, analogy conceptualization, and synthesizing in the incubation and idea creation stages. So, to become more creative, it is necessary to practice and develop both right- and left-hemisphere skills. The following problem-solving exercise is designed to demonstrate the effectiveness of combining the skills of both hemispheres when solving problems.

A Creative Exercise

Assume you have an idea that will save your organization time and money on processing customer complaints. Your supervisor has been extremely busy and has been unwilling to stop and listen to your idea.

1. Write down all of the left-hemisphere-type solutions to this problem you can think of in five minutes.

2. Write down all of the right-hemisphere-type solutions to this problem you can think of in five minutes.

3. Compare these lists and combine two or more solutions from each list that will result in a unique and innovative way to solve this problem.

4. Repeat steps 1, 2, and 3 using a current problem you are facing at work or at home.

Our society and its educational institutions reward individuals who have been successful at developing their logical, analytical, and rational left-brain skills. Little emphasis, however, has been placed on practicing and using right-brain skills. Table 5.5 represents some ways you can practice developing both left- and right-hemisphere skills.[29]

Table 5.4	Processes Associated with the Two Brain Hemispheres

Left Hemisphere	Right Hemisphere
Verbal	Nonverbal
Analytical	Synthesizing
Abstract	Seeing analogies
Rational	Nonrational
Logical	Spatial
Linear	Intuitive
	Imaginative

Source: Betty Edwards, *Drawing on the Right Side of the Brain* (Los Angeles: Tarcher, 1979).

the entrepreneurial process

Developing Creativity

What color is the sky when you dream? Do you consider yourself to be creative? *Creativity* has been defined as having the quality or power of creating. People are innately creative. Really. Let your creativity out of the playpen! Millions of dollars are made from truly simple creative endeavors. You can cash in too if you use some of these methods to boost your creativity.

1. **Brainstorm!** This is the old-school way to drum up creative ideas and solve problems, but it's still by far the best. The corporate world was woken up when Alex Osborn introduced this concept in the 1950s. Established rules were easy to follow:

   - *Shout out or write down every solution that comes to mind.*
   - *Off-the-wall ideas are welcome.*
   - *Criticize nothing.*
   - *Organize later.*

2. **Opposites attract.** Here's an interesting concept: synectics. Similar to the word itself, *synectics* involves putting two "nonsensical" things together to see what happens. Examples include: "Imagine a restaurant with no waiters, tables, or silverware" (McDonald's); "Imagine a bookstore with no books—and no store" (Amazon.com); "Imagine moving trucks with no movers" (U-Haul). Don't hesitate to explore that which is strange!

3. **THINKubate.** Gerald Haman created (there's that word again) the "THINKubator"—a playground where businesspeople, entrepreneurs, and the like can go to escape the humdrum environment of offices and "can't doers." The playground houses comfortable seating, toys, and fun pictures, and it offers an environment that favors brain stimulation and idea creation. It must work, because Haman has developed numerous products for Procter & Gamble and Arthur Andersen.

4. **Trigger great ideas.** Triggers are everyday items that can be used to stimulate the brain: abstract photos, inspiring quotes, uncompleted ideas, tips, and so on. Place trigger items in various places you look or visit often—for example, the refrigerator door, your dashboard, or your phone. You never know when a connection will be made.

5. **Connect.** Every person you meet or place you visit might be an opportunity waiting to happen. The key is to be prepared for that opportunity when it arises. Creativity consultant Jordan Ayan suggests building up your CORE: curiosity, openness, risk, and energy. These traits can be enhanced by reading up on trends, attending trade shows, browsing, and trying new things. Spotting open windows isn't necessarily easy, but increasing the number of windows can be.

6. **Always celebrate failure.** Try and try again. What doesn't kill you only makes you stronger. Dare to be great! Get the idea? Don't suffer from insanity! Enjoy every minute of it!

7. **Make 'em laugh.** Humor is a great way to relieve stress. Use it in your creative endeavors. Can you imagine Dennis the Menace helping you build your prototype? How about letting the Disney World characters coauthor your business plan? Let your youngest relative in on your invention. Humor and laughter certainly encourage creativity.

8. **Sweat it.** Yes! Sweat it out! Exercise gets the creative juices—endorphins—flowing. Let the mind wander while you're jogging, or ride the exercise bike while reading the year-end reports. Just be sure to keep a notepad handy to jot down all of your great ideas!

9. **Remember your wildest dreams.** Has anyone ever replied to you with this statement? "In your dreams!" Well, go figure. Dreams are a great place to start when it comes to unleashing creativity. Elias Howe once had a dream in which cannibals were piercing his flesh with spears. Thus, the sewing machine was invented. Don't ignore daydreams or spur-of-the-moment ideas, either. Your subconscious could be trying to tell you something.

Source: Adapted from Nick D'Alto, "Think Big," *Business Start Ups* (January 2000): 61–65.

Table 5.5	Ways to Develop Left- and Right-Hemisphere Skills	

Left-Hemisphere Skills	Right-Hemisphere Skills
1. Step-by-step planning of your work and life activities	1. Using metaphors and analogies to describe things and people in your conversations and writing
2. Reading ancient, medieval, and scholastic philosophy, legal cases, and books on logic	2. Taking off your watch when you are not working
3. Establishing timetables for all of your activities	3. Suspending your initial judgment of ideas, new acquaintances, movies, TV programs, and so on
4. Using and working with a computer program	4. Recording your hunches, feelings, and intuitions and calculating their accuracy
5. Detailed fantasizing and visualizing of things and situations in the future	
6. Drawing faces, caricatures, and landscapes	

ELIMINATING MUDDLING MIND-SETS

A number of mental habits block or impede creative thinking. It has been estimated that adults use only 2 to 10 percent of their creative potential.[30] For example, many individuals tend to make quick judgments about new things, people, and ideas. Another inclination is to point out the negative components of a new or different idea because of the psychological discomfort associated with change. Some common mental habits that inhibit creativity and innovation are "either/or" thinking, security hunting, stereotyping, and probability thinking. These habits, or muddling mind-sets, tend to hinder creative thought processes, and different thought processes must be used to enhance creative thinking.[31]

- *Either/Or Thinking* Because of the speed of change in the modern world, personal lives are filled with a great deal of uncertainty and ambiguity. People often get bogged down with striving for an unreasonable amount of certainty in their lives. But the creative person learns to accept a reasonable amount of ambiguity in his or her work and life. In fact, many exceptionally creative people thrive in an uncertain environment and find it exhilarating.[32]

- *Security Hunting* Many people try to make the right decision or take the correct action every time. In doing so, they rely on averages, stereotypes, and probability theory to minimize their risks. Although this strategy often is appropriate, at times a creator or innovator must take some calculated risks.[33] Sometimes these risks result in the innovator's being wrong and making mistakes. Yet by recognizing this as part of the innovation game, the creative person learns from his or her mistakes and moves on to create bigger and better things. We all know that Thomas Edison failed numerous times when searching for the correct materials to use inside the incandescent light bulb.

- *Stereotyping* It is ironic that, although averages and stereotypes are fabricated abstractions, people act and make decisions based on them as if these were data entities that exist in the real world. For example, one could hypothesize that the average homemaker is female, 38 years old, and 5'4" tall; weighs 120 pounds; and has two children, a part-time job, and 14.5 years of formal education. If one tried to find a person who fits this description, however, the chances of success would be small. In short, the more descriptive the abstraction or stereotype, the less real it becomes. Predicating actions from stereotypes and averages can cause an individual to act on the basis of a distorted picture of reality. More important, relying on these abstractions can limit a person's perception of the real entities and possibilities in the world. Creativity expert Edward deBono argues that people must alter their thinking to enhance their creativity; only new patterns of thinking will lead to new ideas and innovations.[34]

- *Probability Thinking* In their struggle to achieve security, many people also tend to rely on the theory of probability thinking to make decisions. An overreliance on this decision-making method, however, can distort reality and prohibit one from taking calculated risks that may lead to creative endeavors.

    Probability experts report that the predictive power of probability theory increases in proportion to the number of times an event is repeated. If a person wishes to predict the probability of tossing the number 3 when rolling dice a certain number of times, probability theory is extremely useful. However, if the person wishes to know the likelihood of rolling a 4 with one roll of the dice, the predictive ability of probability theory is much less valuable.

In the creative game, often an individual is looking at an opportunity or situation that may occur only once in a lifetime. In a single-event situation, intuition and educated guesses are just as useful, if not more useful, than logic and probability.[35] One way of increasing your creative capacities is to practice looking at some of the situations in your life as a 50/50 game, and then begin to take some risks. Additionally, the following problem-solving exercises are designed to help eliminate muddling mind-sets:

- Practice taking small risks in your personal life and at work, relying on your intuition and hunches. Keep a log of these risks, and chart their accuracy and consequences. For example, try to draw to an inside straight in your next family poker game.

- Go out of your way to talk to people who you think conform to a commonly accepted stereotype.

- Take on a number of complex projects at work and at home that do not lend themselves to guaranteed and predictable results. Allow yourself to live with a manageable amount of ambiguity. Notice how you react to this ambiguity.

- When an idea is presented to you, first think of all the positive aspects of the idea, then of all the negative aspects, and finally of all the interesting aspects.

- When listening to people, suspend initial judgment of them, their ideas, and their information, and simply listen.

- Try making some decisions in the present. That is, do not let your personal history or your estimates about the future dominate your decision-making process.[36]

Arenas in Which People Are Creative

Remember, people are inherently creative. Some act on that creativity all of the time while others stifle it, and most of us fall somewhere in between the two. The reality is that people often do not recognize when or how they are being creative. Furthermore, they fail to recognize the many opportunities for creativity that arise within their jobs on a daily basis. Creativity researcher William Miller argues that people often do not recognize when they are being creative, and they frequently overlook opportunities to be creative. He suggests that the path to creativity begins by first recognizing all of the ways in which we are or can be creative. People in organizations can channel their creativity into seven different arenas:

- *Idea creativity:* thinking up a new idea or concept, such as an idea for a new product or service or a way to solve a problem.

- *Material creativity:* inventing and building a tangible object such as a product, an advertisement, a report, or a photograph.

- *Organization creativity:* organizing people or projects and coming up with a new organizational form or approach to structuring things. Examples could include organizing a project, starting a new type of venture, putting together or reorganizing a work group, and changing the policies and rules of a group.

- *Relationship creativity:* an innovative approach to achieving collaboration, cooperation, and win-win relationships with others. The person who handles a difficult situation well or deals with a particular person in an especially effective manner is being creative in a relationship or one-on-one context.

- *Event creativity:* producing an event such as an awards ceremony, team outing, or annual meeting. The creativity here also encompasses décor, ways in which people are involved, sequence of happenings, setting, and so forth.

- *Inner creativity:* changing one's inner self; being open to new approaches to how one does things and thinking about oneself in different ways; achieving a change of heart or finding a new perspective or way to look at things that is a significant departure from how one has traditionally looked at them.

- *Spontaneous creativity:* acting in a spontaneous or spur-of-the-moment manner, such as coming up with a witty response in a meeting, an off-the-cuff speech, a quick and simple way to settle a dispute, or an innovative appeal when trying to close a sale.[37]

The Creative Climate

Creativity is most likely to occur when the business climate is right. No enterprise will have creative owners and managers for long if the right climate is not established and nurtured. Following are some important characteristics of this climate:

- A trustful management that does not overcontrol the personnel
- Open channels of communication among all business members
- Considerable contact and communication with outsiders
- A large variety of personality types
- A willingness to accept change
- An enjoyment in experimenting with new ideas
- Little fear of negative consequences for making a mistake
- The selection and promotion of employees on the basis of merit
- The use of techniques that encourage ideas, including suggestion systems and brainstorming
- Sufficient financial, managerial, human, and time resources for accomplishing goals[38]

Innovation and the Entrepreneur

Innovation is a key function in the entrepreneurial process. Researchers and authors in the field of entrepreneurship agree, for the most part, with the renowned consultant and author, Peter F. Drucker, about the concept of innovation: "Innovation is the specific function of entrepreneurship. . . . It is the means by which the entrepreneur either creates new wealth-producing resources or endows existing resources with enhanced potential for creating wealth."[39]

Innovation is the process by which entrepreneurs convert opportunities (ideas) into marketable solutions. It is the means by which they become catalysts for change.[40] We demonstrated in the earlier parts of this chapter that the innovation process starts with a good idea. The origin of an idea is important, and the role of creative thinking may be vital to that development.[41] A major difference exists between an idea that arises from mere speculation and one that is the product of extended thinking, research, experience, and work. More important, a prospective entrepreneur must have the desire to bring a good idea through the development stages. Thus, innovation is a combination of the vision to create a good idea and the perseverance and dedication to remain with the concept through implementation.

The Innovation Process

Most innovations result from a conscious, purposeful search for new opportunities.[42] This process begins with the analysis of the sources of new opportunities. Drucker has noted that, because innovation is both conceptual and perceptual, would-be innovators must go out and look, ask, and listen. Successful innovators use both the right and left sides of their brains. They look at figures. They look at people. They analytically work out what the innovation has to be to satisfy the opportunity. Then they go out and look at potential product users to study their expectations, values, and needs.[43]

Most successful innovations are simple and focused. They are directed toward a specific, clear, and carefully designed application. In the process, they create new customers and markets. Today's mobile technology (cell phones) is a good example. Although this technology is highly sophisticated, it has become easy to use and it appeals to a specific market niche: people who want their technology all in one and on the go.

Above all, innovation often involves more work than genius. As Thomas Edison once said, "Genius is 1 percent inspiration and 99 percent perspiration." Moreover, innovators rarely work in more than one area. For all his systematic innovative accomplishments, Edison worked only in the electricity field.

Types of Innovation

Four basic types of innovation exist (Table 5.6). These extend from the totally new to modifications of existing products or services. Following are the four types, in order of originality:

- Invention: the creation of a new product, service, or process—often one that is novel or untried. Such concepts tend to be "revolutionary."
- Extension: the expansion of a product, service, or process already in existence. Such concepts make a different application of a current idea.
- Duplication: the replication of an already existing product, service, or process. The duplication effort, however, is not simply copying but adding the entrepreneur's own creative touch to enhance or improve the concept and beat the competition.
- Synthesis: the combination of existing concepts and factors into a new formulation. This involves taking a number of ideas or items already invented and finding a way that they can form a new application.[44]

Table 5.6   Innovation in Action

Type	Description	Examples
Invention	Totally new product, service, or process	Wright brothers—airplane Thomas Edison—light bulb Alexander Graham Bell—telephone
Extension	New use or different application of an already existing product, service, or process	Ray Kroc—McDonald's Mark Zuckerberg, Facebook Barry Sternlicht, Starwood Hotels & Resorts
Duplication	Creative replication of an existing concept	Wal-Mart—department stores Gateway—personal computers Pizza Hut—pizza parlor
Synthesis	Combination of existing concepts and factors into a new formulation or use	Fred Smith—FedEx Howard Schultz, Starbucks

The Major Misconceptions of Innovation

The entire concept of innovation conjures up many thoughts and misconceptions; it seems that everyone has an opinion as to what innovation entails. In this section, we outline some of the commonly accepted innovation misconceptions and provide reasons why these are misconceptions and not facts.[45]

- *Innovation is planned and predictable.* This statement is based on the old concept that innovation should be left to the research and development (R&D) department under a planned format. In truth, innovation is unpredictable and may be introduced by anyone.

- *Technical specifications must be thoroughly prepared.* This statement comes from the engineering arena, which drafts complete plans before moving on. Thorough preparation is good, but it sometimes takes too long. Quite often, it is more important to use a try/test/revise approach.

- *Innovation relies on dreams and blue-sky ideas.* As we have demonstrated in this chapter, the creative process is extremely important to recognizing innovative ideas. However, accomplished innovators are very practical people and create from opportunities grounded in reality—not daydreams.

- *Big projects will develop better innovations than smaller ones.* This statement has been proven false time and time again. Larger firms are now encouraging their people to work in smaller groups, where it often is easier to generate creative ideas. In Chapter 3, we discussed the importance of I-teams as a method of getting smaller teams to work on innovative projects.

- *Technology is the driving force of innovation success.* Technology is certainly one source for innovation, but it is not the only one. As we outlined earlier in this chapter, numerous sources exist for innovative ideas; technology is certainly a driving factor in many innovations, but it is not the only success factor. Moreover, the customer or market is the driving force behind any innovation. Market-driven or customer-based innovations have the highest probability of success.

Principles of Innovation

Potential entrepreneurs need to realize that innovation principles exist. These principles can be learned and—when combined with opportunity—can enable individuals to innovate. The major motivation principles are as follows:

- *Be action oriented.* Innovators always must be active and searching for new ideas, opportunities, or sources of innovation.

- *Make the product, process, or service simple and understandable.* People must readily understand how the innovation works.

- *Make the product, process, or service customer-based.* Innovators always must keep the customer in mind. The more an innovator has the end user in mind, the greater the chance the concept will be accepted and used.

- *Start small.* Innovators should not attempt a project or development on a grandiose scale. They should begin small and then build and develop, allowing for planned growth and proper expansion in the right manner and at the right time.

- *Aim high.* Innovators should aim high for success by seeking a niche in the marketplace.

- *Try/test/revise.* Innovators always should follow the rule of *try, test, and revise.* This helps work out any flaws in the product, process, or service.

- *Learn from failures.* Innovation does not guarantee success. More important, failures often give rise to innovations.[46]

- *Follow a milestone schedule.* Every innovator should follow a schedule that indicates milestone accomplishments. Although the project may run ahead or behind schedule, it still is important to have a schedule in order to plan and evaluate the project.

- *Reward heroic activity.* This principle applies more to those involved in seeking and motivating others to innovate. Innovative activity should be rewarded and given the proper amount of

entrepreneurship in practice

Terrorism Ignites Innovation

Ask not how America can innovate; ask what you can do to innovate America—this might as well have been the slogan on a war poster with Uncle Sam pointing his finger at us. Only days after September 11, 2001 the still-smoldering Pentagon advertised for the help of American citizens, asking them to send new ideas to combat the threat of terrorism. The Pentagon's Technical Support Working Group (TSWG) usually receives around 900 proposals a year for new technology and ideas to aid the world's most powerful military force; that October, they received 12,500. The TSWG agencies range from the Energy Department to the Federal Bureau of Investigation (FBI), Central Intelligence Agency (CIA), and Federal Aviation Administration, as well as local police and fire departments. The group sends out an annual list of problems it is interested in solving and then evaluates the proposals it receives. They will then choose only 100 to 200 proposals for research each year and fund $50 to $100 million for the projects.

One company that proposes their products to TSWG is Equator Technologies, Inc. Equator makes superfast digital signal processors used in video cameras and is

creating an automated baggage inspection system that would use a database of weapons images rotated on all possible planes of vision. It has been shown that a gun—laid on end—can be mistaken for a shaving-cream can when traditional baggage scanners are used. Another company envisions the use of surveillance cameras equipped with software to identify terrorists whose facial measurements match those found in police files, photos of known terrorists, and possibly FBI records.

Many of the TSWG's projects end up in local firehouses, police stations, airports, and border crossings. Some projects, such as handheld radiation detectors and bomb-resistant building plans, proved successful during the 2002 Olympics and at the Pentagon.

However, the group isn't without failure. They once funded a special radio antenna that picked up signals no better than a chain-link fence. The unofficial motto at TSWG is "If you fail, fail right . . . don't just fail because you didn't try everything or you stopped short."

Source: Paul Magnusson, "Small Biz vs. the Terrorists," *BusinessWeek Online,* March 4, 2002, http://www.businessweek.com/magazine/content/02_09/b3772087.htm (accessed March 18, 2008).

respect. This also means tolerating and, to a limited degree, accepting failures as a means of accomplishing innovation. Innovative work must be viewed as a heroic activity that will reveal new horizons for the enterprise.

- *Work, work, work.* This is a simple but accurate exhortation with which to conclude the innovation principles. It takes work—not genius or mystery—to innovate successfully.[47]

Summary

This chapter examined the importance of creative thinking and innovation to the entrepreneur. Opportunity identification was discussed in relation to the knowledge and learning needed to recognize good ideas. The sources of innovative ideas were outlined and examined. The creativity process was then described, and ways to develop creativity were presented. Exercises and suggestions were included to help the reader increase the development of his or her creativity. The nature of the creative climate also was presented.

The four basic types of innovation—invention, extension, duplication, and synthesis—were explained. The last part of the chapter reviewed the misconceptions commonly associated with innovation and presented the major innovation principles.

Key Terms and Concepts

appositional relationship

creative process

creativity

duplication

extension

functional perspective

incongruities

innovation

invention

left brain

muddling mind-sets

opportunity identification

probability thinking

right brain

stereotype

synthesis

Review and Discussion Questions

1. Describe opportunity identification for the entrepreneur.
2. How are prior knowledge and learning important to the recognition of opportunities?
3. What are the major sources of innovative ideas? Explain and give an example of each.
4. What is the difference between an adaptor and an innovator?
5. What are four major components in the creative process?

6. What are the four steps involved in developing personal creativity?
7. In your own words, state what is meant by the term *innovation*.
8. What are four major types of innovation?
9. Briefly describe the five major misconceptions commonly associated with innovation.
10. Identify and describe five of the innovation principles.

Experiential Exercise

DEVELOPING YOUR PERSONAL CREATIVITY

This exercise is designed to help you develop your personal creativity. To enhance your creativity, you should make improvements in the following areas:

1. *Personal development* (self-discipline, self-awareness, self-confidence, improvement in energy level)

2. *Problem-solving skills* (problem recognition)

3. *Mental fluency* (quantity of thoughts/ideas)

4. *Mental flexibility* (switching gears/approaches)

5. *Originality* (unusual thoughts and ideas)

It is best to start small and work on a few things at a time. Follow the step-by-step approach listed next. Use the accompanying worksheet to help you design a personal creativity program.

1. Choose one of the five areas for improvement listed (for example, mental fluency).

2. Establish a specific objective for this area (for example, to increase your ability to generate logical and intuitive solutions to problems at work).

3. Decide how much time you will give to this program (for example, three hours per week).

4. Decide how long you will work in this area (for example, one month, two months, etc.).

5. Decide what actions you will take and what exercises you will perform to improve in this area (for example, sentence-creation exercises, usage ideas, meditation, suspension of initial judgments, etc.).

6. Set up an outline of your program (that is, day of week, time of day, place, and what you will do during this time).

7. Review your program after completion, and write a similar program for another one of the five areas for improvement.

PERSONAL CREATIVITY PROGRAM WORKSHEET

Area of improvement _____

Specific objective _____

_____

_____

Number of hours per week _____

Duration of program _____

Actions/exercises _____

_____

_____

_____

OUTLINE OF PROGRAM

Day of the week				
Time of day				
Place				
Actions that day				

Case 5.1

POST-IT® NOTES

One way new products are developed is to take a current product and modify it in some form. Another way is to determine how a previously developed product can be marketed or used by a particular group of customers.

The 3M Company is famous for many products, among them adhesives and abrasives. In one of 3M's most famous innovative stories from the 1980s, a 3M manager, who was a member of a church choir, wanted to mark the pages of his hymnal so he could quickly find them. A bookmark would not do, because the piece of paper could easily fall out. The manager needed something that would adhere to the page but not tear it. Back at work, the manager asked one of the members of the research and development department if an adhesive existed that would do this. One did, but it never had been marketed because the company found that the adhesive was not strong enough for industrial use. At the manager's request, a batch of the glue was prepared and applied to small pieces of paper that could be used as bookmarks.

As the manager who had requested the product began to think about the new product, he concluded it had uses other than as a bookmark. Secretaries could use it to attach messages to files, and managers could use it to send notes along with letters and memos. In an effort to spur interest in the product, the manager had a large batch of these "attachable" notes—now called Post-it notes—made, and he began distributing them to secretaries throughout the company. Before long, more people began to ask for them. The manager then ordered the supply cut off and told everyone who wanted them that they would have to contact the marketing department. When that department became inundated with calls for Post-it notes, it concluded that a strong demand existed throughout the industry for these notes, and full production began. Today, Post-it notes are one of the largest and most successful product lines at the 3M Company.

QUESTIONS

1. How did the creative thinking process work in the development of this product? Describe what took place in each of the four steps.

2. Why did the manager have the Post-it notes sent to secretaries throughout the company? What was his objective in doing this?

3. What type of innovation was this—invention, extension, duplication, or synthesis? Defend your answer.

4. Which of the sources of innovative ideas discussed in the chapter help account for this product's success? Explain in detail.

Notes

1. S. Venkataraman, "The Distinctive Domain of Entrepreneurship Research," in *Advances in Entrepreneurship, Firm Emergence, and Growth,* vol. 3, ed. J. A. Katz (Greenwich, CT: JAI Press, 1997): 119–38.

2. Connie M. Gaglio and Jerome A. Katz, "The Psychological Basis of Opportunity Identification: Entrepreneurial Alertness," *Journal of Small Business Economics* 16 (2001): 11–95; see also Dean A. Shepherd and Dawn DeTienne, "Prior Knowledge, Potential Financial Reward, and Opportunity Identification," *Entrepreneurship Theory and Practice* 29, no. 1 (January 2005): 91–112.

3. A. Ardichvili, R. Cardozo, and S. Ray, "A Theory of Entrepreneurial Opportunity Identification and Development," *Journal of Business Venturing* 18, no. 1 (2003): 105–23; and Per Davidsson and Benson Honig, "The Role of Social and Human Capital Among Nascent Entrepreneurs," *Journal of Business Venturing* 18, no. 3 (2003): 301–31.

4. Andrew C. Corbett, "Experiential Learning within the Process of Opportunity Identification and Exploitation," *Entrepreneurship Theory and Practice* 29, no. 4 (2005): 473–91; and Andrew C. Corbett, "Learning Asymmetries and the Discovery of Entrepreneurial Opportunities," *Journal of Business Venturing* 22, no. 1 (2007): 97–118.

5. Lloyd W. Fernald, Jr., "The Underlying Relationship between Creativity, Innovation, and Entrepreneurship," *Journal of Creative Behavior* 22, no. 3 (1988): 196–202; and Thomas B. Ward, "Cognition, Creativity, and Entrepreneurship," *Journal of Business Venturing* 19, no. 2 (March 2004): 173–88.

6. Timothy A. Matherly and Ronald E. Goldsmith, "The Two Faces of Creativity," *Business Horizons* (September/October 1985): 8; see also Bruce G. Whiting, "Creativity and Entrepreneurship: How Do They Relate?" *Journal of Creative Behavior* 22 no. 3 (1988): 178–83.

7. Michael Kirton, "Adaptors and Innovators: A Description and Measure," *Journal of Applied Psychology* (October 1976): 622–29.

8. E. Holly Buttner and Nur Gryskiewicz, "Entrepreneurs' Problem-Solving Styles: An Empirical Study Using the Kirton Adaption/Innovation Theory," *Journal of Small Business Management* (January 1993): 22–31.

9. See Edward deBono, *Serious Creativity: Using the Power of Creativity to Create New Ideas* (New York: HarperBusiness, 1992).

10. Eleni Mellow, "The Two Conditions View of Creativity," *Journal of Creative Behavior* 30, no. 2 (1996): 126–43.

11. H. J. Eysenck, *Genius: The Nature of Creativity* (New York: Cambridge University Press, 1995); and B. Taylor, *Into the Open: Reflections on Genius and Modernity* (New York: New York University Press, 1995).

12. Teresa Amabile, "How to Kill Creativity," *Harvard Business Review* 76 (September/October 1998): 77–87.

13. See Dale Dauten, *Taking Chances: Lessons in Putting Passion and Creativity in Your Work Life* (New York: New Market Press, 1986).

14. Edward deBono, *Six Thinking Hats* (Boston: Little, Brown, 1985); and Edward deBono, "Serious Creativity," *The Journal for Quality and Participation* 18, no. 5 (1995): 12.

15. For a discussion of the development of creativity, see Eugene Raudsepp, *How Creative Are You?* (New York: Perigee Books, 1981); Arthur B. Van Gundy, *108 Ways to Get a Bright Idea and Increase Your Creative Potential* (Englewood Cliffs, NJ: Prentice Hall, 1983); and Roger L. Firestien, *Why Didn't I Think of That?* (Buffalo, NY: United Education Services, 1989).

16. T. A. Nosanchuk, J. A. Ogrodnik, and Tom Henigan, "A Preliminary Investigation of Incubation in Short Story Writing," *Journal of Creative Behavior* 22, no. 4 (1988): 279–80.

17. W. W. Harman and H. Rheingold, *Higher Creativity: Liberating the Unconscious for Breakthrough Insights* (Los Angeles: Tarcher, 1984); and Daniel Goleman, Paul Kaufman, and Michael Ray, *The Creative Spirit* (New York: Penguin Books, 1993).

18. See J. Conrath, "Developing More Powerful Ideas," *Supervisory Management* (March 1985): 2–9; Denise Shekerjian, *Uncommon Genius: How Great Ideas Are Born* (New York: Viking Press, 1990); and Keng L. Siau, "Group Creativity and Technology," *Journal of Creative Behavior* 29, no. 3 (1995): 201–216.

19. Deborah Funk, "I Was Showering When . . .," *Baltimore Business Journal* 12, no. 46 (March 1995): 13–14.

20. For more on idea development, see A. F. Osborn, *Applied Imagination*, 3rd ed. (New York: Scribner's, 1963); William J. Gordon, *Synectics* (New York: Harper & Row, 1961); and Ted Pollock, "A Personal File of Stimulating Ideas, Little-Known Facts and Daily Problem-Solvers," *Supervision* 4 (April 1995): 24.

21. Martin F. Rosenman, "Serendipity and Scientific Discovery," *Journal of Creative Behavior* 22, no. 2 (1988): 132–38.

22. For more on implementation, see John M. Keil, *The Creative Mystique: How to Manage It, Nurture It, and Make It Pay* (New York: Wiley, 1985); and James F. Brandowski, *Corporate Imagination Plus: Five Steps to Translating Innovative Strategies into Action* (New York: The Free Press, 1990).

23. J. Wajec, *Five Star Minds: Recipes to Stimulate Your Creativity and Imagination* (New York: Doubleday, 1995); and Frank Barron, *No Rootless Flower: An Ecology of Creativity* (Cresskill, NJ: Hampton Press, 1995).

24. See Dale Dauten, *Taking Chances: Lessons in Putting Passion and Creativity into Your Work Life* (New York: Newmarket Press, 1986); and Gary A. Davis, *Creativity Is Forever* (Dubuque, IA: Kendall/Hunt, 1986).

25. Sidney J. Parnes, *Visionizing: State-of-the-Art Processes for Encouraging Innovative Excellence* (East Aurora, NY: D.O.K., 1988).

26. See E. Paul Torrance, *The Search for Sartori and Creativity* (Buffalo, NY: Creative Education Foundations, 1979); Erik K. Winslow and George T. Solomon, "Further Development of a Descriptive Profile of Entrepreneurs," *Journal of Creative Behavior* 23, no. 3 (1989): 149–61; and Roger von Oech, *A Whack on the Side of the Head* (New York: Warner Books, 1998).

27. Tony Buzan, *Make the Most of Your Mind* (New York: Simon & Schuster, 1984).

28. Weston H. Agor, *Intuitive Management: Integrating Left and Right Brain Management Skills* (Englewood Cliffs, NJ: Prentice Hall, 1984); Tony Buzan, *Using Both Sides of Your Brain* (New York: Dutton, 1976); and D. Hall, *Jump Start Your Brain* (New York: Warner Books, 1995).

29. For more on this topic, see Jacquelyn Wonder and Priscilla Donovan, *Whole-Brain Thinking* (New York: Morrow, 1984), 60–61.

30. Doris Shallcross and Anthony M. Gawienowski, "Top Experts Address Issues on Creativity Gap in Higher Education," *Journal of Creative Behavior* 23, no. 2 (1989): 75.

31. Vincent Ryan Ruggiero, *The Art of Thinking: A Guide to Critical and Creative Thought* (New York: HarperCollins, 1995).

32. David Campbell, *Take the Road to Creativity and Get Off Your Dead End* (Greensboro, NC: Center for Creative Leadership, 1985).

33. James O'Toole, *Vanguard Management: Redesigning the Corporate Future* (New York: Berkley Books, 1987).

34. Edward deBono, *Lateral Thinking: Creativity Step by Step* (New York: Harper & Row, 1970).

35. Zoa Rockenstein, "Intuitive Processes in Executive Decision Making," *Journal of Creative Behavior* 22, no. 2 (1988): 77–84.

36. Adapted from deBono, *Lateral Thinking;* and Eugene Raudsepp, *How to Create New Ideas: For Corporate Profit and Personal Success* (Englewood Cliffs, NJ: Prentice Hall, 1982).

37. William C. Miller, *Flash of Brilliance* (Reading, PA: Perseus Books, 1999).

38. Karl Albrecht, *The Creative Corporation* (Homewood, IL: Dow Jones-Irwin, 1987); see also William C. Miller, *The Creative Edge: Fostering Innovation Where You Work* (New York: Addison-Wesley, 1987); K. Mark Weaver, "Developing and Implementing Entrepreneurial Cultures," *Journal of Creative Behavior* 22, no. 3 (1988): 184–95; American Management Association, *Creative Edge: How Corporations Support Creativity and Innovation* (New York: AMA, 1995); D. Leonard and S. Straus, "Putting the Company's Whole Brain to Work," *Harvard Business Review* 75 (July/August 1997): 111–21; and J. Hirshberg, *The Creative Priority* (New York: Harper & Row, 1998).

39. Peter F. Drucker, *Innovation and Entrepreneurship* (New York: Harper & Row, 1985), 20.

40. Jane M. Howell and Christopher A. Higgins, "Champions of Change: Identifying, Understanding, and Supporting Champions of Technological Innovations," *Organizational Dynamics* (Summer 1990): 40–55; see also Dean M. Schroeder, "A Dynamic Perspective on the Impact of Process Innovation upon Competitive Strategies," *Strategic Management Journal* 11 (1990): 25–41.

41. Peter F. Drucker, "The Discipline of Innovation," *Harvard Business Review* (May/June 1985): 67–72.

42. See Peter L. Josty, "A Tentative Model of the Innovation Process," *R & D Management* (January 1990): 35–44.

43. Drucker, "The Discipline of Innovation," 67.

44. Adapted from Richard M. Hodgetts and Donald F. Kuratko, *Effective Small Business Management,* 7th ed. (Fort Worth, TX: Harcourt College Publishers, 2001), 21–23.

45. Adapted from Drucker, *Innovation and Entrepreneurship;* and Thomas J. Peters and Nancy J. Austin, *A Passion for Excellence* (New York: Random House, 1985).

46. For a good example, see Ronald A. Mitsch, "Three Roads to Innovation," *Journal of Business Strategy* (September/October 1990): 18–21.

47. William Taylor, "The Business of Innovation," *Harvard Business Review* (March/April 1990): 97–106.

CHAPTER 6

Methods to Initiate Ventures

Entrepreneurial Thought

Every large and successful company was once a startup struggling to survive. Some of these successful companies were conceived in a flash of inspiration and planned on the back of a napkin in a coffee shop. Others took shape painstakingly over time in a basement or a garage. Some startups were created and then flourished overnight, while others achieved success only through a long series of painful fits and starts. The point is, every company that exists today began rather small.

— **JOEL KURTZMAN** *Startups That Work*

Chapter Objectives

1 To describe the major pathways and structures for entrepreneurial ventures

2 To present the factors involved in creating a new venture

3 To identify and discuss the elements involved in acquiring an established venture

4 To outline ten key questions to ask when buying an ongoing venture

5 To define a franchise and outline its structure

6 To examine the benefits and drawbacks of franchising

7 To present the Uniform Franchise Offering Circular (UFOC) as a key item in franchises

The Pathways to New Ventures for Entrepreneurs

Every prospective entrepreneur wants to know the best methods for entering business. In other words, what are the ideal pathways to starting a venture for oneself? In this chapter, we examine the three most common methods: creating a new venture, acquiring an existing venture, or obtaining a franchise. Each pathway has its own particular advantages and disadvantages. In addition, each method has a variety of issues that need to be understood by the entrepreneur. It is always unwise for an entrepreneur to rush into a decision for a venture without the proper understanding of the particular form of entry. This chapter is devoted to outlining some of the particular issues related to each form.

Creating New Ventures

The most effective way to approach a new business venture is to create a unique product or service—one that is not being offered today but would be in great demand if it were. The next-best way is to adapt something that is currently on the market or extend the offering into an area in which it is not presently available. The first approach is often referred to as *new-new*, the second as *new-old*.

New–New Approach

New products or services frequently enter the market. Typical examples include smartphones, MP3 players, plasma televisions, and global positioning systems (GPS). All of these products and more have been introduced as a result of research and development (R&D) efforts by major corporations (see Table 6.1 for a list of emerging ideas). What we must realize, however, is that unique ideas are not produced only by large companies. Moreover, the rate at which new products enter the market has caused the public to expect many of their household goods to improve continually.

How does one discover or invent new products? One of the easiest ways is to make a list of annoying experiences or hazards encountered with various products or services during a given period of time. Common examples include objects that fall out of one's hand, household chores that are difficult to do, and items that are hard to store. Can certain innovations alleviate these problems? This is how some people get ideas for new products. For example, an engineer once observed the mechanism for recording the revolutions of a ship's propeller. As he watched the device tally the propeller's revolutions, he realized that the idea could be adapted to the recording of sales transactions—a problem he had been trying to solve for some time. The result led eventually to development of the traditional cash register.

Most business ideas tend to come from people's experiences. Figure 6.1 illustrates the sources of new business ideas from a study conducted by the National Federation of Independent Business.

One hot area is Internet social utilities, such as Facebook and MySpace. Facebook was founded by Mark Zuckerberg, a Harvard University student who was frustrated by the lack of networking facilities on campus. The company was founded in February 2004 and is now the largest source for photos and one of the most trafficked sites on the Internet. In two short years, the company has attracted offers of $750 million from Viacom[1] and $900 million from Yahoo.[2] In general, the main sources for both men and women are prior jobs, hobbies or interests, and personally identified problems. This new-new approach indicates the importance of people's awareness of their daily lives (work and free time) for developing new business ideas.

New–Old Approach

Most small ventures do not start with a totally unique idea. Instead, an individual "piggy-backs" on someone else's idea by either improving a product or offering a service in an area in which it is not currently available—hence the term new-old approach. Some of the most

| *Table* 6.1 | Trends Creating Business Opportunities |

Emerging Opportunities

Green Products
- Organic foods
- Organic fibers/textiles

Alternative Energy
- Solar
- Biofuel
- Fuel cells
- Energy conservation

Health Care
- Healthy food
- School- and govt.-sponsored programs
- Exercise
- Yoga
- Niche gyms
- Children
- Nonmedical
- Pre-assisted living
- Assisted living transition services

Niche Consumables
- Wine
- Chocolate
- Burgers
- Coffee houses
- Exotic salads

Home Automation and Media Storage
- Lighting control
- Security systems
- Energy management
- Comfort management
- Entertainment systems
- Networked kitchen appliances

Emerging Internet Opportunities

Mobile Advertising
- Cell phones
- PDAs

Concierge Services

Niche Social Networks
- Seniors
- Music fans
- Groups of local users
- Pet owners
- Dating groups

Virtual Economies — Online auctions

Educational Tutoring

Human Resources Services
- Matchmaking
- Virtual HR
- Online Staffing

Emerging Technology Opportunities

Nanotechnology

Wireless Technology

Source: Steve Cooper, Amanda C. Kooser, Kristin Ohlson, Karen E. Spaeder, Nichole L. Torres, and Sara Wilson, "2007 Hot List," *Entrepreneur* (December 2006): 80–93.

| *Figure* | **6.1** | **Sources of New Business Ideas Among Men and Women** |

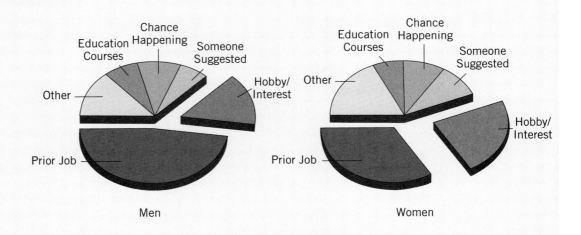

Source: William J. Dennis, *A Small Business Primer* (Washington, DC: National Federation of Independent Business, 1993), 27. Reprinted with permission.

common examples are setting up restaurants, clothing stores, or similar outlets in sprawling suburban areas that do not have an abundance of these stores. Of course, these kinds of operations can be risky because competitors can move in easily. Potential owners considering this kind of enterprise should try to offer a product or service that is difficult to copy. For example, a computerized billing and accounting service for medical doctors can be successful if the business serves a sufficient number of doctors to cover the cost of computer operators and administrative expenses in order to turn an adequate profit. Or perhaps another type of enterprise is likely to be overlooked by other would-be entrepreneurs.

Regardless of whether the business is based on a new-new or a new-old idea, the prospective owner cannot rely exclusively on gut feeling or intuition to get started. As we demonstrate in Part III of this book, proper planning and analysis are the keys to any successful venture.

Examination of the Financial Picture

If, through a thorough analysis and business plan (covered in detail in Chapter 12), a prospective entrepreneur decides that a new venture is a wise one, it is imperative to remember that the plan may not work perfectly. Some modification may be necessary. Thus, the entrepreneur has to be flexible. If something does not work out, a contingency or backup plan should be available. The worst thing the entrepreneur could do is adopt an "all or nothing" strategy. The prospective entrepreneur of a new venture must evaluate the enterprise's financial picture. How much will it cost to stay in business for the first year? How much revenue will the firm generate during this time period? If the outflow of cash is greater than the inflow, how long will it take before the business turns the corner?

Answering these questions requires consideration of two kinds of expenses: start-up and monthly. Table 6.2 illustrates a typical worksheet for making the necessary calculations of start-up expenses. Notice that this worksheet is based on the assumption that no money will flow in for about three months. Also, all start-up costs are totally covered. If the firm is in the manufacturing business, however, it will be three to four months before any goods are produced and sold, so the factors in Column 3 have to be doubled, and the amount of cash needed for start-up will be greater. Much of the information needed to fill in this worksheet already should have been gathered and at least partially analyzed. Now, however, it can be put into a format that allows the owner to look at the overall financial picture.

entrepreneurship in practice

The "Real" Opportunities in Virtual Worlds

As the online gaming population continues to grow, opportunities for entrepreneurs will grow as well. Approximately 34 percent of adult Internet users play online games on a weekly basis, which is more than the percentage of adults who use social networking sites and watch videos, according to a report from Parks Associates. As casual and hard-core gamers continue to move to the Internet, virtual economies have begun to develop, allowing them to buy virtual goods with virtual currency converted from real money; herein lies the business opportunity.

Historically, gamers have informally traded, bought, and sold their virtual wares, but companies like Sparter are changing the landscape. The company provides a formalized market in which players of games like Everquest and World of Warcraft can exchange virtual currencies from virtual worlds and online games. The Web site was officially launched in February 2007, with $250,000 in expected sales for the first year.

The company's founders, Dan Kelly and Boris Putanec, attribute their success to conducting significant market research. They discovered that people already were actively buying and selling virtual goods. By taking a commission from each seller's transaction, the company can afford to offer the service to buyers at no charge. The founders decided to offer the service for multiple online games and to provide service for international transactions, which has allowed the company to diversify and hedge against flagging interest in any one game or from a given country.

Sparter chose to focus on virtual currency exchange; however, this is just one business need that gamers will have as their communities continue to grow. Kelly suggests that micropayments and cyber-currency fraud will present new challenges and, in turn, new opportunities. Another opportunity that Kelly believes will always exist is providing informational services for games, such as forums and guides.

For those entrepreneurs interested in starting a business serving online gamers, the following steps will help to ensure success in the industry:

1. *Keep the international nature of the industry in mind.* One of the benefits of virtual worlds is the complete anonymity that is provided to gamers, which allows not only for greater freedom in social interactions but also for the disappearance of all territorial boundaries. Companies that hope to address the needs of these customers must be aware of the global community.

2. *Be prepared for a rapidly changing marketplace.* Another benefit of virtual worlds is their almost complete flexibility. After all, they are digital representations of real-world items, but the only engineering limitations are those imposed by the companies hosting the games. This versatility makes for a better gaming experience, but it complicates the process of tracking the market for businesses that hope to have gamers as customers. Putanec suggests building a scalable business to take advantage of the currently fragmented market and to allow for better positioning when trends present themselves.

3. *Be willing to speak with the online game developers.* The gods of these virtual worlds are the developers who create the environments and artifacts available to gamers. It is in the best interest of these developers to encourage new service providers to enter the scene, given that such services will enhance the game play. By getting their feedback regarding your business concept, you will not only get an expert's opinion, which is useful in honing your offerings, but you might even get an endorsement from an industry insider.

Source: Adapted from: Amanda C. Kooser, "Out of This World," *Entrepreneur* (February 2008): 124.

Table	6.2	Checklist for Estimating Start-Up Expenses

MONTHLY	EXPENSES	CASH NEEDED TO START THE BUSINESS	WHAT TO PUT IN COLUMN 2
			(These figures are estimates. The owner/ manager decided how many months to allow, depending on the type of business)
Item	Estimate based on sales of $____ per year	(see Column 3)	
Salary of owner/manager	Column 1	Column 2	Column 3
	$	$	3 times Column 1
Other salaries and wages			3 times Column 1
Rent			3 times Column 1
Advertising			3 times Column 1
Delivery expense			3 times Column 1
Supplies			3 times Column 1
Telephone and telegraph			3 times Column 1
Other utilities			3 times Column 1
Insurance			6 times Column 1
Taxes, Social Security			4 times Column 1
Interest			3 times Column 1
Maintenance			3 times Column 1
Legal and other professional assistance			3 times Column 1
Miscellaneous			3 times Column 1

START-UP COSTS

Item	Estimate	TO ARRIVE AT ESTIMATE
Fixtures and equipment	$	Determine what is typical for this kind of business; talk to suppliers.
Decorating and remodeling		Talk to a contractor.
Installation of fixtures, equipment		Talk to suppliers.
Starting inventory		Talk to suppliers.
Deposits with public utilities		Talk to utility companies.
Legal and other professional fees		Talk to a lawyer, accountant, or other professional.
Licenses and permits		Contact appropriate city offices.

Table **6.2**	Checklist for Estimating Start-Up Expenses *(Continued)*

START-UP COSTS

Item	Estimate	TO ARRIVE AT ESTIMATE
Advertising and promotion		Decide what will be used; talk to media.
Accounts receivable		Estimate how much will be tied up in receivables by credit customers and for how long.
Cash		Allow for unexpected expenses and losses, special purchases, and other expenditures.
Other Expenses		List them and estimate costs.
TOTAL CASH NEEDED TO START	$_____	Add all estimated amounts.

Source: U.S. Small Business Administration, "Management Aids" MA. 2.025 (Washington, DC: U.S. Government Printing Office).

At this point, the individual should be concerned with what is called upside gain and downside loss. This term refers to the profits the business can make and the losses it can suffer. How much money will the enterprise take in if everything goes well? How much will it gross if operations run as expected? How much will it lose if operations do not work out well? Answers to these questions provide a composite picture of the most optimistic, the most likely, and the most pessimistic results. The owner has to keep in mind that the upside gain may be minimal, whereas the downside loss may be great.

It is necessary to examine overall gains and losses. This kind of analysis is referred to as risk vs. reward analysis and points out the importance of getting an adequate return on the amount of money risked.

the global perspective

Taking Cues from the Third World

Indian consumers currently use smart cards in conjunction with their mobile phones to make financial transactions, a technological development that currently eludes consumers in the United States and Europe. This phenomenon is more than a fluke. Surprisingly, consumers in the third world are beginning to demonstrate to those in the first the radical effects such developments can have. From buying groceries to withdrawing cash from an ATM, mobile technologies are destined to revolutionize the way people think about money.

How are countries such as Africa, Latin America, and India leading the charge in introducing new technologies when—until recently—those same countries were using the antiquated technology abandoned by more developed countries? Ironically, their lack of infrastructure has led to their ability to quickly adopt more flexible options. For instance, as countries without basic phone service have begun to consider technical solutions, the cost savings

Continued

associated with implementing an all-mobile system has made installing a network of telephone wires unattractive. Moreover, now that LEDs and fluorescent bulbs are readily available as a more eco-friendly alternative to incandescent bulbs, countries that need to electrify rural areas are in a position to embrace the most advanced offerings.

An interesting result of this transition has been companies' willingness to shift their focus away from consumers in the more developed countries. For instance, Intel has been working on a wireless broadband standard designed to connect billions of citizens in the developing world cost-effectively to the Internet. If the project is a success, the standard will soon be implemented in the United States and Europe. Another example of this unprecedented shift can be found with Motorola's Motofone. The phone is designed to provide up to 400 hours of standby on a single battery charge, and it retails for only $30. The lack of electrical infrastructure in developing countries led the company to engineer the phone without an internal lamp, resulting in a significant reduction in energy use.

Despite the new focus on relatively undeveloped countries, companies will continue to consider developed countries when innovating; yet, the influence that consumers in the third world now have on new product development will forever change the process of how products are brought to market. Companies that refuse to acknowledge this transition will risk ignoring billions of potential customers.

Source: Adapted from Jeremy Kahn, "Third World First: The Rise of Cell Phone Banking in India Highlights a New Trend," *Boston Globe,* January 20, 2008, sec. Ideas, K1.

Acquiring an Established Entrepreneurial Venture

A prospective entrepreneur may seek to purchase a business venture rather than start an enterprise. This can be a successful method of getting into business, but numerous factors need to be analyzed. Purchasing a business venture is a complex transaction, and the advice of professionals always should be sought. However, a few basic steps that can be easily understood are presented here, including the entrepreneur's personal preferences, examination of opportunities, evaluation of the selected venture, and key questions to ask.

Personal Preferences

Entrepreneurs need to recognize certain personal factors and to limit their choices of ventures accordingly. An entrepreneur's background, skills, interests, and experience are all important factors in selecting the type of business to buy. In addition, personal preferences for location and size of a business should guide the selection process. If an entrepreneur always has desired to own a business in the South or West, then that is exactly where the search should begin.

Examination of Opportunities

Entrepreneurs in search of a possible venture to buy need to examine the available opportunities through various sources:

- *Business brokers.* Professionals specializing in business opportunities often can provide leads and assistance in finding a venture for sale. However, the buyer should evaluate the broker's reputation, services, and contacts. The entrepreneur also should remember that the broker usually represents—and gets a commission on the sale from—the seller.
- *Newspaper ads.* "Business Opportunity" classified ads are another source. Because an ad often will appear in one paper and not another, it may be necessary to check the classified sections of all the papers in the area.
- *Trade sources.* Suppliers, distributors, manufacturers, trade publications, trade associations, and trade schools may have information about businesses for sale.
- *Professional sources.* Professionals such as management consultants, attorneys, and accountants often know of businesses available for purchase.

Advantages of Acquiring an Ongoing Venture

Of the numerous advantages to buying an ongoing venture, three of the most important are as follows:

1. Because the enterprise is already in operation, its successful future operation is likely.

2. The time and effort associated with starting a new enterprise are eliminated.

3. It sometimes is possible to buy an ongoing business at a bargain price.

Each of these three advantages is discussed next.

LESS FEAR ABOUT SUCCESSFUL FUTURE OPERATION

A new business faces two great dangers: the possibility that it will not find a market for its goods or services, and the chance that it will not be able to control its costs. If either event occurs, the new business will go bankrupt.

Buying an existing concern, however, alleviates most of these fears. A successful business already has demonstrated the ability to attract customers, control costs, and make a profit. Additionally, many of the problems a newly formed firm faces are sidestepped. For example: Where should the company be located? How should it advertise? What type of plant or merchandise layout will be the most effective? How much should be reordered every three months? What types of customers will this business attract? What pricing strategy should the firm use? Questions such as these already have been asked and answered. Thus, when a new owner buys an ongoing operation, he or she is often purchasing a known quantity. Of course, it is important to check whether hidden problems exist in the operation. Barring something of this nature, however, the purchase of an existing successful operating venture can be a wise investment.

REDUCED TIME AND EFFORT

An ongoing enterprise already has assembled the inventory, equipment, personnel, and facilities necessary to run it. In many cases, this has taken the owners a long time to do. They have spent countless hours "working out the bugs" so that the business is as efficient as possible. Likewise, they probably have gone through a fair number of employees before getting the right type of personnel. Except for the top management in an operating venture, the personnel usually stay with the sale. Therefore, if the new owners treat the workers fairly, they should not have to worry about hiring, placing, and training personnel.

In addition, the previous owners undoubtedly have established relations with suppliers, bankers, and other businesspeople. These individuals often can be relied on to provide assistance to the new owners. The suppliers know the type of merchandise the business orders and how often it needs to be replenished. They can be a source of advice about managing the operation, as can the bankers with whom the enterprise has been doing business. These individuals know the enterprise's capital needs and often provide new owners with the same credit line and assistance they gave the previous owners. The same holds true for the accountant, the lawyer, and any other professionals who served the business in an advisory capacity. Naturally, the new owners may have their own bankers, accountant, or lawyer, but these old relationships are there if the new owners need them.

A GOOD PRICE

Sometimes it is possible to buy an ongoing operating venture at a very good price. The owner may want to sell quickly because of a retirement decision or illness. Or the owner may be forced to sell the business to raise money for some emergency that has occurred. Or the owner may seek a greater opportunity in another type of business and therefore be willing to sell at a low price in order to take advantage of the new opportunity.

Ideally, when one is looking to buy an ongoing, successful operating venture, one of these three advantages (especially the last one) is present. However, seldom does someone in business sell a successful firm at an extraordinarily low price. The owner of a successful small venture built the enterprise through skillful business practices, knows how to deal with people, and has a good idea of the operation's fair market value. That person will rarely sell for much below the fair market value. Therefore, the prospective owner must avoid bidding high on a poor investment or walking away from a good bargain because "it smells fishy." The way to prevent making the wrong decision is to evaluate the existing operation in a logical manner.

Evaluation of the Selected Venture

After the entrepreneur considers personal preferences and examines information sources, the next step is to evaluate the specific factors of the venture being offered for sale:

- *The business environment.* The local environment for business should be analyzed to establish the potential of the venture in its present location.

- *Profits, sales, and operating ratios.* The business's profit potential is a key factor in evaluating the venture's attractiveness and in later determining a reasonable price for it. To estimate the potential earning power of the business, the buyer should review past profits, sales, and operating ratios, and project sales and profits for the next one to two years. Valuation will be further discussed later in the chapter.

- *The business assets.* The tangible (physical) and intangible (for example, reputation) assets of the business need to be assessed. The following assets should be examined:

  - Inventory (age, quality, salability, condition)
  - Furniture, equipment, fixtures (value, condition, leased or owned)
  - Accounts receivable (age of outstanding debts, past collection periods, credit standing of customers)
  - Trademarks, patents, copyrights, business name (value, role in the business's success, degree of competitive edge)
  - Goodwill (reputation, established clientele, trusted name)

A lot of headaches can be avoided by taking the approach of purchasing an existing venture. For example, start-up problems will have been taken care of by previous owners. Additionally, the business has a track record the buyer can examine to determine the types of products to sell, the prices to charge, and so on. But buying an existing business also has potential pitfalls. Examples include buying a company whose success has been due to the personality and charisma of the owner/manager, buying a company when the market for its product has peaked, and paying too much for a company.

Key Questions to Ask

When deciding whether to buy, the astute prospective owner needs to ask and answer a series of "right questions."[3] The following section discusses questions and provides insights into the types of actions to take for each response.

WHY IS THE BUSINESS BEING SOLD?

One of the first questions that should be asked is *why* the owner is selling the business.[4] Quite often, a difference exists between the reason given to prospective buyers and the real reason. Typical responses include "I'm thinking about retiring," "I've proven to myself that I can be successful in this line of business, so now I'm moving to another operation that will provide me with new challenges," and "I want to move to California and go into business with my brother-in-law there."

Any of these statements may be accurate, and—if they can be substantiated—the buyer may find that the business is indeed worth purchasing. However, because it is difficult to substantiate this sort of personal information, the next best thing to do is to check around and gather business-related information. Is the owner in trouble with the suppliers? Is the lease on the building due for renewal and the landlord planning to triple the rent? Worse yet, is the building about to be torn down? Other site-location problems may relate to competition in the nearby area or zoning changes. Is a new shopping mall about to be built nearby that will take much of the business away from this location? Has the city council passed a new ordinance that calls for the closing of business on Sunday, the day of the week when this store does 25 percent of its business?

Financially, what is the owner going to do after selling the business? Is the seller planning to stay in town? What employment opportunities does he or she have? The reason for asking these questions is that the new owner's worst nightmare is to find that the previous owner has set up a similar business a block away and is drawing back all of the customers. One way to prevent this from happening is to have an attorney write into the contract an agreement that the previous owner will refrain from conducting the same business within a reasonable distance for a period of at least five years. This is known as a **legal restraint of trade**—an agreement not to compete or "**non-compete clause**". Doing this helps the new owner retain the business's customers.

WHAT IS THE CURRENT PHYSICAL CONDITION OF THE BUSINESS?

Even if the asking price for the operation appears to be fair, it is necessary to examine the *physical condition of the assets*. Does the company own the building? If it does, how much repair work needs to be done? If the building is leased, does the lease provide for the kinds of repairs that will enhance the successful operation of the business? For example, if a flower shop has a somewhat large refrigerator for keeping flowers cool, who has to pay to expand the size of the refrigerator? If the landlord agrees to do so and to recover the investment through an increase in the lease price, the total cost of the additional refrigerated space must be compared to the expected increase in business. Meanwhile, if the landlord does not want to make this type of investment, the new owners must realize that any *permanent additions to the property remain with the property*. This means that if something simply cannot be carried out of the building, it stays. Pictures on the walls, chairs, and desks the previous business owner purchased can be removed. However, new bookshelves nailed to the wall, carpeting attached to the floor, a new acoustic ceiling installed to cut down on noise in the shop, and the new refrigerated area all become permanent property of the building owner. Therefore, the overriding question while examining the physical facilities is, "How much will it cost to get things in order?"

WHAT IS THE CONDITION OF THE INVENTORY?

How much inventory does the current owner show on the books? Does a physical check show that inventory actually exists? Additionally, is inventory salable, or is it out-of-date or badly deteriorated?

WHAT IS THE STATE OF THE COMPANY'S OTHER ASSETS?

Most operating ventures have assets in addition to the physical facilities and the inventory. A machine shop, for example, may have various types of presses and other machinery. An office may have computers, copiers, and other technology that belong to the business. The question to ask about all of this equipment is, "Is it still useful, or has it been replaced by more modern technology?" In short, are these assets obsolete?

Another often overlooked asset is the firm's records. If the business has kept careful records, it may be possible to determine who is a good credit risk and who is not. Additionally, these records make it easy for a new owner to decide how much credit to extend to the prior customers. Likewise, sales records can be very important because they show seasonal demands and peak periods. This can provide the new owner with information for inventory-control purposes and can greatly reduce the risks of over- or under-stocking.

Still another commonly overlooked asset is past contracts. What type of lease does the current owner have on the building? If the lease was signed three years ago and is a seven-year lease with a fixed rent, it may have been somewhat high when it came into effect but could be somewhat on the low side for comparable facilities today. Furthermore, over the next four years the rent should prove to be quite low considering what competitors will be paying. Of course, if the lease is about to expire, this is a different story. Then the prospective owner has to talk to the landlord to find out what the terms of the lease will be. Additionally, a prospective owner's lawyer should look at the old lease to determine if it can be passed on to a new owner and, regardless of the rent, how difficult it is to break the lease if the business should start to fail.

Finally, the prospective buyer must look at an intangible asset called **goodwill**. Goodwill is often defined as the value of the company beyond what is shown on the books. For example, if a software company has a reputation for quick and accurate service, the company has built up goodwill among its customers. If the owners were to sell the business, the buyer would have to pay not only for the physical assets in the software company (office furniture, computers, etc.) but also for the goodwill the firm has accumulated over the years. The reputation of the business has a value.[5]

HOW MANY OF THE EMPLOYEES WILL REMAIN?

It is often difficult to give customers the good service they have come to expect if seasoned employees decide they do not want to remain with the new owner. The owner is certainly an important asset of the firm, but so are the employees; they play a role in making the business a success. Therefore, one question the prospective buyer must ask is, "If some people will be leaving, will enough be left to maintain the type of service the customer is used to getting?" In particular, the new owner must be concerned about key people who are not staying. Key employees are part of the value of the business. If it is evident that these people will not be staying, the prospective buyer must subtract something from the purchase price by making some allowance for the decline in sales and the accompanying expense associated with replacing key personnel.

When purchasing an existing business, the prospective owner should conduct an assessment of the current group of employees. He or she should review existing performance evaluations and talk with the current owners about the quality of each employee and his or her value to the business. It may be easier to retain valuable employees by seeking them out before the purchase to ensure their feelings of security. The incoming owner should interview all of the current employees and make decisions about who to keep and who to let go before actually taking over the enterprise.

WHAT TYPE OF COMPETITION DOES THE BUSINESS FACE?

No matter what goods or service the business provides, the number of people who will want it and the total amount of money they will spend for it is limited. Thus, the greater the competition, the less the business's chance of earning large profits. As the number of competitors increases, the cost of fighting them usually goes up. More money must be spent on advertising. Price competition must be met with accompanying reductions in overall revenue. Simply too many companies are pursuing the same market.

Additionally, the quality of competition must be considered. If nine competitors exist, a new owner could estimate a market share of 10 percent. However, some of these competitors undoubtedly will be more effective than others. One or two may have very good advertising and know how to use it to capture 25 percent of the market. A few others may offer outstanding service and use this advantage to capture 20 percent of the market. Meanwhile, the remaining six fight for what is left.

Then the location of the competition must be considered. In many instances, a new venture does not offer anything unique, so people buy on the basis of convenience. A service located on the corner may get most of the business of local residents. One located across town will get virtually none. Because the product is the same at each location, no one is going to drive across town for it. This analogy holds true for groceries, notions, drugs, and hardware. If competitors are located near one another, each will take some of the business the others could have expected, but none is going to maximize its income. But if the merchandise is an item that people shop for very carefully—furniture, for example—a competitor in the immediate area can be a distinct advantage. For example, two furniture stores located near each other tend to draw a greater number of customers than they would if located ten blocks apart. When people shop for furniture, they go where a large selection is available. With adjacent stores, customers will reason that if the furniture they are looking for is not in one, it might be in the other. Additionally, since they can step from one store to the next, they can easily compare prices and the sale terms.

Finally, any analysis of competition should look for unscrupulous practices. How cutthroat are the competitors? If they are very cutthroat, the prospective buyer will have to be continually alert for practices such as price fixing and kickbacks to suppliers for special services. Usually, if the company has been around for a couple of years, it has been successful dealing with these types of practices. However, if some competitors are getting bad reputations, the new owner will want to know this. After all, over time the customers are likely to form a stereotyped impression of enterprises in a given geographic area and will simply refuse to do business with any of them ("It's no use looking for clothing in the Eighth Street area"). In this case, the customers retaliate against unethical business practices by boycotting the entire area in which these firms are located. In short, an unethical business competitor can drag down other firms as well.

WHAT DOES THE FIRM'S FINANCIAL PICTURE LOOK LIKE?

It may be necessary for a prospective buyer to hire an accountant to look over the company's books. It is important to get an idea of how well the firm is doing financially. One of the primary areas of interest should be the company's profitability.[6] Is the business doing anything wrong that can be spotted from the statements? If so, can the prospective buyer eliminate these problems?

Individuals who are skilled in buying companies that are in trouble, straightening them out, and reselling them at a profit know what to look for when examining the books. So do good accountants. Both also know that the seller's books alone should not be taken as proof of sales or profits. One should insist on seeing records of bank deposits for the past two to three years. If the current owner has held the firm for only a short time, the records of the previous owner also should be examined. In fact, it is not out of line to ask for the owner's income tax return. The astute buyer knows that the firm's records reflect its condition.

Another area of interest is the firm's profit trend. Is it making more money year after year? More important, are profits going up as fast as sales, or is more and more revenue necessary to attain the same profit? If the latter is true, this means the business may have to increase sales 5 to 10 percent annually to net as much as it did the previous year. This spells trouble and is often a sign that the owner is selling because "there are easier ways to make a living."

Finally, even if the company is making money, the prospective buyer should compare the firm's performance to that of similar companies. For example, if a small retail shop is making a 22 percent return in investment this year in contrast to 16 percent two years ago, is this good or bad? It certainly appears to be good, but what if competing stores are making a 32 percent return on investment? Given this information, the firm is not doing as well.

One way to compare a company to the competition is to obtain comparative information put out by firms such as Dun & Bradstreet that gather data on retail and wholesale firms in various fields and provide businesspeople with an overall view of many key financial ratios. For example, one of the most important is the comparison of current assets (cash, or items that can be turned into cash in the short run) to current liabilities (debts that will come due in the short run). This key ratio reflects a business's ability to meet its current obligations. A second key ratio is the comparison of net profits to net sales (net profit margin). How much profit is the owner making for every dollar in sales? A third key ratio is net profit to net worth (return on net worth). How much profit is the individual making for every dollar invested in the firm?

By comparing the accounting information obtained from a business's books to external financial comparison data (industry ratios, industry multiples used for valuation, etc.), it is possible to determine how well the business is doing. If the facts look good, then the prospective buyer can turn to the question of how much to offer the seller.

Negotiating the Deal

The potential buyer must negotiate the final deal.[7] This negotiation process, however, involves a number of factors. Four critical elements should be recognized: information, time, pressure, and alternatives.

Information may be the most critical element during negotiations. The performance of the company, the nature of its competition, the condition of the market, and clear answers to all of the key questions presented earlier are all vital components in the determination of the business's real potential. Without reliable information, the buyer is at a costly disadvantage. The seller never should be relied on as the sole information source. Although the seller may not falsify any information, he or she is likely to make available only the information that presents the business in the most favorable light. Therefore, the buyer should develop as many sources as possible. The rule should be to investigate every possible source.

Time is also a critical element. If the seller already has purchased another business and a potential buyer is the only prospect to buy the existing firm, then that buyer has the power to win some important concessions from the seller. If, however, the owner has no such deadline but simply is headed to retirement, or if the buyer's financial sources wish to invest in the project quickly, then the buyer is at a serious disadvantage. In short, having more time than the other party can be very beneficial.

Pressure from others also will affect the negotiation process. If the company is owned by several partners, then the individual who is selling the company may not have complete autonomy. If one of the owners is in favor of accepting an offer, the negotiator for the company must decide whether to accept the bid on behalf of all owners or attempt to hold out for more money. This causes a distraction during the negotiation process.

Finally, the alternatives available to each party become important factors. The party with no other alternatives has a great deal of interest in concluding negotiations quickly. Table 6.3 outlines some additional considerations that a person should keep in mind when purchasing a business.

For the seller, alternatives include finding another buyer in the near future or not selling at all. He or she may continue to run the business, hire a manager to do so, or sell off parts of the company. Likewise, the buyer may choose not to purchase the business or may have alternative investment opportunities available. In any event, the negotiating parties' alternatives should be recognized because they impact the ability to reach an agreement.

Table **6.3**   **Dos and Don'ts of Buying a Business**

Buying an ongoing business provides many advantages for a prospective purchaser, such as a proven track record, established credit, ongoing operations, and a significantly lower chance for failure. However, without careful analysis, a person buying an ongoing business may suffer from hidden problems inherited with the business. The following list of dos and don'ts provides some practical tips to consider before signing over the check.

1. *Have a seller retain a minority interest in the business.* If a seller walks with 100 percent of the purchase money, it is highly unlikely that he or she will give you any help running the business in the future. Another option would be to have the ultimate purchase price of the business dependent on the performance of the business over the next three-to-five-year period.

2. *Never rely on oral statements.* Get everything in writing; oral promises count for little after you have bought the business.

3. *Have an accountant examine the books and check the cash flow.* Your accountant must reconstruct the seller's financial statements to determine exactly how much cash is available to you.

4. *Investigate, investigate, investigate!* Find out as much as you can about the business before you fork over your hard-earned cash. Talk to vendors, suppliers, customers, and even the competition to get the real story. Go beyond the list of references the seller provides you. Investigate the entire industry, looking for possible major shifts that could affect future business. The more time you devote to such research, the better decision you'll make.

5. *Interview the employees.* All employees have valuable information about the company they work for. If the seller is serious about selling, he or she should not be afraid to let buyers communicate with employees. Try to do interviews in a confidential situation; otherwise, any information you gain may be incorrect or misleading.

6. *Find out the real reason the company is for sale.* True, many people want out of a successful business for legitimate reasons. Just make sure the reasons are legitimate.

Source: Adapted from Bruce J. Blechman, "Good Buy," *Entrepreneur* (February 1994): 22–25. Reprinted with permission from *Entrepreneur* magazine, February 1994.

Franchising: The Hybrid

One form of business that incorporates some of the independence of an entrepreneur with the larger umbrella of a corporation is the franchise. Thus, it is a "hybrid" form of entering business for oneself. Today, more than a third of all retail sales and an increasing part of the gross domestic product are generated by private franchises. A franchise is any arrangement in which the owner of a trademark, trade name, or copyright has licensed others to use it in selling goods or services. A franchisee (a purchaser of a franchise) generally is legally independent but economically dependent on the integrated business system of the franchisor (the seller of the franchise). In other words, a franchisee can operate as an independent businessperson but still realize the advantages of a regional or national organization.[8]

How a Franchise Works

Business franchise systems for goods and services generally work the same way. The franchisee, an independent businessperson, contracts for a complete business package. This usually requires the individual to do one or more of the following:

1. Make a financial investment in the operation

2. Obtain and maintain a standardized inventory and/or equipment package usually purchased from the franchisor

3. Maintain a specified quality of performance

4. Follow a franchise fee as well as a percentage of the gross revenues

5. Engage in a continuing business relationship

In turn, the franchisor provides the following types of benefits and assistance:

1. The company name. For example, if someone bought a Burger King franchise, this would provide the business with drawing power. A well-known name, such as Burger King, ensures higher sales than an unknown name, such as Ralph's Big Burgers.

2. Identifying symbols, logos, designs, and facilities. For example, all McDonald's units have the same identifying golden arches on the premises. Likewise, the facilities are similar inside.

3. Professional management training for each independent unit's staff.

4. Sale of specific merchandise necessary for the unit's operation at wholesale prices. Usually provided is all of the equipment to run the operation and the food or materials needed for the final product.

5. Financial assistance, if needed, to help the unit in any way possible.

6. Continuing aid and guidance to ensure that everything is done in accordance with the contract.[9]

Advantages of Franchising

A number of advantages are associated with franchising. In the following section, we describe four of the most well-known advantages: training and guidance, brand-name appeal, a proven track record, and financial assistance.

TRAINING AND GUIDANCE

Perhaps the greatest advantage of buying a franchise, as compared to starting a new business or buying an existing one, is that the franchisor usually will provide both training and guidance to the franchisee. As a result, the likelihood of success is much greater for national

Top 10 Franchises

1. 7-Eleven Inc.
2. Subway
3. Dunkin' Donuts
4. Pizza Hut
5. McDonald's

6. Sonic Drive-In Restaurants
7. KFC Corp.
8. InterContinental Hotels
9. Domino's Pizza LLC
10. RE/MAX

Source: "Top 10 Lists for 2008," *Entrepreneur,* http://www.entrepreneur.com/franchises/toplists/2008.html (accessed April 8, 2008).

franchisees who receive this assistance than for small-business owners in general. For example, it has been reported that the ratio of failure for small enterprises in general to franchised businesses may be as high as 4:1 or 5:1.

BRAND-NAME APPEAL

An individual who buys a well-known national franchise, especially a big-name one, has a good chance to succeed. The franchisor's name is a drawing card for the establishment. People are often more aware of the product or service offered by a national franchise and prefer it to those offered by lesser-known outlets.

A PROVEN TRACK RECORD

Another benefit of buying a franchise is that the franchisor has already proved that the operation can be successful. Of course, if someone is the first individual to buy a franchise, this is not the case. However, if the organization has been around for five to ten years and has 50 or more units, it should not be difficult to see how successful the operations have been. If all of the units are still in operation and the owners report they are doing well financially, one can be certain the franchisor has proved that the layout and location of the store, the pricing policy, the quality of the goods or service, and the overall management system are successful.

FINANCIAL ASSISTANCE

Another reason a franchise can be a good investment is that the franchisor may be able to help the new owner secure the financial assistance needed to run the operation. In fact, some franchisors have personally helped the franchisee get started by lending money and not requiring any repayment until the operation is running smoothly. In short, buying a franchise is often an ideal way to ensure assistance from the financial community.

Disadvantages of Franchising

The prospective franchisee must weigh the advantages of franchising against the accompanying disadvantages. Some of the most important drawbacks are franchise fees, the control exercised by the franchisor, and unfulfilled promises by some franchisors. The following sections examine each of these disadvantages.

FRANCHISE FEES

In business, no one gets something for nothing. The larger and more successful the franchisor, the greater the franchise fee. For a franchise from a national chain, it is not uncommon for a buyer to be faced with a fee of $5,000 to $100,000. Smaller franchisors or those who have not had great success charge less. Nevertheless, entrepreneurs deciding whether or not to take the franchise route into small business should weigh the fee against the return they could get putting the money into another type of business. Also, remember that this fee covers only the benefits discussed in the previous section. The prospective franchisee also must pay to build the unit and stock it, although the franchisor may provide assistance in securing a bank loan. Additionally, a fee is usually tied to gross sales. The franchise buyer typically pays an initial franchise fee, spends his or her own money to build a store, buys the equipment and inventory, and then pays a continuing royalty based on sales (usually between 5 and 12 percent). Most franchisors require buyers to have 25 to 50 percent of the initial costs in cash. The rest can be borrowed—in some cases, from the franchising organization itself.[10] Table 6.4 presents a list of the costs involved in buying a franchise.

FRANCHISOR CONTROL

In a large corporation, the company controls the employee's activities. If an individual has a personal business, he or she controls his or her own activities. A franchise operator is

Table **6.4**	**The Cost of Franchising**

Don't let the advantages of franchising cloud the significant costs involved. Although the franchise fee may be $75,000, the actual cost of "opening your doors for business" can be more than $200,000! Depending on the type of franchise, the following expenditures are possible:

1. *The basic franchising fee.* For this, you may receive a wide range of services: personnel training, licenses, operations manuals, training materials, site selection and location preparation assistance, and more. Or you may receive none of these.

2. *Insurance.* You will need coverage for a variety of items, such as plate glass, office contents, vehicles, and others. You also should obtain so-called "umbrella" insurance. It is inexpensive and is meant to help out in the event of crippling million- or multimillion-dollar lawsuits.

3. *Opening product inventory.* If initial inventory is not included in your franchise fee, you will have to obtain enough to open your franchise.

4. *Remodeling and leasehold improvements.* Under most commercial leases, you are responsible for these costs.

5. *Utility charges.* Deposits to cover the first month or two are usually required for electricity, gas, oil, telephone, and water.

6. *Payroll.* This should include the costs of training employees before the store opens. You should include a reasonable salary for yourself.

7. *Debt service.* This includes principal and interest payments.

8. *Bookkeeping and accounting fees.* In addition to the services the franchisor may supply in this area, it is always wise to use your own accountant.

9. *Legal and professional fees.* The cost of hiring an attorney to review the franchise contract, to file for and obtain any necessary zoning or planning ordinances, and to handle any unforeseen conflicts must be factored into your opening costs projections.

10. *State and local licenses, permits, and certificates.* These run the gamut from liquor licenses to building permits for renovations.

Source: Donald F. Kuratko, "Achieving the American Dream as a Franchise," *Small Business Network* (July 1987): 2. updated by author, April, 2008.

entrepreneurship in practice

To Franchise or Not to Franchise: That Is the Question

Franchises are a vehicle for those individuals with entrepreneurial tendencies but without the desire to base a business on their own idea. Given this fact, franchising would seem a logical fit for young entrepreneurs fresh from college. Experts differ on the merits of such an approach. Following are reasons for and against becoming a franchisee straight out of college:

For

- *Students learn best in structured learning environments, as provided by franchising.* The support structure provided by franchisors makes franchising an ideal option for students looking to experience entrepreneurship with a proven formula. The educational materials provided to new franchisees extend the classroom environment to a real-world application.

- *Students are experienced customers and, in many cases, employees of franchises.* Because fewer families have stay-at-home parents, today's students have experienced an active childhood, which often involved relying on "fast" food between appointments. Many students also have taken part-time positions with these franchises, which has given them a behind-the-scenes look at how they are run.

- *So-called "helicopter parents" often continue to provide support beyond college.* The support that students require when starting their first business extends beyond financial needs. Having parents who are actively involved can give students the boost they need to venture out on their own, knowing that there is a safety net in the event that they fail. Although some would argue that the limited financial contribution of the students inevitably leads to a lack of accountability, others argue that having the investments from family and friends on the line further motivates the students to succeed.

- *Students are accustomed to being visionary, which fuels innovation.* The Internet has given students a venue for self-expression on a grand scale. The immediacy of results from the digitization of society has taught students how to generate an idea, implement it, and assess the results. This enthusiasm often translates to ambition that franchisors look for in their franchisees.

Against

- *Few college students have the financial wherewithal to start a franchise.* Although the costs associated with starting a franchise in the long run can be less than those for developing a new concept, the upfront franchising fees can cost several hundred thousand dollars, making the financial requirements a significant hurdle for individuals without the credit history to acquire a bank loan without a cosigner.

- *Students usually find staying motivated difficult when the business struggles.* Business concepts that initially were exciting can quickly lose their luster when they lose momentum. Given that most students will have had financial assistance from family or friends, they have little to no financial commitment to the business, which can lead to a lack of ownership when problems arise.

- *Lack of management experience makes dealing with employees a challenge.* Franchisors will provide marketing materials, supplier connections, and operational plans, but the responsibility for managing employees falls squarely on the shoulders of the franchisees. The recruitment, management, and retention of employees can be stressful for even the most seasoned manager, so students with no experience in management find it difficult to keep employees motivated and committed. Gaining experience through trial and error as a manager in a large corporation is unlikely to lead to the collapse of the entire organization, whereas franchises are far more susceptible to management mistakes.

In the end, students have to determine what makes the most sense for their career aspirations as well as for their management style. Although there is more risk inherent with a new concept, franchising is not for everyone. Some entrepreneurs have concluded that franchisor agreements are too restrictive, relegating them to what they consider to be mere employees; however, all franchisors stipulate different policies and procedures. Deciding whether to purchase a franchise is only the beginning of the process. The real work begins when an entrepreneur decides what franchise to purchase.

Source: Adapted from Jeff Elgin and Jennifer Kushell, "He Said, She Said," *Entrepreneur*, January 2008, https://www .entrepreneur.com/magazine/entrepreneur/2008/ January/ 187674.html (accessed March 16, 2008).

somewhere between these extremes. Under franchisor control the franchisor generally exercises a fair amount of control over the operation in order to achieve a degree of uniformity. If entrepreneurs do not follow franchisor directions, they may not have their franchise license renewed when the contract expires.

UNFULFILLED PROMISES

In some cases, especially among less-known franchisors, the franchisees have not received all they were promised.[11] For example, many franchisees have found themselves with trade names that have no drawing power. Also, many franchisees have found that the promised assistance from the franchisor has not been forthcoming. For example, instead of being able to purchase supplies more cheaply through the franchisor, many operators have found themselves paying exorbitant prices for supplies. If franchisees complain, they risk having their agreement with the franchisor terminated or not renewed.

Franchise Law

The growth in franchise operations has outdistanced laws about franchising. A solid body of appellate decisions under federal or state laws that relate to franchises has yet to be developed.[12] In the absence of case law that precisely addresses franchising, the courts tend to apply general common-law principles and appropriate federal or state statutory definitions and rules. Characteristics associated with a franchising relationship are similar in some respects to those of principal/agent, employer/employee, and employer/independent-contractor relationships, yet a franchising relationship does not truly fit into any of these traditional classifications. (See The Entrepreneurial Process: The Uniform Franchise Offering Circular).

Much franchise litigation has arisen over termination provisions. Because the franchise agreement is normally a form contract the franchisor draws and prepares, and because the bargaining power of the franchisee is rarely equal to that of the franchisor, the termination provisions of contracts are generally more favorable to the franchisor. This means that the franchisee, who normally invests a substantial amount of time and money in the franchise operation to make it successful, may receive little or nothing for the business upon termination. The franchisor owns the trademark and hence the business.[13]

Evaluating the Opportunities

How can the average entrepreneur evaluate a franchise operation and decide if it is a good deal? Unfortunately, no mathematical formula exists (although the best valuation methods are presented in Chapter 14). Nor is it possible simply to ask a friend, because the most popular franchises, which are probably the only ones the individual is familiar with, do not give franchises to people seeking to enter the field. This leaves only the smaller, lesser-known, and more risky franchise operations.[14]

One research study examined the relationship between the base fees and royalties paid to the franchise's overall value. The findings indicated that the age of a franchise, number of retail units, concentration in the state, and national representation are all reflected in the size

the entrepreneurial process

The Uniform Franchise Offering Circular

In 1979, the Federal Trade Commission established a Franchise Disclosure Rule that required franchisors to make full presale disclosure nationwide. To comply with this ruling, the Uniform Franchise Offering Circular (UFOC) was developed.

The UFOC is divided into 23 items that provide different segments of information for prospective franchisees. In summary form, the major sections are as follows:

Sections I–IV: Cover the franchisor, the franchisor's background, and the franchise being offered.

Sections V–VI: Delineate the franchise fees, both initial and ongoing.

Section VII: Sets forth all of the initial expenses involved to establish the entire franchise.

Sections VIII–IX: Detail the franchisee's obligation to purchase specific goods, supplies, services, and so forth from the franchisor.

Section X: Provides information on any financing arrangements available to franchisees.

Section XI: Describes in detail the contractual obligations of the franchisor to the franchisee.

Section XII: Clearly outlines the geographic market within which the franchisee must operate.

Sections XIII–XIV: Disclose all pertinent information regarding trademarks, trade names, patents, and so forth.

Section XV: Outlines the franchisor's expectations of the franchisee (day-to-day operations).

Section XVI: Explains any restrictions or limitations.

Section XVII: Sets forth the conditions for the franchise's renewal, termination, or sale.

Section XVIII: Discloses the actual relationship between the franchise and any celebrity figure used in advertising for the franchise.

Section XIX: Provides a factual description of any potential "earnings claims," including their assumptions and actual figures.

Section XX: Lists the names and addresses of all existing franchises in the state where the proposed franchise is to be located.

Sections XXI–XXIII: Provides certified financial statements for the previous three fiscal years and a copy of the actual franchise contract.

The UFOC must be given to a prospective franchisee at least ten days prior to the payment of any fees or contracts signed. It is the responsibility of the franchisee to read and understand the various sections delineated in this document.

_____

Source: Adapted from the Federal Trade Commission, 2008.

of base fees and royalties. However, the key to examining the value of a prospective franchise is a proper information search.[15] In addition, to ensure an adequately protected investment, an evaluation of all franchise opportunities must be undertaken. Figure 6.2 illustrates a complete process model for analyzing the purchase of a franchise.

LEARN OF OPPORTUNITIES

One of the first things a prospective franchisee must do is to find a reliable source of information about franchising opportunities. Some of the most readily available sources are newspapers, trade publications, and the Internet (see Table 6.5 for a list of useful Web sites). *Entrepreneur* magazine carries advertisements of franchise opportunities, and exhibitions and trade shows are held by franchisors from time to time in various cities. Entrepreneur.com annually lists the top franchises and the fastest-growing franchises. Finally, franchisors themselves offer information on specific opportunities—although, in this case, one needs to beware of promises that exceed what may be delivered.

Figure **6.2** The Decision to Purchase a Franchise: Process Model

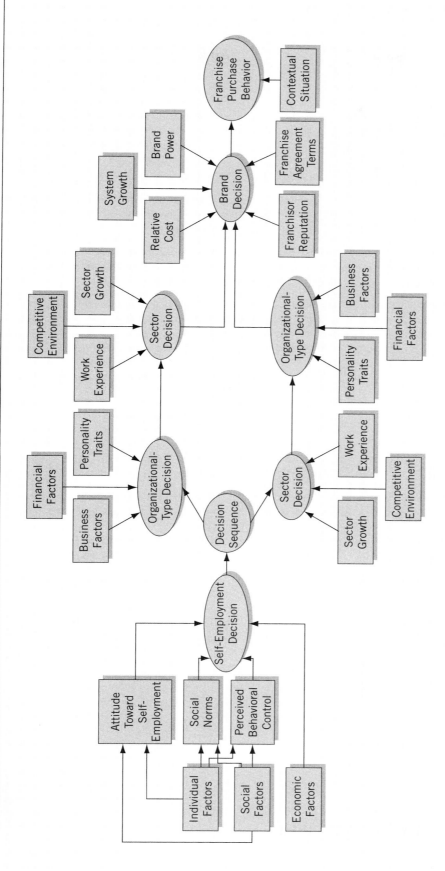

Source: Patrick J. Kaufmann, "Franchising and the Choice of Self Employment," *Journal of Business Venturing,* 14, no. 4 (1999): 348.

Table	**6.5**	**World Wide Web Franchise Sites**

The Internet has become the foremost source of information for people of all ages, trades, and interests. Short of handing over the funds, the prospective franchisee can find everything he or she needs to ensure the successful research, selecting, and planning of a franchise business in the comfort of his or her own home.

You can search for the perfect match by location, category, investment, and actual franchise at http://www.betheboss.com. This site allows you to obtain pertinent information about certain franchises via "showcases" that provide histories, business summaries, frequently asked questions, and investment requirements. Basic franchise information, including interactive financial worksheets, ways to select the right franchise, expo information, and links to other valuable Web resources are also available.

Multiple links from http://franchise1.com, the Franchise Handbook, offer the serious person serious answers to his or her questions. Directories, associations, a message board, and industry news are just a few of the resources available on the Web's most popular franchise site.

Franchise Works can be found at http://www.franchiseworks.com/. Here you will find different franchises listed by category, as well as other available business opportunities. Also on the site are resources that can be used to cover all aspects of the start of a business.

The International Franchise Association is a premier source for industry data. Browse http://franchise.org to stay on top of the latest government developments and hot topics that affect franchisees and franchisors worldwide.

Other Valuable Sites:

American Bar Association Forum on Franchising	www.abanet.org/forums/franchising
U.S. Small Business Administration	www.sba.gov
Statistics—USA	www.stat-usa.gov
Entrepreneur Magazine	www.entrepreneur.com/franchises/bestofthe-best/index.html
Minority Business Entrepreneur Magazine	www.mbemag.com
Franchise Times	www.franchisetimes.com
Franchise Update	www.franchise-update.com
Restaurant Business Magazine	www.restaurantbiz.com
Source Book Publications	www.franchisordatabase.com
Federal Trade Commission	http://www.ftc.gov/bcp/franchise/netfran.shtm
Franchise.com	http://www.franchise.com
World Franchising	http://www.worldfranchising.com
Franchise Solutions	http://www.franchisesolutions.com
Franchise Opportunities	http://www.franchiseopportunities.com
Franchise Trade	http://www.franchisetrade.com
The Franchise Magazine	http://www.thefranchisemagazine.net
Franchise Info Mall	http://www.franchiseinfomall.com
Franchise Advantage	http://www.franchiseadvantage.com
U.S. Franchise News	http://www.usfranchisenews.com

INVESTIGATE THE FRANCHISOR

The prospective investor should get as much information as possible on the franchisor. So many people have lost their life savings in franchise schemes that, except when dealing with a long-established franchisor, one is best advised to enter the investigation prepared for the worst. In particular, if the franchisor seems too eager to sell dealerships or units, it is cause for alarm. Likewise, if the franchisor does not make a vigorous effort to check out prospective investors, it is usually a sign that the seller does not think the operation will last long and probably is interested in just taking the franchise fees and absconding with them. Remember: No reputable franchisor will sell a franchise without ensuring that the buyer is capable of operating it successfully. McDonald's—one of the most cautious of all franchisors—carefully screens all applicants, and it claims it has never had a unit go bankrupt.

SEEK PROFESSIONAL HELP

If the franchisor passes the initial investigation and offers a franchise contract, the prospective franchisee should first take it to a qualified attorney. The attorney will understand the terms of the agreement and can explain any penalties or restrictive clauses that limit what the franchisee can do.

Of major importance are contract provisions related to cancellation and renewal of the franchise. Can the franchisor take away the franchise for some minor rule infraction? More important, if the agreement is canceled, how much of the initial franchise fee will be refunded to the individual? If the franchise can be purchased back by the franchisor at 20 percent of the initial fee, the lawyer will need to examine carefully how easily the franchisor can terminate the agreement.

Other considerations include the franchise fee, the percentage of gross revenues to be paid to the franchisor, the type and extent of training to be provided, the territorial limits of the franchise, and the provisions for supplying materials to the unit. In addition, the lawyer needs to examine the degree of control the franchisor will have over operations, including price requirements, performance standards, and the required days and hours of operation. The individual also should seek financial counsel. A good banker should be able to look over the franchisor's prospectus and give an opinion regarding its feasibility. Is the projected revenue too high for a new unit? Is the return on investment overly optimistic? Would the bank be prepared to advance a loan on this type of business undertaking?

Finally, the investor should talk to a certified public accountant (CPA), who can review the data and construct a projected income statement for the first few years. Does the investment look promising? What might go wrong and jeopardize the investment? How likely are those developments? Is this the type of investment that constitutes an acceptable risk for the prospective buyer, or should the individual walk away from the deal?

Legal and financial professionals will help the prospective franchisee answer some very important questions. In particular, they will force the individual to face the risks inherent in a franchise and answer the question, "Am I willing to take this type of risk?"

THE DECISION: IT'S UP TO THE ENTREPRENEUR

After the prospective entrepreneur has gathered all of the necessary information, it is up to him or her to make the final decision on the matter. As with buying an ongoing business, however, the series of "right questions" outlined previously can help.

Summary

The easiest and best way to approach a new business venture is to design a unique product or service. Sometimes this involves what is called a new-new approach—that is, the development of an entirely new idea for a product or service (as was the case with MySpace and Google). In most instances, however, the prospective owner/manager must be content to use a new-old approach by "piggybacking" on someone else's ideas. This involves either expanding on what the competition is doing or offering a product or service in an area in which it is not presently available.

On the financial side, the prospective owner/manager needs to examine the enterprise's financial picture and determine the costs of setting up the operation and the amount of revenue that will be generated during the initial period. Finally, the prospective owner/manager must review a series of other operational considerations ranging from the building, merchandise, and equipment needed for operations to record keeping, insurance, legal, marketing, and personal matters.

Another opportunity is the purchase of an existing successful firm, which has a number of advantages. Three of the most important are that its successful future operation is likely, the time and effort associated with starting a new enterprise are eliminated, and a bargain price may be possible.

Before deciding whether to buy, however, the prospective owner needs to ask and answer a series of "right questions." These include: Why is the business being sold? What is the physical condition of the business? What is the condition of the inventory? What is the state of the company's other assets? How many of the employees will remain? What competition does the business face? What is the firm's financial picture?

After all questions have been answered satisfactorily, the prospective buyer must negotiate for the business. In the final analysis, however, the prospective owner should be concerned with buying the company's assets at *market value* and then paying something for *goodwill* if it is deemed an asset. Valuation is discussed further in Chapter 14.

Key Terms and Concepts

business broker	goodwill	risk vs. reward
franchise	legal restraint of trade	Uniform Franchise Offering Circular (UFOC)
franchisee	new-new approach	unscrupulous practices
franchise fee	new-old approach	upside gain and downside loss
franchisor	non-compete clause	
franchisor control	profit trend	

Review and Discussion Questions

1. Identify the three main pathways to entering business for a prospective entrepreneur.
2. What is the new-new approach to starting a new venture? How does this approach differ from a new-old approach?
3. How can an individual who is thinking of going into business evaluate the financial picture of the enterprise? Use the methodology of Table 5.2 to prepare your answer.
4. In addition to personal and financial issues, what other factors should the prospective owner be concerned with? Describe at least four.
5. What are the advantages of buying an ongoing business? Explain them.
6. What "right questions" need to be answered when deciding whether to buy a business?
7. How should a prospective buyer examine the assets of a company? Explain.
8. What is meant by the term *franchise*?
9. In a franchising agreement, what is the franchisee often called on to do? What responsibility does the franchisor assume?
10. What are some of the major advantages of franchising? Cite and explain three.
11. What are some of the major disadvantages of franchising? Cite and explain at least two.
12. How can a prospective franchisee evaluate a franchise opportunity? Explain.
13. In evaluating whether or not to buy a franchise operation, the potential investor should ask a series of questions. What questions should the potential investor ask about the franchisor, the franchise, the market, and the potential investor (himself or herself)?
14. What are the advantages and disadvantages of franchising?
15. Identify the UFOC. Explain why it is important in franchising.

Experiential Exercise

THE PERSONAL ENTREPRENEURIAL ACTION PLAN

Before making the final decision about going into business, a prospective entrepreneur needs to ask a number of personal questions. Ten of the most important ones are listed here. As you read, mark the response that best describes you.

1. Are you a self-starter?
   - ☐ I can get going without help from others.
   - ☐ Once someone gets me going, I am just fine.
   - ☐ I take things easy and do not move until I have to.

2. How do you feel about others?
   - ☐ I can get along with just about anyone.
   - ☐ I do not need anyone else.
   - ☐ People irritate me.

3. Can you lead people?
   - ☐ I can get most people to go along with me once I start something.
   - ☐ I can give the orders if someone tells me what should be done.
   - ☐ I let someone else get things done and go along if I like it.

4. Can you take responsibility?
   - ☐ I take charge and see things through.
   - ☐ I'll take over if necessary but would rather let someone else be responsible.
   - ☐ If someone is around who wants to do it, I let him or her.

5. Are you an organizer?
   - ☐ I like to have a plan before I begin.
   - ☐ I do all right unless things get too confusing, in which case I quit.
   - ☐ Whenever I have things all set up, something always comes along to disrupt the plan, so I take things as they come.

6. Are you a hard worker?
   - ☐ I can keep going as long as necessary.
   - ☐ I work hard for a while, but then that's it.
   - ☐ I cannot see that hard work gets you anywhere.

7. Can you make decisions?
   - ☐ I can make decisions, and they usually turn out pretty well.
   - ☐ I can make decisions if I have plenty of time, but fast decision making upsets me.
   - ☐ I do not like to be the one who has to decide things.

8. Can people rely on your word?
   - ☐ Yes, I do not say things I do not mean.
   - ☐ I try to level with people, but sometimes I say what is easiest.
   - ☐ Why bother? The other person does not know the difference.

9. Can you stick with it?
   - ☐ When I make up my mind to do something, nothing stops me.
   - ☐ I usually finish what I start.
   - ☐ If things start to go awry, I usually quit.

10. How good is your health?
    - ☐ Excellent.
    - ☐ Pretty good.
    - ☐ Okay, but it has been better.

Now count the number of checks you have made next to the first responses and multiply this number by 3. Count the checks next to the second responses and multiply by 2. Count the number of times you checked the third answer. Total these three numbers. Of a possible 30 total points, a potentially successful entrepreneur should have at least 25 points. If not, the prospective entrepreneur should consider bringing in a partner or abandoning the idea of going into business alone. The potential entrepreneur should always keep in mind these personal factors while formulating the action plan.

Case 6.1

AN IDEA FOR THE DOGS!

Chris Wasserberg is a salesperson for a *Fortune* 100 firm. He has a bachelor's degree in marketing and is one of the firm's best salespeople. It is likely that Chris will one day become a sales manager if he stays with the firm. This is doubtful, however, because he hopes to start his own business.

Since he was hired seven years ago, Chris has managed to build a nest egg of $160,000. He now is looking for a business that would require no more than $60,000–$70,000 to get started. The rest would be used for operating capital and to keep him going until the company turns profitable. In the past, Chris has gathered ideas by reading magazines such as *Entrepreneur* and *Inc.*, which report new types of businesses.

Last week, Chris read a story that intrigued him. A man on the West Coast has been building custom doghouses out of expensive materials and selling then for $5,000 to $15,000 each. Chris realizes that few people can afford to pay this much for a doghouse. Yet most doghouses are not distinctive, and owners simply pay $50 to $150 for basic doghouses. Chris believes a market may exist for doghouses between these two extremes, in the range of $250 to $500. Chris has done the research and believes it would not be too difficult to differentiate his product from the standard doghouse. In particular, he is considering building a house that is slightly larger than the typical one, well insulated, and floored with washable vinyl; he would put the dog's name above the door and shingle the roof. Additionally, he believes that it would be more appealing if the house has the same basic design as the owner's. The two biggest obstacles will be marketing and production—that is, getting people to order houses for their dogs and then building the houses. Chris believes that, with his background, he can handle the marketing, and it should not be too difficult to find someone to handle the construction. Moreover, until the business takes off, he believes he can continue with his sales job.

QUESTIONS

1. Is anything unique about Chris's idea? Explain.

2. What is the first thing Chris should do to follow up on his idea? Explain.

3. When this is done, what else should Chris do? Outline a general course of action for him.

Case 6.2

CHECKING IT OUT

When Arlene Ryan inherited $150,000 from her grandfather, she decided to use the money to start her own business. Arlene has been a legal secretary for 14 years and feels she knows quite a lot about business. "Every day I take depositions and type legal memoranda," she noted to a friend. "And I've seen lots of businesses fail because they didn't have adequate capital or proper management. Believe me, when you work for a law firm, you see—and learn—plenty."

Almost six months passed before Arlene decided on a business to pursue. A franchise ad in a business magazine caught her attention; Arlene called and found out that the franchisor was selling fast-food franchises in her area. "We are in the process of moving into your section of the country," the spokesperson told her. "We have 111 franchisees throughout the nation and want to sell 26 in your state." Arlene went to a meeting that the franchisor held at a local hotel and, along with a large number of other potential investors, listened to the sales pitch. It all sounded very good. The cost of the franchise was $75,000 plus 4 percent of gross revenues. The franchisor promised assistance with site location and personnel training and encouraged the prospective franchisees to ask questions and investigate the organization. "If you don't feel this is a good deal for you, it's not a good deal for us either; good business is a two-way street," the spokesperson pointed out. "We are going to be looking very carefully at all franchise applications, and you ought to be giving us the same degree of scrutiny."

Arlene liked what she heard but felt it would be prudent to do some checking on her own. Before leaving the meeting, she asked the spokesperson for the names and addresses of some current franchisees. "I don't have a list with me," he said, "but I can write down some that I know of, and you can get their numbers from the operator." He then scribbled four names and locations on a piece of paper and handed it to her.

Arlene called information and was able to get telephone numbers for only two of the franchises. The other addresses apparently were wrong. She then placed calls to the two franchisees. The first person said she had owned her franchise for one year and felt it was too early to judge the success of the operation. When she found out Arlene was thinking about buying a franchise, she asked if Arlene would consider buying hers. The price the woman quoted was $5,000 less than what the company currently was quoting. The second person told Arlene he simply did not give out information over the phone. He seemed somewhat edgy about talking to her and continually sidestepped Arlene's requests for specific financial information. Finally, he told her, "Look, if you really want this information, I think you should talk to my attorney. If he says it's okay to tell you, I will." He then gave Arlene the attorney's number. Before she could call the lawyer, Arlene left for lunch. When she returned, one of the partners of her firm was standing beside her desk. "Hey, Arlene, what are you doing calling this guy?" he asked, holding up the telephone number of the franchisee's attorney. "Are you planning to sue someone? That's his specialty, you know." Arlene smiled. "As a matter of fact, I am. I'm thinking of suing you guys for back wages." The attorney laughed along with her and then walked back into his office.

QUESTIONS

1. What is your appraisal of the situation? Does it look good or bad?

2. Would you recommend that Arlene buy the franchise from the woman who has offered to sell? Why or why not?

3. What would you recommend Arlene do now? Be complete in your answer.

Notes

1. Steve Rosenbush, "Facebook's on the Block," *BusinessWeek Online*, March 28, 2006, http://www.businessweek.com/technology/content/mar2006/tc20060327_215976.htm (accessed October 3, 2006).

2. Saul Hansell, "Yahoo Woos a Social Networking Site," *New York Times Online*, September 22, 2006, http://www.nytimes.com/2006/09/22/technology/22facebook.html?ex=1316577600&en=09f3d5e70aa0f977&ei=5088&partner=rssnyt&emc=rss (accessed October 3, 2006).

3. Donald F. Kuratko and Jeffrey S. Hornsby, *New Venture Management* (Upper Saddle River, NJ: Pearson/Prentice Hall, 2009), 33–38.

4. Fred Steingold and Emily Dostow, *The Complete Guide to Buying a Business* (Berkeley CA: Nolo Press, 2005).

5. Jay B. Abrams, *How to Value Your Business and Increase Its Potential* (New York: McGraw-Hill, 2005).

6. For a good discussion of buying or selling a small business, see Rene V. Richards, *How to Buy and/or Sell a Small Business for Maximum Profit* (Charleston, SC: Atlantic, 2006).

7. See Roy J. Lewicki, David M. Saunders, and John W. Minton, *Negotiation,* 3rd ed. (New York: McGraw Hill/Irwin, 2002). This paperback gives practical examples and advice about negotiating. Also see Michael Watkins, *Negotiation: Harvard*

Business Essentials (Boston: Harvard Business School Press, 2003).

8. For an excellent overview of franchises, see Rupert Barkoff, *Fundamentals of Business Franchising,* 2nd ed. (Chicago: American Bar Association, 2005); and Gaylord A. Jentz, Roger LeRoy Miller, and Frank B. Cross, *West's Business Law,* 10th ed. (Mason, OH: South-Western/Cengage Learning, 2007).

9. Patrick J. Kaufmann, "Franchising and the Choice of Self-Employment," *Journal of Business Venturing* (July 1999): 345–62.

10. Robert T. Justis and Richard J. Judd, *Franchising,* 3rd ed. (Mason, OH: South-Western/Cengage Learning, 2004); and Joe Mathews, Don DeBolt, and Deb Percival, *Street Smart Franchising* (Irvine, CA: Entrepreneur Press, 2006).

11. Darrell L. Williams, "Why Do Entrepreneurs Become Franchisees? An Empirical Analysis of Organizational Choice," *Journal of Business Venturing* (January 1999): 103–24.

12. Jentz, Miller, and Cross, *West's Business Law,* 10th ed.

13. See Steven C. Michael, "To Franchise or Not to Franchise: An Analysis of Decision Rights and Organizational Form Shares," *Journal of Business Venturing* (January 1996): 59–71; also see Nerilee Hing, "Franchisee Satisfaction: Contributors and Consequences," *Journal of Small Business Management* (April 1995): 12–25; Marko Grunhagen and Robert A. Mittelstaedt, "Entrepreneurs or Investors: Do Multi-unit Franchisees Have Different Philosophical Orientations?" *Journal of Small Business Management,* 43, no. 3 (July 2005): 207–25.

14. Thani Jambulingam and John R. Nevin, "Influence of Franchisee Selction Criteria of Outcomes Desired by the Franchisor," *Journal of Business Venturing* (July 1999): 363–96; see also Gary J. Castrogiovanni, James G. Combs, and Robert T. Justis, "Shifting Imperatives: An Integrative View of Resource Scarcity and Agency Reasons for Franchising," *Entrepreneurship Theory & Practice,* 30, no. 1 (January 2006): 23–40; and Roland E. Kidwell, Arne Nygaard, and Ragnhild Silkoset, "Antecedents and Effects of Free Riding in the Franchisor–Franchisee Relationship," *Journal of Business Venturing* 22, no. 4 (July 2007): 522–44.

15. David A. Baucus, Melissa S. Baucas, and Sherrie E. Human, "Choosing a Franchise: How Base Fees and Royalties Relate to the Value of the Franchise," *Journal of Small Business Management* (April 1993): 91–104; see also Andrew J. Sherman, *Franchising & Licensing: Two Powerful Ways to Grow Your Business in Any Economy,* 3rd ed. (New York: AMACOM Books, 2004).

7

Legal Challenges in Entrepreneurship

Entrepreneurial Thought

A major difficulty for the inexperienced entrepreneur is the host of strange terms and phrases which are scattered throughout most legal documents. The novice in this kind of reading should have some understanding not only of what is contained in such documents, but also why these provisions have been included. If an entrepreneur cannot find the time or take the interest to read and understand the major contracts into which his company will enter, he should be very cautious about being an entrepreneur at all.

— **PATRICK R. LILES** *Harvard Business School*

Chapter Objectives

1   To introduce the importance of legal issues to entrepreneurs

2   To examine patent protection, including definitions and preparation

3   To review copyrights and their relevance to entrepreneurs

4   To study trademarks and their impact on new ventures

5   To examine the legal forms of organization—sole proprietorship, partnership, and corporation

6   To illustrate the advantages and disadvantages of each of these three legal forms

7   To explain the nature of the limited partnership and limited liability partnerships (LLPs)

8   To examine how an S corporation works

9   To define the additional classifications of corporations, including limited liability companies (LLCs)

10   To present the major segments of the bankruptcy law that apply to entrepreneurs

Legal Challenges for the Entrepreneurial Venture

Entrepreneurs cannot hope to have the legal expertise or background of an attorney, of course, but they should be sufficiently knowledgeable about certain legal concepts that have implications for the business venture.[1]

Table 7.1 sets forth some of the major legal concepts that can affect entrepreneurial ventures. These concepts can be divided into three groups: (1) those that relate to the inception of the

Table 7.1	Major Legal Concepts and Entrepreneurial Ventures

I. Inception of an Entrepreneurial Venture
   A. Laws governing intellectual property
      1. Patents
      2. Copyrights
      3. Trademarks
   B. Forms of business organization
      1. Sole proprietorship
      2. Partnership
      3. Corporation
      4. Franchise
   C. Tax considerations
   D. Capital formation
   E. Liability questions

II. An Ongoing Venture: Business Development and Transactions
   A. Personnel law
      1. Hiring and firing policies
      2. Equal Employment Opportunity Commission
      3. Collective bargaining
   B. Contract law
      1. Legal contracts
      2. Sales contracts
      3. Leases

III. Growth and Continuity of a Successful Entrepreneurial Venture
   A. Tax considerations
      1. Federal, state, local
      2. Payroll
      3. Incentives
   B. Governmental regulations
      1. Zoning (property)
      2. Administrative agencies (regulatory)
      3. Consumer law
   C. Continuity of ownership rights
      1. Property laws and ownership
      2. Wills, trusts, estates
      3. Bankruptcy

venture, (2) those that relate to the ongoing venture, and (3) those that relate to the growth and continuity of the venture. The focus of this chapter will be on the legal concepts related to the first and third groups. Specifically, we shall examine intellectual property protection (patents, copyrights, trademarks), the legal forms of organization, and bankruptcy law.

Intellectual Property Protection: Patents

A patent provides the owner with exclusive rights to hold, transfer, and license the production and sale of the product or process. Design patents last for 14 years; all others last for 20 years. The objective of a patent is to provide the holder with a temporary monopoly on his or her innovation and thus to encourage the creation and disclosure of new ideas and innovations in the marketplace. Securing a patent, however, is not always an easy process.

A patent is an intellectual property right. It is the result of a unique discovery, and patent holders are provided protection against infringement by others. In general, a number of items can qualify for patent protection, among them processes, machines, products, plants, compositions of elements (chemical compounds), and improvements on already existing items.[2]

Securing a Patent

Because quite often the patent process is complex (see Figure 7.1), careful planning is required. For pursuing a patent, the following basic rules are recommended by the experts:

Rule 1: Pursue patents that are broad, are commercially significant, and offer a strong position. This means that relevant patent law must be researched to obtain the widest coverage possible on the idea or concept. In addition, there must be something significantly novel or proprietary about the innovation. Record all steps or processes in a notebook and have them witnessed so that documentation secures a strong proprietary position.

Rule 2: Prepare a patent plan in detail. This plan should outline the costs to develop and market the innovation as well as analyze the competition and technological similarities to your idea. Attempt to detail the precise value of the innovation.

Rule 3: Have your actions relate to your original patent plan. This does not mean a plan cannot be changed. However, it is wise to remain close to the plan during the early stages of establishing the patent. Later, the path that is prepared may change—for example, licensing out the patent versus keeping it for yourself.

Rule 4: Establish an infringement budget. Patent rights are effective only if potential infringers fear legal damages. Thus, it is important to prepare a realistic budget for prosecuting violations of the patent.

Rule 5: Evaluate the patent plan strategically. The typical patent process takes three years. This should be compared to the actual life cycle of the proposed innovation or technology. Will the patent be worth defending in three years, or will enforcement cost more than the damages collected?[3]

These rules about proper definition, preparation, planning, and evaluation can help entrepreneurs establish effective patent protection. In addition, they can help the patent attorney conduct the search process.

Patent applications must include detailed specifications of the innovation that any skilled person in the specific area can understand. A patent application has two parts:

1. Specification is the text of a patent and may include any accompanying illustrations. Because its purpose is to teach those fluent in this area of technology all they need to understand, duplicate, and use the invention, it may be quite long. The specification typically includes:

   a. An introduction explaining why the invention will be useful.

   b. Description of all prior art that you are aware of and that could be considered similar to the invention. The specification usually lists other patents by number—with a brief description of each—but you can cite and describe unpatented technology as well.

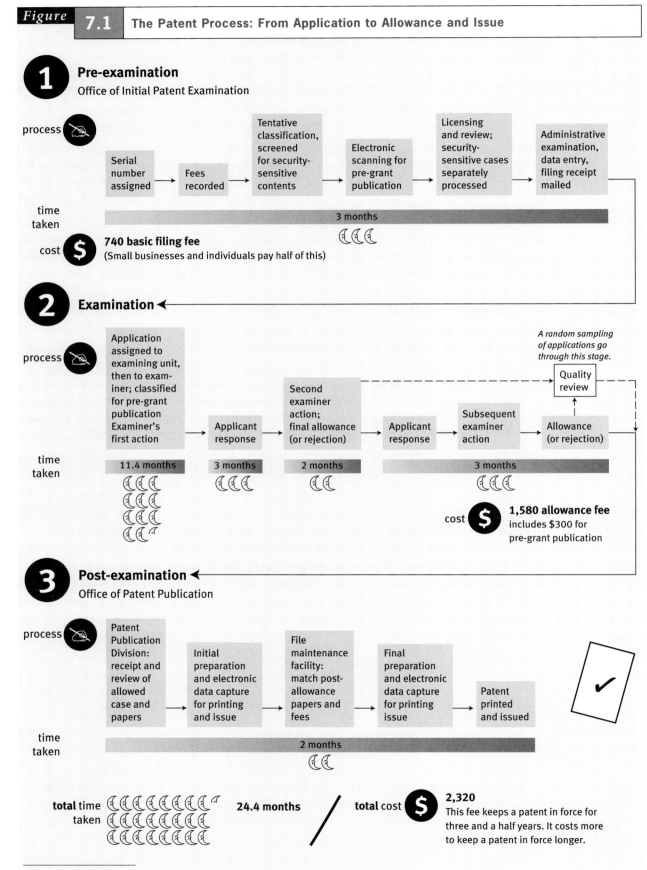

Figure 7.1   The Patent Process: From Application to Allowance and Issue

Source: United States Patent Office, 2005.

entrepreneurship in practice

Patent Protection—A Practical Perspective

Most people do not realize that just 2 percent of all patents ever realize any profits. Considering the cost of the patent process and the amount of time and resources it takes to protect patents, actually getting patent protection may not even be the best way to go. Because of this, many experts suggest that inventors consider licensing their product rather than marketing it themselves. In addition, many experts suggest that a venture capitalist, financially secure business partner, or consultant may be the best way to ensure success. The United States Patent and Trademark Office (USPTO) also gives priority to individuals who can prove that they came up with an idea first. This is difficult to prove, and again, the bigger, more established companies likely have an advantage on the average inventor. Just $10 allows the inventor to file a disclosure agreement with the USPTO. The next step is to file for a "patent pending" status, or a "provisional patent." This filing costs just $80 and lasts for one year. It allows the inventor to further test the product and to seek legal advice regarding the product. More information regarding provisional patents can be found on the USPTO Web site at http://www.uspto.gov/web/offices/pac/provapp.htm. Avoid the TV commercials that offer patent assistance for as much as a $13,000 fee—they usually offer only a design patent (when a utility patent is most often needed). They also offer to submit the invention to industry. However, this does not mean that they will submit the invention to the correct industry or really do any "legwork" for the inventor. Finally, examine the many resources on the Internet that can help inventors take the best route toward success. Some examples are:

    http://www.patentcafe.com
    http://www.inventnet.com
    http://www.inventorfraud.com
    http://www.wini2.com
    http://www.inventorfraud.com/helpers.htm
    http://www.uspto.gov

Source: Adapted from Michael Boland, "ASAP Inventor's Guide to the Fast Lane," *Forbes* (June 24, 2002): 72.

c. A summary of the invention that describes the essence of the new technology and emphasizes its difference from prior art, while including all its requisite features, whether novel or not.

d. A detailed description of the invention, including anything that could be remotely relevant, reference to all reasonable variations, and number bounds. Take as much space as you like. Use as many numbers as necessary, including close or tight limits based on experience, as well as loose ones based on what might be possible. This section should be detailed enough to really teach a skilled practitioner.

e. Examples and/or experimental results, in full detail.

The specification is inherently broad because its intent is to teach and also, as a practical matter, to allow some flexibility in the claims that are based on it.

2. Claims are a series of short paragraphs, each of which identifies a particular feature or combination of features that is protected by the patent. The entire claims section, at the end of the patent, is typically about one page long or less.

Claims define and limit the patented invention. The invention can be broad (a process requiring an "inorganic, nonmetal solid" would cover a lot of possibilities, for example) but sharply limited not to cover anything in prior art (other existing processes that use organics or metals).[4]

Once the application is filed with the **Patent and Trademark Office** of the Department of Commerce, an examiner will determine whether the innovation qualifies for patentability. The examiner will do this by researching technical data in journals as well as previously issued patents. Based on the individual's findings, the application will be rejected or accepted.

Only a small percentage of issued patents are commercially valuable. Consequently, the entrepreneur must weigh the value of the innovation against the time and money spent to obtain the patent. Also, it is important to remember that many patents granted by the Patent and Trademark Office have been declared invalid after being challenged in court. This occurs for several reasons. One is that the patent holder waited an unreasonable length of time before asserting his or her rights. A second is that those bringing suit against the patent holder are able to prove that the individual misused the patent rights—for example, by requiring certain purchases of other goods or services as part of the patent-use arrangement. A third is that other parties are able to prove that the patent itself fails to meet tests of patentability and is therefore invalid.[5]

If, after careful review, an entrepreneur concludes that the innovation will withstand any legal challenge and is commercially worthwhile, a patent should be pursued. If a challenge is mounted, legal fees may be sizable, but a successful defense can result in damages sufficient to compensate for the infringement plus court costs and interest. In fact, the court may award damages of up to three times the actual amount. In addition, a patent infringer can be liable for all profits resulting from the infringement as well as for legal fees.[6]

Intellectual Property Protection: Copyrights

A **copyright** provides exclusive rights to creative individuals for the protection of their literary or artistic productions. It is not possible to copyright an idea, but the particular mode for expression of that idea often can be copyrighted. This expression can take many forms, including books, periodicals, dramatic or musical compositions, art, motion pictures, lectures, sound recordings, and computer programs.

Any works created after January 1, 1978, and receiving a copyright are protected for the life of the author plus 70 years. The owner of this copyright may (1) reproduce the work, (2) prepare derivative works based on it (for example, a condensation or movie version of a novel), (3) distribute copies of the work by sale or otherwise, (4) perform the work publicly, and (5) display the work publicly. Each of these rights, or a portion of each, also may be transferred.[7]

Understanding Copyright Protection

For the author of creative material to obtain copyright protection, the material must be in a tangible form so it can be communicated or reproduced. It also must be the author's own work and thus the product of his or her skill or judgment. Concepts, principles, processes, systems, or discoveries are not valid for copyright protection until they are put in tangible form—written or recorded.

Formal registration of a copyright with the Copyright Office of the Library of Congress is a requirement before an author can begin a lawsuit for infringement. In addition, an author can find his or her copyright invalidated if proper notice isn't provided.

Anyone who violates an author's exclusive rights under a copyright is liable for infringement. However, because of the **fair use doctrine**, it is sometimes difficult to establish infringement. Fair use is described as the reproduction of a copyrighted work for purposes such as criticism, comment, news reporting, teaching (including multiple copies for classroom use), scholarship, or research. These uses may be good candidates for the fair use defense, as they may be deemed not an infringement of copyright. In determining whether the use made of a work in any particular case is a fair use, the factors to be considered include (1) the purpose and character of the use, including whether such use is of a commercial

entrepreneurship in practice

Watch What You Say

The government can't help protect your business from the competition if your employees willingly share valuable information. Copious amounts of sensitive and confidential information are being made public every day by business travelers who pay no heed to the fact that people have ears. Carrying on a seemingly harmless conversation with a co-worker on an airplane, in a bus, or in a restaurant has wreaked havoc for more than one company. An employee of Fuld & Company, a management consulting firm, was riding a shuttle bus when he heard every bit of a company's distribution strategy being discussed in the seat in front of him. Luckily for the two talkers, he wasn't competition. He did, however, let it be known what had just occurred.

Protecting trade secrets is not a new concept, but with the amount of businesspeople traveling every day and the development of technology, the smallest slip can be dangerous. Leonard Fuld, a competitive intelligence expert, states that it's common for companies to overlook the human factor when it comes to information leaking out. He emphasizes the point by talking about the "Nerd Bird," a frequent shuttle flight from Austin, Texas, to San Jose, California, that carries mostly engineers and executives from the semiconductor and software industries. "I was even told an anecdote about an executive who waited until passengers had disembarked and then quickly roamed the aisle to see if any documents had been left behind." "I know of people in firms who justify booking first-class airfare based on the quality of information they might be able to pick up that way," states a Silicon Valley businessperson.

Verbal exchanges aren't the only way travelers hurt themselves. Rental car trunks, stolen briefcases,

and the simple misplaced memo are known to be gold mines as well.

Business travelers should keep the following in mind to protect intellectual property that can't be protected by the government:

1. **Avoid talking shop in public areas where competitors are likely to be present.** Business jargon isn't a code when the executive sitting right beside you is in the same industry.

2. **Never expose laptop screens on airplanes, buses, or other conveyances when working on confidential facts and figures.** If the work is unavoidable, ask for a window seat and use smaller font sizes.

3. **Be particularly vigilant at trade shows.** Proprietary technology, new-product releases, and the like should be discussed in detail only behind closed doors.

4. **Pay phones and cell phones pose an amazing opportunity for others to partake in the conversation.** Be cautious of your surroundings when making important phone calls.

5. **Protect the files on your computer by purchasing a cable lock or security software.** Help deter computer theft by labeling both the case and computer and never letting them out of your sight.

6. **Keep unnecessary documentation at the office.** Also check your work area and account for all paperwork after handling important documents to see if anything has "mysteriously" landed on the floor.

Source: David Barber, "Loose Lips Sink You," *Inc.*, June 1999, http://www.inc.com/magazine/19990601/4628.html (accessed April 2, 2008).

nature or is for nonprofit educational purposes; (2) the nature of the copyrighted work; (3) the amount and substantiality of the portion used in relation to the copyrighted work as a whole; and (4) the effect of the use upon the potential market for a value of the copyrighted work.[8]

If, however, an author substantiates a copyright infringement, the normal remedy is recovery of actual damages plus any profits the violator receives. Keep in mind that there is absolutely no cost or risk involved in protecting material that you generate by copyright. Therefore, as a matter of course, any writing that you prepare and spend a lot of time on should be copyrighted by putting the copyright notice (©) on it. Also, it is not necessary to register copyrights with the Copyright Office unless and until you want to sue somebody for infringement. In the overwhelming majority of cases—assuming you are not in the publishing business—you can simply use the copyright notice and do not need to spend the time and effort necessary to register copyrights with the U.S. Copyright Office.

Protected Ideas?

The Copyright Act specifically excludes copyright protection for any "idea, procedure, process, system, method of operation, concept, principle, or discovery, regardless of the form in which it is described, explained, illustrated, or embodied." Note that it is not possible to copyright an *idea*—the underlying ideas embodied in a work may be used freely by others. What is copyrightable is the particular way an idea is expressed. Whenever an idea and an expression are inseparable, the expression cannot be copyrighted.

Generally, anything that is not an original expression will not qualify for copyright protection. Facts widely known to the public are not copyrightable. Page numbers are not copyrightable because they follow a sequence known to everyone. Mathematical calculations are not copyrightable. Compilations of facts, however, are copyrightable. The Copyright Act defines a compilation as "a work formed by the collection and assembling of preexisting materials of data that are selected, coordinated, or arranged in such a way that the resulting work as a whole constitutes an original work of authorship."[9]

Intellectual Property Protection: Trademarks

A **trademark** is a distinctive name, mark, symbol, or motto identified with a company's product(s) and registered at the Patent and Trademark Office. Thanks to trademark law, no confusion should result from one venture's using the symbol or name of another.

Specific legal terms differentiate the exact types of marks. For example, trademarks identify and distinguish goods. Service marks identify and distinguish services. Certification marks denote the quality, materials, or other aspects of goods and services and are used by someone other than the mark's owner. Collective marks are trademarks or service marks that members of groups or organizations use to identify themselves as the source of goods or services.[10]

Usually, personal names or words that are considered generic or descriptive are not trademarked, unless the words are in some way suggestive or fanciful, or the personal name is accompanied by a specific design. For example, English Leather may not be trademarked to describe a leather processed in England; however, English Leather is trademarked as a name for aftershave lotion, because this constitutes a fanciful use of the words. Consider also that even the common name of an individual may be trademarked if that name is accompanied by a picture or some fanciful design that allows easy identification of the product, such as Smith Brothers Cough Drops.

In most cases, the Patent and Trademark Office will reject an application for marks, symbols, or names that are flags or insignias of governments, portraits or signatures of living persons, immoral or deceptive, or items likely to cause problems because of resemblance to a previously registered mark. Once issued, the trademark is listed in the Principal Register of the Patent and Trademark Office. This listing offers several advantages: (1) nationwide constructive notice of the owner's right to use the mark (thus eliminating the need to show that the defendant in an infringement suit had notice of the mark), (2) Bureau of Customs protection against importers using the mark, and (3) incontestability of the mark after five years.[11]

In 1995, Congress amended the Trademark Act by passing the Federal Trademark Dilution Act, which extended the protection available to trademark owners by creating a

the entrepreneurial process

Nike vs. Mike: A Parody on Trademark Infringement

Mike Stanard had a great idea for his daughter to try during summer vacation: Establish an enterprise called "Just Did It" (a spoof on Nike's "Just Do It" slogan) and sell tee shirts with the famous swoosh design (identical to Nike's) accompanied by the word *Mike* instead of *Nike*. The tee shirts would be sold for $19.95 (or $24.95 for the long-sleeved version). They would send out 1,400 brochures to college athletes and celebrities named Michael. What a great idea!

Nike did not think so. From 1971 to 1994, Nike had invested more than $300 million advertising its trademarks. Aggregate sales revenues from Nike trademarked apparel had exceeded $10 billion. The "Just Do It" slogan alone produced 1989–1994 revenue exceeding $15 million. Nike sued Stanard for trademark infringement.

Stanard's defense was parody. A parody must convey two simultaneous and contradictory messages: that it is the original, but also that it is not the original and is instead a parody. The customer must be amused and not confused.

To assess whether a trademark infringement has occurred, the courts consider seven factors: (1) the degree of similarity between the trademarks, (2) the similarity of the products for which the name is used, (3) the area and manner of concurrent use, (4) the degree of care likely to be exercised by consumers, (5) the strength of the complainant's trademark, (6) whether actual product confusion exists among buyers, and (7) an intent on the part of the alleged infringer to palm off his or her products as those of another.

Because Stanard sold the shirts by mail (customers had to write a check to "Just Did It") and had no apparent intent to copy Nike's products specifically, the court concluded that no confusion existed. Thus, the parody defense succeeded. The parody defense doesn't always work, however. Marketers will have to decide whether the legal risk involved in parody marketing is worth unknown sales results.

Examples of court rulings include:

- Miami Mice was a valid parody of Miami Vice.
- Hard Rain Cafe was likely to confuse consumers regarding the Hard Rock Cafe.
- Enjoy Cocaine was not a valid parody of Enjoy Coca-Cola, where both used the familiar red-and-white logo.
- Stop the Olympic Prison, which used the five-interlocking-rings logo, was not considered confusing with the Olympic Committee's trademark.
- Lardash was considered a valid parody of Jordache.
- Mutant of Omaha and the subtitle Nuclear Holocaust Insurance was not a valid parody of Mutual of Omaha.
- Bagzilla was a permissible pun of Godzilla and would not confuse consumers.
- Spy Notes was a valid parody of CliffsNotes.

Source: Maxine S. Lans, "Parody as a Marketing Strategy," *Marketing News* (January 3, 1994): 20.

federal cause of action for trademark dilution. Until the passage of this amendment, federal trademark law prohibited only the unauthorized use of the same mark on competing—or on noncompeting but "related"—goods or services when such use would likely confuse consumers as to the origin of those goods and services. Trademark dilution laws that also have been enacted by about half of the states protect "distinctive" or "famous" trademarks (such as Jergens, McDonald's, RCA, and Macintosh) from certain unauthorized uses of the marks *regardless* of a showing of competition or a likelihood of confusion.[12]

Historically, a trademark registration lasted 20 years; however, the current registrations are good for only 10 years, with the possibility for continuous renewal every

the entrepreneurial process

Internet Intellectual Property Information Sources

http://www.uspto.gov

The United States Patent and Trademark Office Web site provides a wealth of valuable information for entrepreneurs. Users can locate patent and trademark information, such as registration forms, international patents, legal issues, and frequently asked questions (FAQs). Users can also check the status of a trademark or patent application on this site.

http://www.patents.com

This site, provided by the law offices of Oppedahl and Larson, provides basic patent information in a very organized manner. It is also updated frequently.

http://www.bustpatents.com

This site, sponsored by Source Translation and Optimization, offers assistance with Internet, biotech, and e-commerce patents. Users also can sign up for the free daily information e-mail, Internet Patent News Service, at this site.

http://www.copyright.gov/

The United States Copyright Office at the Library of Congress Web site provides information on copyright protecting works, licensing, and legal issues. Users also can search copyright records on the site.

http://www.law.cornell.edu/

The Web site for the Legal Information Institute at the Cornell School of Law provides legal documentation and a history of copyright law. It also offers information on international copyrights and links to other copyright information resources.

http://www.findlaw.com

This site allows the user to search for any topic and yield returns of the actual written law, court precedence, and current cases and interpretations. The site also provides topical searches that aid the user in getting started as well as a business section to help put the laws into more practical applications.

http://academic.cengage.com/blaw/wbl/chooseyourbook.html

West's Business Law textbook's Web site offers an overview of the book, cases, and updates that allow surfers to check contents before purchasing.

---

10 years. It is most important to understand that a trademark may be invalidated in four specific ways:

1. **Cancellation proceedings:** a third party's challenge to the mark's distinctiveness within five years of its issuance.

2. **Cleaning-out procedure:** the failure of a trademark owner to file an affidavit stating it is in use or justifying its lack of use within six years of registration.

3. **Abandonment:** the nonuse of a trademark for two consecutive years without justification or a statement regarding the trademark's abandonment.

4. **Generic meaning:** the allowance of a trademark to represent a general grouping of products or services. For example, cellophane has come to represent plastic wrap, and Scotch tape has come to represent adhesive tape. Xerox is currently seeking, through national advertising, to avoid having its name used to represent copier machines.

If a trademark is properly registered, used, and protected, the owner can obtain an injunction against any uses of the mark that are likely to cause confusion. Moreover, if infringement and damages can be proven in court, a monetary award may be given to the trademark holder.

Avoiding the Trademark Pitfalls

Trademark registration and search can be costly, sometimes ranging into the thousands of dollars. Trademark infringement can be even more expensive. To avoid these pitfalls, one author has noted five basic rules that entrepreneurs should follow when selecting trademarks for their new ventures, as follows:

- Never select a corporate name or a mark without first doing a trademark search.
- If your attorney says you have a potential problem with a mark, trust his or her judgment.
- Seek a coined or fanciful name or mark before you settle for a descriptive or highly suggestive one.
- Whenever marketing or other considerations dictate the use of a name or mark that is highly suggestive of the product, select a distinctive logotype for the descriptive or suggestive words.
- Avoid abbreviations and acronyms wherever possible, and when no alternative is acceptable, select a distinctive logotype in which the abbreviation or acronym appears.[13]

Trade Secrets

Certain business processes and information cannot be patented, copyrighted, or trademarked. Yet they may be protected as trade secrets. Customer lists, plans, research and development, pricing information, marketing techniques, and production techniques are examples of potential trade secrets. Generally, anything that makes an individual company unique and has value to a competitor could be a trade secret.[14]

Protection of trade secrets extends both to ideas and to their expression. For this reason, and because a trade secret involves no registration or filing requirements, trade-secret protection is ideal for software. Of course, the secret formula, method, or other information must be disclosed to key employees. Businesses generally attempt to protect their trade secrets by having all employees who use the process or information agree in their contracts never to divulge it. Theft of confidential business data by industrial espionage—such as stealing a competitor's documents—is a theft of trade secrets without any contractual violation and is actionable in itself.

The law clearly outlines the area of trade secrets: Information is a trade secret if (1) it is not known by the competition, (2) the business would lose its advantage if the competition were to obtain it, and (3) the owner has taken reasonable steps to protect the secret from disclosure.[15] Keep in mind that prosecution is still difficult in many of these cases.

Trademark Protection on the Internet

Because of the unique nature of the Internet, its use creates unique legal questions and issues—particularly with respect to intellectual property rights. The emerging body of law governing cyberspace is often referred to as *cyberlaw*.

One of the initial trademark issues involving intellectual property in cyberspace has been whether domain names (Internet addresses) should be treated as trademarks or simply as a means of access, similar to street addresses in the physical world. Increasingly, the courts are holding that the principles of trademark law should apply to domain names. One problem in applying trademark law to Internet domain names, however, is that trademark law allows multiple parties to use the same mark—as long as the mark is used for different goods or services and will not cause customer confusion. On the Internet as it is currently structured, only one party can use a particular domain name, regardless of the type of goods or services offered. In other words, although two or more businesses can own the trademark Entrevision, only one business can operate on the Internet with the domain name Entrevision.com. Because of this restrictive feature of domain names, a question has arisen as to whether domain names should function as trademarks. To date, the courts that have considered this question have held that the unauthorized use of another's mark in a domain name may constitute trademark infringement.[16]

Table 7.2 provides a comprehensive outline of the forms of intellectual property protection.

Table **7.2**	**Forms of Intellectual Property**			
	Patent	**Copyright**	**Trademarks (Service Marks and Trade Dress)**	**Trade Secrets**
DEFINITION	A grant from the government that gives an inventor exclusive rights to an invention.	An intangible property right granted to authors and originators of a literary work or artistic production that falls within specified categories.	Any distinctive word, name, symbol, or device (image or appearance), or combination thereof, that an entity uses to identify and distinguish its goods or services from those of others.	Any information (including formulas, patterns, programs, devices, techniques, and processes) that a business possesses and that gives the business an advantage over competitors who do not know the information or process.
REQUIREMENTS	An invention must be: 1. Novel. 2. Not obvious. 3. Useful.	Literary or artistic works must be: 1. Original. 2. Fixed in a durable medium that can be perceived, reproduced, or communicated. 3. Within a copyrightable category.	Trademarks, service marks, and trade dresses must be sufficiently distinctive (or must have acquired a secondary meaning) to enable consumers and others to distinguish the manufacturer's, seller's, or business user's products or services from those of competitors.	Information and processes that have commercial value, that are not known or easily ascertainable by the general public or others, and that are reasonably protected from disclosure.
TYPES OR CATEGORIES	1. Utility (general). 2. Design. 3. Plant (flowers, vegetables, and so on).	1. Literary works (including computer programs). 2. Musical works. 3. Dramatic works. 4. Pantomime and choreographic works. 5. Pictorial, graphic, and sculptural works. 6. Films and audiovisual works. 7. Sound recordings.	1. Strong, distinctive marks (such as fanciful, arbitrary, or suggestive marks). 2. Marks that have acquired a secondary meaning by use. 3. Other types of marks, including certification marks and collective marks. 4. Trade dress (such as a distinctive decor, menu, style, or type of service).	1. Customer lists. 2. Research and development. 3. Plans and programs. 4. Pricing information. 5. Production techniques. 6. Marketing techniques. 7. Formulas. 8. Compilations.
HOW ACQUIRED	By filing a patent application with the U.S. Patent and Trademark Office and receiving that office's approval.	Automatic (once in tangible form); to recover for infringement, the copyright must be registered with the U.S. Copyright Office.	1. At common law, ownership is created by use of mark. 2. Registration (either with the U.S. Patent and Trademark Office or with the appropriate state office) gives constructive notice of date of use.	Through the originality and development of information and processes that are unique to a business, that are unknown by others, and that

Table 7.2	Forms of Intellectual Property *(Continued)*

	Patent	Copyright	Trademarks (Service Marks and Trade Dress)	Trade Secrets
			3. Federal registration is permitted if the mark is currently in use or if the applicant intends use within six months (period can be extended to three years). 4. Federal registration can be renewed between the fifth and sixth years and, thereafter, every ten years.	would be valuable to competitors if they knew of the information and processes.
RIGHTS	An inventor has the right to make, use, sell, assign, or license the invention during the duration of the patent's term. The first to invent has patent rights.	The author or originator has the exclusive right to reproduce, distribute, display, license, or transfer a copyrighted work.	The owner has the right to use the mark or trade dress and to exclude others from using it. The right of use can be licensed or sold (assigned) to another.	The owner has the right to sole and exclusive use of the trade secrets and the right to use legal means to protect against misappropriation of the trade secrets by others. The owner can license or assign a trade secret.
DURATION	20 years from the date of application; for design patents, 14 years.	1. For authors: the life of the author, plus 70 years. 2. For publishers: 95 years after the date of publication or 120 years after creation.	Unlimited, as long as it is in use. To continue notice by registration, the registration must be renewed by filing.	Unlimited, as long as not revealed to others.
CIVIL REMEDIES FOR INFRINGEMENT	Monetary damages, which include reasonable royalties and lost profits, *plus* attorneys' fees. (Treble damages are available for intentional infringement.)	Actual damages, plus profits received by the infringer; *or* statutory damages of not less than $500 and not more than $20,000 ($100,000, if infringement is willful); *plus* costs and attorneys' fees.	1. Injunction prohibiting future use of mark. 2. Actual damages, *plus* profits received by the infringer (can be increased to three times the actual damages under the Lanham Act). 3. Impoundment and destruction of infringing articles. 4. *Plus* costs and attorneys' fees.	Monetary damages for misappropriation (the Uniform Trade Secrets Act permits punitive damages up to twice the amount of actual damages for willful and malicious misappropriation); *plus* costs and attorneys' fees.

Source: Kenneth W. Clarkson, Roger LeRoy Miller, Gaylord A. Jentz, and Frank B. Cross, *West's Business Law: Legal, Ethical, International, and E-Commerce Environment*, 8th ed. (Mason, OH: South-Western/Cengage Learning, http://permission.cengage.com/permissions/action/start, 2001), 125–26. Reprinted with permission.

Identifying Legal Structures for Entrepreneurial Ventures

Prospective entrepreneurs need to identify the legal structure that will best suit the demands of the venture. The necessity for this derives from changing tax laws, liability situations, the availability of capital, and the complexity of business formation.[17] When examining these legal forms of organizations, entrepreneurs need to consider a few important factors:

- How easily the form of business organization can be implemented
- The amount of capital required to implement the form of business organization
- Legal considerations that might limit the options available to the entrepreneur
- The tax effects of the form of organization selected
- The potential liability to the owner of the form of organization selected

Three primary legal forms of organization are the sole proprietorship, the partnership, and the corporation. Because each form has specific advantages and disadvantages, it is impossible to recommend one form over the other. The entrepreneur's specific situation, concerns, and desires will dictate this choice.[18]

Sole Proprietorships

A **sole proprietorship** is a business that is owned and operated by one person. The enterprise has no existence apart from its owner. This individual has a right to all of the profits and bears all of the liability for the debts and obligations of the business. The individual also has **unlimited liability**, which means that his or her business and personal assets stand behind the operation. If the company cannot meet its financial obligations, the owner may be forced to sell the family car, house, and whatever assets would satisfy the creditors.

To establish a sole proprietorship, a person merely needs to obtain whatever local and state licenses are necessary to begin operations. If the proprietor chooses a fictitious or assumed name, he or she also must file a *certificate of assumed business name* with the county. Because of its ease of formation, the sole proprietorship is the most widely used legal form of organization.[19]

Advantages of Sole Proprietorships

Some of the advantages associated with sole proprietorships are as follows:

- *Ease of formation.* Less formality and fewer restrictions are associated with establishing a sole proprietorship than with any other legal form. The proprietorship needs little or no governmental approval, and it usually is less expensive than a partnership or corporation.
- *Sole ownership of profits.* The proprietor is not required to share profits with anyone.
- *Decision making and control vested in one owner.* No co-owners or partners must be consulted in the running of the operation.
- *Flexibility.* Management is able to respond quickly to business needs in the form of day-to-day management decisions as governed by various laws and good sense.
- *Relative freedom from governmental control.* Except for requiring the necessary licenses, very little governmental interference occurs in the operation.
- *Freedom from corporate business taxes.* Proprietors are taxed as individual taxpayers and not as businesses.

entrepreneurship in practice

Entrepreneurs Fighting Back (Legally) Against the IRS

When it comes to generating wealth, you can either earn more or keep more. As the federal deficit has climbed to record levels, the federal government has begun to try to "earn" more by focusing on small businesses and the taxes they are currently paying. In order to survive, entrepreneurs will have to reciprocate by being diligent about taking every credit and deduction that is legally allowable. Earning more comes naturally to entrepreneurs, given that the very nature of business is to develop a product or service in order to generate revenue. In addition, entrepreneurs understand that minimizing expenses leads to greater profits; however, most business owners find thinking of the taxes they pay on their business as a reducible expense to be less intuitive.

From 2004 to 2006, the number of small business audited by the IRS climbed from 7,000 to 18,000, which makes the risk of paying penalties for misrepresenting your tax liability a serious concern. The issue is that entrepreneurs fearful of being audited often avoid legitimate deductions in an attempt to be as conservative as possible, giving away their sorely needed capital in the process. No verifiable statistics exist to indicate exactly how much entrepreneurs are overpaying in taxes or what is leading to the overpayment; however, several steps are consistently cited as being overlooked by entrepreneurs when filing their annual taxes.

For example, many tax deductions are given exotic names, such as the domestic-production break. The fact that manufacturers often take advantage of this deduction is not particularly surprising; however, the fact that software companies and agricultural businesses are also eligible is one example of an application that is commonly missed. In addition, the Work Opportunity Tax Credit (WOTC) can be forgotten, most likely due to the fact that the criteria are in constant flux; yet, this credit can amount to as much as $4,800 per employee. Eligible employees usually include discharged veterans, ex-felons, and hires living in an enterprise community, as designated by the federal government.

Given the complexity and sheer volume of tax regulations, few entrepreneurs feel qualified to push their tax preparers to ensure that no deductions have been overlooked. Of course, entrepreneurs need to make certain that they are working with a legitimate professional and—just as important—someone they trust when preparing their taxes; however, if a company's tax preparer regularly appears too conservative when considering deductions, management would be remiss not to consider other preparers. The cost of an overly cautious preparer can quickly exceed the cost of an audit.

In the end, the most important point to remember is that the onus of legally filing the company's taxes falls on the entrepreneur. The most important step that an entrepreneur can take is to develop a system to ensure that all of the paperwork needed to verify the expenses generated over the course of the year are kept organized. Keeping receipts in a shoebox is not an effective solution; moreover, filing receipts without noting the associated purpose of the purchases will lead to the nightmarish task of recalling the purpose of every excursion made over the last year. Annotating receipts and filing them in an intuitively labeled filing system is the best measure to take to save countless hours of frustration at tax time. Additionally, in the event that your company is audited, you will be in a position to readily provide documentation for every detail of your tax filing.

As the IRS shifts its focus to small businesses, entrepreneurs need to do what they do best: innovate. Buried in the tax laws is a multitude of ways for businesses to reduce their tax liability legally. Leaving money on the table when negotiating with business partners is never a strategy for financial success; dealing with the government is no different.

Adapted from Justin Martin, "Stop Overpaying the IRS," *Fortune Small Business*, February 25, 2008, http://money.cnn.com/2008/02/22/smbusiness/overpaying_IRS_cover.fsb/index.htm (accessed April 4, 2008).

Disadvantages of Sole Proprietorships

Sole proprietorships also have disadvantages. Some of these are as follows:

- *Unlimited liability.* The individual proprietor is personally responsible for all business debts. This liability extends to *all* of the proprietor's assets.
- *Lack of continuity.* The enterprise may be crippled or terminated if the owner becomes ill or dies.
- *Less available capital.* Ordinarily, proprietorships have less available capital than other types of business organizations, such as partnerships and corporations.
- *Relative difficulty obtaining long-term financing.* Because the enterprise rests exclusively on one person, it often has difficulty raising long-term capital.
- *Relatively limited viewpoint and experience.* The operation depends on one person, and this individual's ability, training, and expertise will limit its direction and scope.

Partnerships

A **partnership**, as defined by the **Revised Uniform Partnership Act (RUPA)**, is an association of two or more persons who act as co-owners of a business for profit. Each partner contributes money, property, labor, or skills, and each shares in the profits (as well as the losses) of the business.[20] Though not specifically required, written articles of partnership are usually executed and are always recommended. This is because, unless otherwise agreed to in writing, the courts assume equal partnership—that is, equal sharing of profits, losses, assets, management, and other aspects of the business.

The articles of partnership clearly outline the financial and managerial contributions of the partners and carefully delineate the roles in the partnership relationship, including such items as: duration of agreement; character of partners (general or limited, active or silent); division of profits and losses; salaries; death of a partner (dissolution and windup); authority (individual partner's authority on business conduct); settlement of disputes; and additions, alterations, or modifications of partnership.

In addition to the written articles, entrepreneurs must consider a number of different types of partnership arrangements. Depending on the needs of the enterprise, one or more of these may be used. Examples include the percentage of financial investment of each partner, the amount of managerial control of each partner, and the actual duties assigned to each partner. It is important to remember that, in a typical partnership arrangement, at least one partner must be a general partner who is responsible for the debts of the enterprise and who has unlimited liability.[21]

Advantages of Partnerships

The advantages associated with the partnership form of organization are as follows:

- *Ease of formation.* Legal formalities and expenses are few compared with those for creating a more complex enterprise, such as a corporation.
- *Direct rewards.* Partners are motivated to put forth their best efforts by direct sharing of the profits.
- *Growth and performance facilitated.* It often is possible to obtain more capital and a better range of skills in a partnership than in a sole proprietorship.
- *Flexibility.* A partnership often is able to respond quickly to business needs in the form of day-to-day decisions.
- *Relative freedom from governmental control and regulation.* Very little governmental interference occurs in the operation of a partnership.
- *Possible tax advantage.* Most partnerships pay taxes as individuals, thus escaping the higher rate assessed against corporations.

Disadvantages of Partnerships

Partnerships also have disadvantages. Some of these are as follows:

- *Unlimited liability of at least one partner.* Although some partners can have limited liability, at least one must be a general partner who assumes unlimited liability.

- *Lack of continuity.* If any partner dies, is adjudged insane, or simply withdraws from the business, the partnership arrangement ceases. However, operation of the business can continue based on the right of survivorship and the possible creation of a new partnership by the remaining members or by the addition of new members.

- *Relative difficulty obtaining large sums of capital.* Most partnerships have some problems raising a great deal of capital, especially when long-term financing is involved. Usually the collective wealth of the partners dictates the amount of total capital the partnership can raise, especially when first starting out.

- *Bound by the acts of just one partner.* A general partner can commit the enterprise to contracts and obligations that may prove disastrous to the enterprise in general and to the other partners in particular.

- *Difficulty of disposing of partnership interest.* The buyout of a partner may be difficult unless specifically arranged for in the written agreement.

Corporations

According to Supreme Court Justice John Marshall (1819), a corporation is "an artificial being, invisible, intangible, and existing only in contemplation of the law." As such, a corporation is a separate legal entity apart from the individuals who own it. A corporation is created by the authority of state laws and usually is formed when a transfer of money or property by prospective shareholders (owners) takes place in exchange for capital stock (ownership certificates) in the corporation.[22] The procedures ordinarily required to form a corporation are (1) subscriptions for capital stock must be taken and a tentative organization created, and (2) approval must be obtained from the secretary of state in the state in which the corporation is to be formed. This approval is in the form of a charter for the corporation, which states the powers and limitations of the particular enterprise. Corporations that do business in more than one state must comply with federal laws regarding interstate commerce and with the varying state laws that cover foreign (out-of-state) corporations.

Advantages of Corporations

Some of the advantages associated with corporations are as follows:

- *Limited liability.* The stockholder's liability is limited to the individual's investment. This is the most money the person can lose.

- *Transfer of ownership.* Ownership can be transferred through the sale of stock to interested buyers.

- *Unlimited life.* The company has a life separate and distinct from that of its owners and can continue for an indefinite period of time.

- *Relative ease of securing capital in large amounts.* Capital can be acquired through the issuance of bonds and shares of stock and through short-term loans made against the assets of the business or personal guarantees of the major stockholders.

- *Increased ability and expertise.* The corporation is able to draw on the expertise and skills of a number of individuals, ranging from the major stockholders to the professional managers who are brought on board.

Disadvantages of Corporations

Corporations also have disadvantages. Some of these are as follows:

- *Activity restrictions.* Corporate activities are limited by the charter and by various laws.
- *Lack of representation.* Minority stockholders are sometimes outvoted by the majority, who force their will on the others.
- *Regulation.* Extensive governmental regulations and reports required by local, state, and federal agencies often result in a great deal of paperwork and red tape.
- *Organizing expenses.* A multitude of expenses are involved in forming a corporation.
- *Double taxation.* Income taxes are levied both on corporate profits and on individual salaries and dividends.

Table 7.3 compares the characteristics of sole proprietorships, partnerships, and corporations.

---

the entrepreneurial process

Incorporating on the Web

Today, forming a corporation is easier than ever. Individuals who wish to form a corporation can simply access the services of one of the many companies that provide online incorporation services. Although one has always been able to incorporate in states outside of his or her residence, online incorporation service providers have made this process much more simple. Delaware has been the favorite of many out-of-state incorporations over the past several years. This is due, in large part, to the state's limited restrictions on the formation and operation of corporations.

Web Incorporation Firms

Hundreds of firms offer online incorporation services, and most of these firms offer a very simple process for incorporation in any state. Most of these sites also offer valuable information, such as the various forms of corporation and the positives and negatives of the different options, FAQs on incorporation, the cost of incorporation and maintenance of a corporation, and advantages and disadvantages of incorporation. Harvard Business Services (http://www.delawareinc.com), The Company Corporation (http://www.incorporate.com), and American Incorporators Ltd. (http://www.ailcorp.com)

are a few examples of these online incorporation firms. Entrepreneurs also can simply search using a search engine by typing in the word "incorporation" to locate other online incorporation firms.

Considerations for the Entrepreneur

The entrepreneur must consider the future of the business that he or she wishes to incorporate. In most cases, online incorporation is fine for individuals who are interested in starting smaller businesses with limited growth potential, but other avenues are recommended for entrepreneurs who plan to start a business with higher growth potential. If high growth is possible and large amounts of funding is likely necessary, then entrepreneurs are recommended to seek legal counsel through the process of incorporation.

How to Incorporate on the Web

In most cases, filing for incorporation on the Web is as simple as filling out an online incorporation form on one of these firm's Web sites. The firms then take this information and file the necessary forms at the state office in which the entrepreneur wishes to incorporate. The given state will then issue a certificate of incorporation.

Table 7.3 General Characteristics of Forms of Business

	Sole Proprietorship	Partnership	Limited Liability Partnership	Limited Partnership	Limited Liability Limited Partnership	Corporation	S Corporation	Limited Liability Company
Formation	When one person owns a business without forming a corporation or LLC	By agreement of owners or by default when two or more owners conduct business together without forming a limited partnership, an LLC, or a corporation	By agreement of owners; must comply with limited liability partnership statute	By agreement of owners; must comply with limited partnership statute	By agreement of owners; must comply with limited liability limited partnership statute	By agreement of owners; must comply with corporation statute	By agreement of owners; must comply with corporation state; must elect S Corporation status under Subchapter S of Internal Revenue Code	By agreement of owners; must comply with limited liability company statute
Duration	Terminates on death or withdrawal of sole proprietor	Usually unaffected by death or withdrawal of partner	Unaffected by death or withdrawal of partner	Unaffected by death or withdrawal of partner, unless sole general partner dissociates	Unaffected by death or withdrawal of partner, unless sole general partner dissociates	Unaffected by death or withdrawal of shareholder	Unaffected by death or withdrawal of shareholder	Usually unaffected by death or withdrawal of member
Management	By sole proprietor	By partners	By partners	By general partners	By general partners	By board of directors	By board of directors	By managers or members

(Continued)

Table 7.3 General Characteristics of Forms of Business (Continued)

	Sole Proprietorship	Partnership	Limited Liability Partnership	Limited Partnership	Limited Liability Limited Partnership	Corporation	S Corporation	Limited Liability Company
Owner Liability	Unlimited	Unlimited	Mostly limited to capital contribution	Unlimited for general partners; limited to capital contribution for limited partners	Limited to capital contribution	Limited to capital contribution	Limited to capital contribution	Limited to capital contribution
Transferability of Owners' Interest	None	None	None	None, unless agreed otherwise	None, unless agreed otherwise	Freely transferable, although shareholders may agree otherwise	Freely transferable, although shareholders usually agree otherwise	None, unless agreed otherwise
Federal Income Taxation	Only sole proprietor taxed	Only partners taxed	Usually only partners taxed; may elect to be taxed like a corporation	Usually only partners taxed; may elect to be taxed like a corporation	Usually only partners taxed; may elect to be taxed like a corporation	Corporation taxed; shareholders taxed on dividends (double tax)	Only shareholders taxed	Usually only members taxed; may elect to be taxed like a corporation

Source: Jane P. Mallor, A. James Barnes, Thomas Bowers, and Arlen W. Langvardt, *Business Law: The Ethical, Global, and E-Commerce Environment,* 13th ed. (New York: McGraw-Hill Irwin, 2007), 897.

Specific Forms of Partnerships and Corporations

A number of specific forms of partnerships and corporations warrant special attention. The following sections examine these.

Limited Partnerships

Limited partnerships are used in situations where a form of organization is needed that permits capital investment without responsibility for management *and* without liability for losses beyond the initial investment. Such an organization allows the right to share in the profits with limited liability for the losses.

Limited partnerships are governed by the Revised Uniform Limited Partnership Act (RULPA).[23] The act contains 11 articles and 64 sections of guidelines covering areas such as (1) general provisions, (2) formation, (3) limited partners, (4) general partners, (5) finance, (6) distributions and withdrawals, (7) assignment of partnership interest, (8) dissolution, (9) foreign limited partnerships, (10) derivative actions, and (11) miscellaneous. If a limited partnership appears to be the desired legal form of organization, the prospective partners must examine these RULPA guidelines.

Limited Liability Partnerships

The limited liability partnership (LLP) is a relatively new form of partnership that allows professionals the tax benefits of a partnership while avoiding personal liability for the malpractice of other partners. If a professional group organizes as an LLP, innocent partners are not personally liable for the wrongdoing of the other partners.

The LLP is similar to the *limited liability company (LLC)* discussed later. The difference is that LLPs are designed more for professionals who normally do business as a partnership. As with limited liability companies, LLPs must be formed and operated in compliance with state statutes.

One of the reasons why LLPs are becoming so popular among professionals is that most statutes make it relatively easy to establish an LLP. This is particularly true for an already formal partnership. For example, to become an LLP in Texas, all a partnership must do is fulfill the following requirements:

1. File the appropriate form with the secretary of state

2. Pay an annual fee of $200 per partner

3. Maintain at least $100,000 in professional liability insurance

4. Add either "LLP" or "Registered Limited Liability Partnership" to its name

Converting from a partnership to an LLP also is easy because the firm's basic organizational structure remains the same. Additionally, all of the statutory and common-law rules governing partnerships still apply (apart from those modified by the LLP statute). Normally, LLP statutes are simply amendments to a state's already existing partnership law.[24]

The limited liability limited partnership (LLLP) is a relatively new variant of the limited partnership. An LLLP has elected limited liability status for all of its partners, including general partners. Except for this liability status of general partners, limited partnerships and LLLPs are identical (see Table 7.4 for characteristics of limited partnerships and LLLPs).

S Corporations

Formerly termed a Subchapter S corporation, the S corporation takes its name from Subchapter S of the Internal Revenue Code, under which a business can seek to avoid the imposition of income taxes at the corporate level yet retain some of the benefits of a corporate form (especially the limited liability).

Table 7.4	Principal Characteristics of Limited Partnerships and LLLPs

1. A limited partnership or LLLP may be *created only in accordance with a statute.*

2. A limited partnership or LLLP has two types of partners: *general partners* and *limited partners.* It must have one or more of each type.

3. All partners, limited and general, *share the profits* of the business.

4. Each limited partner has liability *limited to his capital contribution* to the business. Each general partner of a limited partnership has *unlimited liability* for the obligations of the business. A general partner in an LLLP, however, has liability *limited to his capital contribution.*

5. Each general partner has a *right to manage* the business, and she is an agent of the limited partnership or LLLP. A limited partner has *no right to manage* the business or to act as its agent, but he does have the right to vote on fundamental matters. A limited partner may manage the business yet retain limited liability for partnership obligations.

6. General partners, as agents, are *fiduciaries* of the business. Limited partners are not fiduciaries.

7. A partner's rights in a limited partnership or LLLP *are not freely transferable.* A transferee of a general or limited partnership interest in not a partner, but is entitled only to the transferring partner's share of capital and profits.

8. The death or other withdrawal of a partner does not dissolve a limited partnership or LLLP, unless there is no surviving general partner.

9. Usually, a limited partnership or LLLP is taxed like a partnership.

Source: Adapted from Jane P. Mallor, A. James Barnes, Thomas Bowers, and Arlen W. Langvardt, *Business Law: The Ethical, Global, and E-Commerce Environment,* 13 ed. (New York: McGraw-Hill Irwin, 2007), 953.

Commonly known as a "tax option corporation," an S corporation is taxed similarly to a partnership. Only an information form is filed with the IRS to indicate the shareholders' income. In this manner, the double-taxation problem of corporations is avoided. Corporate income is not taxed but instead flows to the personal income of shareholders of businesses and is taxable at that point.

Although this is very useful for small businesses, strict guidelines must be followed:

1. The corporation must be a domestic corporation.

2. The corporation must not be a member of an affiliated group of corporations.

3. The shareholders of the corporation must be individuals, estates, or certain trusts. Corporations, partnerships, and nonqualifying trusts cannot be shareholders.

4. The corporation must have 100 or fewer shareholders.

5. The corporation must have only one class of stock, although not all shareholders need have the same voting rights.

6. No shareholder of the corporation may be a nonresident alien.

BENEFITS FROM ELECTING S CORPORATIONS

The S corporation offers a number of benefits. For example, when the corporation has losses, Subchapter S allows the shareholders to use these losses to offset taxable income. Also, when the stockholders are in a tax bracket lower than that of the corporation, Subchapter S causes the company's entire income to be taxed in the shareholders' bracket, whether or not it is distributed. This is particularly attractive when the corporation wants to accumulate earnings for future business purposes.

The taxable income of an S corporation is taxable only to those who are shareholders at the end of the corporate year when that income is distributed. The S corporation can choose a fiscal year that will permit it to defer some of its shareholders' taxes. This is important because undistributed earnings are not taxed to the shareholders until after the corporation's (not the shareholders') fiscal year. In addition, the shareholder in an S corporation can give some of his or her stock to other members of the family who are in a lower tax bracket. Additionally, up to six generations of one family may elect to be treated as one shareholder. Finally, an S corporation can offer some tax-free corporate benefits. These benefits typically mean federal tax savings to the shareholders.

Limited Liability Companies

Since 1977, an increasing number of states have authorized a new form of business organization called the limited liability company (LLC). The LLC is a hybrid form of business enterprise that offers the limited liability of a corporation but the tax advantages of a partnership.

A major advantage of the LLC is that it does not pay taxes on an entity; rather, profits are "passed through" the LLC and paid personally by company members. Another advantage is that the liability of members is limited to the amount of their investments. In an LLC, members are allowed to participate fully in management activities, and—under at least one state's statute—the firm's managers need not even be LLC members. Yet another advantage is that corporations and partnerships, as well as foreign investors, can be LLC members. Also, no limit exists on the number of LLC shareholder members.

The disadvantages of the LLC are relatively few. Perhaps the greatest disadvantage is that LLC statutes differ from state to state, and thus any firm engaged in multistate operations may face difficulties. In an attempt to promote some uniformity among the states in respect to LLC statutes, the National Conference of Commissioners on Uniform State Laws drafted a uniform limited liability company statute for submission to the states to consider for adoption. Until all of the states have adopted the uniform law, however, an LLC in one state will have to check the rules in the other states in which the firm does business to ensure that it retains its limited liability.[25]

Final Thoughts on Legal Forms

As mentioned earlier, an entrepreneur always should seek professional legal advice to avoid misunderstandings, mistakes and, of course, added expenses. The average entrepreneur encounters many diverse problems and stumbling blocks in venture formation. Because he or she does not have a thorough knowledge of law, accounting, real estate, taxes, and governmental regulations, an understanding of certain basic concepts in these areas is imperative.

The material in this chapter is a good start toward understanding the legal forms of organizations. It can provide entrepreneurs with guidelines for seeking further and more specific advice on the legal form that appears most applicable to their situation.

Understanding Bankruptcy

Bankruptcy occurs when a venture's financial obligations are greater than its assets. No entrepreneur intentionally seeks bankruptcy. Although problems occasionally can arise out of the blue, following are several ways to foresee impending failure: (1) New competition enters the market, (2) other firms seem to be selling products that are a generation ahead, (3) the research and development budget is proportionately less than the competition's, and (4) retailers always seem to be overstocked.[26]

The Bankruptcy Act

The Bankruptcy Act is a federal law that provides for specific procedures to handle insolvent debtors—those who are unable to pay debts as they become due. The initial act of 1912 was amended in 1938 and then completely revised in 1978; significant amendments were added in 1984. The purposes of the Bankruptcy Act are (1) to ensure that the property of the debtor is distributed fairly to the creditors, (2) to protect creditors from having debtors unreasonably diminish their assets, and (3) to protect debtors from extreme demands by creditors. The law was set up to provide assistance to both debtors and creditors.

Each of the various types of bankruptcy proceedings has its own particular provisions. For purposes of business ventures, the three major sections are called straight bankruptcy (Chapter 7), reorganization (Chapter 11), and adjustment of debts (Chapter 7). Table 7.5 provides a comparison of these three types of bankruptcies. The following sections examine each type.

Chapter 7: Straight Bankruptcy

Chapter 7 bankruptcy, sometimes referred to as **liquidation**, requires the debtor to surrender all property to a trustee appointed by the court. The trustee then sells the assets and turns the proceeds over to the creditors. The remaining debts (with certain exceptions) are then discharged, and the debtor is relieved of his or her obligations.

Table **7.5**	Bankruptcy: A Comparison of Chapters 7, 11, and 13		
	Chapter 7	**Chapter 11**	**Chapter 13**
Purpose	Liquidation	Reorganization	Adjustment
Who Can Petition	Debtor (voluntary) or creditors (involuntary)	Debtor (voluntary) or creditors (involuntary)	Debtor (voluntary) only
Who Can Be a Debtor	Any "person" (including partnerships and corporations) except railroads, insurance companies, banks, savings and loan institutions, and credit unions. Farmers and charitable institutions cannot be involuntarily petitioned.	Any debtor eligible for Chapter 7 relief; railroads are also eligible.	Any individual (not partnerships or corporations) with regular income who owes fixed unsecured debt of less than $290,525 or secured debt of less than $871,550.
Procedure Leading to Discharge	Nonexempt property is sold with proceeds to be distributed (in order) to priority groups. Dischargeable debts are terminated.	A plan is submitted and, if it is approved and followed, debts are discharged.	A plan is submitted (must be approved if debtor turns over disposable income for three-year period) and, if it is approved and followed, debts are discharged.
Advantages	On liquidation and distribution, most debts are discharged, and the debtor has an opportunity for a fresh start.	The debtor continues in business. Creditors can accept the plan, or it can be "crammed down" on them. The plan allows for a reorganization and liquidation of debts over the plan period.	The debtor continues in business or keeps possession of assets. If the plan is approved, most debts are discharged after a three-year period.

Source: Roger LeRoy Miller and Gaylord A. Jentz, *Fundamentals of Business Law,* 6th ed. (Mason, OH: South-Western/ Cengage Learning, http://permission.cengage.com/permissions/action/start, 2005), 438. Reprinted with permission.

A liquidation proceeding may be voluntary or involuntary. In a voluntary bankruptcy, the debtor files a petition with the bankruptcy court that provides a list of all creditors, a statement of financial affairs, a list of all owned property, and a list of current income and expenses. In an involuntary bankruptcy, the creditors force the debtor into bankruptcy. For this to occur, 12 or more creditors (of which at least 3 have a total of $5,000 of claims) must exist; if fewer than 12 exist, 1 or more creditors must have a claim of $5,000 against the debtor.[27]

Chapter 11: Reorganization

Reorganization is the most common form of bankruptcy. Under this format, a debtor attempts to formulate a plan to pay a portion of the debts, have the remaining sum discharged, and continue to stay in operation. The plan is essentially a contract between the debtor and creditors. In addition to being viewed as "fair and equitable," the plan must (1) divide the creditors into classes, (2) set forth how each creditor will be satisfied, (3) state which claims or classes of claims are impaired or adversely affected by the plan, and (4) provide the same treatment to each creditor in a particular class.

The same basic principles that govern Chapter 7 bankruptcy petitions also govern the Chapter 11 petitions. The proceedings may be either voluntary or involuntary, and the provisions for protection and discharge are similar to the Chapter 7 regulations.

Once an order for relief (the petition) is filed, the debtor in a Chapter 11 proceeding continues to operate the business as a **debtor-in-possession**, which means that the court appoints a trustee to oversee the management of the business. The plan is then submitted to the creditors for approval. Approval generally requires that creditors holding two-thirds of the amount and one-half of the number of each class of claims impaired by the plan must accept it. Once approved, the plan goes before the court for confirmation. If the plan is confirmed, the debtor is responsible for carrying it out.[28]

Once the plan is confirmed by the creditors, it is binding for the debtor. This type of bankruptcy provides an alternative to liquidating the entire business and thus extends to the creditors and debtor the benefits of keeping the enterprise in operation.

Chapter 13: Adjustment of Debts

Under this arrangement, individuals are allowed to (1) avoid a declaration of bankruptcy, (2) pay their debts in installments, and (3) be protected by the federal court. Individuals or sole proprietors with unsecured debts of less than $100,000 or secured debts of less than $350,000 are eligible to file under a Chapter 13 procedure. This petition must be voluntary only; creditors are not allowed to file a Chapter 13 proceeding. In the petition, the debtor declares an inability to pay his or her debts and requests some form of extension through future earnings (longer period of time to pay) or a composition of debt (reduction in the amount owed).

The individual debtor then files a plan providing the details for treatment of the debts. A Chapter 13 plan must provide for (1) the turnover of such future earnings or income of the debtor to the trustee as is necessary for execution of the plan, (2) full payment in deferred cash payments of all claims entitled to priority, and (3) the same treatment of each claim within a particular class (although the 1984 amendments permit the debtor to list co-debtors, such as guarantors or sureties, as a separate class).[29] The plan must provide for payment within three years unless the court specifically grants an extension to five years.

Once the debtor has completed all scheduled payments scheduled, the court will issue a discharge of all other debts provided for in the plan. As always, some exceptions to the discharge exist, such as child support and certain long-term debts. In addition, the debtor can be discharged even though he or she does not complete the payments within the three years if the court is satisfied that the failure is due to circumstances for which the debtor cannot justly be held accountable. During a Chapter 13 proceeding, no other bankruptcy petition (Chapter 7 or 11) may be filed against the debtor. Thus, an individual has an opportunity to relieve a debt situation without liquidation or the stigma of bankruptcy. In addition, the creditors may benefit by recovering a larger percentage than they would through a liquidation.

the global perspective

The Other Side of the Outsourcing Conundrum

Outsourcing work overseas has become a highly politicized subject in the United States. Countless manufacturing jobs have been lost as domestic operations are shuttled and reestablished in foreign countries. The side of the topic that is rarely discussed is the dependence of domestic companies on technical workers who provide services that would otherwise be unavailable. For those organizations, federal regulations introduced to provide barriers to the loss of domestic jobs are counterproductive.

H-1B visas, the documents needed for foreign workers to be employed temporarily in the United States, have become increasingly more difficult to get. In turn, entrepreneurs who depend on highly technical workers are now having trouble finding people with the skills they need. This situation has led entrepreneurs to lobby Congress to raise the number of H-1B visas issued. Ironically, their argument is that such measures will improve the economy. Proponents suggest that speeding the delivery of green cards to highly skilled workers already in the United States will help to remedy the situation.

Although governors from 13 states are considering the issue, not everyone supports the H-1B program. Domestic technology workers argue that the real issue at hand is not losing highly skilled workers from overseas to foreign competitors but rather that it is an attempt to lower the wages of current domestic employees by flooding the market with talent. Some domestic employers also oppose the program, suggesting that efforts by competition to employ foreign workers will force them to offer lower salaries for existing employees in order to remain competitive.

On the first day of the H-1B application filing period for 2008, the U.S. Citizen and Immigration Services (USCIS) received over 130,000 applications, requiring the agency to enter all applications into a lottery. The current cap of 65,000 visas was set by Congress in 1990 and was temporarily raised to 195,000 from 2001 to 2003; however, it has since returned to the set number of 65,000. Because American-born workers have not sought out the technical skills required for the positions that need to be filled, the gap between supply and demand has continued to widen.

As a result of the depleted technical workforce in the United States, the lack of visas for foreign workers, and the steep costs of opening satellite offices overseas in order to employ cheaper, highly skilled workers directly in their home countries, new ventures certainly will be the most affected by the labor shortage. Unless there is a shift in federal policies toward allowing more foreign workers into the United States or an increase in domestic employees' interest in obtaining the necessary technical skills, small businesses will be ineffective when trying to compete on a global scale.

Adapted from Eilene Zimmerman, "Wanted: Foreign Tech Workers," *Fortune Small Business*, September 26, 2007, http://money.cnn.com/2007/09/25/smbusiness/h1b_cap.fsb/index.htm (accessed March 30, 2008).

Keeping Legal Expenses Down

Throughout any legal proceedings, the entrepreneur can run up large legal bills. Following are some suggestions for minimizing these expenses:

- Establish a clear fee structure with an attorney before any legal matters are handled. This structure may be based on an hourly charge, a flat fee (straight contract fee), or a contingent fee (percentage of negotiated settlement).
- Attorneys also operate in a competitive environment; thus, fee structures are negotiable.

- Establish clear written agreements on all critical matters that affect business operations, including agreements between principals, employment agreements, confidentiality agreements, and noncompete agreements.
- Always attempt to settle any dispute rather than litigate.
- Have your attorney share forms in electronic format that you can use in routine transactions.
- Use a less expensive attorney for smaller transactions.
- Suggest cost-saving methods to your attorney for ordinary business matters.
- Always check with your attorney during normal business hours.
- Client inefficiency rewards attorneys: Consult with your attorney on several matters at one time.
- Keep abreast of legal developments in your field.
- Handle matters within your "comfort zone" yourself.
- Involve attorneys early on when it is feasible: An ounce of prevention is worth a pound of cure.
- Shop around, but don't attorney-hop. Once you find a good attorney, stick with that person. An attorney who is familiar with your business can handle your affairs much more efficiently than a succession of attorneys, each of whom must research your case from scratch.[30]

Summary

A patent is an intellectual property right that is a result of a unique discovery. Patent holders are provided protection against infringement by others. This protection lasts for 14 years in the case of design patents and for 20 years in all other cases.

Securing a patent can be a complex process, and careful planning is required. Some of the useful rules to follow in acquiring a patent were set forth in this chapter.

A patent may be declared invalid for several reasons: failure to assert the property right for an unreasonable length of time, misuse of the patent, and inability to prove that the patent meets patentability tests. On the other hand, if a patent is valid, the owner can prevent others from infringing on it; if they do infringe on it, the owner can bring legal action to prevent the infringement as well as, in some cases, obtain financial damages.

A copyright provides exclusive rights to creative individuals for the protection of their literary or artistic productions. This protection lasts for the life of the author plus 70 years. In case of infringement, the author (or whoever holds the copyright) can initiate a lawsuit for infringement. This action can result in an end to the infringement and, in some cases, the awarding of financial damages.

A trademark is a distinctive name, mark, symbol, or motto identified with a company's product(s). When an organization registers a trademark, it has the exclusive right to use that mark. Registration acquired before 1989 lasts for 20 years. However, after 1989, registration lasts for 10 years and is renewable every 10 years thereafter. In case of infringement, the trademark holder can seek legal action and damages.

This chapter examined the three major forms of legal organization: sole proprietorship, partnership, and corporation. The advantages and disadvantages of each form were highlighted and compared. In addition, the characteristics and tax considerations of partnerships were compared with those of corporations.

The specific forms of partnerships and corporations were examined. In particular, the requirements and benefits of limited partnerships, limited liability partnerships, S corporations, and limited liability companies were presented.

During the last two decades, numerous business failures have occurred. Three major sections of the Bankruptcy Act are of importance to entrepreneurs. Chapter 7 deals with straight bankruptcy and calls for a liquidation of all assets to satisfy outstanding debts. Chapter 11 deals with reorganization, a format wherein a business continues operating and attempts to formulate a plan to pay a portion of the debts, to have the remaining sum discharged, and to continue to pay the debt in installments. Chapter 13 deals with individual debtors who file a plan for adjustment of their debts. This would apply to sole proprietorships because they are individually owned. More business bankruptcies are handled under Chapter 11 than under the other two sections.

Key Terms and Concepts

abandonment

bankruptcy

Bankruptcy Act

cancellation proceedings

claims

cleaning-out procedure

copyright

corporation

debtor-in-possession

fair use doctrine

generic meaning

infringement budget

insolvent debtors

intellectual property right

limited liability company (LLC)

limited liability limited partnership (LLLP)

limited liability partnership (LLP)

limited partnership

liquidation

partnership

patent

Patent and Trademark Office

Revised Uniform Limited Partnership Act (RULPA)

S corporation

sole proprietorship

specification

trademark

trade secrets

unlimited liability

Review and Discussion Questions

1. In your own words, what is a patent? Of what value is a patent to an entrepreneur? What benefits does it provide?

2. What are four basic rules entrepreneurs should remember about securing a patent?

3. When can a patent be declared invalid? Cite two examples.

4. In your own words, what is a copyright? What benefits does a copyright provide?

5. How much protection does a copyright afford the owner? Can any of the individual's work be copied without paying a fee? Explain in detail. If an infringement of the copyright occurs, what legal recourse does the owner have?

6. In your own words, what is a trademark? Why are generic or descriptive names or words not given trademarks?

7. When may a trademark be invalidated? Explain.

8. What are three of the pitfalls individuals should avoid when seeking a trademark?

9. Identify the legal forms available for entrepreneurs structuring their ventures: sole proprietorship, partnership, and corporation.

10. What are the specific advantages and disadvantages associated with each primary legal form of organization?

11. What is the ULPA? Describe it.

12. Explain the limited liability partnership.

13. What is the nature of an S corporation? List five requirements for such a corporation.

14. What is a limited liability company?

15. How can an entrepreneur find out if the business is going bankrupt? What are three early warning signs?

16. What type of protection does Chapter 7 offer to a bankrupt entrepreneur?

17. What type of protection does Chapter 11 offer to a bankrupt entrepreneur? Why do many people prefer Chapter 11 to Chapter 7?

18. What type of protection does Chapter 13 offer to a bankrupt entrepreneur? How does Chapter 13 differ from Chapter 7 or Chapter 11?

Experiential Exercises

PROTECTING YOUR LEGAL INTERESTS

Entrepreneurs need to know how to legally protect their interests in a property or work. The most effective way to gain legal protection is to obtain a copyright or a trademark. Two definitions are given here. Place a *C* next to the one that defines a copyright; place a *T* next to the one that defines a trademark. Then, on the list that follows (a. through j.), place a *C* next to each item that could be protected with a copyright and a *T* next to each item that could be protected with a trademark. Answers are provided at the end of the exercise.

1. _____ A distinctive name, mark, symbol, or motto identified with a company's product

2. _____ An exclusive protection of a literary or an artistic production

    a. _____ Best-selling novel

    b. _____ Logo

    c. _____ Company's initials (such as IBM or ITT)

    d. _____ Motion picture

    e. _____ Word (such as *Coke* or *Pepsi*)

    f. _____ Computer program

    g. _____ Musical comedy

    h. _____ Slogan

    i. _____ Stage play

    j. _____ Symbol

Answers: 1. T; 2. C; a. C; b. T; c. T; d. C; e. T; f. C; g. C; h. T; i. C; j. T

GETTING IT RIGHT

The following list of advantages and disadvantages is associated with sole proprietorships, partnerships, and corporations. Place an *S* next to those that relate to sole proprietorships, a *P* next to those that relate to partnerships, and a *C* next to those that relate to corporations. If the advantage or disadvantage applies to more than one type of organizational form, put all answers on the accompanying line. Answers are provided at the end of the exercise.

Advantages	Disadvantages
1. Limited liability _____	1. Unlimited liability _____
2. Sole ownership of profits _____	2. Governmental regulation _____
3. Unlimited life _____	3. Lack of continuity _____
4. Ease of formation _____	4. Double taxation _____
5. Flexibility _____	5. Difficulty obtaining large sums of capital _____
6. Transfer of ownership _____	6. Organizing expenses _____
7. Relative freedom from governmental control _____	7. Relatively limited viewpoint and experience _____
8. Increased ability and expertise _____	8. Activity restrictions _____

Answers: Advantages: 1. C; 2. S; 3. C; 4. S, P; 5. S, P; 6. C; 7. S, P; 8. C
Disadvantages: 1. S, P; 2. C; 3. S, P; 4. C; 5. S, P; 6. C; 7. S; 8. C

Case 7.1

A PATENT MATTER

Technological breakthroughs in the machine industry are commonplace. Thus, whenever one company announces a new development, some of the first customers are that company's competitors. The latter will purchase the machine, strip it down, examine the new technology, and then look for ways to improve it. The original breakthroughs always are patented by the firm that discovers them, even though the technology is soon surpassed.

A few weeks ago, Tom Farrington completed the development of a specialized lathe machine that is 25 percent faster and 9 percent more efficient than anything currently on the market. This technological breakthrough was a result of careful analysis of competitive products. "Until I saw some of the latest developments in the field," Tom told his wife, "I didn't realize how easy it would be to increase the speed and efficiency of the machine. But once I saw the competition's products, I knew immediately how to proceed."

Tom has shown his machine to five major firms in the industry, and all have placed orders with him. Tom has little doubt that he will make a great deal of money from his invention. Before beginning production, however, Tom intends to get a patent on his invention. He believes his machine is so much more sophisticated and complex than any other machine on the market that it will take his competitors at least four years to develop a better product. "By that time, I hope to have improved on my invention and to continue to remain ahead of them," he noted.

Tom has talked to an attorney about filing for a patent. The attorney believes that Tom should answer two questions before proceeding: (1) How long will it take the competition to improve on your patent? (2) How far are you willing to go to defend your patent right? Part of the attorney's comments were as follows: "It will take us about three years to get a patent. If, during this time, the competition is able to come out with something that is better than what you have, we will have wasted a lot of time and effort. The patent will have little value because no one will be interested in using it. Since some of your first sales will be to the competition, this is something to which you have to give serious thought. Second, even if it takes four years for the competition to catch up, would you be interested in fighting those who copy your invention after, say, two years? Simply put, we can get you a patent, but I'm not sure it will provide you as much protection as you think."

QUESTIONS

1. Given the nature of the industry, how valuable will a patent be to Tom? Explain.

2. If Tom does get a patent, can he bring action against infringers? Will it be worth the time and expense? Why or why not?

3. What do you think Tom should do? Why?

Case 7.2

A QUESTION OF INCORPORATION

The Harlow family opened its first motel in 1992. Initially, business was slow. It took almost 11 months to break even and three years for the Harlows to feel that the operation was going to be a success. They stuck with it, and by 1997 they were able to increase the size of the motel from 28 to 50 rooms. They expanded again in 1999, this time to 100 rooms. In each case, the motel's occupancy rate was so high that the Harlows had to turn people away during the months of April to September, and the occupancy rate was 85 percent during the other months. By industry standards, their business was one of the most successful motels in the country.

As they entered the 2000s, Harold and Becky Harlow decided that, rather than expanding, they would be better off buying another motel, perhaps in a nearby locale. They chose to hire someone to run their current operation and spend most of their time at the new location until they had it running properly. In 2002, they made their purchase. Like their first motel, the second location was an overwhelming success within a few years. From then on, the Harlows bought a number of new motels. By 2008, they had seven motels with an average of 100 rooms per unit.

During all of this time, Becky and Harold kept their own financial records, bringing in a certified public accountant only once a year to close the books and prepare their income tax returns. Last week, the new accountant asked them how long they intended to keep running seven motels. The Harlows told him that they enjoyed the operation and hoped to keep at it for another ten years, when they planned to sell out and retire.

Harold admitted that trying to keep all of the motels going at the same time was difficult but noted that he had some excellent managers working for him. The accountant asked him whether he would consider incorporating. "If you incorporate," he said, "you could sell stock and use the money to buy more motels. Additionally, you could keep some of the stock for yourself so you could maintain control of the operation, sell some for expansion purposes, and sell the rest to raise some money you can put aside in a savings account or some conservative investment. That way, if things go bad, you still will have a nest egg built up." The accountant also explained to Harold and Becky that, as a partnership, they currently are responsible for all business debts. With a corporation, they would have limited liability; that is, if the corporation failed, the creditors could not sue them for their personal assets. In this way, their assets would be protected, so the money Harold would get for selling the stock would be safely tucked away.

The Harlows admitted that they had never really considered another form of organization. They always assumed that a partnership was the best form for them. Now they are willing to examine the benefits of a corporation, and they will go ahead and incorporate their business if this approach promises them greater advantages.

QUESTIONS

1. What are the advantages and disadvantages of a partnership?

2. Contrast the advantages and disadvantages of a partnership with those of a corporation.

3. Provide your opinion on whether the Harlows should incorporate.

4. Would the LLC option be of value to them? Explain.

Case 7.3

ALL SHE NEEDS IS A LITTLE BREATHING ROOM

When Debbie Dawson started her business 12 months ago, she estimated that it would be profitable within 8 months. That is not what happened. During the first 6 months, she lost $18,000; during the next 6 months, she lost an additional $14,000. Debbie believes that the business is going to get better during the next 6 months and that she will be able to break even by the end of the second year. However, her creditors are not sure. Debbie's business owes the two largest creditors a total of $48,000. The others are owed a total of $38,000.

Debbie believes that, if she can postpone paying her creditors for a period of one year, her company will be strong enough to pay off all of its debts. On the other hand, if she has to pay the creditors now, she will be too weak financially to continue and will have to declare bankruptcy. "I really think it's in everyone's best interest to give me 12 months of breathing room," she explained to her husband. "If they will do this, everyone is going to come out on top. Otherwise, we are all going to take a financial bath."

Debbie has considered broaching the subject with her two major creditors. However, she is not sure whether this suggestion would be accepted or would be used as a basis for their bringing legal action against her. "If they think I am trying to stall them, they just might demand repayment immediately and force me into bankruptcy," she explained to a close friend. "Of course, if they see things my way, that's a different story. In any event, I'm reluctant to pursue this line of action without talking to my attorney."

Debbie hopes she and her attorney, Juan, can work out a plan of action that will prevent her from having to declare bankruptcy and liquidate the firm. During her phone call to set up a meeting with Juan, she comments, "If everyone remains calm and looks the situation over very carefully, I think they'll agree that my suggestion is a good one. After all, I'm not asking them to put any more money in the business, so the most they can lose is what they are owed currently. On the other hand, if they force my hand, they'll probably be lucky to get 40 cents on the dollar. If they wait, they could end up with all of their money. All I'm asking for is a little breathing room." Juan suggests that they meet later in the week to talk about it. "I'm sure we can think of something," he tells her.

QUESTIONS

1. What type of bankruptcy agreement would you recommend? Why?

2. Why would you not recommend the other types of bankruptcy? Be complete in your answer.

3. When selling the creditors on your recommendation, what argument(s) would you use?

Notes

1. Marianne M. Jennings, *Business: Its Legal, Ethical, and Global Environment,* 7th ed., (Mason, OH: South-Western/Cengage Learning, 2006).

2. See Constance E. Bagley and Craig E. Dauchy, *The Entrepreneur's Guide to Business Law,* (Mason, OH: South-Western/Cengage Learning, 2003).

3. Reprinted by permission of the *Harvard Business Review.* An excerpt from "Making Patents Work for Small Companies," by Ronald D. Rothchild, July/August 1987, 24–30. Copyright © 1987 by the President and Fellows of Harvard College; all rights reserved.

4. Ibid., 28.

5. Gaylord A. Jentz, Roger LeRoy Miller, and Frank B. Cross, *West's Business Law,* 10th ed. (Mason, OH: South-Western/Cengage Learning, 2007), 131–36.

6. See Jane P. Mallor, A. James Barnes, Thomas Bowers, and Arlen W. Langvardt, *Business Law: The Ethical, Global, and E-Commerce Environment,* 13th ed. (New York: McGraw-Hill Irwin, 2007), 234–38.

7. Ibid., 238–50.

8. Ibid., 246.

9. Jentz et al., *West's Business Law,* 134–35.

10. See Thomas G. Field, Jr., *Trademarks and Business Goodwill* (Washington, DC: Office of Business Development, Small Business Administration, 1990).

11. Dorothy Cohen, "Trademark Strategy," *Journal of Marketing* (January 1986): 61–74.

12. Jentz et al., *West's Business Law,* 128.

13. Thomas M. S. Hemnes, "How Can You Find a Safe Trademark?" *Harvard Business Review* (March/April 1985): 40–48; see also Michael Finn, "Everything You Need to Know about Trademarks and Publishing," *Publishers Weekly* (January 6, 1992): 41–44.

14. Jentz et al., *West's Business Law,* 137.

15. See Jane P. Mallor, A. James Barnes, Thomas Bowers, and Arlen W. Langvardt, *Business Law: The Ethical, Global, and E-Commerce Environment,* 12th ed. (New York: McGraw-Hill Irwin, 2004).

16. Jentz et al., *West's Business Law,* 544–63.

17. David S. Hulse and Thomas R. Pope, "The Effect of Income Taxes on the Preference of Organizational Form for Small Businesses in the United States," *Journal of Small Business Management* 34, no. 1 (1996): 24–35. See also Sandra Malach, Peter Robinson, and Tannis Radcliffe, "Differentiating Legal Issues by Business Type," *Journal of Small Business Management,* 44, no. 4 (2006): 563–76.

18. For a detailed discussion of each form, see Kenneth W. Clarkson, Roger LeRoy Miller, Gaylord A. Jentz, and Frank B. Cross, *West's Business Law,* 9th ed. (Mason, OH: South-Western/Cengage Learning, 2004), 615–737.

19. For further discussion on the legal aspects of proprietorships, see Gaylord A. Jentz, Roger LeRoy Miller, and Frank B. Cross, *West's Business Law,* 10th ed. (Mason, OH: South-Western/Cengage Learning, 2007), 652.

20. For a good analysis of partnerships, see Roger LeRoy Miller and Gaylord A. Jentz, *Business Law Today* (Mason, OH: South-Western/Cengage Learning, 2006); see also Jentz et al., *West's Business Law,* 10th ed., 663–83.

21. For the complete Revised Uniform Partnership Act, see Jentz et al., *West's Business Law,* 10th ed., A203–A212.

22. For a detailed discussion of corporate laws and regulations, see Mallor et al., *Business Law: The Ethical, Global, and E-Commerce Environment,* 13th ed., 968–1286.

23. For the complete Revised Uniform Partnership Act, see Jentz et al., *West's Business Law,* 10th ed., A203–A212.

24. For more detail on limited partnerships, see Richard A. Mann and Barry S. Roberts, *Smith and Roberson's Business Law,* 13th ed. (Mason, OH: South-Western/Cengage Learning, 2006).

25. See Constance E. Bagley and Craig E. Dauchy, *The Entrepreneur's Guide to Business Law,* (Mason, OH: South-Western/Cengage Learning, 2003). See also Mary Sprouse, "The Lure of Limited Liability Companies," *Your Company* (Fall 1995): 19. For further discussion on the legal aspects of LLPs, see Jentz et al., *West's Business Law,* 10th ed., 675.

26. Harlan D. Platt, *Why Companies Fail* (Lexington, MA: Lexington Books, 1985), 83.

27. Mallor et al., *Business Law: The Ethical, Global, and E-Commerce Environment,* 13th ed., 737–71.

28. For a detailed discussion of Chapter 11 bankruptcy, see Mallor et al., *Business Law: The Ethical, Global, and E-Commerce Environment,* 13th ed., 757–62.

29. Ibid., 764–68.

30. Interview with Mark E. Need, JD/MBA, Director, Elmore Entrepreneurship Law Clinic, Indiana University, April 2008.

The Search For Entrepreneurial Capital

Entrepreneurial Thought

Money is like a sixth sense without which you cannot make a complete use of the other five.

— **WILLIAM SOMERSET MAUGHAM** *Of Human Bondage*

Chapter Objectives

1 To differentiate between debt and equity as methods of financing

2 To examine commercial loans and public stock offerings as sources of capital

3 To discuss private placements as an opportunity for equity capital

4 To study the market for venture capital and to review venture capitalists' evaluation criteria for new ventures

5 To discuss the importance of evaluating venture capitalists for a proper selection

6 To examine the existing informal risk-capital market ("angel capital")

The Entrepreneur's Search for Capital

Every entrepreneur planning a new venture confronts the dilemma of where to find start-up capital. Entrepreneurs usually are not aware that numerous possibilities and combinations of financial packages may be appropriate for new ventures.

It is important, therefore, to understand not only the various sources of capital but also the expectations and requirements of these sources. Without this understanding, an entrepreneur may be frustrated with attempts to find appropriate start-up capital.

Commercial loans, public offerings, private placements, convertible debentures, venture capital, and informal risk capital are some of the major terms used in the search for capital. But what exactly are they, and what is expected of an entrepreneur applying for these funds?

Studies have investigated the various sources of capital preferred by entrepreneurs.[1] These sources range from debt to equity, depending on the type of financing that is arranged. As illustrated in Figure 8.1, entrepreneurs have a number of sources of capital as their ventures develop. Notice that the level of risk and the stage of the firm's development impact the appropriate source financing for the entrepreneurial ventures.

In this chapter, we examine the various sources of capital available to new ventures, along with some insights into the processes expected of the entrepreneur. We begin with an examination of the differences between debt and equity financing.

Debt Versus Equity

The use of *debt* to finance a new venture involves a payback of the funds plus a fee (interest) for the use of the money. *Equity* financing involves the sale of some of the ownership in the venture. Debt places a burden of repayment and interest on the entrepreneur, whereas equity

---

Figure 8.1   Who Is Funding Entrepreneurial Start-Up Companies?

Financing Continuum

The following diagram depicts the typical financing for start-up companies.

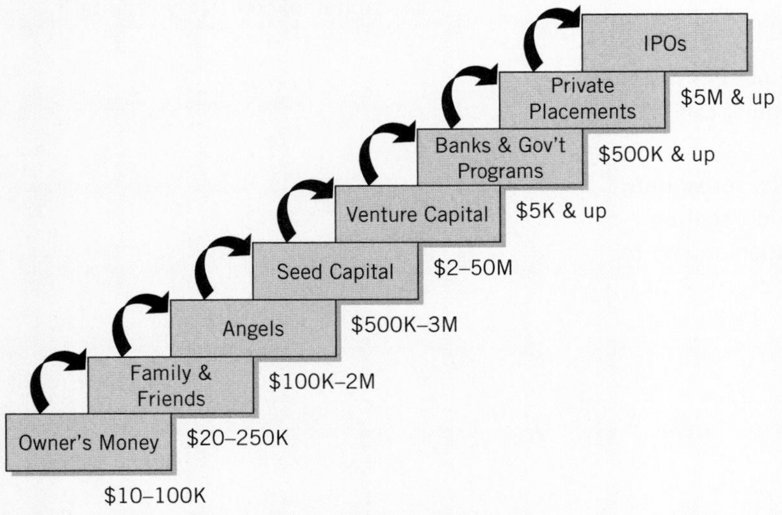

IPOs

Private Placements — $5M & up

Banks & Gov't Programs — $500K & up

Venture Capital — $5K & up

Seed Capital — $2–50M

Angels — $500K–3M

Family & Friends — $100K–2M

Owner's Money — $20–250K

$10–100K

Source: "Successful Angel Investing," Indiana Venture Center, March 2008.

financing forces the entrepreneur to relinquish some degree of control. In the extreme, the choice for the entrepreneur is (1) to take on debt without giving up ownership in the venture or (2) to relinquish a percentage of ownership in order to avoid having to borrow. In most cases, a combination of debt and equity proves most appropriate.

Debt Financing

Many new ventures find that **debt financing** is necessary. Short-term borrowing (one year or less) is often required for working capital and is repaid out of the proceeds from sales. Long-term debt (term loans of one to five years or long-term loans maturing in more than five years) is used to finance the purchase of property or equipment, with the purchased asset serving as collateral for the loans. The most common sources of debt financing are commercial banks.[2]

COMMERCIAL BANKS

About 8,528 commercial banks operate in the United States today.[3] Although some banks will make unsecured short-term loans, most bank loans are secured by receivables, inventories, or other assets. Commercial banks also make a large number of intermediate-term loans with maturities of one to five years. In about 90 percent of these cases, the banks require collateral—which generally consists of stocks, machinery, equipment, and real estate—and systematic payments over the life of the loan are required. Apart from real estate mortgages and loans guaranteed by the Small Business Administration (SBA) or a similar organization, commercial banks make few loans with maturities greater than five years. Banks also may offer a number of services to a new venture, including computerized payroll preparation, letters of credit, international services, lease financing, and money market accounts.

To secure a bank loan, an entrepreneur typically will have to answer a number of questions. Five of the most common questions, together with descriptive commentaries, follow.

1. *What do you plan to do with the money?* Do not plan on using funds for a high-risk venture. Banks seek the most secure venture possible.

2. *How much do you need?* Some entrepreneurs go to their bank with no clear idea of how much money they need. All they know is that they want money. The more precisely the entrepreneur can answer this question, the more likely the loan will be granted.

3. *When do you need it?* Never rush to the bank with immediate requests for money with no plan. Such a strategy shows that the entrepreneur is a poor planner, and most lenders will not want to get involved.

4. *How long will you need it?* The shorter the period of time the entrepreneur needs the money, the more likely he or she is to get the loan. The time at which the loan will be repaid should correspond to some important milestone in the business plan.

5. *How will you repay the loan?* This is the most important question. What if plans go awry? Can other income be diverted to pay off the loan? Does collateral exist? Even if a quantity of fixed assets exists, the bank may be unimpressed because it knows from experience that assets sold at a liquidation auction bring only a fraction of their value—five to ten cents on the dollar is not unusual.[4]

Banks are not the only source of debt financing. Sometimes a new venture can obtain long-term financing for a particular piece of equipment from the manufacturer, which will take a portion of the purchase price in the form of a long-term note. Manufacturers are most willing to do this when an active market exists for their used equipment, so if the machinery must be repossessed, it can be resold. Also, new ventures sometimes can obtain short-term debt financing by negotiating extended credit terms with suppliers. However, this kind of trade credit restricts the venture's flexibility with selecting suppliers and may reduce its ability to negotiate supplier prices.

Debt financing has both advantages and disadvantages, as follows.

Advantages
- No relinquishment of ownership is required.
- More borrowing allows for potentially greater return on equity.
- During periods of low interest rates, the opportunity cost is justified because the cost of borrowing is low.

Disadvantages
- Regular (monthly) interest payments are required.
- Continual cash-flow problems can be intensified because of payback responsibility.
- Heavy use of debt can inhibit growth and development.

entrepreneurship in practice

Social Lending Provides Capital When Commercial Lenders Won't

A new phenomenon that provides capital for both existing ventures and start-ups is social lending, also known as peer-to-peer (P2P) lending or Banking 2.0. Often, commercial lenders are unwilling to lend to unproven enterprises, leaving entrepreneurs little recourse when they are desperate for funding. Michael and Amy DeFabio netted a $15,000 loan through the social lending site Lending Club after struggling for three months to convince commercial lenders that their holistic health care business was financially viable.

As the movement has gained momentum, several social lending sites have sprung up, with Virgin Money, Prosper, Lending Club, Zopa, and GlobeFunder being the most popular. Once thought of as an alternative funding option for entrepreneurs unable to qualify for a commercial loan, social lending has begun to offer established entrepreneurs quick capital without the administrative overhead required with traditional loans. Lending Club, Virgin Money, and Prosper report that a minimum of 20 percent of the loans made through their sites are for business purposes and consist of loans ranging from $9,000 to $21,000.

Some analysts attribute the success of social lending to the weakening economy. Commercial lenders have been forced to be more conservative in their lending practices, which has led to a depleted pool of capital for entrepreneurs. Most of the businesses that utilize social lending sites are start-ups, largely due to the fact that the most popular sites, with the exclusion of Virgin Money, set the maximum loan amount at $25,000. The relatively small loan amounts and the ease with which people can submit their ideas has led many individuals—who otherwise would have avoided pursuing their business venture due to a lack of confidence in their ability to obtain a commercial loan—to view social lending as a low-risk mechanism for getting started.

Social lending is very similar to other social networking phenomena in that it is largely dependent on the site providers' ability to provide a forum in which an open, trusting community can be built. Madeline Smith organized a community pet show in 2007, which led her to consider opening a pet boutique. She was leery about putting together a business plan and presenting the idea to commercial lenders. After a friend suggested that she post her concept on Prosper.com, Madeline was offered a $5,000 loan within weeks. Interestingly, Madeline found that pursuing a social loan provided benefits beyond the capital. The lender, a woman who had also dreamt of opening a pet boutique, indicated that the reason for making the loan was so that she could experience the thrill of building a business through Madeline. The interaction between members of social lending communities provides psychological benefits that are not available through commercial lenders.

Another interesting result of social lending is that entrepreneurs who receive loans often become lenders. The sense of camaraderie and goodwill that is developed by helping others fulfill their dreams makes the lending process far more personal, for both the loan recipient and the lender. Despite the emotional benefits of working through social lending sites, the fact that businesses are taking on debt should not be dismissed. Chayah Masters, the owner of Gittel on the Go, Inc.—a staffing agency for part-time assistants based in Los Angeles—was in need of $5,000 to revamp her company's Web site. When researching her funding options, she found Zopa; within days, she had the money in hand. Before starting the process of searching for the loan, Masters made sure to have her repayment plan in place, which consisted of paying back her loan with her upcoming tax return.

If the social lending movement continues, entrepreneurs will have an effective weapon in their arsenal to combat the cash-flow issues inherent in running a business. As should be done with all lenders, entrepreneurs need to carefully review the policies and procedures as well as the reputation for any social lender they are considering taking a loan through. For those individuals who have been putting their entrepreneurial aspirations on hold due to financial fears, social lending could provide the peace of mind needed for them to dust off their ideas and put them into action.

Source: Adapted from Kristin Edelhauser Chessman, "Business Loans Get Personal," *Entrepreneur,* March 19, 2008, http://www.entrepreneur.com/money/financing/article191726.html (accessed April 1, 2008).

OTHER DEBT-FINANCING SOURCES

In addition to commercial banks, other debt-financing sources include trade credit, accounts receivable factoring, finance companies, leasing companies, mutual savings banks, savings and loan associations, and insurance companies. Table 8.1 provides a summary of these sources, the business types they often finance, and their financing terms.

Table **8.1** **Common Debt Sources**

	Business Type Financed			Financing Term	
Source	Start–Up Firm	Existing Firm	Short Term	Intermediate Term	Long Term
Trade credit	Yes	Yes	Yes	No	No
Commercial banks	Sometimes, but only if strong capital or collateral exists	Yes	Frequently	Sometimes	Seldom
Finance companies	Seldom	Yes	Most frequent	Yes	Seldom
Factors	Seldom	Yes	Most frequent	Seldom	No
Leasing companies	Seldom	Yes	No	Most frequent	Occasionally
Mutual savings banks and savings-and-loan associations	Seldom	Real estate ventures only	No	No	Real estate ventures only
Insurance companies	Rarely	Yes	No	No	Yes

Trade credit is credit given by suppliers who sell goods on account. This credit is reflected on the entrepreneur's balance sheet as accounts payable, and in most cases it must be paid in 30 to 90 days. Many small, new businesses obtain this credit when no other form of financing is available to them. Suppliers typically offer this credit as a way to attract new customers.

Accounts receivable financing is short-term financing that involves either the pledge of receivables as collateral for a loan or the sale of receivables (factoring). Accounts receivable loans are made by commercial banks, whereas factoring is done primarily by commercial finance companies and factoring concerns.

Accounts receivable bank loans are made on a discounted value of the receivables pledged. A bank may make receivable loans on a notification or non-notification plan. Under the notification plan, purchasers of goods are informed that their accounts have been assigned to the bank. They then make payments directly to the bank, which credits them to the borrower's account. Under the non-notification plan, borrowers collect their accounts as usual and then pay off the bank loan.

Factoring is the sale of accounts receivable. Under this arrangement, the receivables are sold, at a discounted value, to a factoring company. Some commercial finance companies also do factoring. Under a standard arrangement, the factor will buy the client's receivables outright, without recourse, as soon as the client creates them by its shipment of goods to customers. Factoring fits some businesses better than others, and it has become almost traditional in industries such as textiles, furniture manufacturing, clothing manufacturing, toys, shoes, and plastics.

Finance companies are asset-based lenders that lend money against assets such as receivables, inventory, and equipment. The advantage of dealing with a commercial finance company is that it often will make loans that banks will not. The interest rate varies from 2 to 6 percent over that charged by a bank. New ventures that are unable to raise money from banks and factors often turn to finance companies.

Other financial sources include equity instruments (discussed in the next section), which give investors a share of the ownership. Examples of these follow.

- *Loan with warrants* provides the investor with the right to buy stock at a fixed price at some future date. Terms on the warrants are negotiable. The warrant customarily provides for the purchase of additional stock, such as up to 10 percent of the total issue at 130 percent of the original offering price within a five-year period following the offering date.

- *Convertible debentures* are unsecured loans that can be converted into stock. The conversion price, the interest rate, and the provisions of the loan agreement are all areas for negotiation.

- *Preferred stock* is equity that gives investors a preferred place among the creditors in the event the venture is dissolved. The stock also pays a dividend and can increase in price, thus giving investors an even greater return. Some preferred stock issues are convertible to common stock, a feature that can make them even more attractive.

- *Common stock* is the most basic form of ownership. This stock usually carries the right to vote for the board of directors. If a new venture does well, common-stock investors often make a large return on their investment. These stock issues often are sold through public or private offerings.

Equity Financing

Equity financing is money invested in the venture with no legal obligation for entrepreneurs to repay the principal amount or pay interest on it. The use of equity funding thus requires no repayment in the form of debt. It does, however, require sharing the ownership and profits with the funding source. Because no repayment is required, equity capital can be much safer for new ventures than debt financing. However, the entrepreneur must consciously decide to give up part of the ownership in return for this funding.[5]

During the past 30 years, a tremendous boom has taken place in the private equity industry. The pool of U.S. private equity funds—partnerships that specialize in venture capital, leveraged buyouts, mezzanine investments, build-ups, distressed debt, and related investments—grew from $5 billion in 1980 to more than $302 billion in 2007.[6]

Equity capital can be raised through two major sources: public stock offerings and private placements. In both cases, entrepreneurs must follow the state laws pertaining to the raising of such funds and must meet the requirements set forth by the Securities and Exchange Commission (SEC). This entire process can be difficult, expensive, and time consuming. The laws and regulations are complex and often vary from state to state. On the other hand, successful stock offerings can help a fledgling enterprise raise a great deal of money.

PUBLIC OFFERINGS

Going public is a term used to refer to a corporation's raising capital through the sale of securities on the public markets. Following are some of the advantages to this approach.

- *Size of capital amount.* Selling securities is one of the fastest ways to raise large sums of capital in a short period of time.
- *Liquidity.* The public market provides liquidity for owners since they can readily sell their stock.
- *Value.* The marketplace puts a value on the company's stock, which in turn allows value to be placed on the corporation.
- *Image.* The image of a publicly traded corporation often is stronger in the eyes of suppliers, financiers, and customers.[7]

During the last decade, many new ventures have sought capital through the public markets. The term **initial public offering (IPO)** is used to represent the registered public offering of a company's securities for the first time. In 2006, for example, there were 241 IPOs accounting for $50.5 billion. The year 2007 witnessed an increase to 275 IPOs, and the amount raised soared to $65.7 billion. Many times, the number of companies "going public" does not vary much, but the amount of financing raised certainly does. In addition, the economy has a major effect on the IPO markets—as evidenced by the huge upswing in IPOs from 1995 to 1999, when 2,994 companies went public during an economic period of continual growth and prosperity. The year 2000 introduced a correction on the economy, and everything began to constrict, including the IPO market. By 2001, only 91 firms went public, raising $37.1 billion—quite a slump from the all-time high of 868 IPOs in 1996. Today we see much more stable and conservative activity among the IPO markets, as evidenced by the four-year average of 249 IPOs between 2004 and 2007.[8]

These figures reflect the tremendous *volatility* that exists within the stock market over the years and, thus, entrepreneurs should be aware of the concerns that confront them when they pursue the IPO market. In addition, many new ventures have begun to recognize some other disadvantages of going public. Several of these follow.

- *Costs.* The expenses involved with a public offering are significantly higher than for other sources of capital. Accounting fees, legal fees, and prospectus printing and distribution, as well as the cost of underwriting the stock, can result in high costs.
- *Disclosure.* Detailed disclosures of the company's affairs must be made public. New-venture firms often prefer to keep such information private.
- *Requirements.* The paperwork involved with SEC regulations, as well as continuing performance information, drains large amounts of time, energy, and money from management. Many new ventures consider these elements better invested in helping the company grow.
- *Shareholder pressure.* Management decisions are sometimes short term in nature to maintain a good performance record for earnings and dividends to the shareholders. This pressure can lead to a failure to give adequate consideration to the company's long-term growth and improvement.[9]

The advantages and disadvantages of going public must be weighed carefully. If the decision is to undertake a public offering, it is important that the entrepreneur understand the process involved. Chapter 15 presents some of the complex requirements involved in the IPO process. Here, we summarize by saying that entrepreneurs who pursue the public securities route should be prepared for reporting requirements, disclosure statements, and the shared control and ownership with outside shareholders.

PRIVATE PLACEMENTS

Another method of raising capital is through the private placement of securities. Small ventures often use this approach.

The SEC provides **Regulation D**, which eases the regulations for the reports and statements required for selling stock to private parties—friends, employees, customers, relatives, and local professionals. Regulation D defines four separate exemptions, which are based on the amount of money being raised. Along with their accompanying rule, these exemptions follow.

1. *Rule 504a—placements of less than $500,000:* No specific disclosure/information requirements and no limits on the kind or type of purchasers exist. This makes marketing offerings of this size easier than it was heretofore.

2. *Rule 504—placements up to $1,000,000:* Again, no specific disclosure/information requirements and no limits on the kind or type of purchasers exist.

3. *Rule 505—placements of up to $5 million:* The criteria for a public offering exemption are somewhat more difficult to meet than those for smaller offerings. Sales of securities can be made to not more than 35 nonaccredited purchasers and to an unlimited number of accredited purchasers. If purchasers are nonaccredited as well as accredited, then the company must follow specified information disclosure requirements. Investors must have the opportunity to obtain additional information about the company and its management.

4. *Rule 506—placements in excess of $5 million:* Sales can be made to no more than 35 nonaccredited purchasers and an unlimited number of accredited purchasers. However, the nonaccredited purchasers must be "sophisticated" in investment matters. Also, the specific disclosure requirements are more detailed than those for offerings between $500,000 and $5 million. Investors must have the opportunity to obtain additional information about the company and its management.[10]

the entrepreneurial process

Going Public: The Acid Test

For most entrepreneurs, an IPO is the ultimate achievement. The process of going public is a coming of age for companies during which a new world of financial and, in turn, growth opportunities are revealed; yet, not all companies are prepared for the transition to public ownership. Following are the five steps of an IPO to keep in mind when deciding whether you and your company are well-suited for the public stage.

1. **Hiring a Team**

   Given the overwhelming amount of preparation, paperwork and meetings required from a CEO, the IPO process entails a coordinated effort from a carefully constructed team. The job of the CEO is to hire the people most capable of ensuring the success of the offering. This group will include a lead investment bank, secondary bankers, auditors, securities lawyers and analysts.

2. **Preparing the Document**

   The S-1, the SEC filing document to be filed by companies intending to go public, will need to be written by your team, with the CEO and CFO guiding the process to guarantee that all parties are consistent and timely when assembling their respective parts. The key is to begin the process by meeting with everyone involved to ensure that they know where the company is and where it is going. This process can take two to three months to complete. Once you have completed the S-1, you will need to send it to a financial printer to be put into its final format for electronic submission to the SEC. This step also requires fine-tuning the document's formatting as well as incorporating any last-minute edits from the team. Expect to spend two to four days completing this activity.

3. **SEC Review**

The most painstaking step in the process is the SEC review of your filing. 30- to 45-day cycles of the SEC posing questions and you responding can be repeated as many as six to eight times. Once the SEC has approved your filing, you will then have a prospectus to show investors, which is known as a "red herring."

4. **The Investor Roadshow**

Traveling to meet potential investors may seem glamorous, but months of meetings and travel can quickly wear on you. Investors are prone to change their minds, even after you have spent hours convincing them of the merits of your company, which requires subsequent trips back to previously committed buyers. Within 135 days of the last official filing of your company's financials, the roadshow, investor commitments and pricing have to be completed; otherwise, your financials will be considered stale, and you will be required to resubmit them, adding as much as another quarter if not an entire year to the process.

5. **Cashing Out**

Before your stock can be traded, the SEC has to declare your application "effective", which takes place once your stock price has been determined and all S-1 amendments have been filed. Despite the extensive coverage of entrepreneurs striking it rich after taking their company public, various SEC rules and SOX legislation specify when executives can sell shares, which implies that you will not receive your money immediately following your IPO.

Given the time and effort required in going public, some entrepeneurs opt for a simpler path, such as a strategic acquisition; yet, when entrepreneurs want to retain control of their company while raising capital, an IPO is still the most effective route to take.

Source: Adapted from David Worrell, (2007, December). Your Best Offering. Retrieved August 4, 2008, from *Entrepreneur* Magazine Website: http://www.entrepreneur.com/magazine/entrepreneur/2007/december/186560.html; see also Walter G. Kortschak, (2007, May). Strategic Acquisition or IPO? Retrieved August 4, 2008, from *Inc.* Magazine Website: http://www.inc.com/inc5000/articles/20070501/kortschak.html)

As noted in Rules 505 and 506, Regulation D uses the term accredited purchaser. Included in this category are institutional investors such as banks, insurance companies, venture capital firms, registered investment companies, and small-business investment companies (SBICs), wealthy individuals, and certain tax-exempt organizations with more than $5 million in assets. Everyone not covered in these descriptions is regarded as a nonaccredited purchaser.

"Sophisticated" investors are wealthy individuals who invest more or less regularly in new and early- and late-stage ventures. They are knowledgeable about the technical and commercial opportunities and risks of the businesses in which they invest. They know the kind of information they want about their prospective investment, and they have the experience and ability needed to obtain and analyze the data provided.

The objective of Regulation D is to make it easier and less expensive for small ventures to sell stock. However, many states have not kept pace with these rules. Consequently, many new ventures still find it costly and time consuming to try to clear their offerings in some states. In addition, many are discouraged by the disclosure requirements for offerings of $500,000 and over, which are cited under Rules 505 and 506. Despite these difficulties, Regulation D does a lot to simplify small-company financing.[11]

Fighting Terrorism with Financial Opportunity

Ronald Bruder, an American entrepreneur, started the Education for Employment Foundation (EFE) to teach young Jordanians the fundamentals of finding and keeping a job. Skills taught include how to write a résumé, make presentations to audiences, and handle job interviews. In a former life, Bruder was a real estate developer in New York City. Now, at age 60, he spends his time working in the Middle East to do what he can to improve living conditions. His theory is that Muslims are enraged and driven to terrorism not by their ideology, as suggested by most experts, but by their lack of economic opportunity. Without any hope of financial stability in a war-torn environment, young adults have limited alternatives. The logic is simple: provide opportunities for citizens to find gainful employment and eliminate the pool of soldiers for al Qaeda to recruit.

Bruder's efforts are made more extraordinary by the fact that he is Jewish. Feelings of anti-Semitism run deep in many of the countries in which EFE operates; yet, Bruder does not let religious beliefs stand in the way of his mission. As a serial entrepreneur who has started businesses as diverse as a medical technology company, an oil-and-gas business, and a shopping mall development company, he is experienced in overcoming obstacles. Bruder founded EFE by committing $10 million of his own money. The organization currently operates in Morocco, Yemen, Gaza, and Egypt. EFE partners with local businesses in each country, which fund and hire the students of Bruder's program. The first training program was launched in Jordan in 2005.

With approximately 10,000 college graduates waiting an average of 3 to 4 years to find employment, EFE has its work cut out for it. The group's efforts are already showing results—hundreds of young Jordanians, Moroccans, and Palestinians have been placed in gainful employment through the EFE. The organization has placed 980 program graduates since its inception. Bruder, being the successful entrepreneur that he is, has grand visions for any endeavor he undertakes. His overarching goal for the EFE is no different: the social and economic transformation of the Islamic world.

Source: Adapted from Richard McGill Murphy, "Bruder's Vision Gets Results," *Fortune Small Business,* April 3, 2008, http://money.cnn.com/2008/04/02/smbusiness/jihad_jobs.fsb/index2.htm (accessed April 3, 2008).

The Venture Capital Market

Venture capitalists are a valuable and powerful source of equity funding for new ventures. These experienced professionals provide a full range of financial services for new or growing ventures, including the following.

- Capital for start-ups and expansion
- Market research and strategy for businesses that do not have their own marketing departments
- Management-consulting functions and management audit and evaluation
- Contacts with prospective customers, suppliers, and other important businesspeople
- Assistance in negotiating technical agreements
- Help in establishing management and accounting controls
- Help in employee recruitment and development of employee agreements

- Help in risk management and the establishment of an effective insurance program
- Counseling and guidance in complying with a myriad of government regulations

Recent Developments in Venture Capital

Following a three-year downward trend from 2001 to 2004, venture capital began to level off with regard to the amount and size of investments. Venture capitalists (VCs) invested $21 billion into 2,873 deals in 2004; $22.9 billion into 3,138 deals in 2005; $26.5 billion into 3,630 deals in 2006; and $29.4 billion into 3,813 deals in 2007. However, it should be understood that the VCs raised their investments in later-stage companies and not start-ups or early-stage ventures. Table 8.2 illustrates the stages of VC investment in 2007. Notice the smaller amount of activity associated with the start-up and seed-stage companies: There were only 415 seed-stage deals compared to 1,168 later-stage deals. Therefore, it must be understood that today's venture capitalists are far less inclined to finance a start-up firm as opposed to a firm in its more mature stages of development.

In addition to these developments, a number of major trends have occurred in venture capital over the last few years.

First, the predominant investor class is changing from individuals, foundations, and families to pension institutions. Therefore, sources of capital commitments will continue to shift away from the less-experienced venture capital firm (less than three years) to the more-experienced firm (greater than three years).

Second, funds are becoming more specialized and less homogeneous. The industry has become more diverse, more specialized, and less uniform than is generally thought. Sharp differences are apparent in terms of investing objectives and criteria, strategy, and focusing on particular stages, sizes, and market technology niches.[12]

Third, feeder funds are emerging. Accompanying this specialization is a new farm team system. Large, established venture capital firms have crafted both formal and informal relationships with new funds as feeder funds. Often, one general partner of the established fund will provide time and know-how to the new fund. The team may share deal flow and co-invest in a syndicated deal. More often than not, these new funds focus on seed-stage or start-up deals that can feed later deals to the more conventional, mainstream venture capital firm with which they are associated.[13]

Fourth, small start-up investments are drying up. Many venture capital firms have experienced high-risk ventures in today's technological environment in their portfolios. As a result, general partners—who are often the most experienced and skillful at finding and nurturing innovative technological ventures—are allocating premium time to salvaging or turning around problem ventures. In addition, because start-up and first-stage investing demands the greatest intensity of involvement by venture capital investors, this type of venture has felt the greatest effects. Finally, other venture capital funds lack professionals

Table 8.2	Venture Capital Investments Comparison by Stages	
Stage	**Amount**	**Deals**
Expansion	$10.8 billion	1,235
Later Stage	$12.2 billion	1,168
Early Stage	$5.2 billion	995
Start-Up/Seed	$1.2 billion	415

Source: PricewaterhouseCoopers/National Venture Capital Association, MoneyTree™ Report, 2007.

who have experience with start-ups and first-stage ventures. Consequently, the level of seed and start-up financing is lower in comparison to the financing available for early stages, expansion, and acquisition.[14]

Fifth, the trend is toward a new legal environment. The heated competition for venture capital in recent years has resulted in a more sophisticated legal and contractual environment. The frequency and extent of litigation are rising. As an example, the final document governing the investor/entrepreneur relationship—called the investment agreement—can be a few inches thick and can comprise two volumes. In this regard, legal experts recommend that the following provisions be carefully considered in the investment agreement: choice of securities (preferred stock, common stock, convertible debt, and so forth), control issues (who maintains voting power), evaluation issues and financial covenants (ability to proceed with mergers and acquisitions), and remedies for breach of contract (rescission of the contract or monetary damages).[15]

Dispelling Venture Capital Myths

Because many people have mistaken ideas about the role and function of venture capitalists, a number of myths have sprung up about them. Some of these, along with their rebuttals, follow.

MYTH 1: VENTURE CAPITAL FIRMS WANT TO OWN CONTROL OF YOUR COMPANY AND TELL YOU HOW TO RUN THE BUSINESS

No venture capital firm intentionally sets out to own control of a small business. Venture capitalists have no desire to run the business. They do not want to tell entrepreneurs how to make day-to-day decisions and have the owner report to them daily. They want the entrepreneur and the management team to run the company profitably. They do want to be consulted on any major decision, but they want no say in daily business operations.[16]

MYTH 2: VENTURE CAPITALISTS ARE SATISFIED WITH A REASONABLE RETURN ON INVESTMENTS

Venture capitalists expect very high, exorbitant, unreasonable returns. They can obtain reasonable returns from hundreds of publicly traded companies. They can obtain reasonable returns from many types of investments that do not have the degree of risk involved in financing a small business. Because every venture capital investment involves a high degree of risk, it must have a correspondingly high return on investment.[17]

MYTH 3: VENTURE CAPITALISTS ARE QUICK TO INVEST

It takes a long time to raise venture capital. On the average, it will take six to eight weeks from the initial contact to raise venture capital. If the entrepreneur has a well-prepared business plan, the investor will be able to raise money in that time frame. A venture capitalist will see from 50 to 100 proposals a month; of that number, 10 will be of some interest. Of those, 2 or 3 will receive a fair amount of analysis, negotiation, and investigation. Of the 2 or 3, just 1 may be funded. This funneling process of selecting 1 out of 100 takes a great deal of time. Once the venture capitalist has found that 1, he or she will spend a significant amount of time investigating possible outcomes before funding it.

MYTH 4: VENTURE CAPITALISTS ARE INTERESTED IN BACKING NEW IDEAS OR HIGH-TECHNOLOGY INVENTIONS—MANAGEMENT IS A SECONDARY CONSIDERATION

Venture capitalists back only good management. If an entrepreneur has a bright idea but a poor managerial background and no experience in the industry, the individual should try to find someone in the industry to bring onto the team. The venture capitalist will have a hard time believing that an entrepreneur with no experience in that industry and no managerial ability in his or her background can follow through on a business plan. A good idea is important, but a good management team is even more important.[18]

the entrepreneurial process

Venture Capitalist' Due Diligence "Deal Killers"

When venture capitalists examine a business plan and then conduct their own "due diligence" on a proposed venture, certain areas stand out immediately as negative. These are referred to as "deal killers," because it is sometime impossible to get a deal done if any one of these items is identified.

An arrogant management team. This is a team that will not listen, one that has displayed a lack of integrity, or one that is preoccupied with complete control.

No defendable market position. This occurs when there is no identified intellectual property to defend or any specific market niche to occupy.

Excessive founder salaries. If the focus seems to be on the founders' distributing the proceeds to themselves quickly (or bonuses), then there is a problem of commitment to the venture.

Vulnerability of the founder. Whenever there is overdependence on one person (a particular founder)

for his or her skills or persona, there could be a major issue.

Yesterday's news. If a business plan is perceived as "overshopped" or simply presented too much over a short period of time, then it may be perceived as an "old idea."

Ignorance of the competitive landscape. Whenever the team lacks the understanding of the real strengths and weaknesses of the competition, a major red flag goes up for the VC.

Unrealistic expectations. A typical problem of entrepreneurs is their lack of understanding of the valuation of their venture and the deal terms involved in the VC investment proposal. Usually the entrepreneurs think that their venture is worth far more than the VC does.

Source: Adapted from: Andrew J. Sherman, *Raising Capital,* 2nd ed. (New York: AMACOM Books, 2005), 182.

MYTH 5: VENTURE CAPITALISTS NEED ONLY BASIC SUMMARY INFORMATION BEFORE THEY MAKE AN INVESTMENT

A detailed and well-organized business plan is the only way to gain a venture capital investor's attention and obtain funding. Every venture capitalist, before becoming involved, wants the entrepreneur to have thought out the entire business plan and to have written it down in detail.[19]

Venture Capitalists' Objectives

Venture capitalists have different objectives from most others who provide capital to new ventures. Lenders, for example, are interested in security and payback. As partial owners of the companies they invest in, venture capitalists, however, are most concerned with return on investment. As a result, they put a great deal of time into weighing the risk of a venture against the potential return. They carefully measure both the product/service and the management. Figure 8.2 illustrates an evaluation system for measuring these two critical factors—status of product/service and status of management—on four levels. The figure demonstrates that ideas as well as entrepreneurs are evaluated when the viability of a venture proposal is determined.

Venture capitalists are particularly interested in making a large return on investment (ROI). Table 8.3 provides some commonly sought targets. Of course, these targets are flexible. They would be reduced, for example, in cases where a company has a strong market potential, is able to generate good cash flow, or the management has invested a sizable portion of its own funds in the venture. However, an annual goal of 20 to 30 percent ROI would not be considered too high, regardless of the risks involved.

Figure	8.2	Venture Capitalist System of Evaluating Product/Service and Management

<table>
<tr><td rowspan="10">Status of Product/Service</td><td rowspan="2">Riskiest</td><td colspan="5"></td></tr>
<tr><td>Level 4
Fully developed product/service
Established market
Satisfied users</td><td>4/1</td><td>4/2</td><td>4/3</td><td>4/4</td></tr>
<tr><td>Level 3
Fully developed product/service
Few users as of yet
Market assumed</td><td>3/1</td><td>3/2</td><td>3/3</td><td>3/4</td></tr>
<tr><td>Level 2
Operable pilot or prototype
Not yet developed for production
Market assumed</td><td>2/1</td><td>2/2</td><td>2/3</td><td>2/4</td></tr>
<tr><td>Level 1
Product/service idea
Not yet operable
Market assumed</td><td>1/1</td><td>1/2</td><td>1/3</td><td>1/4</td></tr>
</table>

	Level 1	**Level 2**	**Level 3**	**Level 4**
	Individual founder/entrepreneur	Two founders Other personnel not yet identified	Partial management team Members identified to join company when funding is received	Fully staffed, experienced management team

◄───────────────── **Riskiest** ─────────────────►

Status of Management

Source: Stanley Rich and David Gumpert, *Business Plans That Win $$$* (New York: Harper & Row, 1985), 169. Reprinted by permission of Sterling Lord Literistic, Inc. Copyright © 1985 by Stanley Rich and David Gumpert.

Criteria for Evaluating New-Venture Proposals

In addition to the evaluation of product ideas and management strength, numerous criteria are used to evaluate new-venture proposals. Researcher Dean A. Shepherd developed a list of eight critical factors that venture capitalists use in the evaluation of new ventures, as follows:

- Timing of entry
- Key success factor stability
- Educational capability
- Lead time
- Competitive rivalry

Table	8.3	Returns on Investment Typically Sought by Venture Capitalists

Stage of Business	Expected Annual Return on Investment	Expected Increase on Initial Investment
Start-up business (idea stage)	60% +	10–15 × investment
First-stage financing (new business)	40%–60%	6–12 × investment
Second-stage financing (development stage)	30%–50%	4–8 × investment
Third-stage financing (expansion stage)	25%–40%	3–6 × investment
Turnaround situation	50% +	8–15 × investment

Source: W. Keith Schilit, "How to Obtain Venture Capital," *Business Horizons* (May/June 1987): 78. Copyright © 1987 by the Foundation for the School of Business at Indiana University. Reprinted by permission.

- Entry wedge imitation
- Scope
- Industry-related competence[20]

Each factor was defined from the high/low perspective (see Table 8.4 for definitions). Another set of researchers developed 28 of these criteria, grouped into six major categories:

- Entrepreneur's personality
- Entrepreneur's experience
- Product or service characteristics
- Market characteristics
- Financial considerations
- Nature of the venture team[21]

Table	8.4	Factors in Venture Capitalists' Evaluation Process

Attribute	Level	Definition
Timing of entry	Pioneer	Enters a new industry first
	Late follower	Enters an industry late in the industry's stage of development
Key success factor stability	High	Requirements necessary for success will not change radically during industry development
	Low	Requirements necessary for success will change radically during industry development
Educational capability	High	Considerable resources and skills available to overcome market ignorance through education
	Low	Few resources or skills available to overcome market ignorance through education

Continued

Table **8.4**   **Factors in Venture Capitalists' Evaluation Process (Continued)**

Attribute	Level	Definition
Lead time	Long	An extended period of monopoly for the first entrant prior to competitors entering the industry
	Short	A minimal period of monopoly for the first entrant prior to competitors entering this industry
Competitive rivalry	High	Intense competition among industry members during industry development
	Low	Little competition among industry members during industry development
Entry wedge mimicry	High	Considerable imitation of the mechanisms used by other firms to enter this, or any other, industry—for example, a franchisee
	Low	Minimal imitation of the mechanisms used by other firms to enter this, or any other, industry—for example, introducing a new product
Scope	Broad	A firm that spreads its resources across a wide spectrum of the market—for example, many segments of the market
	Narrow	A firm that concentrates on intensively exploiting a small segment of the market—for example, targeting a niche
Industry-related competence	High	Venturer has considerable experience and knowledge with the industry being entered or a related industry
	Low	Venturer has minimal experience and knowledge with the industry being entered or a related industry

Source: Dean A. Shepherd, "Venture Capitalists' Introspection: A Comparison of 'In Use' and 'Espoused' Decision Policies," *Journal of Small Business Management* (April 1999): 76–87; and "Venture Capitalists' Assessment of New Venture Survival," *Management Science* (May 1999): 621–32. Reprinted by permission. Copyright 1999, the Institute for Operation Research and the Management Sciences (INFORMS), 7240 Parkway Drive, Suite 310, Hanover MD 21076 USA.

The study surveyed more than 100 venture capitalists regarding these criteria and found that they most frequently rated ten of the criteria as essential when reviewing new-venture proposals (Table 8.5). Six of these ten relate to the entrepreneur personally, three deal with the investment in and growth of the project, and one relates to the venture's patent or copyright position.

Other researchers have uncovered similar results. For example, one study examined the criteria venture capitalists use during a proposal screening and evaluation. Table 8.6 outlines the factors used in the study.[22] Their results showed that venture capitalists reached a "go/no go" decision in an average of 6 minutes on the initial screening and in less than 21 minutes on the overall proposal evaluation. They found that the venture capital firm's requirements and the long-term growth and profitability of the proposed venture's industry were the critical factors for initial screening. In the more-detailed evaluation, the background of the entrepreneurs as well as the characteristics of the proposal itself were important.

In a study that examined the "demand side" of venture capital, researchers surveyed 318 private entrepreneurs who sought out venture capital in amounts of $100,000 or more. The study found that entrepreneurs' success with acquiring funding is related to four general, variable categories: (1) characteristics of the entrepreneurs, including education, experience, and age; (2) characteristics of the enterprise, including stage, industry type, and location (for example, rural or urban); (3) characteristics of the request, including amount, business plan,

Table **8.5**	Ten Criteria Most Frequently Rated Essential in New-Venture Evaluation

Criterion	Percentage
Capable of sustained intense effort	64
Thoroughly familiar with market	62
At least ten times return in five to ten years	50
Demonstrated leadership in past	50
Evaluates and reacts to risk well	48
Investment can be made liquid	44
Significant market growth	43
Track record relevant to venture	37
Articulates venture well	31
Proprietary protection	29

Source: Reprinted by permission of the publisher from Ian C. MacMillan, Robin Siegel, and P. N. Subba Narasimha, "Criteria Used by Venture Capitalists to Evaluate New Venture Proposals," *Journal of Business Venturing* (Winter 1985): 123. Copyright © 1985 by Elsevier Science Publishing Co., Inc.

and prospective capital source; and (4) sources of advice, including technology, preparation of the business plan, and places to seek funding.[23]

The business plan is a critical element in a new-venture proposal and should be complete, clear, and well presented. Venture capitalists generally will analyze five major aspects of the plan: (1) the proposal size, (2) financial projections, (3) investment recovery, (4) competitive advantage, and (5) company management.

Table **8.6**	Venture Capitalists' Screening Criteria

Venture Capital Firm Requirements

Must fit within lending guidelines of venture firm for stage and size of investment

Proposed business must be within geographic area of interest

Prefer proposals recommended by someone known to venture capitalist

Proposed industry must be kind of industry invested in by venture firm

Nature of the Proposed Business

Projected growth should be relatively large within five years of investment

Economic Environment of Proposed Industry

Industry must be capable of long-term growth and profitability

Economic environment should be favorable to a new entrant

Continued

Table 8.6	Venture Capitalists' Screening Criteria (Continued)

Proposed Business Strategy

Selection of distribution channel(s) must be feasible

Product must demonstrate defendable competitive position

Financial Information on the Proposed Business

Financial projections should be realistic

Proposal Characteristics

Must have full information

Should be a reasonable length, be easy to scan, have an executive summary, and be
professionally presented

Must contain a balanced presentation

Use graphics and large print to emphasize key points

Entrepreneur/Team Characteristics

Must have relevant experience

Should have a balanced management team in place

Management must be willing to work with venture partners

Entrepreneur who has successfully started previous business given special consideration

Source: John Hall and Charles W. Hofer, "Venture Capitalists' Decision Criteria in New Venture Evaluation,"
Journal of Business Venturing (January 1993): 37.

The evaluation process typically takes place in stages. The four most common stages
follow.

STAGE 1: INITIAL SCREENING

This is a quick review of the basic venture to see if it meets the venture capitalist's particular
interests.

STAGE 2: EVALUATION OF THE BUSINESS PLAN

A detailed reading of the plan is done to evaluate the factors mentioned earlier.

STAGE 3: ORAL PRESENTATION

The entrepreneur verbally presents the plan to the venture capitalist. See Table 8.7 for a
thorough understanding of the key elements necessary in presenting to a venture capitalist.

STAGE 4: FINAL EVALUATION

After analyzing the plan and visiting with suppliers, customers, consultants, and others, the
venture capitalist makes a final decision.

This four-step process screens out approximately 98 percent of all venture plans. The rest
receive some degree of financial backing.

Evaluating the Venture Capitalist

The venture capitalist will evaluate the entrepreneur's proposal carefully, and the entrepreneur should not hesitate to evaluate the venture capitalist. Does the venture capitalist

Table	8.7	Essential Elements for a Successful Presentation to a Venture Capitalist

Team Must:

- Be able to adapt
- Know the competition
- Be able to manage rapid growth
- Be able to manage an industry leader
- Have relevant background and industry experience
- Show financial commitment to company, not just sweat equity
- Be strong with a proven track record in the industry unless the company is a start-up or seed investment

Product Must:

- Be real and work
- Be unique
- Be proprietary
- Meet a well-defined need in the marketplace
- Demonstrate potential for product expansion, to avoid being a one-product company
- Emphasize usability
- Solve a problem or improve a process significantly
- Be for mass production with potential for cost reduction

Market Must:

- Have current customers and the potential for many more
- Grow rapidly (25% to 45% per year)
- Have a potential for market size in excess of $250 million
- Show where and how you are competing in the marketplace
- Have potential to become a market leader
- Outline any barriers to entry

Business Plan Must:

- Tell the full story, not just one chapter
- Promote a company, not just a product
- Be compelling
- Show the potential for rapid growth and knowledge of your industry, especially competition and market vision
- Include milestones for measuring performance
- Show how you plan to beat or exceed those milestones
- Address all of the key areas
- Detail projections and assumptions; be realistic
- Serve as a sales document
- Include a strong and well-written executive summary
- Show excitement and color
- Show superior rate of return (a minimum of 30% to 40% per year) with a clear exit strategy

Source: Andrew J. Sherman, *Raising Capital*, 2nd ed. AMACOM Books, 2005; p.175.

understand the proposal? Is the individual familiar with the business? Is the person someone with whom the entrepreneur can work? If the answers reveal a poor fit, it is best for the entrepreneur to look for a different venture capitalist.

One researcher found that venture capitalists do add value to an entrepreneurial firm beyond the money they supply, especially in high-innovation ventures. Because of this finding, entrepreneurs need to choose the appropriate venture capitalist at the outset, and, most important, they must keep the communication channels open as the firm grows.[24]

On the other hand, it is important to realize that the choice of a venture capitalist can be limited. Although funds are available today, they tend to be controlled by fewer groups, and the quality of the venture must be promising. Even though two and one-half times more money is available today for seed financing than was available ten years ago, the number of venture capital firms is not increasing. In addition, the trend toward concentration of venture capital under the control of a few firms is increasing.[25]

Nevertheless, the entrepreneur should not be deterred from evaluating prospective venture capitalists. "Entrepreneurship in Practice: Asking the Right Questions" provides a list of important questions that a prospective venture capital firm should answer. Evaluating and even negotiating with the venture capitalist are critical to establishing the best equity funding:

You may worry that if you rock the boat by demanding too much, the venture capital firm will lose interest. That's an understandable attitude; venture capital is hard to

Asking the Right Questions

There are a number of important questions that entrepreneurs should ask of venture capitalists. Following are seven of the most important, along with their rationales.

1. Does the venture capital firm in fact invest in your industry? How many deals has the firm actually done in your field?

2. What is it like to work with this venture capital firm? Get references. (An unscreened list of referrals, including CEOs of companies that the firm has been successful with—as well as those it has not—can be very helpful.)

3. What experience does the partner doing your deal have, and what is his or her clout within the firm? Check out the experiences of other entrepreneurs.

4. How much time will the partner spend with your company if you run into trouble? A seed-stage company should ask, "You guys are a big fund, and you say you can seed me a quarter of a million

dollars. How often will you be able to see me?" The answer should be at least once a week.

5. How healthy is the venture capital fund, and how much has been invested? A venture firm with a lot of troubled investments will not have much time to spare. If most of the fund is invested, there may not be much money available for your follow-on rounds.

6. Are the investment goals of the venture capitalists consistent with your own?

7. Have the venture firm and the partner championing your deal been through any economic downturns? A good venture capitalist won't panic when things get bad.

Source: Reprinted from Marie-Jeanne Juilland, "What Do You Want from a Venture Capitalist?" August 1987 issue of *Venture, For Entrepreneurial Business Owners & Investors*, by special permission. Copyright © 1987 Venture Magazine, Inc., 521 Fifth Ave., New York, NY 10175-0028.

---

get and if you've gotten as far as the negotiating process, you're already among the lucky few.

But that doesn't mean you have to roll over and play dead. A venture capital investment is a business deal that you may have to live with for a long time. Although you'll have to give ground on many issues when you come to the bargaining table, there is always a point beyond which the deal no longer makes sense for you. You must draw a line and fight for the points that really count.[26]

Informal Risk Capital: "Angel" Financing

Not all venture capital is raised through formal sources such as public and private placements. Many wealthy people in the United States are looking for investment opportunities; they are referred to as business angels or informal risk capitalists. These individuals constitute a huge potential investment pool, as the following calculations show.

- The *Forbes* 400 richest people in America represent a combined net worth of approximately $125 billion (an average of $315 million per person).

- Forty percent of the 400 are self-made millionaires, with a combined net worth of approximately $50 billion.

- If 10 percent of the self-made wealth were available for venture financing, the pool of funds would amount to $5 billion.

- More than 500,000 individuals in America have a net worth in excess of $1 million. If 40 percent of these individuals were interested in venture financing, 200,000 millionaires would be available.

- Assuming only one-half of those 200,000 millionaires would actually consider investment in new ventures at a rate of $50,000 per person, 100,000 investors would provide a pool of $5 billion.

- If the typical deal took four investors with $50,000 each (from the pool of $5 billion), then a potential 25,000 ventures could be funded at $200,000 apiece.[27]

William E. Wetzel, Jr., a noted researcher in the field of informal risk capital, has defined this type of investor as someone who has already made his or her money and now seeks out promising young ventures to support financially. "Angels are typically entrepreneurs, retired corporate executives, or professionals who have a net worth of more than $1 million and an income of more than $100,000 a year. They're self-starters. And they're trying to perpetuate the system that made them successful."[28] If entrepreneurs are looking for such an angel, Wetzel advises them, "Don't look very far away—within 50 miles or within a day's drive at most. And that's because this is not a full-time profession for them."[29]

Why would individuals be interested in investing in a new venture from which professional venture capitalists see no powerful payoff? It may be, of course, that the reduced investment amount reduces the total risk involved in the investment. However, informal investors seek other, nonfinancial returns—among them the creation of jobs in areas of high unemployment, development of technology for social needs (for example, medical or energy), urban revitalization, minority or disadvantaged assistance, and personal satisfaction from assisting entrepreneurs.[30] Table 8.8 describes the major differences between business angels and venture capitalists.

How do informal investors find projects? Research studies indicate that they use a network of friends. Additionally, many states are formulating venture capital networks, which attempt to link informal investors with entrepreneurs and their new or growing ventures.

Table **8.8**	Main Differences Between Business Angels and Venture Capitalists

Main Differences	Business Angels	Venture Capitalists
Personal	Entrepreneurs	Investors
Firms funded	Small, early stage	Large, mature
Due diligence done	Minimal	Extensive
Location of investment	Of concern	Not important
Contract used	Simple	Comprehensive
Monitoring after investment	Active, hands-on	Strategic
Exiting the firm	Of lesser concern	Highly important
Rate of return	Of lesser concern	Highly important

Source: Mark Van Osnabrugge and Robert J. Robinson, *Angel Investing* (San Francisco: Jossey-Bass, 2000), 111. This material is used by permission of John Wiley & Sons, Inc.

Types of Angel Investors

Angel investors can be classified into five basic groups:

- **Corporate angels.** Typically, so-called "corporate angels" are senior managers at *Fortune* 1000 corporations who have been laid off with generous severances or have taken early retirement. In addition to receiving the cash, an entrepreneur may persuade the corporate angel to occupy a senior management position.

- **Entrepreneurial angels.** The most prevalent type of investors, most of these individuals own and operate highly successful businesses. Because these investors have other sources of income, and perhaps significant wealth from IPOs or partial buyouts, they will take bigger risks and invest more capital. The best way to market your deal to these angels, therefore, is as a synergistic opportunity. Reflecting this orientation, entrepreneurial angels seldom look at companies outside of their own area of expertise and will participate in no more than a handful of investments at any one time. These investors almost always take a seat on the board of directors but rarely assume management duties. They will make fair-sized investments—typically $200,000 to $500,000—and invest more as the company progresses.

- **Enthusiast angels.** Whereas entrepreneurial angels tend to be somewhat calculating, enthusiasts simply like to be involved in deals. Most enthusiast angels are age 65 or older, independently wealthy from success in a business they started, and have abbreviated work schedules. For them, investing is a hobby. As a result, they typically play no role in management and rarely seek to be placed on a board. Because they spread themselves across so many companies, the size of their investments tends to be small—ranging from as little as $10,000 to perhaps a few hundred thousand dollars.

- **Micromanagement angels.** Micromanagers are very serious investors. Some of them were born wealthy, but the vast majority attained wealth through their own efforts. Unfortunately, this heritage makes them dangerous. Because most have successfully built a company, micromanagers attempt to impose the tactics that worked for them on their portfolio companies. Although they do not seek an active management role, micromanagers usually demand a seat on the board of directors. If business is not going well, they will try to bring in new managers.

- **Professional angels.** The term *professional* in this context refers to the investor's occupation, such as doctor, lawyer and, in some very rare instances, accountant. Professional angels like to invest in companies that offer a product or service with which they have some experience. They rarely seek a board seat, but they can be unpleasant to deal with when the going gets rough and may believe that a company is in trouble before it actually is. Professional angels will invest in several companies at one time, and their capital contributions range from $25,000 to $200,000.[31]

The importance of understanding the role of informal risk capital is illustrated by the fact that the pool of today's angel capital is five times the amount in the institutional venture capital market, providing money to 20 to 30 times as many companies. Angels invest more than $25 billion a year in 50,000 to 60,000 companies nationwide, twice the amount of money and twice the number of companies as ten years ago.[32]

Recent research by Jeffrey Sohl, who worked with William E. Wetzel, Jr., on angel capital, shows a marked increase in angel investing activity over the past few years. A total of 57,120 entrepreneurial ventures received angel funding in 2007 totaling more than $26 billion. In addition, 258,200 individual angel investors were active in 2007, which demonstrates the huge expansion of angel activity in the United States during the last few years.[33]

Another important consideration for *angel capital* is that 60 percent of informal investment is devoted to seed a start-up business as opposed to 28 percent of venture capital. Of those initial deals, 82 percent were for less than $500,000, whereas only 13 percent of venture capital handled deals that small. The average size of an informal investment is $250,000, which indicates the importance of informal risk capital to entrepreneurs seeking small amounts of start-up financing.[34] (See Table 8.9 for some "angel stats.") Obviously, informal networks are a major potential capital source for entrepreneurs. However, every entrepreneur should be careful and thorough in his or her approach to business angels—there are advantages and disadvantages associated with angel financing. Figure 8.3 illustrates some of the critical pros and cons of dealing with business angels. Only through recognition of these issues will entrepreneurs be able to establish the best relationship with a business angel.

Table 8.9	"Angel Stats"	
Typical deal size	$250,000–$500,000
Typical recipient	Start-up firms
Cash-out time frame	5 to 7 years
Expected return	35 to 50% a year
Ownership stake	Less than 50%

Source: William E. Wetzel, University of New Hampshire's Center for Venture Research, and the Indiana Venture Center, 2008.

Figure 8.3	The Pros and Cons of Business Angel Investments

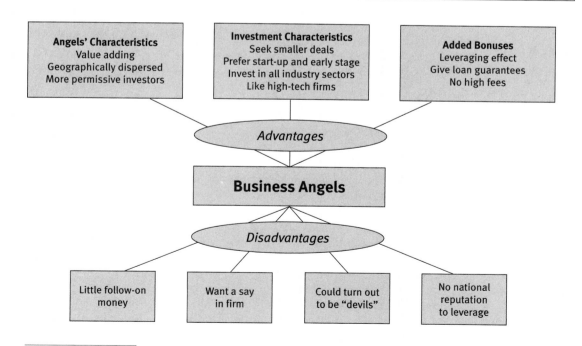

Source: Mark Van Osnabrugge and Robert J. Robinson, *Angel Investing* (San Francisco: Jossey-Bass, 2000), 64. This material is used by permission of John Wiley & Sons, Inc.

the entrepreneurial process

Why Are Angels Joining Angel Organizations?

Angel Investing Early On

In the 1980s, networking was very difficult. Deal flow was low and syndication impossible. In addition, the process was not very well defined. Consequently:

- Angel investing was too much work
- Angels hid from entrepreneurs
  - To avoid reading 100 plans per year
  - Preferring deals from trusted sources only

Angel Investing Today

Today the process is well documented with an explosive growth in angel organizations, from 10 to over 200 angel groups in the United States in eight years! Consequently:

- Deal flow is up, encouraged by new originations and high-profile successes
- Angels are rather easy to access in multiple markets
- Training and education is available for both entrepreneurs and angels

- VCs are more willing to work with angels (love/hate relationship)
- Significantly more capital in play

Outcomes

The proliferation of formal angel networks results in:

- Increased visibility of angels
  - Understanding level of activity
  - Recruiting new angel members
- Finding quality angels more easily, thereby increasing deal flow
- Availability of best practices and organizational models
- Avoiding burnout through division of labor
- Eliminating the need to fly solo

Source: "Successful Angel Investing," Indiana Venture Center, March 2005.

Summary

This chapter has examined the various forms of capital formation for entrepreneurs. Initial consideration was given to debt and equity financing in the form of commercial banks, trade credit, accounts receivable financing, factoring and finance companies, and various forms of equity instruments.

Public stock offerings have advantages and disadvantages as a source of equity capital. Although large amounts of money can be raised in short periods of time, the entrepreneur must sacrifice a degree of control and ownership. In addition, the Securities and Exchange Commission has myriad requirements and regulations that must be followed.

Private placements are an alternative means of raising equity capital for new ventures. This source is often available to entrepreneurs who seek venture capital in amounts of less than $500,000, although it is possible that up to $5 million could be raised with no more than 35 nonaccredited purchasers. The SEC's Regulation D clearly outlines the exemptions and requirements involved in a private placement. This placement's greatest advantage to the entrepreneur is limited company disclosure and only a small number of shareholders.

In recent years, the venture capital market has grown dramatically. Billions of dollars are now invested annually to seed new ventures or help fledgling enterprises grow. The individuals who invest these funds are known as venture capitalists. A number of myths that have sprung up about these capitalists were discussed and refuted.

Venture capitalists use a number of different criteria when evaluating new-venture proposals. In the main, these criteria focus on two areas: the entrepreneur and the investment potential of the venture. The evaluation process typically involves four stages: initial screening, business plan evaluation, oral presentation, and final evaluation.

In recent years, informal risk capital has begun to play an important role in new-venture financing. Everyone with money to invest in new ventures can be considered a source for this type of capital. Some estimates put the informal risk capital pool at more than $5 billion. Entrepreneurs who are unable to secure financing through banks or through public or private stock offerings typically will turn to the informal risk capital market by seeking out friends, associates, and other contacts who may have (or know of someone who has) money to invest in a new venture.

Key Terms and Concepts

accounts receivable financing	equity financing	private placement
accredited purchaser	factoring	Regulation D
angel capital	finance companies	sophisticated investors
business angel	informal risk capitalist	trade credit
debt financing	initial public offering (IPO)	venture capitalist

Review and Discussion Questions

1. Using Figure 8.1, describe some of the sources of capital available to entrepreneurs, and discuss how they correlate to the varying levels of risk involved with each stage of the venture.
2. What are the benefits and drawbacks of equity and of debt financing? Briefly discuss both.
3. Identify and describe four types of debt financing.
4. If a new venture has its choice between long-term debt and equity financing, which would you recommend? Why?
5. Why would a venture capitalist be more interested in buying a convertible debenture for $50,000 than in lending the new business $50,000 at a 10 percent interest rate?
6. What are some of the advantages of going public? What are some of the disadvantages?
7. What is the objective of Regulation D?
8. If a person inherited $100,000 and decided to buy stock in a new venture through a private placement, how would Regulation D affect this investor?
9. How large is the venture capital pool today? Is it growing or shrinking?
10. Is it easier or more difficult to get new-venture financing today? Why?
11. Some entrepreneurs do not like to seek new-venture financing because they feel that venture capitalists are greedy. In your opinion, is this true? Do these capitalists want too much?
12. Identify and describe three objectives of venture capitalists.
13. How would a venture capitalist use Figure 8.2 to evaluate an investment? Use an illustration in your answer.
14. Identify and describe four of the most common criteria venture capitalists use to evaluate a proposal.
15. Of what practical value is Table 8.3 to new-venture entrepreneurs?
16. In a new-venture evaluation, what are the four stages through which a proposal typically goes? Describe each in detail.
17. An entrepreneur is in the process of contacting three different venture capitalists and asking each to evaluate her new business proposal. What questions should she be able to answer about each of the three?
18. An entrepreneur of a new venture has had no success in getting financing from formal venture capitalists. He now has decided to turn to the informal risk capital market. Who is in this market? How would you recommend that the entrepreneur contact these individuals?

19. How likely is it that the informal risk capital market will grow during the next five years? Defend your answer.

20. Of all the sources of capital formation, which is ideal? Why?

Experiential Exercise

ANALYZING THE FUNDING SOURCES

For each funding source, write down what the text says about its usefulness for small firms. Then seek out and interview a representative of each source to find out the person's point of view of his or her relationship to small firms.

Source	What the Text Says	Source's Point of View
Banks		
Long-term loans		
Short-term loans		
Intermediate-term loans		
Private placement (Regulation D)		
Public offerings (IPO)		
Finance company		
Factor		
Trade credit		
State or local development companies		
Small Business Investment Company (SBIC)		
Informal risk capital (angel capital network)		
Venture capitalist		

Case 8.1

LOOKING FOR CAPITAL

When Joyce and Phil Abrams opened their bookstore one year ago, they estimated it would take them six months to break even. Because they had gone into the venture with enough capital to keep them afloat for nine months, they were sure they would need no outside financing. However, sales have been slower than anticipated, and most of their funds now have been used to purchase inventory or meet monthly expenses. On the other hand, the store is doing better each month, and the Abramses are convinced they will be able to turn a profit within six months.

At present, Joyce and Phil want to secure additional financing. Specifically, they would like to raise $100,000 to expand their product line. The store currently focuses most heavily on how-to-do-it books and is developing a loyal customer following. However, this market is not large enough to carry the business. The Abramses feel that if they expand into an additional market such as cookbooks, they can develop two market segments that—when combined—would prove profitable. Joyce is convinced that cookbooks are an important niche, and she has saved a number of clippings from national newspapers and magazines reporting that people who buy cookbooks tend to spend more money per month on these purchases than does the average book buyer. Additionally, customer loyalty among this group tends to be very high.

The Abramses own their entire inventory, which has a retail market value of $280,000. The merchandise cost them $140,000. They also have at a local bank a line of credit of $10,000, of which they have used $4,000. Most of their monthly expenses are covered out of the initial capital with which they started the business ($180,000 in all). However, they will be out of money in three months if they are not able to get additional funding.

The owners have considered investigating a number of sources. The two primary ones are a loan from their bank and a private stock offering to investors. They know nothing about how to raise money, and these are only general ideas they have been discussing with each other. However, they do have a meeting scheduled with their accountant, a friend, who they hope can advise them on how to raise more capital. For the moment, the Abramses are focusing on writing a business plan that spells out their short business history and objectives and explains how much money they would like to raise and where it would be invested. They hope to have the plan completed before the end of the week and take it with them to the accountant. The biggest problem they are having in writing the plan is that they are unsure of how to direct their presentation. Should they aim it at a banker or a venture capitalist? After their meeting with the accountant, they plan to refine the plan and direct it toward the appropriate source.

QUESTIONS

1. Would a commercial banker be willing to lend money to the Abramses? How much? On what do you base your answer?

2. Would this venture have any appeal for a venture capitalist? Why or why not?

3. If you were advising the Abramses, how would you recommend they seek additional capital? Be complete in your answer.

Case 8.2

THE $3 MILLION VENTURE

The Friendly Market is a large supermarket located in a city in the Southwest. "Friendly's," as it is popularly known, has more sales per square foot than any of its competitors because it lives up to its name. The personnel go out of their way to be friendly and helpful. If someone asks for a particular brand-name item and the store does not carry it, the product will be ordered. If enough customers want a particular product, it is added to the regular line. Additionally, the store provides free delivery of groceries for senior citizens, check-cashing privileges for its regular customers, and credit for those who have filled out the necessary application and have been accepted into the "Friendly Credit" group.

The owner, Charles Beavent, believes that his marketing-oriented approach can be successfully used in any area of the country. He therefore is thinking about expanding and opening two new stores, one in the northern part of the city and the other in a city located 50 miles east. Locations have been scouted, and a detailed business plan has been drawn up. However, Charles has not approached anyone about providing the necessary capital. He estimates he will need about $3 million to get both stores up and going. Any additional funding can come from the current operation, which throws off a cash flow of about $100,000 monthly.

Charles feels that two avenues are available to him: debt and equity. His local banker has told him the bank would be willing to look over any business plan he submits and would give him an answer within five working days. Charles is convinced he can get the bank to lend him $3 million. However, he does not like the idea of owing that much money. He believes he would be better off selling stock to raise the needed capital. Doing so would require him to give up some ownership, but this is more agreeable to him than the alternative.

The big question now is, How can the company raise $3 million through a stock offering? Charles intends to check into this over the next four weeks and make a decision within eight weeks. A number of customers have approached him during the past year and have asked him if he would consider making a private stock offering. Charles is convinced he can get many of his customers to buy into the venture, although he is not sure he can raise the full $3 million this way. The other approach he sees as feasible is to raise the funds through a venture capital company. This might be the best way to get such a large sum, but Charles wonders how difficult it would be to work with these people on a long-term basis. In any event, as he said to his wife yesterday, "If we're going to expand, we have to start looking into how we can raise more capital. I think the first step is to identify the best source. Then we can focus on the specifics of the deal."

QUESTIONS

1. What would be the benefits of raising the $3 million through a private placement? What would be the benefits of raising the money through a venture capitalist?

2. Of these two approaches, which would be best for Charles? Why?

3. What would you recommend Charles do now? Briefly outline a plan of action he can use to get the financing process started.

Notes

1. Gavin Cassar, "The Financing of Business Start-Ups," *Journal of Business Venturing* 19, no. 2 (March 2004): 261–83; Brian T. Gregory, Matthew W. Rutherford, Sharon Oswald, and Lorraine Gardiner, "An Empirical Investigation of the Growth Cycle Theory of Small Firm Financing," *Journal of Small Business Management,* 43, no. 4 (2005): 382–92; Jay Ebben and Alec Johnson, "Bootstrapping in Small Firms: An Empirical Analysis of Change over Time," *Journal of Business Venturing* 21, no. 6 (November 2006): 851–65; and Armin Schweinbacher, "A Theoretical Analysis of Optimal Financing Strategies for Different Types of Capital Constrained Entrepreneurs," *Journal of Business Venturing* 22, no. 6 (2007): 753–81.

2. *The State of Small Business: A Report of the President,* 2007 (Washington, DC: Government Printing Office, 2007), 25–48; Jean-Etienne de Bettignies and James A. Brander, "Financing Entrepreneurship: Bank Finance versus Venture Capital, *Journal of Business Venturing* 22, no. 6 (2007): 808–32; see also http://www.sba.gov (Services-Financial Assistance), 2008.

3. http://www.referenceforbusiness.com/industries/ Finance-Insurance-Real-Estate/National-Commercial-Banks.html (accessed April 4, 2008).

4. A complete explanation can be found in Ralph Alterowitz and Jon Zonderman, *Financing Your New or Growing Business* (Canada: Entrepreneur Press, 2002); see also Elijah Brewer III, "On Lending to Small Firms" *Journal of Small Business Management* 45, no. 1 (2007) 42–46.

5. Truls Erikson, "Entrepreneurial Capital: The Emerging Venture's Most Important Asset and Competitive Advantage," *Journal of Business Venturing* 17, no. 3 (2002): 275–90; see also Larry

D. Wall, "On Investing in the Equity of Small Firms," *Journal of Small Business Management* 45, no. 1 (2007): 89–93.

6. PriceWaterhouseCoopers, MoneyTree Survey 2005, http://www.nvca.com.

7. See *"Going Public,"* (New York: NASDAQ Stock Market, 2005). http://www.nasdaq.com/about/ GP2005_cover_toc.pdf.

8. See "Global IPOs hit record levels in 2007," *Ernst & Young,* December 17, 2007, http://www.ey.com/ global/content.nsf/UK/Media_-_07_12_17_DC_-_ Global_IPOs_hit_record_levels_in_2007 (accessed April 11, 2008).

9. See *"Going Public,"* (New York: NASDAQ Stock Market, 2005). http://www.nasdaq.com/about/ GP2005_cover_toc.pdf.

10. A summary can be found in business law texts such as Jane P. Mallor, A. James Barnes, Thomas Bowers, and Arlen W. Langvardt, *Business Law: The Ethical, Global, and E-Commerce Environment,* 13th ed. (New York: McGraw-Hill Irwin, 2007), 1079–1103.

11. For a good source of firms involved in private placements, see David R. Evanson, *Where to Go When the Bank Says No: Alternatives for Financing Your Business* (Princeton, NJ: Bloomberg Press, 1998); see also T. B. Folta and J. J. Janney, "Strategic Benefits to Firms Issuing Private Equity Placements," *Strategic Management Journal* 25, no. 3 (March 2004): 223–42.

12. Edgar Norton and Bernard H. Tenenbaum, "Specialization versus Diversification as a Venture Capital Investment Strategy," *Journal of Business Venturing* 8, no. 5, (September 1993): 431–42.

13. Dirk De Clercq, Vance H. Fried, Oskari Lehtonen, and Harry J. Sapienza, "An Entrepreneur's Guide to the Venture Capital Galaxy," *Academy of Management Perspectives* 20 (August 2006): 90–112.

14. S. Michael Camp and Donald L. Sexton, "Trends in Venture Capital Investment: Implications for High Technology Firms," *Journal of Small Business Management* (July 1992): 11–19; Raphael Amit, James Brander, and Christoph Zott, "Why Do Venture Capital Firms Exist? Theory and Canadian Evidence," *Journal of Business Venturing* 13, no. 6 (1998: 441–66; and PriceWaterhouseCoopers, MoneyTree Report, 2007.

15. Ghislaine Bouillet-Cordonnier, "Legal Aspects of Start-Up Evaluation and Adjustment Methods," *Journal of Business Venturing* 7, no. 2, (March 1992): 91–102; and PriceWaterhouseCoopers, MoneyTree Report, 2007.

16. Ian C. MacMillan, David M. Kulow, and Roubina Khoylian, "Venture Capitalists' Involvement in Their Investments: Extent and Performance," *Journal of Business Venturing* 4, no. 1, (January 1989): 27–47; Sharon Gifford, "Limited Attention and the Role of the Venture Capitalist," *Journal of Business Venturing* 12, no. 6 (1997): 459–82; and Dimo Dimov, Dean A. Shepherd, and Kathleen M. Sutcliffe, "Requisite Expertise, Firm Reputation, and Status in Venture Capital Investment Allocation Decisions," *Journal of Business Venturing* 22, no. 4 (2007): 481–502.

17. Gregory F. Chiampou and Joel J. Kallet, "Risk/Return Profile of Venture Capital," *Journal of Business Venturing* 4, no.1 (January 1989): 1–10; Jonathan D. Arthurs and Lowell W. Busenitz, "Dynamic Capabilities and Venture Performance: The Effects of Venture Capitalists," *Journal of Business Venturing* 21, no. 2 (March 2006): 195–216; and Dirk De Lercq and Harry J. Sapienza, "Effects of Relational Capital and Commitment on Venture Capitalists' Perception of Portfolio Company Performance," *Journal of Business Venturing* 21, no. 3 (May 2006): 326–47. See also, Charles Baden-Fuller, Alison Dean, Peter McNamara, and Bill Hilliard, "Raising the Returns to Venture Finance," *Journal of Business Venturing* 21, no. 3 (May 2006): 265–85.

18. Howard E. Van Auken, "Financing Small Technology-Based Companies: The Relationship Between Familiarity with Capital and Ability to Price and Negotiate Investment," *Journal of Small Business Management* 39, no. 3 (2001): 240–58.

19. De Clercq et al., "An Entrepreneur's Guide to the Venture Capital Galaxy"; see also Andrew J. Sherman, *Raising Capital,* 2nd ed. (New York: AMACOM Books, 2005).

20. Dean A. Shepherd, "Venture Capitalists' Introspection: A Comparison of 'In Use' and 'Espoused' Decision Policies," *Journal of Small Business Management* (April 1999): 76–87; and Dean A. Shepherd "Venture Capitalists' Assessment of New Venture Survival," *Management Science* (May 1999): 621–32.

21. Ian C. MacMillan, Robin Siegel, and P. N. Subba Narasimha, "Criteria Used by Venture Capitalists to Evaluate New Venture Proposals," *Journal of Business Venturing* 1, no. 1 (Winter 1985): 119–28.

22. John Hall and Charles W. Hofer, "Venture Capitalist's Decision Criteria in New Venture Evaluation," *Journal of Business Venturing* 8, no. 1, (January 1993): 25–42; see also Nikolaus Franke, Marc Gruber, Dietmar Harhoff, and Joachim Henkel, "What You Are Is What You Like—Similarity Biases in Venture Capitalists' Evaluations of Start Up Teams," *Journal of Business Venturing* 21, no. 6 (2006): 802–26.

23. Ronald J. Hustedde and Glen C. Pulver, "Factors Affecting Equity Capital Acquisition: The Demand Side," *Journal of Business Venturing* 7, no. 5, (September 1992): 363–74.

24. Harry J. Sapienza, "When Do Venture Capitalists Add Value?" *Journal of Business Venturing* 7, no. 1, (January 1992): 9–28; see also Juan Florin, "Is Venture Capital Worth It? Effects on Firm Performance and Founder Returns," *Journal of Business Venturing* 20, no. 1 (January 2005): 113–35; and Lowell W. Busenitz, James O. Fiet, and Douglas D. Moesel, "Reconsidering the Venture Capitalists' 'Value Added' Proposition: An Interorganizational Learning Perspective," *Journal of Business Venturing* 19, no. 6 (November 2004): 787–807.

25. B. Elango, Vance H. Fried, Robert D. Hisrich, and Amy Polonchek, "How Venture Capital Firms Differ," *Journal of Business Venturing* (March 1995): 157–79; Dean A. Shepherd and Andrew L. Zacharakis, "Venture Capitalists' Expertise: A Call for Research into Decision Aids and Cognitive Feedback," *Journal of Business Venturing* 17, no. 1 (2002): 1–20; and Dick De Clercq and Harry J. Sapienza, "When Do Venture Capitalists Learn from Their Portfolio Companies?" *Entrepreneurship Theory and Practice* 29, no. 4 (2005): 517–35.

26. Harold M. Hoffman and James Blakey, "You Can Negotiate with Venture Capitalists," *Harvard Business Review* (March/April 1987): 16; Andrew L. Zacharakis and Dean A. Shepherd, "The Nature of Information and Overconfidence on Venture Capitalist's Decision Making," *Journal of Business Venturing* 16, no. 4 (July 2001): 311–32; James C. Brau, Richard A. Brown, and Jerome S. Osteryoung, "Do Venture Capitalists Add Value to Small Manufacturing Firms? An Empirical Analysis of Venture and Nonventure Capital-Backed Initial Public Offerings," *Journal of Small Business Management* 42, no. 1 (January 2004): 78–92; and Lowell W. Busenitz, James O. Fiet, and Douglas D. Moesel, "Signaling in Venture Capitalist—New Venture Team Funding Decisions: Does It Indicate Long-Term Venture Outcomes?" *Entrepreneurship Theory and Practice* 29, no. 1 (January 2005): 1–12.

27. William E. Wetzel, Jr., "Informal Risk Capital: Knowns and Unknowns," in *The Art and Science of Entrepreneurship,* ed. Donald L. Sexton and Raymond W. Smilor (Cambridge, MA: Ballinger, 1986), 88.

28. William E. Wetzel, Jr., as quoted by Dale D. Buss, "Heaven Help Us," *Nation's Business* (November 1993): 29.

29. William E. Wetzel, Jr., "Angel Money," *In-Business* (November/December 1989): 44.

30. William E. Wetzel, Jr., "Angels and Informal Risk Capital," *Sloan Management Review* (Summer 1983); see also John Freear, Jeffrey E. Sohl, and William E. Wetzel, Jr., "Angels and Non-angels: Are There Differences?" *Journal of Business Venturing* (March 1994): 109–23.

31. Evanson, *Where to Go When the Bank Says No,* 40–44.

32. Buss, "Heaven Help Us," 29–30; see also John Freear, Jeffrey E. Sohl, and William E. Wetzel, Jr., "Angels:

Personal Investors in the Venture Capital Market," *Entrepreneurship & Regional Development* 7 (1995): 85–94; and Jeffrey Sohl, "The Angel Investor Market in 2007," Center for Venture Research, University of New Hampshire, May 2008.

33. Jeffrey Sohl, "The Angel Investor Market in 2007," Center for Venture Research, University of New Hampshire, May 2008.

34. Wetzel, "Angel Money," 42–44; and Colin M. Mason and Richard T. Harrison, "Is It Worth It? The Rates of Return from Informal Venture Capital Investments," *Journal of Business Venturing* 17, no. 3 (2002): 211–36.

Angel Investor vs. Venture Capitalist

DIRECTIONS:

Contact a local venture capital firm to schedule an interview with one of the partners. Then contact the local angel network to schedule an interview with an angel investor. If there is no local angel network, contact one of the respected law firms in your area and ask for a recommended source that could serve as an angel investor for the purposes of this exercise. For each interview, simply find out the answer to each component of the comparison table below.

Total Annual Investment in Start-Up Ventures

	Angel	Venture Capitalist
Total Dollars:		
Number of Investments:		
Number of Investors:		
Per Round:		
Entities per Round:		

Individual Investments in Start-Up Ventures

	Angel	Venture Capitalist
Investment Size per Round:		
Each Investor:		
Typical Investment Stage:		

Formulation of the Entrepreneurial Plan

part

3

9

The Assessment Function with Opportunities

Entrepreneurial Thought

To avoid all mistakes in the conduct of a great enterprise is beyond man's powers. . . . But, when a mistake has once been made, to use his reverses as lessons for the future is the part of a brave and sensible man.

— MINUCIUS (A.D. 209)

Chapter Objectives

1 To explain the challenge of new-venture start-ups

2 To review common pitfalls in the selection of new-venture ideas

3 To present critical factors involved in new-venture development

4 To examine why new ventures fail

5 To study certain factors that underlie venture success

6 To analyze the evaluation process methods: profile analysis, feasibility criteria approach, and comprehensive feasibility method

7 To outline the specific activities involved in a comprehensive feasibility evaluation

The Challenge of New-Venture Start-Ups

During the past two decades, the number of new-venture start-ups has been consistently high. It is reported that more than 600,000 new firms have emerged in the United States every year since the mid-1990s; that works out to approximately 1,500 business start-ups per day. In addition, the ideas for potential new businesses are also surfacing in record numbers; the U.S. Patent Office currently reviews more than 375,000 patent applications per year.[1]

The reasons that entrepreneurs start new ventures are numerous. One study reported seven components of new-venture motivation: (1) the need for approval, (2) the need for independence, (3) the need for personal development, (4) welfare (philanthropic) considerations, (5) perception of wealth, (6) tax reduction and indirect benefits, and (7) following role models.[2] These components are similar to the characteristics discussed in Chapter 3 concerning the "entrepreneurial mind-set." Although researchers agree that many reasons exist for starting a venture, the entrepreneurial motivations of individuals usually relate to the *personal characteristics* of the entrepreneur, the *environment*, and the *venture* itself. The complexity of these key factors makes the assessment of new ventures extremely difficult. One recent study examined the importance of start-up activities to potential entrepreneurs (those attempting to start a venture). Entrepreneurs who successfully started a business "were more aggressive in making their business real; that is, they undertook activities that made their businesses tangible to others: they looked for facilities and equipment, sought and got financial support, formed a legal entity, organized a team, bought facilities and equipment, and devoted full time to the business. Individuals who started businesses seemed to act with a greater level of intensity. They undertook more activities than those individuals who did not start their businesses. The pattern of activities seems to indicate that individuals who started firms put themselves into the day-to-day process of running an ongoing business as quickly as they could and that these activities resulted in starting firms that generated sales (94 percent of the entrepreneurs) and positive cash flow (50 percent of the entrepreneurs)."[3] Another study examined the quantitative and qualitative managerial factors that contribute to the success or failure of a young firm, and the results showed that firms do not have equal resources starting out. More importantly, the successful firms made greater use of professional advice and developed more detailed business plans.[4] Yet another recent study examined the importance of obtaining legitimacy with the early stakeholders as a prerequisite to venture survival.[5] As researcher Arnold C. Cooper points out, the challenges to predicting new-firm performance include environmental effects (the risk of new products or services, narrow markets, and scarce resources), the entrepreneur's personal goals and founding processes (reasons for start-up), and the diversity of the ventures themselves (differing scales and potential).[6] (See Figure 9.1 for illustration.) Some of the latest research studies are emphasizing the importance of "fit"

Figure 9.1   The Elements Affecting New-Venture Performance

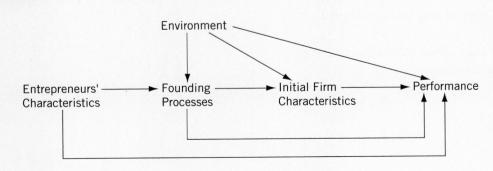

Source: Arnold C. Cooper, "Challenges in Predicting New Firm Performance," *Journal of Business Venturing* (May 1993): 243. Reprinted with permission.

for the entrepreneur with the organization—the idea that an individual's cognitive abilities must match with the organization or venture that he or she is attempting to develop.[7]

In addition to the problems presented by the complexity of the factors in new-venture performance, it is difficult to obtain reliable data concerning start-up, performance, and failure. Surveys by phone and mail have been used with owners, employees, and competitors to obtain measures of sales, profit, technology, market share, and so forth.[8] The results are not completely comparable to all ventures or all industries. It is from this pioneering work, however, that more and better data are being gathered for the evaluation of new ventures.

It should be understood that new-venture assessment begins with the idea and venture selection stage. However, most studies of new-venture development deal with established start-up businesses. A "fully developed new firm" has been described as one that requires the full-time commitment of one or more individuals, is selling a product or service, has formal financial support, and has hired one or more individuals.[9]

Therefore, as ideas develop into new-venture start-ups, the real challenge is for those firms to survive and grow. In order to do this, they need to have a clear understanding of the critical factors for selecting ventures, the known reasons for venture failure, and an effective evaluation process for new ventures.

Pitfalls in Selecting New Ventures

The first key area of analysis is the selection of a new venture. This stage of transition—from an idea to a potential venture—can be the most critical for understanding new-venture development. Following are six of the most important pitfalls commonly encountered in the process of selecting a new venture.

Lack of Objective Evaluation

Many entrepreneurs lack objectivity. Engineers and technically trained people are particularly prone to falling in love with an idea for a product or service. They seem unaware of the need for the scrutiny they would give to a design or project in the ordinary course of their professional work. The way to avoid this pitfall is to subject all ideas to rigorous study and investigation.[10]

No Real Insight into the Market

Many entrepreneurs do not realize the importance of developing a marketing approach in laying the foundation for a new venture. They show a managerial shortsightedness.[11] Also, they do not understand the life cycle that must be considered when introducing a new product or service.

No product is instantaneously profitable, nor does its success endure indefinitely. Entrepreneurs must not only project the life cycle of the new product, they must also recognize that introducing the product at the right time is important to its success. Timing is critical. Action taken too soon or too late will often result in failure.

Inadequate Understanding of Technical Requirements

The development of a new product often involves new techniques. Failure to anticipate the technical difficulties related to developing or producing a product can sink a new venture. Entrepreneurs cannot be too thorough when studying the project before initiating it. Encountering unexpected technical difficulties frequently poses time-consuming and costly problems.

Poor Financial Understanding

A common difficulty with the development of a new product is an overly optimistic estimate of the funds required to carry the project to completion. Sometimes entrepreneurs are ignorant of costs or are victims of inadequate research and planning. Quite often they tend to underestimate development costs by wide margins. It is not unusual for estimates to be less than half of what is eventually required.

eBay Entrepreneurship

Fledgling entrepreneurs are flocking to eBay because of the ease with which the site's users can start a business. Currently, more than 247 million registered users do business on eBay, which has led to $60 billion in sales annually. Taking the following nine steps will get you well on your way to starting a successful eBay business.

Start with used items. Given most people's access to used items in their homes, cleaning out storage is a natural way to get started selling. The problem with such an approach can be the time that it takes to find and clean merchandise; however, the low costs and risks associated with selling used products, at least in the beginning, far outweigh the time commitment required.

Develop a specialty. The more specialized your business becomes, the more confidence your customers will have in your offerings and the less time you will spend addressing questions about the random products you found in your basement. Most sellers start by selling used items, but eventually, the successful eBay seller will develop a niche to allow for greater economies of scale.

Research the market. Selling on eBay does not excuse you from the usual legwork involved in starting a business. In order to determine the right market for you, conduct research on how much items in a given category are selling for on eBay as well as elsewhere. Marketplace Research is a subscription-based tool available through eBay that allows you to view historical pricing information for products.

Access assistance. You will certainly make mistakes as you build your eBay business, but many of your questions can be answered by accessing eBay's help files or by reading the discussion boards, through which successful sellers provide feedback and advice.

Invest in your business. If you plan to start your eBay business by selling off old items lying around your home, you will not need to invest much, if any, upfront capital; however, as your business grows, a few items will come in handy. First, designating a computer to be used solely for your eBay transactions will allow you to fully deduct it on your taxes. Second, a regulation postal scale will save you several hours waiting in line at the post office. Finally,

a decent camera is a must. Posting poor-quality photos of your merchandise will lead your customers to wonder about the quality of the rest of your business.

Develop a system. As with any business, policies and procedures become increasingly important the larger your business becomes. Standardizing your templates or buying some through eBay's Seller Tools section will help to streamline the process. In addition, establishing a routine for corresponding with your customers regarding their questions and concerns will enable you to prevent any minor issues from escalating into major problems.

Find a reliable product source. In order for your business to grow, you will need to gain access to a reliable source of consistent products. Starting with garage sales might work in the onset, but each product you post will likely be one of a kind, which makes posting and shipping the products time consuming. Developing a relationship with a manufacturer or a master distributor is required to develop a reasonable profit margin; however, avoid overstocking when trying to take advantage of cheap merchandise. Stick to what you know and grow your business slowly to avoid losing track of your customer base.

Manage customer expectations. Make sure to under-promise and over-deliver to guarantee that your customers will not be disappointed when your product is described as "new" but arrives with a mild scratch. Be as forthright as possible. If you notice an imperfection, your customer surely will as well.

Know your numbers. eBay charges listing and final value fees, which can add up if you have to post your merchandise multiple times; however, the cost of gaining access to eBay's customer base is insignificant when compared to the cost of using traditional advertising channels. If you expect your product to take several auctions to sell, cover your costs by charging higher seller fees.

Never misrepresent your products. Customers who have been misled will likely take the issue to eBay for reconciliation, which will most likely result in you reimbursing the customer and potentially being reprimanded.

Offer an unconditional guarantee. This puts the buyer at ease and avoids any complications due to damage during shipping or the customer claiming product misrepresentation.

Offer PayPal. As an accepted form of payment, an estimated 93–95 percent of buyers prefer to pay online. Although less popular, some customers might prefer to pay with personal checks and money orders, so allowing

these forms of payment can make those customers less familiar with online shopping more comfortable.

Source: Adapted from Marcia Layton Turner, "Get Sold on eBay," *Entrepreneur*, March 2008, http://www.entrepreneur.com/magazine/entrepreneur/2008/march/190186.html (accessed March 16, 2008).

Lack of Venture Uniqueness

A new venture should be unique. Uniqueness is the special characteristics and design concepts that draw the customer to the venture, which should provide performance or service that is superior to competitive offerings. The best way to ensure customer awareness of differences between the company's product and competitors' products is through product differentiation. Pricing becomes less of a problem when the customer sees the product as superior to its competitors. A product that is unique in a significant way can gain the advantage of differentiation.

Ignorance of Legal Issues

Business is subject to many legal requirements. One is the need to make the workplace safe for employees. A second is to provide reliable and safe products and services. A third is the necessity for patents, trademarks, and copyrights to protect one's inventions and products. When these legal issues are overlooked, major problems can result.

Critical Factors for New-Venture Development

A number of critical factors are important for new-venture assessment. One way to identify and evaluate them is with a checklist (see Table 9.1). In most cases, however, such a questionnaire approach is too general. The assessment must be tailor-made for the specific venture.

Table 9.1   A New-Venture Idea Checklist

Basic Feasibility of the Venture

1. Can the product or service work?
2. Is it legal?

Competitive Advantages of the Venture

1. What specific competitive advantages will the product or service offer?
2. What are the competitive advantages of the companies already in business?
3. How are the competitors likely to respond?
4. How will the initial competitive advantage be maintained?

Buyer Decisions in the Venture

1. Who are the customers likely to be?
2. How much will each customer buy, and how many customers are there?
3. Where are these customers located, and how will they be serviced?

Continued

Table	9.1	A New-Venture Idea Checklist (*Continued*)

Marketing of the Goods and Services

1. How much will be spent on advertising and selling?
2. What share of market will the company capture? By when?
3. Who will perform the selling functions?
4. How will prices be set? How will they compare with the competition's prices?
5. How important is location, and how will it be determined?
6. What distribution channels will be used—wholesale, retail, agents, direct mail?
7. What are the sales targets? By when should they be met?
8. Can any orders be obtained before starting the business? How many? For what total amount?

Production of the Goods and Services

1. Will the company make or buy what it sells? Or will it use a combination of these two strategies?
2. Are sources of supplies available at reasonable prices?
3. How long will delivery take?
4. Have adequate lease arrangements for premises been made?
5. Will the needed equipment be available on time?
6. Do any special problems with plant setup, clearances, or insurance exist? How will they be resolved?
7. How will quality be controlled?
8. How will returns and servicing be handled?
9. How will pilferage, waste, spoilage, and scrap be controlled?

Staffing Decisions in the Venture

1. How will competence in each area of the business be ensured?
2. Who will have to be hired? By when? How will they be found and recruited?
3. Will a banker, lawyer, accountant, or other advisers be needed?
4. How will replacements be obtained if key people leave?
5. Will special benefit plans have to be arranged?

Control of the Venture

1. What records will be needed? When?
2. Will any special controls be required? What are they? Who will be responsible for them?

Financing the Venture

1. How much will be needed for development of the product or service?
2. How much will be needed for setting up operations?
3. How much will be needed for working capital?
4. Where will the money come from? What if more is needed?
5. Which assumptions in the financial forecasts are most uncertain?
6. What will the return on equity or sales be, and how does it compare with the rest of the industry?
7. When and how will investors get their money back?
8. What will be needed from the bank, and what is the bank's response?

Source: Karl H. Vesper, *New Venture Strategies*, copyright © 1990, 172. Adapted by permission of Prentice Hall, Inc., Englewood Cliffs, New Jersey.

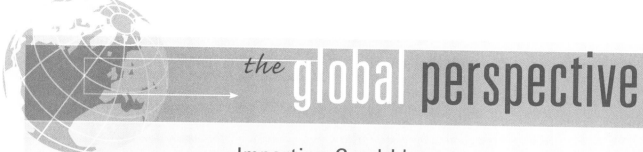

Importing Good Ideas

Some entrepreneurs rack their brains trying to come up with the next big thing. There is no arguing that the thrill of developing an idea, commercializing it, and seeing it blossom into a successful business is the process that drives many people to pursue their entrepreneurial aspirations; however, another path is often left unnoticed: importing someone else's idea.

Many opportunities exist for licensing technology. From large corporations and universities making their intellectual property portfolios available to scientists looking to partner with business people to develop a venture, opportunities for building a business around the ideas of others abound. Some entrepreneurs have begun to discover the potential for taking concepts developed overseas and bringing them to their home market.

Dieter Kondek, a German-born entrepreneur living in Cape Coral, Florida, is one such entrepreneur. He noticed that the new condos being built around his home were using what he considered to be cheap lighting. Given his connection to Germany, he was aware of Moonlight, a German-based manufacturing company specializing in glowing orbs that can be used to light paths, rooms, and pools.

Kondek was curious about the lack of availability of Moonlight's globes in the United States. He began to research the products and became further intrigued by their versatility—they can tolerate environments that range between −40° and 170° Fahrenheit in temperature. He next studied the distribution being used by the company and found that Moonlight had distributors in Europe, the Middle East, and Asia but had yet to enter the United States.

Given that Kondek had spent 30 years working in a high-tech field, he and his wife decided that they were ideally suited to take on the task of introducing Moonlight's globes to the States. They and two of their friends formed Moonlight U.S.A. and gained an exclusive distribution deal with the company. Moonlight has sold 10,000 globes worldwide, ranging in price from $325 to $1,000. Kondek predicts that U.S. sales will soon generate as much as half of Moonlight's sales.

With overseas studies becoming an important part of the educational experience, students are ideally suited to discover opportunities for importing foreign products. The management in foreign manufacturing companies might assume that their products would not sell in a given country or that they do not have strong enough experience doing business in the country to build a successful operation. Those entrepreneurs able to prove that the potential of such a venture would outweigh the risks for these companies could find that they are in a better position to start the business than the manufacturers.

Source: Adapted from Jessica Centers, "Glowing German Orbs Alight in U.S.," *Fortune*, April 1, 2008, http://money.cnn.com/2008/03/27/smbusiness/great_balls_light.fsb/index.htm?postversion=2008040112 (accessed April 9, 2008).

A new venture goes through three specific phases: prestart-up, start-up, and poststart-up. The prestart-up phase begins with an idea for the venture and ends when the doors are opened for business. The start-up phase commences with the initiation of sales activity and the delivery of products and services, and ends when the business is firmly established and beyond short-term threats to survival. The poststart-up phase lasts until the venture is terminated or the surviving organizational entity is no longer controlled by an entrepreneur.

The major focus in this chapter is on the prestart-up and start-up phases, because these are the critical segments for entrepreneurs. During these two phases, five factors are critical: (1) the relative uniqueness of the venture, (2) the relative investment size at start-up, (3) the expected growth of sales and/or profits as the venture moves through its start-up phase, (4) the availability of products during the prestart-up and start-up phases, and (5) the availability of customers during the prestart-up and start-up phases.

Uniqueness

A new venture's range of uniqueness can be considerable, extending from fairly routine to highly nonroutine. What separates the routine from the nonroutine venture is the amount of innovation required during prestart-up. This distinction is based on the need for new process technology to produce services or products and on the need to service new market segments. Venture uniqueness is further characterized by the length of time a nonroutine venture will remain nonroutine. For instance, will new products, new technology, and new markets be required on a continuing basis? Or will the venture be able to "settle down" after the start-up period and use existing products, technologies, and markets?

Investment

The capital investment required to start a new venture can vary considerably. In some industries less than $100,000 may be required, whereas in other industries millions of dollars are necessary. Moreover, in some industries only large-scale start-ups are feasible. For example, in the publishing industry one can start a small venture that can remain small or grow into a larger venture. By contrast, an entrepreneur attempting to break into the airline industry will need a considerable upfront investment.

Another finance-related critical issue is the extent and timing of funds needed to move through the venture process. To determine the amount of needed investment, entrepreneurs must answer questions such as these: Will industry growth be sufficient to maintain break-even sales to cover a high fixed-cost structure during the start-up period? Do the principal entrepreneurs have access to substantial financial reserves to protect a large initial investment? Do the entrepreneurs have the appropriate contacts to take advantage of various environmental opportunities? Do the entrepreneurs have both industry and entrepreneurial track records that justify the financial risk of a large-scale start-up?[12]

Growth of Sales

The **growth of sales** through the start-up phase is another critical factor. Key questions are as follows: What is the growth pattern anticipated for new-venture sales and profits? Are sales and profits expected to grow slowly or level off shortly after start-up? Are large profits expected at some point, with only small or moderate sales growth? Or are both high sales growth and high profit growth likely? Or will initial profits be limited, with eventual high profit growth over a multiyear period? In answering these questions, it is important to remember that most ventures fit into one of the three following classifications.

- Lifestyle ventures appear to have independence, autonomy, and control as their primary driving forces. Neither large sales nor profits are deemed important beyond providing a sufficient and comfortable living for the entrepreneur.

- In small profitable ventures, financial considerations play a major role. Autonomy and control also are important in the sense that the entrepreneur does not want venture sales (and employment) to become so large that he or she must relinquish equity or an ownership position and thus give up control over cash flow and profits—which, it is hoped, will be substantial.

- In high-growth ventures, significant sales and profit growth are expected to the extent that it may be possible to attract venture capital money and funds raised through public or private placements.[13]

Product Availability

Essential to the success of any venture is **product availability**, the availability of a salable good or service at the time the venture opens its doors. Some ventures have problems in this regard because the product or service is still in development and needs further modification or testing. Other ventures find that, because they bring their product to market too soon, it must be recalled for further work. A typical example is the software firm that rushes the development of its product and is then besieged by customers who find "bugs" in the program. Lack of product availability in finished form can affect the company's image and its bottom line.

Customer Availability

If the product is available before the venture is started, the likelihood of venture success is considerably better than it would be otherwise. Similarly, venture risk is affected by **customer availability** for start-up. At one end of the risk continuum is the situation where customers are willing to pay cash for products or services before delivery. At the other end of the continuum is the enterprise that gets started without knowing exactly who will buy its product. A critical consideration is how long it will take to determine who the customers are, as well as their buying habits. As one researcher noted:

> The decision to ignore the market is an extremely risky one. There are, after all, two fundamental criteria for entrepreneurial success. The first is having a customer who is willing to pay you a profitable price for a product or a service. The second is that you must actually produce and deliver the product or service. The farther a venture removes itself from certainty about these two rules, the greater the risk and the greater the time required to offset this risk as the venture moves through the prestart-up and start-up periods.[14]

Why New Ventures Fail

Every year, many millions of dollars are spent on starting new enterprises. Many of these newly established businesses vanish within a year or two; only a small percentage succeed. Most studies have found that the factors underlying the failure of new ventures are, in most cases, within the control of the entrepreneur. Some of the major reasons for the failure of new ventures follow.

One research study examined 250 high-tech firms and found three major categories of causes for failure: product/market problems, financial difficulties, and managerial problems.[15]

Product/market problems involved the following factors:

- *Poor timing.* A premature entry into the marketplace contributed to failure in 40 percent of the cases studied.

- *Product design problems.* Although these may be related to timing, product design and development became key factors at earlier stages of the venture; when the essential makeup of the product or service changed, failure resulted.

- *Inappropriate distribution strategy.* Whether it was based on commissioned sales representatives or direct sales at trade shows, the distribution strategy had to be geared toward the product and customer.

- *Unclear business definition.* Uncertainty about the "exact" business they were in caused these firms to undergo constant change and to lack stabilization.

- *Overreliance on one customer.* This resulted in a failure to diversify and brought about the eventual demise of some of the firms.

The financial difficulties category involved the following factors:

- *Initial undercapitalization.* Undercapitalization contributed to failure in 30 percent of the case studies.

- *Assuming debt too early.* Some of the firms attempted to obtain debt financing too soon and in too large an amount. This led to debt service problems.

- *Venture capital relationship problems.* Differing goals, visions, and motivations of the entrepreneur and the venture capitalist resulted in problems for the enterprise.

Managerial problems involved two important factors:

- *Concept of a team approach.* The following problems associated with the managerial team were found: (1) hirings and promotions on the basis of nepotism rather than qualifications, (2) poor relationships with parent companies and venture capitalists, (3) founders who focused on their weaknesses rather than on their strengths (though weakening the company, they supposedly were building their skills), and (4) incompetent support professionals (for example, attorneys who were unable to read contracts or collect on court judgments that already had been made).

- *Human resource problems.* Inflated owner ego, employee-related concerns, and control factors were all problems that led to business failure. The study also revealed such interpersonal problems as (1) kickbacks and subsequent firings that resulted in an almost total loss of customers, (2) deceit on the part of a venture capitalist in one case and on the part of a company president in another, (3) verbal agreements between the entrepreneur and the venture capitalists that were not honored, and (4) protracted lawsuits around the time of discontinuance.

In a more recent study of successful ventures (firms listed in the *Inc. 500* group of fastest-growing privately held companies), the most significant problems encountered at start-up were researched in order to systematically sort them into a schematic. Table 9.2 lists the types and classes of problems identified during the first year of operation. The researcher also surveyed the current problems the owners of these successful firms encountered in order to explore the possible changes in problem patterns of new firms. It was found that dominant problems at start-up related to sales/marketing (38 percent), obtaining external financing (17 percent), and internal financial management (16 percent). General management problems were also frequently cited in the start-up stage (11 percent). Sales/marketing remained the most dominant problem (22 percent) in the growth stage, but it was less important than in the start-up stage. Internal financial management (21 percent) continued to be a dominant problem, as were human resource management (17 percent) and general management (14 percent). Additionally, more regulatory environment problems occurred in the growth stage (8 percent) than were mentioned in the start-up stage (1 percent). Finally, organizational structure/design (6 percent) emerged as a problem in the growth stage.[16] It is important for entrepreneurs to recognize these problem areas at the outset because they remain challenges to the venture as it grows.

Table 9.2   Types and Classes of First-Year Problems

1. *Obtaining external financing*
   Obtaining financing for growth
   Other or general financing problems
2. *Internal financial management*
   Inadequate working capital
   Cash-flow problems
   Other or general financial management problems
3. *Sales/marketing*
   Low sales
   Dependence on one or few clients/customers
   Marketing or distribution channels
   Promotion/public relations/advertising
   Other or general marketing problems
4. *Product development*
   Developing products/services
   Other or general product development problems
5. *Production/operations management*
   Establishing or maintaining quality control
   Raw materials/resources/supplies

   Other or general production/operations management problems
6. *General management*
   Lack of management experience
   Only one person/no time
   Managing/controlling growth
   Administrative problems
   Other or general management problems
7. *Human resource management*
   Recruitment/selection
   Turnover/retention
   Satisfaction/morale
   Employee development
   Other or general human resource management problems
8. *Economic environment*
   Poor economy/recession
   Other or general economic environment problems
9. *Regulatory environment*
   Insurance

Source: David E. Terpstra and Philip D. Olson, "Entrepreneurial Start-Up and Growth: A Classification of Problems," *Entrepreneurship Theory and Practice* (Spring 1993): 19.

Another study of 645 entrepreneurs focused on the classification of start-up and growth problems experienced internally versus externally.[17] Figure 9.2 depicts the types of problems and the percentage of firms that reported these problems. Internal problems involved adequate capital, cash flow, facilities/equipment, inventory control, human resources, leadership, organizational structure, and accounting systems. External problems were related to customer contact, market knowledge, marketing planning, location, pricing, product considerations, competitors, and expansion. The researchers found that the "intensity of competition" rather than life-cycle stages was crucial in changing the relative importance of the problem areas. Thus, entrepreneurs need to recognize not only that start-up problems remain with the venture but also that the increasing competition will adjust the relative importance of the problems.

The differing perceptions of new-venture failure were examined in another study conducted by researchers Andrew Zacharakis, G. Dale Meyer, and Julio DeCastro. Internal and external factors were identified and ranked by a sample of venture capitalists as well as a sample of entrepreneurs. Entrepreneurs attributed new-venture failure in general to

Figure 9.2   Internal and External Problems Experienced by Entrepreneurs

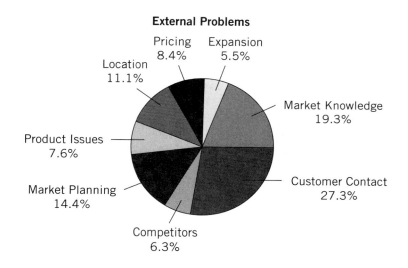

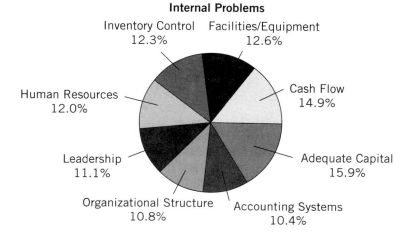

Source: H. Robert Dodge, Sam Fullerton, and John E. Robbins, "Stage of Organization Life Cycle and Competition as Mediators of Problem Perception for Small Businesses," *Strategic Management Journal* 15 (1994): 129. Reprinted by permission of John Wiley & Sons, Ltd.

internal factors 89 percent of the time. In the same vein, venture capitalists overwhelmingly attributed the failure of most new ventures to *internal* causes (84 percent).[18] (See Table 9.3.)

A fourth "failure" or problem study dealt with a proposed failure prediction model based on financial data from newly founded ventures. The study assumed that the financial failure process was characterized by too much initial indebtedness and too little revenue financing. As shown by the failure process schematic in Table 9.4, the risk of failure can be reduced by using less debt as initial financing and by generating enough revenue in the initial stages. Furthermore, the study recognized the risk associated with the initial size of the venture being developed. Specific applications of the model included the following:[19]

1. *Role of profitability and cash flows.* The entrepreneur and manager should ensure that the products are able to yield positive profitability and cash flows in the first years.

2. *Role of debt.* The entrepreneur and manager should ensure that enough stockholders' capital is in the initial balance sheet to buffer future losses.

3. *Combination of both.* The entrepreneur and manager should not start a business if the share of stockholders' capital in the initial balance sheet is low and if negative cash flows in the first years are probable.

4. *Role of initial size.* The entrepreneur and manager should understand that the more probable the negative cash flows and the larger the debt share in the initial balance sheet, the smaller the initial size of the business should be.

5. *Role of velocity of capital.* The entrepreneur and manager should not budget for fast velocity of capital in the initial years if the risk of negative cash flows is high. More sales in comparison to capital results in more negative cash flows and poorer profitability.

6. *Role of control.* The entrepreneur and manager should monitor financial ratios from the first year, especially the cash-flow-to-total-debt ratio. Risky combinations of ratios—especially negative cash flows, a low stockholders' capital-to-total-capital ratio, and a high velocity of capital—should be monitored and compared with industrial standards. The entrepreneur should try to identify the reasons for poor ratios and pay special attention to keeping profitability at the planned level (with control ratios).

Table 9.3   Determinants of New-Venture Failures

Entrepreneur	Rank	Venture Capitalist	Rank
I—Lack of management skill	1	I—Lack of management skill	1
I—Poor management strategy	2	I—Poor management strategy	2
I—Lack of capitalization	3	I—Lack of capitalization	3
I—Lack of vision	4	E—Poor external market conditions	4
I—Poor product design	5	I—Poor product design	5
I—Key personnel incompetent	6	I—Poor product timing	6

E = External factor; I = Internal factor

Source: Andrew L. Zacharakis, G. Dale Meyer, and Julio DeCastro, "Differing Perceptions of New Venture Failure: A Matched Exploratory Study of Venture Capitalists and Entrepreneurs," *Journal of Small Business Management* (July 1999): 8.

Table	**9.4**	**The Failure Process of a Newly Founded Firm**

1. Extremely high indebtedness (poor static solidity) and small size
2. Too slow velocity of capital, too fast growth, too poor profitability (as compared to the budget), or some combination of these
3. Unexpected lack of revenue financing (poor dynamic liquidity)
4. Poor static liquidity and debt service ability (dynamic solidity)

A. Profitability

1. Return on investment ratio defined on end-of-the-year basis
$$= \frac{\text{Net Profit} + \text{Interest Expenses}}{\text{Total Capital at the End of the Year}} \times 100$$

B. Liquidity

Dynamic

2. Cash flow to net sales
$$= \frac{\text{Net Profit} + \text{Depreciations}}{\text{Net Sales}} \times 100$$

Static

3. Quick ratio
$$= \frac{\text{Financial Assets}}{\text{Current Debt}}$$

C. Solidity

Static

4. Stockholders' capital to total capital
$$= \frac{\text{Total Capital} - \text{Debt Capital}}{\text{Total Capital}} \times 100$$

Dynamic

5. Cash flow to total debt
$$= \frac{\text{Net Profit} + \text{Depreciations}}{\text{Total Debt}} \times 100$$

D. Other Factors

Growth or Dynamic Size

6. Rate of annual growth in net sales
$$= \frac{\text{Net Sales in year } t}{\text{Net Sales in year } t-1} \times 100$$

Size

7. Logarithmic net sales
$$= \ln(\text{Net Sales})$$

Velocity of Capital

8. Net sales to total capital
$$= \frac{\text{Net Sales}}{\text{Total Capital at the End of the Year}} \times 100$$

Source: Erkki K. Laitinen, "Prediction of Failure of a Newly Founded Firm," *Journal of Business Venturing* (July 1992): 326–28. Reprinted with permission.

The Evaluation Process

A critical task of starting a new business enterprise is conducting solid analysis and evaluation of the feasibility of the product/service idea getting off the ground. Entrepreneurs must put their ideas through this analysis to discover if the proposals contain any fatal flaws.

Profile Analysis

A single strategic variable seldom shapes the ultimate success or failure of a new venture. In most situations, a combination of variables influences the outcome. Thus, it is important to identify and investigate these variables before the new idea is put into practice. The results of such a profile analysis enable the entrepreneur to judge the business's potential.

The internal profile analysis in the Experiential Exercise at the end of this chapter is one method of determining the resources available to a new venture. This checklist approach allows entrepreneurs to identify major strengths and weaknesses in the financial, marketing, organizational, and human resource factors needed for the venture to progress successfully. In this manner, entrepreneurs can prepare for possible weaknesses that may inhibit the growth of their ventures. More importantly, many of the reasons cited for venture failure earlier in this chapter can be avoided through a careful profile analysis.

Feasibility Criteria Approach

Another method, the feasibility criteria approach, was developed as a criteria selection list from which entrepreneurs can gain insights into the viability of their venture; this approach is based on the following questions:

- *Is it proprietary?* The product does not have to be patented, but it should be sufficiently proprietary to permit a long head start against competitors and a period of extraordinary profits early in the venture to offset start-up costs.

- *Are the initial production costs realistic?* Most estimates are too low. A careful, detailed analysis should be made so that no large, unexpected expenses arise.

- *Are the initial marketing costs realistic?* This answer requires the venture to identify target markets, market channels, and promotional strategy.

- *Does the product have potential for very high margins?* This is almost a necessity for a fledgling company. Gross margins are one thing the financial community understands. Without them, funding can be difficult.

- *Is the time required to get to market and to reach the break-even point realistic?* In most cases, the faster the better. In all cases, the venture plan will be tied to this answer, and an error here can spell trouble later on.

- *Is the potential market large?* In determining the potential market, entrepreneurs must look three to five years into the future, because some markets take this long to emerge. The cellular telephone, for example, had an annual demand of approximately 400,000 units in 1982. However, in the twenty-first century, this market has grown exponentially.

- *Is the product the first of a growing family?* If it is, the venture is more attractive to investors. If they do not realize a large return on the first product, they might on the second, third, or fourth.

- *Does an initial customer exist?* It is certainly impressive to financial backers when a venture can list its first ten customers by name. This pent-up demand also means the first quarter's results are likely to be good and the focus of attention can be directed to later quarters.

- *Are the development costs and calendar times realistic?* Preferably, they are zero. A ready-to-go product gives the venture a big advantage over competitors. If costs exist, they should be complete, detailed, and tied to a month-by-month schedule.

- *Is this a growing industry?* This is not absolutely essential if the profits and company growth are there, but it means less room for mistakes. In a growing industry, good companies do even better.

- *Can the product—and the need for it—be understood by the financial community?* If the financiers can grasp the concept and its value, the chances for funding will increase. For example, a portable heart-monitoring system for postcoronary monitoring is a product many will understand. Undoubtedly, some of those hearing the presentation will already have had coronaries or heart problems of some sort.[20]

This criteria selection approach provides a means of analyzing the internal strengths and weaknesses that exist in a new venture by focusing on the marketing and industry potential critical to assessment. If the new venture meets fewer than six of these criteria, it typically lacks feasibility for funding. If the new venture meets seven or more of the criteria, it may stand a good chance of being funded.

Comprehensive Feasibility Approach

A more comprehensive and systematic feasibility analysis, a comprehensive feasibility approach, incorporates external factors in addition to those included in the criteria questions.

Figure 9.3 presents a breakdown of the factors involved in a comprehensive feasibility study of a new venture: technical, market, financial, organizational, and competitive. A more detailed feasibility analysis guide is provided in Table 9.5, which identifies the specific activities involved in each feasibility area. Although all five of the areas presented in Figure 9.3 are important, two merit special attention: technical and market.

TECHNICAL FEASIBILITY

The evaluation of a new-venture idea should start with identifying the technical requirements—the technical feasibility—for producing a product or service that will satisfy the expectations of potential customers. The most important of these are:

- Functional design of the product and attractiveness in appearance
- Flexibility, permitting ready modification of the external features of the product to meet customer demands or technological and competitive changes
- Durability of the materials from which the product is made
- Reliability, ensuring performance as expected under normal operating conditions
- Product safety, posing no potential dangers under normal operating conditions
- Reasonable utility, an acceptable rate of obsolescence
- Ease and low cost of maintenance
- Standardization through elimination of unnecessary variety among potentially interchangeable parts
- Ease of processing or manufacture
- Ease in handling and use[21]

The results of this investigation provide a basis for deciding whether a new venture is feasible from a technical point of view.

MARKETABILITY

Assembling and analyzing relevant information about the marketability of a new venture are vital for judging its potential success. Three major areas in this type of analysis are (1) investigating the full market potential and identifying customers (or users) for the goods or service, (2) analyzing the extent to which the enterprise might exploit this potential market, and (3) using market analysis to determine the opportunities and risks associated with the venture. To address these areas, a variety of informational sources must be found and used. For a market feasibility analysis, general sources would include the following:

- *General economic trends:* various economic indicators such as new orders, housing starts, inventories, and consumer spending
- *Market data:* customers, customer demand patterns (for example, seasonal variations in demand, governmental regulations affecting demand)

Figure **9.3**   **Key Areas for Assessing the Feasibility of a New Venture**

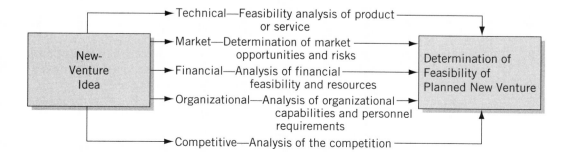

Table 9.5	Specific Activities of Feasibility Analyses			
Technical Feasibility Analysis	**Market Feasibility Analysis**	**Financial Feasibility Analysis**	**Analysis of Organizational Capabilities**	**Competitive Analysis**
Crucial technical specifications	*Market potential*	*Required financial resources for:*	*Personnel requirements*	*Existing competitors*
Design	Identification of potential customers and their dominant characteristics (e.g., age, income level, buying habits)	Fixed assets	Required skill levels and other personal characteristics of potential employees	Size, financial resources, market entrenchment
Durability		Current assets		Potential reaction of competitors to newcomer by means of price cutting, aggressive advertising, introduction of new products, and other actions
Reliability		Necessary working capital	Managerial requirements	
Product safety		*Available financial resources*	Determination of individual responsibilities	
Standardization	Potential market share (as affected by competitive situation)	Required borrowing		
Engineering requirements		Potential sources for funds		
Machines	Potential sales volume	Costs of borrowing	Determination of required organizational relationships	
Tools		Repayment conditions		
Instruments	Sales price projections			
Work flow		Operation cost analysis	Potential organizational development	
Product development	*Market testing*	Fixed costs	Competitive analysis	
Blueprints	Selection of test	Variable costs		
Models	Actual market test	Projected profitability		
Prototypes	Analysis of market			
Product testing	*Marketing planning issues*			
Lab testing				
Field testing	Preferred channels of distribution, impact of promotional efforts, required distribution points (warehouses), packaging considerations, price differentiation			
Plant location				
Desirable characteristics of plant site (proximity to suppliers, customers), environmental regulations				

Source: Hans Schollhammer and Arthur H. Kuriloff, *Entrepreneurship and Small Business Management* (New York: John Wiley & Sons, 1979): 56. Copyright © 1979 by John Wiley & Sons, Inc. Reprinted by permission of John Wiley & Sons, Inc.

- *Pricing data:* range of prices for the same, complementary, and substitute products; base prices; and discount structures
- *Competitive data:* major competitors and their competitive strength

More attention is given to marketing issues in Chapter 10. At this point, it is important to note the value of marketing research in the overall assessment and evaluation of a new venture.[22]

Thus, as demonstrated by Table 9.5, the comprehensive feasibility analysis approach is closely related to the preparation of a thorough business plan (covered in detail in Chapter 12). The approach clearly illustrates the need to evaluate each segment of the venture *before* initiating the business or presenting it to capital sources.

To assist in understanding feasibility analysis, Appendix 9A illustrates a template used for a complete feasibility plan. This template, created in a format to answer specific questions about

entrepreneurship in practice

Facing Your Fears!

The inner journey to the creation of an entrepreneurial venture can be even more fearful than the external process of developing a business plan and searching for capital. Building up the courage to quit a job and start a new venture can sound easy and yet pose enormous emotional challenges when the actual events are about to unfold. One consultant, Suzanne Mulvehill—author of *Employee to Entrepreneur* and host of her own radio talk show—suggests particular strategies to follow when confronting the emotional challenges of entrepreneurial start-ups. She coined the term *Emotional Endurance* to signify the inner strength that is needed to make the jump from job to venture. Following are a few of the more significant strategies that may help entrepreneurs move through the emotional journey.

1. **Say yes to your yearning.** In other words, acknowledge the desire you are experiencing to venture out on your own. It all begins with accepting the possibility that it could happen.

2. **Visualize your success.** Creating a vision of what *could* be may be a powerful motivator to what *will* be. It is important to write down this vision so it has tangible reality in this early stage.

3. **Evaluate your beliefs.** On a sheet of paper, list all of your beliefs about money, business, and yourself. Then, in a similar column, write down how you would *like* to view money, business, and yourself. Compare these beliefs and decide how far apart they are and why.

4. **Do what you love.** There is no replacement for passion. What you love is what will drive you to succeed, even in the tough times. Develop your business ideas around the types of things that you absolutely love to do.

5. **Get educated.** Avoid the myths that education saps out any desire to be an entrepreneur.

That may have been true 20 years ago, but we have come a long way in our approaches to business education. Entrepreneurship education is the hottest subject in universities worldwide. Remember, knowledge is power.

6. **Eliminate excuses.** Whenever you hear yourself make an excuse for not doing something, write it down and examine it later. Become aware of common excuses you may be using that have no real foundation. Turn your "I can'ts" into open-ended questions that allow you to explore the possibilities rather than shut the door.

7. **Know that there is no "right time."** Waiting for the proverbial perfect time is a trap that many people fall into, only to find later that time passed them by. The only guarantee we have about time is that it continues on, with or without us. Rather than wait, you need to proactively move on your idea.

8. **Start small.** It is always better to be realistic and reach for what you can accomplish in the near future. The longer-term future may hold greater things for the venture, but at the beginning you need to avoid being overwhelmed.

9. **Answer the "what ifs."** Stop for a moment and write down all of the "what ifs" that you question yourself with. See if you can begin to logically answer the questions. It's amazing how much courage will be gained by analyzing these contingencies.

10. **Ask for help.** Reach out and find help. The maverick entrepreneur is a myth of the past. Today, there is so much assistance available if you are willing to seek it out. Ignorance is not asking questions; rather, ignorance is being arrogant enough to think you have all the answers.

Source: Adapted from Suzanne Mulvehill, "Fear Factor," *Entrepreneur* (April 2005): 104–11.

the proposed venture idea, allows entrepreneurs the ability to analyze each important segment before moving forward with an idea. Venture capitalists generally agree that the risks in any entrepreneurial venture are you, your management team, and any apparent fundamental flaws in your venture idea. Therefore, you need to make a reasonable evaluation of these risks.

Summary

The complexity of factors involved in new-venture start-up (as shown in Figure 9.1) makes it difficult to clearly assess and evaluate each one. In addition, the difficulty of obtaining reliable data on failed firms adds to this dilemma. Improvements are being made, however, and new-venture assessment is becoming a stronger process.

A number of pitfalls may occur in the selection of a new venture: lack of an objective evaluation of the venture, lack of insight into the market, inadequate understanding of technical requirements, poor financial understanding, lack of venture uniqueness, and failure to be aware of legal issues.

When assessing a new venture, an entrepreneur needs to consider several critical factors: the uniqueness of the good or service, the amount of capital investment required to start the venture, the growth of sales, and the availability of the product.

Some major reasons new ventures fail are inadequate knowledge of the market, faulty product performance, ineffective marketing and sales effort, inadequate awareness of competitive pressures, rapid product obsolescence, poor timing, and undercapitalization. In drawing together these and other reasons, recent research reveals three major categories of causes for failure: product/market problems, financial difficulties, and managerial problems. In addition, entrepreneurs face internal and external problems.

The feasibility of the entrepreneur's product or service can be assessed by asking the right questions, by making a profile analysis of the venture, and by carrying out a comprehensive feasibility study.

Key Terms and Concepts

comprehensive feasibility approach

critical factors

customer availability

external problems

failure prediction model

feasibility criteria approach

growth of sales

growth stage

high-growth ventures

internal problems

lifestyle venture

marketability

product availability

small profitable ventures

start-up problems

technical feasibility

uniqueness

Review and Discussion Questions

1. Explain the challenges involved in new-venture development.
2. Describe some of the key factors involved in new-venture performance (use Figure 9.1).
3. Many entrepreneurs lack objectivity and have no real insight into the market. Why are these characteristics considered pitfalls of selecting new ventures?
4. Many entrepreneurs have a poor understanding of the finances associated with their new venture and/or have a venture that lacks uniqueness. Why are these characteristics considered pitfalls of selecting new ventures?
5. Describe each of the five critical factors involved in the prestart-up and start-up phases of a new venture.
6. Identify and discuss three examples of product/market problems that can cause a venture to fail.
7. Identify and discuss two examples of financial difficulties that can cause a venture to fail.
8. Identify and discuss two examples of managerial problems that can cause a venture to fail.
9. List four major types of problems that new ventures confront.
10. Describe the proposed failure prediction model for newly founded firms.
11. How can asking the right questions help an entrepreneur evaluate a new venture? What types of questions are involved?
12. Explain how a feasibility criteria approach works.
13. Explain how a comprehensive feasibility approach works.

Experiential Exercise

INTERNAL PROFILE ANALYSIS

Choose any emerging company with which you are familiar. If you are not familiar with any, consult magazines such as *Entrepreneur, Fortune Small Business*, and *Business Week*, and gather information on one firm. Then complete the following internal profile analysis by placing a check mark (√) in the appropriate column.

Internal Resource	Strong Weakness	Slight Weakness	Neutral	Slight Strength	Strong Strength
Financial					
Overall performance	_____	_____	_____	_____	_____
Ability to raise capital	_____	_____	_____	_____	_____
Working capital	_____	_____	_____	_____	_____
Position	_____	_____	_____	_____	_____
Marketing					
Market performance	_____	_____	_____	_____	_____
Knowledge of markets	_____	_____	_____	_____	_____
Product	_____	_____	_____	_____	_____
Advertising and promotion	_____	_____	_____	_____	_____
Price	_____	_____	_____	_____	_____
Distribution	_____	_____	_____	_____	_____
Organizational and Technical					
Location	_____	_____	_____	_____	_____
Production	_____	_____	_____	_____	_____
Facilities	_____	_____	_____	_____	_____
Access to suppliers	_____	_____	_____	_____	_____
Inventory control	_____	_____	_____	_____	_____
Quality control	_____	_____	_____	_____	_____
Organizational structure	_____	_____	_____	_____	_____
Rules, policies, and procedures	_____	_____	_____	_____	_____
Company image	_____	_____	_____	_____	_____
Human					
Number of employees	_____	_____	_____	_____	_____
Relevancy of skills	_____	_____	_____	_____	_____
Morale	_____	_____	_____	_____	_____
Compensation package	_____	_____	_____	_____	_____

Based on your analysis, what three recommendations would you make to the company's management?

1. _____

_____

2. _____

_____

3. _____

_____

Case 9.1

NOTHING UNIQUE TO OFFER

During the past four months, George Vazquez has been putting together his plan for a new venture. George wants to open a pizzeria near the local university. The area has three pizza enterprises, but George is convinced that demand is sufficient to support a fourth.

The major competitor is a large national franchise unit that—in addition to its regular food-service menu of pizzas, salads, soft drinks, and desserts—offers door-to-door delivery. This delivery service is very popular with the university students and has helped the franchise unit capture approximately 40 percent of the student market. The second competitor is a "pizza wagon" that carries precooked pizzas. The driver circles the university area and sells pizzas on a first-come, first-served basis. The pizza wagon starts the evening with 50 pizzas of all varieties and sizes and usually sells 45 of them at full price. The last 5 are sold for whatever they will bring. It generally takes the wagon all evening to sell the 50 pizzas, but the profit markup is much higher than that obtained from the typical pizza sales at the franchise unit. The other competitor offers only in-house services, but it is well known for the quality of its food.

George does not believe that it is possible to offer anything unique. However, he does believe that a combination of door-to-door delivery and high-quality, in-house service can help him win 15 to 20 percent of the local market. "Once the customers begin to realize that 'pizza is pizza,'" George told his partner, "we'll begin to get more business. After all, if there is no difference between one pizza place and another, they might just as well eat at our place."

Before finalizing his plans, George would like to bring in one more partner. "You can never have too much initial capital," he said. "You never know when you'll have unexpected expenses." But the individual whom George would like as a partner is reluctant to invest in the venture. "You really don't have anything unique to offer the market," he told George. "You're just another 'me too' pizzeria, and you're not going to survive." George hopes he will be able to change the potential investor's mind, but if he is not, George believes he can find someone else. "I have 90 days before I intend to open the business, and that's more than enough time to line up the third partner and get the venture under way," he told his wife yesterday.

QUESTIONS

1. Is there any truth to the potential investor's comment? Is the lack of uniqueness going to hurt George's chances of success? Explain.

2. If George were going to make his business venture unique, what steps might he take? Be complete in your answer.

3. In addition to the uniqueness feature, what other critical factors is George overlooking? Identify and describe three, and give your recommendations for what to do about them.

Case 9.2

A PRODUCT DESIGN PROBLEM

When Billie Aherne learned that the government was soliciting contracts for the manufacture of microcomputer components, she read the solicitation carefully. Billie's knowledge of microcomputers is extensive, and for the past five years she has been a university professor actively engaged in research in this area. If she could land this government contract, Billie feels certain she would be well on her way to going into business designing microcomputer components.

Billie asked for a leave of absence so she could bid on the microcomputer contract. She then worked up a detailed proposal and submitted it to the government. Eight months ago, she learned that she had been awarded the contract. For the next four months, Billie and two university colleagues who had joined her worked on completing their state-of-the-art components. When private firms learned of their contract, Billie was inundated with requests for components. She realized that as soon as she completed her government contract, she would be free to enter into contracts with private firms. Two months ago, Billie shipped the components to the government. The next week, she began signing contracts with firms in the private sector. In all, Billie signed agreements with six firms to provide each of them an average of $400,000 worth of components during the next four months. Last week, the first shipment of components was delivered to one of the private firms.

In the mail delivered earlier today, Billie received a letter from the government. The communication informed her of quality problems with the components she had manufactured and shipped. Part of the letter read, "It took approximately four weeks of use before it became evident that your components have a quality flaw. We believe the problem is in the basic design. We would like to meet with you at the earliest possible time to discuss your design and to agree on which steps must be taken in order for you to comply with the terms of your contract." Billie hoped to keep this news quiet until she could talk to the government representatives and find out what was going wrong. However, an hour ago she received a call from one of the private firms. "We hear that the microcomputer components you shipped to the government had a quality flaw," the speaker told Billie. "Could you tell us exactly what the problem is?"

QUESTIONS

1. What happened? What mistake did Billie make in terms of the new venture?

2. How could this problem have been prevented? Defend your answer.

3. What lesson about new-venture assessment does this case provide? Be complete in your answer.

Notes

1. Michael S. Malone, "The 200-Year-Old U.S. Patent Office Is Beginning to Show Its Age," *Forbes* (June 24, 2002): 33–40.

2. Sue Birley and Paul Westhead, "A Taxonomy of Business Start-Up Reasons and Their Impact on Firm Growth and Size," *Journal of Business Venturing* 9, no. 1; 11, no. 3, (January 1994): 7–32.

3. Nancy M. Carter, William B. Gartner, and Paul D. Reynolds, "Exploring Start-Up Event Sequences," *Journal of Business Venturing* 11, no. 3 (May 1996): 151–66; see also Benyamin B. Lichtenstein, Kevin J. Dooley, and G.T. Lumpkin, "Measuring Emergence in the Dynamics of New Venture Creation," *Journal of Business Venturing* 21, no. 2 (2006): 153–75.

4. Robert N. Lussier, "A Nonfinancial Business Success versus Failure Prediction Model for Young Firms," *Journal of Small Business Management* (January 1995): 8–20.

5. Frédéric Delmar and Scott Shane, "Legitimating First: Organizing Activities and the Survival of New Ventures," *Journal of Business Venturing* 19, no. 3 (May 2004): 385–410.

6. Arnold C. Cooper, "Challenges in Predicting New Firm Performance," *Journal of Business Venturing* 8, no. 3 (May 1993): 241–53.

7. Keith H. Brigham, Julio O. De Castro, and Dean A. Shepherd, "A Person-Organization Fit Model of Owner-Managers' Cognitive Style and Organizational Demands," *Entrepreneurship Theory and Practice* 31, no. 1 (2007): 29–51; and Dimo Dimov, "From Opportunity Insight to Opportunity Intention: The Importance of Person-Situation Learning Match," *Entrepreneurship Theory and Practice* 31, no. 4 (2007): 561–84.

8. Candida G. Brush and Pieter A. Vanderwerf, "A Comparison of Methods and Sources for Obtaining Estimates of New Venture Performance," *Journal of Business Venturing* 7, no. 2 (March 1992): 157–70; see also Gaylen N. Chandler and Steven H. Hanks, "Measuring the Performance of Emerging Businesses: A Validation Study," *Journal of Business Venturing* 8, no. 5 (September 1993): 391–408; and Scott L. Newbert, "New Firm Formation: A Dynamic Capability," *Journal of Small Business Management* 43, no. 1 (January 2005): 55–77.

9. Paul Reynolds and Brenda Miller, "New Firm Gestation: Conception, Birth, and Implications for Research," *Journal of Business Venturing* 7, no. 5 (September 1992): 405–17.

10. Bhaskar Chakravorti, "The New Rules for Bringing Innovations to the Market," *Harvard Business Review* (March 2004): 58–67; see also Eric A. Morse, Sally B. Fowler, and Thomas B. Lawrence, "The Impact of Virtual Imbeddedness on New Venture Survival: Overcoming the Liabilities of Newness," *Entrepreneurship Theory and Practice* 31, no. 2 (2007): 139–60.

11. Theodore Levitt, "Marketing Myopia," *Harvard Business Review* (July/August 1960): 45–56; see also Eileen Fischer and Rebecca Reuber, "The Good, the Bad, and the Unfamiliar: The Challenges of Reputation Formation Facing New Firms," *Entrepreneurship Theory and Practice* 31, no. 1 (2007): 53–76.

12. Robert C. Ronstadt, *Entrepreneurship* (Dover, MA: Lord Publishing, 1984), 74.

13. Adapted from Ronstadt, *Entrepreneurship*, 75.

14. Ibid., 79.

15. Albert V. Bruno, Joel K. Leidecker, and Joseph W. Harder, "Why Firms Fail," *Business Horizons* (March/April 1987): 50–58. For more recent comparisons, see Fahri Karakaya and Bulent Kobu, "New Product Development Process: An Investigation of Success and Failure in High Technology and Non-High Technology Firms," *Journal of Business Venturing* 9, no. 4 (January 1994): 49–66; Timothy Bates, "Analysis of Young, Small Firms That Have Closed: Delineating Successful from Unsuccessful Closures," *Journal of Business Venturing* 20, no. 3 (May 2005): 343–58; and Steven C. Michael and James G. Combs, "Entrepreneurial Failure: The Case of Franchisees," *Journal of Small Business Management* 46, no. 1 (2008): 75–90.

16. David E. Terpstra and Philip D. Olson, "Entrepreneurial Start-Up and Growth: A Classification of Problems," *Entrepreneurship Theory and Practice* (Spring 1993): 5–20.

17. H. Robert Dodge, Sam Fullerton, and John E. Robbins, "Stage of the Organizational Life Cycle and Competition as Mediators of Problem Perception for Small Businesses," *Strategic Management Journal* 15 (1994): 121–34.

18. Andrew L. Zacharakis, G. Dale Meyer, and Julio DeCastro, "Differing Perceptions of New Venture Failure: A Matched Exploratory Study of Venture Capitalists and Entrepreneurs," *Journal of Small Business Management* (July 1999): 1–14.

19. Erkki K. Laitinen, "Prediction of Failure of a Newly Founded Firm," *Journal of Business Venturing* 7, no. 4 (July 1992): 323–40.

20. Gordon B. Baty, *Entrepreneurship: Playing to Win* (Reston, VA: Reston Publishing, 1974), 33–34.

21. Hans Schollhammer and Arthur H. Kuriloff, *Entrepreneurship and Small Business Management* (New York: John Wiley & Sons, 1979), 58; see also Kwaku Atuahene-Gima and Haiyang Li, "Strategic Decision Comprehensiveness and New Product Development Outcomes in New Technology Ventures," *The Academy of Management Journal* 47, no. 4 (August 2004): 583–97.

22. Frans J. H. M. Verhees and Matthew T. G. Meulenberg, "Market Orientation, Innovativeness, Product Innovation, and Performance in Small Firms," *Journal of Small Business Management* 42, no. 2 (April 2004): 134–54; Minet Schindehutte, Michael H. Morris, and Akin Kocak, "Understanding Market-Driven Behavior: The Role of Entrepreneurship" *Journal of Small Business Management* 46, no. 1 (2008): 4–26; and Gerald E. Hills, Claes M. Hultman, and Morgan P. Miles, "The Evolution and Development of Entrepreneurial Marketing," *Journal of Small Business Management* 46, no. 1 (2008): 99–112.

APPENDIX 9A: Feasibility Plan Outline

This outline provides the needed aspects of a complete feasibility plan. Each section has some of the key material that needs to be included. Following this outline will help the entrepreneur recognize the actual feasibility of the proposed venture as well as the areas that need to be further developed before the concept could ever be considered for potential funding.

Title Page

Name of proposed company: _____

Names and titles of the founding team members:

_____

_____

_____

_____

_____

Relevant contact information (name, title, address, phone, e-mail):

_____

_____

_____

_____

_____

Table of Contents

Make sure that all of the contents in the feasibility plan have page numbers and are listed carefully in the table of contents.

The Sections of a Feasibility Plan

Executive Summary

Explanation: Include the most important highlights from each section of the feasibility study. Be sure to include a clear and concise description of the venture, whatever proprietary aspects it may possess, the target market, the amount of financing needed, and the type of financing that is being requested.

_____

_____

_____

_____

_____

_____

The Business Concept

Explanation: Using the following directions, articulate a compelling story for why this is an excellent concept. This section allows the reader to understand what concept is being proposed and why it has true potential in the marketplace. It also provides an opportunity for the entrepreneur to prove that he or she can articulate this concept in clear and comprehensible terms to people outside their circle of friends and close associates.

KEY CONCEPTS

Describe whether the proposed concept is a retail, wholesale, manufacturing, or service business. Identify the current stage of development for the venture (concept stage, start-up, initial operations, or expansion).

_____

_____

_____

_____

Include a clear description of the targeted customer, the value proposition (in terms of benefits gained) for that customer, and the potential growth opportunities.

_____

_____

_____

_____

Summarize any proprietary rights associated with this concept, whether that be patents, copyrights, licenses, royalties, distribution rights, or franchise agreements.

_____

_____

_____

_____

Industry/Market Analysis

Explanation: The industry/market analysis is critical. Is there a market for the product or service resulting from the venture? What are the current trends in this industry? What are the predicted trends for this industry? Can any of this be substantiated? The market for the product/service may be obvious, yet the feasibility analysis must validate its existence. In the venture feasibility analysis, it may be enough to prove that a sufficient market exists for the venture and that no further in-depth research is warranted. However, entrepreneurs should always study their competitors in the marketplace. Lessons learned from competitors provide opportunities for entrepreneurs to find the unique distinctions in their own concept.

KEY CONCEPTS

Explain the industry that this concept focuses on, as well as whatever trends may exist in that particular industry today.

_____

_____

_____

_____

Discuss the target market analysis that has been used and what specific market niche that has produced. In addition, identify the market size, its growth potential, and your plan for market penetration based on research.

_____

_____

_____

_____

Explain the customer profile in terms of who the specific customer is and—again—what value proposition (in terms of benefits) is being offered the customer.

_____

_____

_____

_____

Finally, be sure to include a competitor analysis that describes thoroughly the competition existing today and how specifically your concept will match up or exceed the competition and why.

_____

_____

_____

_____

Management Team

Explanation: Keep in mind that all new ventures must stand the scrutiny of whether the founding team can really move this idea to market. The experience of the management team may end up being one of the most critical factors to outside investors. Many times, venture capitalists have expressed their belief that they prefer a "B" idea with an "A" team as opposed to an "A" idea with a "B" team. In other words, there is a real concern about the implementation phase of a proposed concept. Does this founding team have the background, experience, skills, and networks to make the concept operationally successfully?

KEY CONCEPTS

Identify the founding team members and the key personnel in place to guide the proposed company.

_____

_____

_____

_____

Explain the team's qualifications and how the critical tasks are being assigned. Also include any board of directors/advisors that are in place.

_____

_____

_____

_____

Finally, outline any "gaps" in the management team (in terms of skills and abilities) and explain how those will be addressed.

_____

_____

_____

_____

Product/Service Development Analysis

Explanation: Before going any further with a conceptual idea, the entrepreneur must determine whether the concept has any practical feasibility. One of the most important questions in this section of the feasibility analysis would be: "What unique features distinguish your product/service?" The more unique the features of a product or service, the better chance the business concept has of being successful.

KEY CONCEPTS

Provide a detailed description of the proposed concept, including any unique features that make it distinctive.

_____

_____

_____

_____

Explain the current status of the project and include a clear timeline of the key tasks to complete.

_____

_____

_____

_____

Identify any intellectual property involved with this potential venture, and discuss the proprietary protection that exists. Any proposed or completed prototype testing should be described here as well.

_____

_____

_____

_____

Finally, identify any anticipated critical risks in terms of potential product liability, governmental regulations, or raw material issues that may hinder this project at any stage.

_____

_____

_____

Financial Analysis

Explanation: Summarize the critical assumptions upon which the financial information is based; in other words, show how the numbers have been derived. A pro forma income statement and a statement of cash flows are the two most critical financial documents to add here—even though they may include preliminary outside sources needed to get some idea of the generation of revenue and the cash position of the venture during the first three years. If possible, provide a break-even analysis to demonstrate where the venture moves from survival to growth.

KEY CONCEPTS

Assumptions:

_____

_____

_____

Pro Forma Income Statement:

_____

_____

_____

Pro Forma Cash-Flow Statement:

_____

_____

_____

Break-Even Analysis:

_____

_____

_____

Timeline

Explanation: Use a graphic representation of the dates and the related tasks in order of their completion until actual concept launch.

_____

_____

_____

_____

Bibliography

Explanation: Provide any key endnotes, footnotes, sources, or extra information that would be critical for a funding source to see in relation to the work you performed in creating this feasibility study.

_____

_____

_____

CHAPTER 10

The Marketing Aspects of New Ventures

Entrepreneurial Thought

The generation and use of market research enables a management team to learn about changes in the market faster than the competition, making it a major component of competitive rationality and competitive advantage.

— **PETER R. DICKSON** *Marketing Management*

Chapter Objectives

1 To review the importance of marketing research for new ventures

2 To identify the key elements of an effective market survey

3 To present factors that inhibit the use of marketing

4 To present the emerging use of Internet marketing for entrepreneurial firms

5 To examine the marketing concept: philosophy, segmentation, and consumer orientation

6 To establish the areas vital to a marketing plan

7 To discuss the key features of a pricing strategy

8 To present a pricing strategy checklist

The Marketing Concept for Entrepreneurs

The marketing concept for entrepreneurs includes knowing what a market consists of, the understanding of marketing research, the development of a marketing plan, and the proper approach to a pricing strategy. In this chapter, we examine each of these key components.

A market is a group of consumers (potential customers) who have purchasing power and unsatisfied needs.[1] A new venture will survive only if a market exists for its product or service.[2] This is so obvious that it would seem every entrepreneur would prepare thoroughly the market analysis needed to establish a target market. However, many entrepreneurs know very little about their market, and some even attempt to launch new ventures without identifying any market. (See Table 10.1 concerning the marketing skills of great entrepreneurs.)

A number of techniques and strategies can assist entrepreneurs to effectively analyze a potential market. By using them, entrepreneurs can gain in-depth knowledge about the specific market and can translate this knowledge into a well-formulated business plan. Effective marketing analysis also can help a new venture position itself and make changes that will result in increased sales.[3] The key to this process is marketing research.

Table **10.1** | **Common Elements in the Marketing Skills of Great Entrepreneurs**

1. They possess unique environmental insight, which they use to spot opportunities that others overlook or view as problems.

2. They develop new marketing strategies that draw on their unique insights. They view the status quo and conventional wisdom as something to be challenged.

3. They take risks that others, lacking their vision, consider foolish.

4. They live in fear of being preempted in the market.

5. They are fiercely competitive.

6. They think through the implications of any proposed strategy, screening it against their knowledge of how the marketplace functions. They identify and solve problems that others do not even recognize.

7. They are meticulous about details and are always in search of new competitive advantages in quality and cost reduction, however small.

8. They lead from the front, executing their management strategies enthusiastically and autocratically. They maintain close information control when they delegate.

9. They drive themselves and their subordinates.

10. They are prepared to adapt their strategies quickly and to keep adapting them until they work. They persevere long after others have given up.

11. They have clear visions of what they want to achieve next. They can see further down the road than the average manager can see.

Source: Peter R. Dickson, *Marketing Management* (Fort Worth, TX: The Dryden Press, 1994), 8. Reprinted with permission of South-Western, a division of Cengage Learning: http://permission.cengage.com/permissions.

Marketing Research

Marketing research involves the gathering of information about a particular market, followed by analysis of that information.[4] A knowledge and understanding of the procedures involved in marketing research can be very helpful to the entrepreneur in gathering, processing, and interpreting market information.

Defining the Research Purpose and Objectives

The first step in marketing research is to define precisely the informational requirements of the decision to be made. Although this may seem too obvious to mention, the fact is that needs are too often identified without sufficient probing. If the problem is not defined clearly, the information gathered will be useless.

In addition, specific objectives should be established. For example, one study has suggested the following set of questions to establish objectives for general marketing research:

- Where do potential customers go to purchase the good or service in question?
- Why do they choose to go there?
- What is the size of the market? How much of it can the business capture?
- How does the business compare with competitors?
- What impact does the business's promotion have on customers?
- What types of products or services are desired by potential customers?[5]

Gathering Secondary Data

Information that has already been compiled is known as secondary data. Generally speaking, secondary data are less expensive to gather than are new, or primary, data. The entrepreneur should exhaust all the available sources of secondary data before going further into the research process. Marketing decisions often can be made entirely with secondary data.

Secondary data may be internal or external. Internal secondary data consist of information that exists within the venture. The records of the business, for example, may contain useful information. External secondary data are available in numerous periodicals, trade association literature, and government publications.

Unfortunately, several problems accompany the use of secondary data. One is that such data may be outdated and, therefore, less useful. Another is that the units of measure in the secondary data may not fit the current problem. Finally, the question of validity is always present. Some sources of secondary data are less valid than others.

Gathering Primary Data

If the secondary data are insufficient, a search for new information, or primary data, is the next step. Several techniques can be used to accumulate primary data; these are often classified as observational methods and questioning methods. Observational methods avoid contact with respondents, whereas questioning methods involve respondents in varying degrees. Observation is probably the oldest form of research in existence. Observational methods can be used very economically, and they avoid a potential bias that can result from a respondent's awareness of his or her participation using questioning methods. A major disadvantage of observational methods, however, is that they are limited to descriptive studies.

Surveys and experimentation are two questioning methods that involve contact with respondents. Surveys include contact by mail, telephone, and personal interviews. Mail surveys are often used when respondents are widely dispersed; however, these are characterized by low response rates. Telephone surveys and personal interview surveys involve verbal communication with respondents and provide higher response rates. Personal interview surveys, however, are more expensive than mail and telephone surveys. Moreover, individuals often are reluctant to grant personal interviews, because they feel a sales pitch is forthcoming. (Table 10.2 describes the major survey research techniques.)

Table **10.2**	**Comparison of Major Survey Research Techniques**				
Criteria	**Direct/ Cold Mailing**	**Mail Panels**	**Telephone**	**Personal In–Home**	**Mall Intercept**
Complexity and versatility	Not much	Not much	Substantial, but complex or lengthy scales difficult to use	Highly flexible	Most flexible
Quantity of data	Substantial	Substantial	Short, lasting typically between15 and 30 minutes	Greatest quantity	Limited, 25 minutes or less
Sample control	Little	Substantial, but representative-ness may be a question	Good, but nonlisted households can be a problem	In theory, provides greatest control	Can be problem-atic; sample representative-ness may be questionable
Quality of data	Better for sensitive or embarrassing questions; however, no interviewer is present to clarify what is being asked		Positive side, interview can clear up any ambiguities; negative side, may lead to socially accepted answers	There is the chance of cheating	Unnatural testing environment can lead to bias
Response	In general, low; as low as 10%	70–80%	60–80%	Greater than 80%	As high as 80%
Speed	Several weeks; completion time will increase with follow-up mailings	Several weeks with no follow-up mailings, longer with follow-up mailings	Large studies can be completed in three to four weeks	Faster than mail but typically slower than telephone surveys	Large studies can be completed in a few days
Cost	Inexpensive; as low as $2.50 per completed interview	Lowest	Not as low as mail; depends on incidence rate and length of question-naire	Can be rela-tively expen-sive, but considerable variability	Less expensive than in-home, but higher than telephone; again, length and incidence rate will determine cost
Uses	Executive, industrial, medical, and readership studies	All areas of mar-keting research, particularly use-ful in low-incidence categories	Particularly effective in studies that require national samples	Still prevalent in product testing and other studies that require visual cues or product	Pervasive-concept tests, name tests, package tests, copy test prototypes

Source: Peter R. Dickson, *Marketing Management* (Fort Worth, TX: The Dryden Press, 1994), 114. Reprinted with permission of South-Western, a division of Cengage Learning: http://permission.cengage.com/permissions.

Experimentation is a form of research that concentrates on investigating cause-and-effect relationships. The goal is to establish the effect an experimental variable has on a dependent variable. For example, what effect will a price change have on sales? Here, the price is the experimental variable, and sales volume is the dependent variable. Measuring the relationship between these two variables would not be difficult were it not for the many other variables involved.[6]

DEVELOPING AN INFORMATION-GATHERING INSTRUMENT

The questionnaire is the basic instrument for guiding the researcher and the respondent through a survey. The questionnaire should be developed carefully before it is used. Several major considerations for designing a questionnaire are as follows:

- Make sure each question pertains to a specific objective that is in line with the purpose of the study.
- Place simple questions first and difficult-to-answer questions later in the questionnaire.
- Avoid leading and biased questions.
- Ask yourself: "How could this question be misinterpreted?" Reword questions to reduce or eliminate the possibility that they will be misunderstood.
- Give concise but complete directions in the questionnaire. Succinctly explain the information desired, and route respondents around questions that may not relate to them.
- When possible, use scaled questions rather than simple yes/no questions to measure intensity of an attitude or frequency of an experience. For example, instead of asking: "Do we have friendly sales clerks?" (yes/no), ask: "How would you evaluate the friendliness of our sales clerks?" Have respondents choose a response on a five-point scale ranging from "Very unfriendly" (1) to "Very friendly" (5).[7]

Interpreting and Reporting the Information

After the necessary data have been accumulated, they should be developed into usable information. Large quantities of data are merely facts. To be useful, they must be organized and molded into meaningful information. The methods of summarizing and simplifying information for users include tables, charts, and other graphic methods. Descriptive statistics—such as the mean, mode, and median—are most helpful in this step of the research procedure.

Marketing Research Questions

The need for marketing research before and during a venture will depend on the type of venture. However, typical research questions might include the following, which are divided by subject:

Sales

1. Do you know all you need to know about your competitors' sales performance by type of product and territory?

2. Do you know which accounts are profitable and how to recognize a potentially profitable one?

3. Is your sales power deployed where it can do the most good and maximize your investment in selling costs?

Distribution

1. If you are considering introducing a new product or line of products, do you know all you should about distributors' and dealers' attitudes toward it?

2. Are your distributors' and dealers' salespeople saying the right things about your products or services?

3. Has your distribution pattern changed along with the geographic shifts of your markets?

the global perspective

The Perils of Marketing

Entrepreneurs know that the best way to get their products and services to market is to have a well-thought-out marketing plan in place; yet, even the best laid plans sometimes go awry. The exposure gained by lavish marketing campaigns can draw light to aspects of a company that the management had not intended. An interesting example of this phenomenon can be observed in the marketing conducted by China leading up to the 2008 Olympics, scheduled to be held in Beijing.

As is customary, the Olympic torch was to be symbolically carried around the globe to generate excitement for the impending games. China's Olympic committee made no exception when planning the marketing activities for the 2008 Olympics, despite recent turmoil that had taken place months before the event. The long, contentious history between Tibet and China had regained international attention when Tibetan protesters began to commit terrorist acts in protest of China's rule over their homeland.

With news of this dispute being broadcast on a global scale, people around the world—most of whom had prior knowledge of the longstanding disagreement—began to debate China's right to hold the Olympics, bringing into question the issue of human rights. Many citizens began to protest their country's involvement in the 2008 Olympics, arguing that it was the moral responsibility of all participants to boycott the event to send a clear message to China.

This drama was unfolding as the Olympic torch relay was set in motion. The torch brought greater tension to the issue as opposed to a sense of peace and hope, as it was intended to do. Demonstrators met the torchbearers at every turn, and they extinguished the flame repeatedly. Protestors grew more aggressive as the torch made its way from Greece to London to Paris, where Parisians forced the torchbearers to be escorted by security forces and to abandon their scheduled routes. In addition, Chinese officials cancelled an Olympic reception to be held in Paris, reportedly because they were insulted by the pro-Tibetan sentiment in the city.

The most elaborate torch relay in Olympics history became a public relations nightmare for China. Chinese officials were forced to seek the help of international public relations firms to attempt to repair the country's image prior to the games. Clearly the campaign had not gone as the Chinese officials had intended. Not only had it *not* led to a positive reflection on the country and its reemergence as a global superpower, it had led to the most intense international protests since the student massacres in Tiananmen Square in 1989.

The lesson to be learned is that the euphemism that there is no such thing as bad press does not always apply. When marketing campaigns lead to negative publicity, companies can be left wondering whether they would have been better off saying nothing at all.

Source: Adapted from Clay Chandler, "The Olympic Torch's World Tour: Is Beijing Playing with Fire?" *Fortune*, April 8, 2008, http://chasingthedragon.blogs.fortune.cnn.com/2008/04/08/the-olympic-torchs-world-tour-is-beijing-playing-with-fire/ (accessed April 9, 2008).

Markets

1. Do you know all that would be useful about the differences in buying habits and tastes by territory and kind of product?

2. Do you have as much information as you need on brand or manufacturer loyalty and repeat purchasing in your product category?

3. Can you now plot, from period to period, your market share of sales by products?

Advertising

1. Is your advertising reaching the right people?

2. Do you know how effective your advertising is compared to that of your competitors?

3. Is your budget allocated appropriately for greater profit—according to products, territories, and market potentials?

Products

1. Do you have a reliable quantitative method for testing the market acceptability of new products and product changes?

2. Do you have a reliable method for testing the effect on sales of new or changed packaging?

3. Do you know whether adding higher or lower quality levels would make new profitable markets for your products?

Inhibitors to Marketing Research

Despite the fact that most entrepreneurs would benefit from marketing research, many fail to do it. A number of reasons exist for this omission, among them cost, complexity, level of need for strategic decisions, and irrelevancy. Several articles have dealt with the lack of marketing research by entrepreneurs in the face of its obvious advantages and vital importance to the success of entrepreneurial businesses.[8]

Cost

Marketing research can be expensive, and some entrepreneurs believe that only major organizations can afford it. Indeed, some high-level marketing research is expensive, but smaller companies can also use very affordable marketing techniques.

Complexity

A number of marketing research techniques rely on sampling, surveying, and statistical analysis. This complexity—especially the quantitative aspects—is frightening to many entrepreneurs, and they shun it. The important point to remember is that the key concern is interpretation of the data, and an entrepreneur always can obtain the advice and counsel of those skilled in statistical design and evaluation by calling on the services of marketing research specialists or university professors trained in this area.

Strategic Decisions

Some entrepreneurs feel that only major strategic decisions need to be supported through marketing research. This idea is tied to the cost and complexity issues already mentioned. The contention is that, because of the cost and statistical complexity of marketing research, it should be conducted only when the decisions to be made are major. The problem lies not only in the misunderstanding of cost and complexity but also in the belief that marketing research's value is restricted to major decisions. Much of the entrepreneur's sales efforts could be enhanced through the results of such research.[9]

Irrelevancy

Many entrepreneurs believe that marketing research data will contain either information that merely supports what they already know or irrelevant information. Although it is true that marketing research does produce a variety of data, some of which may be irrelevant, it is also a fact that much of the information is useful. In addition, even if certain data merely confirm what the entrepreneur already knows, it is knowledge that has been tested and thus allows the individual to act on it with more confidence.

As indicated by these inhibitors, most of the reasons that entrepreneurs do not use marketing research center either on a misunderstanding of its value or on a fear of its cost. However, the approach to marketing does not have to be expensive and can prove extremely valuable.

Internet Marketing

The Internet can assist a new venture's overall marketing strategy in a number of ways. First, Internet marketing allows the firm to increase its presence and brand equity in the marketplace. Company and brand sites provide the opportunity to communicate the overall mission of the company/brand, to provide information on attributes and/or ratings of the company/brand, and to give information on the history of the company/brand. In addition, firms can easily communicate information on the marketing mix offered.

Second, the Internet allows the company to cultivate new customers. Providing important information about both the attributes of the firm's product and those of competitive products can aid in the decision-making process. In addition, the Web site can demonstrate products in actual use. This kind of information builds interest in the brand.

The Internet also allows Web site visitors to match their needs with the offerings of the company. It is extremely important to remember that, while traditional marketing techniques tend to be push-oriented (the company decides what the consumer will see and where), the Internet is pull-oriented (the consumer chooses what, when, and how to look in greater detail). This technique requires Web site designers to think differently about what should or should not appear in the site offering.

Third, the Internet can improve customer service by allowing customers to serve themselves when and where they choose. As more consumers begin to use the Internet, companies can readily serve these individuals without incurring expensive distribution costs. The expansion of the number of customers served requires only that the organization have enough servers available.

The fourth benefit to marketers relates to information transfer. Traditionally, companies have gathered information via focus groups, mail surveys, telephone surveys, and personal interviews. These techniques can be very expensive to implement, however. In contrast, the Web offers a mechanism for the company to collect similar information at a fraction of the cost.

Not only can information be gathered from consumers, it can also be shared with them. For example, the Web can be used to provide expensive or specialized materials to consumers who request such information. The fulfillment of information requests via the Web can offer substantial savings to the company.

Marketing a Web site is not unlike marketing a bricks-and-mortar business in that a budget should be set, a plan should be laid out, and the work remains never-ending. The difference is that the Internet is a direct-sales distribution channel. With Internet marketing, the seller-buyer relationship can be established immediately, and the waiting period that follows a traditional marketing campaign is almost eliminated. This environment therefore requires a top-notch marketing plan. Established Web sites spend a significant amount of money running commercial ads. Experts, however, recommend that start-ups keep their marketing budget at 10 percent of revenues or less. Budget constraints call for creative and cost-effective marketing. Following are three steps to help lure customers to a site once it's up and running.

Step 1:   Co-Marketing Deals and Banner Ads   Banner ads through co-marketing deals are the cheapest and most efficient way for a new site to start down the path toward brand identity and brand loyalty. Banner ads work because they reach the target audience. According to industry gurus, vertical-community sites are the most favored and result-yielding posting sites. In this type of "co-marketing," two or more related sites swap links with each other; the amount of money exchanged depends on the situation. One of the more popular deals is the one between 1-800-Flowers and America Online (AOL): 1-800-Flowers paid AOL $25 million to maintain a four-year status as the AOL florist.

Step 2:   Become a Popular Link The most common approach to marketing a Web site is to get it linked to one of the major search engines: Yahoo, Google, Excite, MSN, and so forth. It is, however, one thing to be linked, and another to make it so the business name pops up more often and under any related search. Keywords are the key! Meta tags are what give the name and description of the storefront and are part of the Web site's software code. The more keywords in the company's meta tags, the greater the chance that the Web site address will pop up when someone is searching for the products or services the company has to offer.

Step 3:   Sponsor Contests, Specials, and Other Interactive Features Contests and specials are the hottest ways to grab Internet users. Successful companies aren't settling for the hits—they're vying for the relationship. The goal is to formulate a site that keeps the product, service, or Web page on the customers' minds after they leave. This goal can be accomplished by interacting with the potential customer—providing an incentive for him or her to return by allowing the visitor to play a fun game, win a prize, and, in the best case, volunteer information for a database. Interactive features that provide the feeling of a "demonstration" will allow the potential buyer to better appreciate the product. An e-mail channel for company and product questions will also aid in establishing a connection with surfers. (See Table 10.3 for Web tips.)

Although numerous advantages are available to companies that market via the Internet, two major concerns have also arisen: the limited target audience and consumer resistance to change. In regard to the first concern, the Internet is popular but not accessible by everyone. Although Internet use is increasing rapidly, until the demographics of Internet usage mirror our society as a whole, companies must use caution in overemphasizing this medium in their overall marketing mix. In regard to the second concern—resistance to change—it should be remembered that changing behavior patterns is difficult and sometimes time consuming.

The change in behavior that will be necessary for Internet marketing to really take off requires that firms understand how to make consumers feel more confident when purchasing over the Internet. One simple solution is to educate consumers about the process—but achieving that goal will take time. Warranties, security measures, and other methods to reduce the perceived risk to consumers must be evaluated by companies that are bent on overcoming consumers' resistance to change.[10]

Table 10.3   Web Design Tips

Things to Do	Things to Avoid
Provide a description of the firm	Scrolling
Ensure fast loading times	Large graphic files
Create consistent navigation pathways	Reliance on one browser
Make the site interactive	Broken links
Register with search engines	Excessive use of plug-ins
Register the domain name	Obscure URLs
Use trademarks appropriately	Copycatting other sites
Market the site in other materials	Allowing the Web site to grow stale

Source: John H. Lindgren, Jr., "Marketing on the Internet," *Marketing Best Practices* (Fort Worth, TX: Harcourt College Publishers, 2000), 559.

Developing the Marketing Concept

Effective marketing is based on three key elements: marketing philosophy, market segmentation, and consumer behavior. A new venture must integrate all three elements when developing its marketing concept and its approach to the market. This approach helps set the stage for how the firm will seek to market its goods and services.

Marketing Philosophy

Three distinct types of marketing philosophies exist among new ventures: production driven, sales driven, and consumer driven.

The **production-driven philosophy** is based on the belief "produce efficiently and worry about sales later." Production is the main emphasis; sales follow in the wake of production. New ventures that produce high-tech, state-of-the-art output sometimes use a production-driven philosophy. A **sales-driven philosophy** focuses on personal selling and advertising to persuade customers to buy the company's output. This philosophy often surfaces when an overabundance of supply occurs in the market. New auto dealers, for example, rely heavily on a sales-driven philosophy. A **consumer-driven philosophy** relies on research to discover consumer preferences, desires, and needs *before* production actually begins. This philosophy stresses the need for marketing research to better understand where or who a market is and to develop a strategy targeted toward that group. Of the three philosophies, a consumer-driven orientation is often most effective, although many ventures do not adopt it.

Three major factors influence the choice of a marketing philosophy:

1. *Competitive pressure.* The intensity of the competition will many times dictate a new venture's philosophy. For example, strong competition will force many entrepreneurs to develop a consumer orientation in order to gain an edge over competitors. If, on the other hand, little competition exists, the entrepreneur may remain with a production orientation in the belief that what is produced will be sold.

2. *Entrepreneur's background.* The range of skills and abilities entrepreneurs possess varies greatly. Whereas some have a sales and marketing background, others possess production and operations experience. The entrepreneur's strengths will influence the choice of a market philosophy.

3. *Short-term focus.* Sometimes a sales-driven philosophy may be preferred due to a short-term focus on "moving the merchandise" and generating sales. Although this focus appears to increase sales (which is why many entrepreneurs pursue this philosophy), it also can develop into a hard-selling approach that soon ignores customer preferences and contributes to long-range dissatisfaction.

Any one of the three marketing philosophies can be successful for an entrepreneur's new venture. It is important to note, however, that over the long run the consumer-driven philosophy is the most successful. This approach focuses on the needs, preferences, and satisfactions of the consumer and works to serve the end user of the product or service.

Market Segmentation

Market segmentation is the process of identifying a specific set of characteristics that differentiates one group of consumers from the rest. For example, although many people eat ice cream, the market for ice cream can be segmented based on taste and price. Some individuals prefer high-quality ice cream made with real sugar and cream because of its taste; many others cannot tell the difference between high-quality and average-quality ingredients and, based solely on taste, are indifferent between the two types. The price is higher for high-quality ice cream such as Häagen-Dazs or Ben & Jerry's, so the market niche is smaller for these offerings than it is for lower-priced competitors. This process of segmenting the market can be critical for new ventures with very limited resources.

the entrepreneurial process

Competitive Information

Felicia Lindau and Jason Monberg run an online retailer of greeting cards. Business was going well when the opportunity to set up a strategic alliance arose. Much to their chagrin, a copy of their business plan also made it to the meeting—but they didn't bring it. It had been obtained by the potential partner from someone Lindau and Monberg thought they could trust with the confidential information.

Following is a list of techniques to use to assess your competition and avoid paying a high-priced market research firm to collect information for you.

1. **Networking.** Speaking with people in the field will help you get a feel for what's going on in your industry. Vendors, customers, and anyone who does business with companies in your field may have information on emerging competition. Venture capitalists can be a great source of information because of the due diligence they must perform with pending venture loans. Much like what happens during the start-up phase of a business, a person can become so immersed in a project that he or she develops tunnel vision. Social networking also can provide a fresh view of the industry.

2. **Related products.** This market is the obvious place to look. Companies that can provide anything that complements your product or service are primed to become competition, because they also know what the customers' needs are and how to fulfill them. Large companies whose customers are businesses will assess this issue very differently from a small business with the average person as its primary consumer. A good example of a complementary relationship is the one that exists among cameras, film, photo disks, and so on. The number and type of photographic products available have increased substantially in recent years, and different fields have capitalized on this trend.

3. **Value chain.** Whereas related products fall on the horizontal axis of an industry, exploring the value chain forces a vertical assessment of potential entrants into your competitive pool. The value chain for a given product or service offers many opportunities for expansion, both for you and for the potential competition. In this situation, the potential competition is fully aware of, and understands, the business environment in which you operate. They already have easy access to suppliers, buyers, and services that you deal with on a daily basis.

4. **Companies with related competencies.** One of the more ignored avenues involves companies that can take their expertise and apply it to an indirectly related field. Competencies can be both technological and nontechnological. Just because one company has unparalleled customer service and sales in the cellular industry doesn't mean the company couldn't use the same spectacular service in the cable business. The perfect example of expanding on technological similarities is Motorola, whose original intent was to focus on the defense industry. Surely that was not an area cellular providers were examining when trying to anticipate potential competition!

5. **Internet.** It goes without saying that the Internet is one of the premiere sources of information available to anyone who knows how to use it. Using search engines to access the 800 million Web pages allows a business to easily scope out anyone that offers similar products or services. Searches can be both broad and defined. Most important, they can be done cheaply and as often as desired. Anderson suggests using words that customers might use and avoiding technological or industry jargon when surfing, but points out that brainstorming all possible relations should ensure a thorough and more effective search.

Once the sufficient information has been gathered, a plan to beat the current and emerging competition should be prepared. The plan created will be analogous to the business's strengths and resources. Issues such as losing sales to another company could be addressed, a SWOT (strengths, weaknesses, opportunities, threats) analysis could be executed, or the plan to offer a new product or change price points could be outlined.

Source: Adapted from Mark Henricks, "Friendly Competition?" *Entrepreneur* (December 1999): 114–17.

To identify specific market segments, entrepreneurs need to analyze a number of variables. As an example, two major variables that can be focused on are demographic and benefit variables. Demographic variables include age, marital status, sex, occupation, income, location, and the like. These characteristics are used to determine a geographic and demographic profile of the consumers and their purchasing potential. The benefit variables help to identify unsatisfied needs that exist within this market. Examples may include convenience, cost, style, trends, and the like, depending on the nature of the particular new venture. Whatever the product or service, it is extremely valuable to ascertain the benefits a market segment is seeking in order to further differentiate a particular target group.

Consumer Behavior

Consumer behavior is defined by the many types and patterns of consumer characteristics. However, entrepreneurs can focus their attention on only two considerations: personal characteristics and psychological characteristics. Table 10.4 provides an example by tying these characteristics to the five types of consumers: (1) innovators, (2) early adopters, (3) early majority, (4) late majority, and (5) laggards.

Table 10.4 Consumer Characteristics

	Innovators (2–3%)	Early Adopters (12–15%)	Early Majority (33%)	Late Majority (34%)	Laggards (12–15%)
Personal Characteristics					
1. Social class	Lower upper	Upper middle	Lower middle	Upper lower	Lower lower
2. Income	High income (inherited)	High income (earned from salary and investment)	Above-average income (earned)	Average income	Below-average income
3. Occupation	Highest professionals Merchants Financiers	Middle management and owners of medium-sized businesses	Owners of small businesses Nonmanagerial office and union managers	Skilled labor	Unskilled labor
4. Education	Private schooling	College	High school Trade school	Grammar school, some high school	Very little—some grammar school
5. Housing	Inherited property Fine mansions	Large homes—good suburbs or best apartments	Small houses Multiple-family dwellings	Low-income housing in urban-renewal projects	Slum apartments
6. Family influence	Not family oriented Children in private school or grown	Children's social advancement important Education important	Child centered and home centered	Children taken for granted	Children expected to raise themselves
7. Time orientation	Present oriented, but worried about impact of time	Future oriented	Present oriented	Present (security) oriented	Tradition oriented, live in the past

Table 10.4	Consumer Characteristics (*Continued*)

	Innovators (2–3%)	Early Adopters (12–15%)	Early Majority (33%)	Late Majority (34%)	Laggards (12–15%)
Psychological Characteristics					
1. Nature of needs	Self-actualization needs (realization of potential)	Esteem needs (for status and recognition by others)	Belonging needs (with others and groups)	Safety needs (freedom from fear)	Survival needs (basic needs)
2. Perceptions	Cosmopolitan in outlook	Prestige. Status conscious. Aspire to upper class	Local aspirations and local social acceptance	Home and product centered	Live from day to day
3. Self-concept	Elite	Social strivers, peer group leaders, venturesome	Respectability from own reference groups and home	Security, home centered, aggressive, apathetic, no hope	Fatalistic, live from day to day
4. Aspiration groups	British upper class	Innovator class	In own social strata, dissociated from upper lower	Others in this classification and in early majority, dissociated from lower lower	Don't aspire
5. Reference groups	Sports, social, and travel groups	Dominate industry and community organizations. Golf, college, and fraternity	Social groups of this strata: chambers of commerce, labor unions, family, church, PTA, auxiliaries	Family, labor unions	Ethnic group oriented

Source: Roy A. Lindberg and Theodore Cohn, *The Marketing Book for Growing Companies That Want to Excel* (New York: Van Nostrand Reinhold, 1986), 80–81. Reprinted with permission.

The differences in social class, income, occupation, education, housing, family influence, and time orientation are illustrated in Table 10.4. So, too, are the psychological characteristics labeled as needs, perceptions, self-concept, aspiration groups, and reference groups. This breakdown can provide an entrepreneur with a visual picture of the type of consumer to target for the sales effort.

The next step is to link the characteristic makeup of potential consumers with buying trends in the marketplace. Table 10.5 shows the changing priorities that have shaped buying decisions. Each of these factors relates to consumer attitudes and behaviors based on education, the economy, the environment, and/or societal changes. By tying together the data in Tables 10.4 and 10.5, the entrepreneur can begin to examine consumer behavior more closely.

An analysis of the way consumers view the venture's product or service provides additional data. Entrepreneurs should be aware of five major consumer classifications:

1. *Convenience goods*—whether staple goods (foods), impulse goods (checkout counter items), or emergency goods and services, consumers will want these goods and services but will not be willing to spend time shopping for them.

Table **10.5**	Changing Priorities and Purchases in the Family Life Cycle

Stage	Priorities	Major Purchases
Fledgling: teens and early 20s	Self; socializing; education	Appearance products, clothing, automobiles, recreation, hobbies, travel
Courting: 20s	Self and other; pair bonding; career	Furniture and furnishings, entertainment and entertaining, savings
Nest building: 20s early 30s	Babies and career	Home, garden, do-it-yourself items, baby-care products, insurance
Full nest: 30–50s	Children and others; career; midlife crisis	Children's food, clothing, education, transportation, orthodontics, career and life counseling
Empty nest: 50–75	Self and others; relaxation	Furniture and furnishings, entertainment, travel, hobbies, luxury automobiles, boats, investments
Sole survivor: 70–90	Self; health; loneliness	Health care services, diet, security and comfort products, TV and books, long-distance telephone services

Source: Peter R. Dickson, *Marketing Management* (Fort Worth, TX: The Dryden Press, 1994), 91. Reprinted with permission of South-Western, a division of Cengage Learning: http://permission.cengage.com/permissions.

2. *Shopping goods*—products consumers will take time to examine carefully and compare for quality and price.

3. *Specialty goods*—consist of products or services consumers make a special effort to find and purchase.

4. *Unsought goods*—items consumers do not currently need or seek. Common examples are life insurance, encyclopedias, and cemetery plots. These products require explanation or demonstration.

5. *New products*—items that are unknown due to lack of advertising or are new products that take time to be understood. When microcomputers were first introduced, for example, they fell into this category.

Developing a Marketing Plan

A marketing plan is the process of determining a clear, comprehensive approach to the creation of customers. The following elements are critical for developing this plan:

- *Current marketing research:* determining who the customers are, what they want, and how they buy
- *Current sales analysis:* promoting and distributing products according to marketing research findings
- *Marketing information system:* collecting, screening, analyzing, storing, retrieving, and disseminating marketing information on which to base plans, decisions, and actions
- *Sales forecasting:* coordinating personal judgment with reliable market information
- *Evaluation:* identifying and assessing deviations from marketing plans[11]

Current Marketing Research

The purpose of current marketing research is to identify customers—target markets—and to fulfill their desires. For current marketing research to be effective for the growing venture, the following areas warrant consideration:

- *The company's major strengths and weaknesses.* These factors offer insights into profitable opportunities and potential problems and provide the basis for effective decision making.

- *Market profile.* A market profile helps a company identify its current market and service needs: How profitable are existing company services? Which of these services offer the most potential? Which (if any) are inappropriate? Which will customers cease to need in the future?

- *Current and best customers.* Identifying the company's current clients allows management to determine where to allocate resources. Defining the best customers enables management to segment this market niche more directly.

- *Potential customers.* By identifying potential customers—either geographically or with an industry-wide analysis of its marketing area—a company increases its ability to target this group, thus turning potential customers into current customers.

- *Competition.* By identifying the competition, a company can determine which firms are most willing to pursue the same basic market niche.

- *Outside factors.* This analysis focuses on changing trends in demographics, economics, technology, cultural attitudes, and governmental policy. These factors may have substantial impact on customer needs and, consequently, expected services.

- *Legal changes.* Marketing research performs the important task of keeping management abreast of significant changes in governmental rates, standards, and tax laws.[12]

the entrepreneurial process

The Guerrilla Marketing Plan

A business plan is essential for any entrepreneur planning to start an initiative; however, by the time you include your market research results, pro forma statements, and critical risks, your business plan will become a dense packet of information to be used when guiding your entire business—a document that few will read in its entirety. Given this fact, entrepreneurs should be able to quickly articulate the key aspects of their venture in a matter of a few minutes. One tool that can be used for this purpose is what is known as a guerrilla marketing plan.

A guerrilla marketing plan forces an entrepreneur to specify the seven most important marketing issues that face her company. Of course, there will most certainly be more than seven key areas to address; however, by going through the exercise of consolidating the marketing topics that require the most focus, an entrepreneur will be better prepared to get to the heart of her concept, both when presenting to potential investors and when managing the business.

The key is to address each area using no more than a sentence. Guerrilla marketing plans give people a quick understanding of exactly what is of the utmost concern to your business by eliminating much of the detail provided in your full business plan. Large companies make use of such plans by developing different ones for different products. For instance, Procter & Gamble develops a guerrilla marketing plan for each of its products.

Although some companies choose to attach several pages of documentation to their plans, the key is to get the seven sentences right. Following are guidelines for developing a guerrilla marketing plan:

- You should begin your guerrilla marketing plan with a sentence that describes the purpose of

Continued

your marketing. This sentence should be very specific and should address what impact your marketing initiative should have on a potential customer. Goals such as "to be more successful than my competitors" or "to be more profitable" are not useful. This sentence should quantify your overarching goal so that it is measurable. The point is to envision exactly what you want your customer to ideally do, and then to establish a goal for ensuring that customers will act in that way.

- The next sentence is meant for you to address the competitive advantages of the enterprise; in other words, what are the characteristics of the business that make it uniquely positioned to offer value to the public? The objective with this sentence is to outline your business's strengths that are the most unique so that you can emphasize them in your marketing materials.

- You will address your target audience in the third sentence. By specifying exactly who will be exposed to a marketing campaign, you will find the process of engineering an effective plan to be much more straightforward. Companies often have more than one target audience, so guerrilla marketing plans should be written to address all potential customers in order to avoid losing sales to competitors.

- For the fourth point, a list is most appropriate. This topic addresses the marketing weapons that you will use. The important idea of this section is to include only those tools that the company can understand, afford, and use properly. Countless tools are now readily available to entrepreneurs, so filtering out those that do not meet these three criteria will help you avoid making poorly directed investments.

- You should discuss the company's market niche in the fifth sentence. Now that you have addressed the

purpose, benefits, and target market, understanding your marketing niche is the next logical step. The market niche should capture what customers most readily associate with your company. It could be speed, value, variety, or any number of other characteristics. You will not be able to please everyone, so defining what your company is and what it is not will help to narrow your focus when promoting it to potential customers.

- The sixth sentence is where you will establish the identity of your company. Entrepreneurs should ensure that the marketing image they broadcast to the world is supported by the identity of their companies, which means that the companies' operating procedures need to reinforce whatever identity they establish.

- The final sentence in your guerrilla marketing plan needs to explicitly state what percentage of projected gross sales you are willing to earmark as your marketing budget. The quality of your marketing materials will clearly reflect on your business, so this step requires a significant amount of research to ensure that the amount you have allotted will be sufficient for supporting all previous steps.

When developing your guerrilla marketing plan, all subsequent steps should be framed by the first sentence you write, which is meant to define the purpose of your plan. Entrepreneurs should theoretically be able to write a plan of this nature within five minutes, given its brevity. The more practice you get at articulating your business objectives, the easier you will find using tools—such as the guerrilla marketing plan—to communicate your business goals.

Source: Adapted from Jay Conrad Levinson and Jeannie Levinson, "Here's the Plan," *Entrepreneur,* February 2008, http://www.entrepreneur.com/magazine/ entrepreneur/2008/ february/188842.html (accessed March 20, 2008).

Marketing research need not be extremely expensive. Presented next are some useful tips regarding low-cost research. These tips can be valuable to entrepreneurs who need research but lack the funds for sophisticated measures.

1. Establish a contest that requires entrants to answer a few simple questions about the quality of your products or services. The entry form is dropped into a convenient deposit box at the exit door of your store or service department, and the drawing is held at month's end.

2. Piggyback a questionnaire about the quality of your products or services onto a company catalog or sales brochure. Be sure also to ask what other items the customer

would like to see the organization offer. Such a system functions as an ongoing program of organizational evaluation.

3. Every organization receives the occasional complaint from a disgruntled customer. Instead of treating such situations casually, many organizations now adopt a management-by-exception philosophy and give grievances a high priority. Management follow-up with an in-depth interview often results in the revelation of unsuspected problems.

4. Develop a standard set of questions regarding the quality of your organization's product and services that is suitable for administration by telephone. Have a secretary or part-time employee set aside a half day each month to call 20 to 30 customers. Such a program often reminds customers to place an order, and many clients feel flattered when their opinions are sought.

5. Some organizations have succeeded by including research questionnaires in various products' packages. In this way, they attempt to determine how a buyer heard about an item, why it was purchased from the firm, and so on. The only difficulty with this approach is that it focuses on customers and neglects research about the potential of sales to those who have not bought.[13]

Current Sales Analysis

An entrepreneur needs to continually review the methods employed for sales and distribution in relation to the market research that has been conducted. Matching the correct customer profile with sales priorities is a major goal in sales analysis. Following is a list of potential questions to be answered by this analysis:

-   Do salespeople call on their most qualified prospects on a proper priority and time-allocation basis?
-   Does the sales force contact decision makers?
-   Are territories aligned according to sales potential and salespeople's abilities?
-   Are sales calls coordinated with other selling efforts, such as trade publication advertising, trade shows, and direct mail?
-   Do salespeople ask the right questions on sales calls? Do sales reports contain appropriate information? Does the sales force understand potential customers' needs?
-   How does the growth or decline of a customer's or a prospect's business affect the company's own sales?

Marketing Information System

A marketing information system compiles and organizes data relating to cost, revenue, and profit from the customer base. This information can be useful for monitoring the strategies, decisions, and programs concerned with marketing. As with all information systems designs, the key factors that affect the value of such a system are (1) data reliability, (2) data usefulness or understandability, (3) reporting system timeliness, (4) data relevancy, and (5) system cost.

Sales Forecasting

Sales forecasting is the process of projecting future sales through historical sales figures and the application of statistical techniques. The process is limited in value due to its reliance on historical data, which many times fail to reflect current market conditions. As a segment of the comprehensive marketing-planning process, however, sales forecasting can be very valuable.

Evaluation

The final critical factor in the marketing planning process is evaluation. Because a number of variables can affect the outcome of marketing planning, it is important to evaluate performance. Most important, reports should be generated from a customer analysis: attraction or loss of customers, with reasons for the gain or loss, as well as established customer preferences and reactions. This analysis can be measured against performance in sales volume, gross sales dollars, or market share. It is only through this type of evaluation that flexibility and adjustment can be incorporated into marketing planning.

Final Considerations for Entrepreneurs

Marketing plans are part of a venture's overall strategic effort.[14] To be effective, these plans must be based on the venture's specific goals. Following is an example of a five-step program designed to help entrepreneurs create a structured approach to developing a market plan:

Step 1:   Appraise marketing strengths and weaknesses, emphasizing factors that will contribute to the firm's "competitive edge." Consider product design, reliability, durability, price/quality ratios, production capacities and limitations, resources, and need for specialized expertise.

Step 2:   Develop marketing objectives, along with the short- and intermediate-range sales goals necessary to meet those objectives. Next, develop specific sales plans for the current fiscal period. These goals should be clearly stated, measurable, and within the company's capabilities. To be realistic, these goals should require only reasonable efforts and affordable expenditures.

Step 3:   Develop product/service strategies. The product strategy begins with identifying the end users, wholesalers, and retailers, as well as their needs and specifications. The product's design, features, performance, cost, and price then should be matched to these needs.

Step 4:   Develop marketing strategies. Strategies are needed to achieve the company's intermediate- and long-range sales goals and long-term marketing objectives. These strategies should include advertising, sales promotion campaigns, trade shows, direct mail, and telemarketing. Strategies also may be necessary to increase the size of the sales force or market new products. Contingency plans will be needed in the event of technological changes, geographic market shifts, or inflation.

Step 5:   Determine a pricing structure. A firm's pricing structure dictates which customers will be attracted, as well as the type or quality of products/services that will be provided. Many firms believe that the market dictates a "competitive" pricing structure. However, this is not always the case—many companies with a high price structure are very successful. Regardless of the strategies, customers must believe that the product's price is appropriate. The price of a product or service, therefore, should not be set until marketing strategies have been developed.[15]

Pricing Strategies

One final marketing issue that needs to be addressed is that of pricing strategies. Many entrepreneurs are unsure of how to price their product or service, even after marketing research is conducted. A number of factors affect this decision: the degree of competitive pressure, the availability of sufficient supply, seasonal or cyclical changes in demand, distribution costs, the product's life-cycle stage, changes in production costs, prevailing economic conditions, customer services provided by the seller, the amount of promotion done, and the market's buying power. Obviously, the ultimate price decision will balance many of these factors and, usually, will not satisfy *all* conditions. However, awareness of the various factors is important.

Other considerations, sometimes overlooked, are psychological in nature:

- In some situations, the quality of a product is interpreted by customers according to the level of the item's price.
- Some customer groups shy away from purchasing a product when no printed price schedule is available.
- An emphasis on the monthly cost of purchasing an expensive item often results in greater sales than an emphasis on total selling price.

- Most buyers expect to pay even-numbered prices for prestigious items and odd-numbered prices for commonly available goods.

- The greater the number of meaningful customer benefits the seller can convey about a given product, the less the price resistance (generally).[16]

Pricing procedures differ depending on the nature of the venture: retail, manufacturing, or service. Pricing for the product life cycle as presented in Table 10.6, however, might be applied to any type of business. The table demonstrates the basic steps of developing a pricing system and indicates how that system should relate to the desired pricing goals.

With this general outline in mind, potential entrepreneurs can formulate the most appropriate pricing strategy. Table 10.7 provides a thorough analysis of pricing strategies and outlines when each strategy is generally used, what the procedures are, and the advantages and disadvantages associated with each. This checklist can provide entrepreneurs with reference points for establishing and evaluating pricing strategies for their ventures.

Table 10.6   Pricing for the Product Life Cycle

Customer demand and sales volume will vary with the development of a product. Thus, pricing for products needs to be adjusted at each stage of their life cycle. The following outline provides some suggested pricing methods that relate to the different stages in the product life cycle.

Product Life-Cycle Stage	Pricing Strategy	Reasons/Effects
Introductory Stage		
Unique product	Skimming—deliberately setting a high price to maximize short-term profits	Initial price set high to establish a quality image, to provide capital to offset development costs, and to allow for future price reductions to handle competition
Nonunique product	Penetration—setting prices at such a low level that products are sold at a loss	Allows quick gains in market share by setting a price below competitors' prices
Growth Stage	Consumer pricing—combining penetration and competitive pricing to gain market share; depends on consumer's perceived value of product	Depends on the number of potential competitors, size of total market, and distribution of that market
Maturity Stage	Demand-oriented pricing—a flexible strategy that bases pricing decisions on the demand level for the product	Sales growth declines; customers are very price-sensitive
Decline Stage	Loss leader pricing—pricing the product below cost in an attempt to attract customers to other products	Product possesses little or no attraction to customers; the idea is to have low prices bring customers to newer product lines

Source: Adapted from Colleen Green, "Strategic Pricing," *Small Business Reports* (August 1989): 27–33.

Table 10.7 Pricing Strategy Checklist

Strategy Objective	When Generally Used	Procedure	Advantages	Disadvantages
Skim the cream of the market for high short-term profit (without regard for long term).	No comparable competitive products. Drastically improved product or new product innovation. Large number of buyers. Little danger of competitor entry due to high price, patent control, high R & D costs, high promotion costs, and/or raw material control. Uncertain costs. Short life cycle. Inelastic demand.	Determine preliminary customer reaction. Charge premium price for product distinctiveness in short run, without considering long-run position. Some buyers will pay more because of higher present value to them. Then gradually reduce price to tap successive market levels (i.e., skimming the cream of a market that is relatively insensitive to price). Finally, tap more sensitive segments.	Cushions against cost overruns. Requires smaller investment. Provides funds quickly to cover new-product promotion and initial development costs. Limits demand until production is ready. Suggests higher value in buyer's mind. Emphasizes value rather than cost as a guide to pricing. Allows initial feeling-out of demand before full-scale production.	Assumes that a market exists at high price. Results in ill will in early buyers when price is reduced. Attracts competition. Likely to underestimate ability of competitors to copy product. Discourages some buyers from trying the product (connotes high profits). May cause long-run inefficiencies.
Slide down demand curve to become established as efficient manufacturer at optimum value before competitors become entrenched, without sacrificing long-term objective (e.g., obtain satisfactory share of market).	By established companies launching innovations. Durable goods. Slight barriers to entry by competition. Medium life span.	Tap successive levels of demand at highest prices possible. Then slide down demand curve faster and farther than forced to in view of potential competition. Rate of price change is slow enough to add significant volume at each successive price level, but fast enough to prevent large competitor from becoming established on a low-cost volume basis.	Emphasizes value rather than cost as a guide to pricing. Provides rapid return on investment. Provides slight cushion against cost overruns.	Requires broad knowledge of competitive product developments. Requires much documented experience. Results in ill will in early buyers when price is reduced. Discourages some buyers from buying at initial high price.
Compete at the market price to encourage others to produce and promote the product to stimulate primary demand.	Several comparable products. Growing market. Medium to long product life span. Known costs.	Start with final price and work back to cost. Use customer surveys and studies of competitors' prices to approximate final price. Deduct selling margins. Adjust product, production, and selling methods to sell at this price ands still make necessary profit margins.	Requires less analysis and research. Existing market requires fewer promotion efforts. Causes no ill will in early buyers because price will not be lowered soon.	Limited flexibility. Limited cushion for error. Slower recovery of investment. Must rely on other differentiating tools.

Table **10.7** **Pricing Strategy Checklist** (*Continued*)

Strategy Objective	When Generally Used	Procedure	Advantages	Disadvantages
Market penetration to stimulate market growth and capture and hold a satisfactory market share at a profit through low prices. Become strongly entrenched to generate profits over long term.	Long product life span. Mass market. Easy market entry. Demand is highly sensitive to price. Unit costs of production and distribution of output increases. Newer product. No "elite" market willing to pay premium for newest and best.	Charge low prices to create a mass market, resulting in cost advantages derived from larger volume. Look at lower end of demand curve to get price low enough to attract a large customer base. Also review past and competitor prices.	Discourages actual and potential competitor inroads because of apparent low profit margins. Emphasizes value more than cost in pricing. Allows maximum exposure and penetration in minimum time. May maximize long-term profits if competition is minimized.	Assumes volume is always responsive to price reductions, which isn't always true. Relies somewhat on glamour and psychological pricing, which doesn't always work. May create more business than production capacity available. Requires significant investment. Small errors often result in large losses.
Preemptive pricing to keep competitors out of market or eliminate existing ones.	Used more often in consumer markets. Manufacturers may use this approach on one or two products, with other prices meeting or higher than those of competitors.	Price at low levels so that market is unattractive to possible competitors. Set prices as close as possible to total unit cost. As increased volume allows lower cost, pass advantage to buyers via lower prices. If cost declines rapidly with increases in volume, can start price below cost (can use price approaching variable costs).	Discourages potential competitors because of apparent low profit margins. Limits competitive activity and expensive requirements to meet them.	Must offer other policies that permit lower price (limited credit, delivery, or promotions). Small errors can result in large losses. Long-term payback period.

Source: Roy A. Lindberg and Theodore Cohn, *The Marketing Book for Growing Companies That Want to Excel* (New York: Van Nostrand Reinhold, 1986), 116–17. Reprinted with permission.

Summary

Marketing research involves the gathering of information about a particular market, followed by analysis of that information. The marketing research process has five steps: (1) Define the purpose and objectives of the research, (2) gather secondary data, (3) gather primary data, (4) develop an information-gathering instrument (if necessary), and (5) interpret and report the information.

Four major reasons that entrepreneurs may not carry out marketing research are: (1) cost, (2) complexity of the undertaking, (3) belief that only major strategic decisions need to be supported through marketing research, and (4) belief that the data will be irrelevant to company operations. Usually they misunderstand the value of marketing research or fear its cost.

The Internet is fast becoming one of the greatest marketing tools of the twenty-first century. It offers numerous benefits for the overall marketing strategy of a company, including brand recognition, information transfer, and customer services. Nevertheless, some concerns have arisen regarding the Internet's limited target audience and the potential for customer resistance to change.

Development of a marketing concept has three important parts. The first part is the formulation of a marketing philosophy. Some entrepreneurs are production driven, others are sales driven, and still others are consumer driven. The entrepreneur's values and the market conditions will help determine this philosophy. The second part is market segmentation, which is the process of identifying a specific set of characteristics that differentiates one group of consumers from the rest. Demographic and benefit variables often are used in this process. The third part is an understanding of consumer behavior. Because many types and patterns of consumer behavior exist, entrepreneurs need to focus on the personal and psychological characteristics of their customers. In this way they can determine a tailor-made, consumer-oriented strategy. This customer analysis focuses on such important factors as general buying trends in the marketplace, specific buying trends of targeted consumers, and the types of goods and services being sold.

A marketing plan is the process of determining a clear, comprehensive approach to the creation of customers. The following elements are critical for developing this plan: current marketing research, current sales analysis, a marketing information system, sales forecasting, and evaluation.

Pricing strategies are a reflection of marketing research and must consider such factors as marketing competitiveness, consumer demand, life cycle of the goods or services being sold, costs, and prevailing economic conditions.

Key Terms and Concepts

consumer-driven philosophy

consumer pricing

demand-oriented pricing

experimentation

Internet marketing

loss leader pricing

market

marketing research

market segmentation

penetration

primary data

production-driven philosophy

sales-driven philosophy

secondary data

skimming

surveys

Review and Discussion Questions

1. In your own words, what is a market? How can marketing research help an entrepreneur identify a market?
2. What are the five steps in the marketing research process? Briefly describe each.
3. Which is of greater value to the entrepreneur, primary or secondary data? Why?
4. Identify and describe three of the primary obstacles to undertaking marketing research.
5. Describe the benefits and concerns of marketing on the Internet. Be specific in your answer.
6. How would an entrepreneur's new-venture strategy differ under each of the following marketing philosophies: production driven,

sales driven, consumer driven? Be complete in your answer.

7. In your own words, what is market segmentation? What role do demographic and benefit variables play in the segmentation process?

8. Identify and discuss three of the most important personal characteristics that help an entrepreneur identify and describe customers. Also, explain how the product life cycle will affect the purchasing behavior of these customers.

9. Identify and discuss three of the psychological characteristics that help an entrepreneur identify and describe customers. Also, explain how the product life cycle will affect the purchasing behavior of these customers.

10. How does the way that consumers view a venture's product or service affect strategy? For example, why would it make a difference to the entrepreneur's strategy if the consumers viewed the company as selling a convenience good as opposed to a shopping good?

11. Identify and describe four of the major forces that shape buying decisions in the new century.

12. What does the entrepreneur of an emerging venture need to know about sales analysis and a marketing information system?

13. What are the five steps that are particularly helpful for developing a marketing plan? Identify and describe each.

14. What are some of the major environmental factors that affect pricing strategies? What are some of the major psychological factors that affect pricing? Identify and discuss three of each.

Experiential Exercise

IDENTIFYING THE CUSTOMER

One of the most important activities for entrepreneurs is identifying their customers. A list of the five basic types of consumers (A through E) and a list of descriptions of these types (a through o) follow. Identify the order in which people adopt new goods by ranking the first list from 1 (first adopters) to 5 (last adopters). Then match the descriptions with the types of consumers by placing a *1* next to those that describe initial adopters, on down to a *5* next to those that describe final adopters. (Three descriptions are listed for each of the five types of consumer.) Answers are provided at the end of the exercise.

A. _____ Early adopters

B. _____ Early majority

C. _____ Laggards

D. _____ Innovators

E. _____ Late majority

    a. _____ High-income people who have inherited their wealth

    b. _____ Future oriented

    c. _____ Below-average-income wage earners

    d. _____ Present (security) oriented

    e. _____ High-income people who have incomes from salary and investment

    f. _____ Highest professionals, including merchants and financiers

    g. _____ Present oriented

    h. _____ Average-income wager earners

    i. _____ Middle managers and owners of medium-sized businesses

    j. _____ Above-average-income wage earners

    k. _____ Present oriented, but worried about the impact of time

    l. _____ Unskilled labor

    m. _____ Skilled labor

    n. _____ Owners of small businesses; nonmanagerial office and union managers

    o. _____ Tradition-oriented people who often live in the past

Answers: A. 2, B. 3, C. 5, D. 1, E. 4, a. 1, b. 2, c. 5, d. 4, e. 1, f. 1, g. 3, h. 4, i. 2, j. 3, k. 1, l. 5, m. 4, n. 3, o. 5

Case 10.1

DEALING WITH THE COMPETITION

Six months ago, Roberta O'Flynn opened a small office supply store. Roberta sells a wide range of general office merchandise, including photocopying and typing paper, writing tablets, envelopes, writing instruments, and computer diskettes, as well as a limited range of office desks, chairs, and lamps.

Several office supply stores in the local area are, in Roberta's opinion, competitors. In an effort to better understand the competition, Roberta has visited four of these stores and pretended to be a customer so she could get information regarding their prices, product offerings, and service. Each has a different strategy. For example, one of them sells strictly on price; it is the customer's responsibility to pick up the merchandise and carry it away. Another relies heavily on service, including a 90-day credit plan for those customers who purchase equipment in excess of $500. This company's prices are the highest of the four stores Roberta visited. The other two stores use a combination of price and service strategies.

Roberta believes that, to get her new venture off the ground, she must develop a marketing strategy that helps her effectively compete with these other firms. Because her store is extremely small, Roberta believes that a certain amount of marketing research could be of value. On the other hand, her budget is extremely limited, and she is not sure how to collect the information. Roberta believes that what she needs to do is develop a market niche that will be loyal to her. In this way, no matter how extensive the competition, she always will have a group of customers who buy from her. Roberta also believes that the focus of this research has to be in two general directions. First, she has to find out what customers look for from an office supply store. How important is price? Service? Quality? Second, she has to determine the general strategy of each of her major competitors so she can develop a plan of action to prevent them from taking away her customers. Right now, however, her biggest question is: How do I go about getting the information I need?

QUESTIONS

1. Will the information Roberta is seeking be of value to her for competing in this market? Why or why not?

2. How would you recommend that Roberta put together her marketing research plan? What should be involved? Be as complete as possible in your answer.

3. How expensive will it be for Roberta to follow your recommendations for her marketing research plan? Describe any other marketing research efforts she could undertake in the near future that would be of minimal cost.

Case 10.2

A NEW SPIN ON MUSIC

Following his graduation from an excellent university with a degree in entrepreneurship, Brian Wright was eager to launch a business. Brian always enjoyed working with new technologies as well as watching movies, playing video games, and listening to music. Because of the proliferation of online movie and video game rental services, he believed that a service providing the online rental of CDs made perfect sense.

Brian was confident that the success of the other online rental services proved that there was a market for the online rental of entertainment media; therefore, renting CDs online would be an easy concept for customers to grasp. Although MP3s and MP3 players were growing in popularity, Brian knew that he and his friends preferred to listen to an album in its entirety; after all, Brian believed that "any true fan of an artist would want the entire album."

When calculating potential revenue, Brian concluded that the average retail price of a CD was approximately $14. If he charged $2 per CD per rental—which would offer an 85 percent savings to the customer based on the full retail price of a CD—he could recoup his costs within seven rentals. In addition, Brian believed that he could negotiate contracts with the music labels to purchase CDs in bulk at a discount, which would in turn reduce the time it would take for him to reach breakeven. He knew enough about music encryption technologies to know that restrictions could be built into the CDs to deter people from copying songs from them. He decided that taking such precautions would alleviate any concerns that the music labels might have regarding piracy.

As Brian began discussing his idea with his friends, their enthusiasm convinced him that he needed to act quickly before someone else seized the opportunity. At $2 per rental and an estimated two rentals per customer per month, he would only need a little over 20,000 customers to reach $1,000,000 in annual revenue. After looking at his financial forecasts, Brian decided that it was time to bring his online CD rental service to market.

QUESTIONS

1. Has Brian completed the proper marketing research for this potential opportunity? Why or why not? Explain.

2. Based on the case, are there key mistakes that you would caution Brian about? Explain.

3. What specific steps would you recommend to Brian for him to better assess this opportunity?

Notes

1. For a discussion of markets, see Peter R. Dickson, *Marketing Management* (Fort Worth, TX: The Dryden Press, 1994); Philip Kotler and Gary Armstrong, *Principles of Marketing.* (Upper Saddle River, NJ: Pearson/Prentice Hall, 2008); and O. C. Ferrell and Michael Hartline, *Marketing Strategy,* 4th ed. (Mason, OH: South-Western/Cengage Learning, 2008).

2. Harriet Buckman Stephenson, "The Most Critical Problem for the Fledgling Small Business: Getting Sales," *American Journal of Small Business* (Summer 1984): 26–33; and Minet Schindehutte, Michael H. Morris, and Akin Kocak, "Understanding Market-Driven Behavior: The Role of Entrepreneurship" *Journal of Small Business Management,* 46, no. 1 (2008): 4–26.

3. Alfred M. Pelham, "Market Orientation and Other Potential Influences on Performance in Small and Medium-Sized Manufacturing Firms," *Journal of Small Business Management* 38, no. 1 (January 2000): 48–67; and Bret Golan, "Achieving Growth and Responsiveness: Process Management and Market Orientation in Small Firms," *Journal of Small Business Management,* 44, no. 3 (2006): 369–85.

4. For a thorough presentation, see Stephen W. McDaniel and A. Parasuraman, "Practical Guidelines for Small Business Marketing Research," *Journal of Small Business Management* 24, no. 1 (January 1986): 1–7; see also R. Ganeshasundaram and N. Henley, "The Prevalence and Usefulness of Market Research: An Empirical Investigation into 'Background' Versus 'Decision' Research." *International Journal of Market Research* 48, no. 5 (2006): 525–50.

5. Timothy M. Baye, "Relationship Marketing: A Six-Step Guide for the Business Start-Up," *Small Business Forum* (Spring 1995): 26–41; and William G. Zikmund and Barry J. Babin, *Exploring Marketing Research,* 9th ed. (Mason, OH: South-Western/Cengage Learning, 2007).

6. Thomas J. Callahan and Michael D. Cassar, "Small Business Owners' Assessments of Their Abilities to Perform and Interpret Formal Market Studies," *Journal of Small Business Management* 33, no. 4 (October 1995): 1–9.

7. McDaniel and Parasuraman, "Practical Guidelines," 5.

8. As an example, see Alan R. Andreasen, "Cost-Conscious Marketing Research," *Harvard Business Review* (July/August 1983): 74–75; and Frank Hoy, "Organizational Learning at the Marketing/ Entrepreneurship Interface," *Journal of Small Business Management* 46, no. 1 (2008): 152–58.

9. John A. Pearce II and Steven C. Michael, "Marketing Strategies That Make Entrepreneurial Firms Recession-Resistant," *Journal of Business Venturing* 12, no. 4 (July 1997): 301–14.

10. For a thorough review of Internet marketing, see John H. Lindgren, Jr., "Marketing on the Internet," *Marketing Best Practices* (Fort Worth, TX: Harcourt College Publishers, 2000), 540–64; see also Charles W. Lamb, Jr., Joseph F. Hair, Jr., and Carl McDaniel, *Essentials of Marketing* (Mason, OH: South-Western/ Cengage Learning, 2005), Chapter 14; and Andy Lockett, "Conducting Market Research Using the Internet: the Case of Xenon Laboratories," *Journal of*

Business & Industrial Marketing 19, no. 3 (2004): 178–87.

11. "Marketing Planning," *Small Business Reports* (April 1986): 68–72.

12. Ibid., 70.

13. *Marketing Tactics Master Guide for Small Business* by Gerald B. McCready, © 1982, 8. Reprinted by permission of the publisher, Prentice Hall, a division of Simon & Schuster, Englewood Cliffs, New Jersey; see also Gerald E. Hills, Claes M. Hultman, and Morgan P. Miles, "The Evolution and Development of Entrepreneurial Marketing," *Journal of Small Business Management* 46, no. 1 (2008): 99–112.

14. Avraham Shama, "Marketing Strategies During Recession: A Comparison of Small and Large Firms," *Journal of Small Business Management* 31, no. 3 (July 1993): 62–72; see also Boyd Cohen and Monika I. Winn, "Market Imperfections, Opportunity, and Sustainable Entrepreneurship," *Journal of Business Venturing* 22, no. 1 (January 2007): 29–49.

15. "Marketing Planning," 71; see also Timothy Matanovich, Gary L. Lilien, and Arvind Rangaswamy, "Engineering the Price-Value Relationship," *Marketing Management* (Spring 1999): 48–53.

16. McCready, *Marketing Tactics,* 79.

11

Financial Statements in New Ventures

Entrepreneurial Thought

Small company managers are too inclined to delegate to outside accountants every decision about their companies' financial statements. Indeed, it is most unfair to suppose that accountants can produce—without management's advice and counsel—the perfect statement for a company. Instead, I contend, top managers of growing small companies must work with their independent accountants in preparing company financial statements to ensure that the right message is being conveyed. . . .

— **JAMES McNEILL STANCILL** *Growing Concerns*

Chapter Objectives

1 To explain the principal financial statements needed for any entrepreneurial venture: the balance sheet, income statement, and cash-flow statement

2 To outline the process of preparing an operating budget

3 To discuss the nature of cash flow and to explain how to draw up such a document

4 To describe how pro forma statements are prepared

5 To explain how capital budgeting can be used in the decision-making process

6 To illustrate how to use break-even analysis

7 To describe ratio analysis and illustrate the use of some of the important measures and their meanings

The Importance of Financial Information for Entrepreneurs

Today's entrepreneur operates in a competitive environment characterized by the constraining forces of governmental regulation, competition, and resources. In regard to the latter, no firm has access to an unlimited amount of resources. So, in order to compete effectively, the entrepreneur must allocate resources efficiently. Three kinds of resources are available to the entrepreneur: human, material, and financial. This chapter focuses on financial resources in the entrepreneurial environment, beginning with a discussion of financial statements as a managerial planning tool. How the budgeting process translates into the preparation of pro forma statements is presented, and attention is also given to break-even analysis and ratio analysis as profit-planning tools.

Financial information pulls together all of the information presented in the other segments of the business: marketing, distribution, manufacturing, and management. It also quantifies all of the assumptions and historical information concerning business operations.[1]

It should be remembered that entrepreneurs make assumptions to explain how numbers are derived, and they correlate these assumptions with information presented in other parts of the business operations. The set of assumptions on which projections are based should be clearly and precisely presented; without these assumptions, numbers will have little meaning. It is only after carefully considering such assumptions that the entrepreneur can assess the validity of financial projections. Because the rest of the financial plan is an outgrowth of these assumptions, they are the most integral part of any financial segment. (See Table 11.1 for a financial glossary for entrepreneurs.)

In order for entrepreneurs to develop the key components of a financial segment, they should follow a clear process, described in the next section.

Table 11.1	A Financial Glossary for the Entrepreneur

Accrual system of accounting A method of recording and allocating income and costs for the period in which each is involved, regardless of the date of payment or collection. For example, if you were paid $100 in April for goods you sold in March, the $100 would be income for March under an accrual system. (Accrual is the opposite of the cash system of accounting.)

Asset Anything of value that is owned by you or your business.

Balance sheet An itemized statement listing the total assets and liabilities of your business at a given moment. It is also called a *statement of condition*.

Capital (1) The amount invested in a business by the proprietor(s) or stockholders. (2) The money available for investment or money invested.

Cash flow The schedule of your cash receipts and disbursements.

Cash system of accounting A method of accounting whereby revenue and expenses are recorded when received and paid, respectively, without regard for the period to which they apply.

Collateral Property you own that you pledge to the lender as security on a loan until the loan is repaid. Collateral can be a car, home, stocks, bonds, or equipment.

Cost of goods sold This is determined by subtracting the value of the ending inventory from the sum of the beginning inventory and purchases made during the period. Gross sales less cost of goods sold gives you gross profit.

Current assets Cash and assets that can be easily converted to cash, such as accounts receivable and inventory. Current assets should exceed current liabilities.

Current liabilities Debts you must pay within a year (also called short-term liabilities).

Depreciation Lost usefulness; expired utility; the diminution of service yield from a fixed asset or fixed asset group that cannot or will not be restored by repairs or by replacement of parts.

Table 11.1	A Financial Glossary for the Entrepreneur (*Continued*)

Equity An interest in property or in a business, subject to prior creditors. An owner's equity in his or her business is the difference between the value of the company's assets and the debt owed by the company. For example, if you borrow $30,000 to purchase assets for which you pay a total of $50,000, your equity is $20,000.

Expense An expired cost; any item or class of cost of (or loss from) carrying on an activity; a present or past expenditure defraying a present operating cost or representing an irrecoverable cost or loss; an item of capital expenditures written down or off; or a term often used with some qualifying expression denoting function, organization, or time, such as a selling expense, factory expense, or monthly expense.

Financial statement A report summarizing the financial condition of a business. It normally includes a balance sheet and an income statement.

Gross profit Sales less the cost of goods sold. For example, if you sell $100,000 worth of merchandise for which you paid $80,000, your gross profit would be $20,000. To get net profit, however, you would have to deduct other expenses incurred during the period in which the sales were made, such as rent, insurance, and sales staff salaries.

Income statement Also called *profit and loss statement.* A statement summarizing the income of a business during a specific period.

Interest The cost of borrowing money. It is paid to the lender and is usually expressed as an annual percentage of the loan. That is, if you borrow $100 at 12%, you pay 1% (.01 $\times$ $100 = $1) interest per month. Interest is an expense of doing business.

Liability Money you owe to your creditors. Liabilities can be in the form of a bank loan, accounts payable, and so on. They represent a claim against your assets.

Loss When a business's total expenses for the period are greater than the income.

Net profit Total income for the period less total expenses for the period. (See *Gross profit.*)

Net worth The same as *equity.*

Personal financial statement A report summarizing your personal financial condition. Normally it includes a listing of your assets, liabilities, large monthly expenses, and sources of income.

Profit (See *Net profit* and *Gross profit.*) "Profit" usually refers to net profit.

Profit and loss statement Same as *income statement.*

Variable cost Costs that vary with the level of production on sales, such as direct labor, material, and sales commissions.

Working capital The excess of current assets over current liabilities.

Understanding the Key Financial Statements

Financial statements are powerful tools that entrepreneurs can use to manage their ventures.[2] The basic financial statements an entrepreneur needs to be familiar with are the balance sheet, the income statement, and the cash-flow statement. The following sections examine each of these in depth, providing a foundation for understanding the books of record all ventures need.

The Balance Sheet

A balance sheet is a financial statement that reports a business's financial position at a specific time. Many accountants like to think of it as a picture taken at the close of business on a particular day, such as December 31. The closing date is usually the one that marks the end of the business year for the organization.

The balance sheet is divided into two parts: the financial resources owned by the firm and the claims against these resources. Traditionally, these claims against the resources come from two groups: creditors who have a claim to the firm's assets and can sue the company if these obligations are not paid, and owners who have rights to anything left over after the creditors' claims have been paid.

The financial resources the firm owns are called assets. The claims that creditors have against the company are called liabilities. The residual interest of the firm's owners is known as owners' equity. When all three are placed on the balance sheet, the assets are listed on the left, and the liabilities and owners' equity are listed on the right.

An asset is something of value the business owns. To determine the value of an asset, the owner/manager must do the following:

1. Identify the resource.

2. Provide a monetary measurement of that resource's value.

3. Establish the degree of ownership in the resource.

Most assets can be identified easily. They are tangible, such as cash, land, and equipment. However, intangible assets also exist. These are assets that cannot be seen; examples include copyrights and patents.

Liabilities are the debts of the business. These may be incurred either through normal operations or through the process of obtaining funds to finance operations. A common liability is a short-term account payable in which the business orders some merchandise, receives it, and has not yet paid for it. This often occurs when a company receives merchandise during the third week of the month and does not pay for it until it pays all of its bills on the first day of the next month. If the balance sheet was constructed as of the end of the month, the account still would be payable at that time.

Liabilities are divided into two categories: short term and long term. Short-term liabilities (also called current liabilities) are those that must be paid during the coming 12 months. Long-term liabilities are those that are not due and payable within the next 12 months, such as a mortgage on a building or a five-year bank loan.

Owners' equity is what remains after the firm's liabilities are subtracted from its assets—it is the claim the owners have against the firm's assets. If the business loses money, its owners' equity will decline. This concept will become clearer when we explain why a balance sheet always balances.[3]

Understanding the Balance Sheet

To fully explain the balance sheet, it is necessary to examine a typical one and determine what each entry means. Table 11.2 provides an illustration. Note that it has three sections: assets, liabilities, and owners' equity. Within each of these classifications are various types of accounts. The following sections examine each type of account presented in the table.

CURRENT ASSETS

Current assets consist of cash and other assets that are reasonably expected to be turned into cash, sold, or used up during a normal operating cycle. The most common types of current assets are those shown in Table 11.2.

Cash refers to coins, currency, and checks on hand. It also includes money that the business has in its checking and savings accounts.

Accounts receivable are claims of the business against its customers for unpaid balances from the sale of merchandise or the performance of services. For example, many firms sell on credit and expect their customers to pay by the end of the month. Or, in many of these cases, they send customers a bill at the end of the month and ask for payment within ten days.

The allowance for uncollectible accounts refers to accounts receivable judged to be uncollectible. How does a business know when receivables are not collectible? This question can be difficult to answer, and a definitive answer is not known. However, assume that the business asks all of its customers to pay within the first ten days of the month following the

Table 11.2 Kendon Corporation Balance Sheet for the Year Ended December 31, 2010

Assets

Current Assets

Cash		$200,000
Accounts receivable	$375,000	
Less: Allowance for uncollectible accounts	$25,000	350,000
Inventory		150,000
Prepaid expenses		35,000
Total current assets		$735,000

Fixed Assets

Land		$330,000
Building	$315,000	
Less: Accumulated depreciation of building	80,000	
Equipment	410,000	
Less: Accumulated depreciation of equipment	60,000	
Total fixed assets		915,000
Total assets		$1,650,000

Liabilities

Current Liabilities

Accounts payable	$150,000	
Notes payable	25,000	
Taxes payable	75,000	
Loan payable	50,000	
Total current liabilities		$300,000
Bank loan		200,000
Total liabilities		$500,000

Owners' Equity

Contributed Capital

Common stock, $10 par, 40,000 shares	$400,000	
Preferred stock, $100 par, 500 shares		
Authorized, none sold	---------	
Retained earnings	750,000	
Total owners' equity		1,150,000
Total liabilities and owners' equity		$1,650,000

purchase. Furthermore, an aging of the accounts receivable shows that the following amounts are due the firm:

Number of Days Outstanding	Amount of Receivables
1–11	$325,000
11–20	25,000
21–30	20,000
31–60	5,000
61–90	7,500
91+	17,500

In this case, the firm might believe that anything more than 60 days old will not be paid and will write it off as uncollectible. Note that, in Table 11.2, the allowance for uncollectible accounts is $25,000, the amount that has been outstanding more than 60 days.

Inventory is merchandise held by the company for resale to customers. Current inventory in our example is $150,000, but this is not all of the inventory the firm had on hand all year. Naturally, the company started the year with some inventory and purchased more as sales were made. This balance sheet figure is what was left at the end of the fiscal year.

Prepaid expenses are expenses the firm already has paid but that have not yet been used. For example, insurance paid on the company car every six months is a prepaid-expense entry because it will be six months before all of the premium has been used. As a result, the accountant would reduce this prepaid amount by one-sixth each month. Sometimes supplies, services, and rent are also prepaid, in which case the same approach is followed.

FIXED ASSETS

Fixed assets consist of land, building, equipment, and other assets expected to remain with the firm for an extended period. They are not totally used up in the production of the firm's goods and services. Some of the most common types are shown in Table 11.2.

Land is property used in the operation of the firm. This is not land that has been purchased for expansion or speculation; that would be listed as an investment rather than a fixed asset. Land is listed on the balance sheet at cost, and its value usually is changed only periodically. For example, every five years, the value of the land might be recalculated so that its value on the balance sheet and its resale value are the same.

Building consists of the structures that house the business. If the firm has more than one building, the total cost of all the structures is listed.

Accumulated depreciation of building refers to the amount of the building that has been written off the books due to wear and tear. For example, referring to Table 11.2, the original cost of the building was $315,000, but accumulated depreciation is $80,000, leaving a net value of $235,000. The amount of depreciation charged each year is determined by the company accountant after checking with the Internal Revenue Service rules. A standard depreciation is 5 percent per year for new buildings, although an accelerated method sometimes is used. In any event, the amount written off is a tax-deductible expense. Depreciation therefore reduces the amount of taxable income to the firm and helps lower the tax liability. In this way, the business gets the opportunity to recover part of its investment.

Equipment is the machinery the business uses to produce goods. This is placed on the books at cost and then depreciated and listed as the accumulated depreciation of equipment. In our example, it is $60,000. The logic behind equipment depreciation and its effect on the firm's income taxes is the same as that for accumulated depreciation on the building.

CURRENT LIABILITIES

Current liabilities are obligations that will become due and payable during the next year or within the operating cycle. The most common current liabilities are listed in Table 11.2.

Accounts payable are liabilities incurred when goods or supplies are purchased on credit. For example, if the business buys on a basis of net 30 days, during that 30 days the bill for the goods will constitute an account payable.

A **note payable** is a promissory note given as tangible recognition of a supplier's claim or a note given in connection with an acquisition of funds, such as for a bank loan. Some suppliers require that a note be given when a company buys merchandise and is unable to pay for it immediately.

Taxes payable are liabilities owed to the government—federal, state, and local. Most businesses pay their federal and state income taxes on a quarterly basis. Typically, payments are made on April 15, June 15, and September 15 of the current year and January 15 of the following year. Then the business closes its books, determines whether it still owes any taxes, and makes the required payments by April 15. Other taxes payable are sales taxes. For example, most states (and some cities) levy a sales tax. Each merchant must collect the taxes and remit them to the appropriate agency.

A **loan payable** is the current installment on a long-term debt that must be paid this year. As a result, it becomes a part of the current liabilities. The remainder is carried as a long-term debt. Note that, in Table 11.2, $50,000 of this debt was paid in 2010 by the Kendon Corporation.

LONG-TERM LIABILITIES

As we have said, long-term liabilities consist of obligations that will not become due or payable for at least one year or not within the current operating cycle. The most common are bank loans.

A **bank loan** is a long-term liability due to a loan from a lending institution. Although it is unclear from the balance sheet in Table 11.2 how large the bank loan originally was, it is being paid down at the rate of $50,000 annually. Thus, it will take four more years to pay off the loan.

CONTRIBUTED CAPITAL

The Kendon Corporation is owned by individuals who have purchased stock in the business. Various kinds of stock can be sold by a corporation, the most typical being common stock and preferred stock. Only common stock has been sold by this company.

Common stock is the most basic form of corporate ownership. This ownership gives the individual the right to vote for the board of directors. Usually, for every share of common stock held, the individual is entitled to one vote. As shown in Table 11.2, the corporation has issued 40,000 shares of $10 par common stock, raising $400,000. Although the term *par value* may have little meaning to most stockholders, it has legal implications: It determines the legal capital of the corporation. This legal capital constitutes an amount that total stockholders' equity cannot be reduced below except under certain circumstances (the most common is a series of net losses). For legal reasons, the total par value of the stock is maintained in the accounting records. However, it has no effect on the market value of the stock.

Preferred stock differs from common stock in that its holders have preference to the assets of the firm in case of dissolution. This means that, after the creditors are paid, preferred stockholders have the next claim on whatever assets are left. The common stockholders' claims come last. Table 11.2 shows that 500 shares of preferred stock were issued, each worth a par value of $100, but none has been sold. Therefore, it is not shown as a number on the balance sheet.

RETAINED EARNINGS

Retained earnings are the accumulated net income over the life of the business to date. In Table 11.2, the retained earnings are shown as $750,000. Every year this amount increases by the profit the firm makes and keeps within the company. If dividends are declared on the stock, they, of course, are paid from the total net earnings. Retained earnings are what remain after that.

Why the Balance Sheet Always Balances

By definition, the balance sheet always balances.[4] If something happens on one side of the balance sheet, it is offset by something on the other side. Hence, the balance sheet remains in balance. Before examining some illustrations, let us restate the balance-sheet equation:

Assets = Liabilities + Owners' Equity

With this in mind, let us look at some typical examples of business transactions and their effect on the balance sheet.

A CREDIT TRANSACTION

The Kendon Corporation calls one of its suppliers and asks for delivery of $11,000 of materials. The materials arrive the next day, and the company takes possession of them.

Watching Your Accounts Receivables

One of the primary issues that plagues start-up companies is poor cash flow, and one of the largest contributors to this problem is uncollected accounts receivables. When the economy is in decline, the first tactic that most businesses will employ is to stretch out the payments on their accounts payables as long as they can, which presents an issue for their vendors. Most entrepreneurs offer credit to their customers to encourage business, but when those customers choose not to pay off that credit in a timely manner, businesses servicing them can face a cash deficit, making payments to their own vendors problematic. In some cases, entrepreneurs are left with no choice but to take on credit cards that charge excessive interest rates just to keep their business afloat.

Avoiding this situation takes significant forethought on the part of the management team. A good rule of thumb is to always secure funding before your company needs it. You will usually find cash when in dire straights, but the cost of that capital can be significant. Securing an operating line of credit and keeping tabs on your accounts receivable will help prevent expensive mistakes when the going gets tough.

Following are five tips for making sure that you are paid what is coming to you:

Develop a process. Customers will stretch out their payments to you if they think they can get away with it; do not let them. Being consistent when dealing with your customers will let them know that you take collecting your receivables seriously. Establish a payment due date and enforce it. If you let your customers slide, you will be sending them the message that they can pay when they want to, which might work fine when your company is flush with cash but will be a significant burden if your business hits a lull.

Make some noise. Once you have provided a product or service, you are entitled to get paid. You should not feel guilty about contacting your customers about a delinquent payment. After all, you have upheld your end of the deal. Your customers are going to pay the vendors who are the most committed to getting paid. If you choose to sit idle, you may never get your money.

Get paid up front. When in doubt, there is no better way to ensure payment than by mandating that your customers pay up front; this is especially useful when working with new clients. You can always charge a percentage so that you and your customers are sharing the burden of responsibility. In the event that you choose to issue credit to a customer, make sure to perform a credit check first.

Find an advocate. The person paying your company is most likely not the entrepreneur. Find out who is responsible for issuing payments in each of your respective customers' businesses so that you get to know her. The order in which payments are submitted will usually be at the discretion of this individual, so you stand a greater chance of being at the top of that list if she knows you.

Know when to walk away. Despite what traditional thinking suggests, customers are not always right and they are not always profitable. The time spent collecting fees from a customer and the cost of carrying the credit for that customer might outweigh the margins that customer's business is generating. If that turns out to be the case, do not be afraid to discontinue the relationship. Often the costs far outweigh what appears on your financial statements, given that time spent on troublesome customers could be spent acquiring new business. To prevent such issues from burdening your company, conduct annual audits of your customers and consider eliminating those that cost you money.

Cash-flow management is a process that never ends for an entrepreneur. Liquidity is an important metric when considering the health of your business; if you are allowing your customers to postpone their payments, you risk them putting your company's life in jeopardy.

Adapted from C. J. Prince, "Time Bomb," *Entrepreneur*, January 2008, http://www.entrepreneur.com/magazine/entrepreneur/2008/january/187658.html (accessed March 16, 2008).

The bill is to be paid within 30 days. How is the balance sheet affected? Inventory goes up by $11,000, and accounts payable rise by $11,000. The increase in current assets is offset by an increase in current liabilities.

Continuing this illustration, what happens when the bill is paid? The company issues a check for $11,000, and cash declines by this amount. At the same time, accounts payable decrease by $11,000. Again, these are offsetting transactions, and the balance sheet remains in balance.

A BANK LOAN

Table 11.2 shows that the Kendon Corporation had an outstanding bank loan of $200,000 in 2010. Assume that the company increases this loan by $110,000 in 2011. How is the balance sheet affected? Cash goes up by $110,000, and bank loan increases by the same amount; again, balance is achieved. However, what if the firm uses this $110,000 to buy new machinery? In this case, cash decreases by $110,000 and equipment increases by a like amount. Again, a balance exists. Finally, what if Kendon decides to pay off its bank loan? In this case, the first situation is reversed; cash and bank loan (long-term liabilities) decrease in equal amounts.

A STOCK SALE

Suppose that the company issues and sells another 40,000 shares of $10 par common stock. How does this action affect the balance sheet? (This answer is rather simple.) Common stock increases by $400,000, and so does cash. Once more, a balance exists.

With these examples in mind, it should be obvious why the balance sheet always balances. Every entry has an equal and offsetting entry to maintain this equation:

Assets = Liabilities + Owners' Equity

Keep in mind that, in accounting language, the terms *debit* and *credit* denote increases and decreases in assets, liabilities, and owners' equity. The following chart relates debits and credits to increases and decreases.

Category	A Transaction Increasing the Amount	A Transaction Decreasing the Amount
Asset	Debit	Credit
Liability	Credit	Debit
Owners' equity	Credit	Debit

Applying this idea to the preceding examples results in the following:

	Debit	Credit
Credit Transaction		
Inventory	$11,000	
Accounts payable		$11,000
Bank Loan		
Cash	110,000	
Bank Loan		110,000
Stock Sale		
Cash	400,000	
Common Stock		400,000
	$511,000	$511,000

The Income Statement

The **income statement** is a financial statement that shows the change that has occurred in a firm's position as a result of its operations over a specific period. This is in contrast to the balance sheet, which reflects the company's position at a particular point in time.

The income statement, sometimes referred to as a "profit and loss statement" or "P&L", reports the success (or failure) of the business during the period. In essence, it shows whether revenues were greater than or less than expenses. These revenues are the monies the small business has received from the sale of its goods and services. The expenses are the costs of the resources used to obtain the revenues. These costs range from the cost of materials used in the products the firm makes to the salaries it pays its employees.

Most income statements cover a one-year interval, but it is not uncommon to find monthly, quarterly, or semiannual income statements. All of the revenues and expenses accumulated during this time are determined, and the net income for the period is identified. Many firms prepare quarterly income statements but construct a balance sheet only once a year. This is because they are interested far more in their profits and losses than in examining their asset, liability, and owners' equity positions. However, it should be noted that the income statement drawn up at the end of the year will coincide with the firm's fiscal year, just as the balance sheet does. As a result, at the end of the business year, the organization will have both a balance sheet and an income statement. In this way, they can be considered together and the interrelationship between them can be studied. A number of different types of income and expenses are reported on the income statement. However, for purposes of simplicity, the income statement can be reduced to three primary categories: (1) revenues, (2) expenses, and (3) net income.

Revenues are the gross sales the business made during the particular period under review. Revenue often consists of the money actually received from sales, but this need not be the case. For example, sales made on account still are recognized as revenue, as when a furniture store sells $500 of furniture to a customer today, delivers it tomorrow, and will receive payment two weeks from now. From the moment the goods are delivered, the company can claim an increase in revenue.

Expenses are the costs associated with producing goods or services. For the furniture store in the preceding paragraph, the expenses associated with the sale would include the costs of acquiring, selling, and delivering the merchandise. Sometimes these are expenses that will be paid later. For example, the people who deliver the furniture may be paid every two weeks, so the actual outflow of expense money in the form of salaries will not occur at the same time the work is performed. Nevertheless, it is treated as an expense.

Net income is the excess of revenue over expenses during the particular period under discussion. If revenues exceed expenses, the result is a net profit. If the reverse is true, the firm suffers a net loss. At the end of the accounting period, all of the revenues and expenses associated with all of the sales of goods and services are added together, and then the expenses are subtracted from the revenues. In this way, the firm knows whether it made an overall profit or suffered an overall loss.[5]

Understanding the Income Statement

To explain the income statement fully, it is necessary to examine one and determine what each account is. Table 11.3 illustrates a typical income statement. It has five major sections: (1) sales revenue, (2) cost of goods sold, (3) operating expenses, (4) financial expense, and (5) income taxes estimated.

REVENUE

Every time a business sells a product or performs a service, it obtains revenue. This often is referred to as *gross revenue* or *sales revenue*. However, it is usually an overstated figure, because the company finds that some of its goods are returned or some customers take advantage of prompt-payment discounts.

In Table 11.3, sales revenue is $1,750,000. However, the firm also has returns and allowances of $50,000. These returns are common for companies that operate on a "satisfaction or your money back" policy. In any event, a small business should keep tabs on these returns

| *Table* **11.3** | Kendon Corporation Income Statement for the Year Ended December 31, 2010 |

Sales Revenue	$1,750,000	
Less: Sales returns and allowances	50,000	
Net sales		$1,700,000
Cost of Goods Sold		
Inventory, January, 2000	$150,000	
Purchases	1,050,000	
Goods available for sale	$1,200,000	
Less: Inventory, December, 2000	200,000	
Cost of goods sold		1,000,000
Gross margin		$700,000
Operating Expenses		
Selling expenses	$150,000	
Administrative expenses	100,000	
Total operating expenses		250,000
Operating income		$450,000
Financial Expenses		$20,000
Income before income taxes		$430,000
Estimated Income Taxes		172,000
Net profit		$258,000

and allowances to see if the total is high in relation to the total sales revenue. If so, the firm will know that something is wrong with what it is selling, and it can take action to correct the situation.

Deducting the sales returns and allowances from the sales revenue, the company finds its net sales. This amount must be great enough to offset the accompanying expenses in order to ensure a profit.

COST OF GOODS SOLD

As the name implies, the cost of goods sold section reports the cost of merchandise sold during the accounting period. Simply put, the cost of goods for a given period equals the beginning inventory plus any purchases the firm makes minus the inventory on hand at the end of the period. Note that, in Table 11.3, the beginning inventory was $150,000 and the purchases totaled $1,050,000. This gave Kendon goods available for sale of $1,200,000. The ending inventory for the period was $200,000, so the cost of goods sold was $1,000,000. This is what it cost the company to buy the inventory it sold. When this cost of goods sold is subtracted from net sales, the result is the gross margin. The gross margin is the amount available to meet expenses and to provide some net income for the firm's owners.

OPERATING EXPENSES

The major expenses, exclusive of costs of goods sold, are classified as operating expenses. These represent the resources expended, except for inventory purchases, to generate the revenue for the period. Expenses often are divided into two broad subclassifications: selling expenses and administrative expenses.

Selling expenses result from activities such as displaying, selling, delivering, and installing a product or performing a service. Expenses for displaying a product include rent for storage space, depreciation on fixtures and furniture, property insurance, and utility and tax expenses. Sales expenses, salaries, commissions, and advertising also fall into this category. Costs associated with getting the product from the store to the customer also are considered selling expenses. Finally, if the firm installs the product for the customer, all costs—including the parts used in the job—are considered in this total. Taken as a whole, these are the selling expenses.

Administrative expenses is a catchall term for operating expenses not directly related to selling or borrowing. In broad terms, these expenses include the costs associated with running the firm. They include salaries of the managers, expenses associated with operating the office, general expenses that cannot be related directly to buying or selling activities, and expenses that arise from delinquent or uncollectible accounts.

When these selling and administrative expenses are added together, the result is total operating expenses. Subtracting them from the gross margin gives the firm its operating income. Note that, in Table 11.3, selling expenses are $150,000, administrative expenses are $100,000, and total operating expenses are $250,000. When subtracted from the gross margin of $700,000, the operating income is $450,000.

FINANCIAL EXPENSE

The **financial expense** is the interest expense on long-term loans. As seen in Table 11.3, this expense is $20,000. Additionally, many companies include their interest expense on short-term obligations as part of their financial expense.

ESTIMATED INCOME TAXES

As noted earlier, corporations pay estimated income taxes; then, at some predetermined time (for example, December 31), the books are closed, actual taxes are determined, and any additional payments are made (or refunds claimed). When these taxes are subtracted from the income before income taxes, the result is the net profit. In our example, the Kendon Corporation made $258,000.

The Cash-Flow Statement

The **cash-flow statement** (also known as *statement of cash flows*) shows the effects of a company's operating, investing, and financing activities on its cash balance. The principal purpose of the statement of cash flows is to provide relevant information about a company's cash receipts and cash payments during a particular accounting period. It is useful for answering such questions as:

* How much cash did the firm generate from operations?
* How did the firm finance fixed capital expenditures?
* How much new debt did the firm add?
* Was the cash from operations sufficient to finance fixed asset purchases?

The statement of cash flows is a supplement to the balance sheet and income statements. One of the limitations of the income and balance sheet statements is that they are based on accrual accounting. In accrual accounting, revenues and expenses are recorded when incurred—not when cash changes hands. For example, if a sale is made for credit, under accrual accounting the sale is recognized but cash has not been received. Similarly, a tax expense may be shown in the income statement, but it may not be paid until later. The statement of cash flows reconciles the accrual-based figures in the income and balance sheet statements to the actual cash balance reported in the balance sheet.

The statement of cash flows is broken down into operating, investing, and financing activities. Table 11.4 provides an outline of a statement of cash flows. **Operating cash flows** refer to cash generated from or used in the course of business operations of the firm. The net operating cash flows will be positive for most firms, because their operating inflows (primarily from revenue collections) will exceed operating cash outflows (for example, payment for raw materials and wages).

Table 11.4	Format of Statement of Cash Flows

Cash flows from operating activities	$50,000
Cash flows from investing activities	($10,000)
Cash flows from financing activities	$5,000
Net increase (decrease) in cash	$45,000
Cash at beginning of period	$400,000
Cash at end of period	$445,000

Investing activities refer to cash-flow effects from long-term investing activities, such as purchase or sale of plant and equipment. The net cash flow from investing activities can be either positive or negative. A firm that is still in the growth phase would be building up fixed assets (installing new equipment or building new plants) and therefore would show negative cash flows from investing activities. On the other hand, a firm that is divesting unprofitable divisions may realize cash inflows from the sale of assets and therefore would show a positive cash flow from investing activities.

Financing activities refer to cash-flow effects of financing decisions of the firm, including sale of new securities (such as stocks and bonds), repurchase of securities, and payment of dividends. Note that payment of interest to lenders is *not* included under financing activities. Accounting convention in determining the statement of cash flows assumes that interest payments are part of operating cash flows. Once the cash flows from the three different sources—operating, investing, and financing—are identified, the beginning and ending cash balances are reconciled.

Because this statement is most frequently used by those analyzing the firm, the use of a cash budget may be the best approach for an entrepreneur starting up a venture. The cash budget procedure will be covered in the next section.

Preparing Financial Budgets

One of the most powerful tools the entrepreneur can use in planning financial operations is a budget.[6] The operating budget is a statement of estimated income and expenses during a specified period of time. Another common type of budget is the cash-flow budget, which is a statement of estimated cash receipts and expenditures during a specified period of time. It is typical for a firm to prepare both types of budgets by first computing an operating budget and then constructing a cash budget based on the operating budget. A third common type of budget is the capital budget, which is used to plan expenditures on assets whose returns are expected to last beyond one year. This section examines all three of these budgets: operating, cash flow, and capital. Then the preparation of pro forma financial statements from these budgets is discussed.

The Operating Budget

Typically, the first step in creating an operating budget is the preparation of the sales forecast.[7] An entrepreneur can prepare the sales forecast in several ways. One way is to implement a statistical forecasting technique such as simple linear regression. Simple linear

292   C H A P T E R   1 1   Financial Statements in New Ventures

regression is a technique in which a linear equation states the relationship among three variables:

$$Y = a + bx$$

Y is a dependent variable (it is dependent on the values of *a, b,* and *x*), *x* is an independent variable (it is not dependent on any of the other variables), *a* is a constant (in regression analysis, Y is dependent on the variable *x*, all other things held constant), and *b* is the slope of the line (the change in Y divided by the change in *x*). For estimating sales, Y is the variable used to represent the expected sales, and *x* is the variable used to represent the factor on which sales are dependent. Some retail stores may believe that their sales are dependent on their advertising expenditures, whereas other stores may believe that their sales are dependent on some other variable, such as the amount of foot traffic past the store.

When using regression analysis, the entrepreneur will draw conclusions about the relationship between, for example, product sales and advertising expenditures. Presented next is an example of how Mary Tindle, owner of a clothing store, used regression analysis.

Mary began with two initial assumptions: (1) If no money is spent on advertising, total sales will be $200,000, and (2) for every dollar spent on advertising, sales will be increased by two times that amount. Relating these two observations yields the following simple linear regression formula:

$$S = \$200,000 + 2A$$

where
   S = Projected Sales
   A = Advertising Expenditures

(Note that it is often easier to substitute more meaningful letters into an equation. In this case, the letter *S* was substituted for the letter Y simply because the word *sales* starts with that letter. The same is true for the letter *A*, which was substituted for the letter X.) In order to determine the expected sales level, Mary must insert different advertising expenditures and complete the simple linear regression formula for each different expenditure. The following data and Figure 11.1 demonstrate the results.

Figure **11.1**   **Regression Analysis**

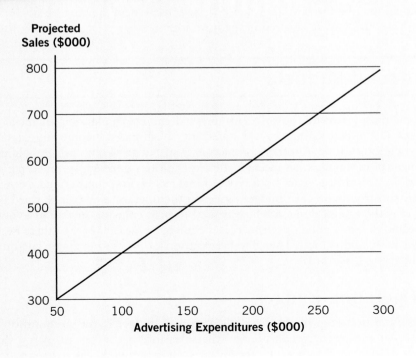

Simple Linear Regression ($000)

A	2A	S = $200 + 2A
$ 50	$100	$300
100	200	400
150	300	500
200	400	600
250	500	700
300	600	800

Another commonly used technique for the preparation of a sales forecast is the estimation that current sales will increase a certain percentage over the prior period's sales. This percentage is based on a trend line analysis that covers the five preceding sales periods and assumes that the seasonal variations will continue to run in the same pattern. Obviously, because it needs five preceding sales periods, trend line analysis is used for more established ventures. It is nevertheless an important tool that entrepreneurs should be aware of as the venture grows and becomes more established. Following is an example of how John Wheatman, owner of North Central Scientific, used trend line analysis to forecast sales for his computer retail store:

> After considerable analysis of his store's sales history, John Wheatman decided to use trend line analysis and estimated that sales would increase 5 percent during the next year, with the seasonal variations following roughly the same pattern. Because he has a personal computer with an electronic spreadsheet program, John chose to use the input of last year's sales figures in the spreadsheet and then to increase each month by 5 percent. The results are shown in Table 11.5.

After a firm has forecast its sales for the budget period, expenses must be estimated. The first type of expenses that should be estimated is the cost of goods sold, which follows sales on the income statement. For retail firms, this is a matter of projecting purchases and the corresponding desired beginning and ending inventories. Many firms prefer to have a certain percentage of the next month's sales on hand in inventory. Here is how John Wheatman determines his store's expected purchases and inventory requirements:

> For determining his purchase requirements, John Wheatman believes that his gross profit will represent 20 percent of his sales dollar. This is based on analysis of the past five years' income statement. Consequently, cost of goods sold will represent 80 percent of the sales for the current month. In addition, John wants to have approximately one week's inventory on hand. Thus, the ending inventory is estimated to be 25 percent of next month's sales. The results are shown in Table 11.6.

Table 11.5   North Central Scientific: Sales Forecast for 2010

	January	February	March	April	May	June
Sales	$300	$350	$400	$375	$500	$450
× 1.05	315	368	420	394	525	473

	July	August	September	October	November	December
Sales	$475	$480	$440	$490	$510	$550
× 1.05	499	504	462	515	536	578

| *Table* **11.6** | **North Central Scientific: Purchase Requirements Budget for 2010** |

	Jan.	Feb.	Mar.	Apr.	May	June	July	Aug.	Sept.	Oct.	Nov.	Dec.
Sales revenue	$315	$368	$420	$394	$525	$473	$499	$504	$462	$515	$536	$578
Cost of goods sold												
Beginning inventory	$63	$74	$84	$79	$105	$95	$100	$101	$92	$103	$107	$116
Purchases	263	305	331	341	410	383	400	395	380	416	437	413
Cost of goods available	$326	$379	$415	$420	$515	$478	$500	$496	$472	$519	$544	$529
Ending inventory	74	85	79	105	95	100	101	92	102	107	116	66
Cost of goods sold	$252	$294	$336	$315	$420	$378	$399	$403	$370	$412	$428	$462
Gross profit	$63	$74	$84	$79	$105	$95	$100	$101	$92	$103	$108	$116

Cost of goods sold = Current period sales × .80

Ending inventory = Next month's sales × (.80)(.25) (since inventory is carried at cost)

Cost of goods available = Cost of goods sold + Ending inventory

Beginning inventory = Prior month's ending inventory or current month's sales × (.80)(.25)

Purchases = Cost of goods available − Beginning inventory

Gross profit = Sales − Cost of goods sold

A manufacturing firm, on the other hand, will need to establish its production budget, a material purchases budget based on the production budget, and the corresponding direct labor budget. The production budget is management's estimate of the number of units that need to be produced in order to meet the sales forecast. This budget is prepared by working backward through the cost of goods sold section. First, the predicted number of units that will be sold during that month is determined. Then the desired ending-inventory-level balance is added to this figure. The sum of these two figures is the number of units that will be needed in inventory. Once the inventory requirements have been determined, the entrepreneur must determine how many of these units will be accounted for by the beginning inventory (which is the prior month's ending inventory) and how many units will have to be produced. The production requirement is calculated by sub-tracting the period's beginning inventory from the inventory needed for that period. For example:

Tom B. Good, president and founder of Dynamic Manufacturing, has decided to imple-ment a budget to help plan for his company's growth. After Tom received the unit sales forecast from his sales manager, he examined last year's product movement reports and determined that he would like to have 11 percent of the next month's sales on hand as a buffer against possible fluctuations in demand. He also has received a report from his production manager that his ending inventory this year is expected to be 12,000 wid-gets, which also will be the beginning inventory for the budget period. Table 11.7 shows the results.

After the production budget has been calculated, the materials required for producing the specified number of units can be determined from an analysis of the bill of materials for the product being manufactured. In addition, by examining the amount of direct labor needed to produce each unit, management can determine the amount of direct labor that will be needed during the forthcoming budget period.

The last step in preparing the operating budget is to estimate the operating expenses for the period. Three of the key concepts in developing an expense budget are fixed, variable,

Table 11.7	Dynamic Manufacturing: Production Budget Worksheet for 2010

	Jan.	Feb.	Mar.	Apr.	May	June	July	Aug.	Sept.	Oct.	Nov.	Dec.
Projected sales (units)	125	136	123	143	154	234	212	267	236	345	367	498
Desired ending inventory	14	12	14	15	23	21	27	24	35	37	50	26
Available for sale	139	148	137	158	177	255	239	291	271	382	417	524
Less: Beginning inventory	12	14	12	14	15	23	21	27	24	35	37	50
Total production requirements	127	134	125	144	162	232	218	264	247	347	380	474

and mixed costs. A fixed cost is one that does not change in response to changes in activity for a given period of time; rent, depreciation, and certain salaries are examples. A variable cost is one that changes in the same direction as, and in direct proportion to, changes in operating activity; direct labor, direct materials, and sales commissions are examples. Mixed costs are a blend of fixed and variable costs. An example is utilities, because part of this expense would be responsive to change in activity, and the rest would be a fixed expense, remaining relatively stable during the budget period. Mixed costs can present a problem for management in that it is sometimes difficult to determine how much of the expense is variable and how much is fixed.

After the expenses have been budgeted, the sales, cost of goods, and expense budget are combined to form the operating budget. Table 11.8 outlines North Central Scientific's anticipated expenses for the budget year and the completed operating budget for the period. Each month represents the pro forma, or projected, income and expenses for that period.

The Cash–Flow Budget

After the operating budget has been prepared, the entrepreneur can proceed to the next phase of the budget process, the cash-flow budget. This budget, which often is prepared with the assistance of an accountant, provides an overview of the cash inflows and outflows during the period. By pinpointing cash problems in advance, management can make the necessary financing arrangements.[8]

The first step in the preparation of the cash-flow budget is the identification and timing of cash inflows. For the typical business, cash inflows will come from three sources: (1) cash sales, (2) cash payments received on account, and (3) loan proceeds. Not all of a firm's sales revenues are cash. In an effort to increase sales, most businesses will allow some customers to purchase goods on account. Consequently, part of the funds will arrive in later periods and will be identified as cash payments received on account. Loan proceeds represent another form of cash inflow that is not directly tied to the sales revenues. A firm may receive loan proceeds for several reasons—for example, the planned expansion of the firm (new building and equipment) or meeting cash-flow problems stemming from an inability to pay current bills.

Some businesses have a desired minimum balance of cash indicated on the cash-flow budget, highlighting the point at which it will be necessary to seek additional financing. Table 11.9 provides an example of how North Central Scientific prepared its cash-flow budget.

| Table 11.8 | North Central Scientific: Expense and Operating Budgets |

In order to identify the behavior of the different expense accounts, John Wheatman decided to analyze the past five years' income statements. Following are the results of his analysis:

- Rent is a constant expense and is expected to remain the same during the next year.

- Payroll expense changes in proportion to sales, because the more sales the store has, the more people it must hire to meet increased consumer demands.

- Utilities are expected to remain relatively constant during the budget period.

- Taxes are based primarily on sales and payroll and are therefore considered a variable expense.

- Supplies will vary in proportion to sales. This is because most of the supplies will be used to support sales.

- Repairs are relatively stable and are a fixed expense. John has maintenance contracts on the equipment in the store, and the cost is not scheduled to rise during the budget period.

North Central Scientific: Expense Budget for 2010

	Jan.	Feb.	Mar.	Apr.	May	June	July	Aug.	Sept.	Oct.	Nov.	Dec.
Anticipated operating expenses												
Rent	$2	$2	$2	$2	$2	$2	$2	$2	$2	$2	$2	$2
Payroll	32	37	42	39	53	47	50	50	46	51	54	58
Utilities	5	5	5	5	5	5	5	5	5	5	5	5
Taxes	3	4	4	4	5	5	5	5	5	5	5	6
Supplies	16	18	21	20	26	24	25	25	23	26	27	29
Repairs	2	2	2	2	2	2	2	2	2	2	2	2
Total expenses	$60	$68	$76	$72	$93	$85	$89	$89	$83	$91	$95	$102
Sales revenue	$315	$368	$420	$394	$525	$473	$499	$504	$462	$515	$536	$578
Cost of goods sold												
Beginning inventory	$63	$74	$84	$79	$105	$95	$100	$101	$92	$103	$107	$116
Purchases	263	305	331	341	410	383	400	395	380	416	437	413
Cost of goods available	$326	$379	$415	$420	$515	$478	$500	$496	$472	$519	$544	$529
Ending inventory	74	85	79	105	95	100	101	92	102	107	116	66
Cost of goods sold	$252	$294	$336	$315	$420	$378	$399	$403	$370	$412	$428	$462
Gross profit	$63	$74	$84	$79	$105	$95	$100	$101	$92	$103	$108	$116
Operating expenses												
Rent	$2	$2	$2	$2	$2	$2	$2	$2	$2	$2	$2	$2
Payroll	32	37	42	39	53	47	50	50	46	51	54	58
Utilities	5	5	5	5	5	5	5	5	5	5	5	5
Taxes	3	4	4	4	5	5	5	5	5	5	5	6
Supplies	16	18	21	20	26	24	25	25	23	26	27	29
Repairs	2	2	2	2	2	2	2	2	2	2	2	2
Total expenses	$60	$68	$76	$72	$93	$85	$89	$89	$83	$91	$95	$102
Net profit	$3	$6	$8	$7	$12	$10	$11	$12	$9	$12	$12	$14

| Table 11.9 | North Central Scientific: Cash-Flow Budget |

John Wheatman has successfully completed his operating budget and is now ready to prepare his cash-flow worksheet. After analyzing the sales figures and the cash receipts, John has determined that 80 percent of monthly sales are in cash. Of the remaining 20 percent, 15 percent is collected in the next month, and the final 5 percent is collected in the month following (see the cash receipts worksheet below). Wheatman's purchases are typically paid during the week following the purchase. Therefore, approximately one-fourth of the purchases are paid for in the following month. Rent expense is paid a month in advance. However, because it is not expected to go up during the budget period, the monthly cash outlay for rent remains the same. All the other expenses are paid in the month of consumption (see the cash disbursements worksheet below). Finally, the cash-flow worksheet is constructed by taking the beginning cash balance, adding the cash receipts for that month, and deducting the cash disbursements for the same month.

North Central Scientific: Cash Receipts Worksheet for 2010

	Jan.	Feb.	Mar.	Apr.	May	June	July	Aug.	Sept.	Oct.	Nov.	Dec.
Sales	$315	$388	$420	$394	$525	$473	$499	$504	$462	$515	$536	$578
Current month	$252	$294	$336	$315	$420	$378	$399	$403	$370	$412	$428	$462
Prior month	82	47	55	63	59	79	71	75	76	69	77	80
Two months back	26	28	16	18	21	19	26	24	24	25	24	26
Cash receipts	$360	$369	$407	$396	$500	$476	$496	$502	$470	$506	$529	$568

North Central Scientific: Cash Disbursements Worksheet for 2010

	Jan.	Feb.	Mar.	Apr.	May	June	July	Aug.	Sept.	Oct.	Nov.	Dec.
Purchases	$263	$305	$331	$341	$410	$383	$400	$395	$380	$416	$437	$413
Current month	$197	$228	$248	$256	$307	$287	$300	$296	$285	$312	$328	$309
Prior month	98	66	76	83	85	102	96	100	99	95	104	109
Purchase payments	$295	$294	$324	$339	$392	$396	$396	$396	$384	$407	$432	$419
Operating expenses	$60	$68	$76	$72	$93	$85	$89	$89	$83	$91	$95	$102
Cash payments	$355	$362	$400	$412	$485	$481	$485	$485	$467	$498	$527	$521

North Central Scientific: Cash-Flow Worksheet for 2010

	Jan.	Feb.	Mar.	Apr.	May	June	July	Aug.	Sept.	Oct.	Nov.	Dec.
Beginning cash	$122	$127	$134	$141	$127	$141	$143	$154	$170	$173	$181	$184
Add: Receipts	360	369	407	396	500	476	496	502	470	506	529	568
Cash available	$482	$496	$541	$537	$627	$617	$639	$656	$640	$679	$710	$752
Less: Payments	355	362	400	411	485	481	485	485	467	498	527	521
Ending cash	$127	$134	$141	$126	$142	$136	$154	$171	$173	$181	$183	$231

the entrepreneurial process

Characteristics of Credible Financials

Although every section of a business plan has its purpose, the financial section bears the most scrutiny. A business's financial statements are deserving of this attention for two reasons: (1) the management team has significant discretion in how the financials are constructed and (2) potential investors reviewing a business plan will be interested in the financial viability of the company's strategy. Following are characteristics that convincing financial statements have in common:

- *Holistic* An income statement tells only part of your business's financial story; the balance sheet and cash-flow statement are necessary to fill in the remaining details. Investors and lenders are interested in every detail of your company's financial health, so never exclude relevant information, such as the amount of and the timeline for the cash you will need.

- *Precise* Although investors will carefully analyze your financial statements, helping them to pinpoint the important details will ensure that they do not lose patience searching through your plan. To aid the readers of your plan, focus your sales and cost of goods sold numbers on major product lines. In addition, pay attention to how you label your line items to ensure that your readers will understand what you are trying to communicate. For instance, "costs" are what you pay for what you are selling while "expenses", like payroll and rent, are overhead charges you would have without sales.

- *Realistic* When you tailor your figures to achieve a predetermined revenue goal, you will have trouble justifying your numbers when questioned. Instead, build your financials by starting with your costs and sales in your local market to anchor your figures in reality. In addition, your projections beyond the first year should be annual or quarterly.

- *Simple* Significant volatility in your industry should be noted, such as your business being impacted by seasonality; however, bogging down your plan with lengthy explanations regarding the probability of your projections will only serve to confuse the reader. By including clarifying statements, such as "most likely", and supporting addendums, such as your break-even analysis, will be sufficient.

- *Accurate* Investors know that your plan will change repeatedly as you build your business; however, overlooking simple expenses, such as interest payments, can cast doubt on your attention to detail. Once you have your financial statements completed, verifying the finer points, such as the accuracy of the interest and tax rates, will show that you are able to take your business from plan to implementation.

Source: Adapted from Tim Berry (2007, May). The Facts About Financial Projections. Retrieved June 21, 2008, from Entrepreneur Magazine Website: https://www.entrepreneur.com/startingabusiness/businessplans/businessplancoachtimberry/article178210.html; and Jim Casparie (2006, April). Realistic Projections That Attract Investors. Retrieved June 21, 2008, from Entrepreneur Magazine Website: http://www.entrepreneur.com/money/financing/raisingmoneycoachjimcasparie/article159516.html.

Pro Forma Statements

The final step in the budget process is the preparation of pro forma statements, which are projections of a firm's financial position during a future period (pro forma income statement) or on a future date (pro forma balance sheet). In the normal accounting cycle, the income statement is prepared first, followed by the balance sheet. Similarly, in the preparation of pro forma statements, the pro forma income statement is followed by the pro forma balance sheet.

In the process of preparing the operating budget, the firm already will have prepared the pro forma income statements for each month in the budget period. Each month presents the anticipated income and expense for that particular period, which is what the monthly pro forma income statements do. To prepare an annual pro forma income statement, the firm combines all months of the year.

The process for preparing a pro forma balance sheet is more complex: The last balance sheet prepared before the budget period began, the operating budget, and the cash-flow budget are needed to prepare it. Starting with the beginning balance sheet balances, the projected changes as depicted on the budgets are added to create the projected balance sheet totals.

After preparing the pro forma balance sheet, the entrepreneur should verify the accuracy of his or her work with the application of the traditional accounting equation:

Assets = Liabilities + Owner's Equity

If the equation is not in balance, the work should be rechecked. Table 11.10 provides a brief account of the process of preparing pro forma financial statements for North Central Scientific.

Table 11.10   North Central Scientific: Pro Forma Statements

At this point in the budget process, John Wheatman has the information necessary to prepare pro forma financial statements. The first set he has decided to prepare is the pro forma income statements. To do this, John simply copies the information from the operating budget (see the comparative income statements below and compare with the operating budget). The next set of pro forma statements is the pro forma balance sheets. In order to compile these, John uses the following information along with the operating budget and the cash-flow worksheet he has prepared:

Cash: the ending cash balance for each month from the cash-flow worksheet

Accounts receivable: 20 percent of the current month's sales plus 5 percent of the preceding month's sales

Inventory: the current month's ending inventory on the pro forma income statements

Prepaid rent: the $2,000 is expected to remain constant throughout the budget period and is always paid one month in advance

Building and equipment: no new acquisitions are expected in this area, so the amount will remain constant

Accumulated depreciation: because no new acquisitions are anticipated, this will stay the same; all buildings and equipment are fully depreciated

Accounts payable: 25 percent of current purchases

Capital: prior month's capital balance plus current month's net income

North Central Scientific: Comparative Pro Forma Income Statements for 2010

	Jan.	Feb.	Mar.	Apr.	May	June	July	Aug.	Sept.	Oct.	Nov.	Dec.
Sales	$315	$388	$420	$394	$525	$473	$499	$504	$462	$515	$536	$578
Cost of goods sold												
Beginning inventory	$63	$74	$84	$79	$105	$95	$100	$101	$92	$103	$107	$116
Purchases	263	305	331	341	410	383	400	395	380	416	437	413
Cost of goods available	$326	$379	$415	$420	$515	$478	$500	$496	$472	$519	$544	$529
Ending inventory	74	85	79	105	95	100	101	92	102	107	116	66
Cost of goods sold	$252	$294	$336	$315	$420	$378	$399	$403	$370	$412	$428	$462
Gross profit	$63	$74	$84	$79	$105	$95	$100	$101	$92	$103	$108	$116

Continued

| Table 11.10 | North Central Scientific: Pro Forma Statements (*Continued*) |

	Jan.	Feb.	Mar.	Apr.	May	June	July	Aug.	Sept.	Oct.	Nov.	Dec.
Operating expenses												
Rent	$2	$2	$2	$2	$2	$2	$2	$2	$2	$2	$2	$2
Payroll	32	37	42	39	53	47	50	50	46	51	54	58
Utilities	5	5	5	5	5	5	5	5	5	5	5	5
Taxes	3	4	4	4	5	5	5	5	5	5	5	6
Supplies	16	18	21	20	26	24	25	25	23	26	27	29
Repairs	2	2	2	2	2	2	2	2	2	2	2	2
Total expenses	$60	$68	$76	$72	$93	$85	$89	$89	$83	$91	$95	$102
Net profit	$3	$6	$8	$7	$12	$10	$11	$12	$9	$12	$12	$14

North Central Scientific: Comparative Pro Forma Balance Sheet

	Jan.	Feb.	Mar.	Apr.	May	June	July	Aug.	Sept.	Oct.	Nov.	Dec.
Assets												
Cash	$127	$134	$141	$126	$142	$136	$154	$171	$173	$181	$183	$231
Accounts receivable	91	89	102	100	125	121	123	126	117	126	133	142
Inventory	74	84	79	105	95	100	101	92	103	107	116	66
Prepaid rent	2	2	2	2	2	2	2	2	2	2	2	2
Building and equipment	350	350	350	350	350	350	350	350	350	350	350	350
Less: Accumulated depreciation	−350	−350	−350	−350	−350	−350	−350	−350	−350	−350	−350	−350
Total assets	$294	$309	$324	$333	$364	$359	$380	$391	$395	$416	$434	$441
Liabilities												
Accounts payable	$66	$76	$83	$85	$102	$96	$100	$99	$95	$104	$109	$103
Capital	228	234	242	249	261	270	280	292	300	312	326	339
Total liabilities and equity	$294	$310	$325	$334	$363	$366	$380	$391	$395	$416	$435	$442

Capital Budgeting

Entrepreneurs may be required to make several investment decisions in the process of managing their firms. The impact of some of these decisions will be felt primarily within one year. Returns on other investments, however, are expected to extend beyond one year. Investments that fit into this second category are commonly referred to as capital investments or capital expenditures. A technique the entrepreneur can use to help plan for capital expenditures is capital budgeting.[9]

The first step in capital budgeting is to identify the cash flows and their timing. The inflows—or returns, as they are commonly called—are equal to net operating income before deduction of payments to the financing sources but after the deduction of applicable taxes and with depreciation added back, as represented by the following formula:

Expected Returns = $X(1 - 2T)$ 1 Depreciation

X is equal to the net operating income, and T is defined as the appropriate tax rate. An illustration follows.

John Wheatman is faced with a dilemma. He has two mutually exclusive projects, both of which require an outlay of $1,000. The problem is that he can afford only one of the projects. After discussing the problem with his accountant, John discovers that the first step he needs to take is to determine the expected return on each project. In order to gather this information, he has studied the probable effect on the store's operations and has developed the data shown in Table 11.11.

Table 11.11 provides a good illustration of the expected returns for John Wheatman's two projects. At this point, however, the cash inflows of each year are shown without consideration of the time value of money. The cash outflow is used to refer to the initial cash outlay that must be made in the beginning (the purchase price). When gathering data to estimate the cash flows over the life of a project, it is imperative to obtain reliable estimates of the savings and expenses associated with the project.

The principal objective of capital budgeting is to maximize the value of the firm. It is designed to answer two basic questions:

1. Which of several mutually exclusive projects should be selected? (Mutually exclusive projects are alternative methods of doing the same job. If one method is chosen, the other methods will not be required.)

2. How many projects, in total, should be selected?[10]

The three most common methods used in capital budgeting are the payback method, the net present value (NPV) method, and the internal rate of return (IRR) method. Each has certain advantages and disadvantages. In this section, the same proposal will be used with each method to more clearly illustrate these three techniques.

Table 11.11 **North Central Scientific: Expected Return Worksheet**

Proposal A

Year	X	$(1 - T)$ $(T = .40)$	$X(1 + T)$	Depreciation	$X(1 - T) +$ Depreciation
1	$500	$0.60	$ 300	$200	$500
2	333	0.60	200	200	400
3	167	0.60	100	200	300
4	−300	0.60	−180	200	20
5	−317	0.60	−190	200	10

Proposal B

Year	X	$(1 - T)$ $(T = .40)$	$X(1 - T)$	Depreciation	$X(1 - T) +$ Depreciation
1	−$167	$0.60	−$100	$200	$100
2	0	0.60	100	200	200
3	167	0.60	100	200	300
4	333	0.60	200	200	400
5	500	0.60	300	200	500

X = Anticipated change in net income

T = Applicable tax rate (.40)

Depreciation = Depreciation (computed on a straight-line basis) = Cost/Life = 1,000/5

Payback Method

One of the easiest capital-budgeting techniques to understand is the payback method or, as it is sometimes called, the payback period. In this method, the length of time required to "pay back" the original investment is the determining criterion. The entrepreneur will select a maximum time frame for the payback period. Any project that requires a longer period will be rejected, and projects that fall within the time frame will be accepted. Following is an example of the payback method used by North Central Scientific:

> John Wheatman has a decision to make. He would like to purchase a new cash register for his store but is unsure about which of two proposals to accept. Each machine costs $1,000. An analysis of the projected returns reveals the following information:

Year	Proposal A	Proposal B
1	$500	$100
2	400	200
3	300	300
4	20	400
5	11	500

> After careful consideration, John decides to use the payback method with a cutoff period of 3 years. In this case, he discovers that Proposal A would pay back his investment in 2 1/3 years; $900 of the original investment will be paid back in the first 2 years, and the last $100 in the third year. Proposal B, on the other hand, will require 4 years for its payback. Using this criterion, John chooses Proposal A and rejects Proposal B.

One of the problems with the payback method is that it ignores cash flows beyond the payback period. Thus, it is possible for the wrong decision to be made. Nevertheless, many companies, particularly entrepreneurial firms, continue to use this method for several reasons: (1) It is very simple to use in comparison to other methods, (2) projects with a faster payback period normally have more favorable short-term effects on earnings, and (3) if a firm is short on cash, it may prefer to use the payback method because it provides a faster return of funds.

Net Present Value

The net present value (NPV) method is a technique that helps to minimize some of the shortcomings of the payback method by recognizing the future cash flows beyond the payback period. The concept works on the premise that a dollar today is worth more than a dollar in the future—how much more depends on the applicable cost of capital for the firm. The cost of capital is the rate used to adjust future cash flows to determine their value in present period terms. This procedure is referred to as discounting the future cash flows, and the discounted cash value is determined by the present value of the cash flow.

To use this approach, the entrepreneur must find the present value of the expected net cash flows of the investment, discounted at the appropriate cost of capital, and subtract from it the initial cost outlay of the project. The result is the net present value of the proposed project. Many financial accounting and finance textbooks include tables (called present value tables) that list the appropriate discount factors to multiply by the future cash flow to determine the present value. In addition, financial calculators are available that will compute the present value given the cost of capital, future cash flow, and the year of the cash flow. Finally, given the appropriate data, electronic spreadsheet programs can be programmed to determine the present value. After the net present value has been calculated for all of the proposals, the entrepreneur can select the project with the highest net present value. Following is an example of the NPV method used by North Central Scientific:

> John Wheatman is not very satisfied with the results he has obtained from the payback method, so he has decided to use the NPV method to see what result it would produce.

After conferring with his accountant, John learns that the cost of capital for his firm is 11 percent. He then prepares the following tables:

Proposal A

Year	Cash Flow	Discount Factor	Present Value
1	$500	0.9091	$454.55
2	400	0.8264	330.56
3	300	0.7513	225.39
4	20	0.6830	13.66
5	11	0.6209	6.21
			$1,030.37
Less: Initial outlay			−1,000.00
Net present value			$30.37

Proposal B

Year	Cash Flow	Discount Factor	Present Value
1	$100	0.9091	$90.91
2	200	0.8264	165.28
3	300	0.7513	225.39
4	400	0.6830	273.20
5	500	0.6209	311.45
			$1,065.23
Less: Initial outlay			−1,000.00
Net present value			$65.23

Because Proposal B has the higher net present value, John selects Proposal B and rejects Proposal A.

Internal Rate of Return

The internal rate of return (IRR) method is similar to the net present value method in that the future cash flows are discounted. However, they are discounted at a rate that makes the net present value of the project equal to zero. This rate is referred to as the internal rate of return of the project. The project with the highest internal rate of return is then selected. Thus, a project that would be selected under the NPV method also would be selected under the IRR method.

One of the major drawbacks to the use of the IRR method is the difficulty that can be encountered when using the technique. Using the NPV method, it is quite simple to look up the appropriate discount factors in the present value tables. When using the IRR concept, however, the entrepreneur must begin with a net present value of zero and work backward through the tables. What this means, essentially, is that the entrepreneur must estimate the approximate rate and eventually try to track the actual internal rate of return for the project. Although this may not seem too difficult for projects with even cash flows (that is, cash flows that are fairly equal over the business periods), projects with uneven cash flows (fluctuating periods of cash inflow and cash outflow) can be a nightmare. Unfortunately, reality dictates that most projects will probably have uneven cash flows. Fortunately, electronic calculators and spreadsheet programs are available that can determine the actual internal rate of return given the cash flows, initial cash outlays, and appropriate cash-flow periods. Following is an example of the IRR method used by North Central Scientific:

Having obtained different results from the payback period and the NPV method, John Wheatman is confused about which alternative to select. To alleviate this confusion, he has chosen to use the internal rate of return to evaluate the two proposals, and he has decided that the project with the higher IRR will be selected (after all, it would win two out of three times). Accordingly, he has prepared the following tables with the help of his calculator:

Proposal A (11.83% IRR)

Year	Cash Flow	Discount Factor	Present Value
1	$500	0.8942	$447.11
2	400	0.7996	319.84
3	300	0.7151	214.53
4	20	0.6394	12.80
5	11	0.5718	5.73
			$1,000.00
Less: Initial outlay			−1,000.00
Net present value			$0.00

Proposal B (12.01% IRR)

Year	Cash Flow	Discount Factor	Present Value
1	$100	0.8928	$89.27
2	200	0.7971	159.42
3	300	0.7117	213.51
4	400	0.6354	254.15
5	500	0.5673	283.65
			$1,000.00
Less: Initial outlay			−1,000.00
Net present value			$0.00

Proposal B is selected because it has the higher IRR. This conclusion supports the statement that the project with the higher NPV will also have the higher IRR.

The North Central Scientific examples illustrate the use of all three capital-budgeting methods. Although Proposal A was chosen by the first method (payback), Proposal B surfaced as the better proposal when the other two methods (net present value and internal rate of return) were used. It is important for entrepreneurs to understand all three methods and to use the one that best fits their needs. If payback had been John Wheatman's only consideration, then Proposal A would have been selected. When future cash flows beyond payback are to be considered, the NPV and IRR methods will determine the best proposal.

The budgeting concepts discussed so far are extremely powerful planning tools. But how can entrepreneurs monitor their progress during the budget period? How can they use the information accumulated during the course of the business to help plan for future periods? Can this information be used for pricing decisions? The answer to the third question is "yes," and the other questions are answered in the following sections.

Break-Even Analysis

In today's competitive marketplace, entrepreneurs need relevant, timely, and accurate information that will enable them to price their products and services competitively and still be able to earn a fair profit. **Break-even analysis** supplies this information.

When Currency Loses Its Global Value

A nation's currency is the bedrock on which its wealth is built. Without it, citizens would be left to barter for products and services. Currency is not inherently valuable. Its worth stems from a nation's citizens' faith in its government's ability to back its currency. As global commerce has become more prevalent, entrepreneurs have been forced to understand the pitfalls and the possibilities of national borders giving way to open trade. One of the repercussions has been the increased volatility of national currency caused by international forces. The precipitous fall in the value of the U.S. dollar is an example of this phenomenon.

The dollar has historically been the world's reserve currency, driving the global economy. Because American consumers have been unable to quench their insatiable hunger for foreign goods, more foreigners are in possession of dollars—which in and of itself is not bad; however, when their faith in the U.S. economy falters, they are inclined to offload dollars in order to hedge against the risk of inflation, which, of course, is self-fulfilling. Due to the subprime lending debacle in the United States, in conjunction with the country carrying record levels of debt, this scenario has begun to play out. For instance, the Chinese government recently announced that it would be moving its reserves into stronger currencies, which most likely translates to abandoning the dollar for the Euro. As other countries follow its lead, the dollar will continue to lose value.

What are entrepreneurs to do when the value of their national currency falls? Ironically, some entrepreneurs can benefit from the situation, at least initially. When a country's currency loses value, revenue generated through tourism tends to increase due to foreigners traveling to the country in order to take advantage of the improved conversion rates. Most business owners are quick to ignore the implications of such a shift as their business prospects improve; however, when foreign companies move from buying products to buying the manufacturers, the national landscape can morph in unpredictable ways. Foreign ownership in the United States has been on the rise during the last couple of decades, and—as the dollar continues its decline—there is no end in sight.

Start-up ventures often have little recourse when their country's currency begins to lose value. While large corporations hedge their bets by converting their capital to foreign currency or by making direct foreign investments, small businesses are left to make the best of a bad situation. Diversifying a company's customer base to include international consumers is one way to help mitigate the risk, but in the end, the factors at play are outside of the control of even the largest companies.

Source: Adapted from Geoff Colvin, "What's Sinking the Dollar?" *Fortune,* November 13, 2007, http://money.cnn .com/magazines/fortune/fortune_archive/2007/11/26/ 101232904/index.htm?postversion=2007111309 (accessed April 9, 2008).

Break-Even Point Computation

Break-even analysis is a technique commonly used to assess expected product profitability. It helps determine how many units must be sold to break even at a particular selling price.

CONTRIBUTION MARGIN APPROACH

A common approach to break-even analysis is the contribution margin approach. Contribution margin is the difference between the selling price and the variable cost per unit. It is the amount per unit that is contributed to covering all other costs.[11] Because the break-even point occurs where income equals expenses, the contribution margin approach formula is

$$0 = (SP - VC)S - FC \text{ or } FC = (SP - VC)S$$

where
SP = Unit selling price
VC = Variable costs per unit
S = Sales in units
FC = Fixed cost

This model also can be used for profit planning by including the desired profit as part of the fixed cost.

GRAPHIC APPROACH

Another approach to break-even analysis taken by entrepreneurial firms is the graphic approach. To use this approach, the entrepreneur needs to graph at least two numbers: total revenue and total costs. The intersection of these two lines (that is, where total revenues are equal to the total costs) is the firm's break-even point. Two additional costs—variable costs and fixed costs—also may be plotted. Doing so enables the entrepreneur to visualize the various relationships in the firm's cost structure.

HANDLING QUESTIONABLE COSTS

Although the first two approaches are adequate for situations in which costs can be broken down into fixed and variable components, some firms have expenses that are difficult to assign. For example, are repairs and maintenance expenses fixed or variable expenses? Can firms that face this type of problem use break-even analysis for profit planning? The answer is "yes," thanks to a new technique designed specifically for entrepreneurial firms. This technique calculates break-even points under alternative assumptions of fixed or variable costs to see if a product's profitability is sensitive to cost behavior. The decision rules for this concept are as follows: If expected sales exceed the higher break-even point, then the product should be profitable, regardless of the other break-even point; if expected sales do not exceed the lower break-even point, then the product should be unprofitable. Only if expected sales are between the two break-even points is further investigation of the questionable cost's behavior needed.[12]

The concept works by substituting the cost in question (QC) first as a fixed cost and then as a variable cost. The break-even formulas presented earlier would have to be modified to determine the break-even levels under the two assumptions. For the fixed-cost assumption, the entrepreneur would use the following equation:

$$0 = (SP - VC)S - FC - QC$$

To calculate the break-even point assuming QC is variable, the following equation would be used:

$$0 = [SP - VC - (QC/U)]S - FC$$

U is the number of units for which the questionable cost normally would be appropriate. What the entrepreneur is determining is the appropriate unit cost that should be used if the cost is a variable cost. Following is an example of how an entrepreneur could use the technique:

> Tim Goodman, president of Dynamic Manufacturing—a small manufacturer of round widgets—has decided to use break-even analysis as a profit-planning tool for his company. He believes that using this technique will enable his firm to compete more effectively in the marketplace. From an analysis of the operating costs, Tim has determined that the variable cost per unit is $9, while fixed costs are estimated to be $1,200 per month. The anticipated selling price per unit is $15. He also has discovered that he is unable to classify one cost as either variable or fixed. It is a $200 repair and maintenance expense allocation. This $200 is appropriate for an activity level of 400 units; therefore, if the cost were variable, it would be $.50 per unit ($200/400). Finally, sales are projected to be 400 units during the next budget period.

The first step in this process is to determine the break-even point assuming the cost in question is fixed. Consequently, Tim would use the following equation:

$$0 = (SC - VC)S - FC - QC$$
$$= (15 - 9)S - 1,200 - 200$$
$$= 6S - 1,400$$
$$1,400 = 6S$$
$$234 = S$$

Figure 11.2 provides a graphic illustration of the results. The final quantity was rounded up to the next unit, because a business normally will not sell part of a unit.

The next step in the process is to calculate the break-even point assuming the cost in question is a variable cost. Tim would use the following equation to ascertain the second break-even point:

$$0 = [SC - VC - (QC/U)]S - FC$$
$$= [15 - 9 - (200/400)]S - 1,200$$
$$= (6 - .50)S - 1,200$$
$$1,200 = 5.50S$$
$$219 = S$$

Figure 11.3 presents a graphic illustration of the results.

Now that the two possible break-even points have been established, Tim must compare them to his projected sales. The variable-cost sales of 400 units are greater than the larger break-even point of 234 units. Therefore, the product is assumed to be profitable regardless of the cost behavior of the repair and maintenance expense. It does not matter whether the cost is variable or fixed; the firm still will be profitable.

Figure **11.2**   **Dynamic Manufacturing: Fixed-Cost Assumption**

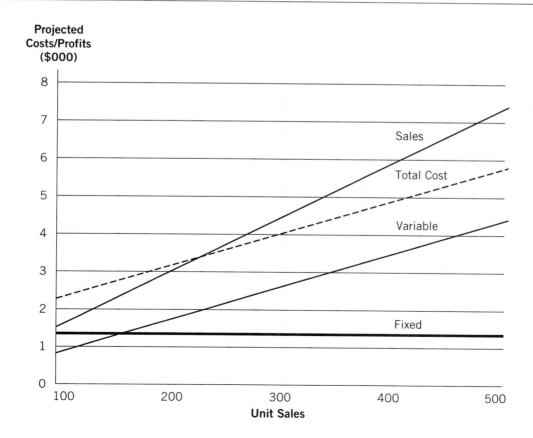

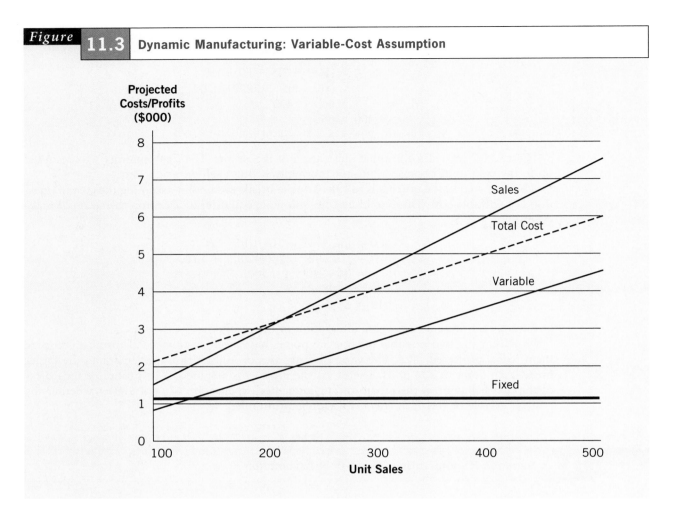

Figure 11.3 Dynamic Manufacturing: Variable-Cost Assumption

Ratio Analysis

Financial statements report on both a firm's position at a point in time and its operations during some past period. However, the real value of financial statements lies in the fact that they can be used to help predict the firm's earnings and dividends. From an investor's standpoint, predicting the future is what financial statement analysis is all about; from an entrepreneur's standpoint, financial statement analysis is useful both as a way to anticipate conditions and, more importantly, as a starting point for planning actions that will influence the course of events.

An analysis of the firm's ratios is generally the key step in a financial analysis. The *ratios* are designed to show relationships among financial statement accounts. For example, Firm A might have a debt of $6,250,000 and interest charges of $520,000, whereas Firm B might have a debt of $62,800,000 and interest charges of $5,840,000. Which company is stronger? The true burden of these debts, and the companies' ability to repay them, can be ascertained (1) by comparing each firm's debt to its assets and (2) by comparing the interest each must pay to the income it has available for interest payment. Such comparisons are made by ratio analysis.[13]

Table 11.12 has been prepared as an entrepreneur's guide to understanding the various ratios. Note that this outline presents the ratio's importance to owners, managers, and creditors. More important than the simple calculation of formulas are the categories that explain what each ratio *measures* and what each ratio *tells* an entrepreneur.

Table **11.12** **Financial Ratios**

Ratio	Formula	What It Measures	What It Tells You
Owners			
Return on investment (ROI)	$\dfrac{\text{Net Income}}{\text{Average Owner's Equity}}$	Return on owner's capital; when compared with return on assets, it measures the extent financial leverage is being used for or against the owner	How well is this company doing as an investment?
Return on assets (ROA)	$\dfrac{\text{Net Income}}{\text{Average Total Assets}}$	How well assets have been employed by management	How well has management employed company assets? Does it pay to borrow?
Managers			
Net profit margin	$\dfrac{\text{Net Income}}{\text{Sales}}$	Operating efficiency; the ability to create sufficient profits from operating activities	Are profits high enough, given the level of sales?
Asset turnover	$\dfrac{\text{Sales}}{\text{Average Total Assets}}$	Relative efficiency in using total resources to produce output	How well are assets being used to generate sales revenue?
Return on assets	$\dfrac{\text{Net Income}}{\text{Sales}} \times \dfrac{\text{Sales}}{\text{Total Assets}}$	Earning power on all assets; ROA ratio broken into its logical parts; turnover and margin	How well has management employed company assets?
Average collection period	$\dfrac{\text{Average Accounts Receivable}}{\text{Annual Credit Sales}} \times 365$	Liquidity of receivables in terms of average number of days receivables are outstanding	Are receivables coming in too slowly?
Inventory turnover	$\dfrac{\text{Cost of Goods Sold Expense}}{\text{Average Inventory}}$	Liquidity of inventory; the number of times it turns over per year	Is too much cash tied up in inventories?
Average age of payables	$\dfrac{\text{Average Accounts Payable}}{\text{Net Purchases}} \times 365$	Approximate length of time a firm takes to pay its bills for trade purchases	How quickly does a prospective customer pay its bills?
Short-Term Creditors			
Working capital	Current Assets − Current Liabilities	Short-term debt-paying ability	Does this customer have sufficient cash or other liquid assets to cover its short-term obligations?
Current ratio	$\dfrac{\text{Current Assets}}{\text{Current Liabilities}}$	Short-term debt-paying ability without regard to the liquidity of current assets	Does this customer have sufficient cash or other liquid assets to cover its short-term obligations?
Quick ratio	$\dfrac{\text{Cash} + \text{Marketable Securities} + \text{Accounts Receivable}}{\text{Current Liabilities}}$	Short-term debt-paying ability without having to rely on inventory sales	Does this customer have sufficient cash or other liquid assets to cover its short-term obligations?

Continued

Table 11.12	Financial Ratios (*Continued*)		
Ratio	**Formula**	**What It Measures**	**What It Tells You**
Long-Term Creditors			
Debt-to-equity ratio	$\dfrac{\text{Total Debt}}{\text{Total Equity}}$	Amount of assets creditors provide for each dollar of assets the owners provide	Is the company's debt load excessive?
Times interest earned	$\dfrac{\text{Net Income} + (\text{Interest} + \text{Taxes})}{\text{Interest Expense}}$	Ability to pay fixed charges for interest from operating profits	Are earnings and cash flows sufficient to cover interest payments and some principal repayments?
Cash flow to liabilities	$\dfrac{\text{Operating Cash Flow}}{\text{Total Liabilities}}$	Total debt coverage; general debt-paying ability	Are earnings and cash flows sufficient to cover interest payments and some principal repayments?

Source: Kenneth M. Macur and Lyal Gustafson, "Financial Statements as a Management Tool," *Small Business Forum* (Fall 1992): 24.

Ratio analysis can be applied from two directions. **Vertical analysis** is the application of ratio analysis to one set of financial statements; an analysis "up and down" the statements is done to find signs of strengths and weaknesses. **Horizontal analysis** looks at financial statements and ratios over time. In horizontal analysis, the trends are critical: Are the numbers increasing or decreasing? Are particular components of the company's financial position getting better or worse?[14]

Summary

Three principal financial statements are important to entrepreneurs: the balance sheet, the income statement, and the cash-flow statement. The budgeting process facilitates financial statement preparation. Some key budgets that entrepreneurs should prepare are the operating budget, the cash-flow budget, and the capital budget. The operating budget typically begins with a sales forecast, followed by an estimation of operating expenses. A cash-flow budget provides an overview of the inflows and outflows of cash during a specific period. Pro forma financial statements then are prepared as projections of the firm's financial position over a future period (pro forma income statement) or on a future date (pro forma balance sheet). The operating and cash-flow budgets often are used to prepare these pro forma statements. The capital budget is used to help entrepreneurs make investment decisions. The three most common methods of capital budgeting are the payback period, the net present value method, and the internal rate of return method.

Another commonly used decision-making tool is break-even analysis, which tells how many units must be sold to break even at a particular selling price. It is possible to use this analysis even when fixed or variable costs can only be estimated. The last part of the chapter examined ratio analysis, which can be a helpful analytical tool for entrepreneurs. Ratios are designed to show relationships between financial statement accounts.

Key Terms and Concepts

accounts payable

accounts receivable

accumulated depreciation of building

administrative expenses

allowance for uncollectible accounts

assets

balance sheet

bank loan

break-even analysis

budget

capital budget

capital budgeting

cash

cash-flow budget

cash-flow statement

contribution margin approach

discounting the future cash flows

expenses

financial expense

fixed assets

fixed cost

horizontal analysis

income statement

internal rate of return (IRR) method

inventory

investing activities

liabilities

loan payable

long-term liabilities

mixed costs

net income

net present value (NPV) method

note payable

operating budget

operating cash flows

operating expenses

owners' equity

payback method

prepaid expenses

pro forma statements

ratios

retained earnings

revenues

sales forecast

selling expenses

short-term liabilities (current liabilities)

simple linear regression

taxes payable

variable cost

vertical analysis

Review and Discussion Questions

1. What is the importance of financial information for entrepreneurs? Briefly describe the key components.
2. What are the benefits of the budgeting process?
3. How is the statistical forecasting technique of simple linear regression used in making a sales forecast?
4. Describe how an operating budget is constructed.
5. Describe how a cash-flow budget is constructed.
6. What are pro forma statements? How are they constructed? Be complete in your answer.
7. Describe how a capital budget is constructed.
8. One of the most popular capital-budgeting techniques is the payback method. How does this method work? Give an example.

9. Describe the net present value method. When would an entrepreneur use this method? Why?
10. Describe the internal rate of return method. When would an entrepreneur use this method? Why?
11. When would an entrepreneur be interested in break-even analysis?
12. If an entrepreneur wants to use break-even analysis but has trouble assigning some costs as either fixed or variable, can break-even analysis still be used? Explain.
13. What is ratio analysis? How is horizontal analysis different from vertical analysis?

Experiential Exercise

THE PROJECT PROPOSAL

Bill Sergent has just received a request for proposal (RFP) from a large computer firm. The firm is looking for a supplier to provide it with high-tech components for a supercomputer being built for the Department of Defense. Bill's firm, which is only eight months old, was founded by a group of scientists and engineers whose primary expertise is in the area of computers and high technology. Bill is thinking about making a reply to the RFP, but first he wants to conduct a break-even analysis to determine how profitable the venture will be. Following is the information he will use in his analysis:

- The computer firm wants 12 different components built, and the purchase price will be $11,000 per component.
- The total cost of building the first component will be $20,000.
- The cost of building each of the 11 other components will be $8,000, $6,000, $5,000, $4,000, $5,000, $6,000, $8,000, $11,000, $28,000, $40,000, and $40,000, respectively.
- Bill's company will not accept any proposal that will give it less than an 11 percent return on sales.

On the basis of this information, complete the following break-even chart, and then answer the two questions.

Revenues ($000)

$150	_____
140	_____
130	_____
120	_____
111	_____
110	_____
90	_____
80	_____
70	_____
60	_____
50	_____
40	_____
30	_____
20	_____
11	_____

    1   2   3   4   5   6   7   8   9 11 11 12

Units

1. Should Bill bid on the contract? Why or why not? _____

_____

2. If Bill has some room for negotiation with the computer firm, what would you recommend he do? Why? _____

_____

_____

Case 11.1

IT'S ALL GREEK TO HER

When Regina McDermott opened her auto repair shop, she thought her 15 years of experience with cars was all she would need. To a degree, she was right—within six months, her shop had more work than it could handle, thanks to her widening reputation. At the same time, however, Regina has found it necessary to spend more and more time dealing with financial planning.

Three weeks ago, her accountant came by to discuss a number of finance-related matters. One of these is the need for cash budgeting. "I can work up a cash budget for you," he explained. "However, I think you should understand what I'm doing so you will realize the importance of the cash budget and be able to visualize your cash inflows and outflows. I think you also need to make a decision regarding the new equipment you are planning to purchase. This machinery is state of the art, but, as we discussed last week, you can buy a number of different types of machinery. You are going to have to decide which is the best choice."

Regina explained to her accountant that she was indifferent about which equipment to buy. "All of this machinery is good. Perhaps I should purchase the cheapest." At this point, the accountant explained to her that she could use a number of ways to evaluate this type of decision. "You can base your choice on the payback method—how long it takes to recover your investment in each of these pieces of equipment. You can base it on net present value by discounting future cash flows to the present. Or you can base it on internal rate of return, under which the cash flows are discounted at a rate that makes the net present value of the project equal to zero."

Regina listened quietly; when the accountant was finished, she said, "Let me think about the various ways of evaluating my capital investment, and I'll get back to you. Then, perhaps you and I can work out the numbers together." Her accountant said this sounded fine to him, and he left. Regina began to wish that she had taken more accounting courses while in college. As she explained to her husband, "When the accountant begins to talk, it's all Greek to me."

QUESTIONS

1. What is the purpose of a cash-flow budget? What does it reveal? Of what value would it be to Regina?

2. How does the payback method work? How does the net present value method work? How would you explain each of these methods to Regina?

3. How does the internal rate of return method work? How would you explain it to Regina?

Case 11.2

THE CONTRACT PROPOSAL

Dennis Darby owns a small manufacturing firm that produces electronic components for use in helicopters. Most of his business is a result of military and aircraft manufacturer contracts, although 11 percent of revenues come from firms that own or rent helicopters. The latter are typically large *Fortune* 500 companies or leasing/rental firms that work on a contractual basis for clients.

Dennis would like to increase his revenues from sales to private corporations that own their own helicopters. Specifically, he would like to do more business with oil companies that maintain helicopter fleets for ferrying people to and from oil rigs in the Gulf of Mexico and other offshore locations. Early this week, Dennis received a request from an oil company for 120 electronic components. He turned the order over to his chief estimator, who estimates that the fixed costs associated with producing these components will be $35,000, the unit variable cost will be $400, and the unit selling price will be $800.

Dennis will not accept any order on which the return on sales is less than 20 percent. Additionally, the estimator has told him that a $1,000 expense can be classified as either fixed or variable. Dennis intends to take this information and make a decision whether to accept the contract from the oil company. He has to make a decision within the next three days.

QUESTIONS

1. What is the break-even point for this project? Will the company make money if it manufactures the components? Show your calculations.

2. If the project will be profitable, will it provide Dennis with the desired 20 percent return? Explain.

3. Of what value is break-even analysis to Dennis? Be complete in your answer.

Notes

1. See Richard G. P. McMahon and Leslie G. Davies, "Financial Reporting and Analysis Practices in Small Enterprises: Their Association with Growth Rate and Financial Performance," *Journal of Small Business Management* 32, no. 1 (January 1994): 9–17; Clyde Stickney, Paul Brown, and James M. Whalen, *Financial Reporting, Financial Statement Analysis, and Valuation: A Strategic Perspective*, 6th ed. (Mason, OH: South-Western/Cengage Learning, 2007).

2. Kenneth M. Macur and Lyal Gustafson, "Financial Statements as a Management Tool," *Small Business Forum* (Fall 1992): 23–34; see also Robert Dove, "Financial Statements," *Accountancy* (January 2000): 7; and W. Steve Albrecht, James D. Stice, Earl K. Stice, and Monte Swain, *Accounting: Concepts and Applications*, 10th ed. (Mason, OH: South-Western/Cengage Learning, 2008).

3. Albrecht et al., *Accounting: Concepts and Applications*, 10th ed.

4. See Jacqueline Emigh, "Balance Sheet," *ComputerWorld*, November 15, 1999, 86.

5. See John Capel, "Balancing the Books," *Supply Management*, November 1999, 94; and Carl S. Warren and James M. Reeve, *Financial & Managerial Accounting* 9th ed. (Mason, OH: South-Western/ Cengage Learning, 2007).

6. Neil C. Churchill, "Budget Choice: Planning vs. Control," *Harvard Business Review* (July/August 1984): 151.

7. Stickney, Brown, and Whalen, *Financial Reporting*, 6th ed.

8. Fred Waedt, "Understanding Cash Flow Statements, or What You Need to Know Before You Ask for a Loan," *Small Business Forum* (Spring 1995): 42–51; see also Ram Mudambi and Monica Zimmerman Treichel, "Cash Crisis in Newly Public Internet-Based Firms: An Empirical Analysis," *Journal of Business Venturing* 20, no. 4 (July 2005): 543–71.

9. See Warren and Reeve, *Financial & Managerial Accounting*, 9th ed.

10. Ibid.

11. Albrecht et al., *Accounting*, 10th ed.

12. Kenneth P. Sinclair and James A. Talbott, Jr., "Using Break-Even Analysis When Cost Behavior Is Unknown," *Management Accounting* (July 1986): 53; see also Stickney, Brown, and Whalen, *Financial Reporting*, 6th ed.

13. See Warren and Reeve, *Financial & Managerial Accounting*, 9th ed.

14. Macur and Lyal, "Financial Statements as a Management Tool"; see also Robert Hitchings, "Ratio Analysis as a Tool in Credit Assessment," *Commercial Lending Review* (Summer 1999): 45–49. For an interesting discussion, see Patricia Lee Huff, "Should You Consider Company Size When Making Ratio Comparisons?" *National Public Accountant* (February/ March 2000): 8–12; see also Krishna G. Palepu and Paul M. Healy, *Business Analysis and Valuation: Using Financial Statements, Text and Cases*, 4th ed. (Mason, OH: South-Western/Cengage Learning, 2008).

12

Business Plan Preparation for New Ventures

Entrepreneurial Thought

It is well established that you can't raise money without a business plan . . . a business plan is a work of art in its own right. It's the document that personifies and expresses your company. Each plan, like every snowflake, must be different. Each is a separate piece of art. Each must be reflective of the individuality of the entrepreneur. Just as you wouldn't copy someone else's romancing techniques, so should you seek to distinguish your plan for its differences.

— **JOSEPH R. MANCUSO** *How to Write a Winning Business Plan*

Chapter Objectives

1 To define a business plan and demonstrate its value

2 To explore the planning pitfalls that plague many new ventures

3 To describe the benefits of a business plan

4 To set forth the viewpoints of those who read a business plan

5 To emphasize the importance of coordinating the business plan segments

6 To review key recommendations by venture capital experts regarding a business plan

7 To present a complete outline of an effective business plan

8 To present some helpful hints for writing an effective business plan

9 To highlight points to remember in the presentation of a business plan

What Is a Business Plan?

A **business plan** is the written document that details the proposed venture. It must describe current status, expected needs, and projected results of the new business. Every aspect of the venture needs to be covered: the project, marketing, research and development, management, critical risks, financial projections, and milestones or a timetable. A description of all of these facets of the proposed venture is necessary to demonstrate a clear picture of what that venture is, where it is projected to go, and how the entrepreneur proposes it will get there. The business plan is the entrepreneur's road map for a successful enterprise.[1]

In some professional areas, the business plan is referred to as a venture plan, a loan proposal, or an investment prospectus. Whatever the name, the business plan is the minimum document required by any financial source. The business plan allows the entrepreneur entrance into the investment process. Although it should be used as a working document once the venture is established, the major thrust of the business plan is to encapsulate the strategic development of the project in a comprehensive document for outside investors to read and understand.

The business plan describes to investors and financial sources all of the events that may affect the proposed venture. Details are needed for various projected actions of the venture, with associated revenues and costs outlined. It is vital to explicitly state the assumptions on which the plan is based. For example, increases/decreases in the market or upswings/downswings in the economy during the start-up period of the new venture should be stated.

The emphasis of the business plan always should be the final implementation of the venture. In other words, it's not just the writing of an effective plan that is important but also the translation of that plan into a successful enterprise.[2]

The comprehensive business plan, which should be the result of meetings and reflections on the direction of the new venture, is the major tool for determining the essential operation of a venture. It also is the primary document for managing the venture. One of the major benefits of this plan is that it helps the enterprise avoid common pitfalls that often undo all previous efforts. The following section describes these pitfalls.

Pitfalls to Avoid in Planning

A number of pitfalls in the business plan process should be avoided. The five pitfalls presented in this section represent the most common errors committed by entrepreneurs. To make these danger areas more easily recognizable, certain indicators or warning signs are presented. We also include a possible solution to each pitfall that will help entrepreneurs avoid the particular trap that limits a new venture's opportunity to succeed.

Pitfall 1: No Realistic Goals

Although this pitfall may sound self-explanatory, the following indicators demonstrate how common and well disguised it can be: lack of any attainable goals, lack of a time frame to accomplish things, lack of priorities, and lack of action steps.

One way to avoid this pitfall is to set up a timetable of specific steps to be accomplished during a specific period.

Pitfall 2: Failure to Anticipate Roadblocks

One of the most common pitfalls occurs when the entrepreneur is so immersed in his or her idea that objectivity goes out the window. In other words, the person does not recognize the possible problems that may arise. Indicators are: no recognition of future problems, no admission of possible flaws or weaknesses in the plan, and no contingency or alternative plans.

The best way to avoid this pitfall is to list (1) the possible obstacles that may arise and (2) the alternatives that state what might have to be done to overcome the obstacles.

Pitfall 3: No Commitment or Dedication

Too many entrepreneurs appear to lack real commitment to their ventures. Although ventures may have started from a hobby or part-time endeavor, entrepreneurs must be careful to avoid the impression that they do not take their ventures seriously. Indicators are: excessive procrastination, missed appointments, no desire to invest personal money, and the appearance of making a "fast buck" from a hobby or a "whim."

The easiest way to avoid this pitfall is to act quickly and to be sure to follow up all professional appointments. Also, be ready and willing to demonstrate a financial commitment to the venture.

Pitfall 4: Lack of Demonstrated Experience (Business or Technical)

Many investors weigh very heavily the entrepreneur's actual experience in a venture, so it is important that entrepreneurs demonstrate what background they possess. Because too many beginners attempt to promote ideas they really have no true knowledge of, they are doomed to fail simply because they are perceived as ignorant of the specifics in the proposed business. Indicators are: no experience in business, no experience in the specific area of the venture, lack of understanding of the industry in which the venture fits, and failure to convey a clear picture of how and why the venture will work and who will accept it.

To avoid this pitfall, entrepreneurs need to give evidence of personal experience and background for the venture. If they lack specific knowledge or skills, they should obtain assistance from those who possess this knowledge or these skills. Demonstrating a team concept about those who help out also may be useful.

Pitfall 5: No Market Niche (Segment)

Many entrepreneurs propose an idea without establishing who the potential customers will be. Just because the entrepreneur likes the product or service does not mean that others will buy it. Numerous inventions at the U.S. Patent Office never reached the marketplace because no customers were targeted to buy them—no market was ever established. Indicators are: uncertainty about who will buy the basic idea(s) behind the venture, no proof of a need or desire for the good or product proposed, and an assumption that customers or clients will purchase just because the entrepreneur thinks so.

The best possible way to avoid this pitfall is to have a market segment specifically targeted and to demonstrate why and how the specific product or service will meet the needs or desires of this target group. (More specific information on market research was developed in Chapter 10.)

The five pitfalls detailed here represent the most common points of failure entrepreneurs experience *before* their business plan ever gets reviewed. In other words, these critical areas must be carefully addressed before a business plan is developed. If these pitfalls can be avoided, the entire business plan will be written more carefully and thus will be reviewed more thoroughly. This preparation helps entrepreneurs establish a solid foundation on which to develop an effective business plan.

Benefits of a Business Plan

The entire business planning process forces the entrepreneur to analyze all aspects of the venture and to prepare an effective strategy to deal with the uncertainties that arise. Thus, a business plan may help an entrepreneur avoid a project doomed to failure. As one researcher states, "If your proposed venture is marginal at best, the business plan will show you why and may help you avoid paying the high tuition of business failure. It is far cheaper not to begin an ill-fated business than to learn by experience what your business plan could have taught you at a cost of several hours of concentrated work."[3]

the entrepreneurial process

Overlooked Research Sources for Business Plans

The first obstacle to overcome when preparing a business plan is a lack of in-depth research resources. The following sources are recommended for entrepreneurs to pursue when seeking some of the basic information needed to prepare the business plan.

Track the Industry. Begin by finding out what North American Industry Classification System (NAICS) code your company may fall under. Look up the appropriate NAICS or SIC code at http://www.census.gov/epcd/www/naics.html. You can now use this code to gain important information on your industry at sites such as Hoover's (http://www.hoovers.com) and ThomasNet (http://www.thomasnet.com/index.html). These sites offer free access to essential statistics and comparisons with both public and private companies. Additional industry sites include Yahoo's finance guide (http://finance.yahoo.com), industry guide (http://biz.yahoo.com/industry), and their list of newspapers and magazines (http://dir.yahoo.com/News_and_Media/Newspapers/By_Region). Chambers of commerce are also a valuable source of information for specific markets. You can begin at the U.S. Chamber of Commerce to find a local chamber's site (http://www.uschamber.com).

Check Your Competition. The art of competitive research has really taken off. Specialized firms now charge exorbitant fees for in-depth research, but you can extract valuable information on your own just by browsing companies' Web sites. You can gain insight on their strategies by perusing their job listings, finding strategic partnerships, and assessing customer relationships. Venture Consult also suggests scanning résumés of people who have worked for your competition; you can learn more about the strategies and weaknesses of the company from the job-hunter's accomplishments.

Search Out Government Resources. Start with FirstGov (http://www.firstgov.com) and the U.S. Small Business Administration (http://www.sba.gov). You also can buy the annual U.S. industry and trade outlook online (http://www.ita.doc.gov/td/industry/otea/outlook/index.html).

Don't Forget Your Customers. Private companies typically have the most in-depth research available; however, the majority of the research is not available to the public. Private associations, industry organizations, and trade shows can offer much of the valuable research that private companies spend thousands to gain. Locate the industry Web site that covers your market, and you will find the top trade shows that cover your company's niche and market. It is often much less expensive to purchase a report than to commission research through a firm. A couple of companies' sites worth checking out are http://www.InfoTechTrends.com and http://www.MarketResearch.com. The absolute best source of information is your current and prospective customers. Listen to what they want, and find out what problems they have with other companies and what they would like to see happen with your company.

Check out Internet sources. For example, the Gale Web site (gale.cengage.com) includes several resources that could be of use. The company maintains over 600 databases online, in print, and in e-book form, offering business plan examples and market research for different industries. Fintel (http://fintel.us) is another resource that can be used to help with the financial issues of putting together a business plan. This site includes current industry reports, financial benchmarking, customized research options, and other resources. Marketresearch.com (http://www.marketresearch.com) is the world's largest collection of market research for different industries. This Web site can provide information such as product trends and analysis of a given market. The American Factfinder Web site (http://factfinder.census.gov/home/saff/main.html) is provided by the U.S. Census Bureau. This is a great resource for information regarding population, housing, economic, business, industry, and geographic data. Small Business Trends (http://www.smallbiztrends.com) is a site that provides updates on trends that affect small and medium-sized businesses. It features traditional Web sites that contain small business data as well as a blog. LogoYes (http://www.logoyes.com)

is a leading provider of do-it-yourself logos for small businesses. Using this site, an entrepreneur can design a logo for his or her business (though downloading the logo may cost some money). Finally, the Claritas site (http://www.claritas.com/MyBestSegments/Default .jsp) defines the market for your business. It offers information on consumer segments as well as defined and described customer segmentation profiling. This site can help answer questions such as: What are these customers like? Where can I find them? How can I reach them?

Source: Adapted from Karen Klein, "Research Resources for Beginners," *Business Week Online*, January 14, 2002, http://www.businessweek.com/smallbiz/content/jan2002/sb20020114_0616.htm?chan=search (accessed April 10, 2008) and Donald F. Kuratko and Jeffrey S. Hornsby, *New Venture Management: The Entrepreneur's Roadmap* (Upper Saddle River, NJ: Pearson/Prentice Hall, 2009).

It is important that entrepreneurs prepare their own business plan. If an entrepreneurial team is involved, then all of the key members should be part of writing the plan; in this case, it is important that the lead entrepreneur understand the contribution of each team member. If consultants are sought to help prepare a business plan, the entrepreneur must remain the driving force behind the plan. Seeking the advice and assistance of outside professionals is always wise, but entrepreneurs need to understand every aspect of the business plan, because they are the ones who come under the scrutiny of financial sources. Thus, the business plan stands as the entrepreneur's description and prediction for his or her venture, and it must be defended by the entrepreneur—simply put, it is the entrepreneur's responsibility.[4]

Other benefits are derived from a business plan, for both the entrepreneur and the financial sources that read it and evaluate the venture. For the entrepreneur, the following benefits are gained:

- The time, effort, research, and discipline needed to put together a formal business plan force the entrepreneur to view the venture critically and objectively.
- The competitive, economic, and financial analyses included in the business plan subject the entrepreneur to close scrutiny of his or her assumptions about the venture's success.
- Because all aspects of the business venture must be addressed in the plan, the entrepreneur develops and examines operating strategies and expected results for outside evaluators.
- The business plan quantifies objectives, providing measurable benchmarks for comparing forecasts with actual results.
- The completed business plan provides the entrepreneur with a communication tool for outside financial sources as well as an operational tool for guiding the venture toward success.[5]

The financial sources that read the plan derive the following benefits from the business plan:

- The business plan provides the details of the market potential and plans for securing a share of that market.
- Through prospective financial statements, the business plan illustrates the venture's ability to service debt or provide an adequate return on equity.
- The plan identifies critical risks and crucial events with a discussion of contingency plans that provide opportunity for the venture's success.
- By providing a comprehensive overview of the entire operation, the business plan gives financial sources a clear, concise document that contains the necessary information for a thorough business and financial evaluation.
- For a financial source with no prior knowledge of the entrepreneur or the venture, the business plan provides a useful guide for assessing the individual entrepreneur's planning and managerial ability.[6]

Developing a Well-Conceived Business Plan

Most investors agree that only a well-conceived and well-developed business plan can gather the necessary support that will eventually lead to financing. The business plan must describe the new venture with excitement and yet with complete accuracy.

Who Reads the Plan?

It is important to understand the audience for whom the business plan is written. Although numerous professionals may be involved with reading the business plan—such as venture capitalists, bankers, angel investors, potential large customers, lawyers, consultants, and suppliers—entrepreneurs need to clearly understand three main viewpoints when preparing the plan.[7]

The first viewpoint is, of course, the entrepreneur's, because he or she is the one developing the venture and clearly has the most in-depth knowledge of the technology or creativity involved. This is the most common viewpoint in business plans, and it is essential. However, too many plans emphasize this viewpoint and neglect the viewpoints of potential customers and investors.

More important than high technology or creative flair is the marketability of a new venture. This type of enterprise, referred to as "market-driven," convincingly demonstrates the benefits to users (the particular group of customers it is aiming for) and the existence of a substantial market. This viewpoint—that of the marketplace—is the second critical emphasis that an entrepreneur must incorporate into a business plan. Yet, although the actual value of this information is considered high, too many entrepreneurs tend to deemphasize in-depth marketing information in their business plans.[8] Establishing an actual market (determining who will buy the product or use the service) and documenting that the anticipated percentage of this market is appropriate for the venture's success are valuable criteria for the business plan.

The third viewpoint is related to the marketing emphasis just discussed. The investor's point of view is concentrated on the financial forecast. Sound financial projections are necessary if investors are to evaluate the worth of their investment. This is not to say that an entrepreneur should fill the business plan with spreadsheets of figures. In fact, many venture capital firms employ a "projection discount factor," which merely represents the belief of venture capitalists that successful new ventures usually reach approximately 50 percent of their projected financial goals.[9] However, a three- to five-year financial projection is essential for investors to use in making their judgment of a venture's future success.

These three viewpoints have been presented in order of decreasing significance to point out the emphasis needed in a well-conceived business plan. If they are addressed carefully in the plan, then the entrepreneur has prepared for what experts term the five-minute reading. The following six steps represent the typical business plan reading process that many venture capitalists use (less than one minute is devoted to each step):

Step 1: Determine the characteristics of the venture and its industry.

Step 2: Determine the financial structure of the plan (amount of debt or equity investment required).

Step 3: Read the latest balance sheet (to determine liquidity, net worth, and debt/equity).

Step 4: Determine the quality of entrepreneurs in the venture (sometimes *the* most important step).

Step 5: Establish the unique feature in this venture (find out what is different).

Step 6: Read over the entire plan lightly (this is when the entire package is paged through for a casual look at graphs, charts, exhibits, and other plan components).[10]

These steps provide insight into how the average business plan is read. It may seem somewhat unjust that so much of the entrepreneur's effort is put into a plan that is given only a five-minute reading. However, that's the nature of the process for many venture capitalists. Other financial or professional sources may devote more time to analyzing the plan. But keep in mind that venture capitalists read through numerous business plans; thus, knowing the steps in their reading process is valuable for developing any plan. Related to the process of venture capitalists is this updated version of an old quote that links entrepreneurs and venture capitalists: "The people who manage people manage people who manage things, *but* the people who manage money manage the people who manage people."[11]

Putting the Package Together

When presenting a business plan to potential investors, the entrepreneur must realize that the entire package is important. Presented next is a summary of key issues that the entrepreneur needs to watch for if his or her plan is going to be viewed successfully. A business plan gives financiers their first impressions of a company and its principals.

Potential investors expect the plan to look good, but not too good; to be the right length; to clearly and concisely explain (early on) all aspects of the company's business; and not to contain bad grammar and typographical or spelling errors.

Investors are looking for evidence that the principals treat their own property with care—and will likewise treat the investment carefully. In other words, form as well as content is important; investors know that good form reflects good content, and vice versa. Among the format issues we think most important are the following:

> **Appearance**—The binding and printing must not be sloppy; neither should the presentation be too lavish. A stapled compilation of photocopied pages usually looks amateurish, whereas bookbinding with typeset pages may arouse concern about excessive and inappropriate spending. A plastic spiral binding, holding together a pair of cover sheets of a single color, provides both a neat appearance and sufficient strength to withstand handling by a number of people without damage.

> **Length**—A business plan should be no more than 50 pages long. The first draft will likely exceed that, but editing should produce a final version that fits within the 40-page ideal. Adherence to this length forces entrepreneurs to sharpen their ideas and results in a document that is likely to hold investors' attention.

> Background details can be included in an additional volume. Entrepreneurs can make this material available to investors during the investigative period, after the initial expression of interest.

> **The Cover and Title Page**—The cover should bear the name of the company, its address and phone number, and the month and year in which the plan is issued. Surprisingly, a large number of business plans are submitted to potential investors without return addresses or phone numbers. An interested investor wants to be able to contact a company easily to request further information or express an interest, either in the company or in some aspect of the plan.

> Inside the front cover should be a well-designed title page on which the cover information is repeated and, in an upper or a lower corner, the "copy number" provided. Besides helping entrepreneurs keep track of plans in circulation, holding down the number of copies outstanding—usually to no more than 20—has a psychological advantage. After all, no investor likes to think that the prospective investment is shopworn.

> **The Executive Summary**—The two to three pages immediately following the title page should concisely explain the company's current status, its products or services, the benefits to customers, the financial forecasts, the venture's objectives in three to seven years, the amount of financing needed, and how investors will benefit.

> This is a tall order for a two-page summary, but it will either sell investors on reading the rest of the plan or convince them to forget the whole thing.

> **The Table of Contents**—After the executive summary, include a well-designed table of contents. List each of the business plan's sections and mark the pages for each section.

An attractive appearance, an effective length, an executive summary, a table of contents, proper grammar, correct typing, and a cover page—all are important factors when putting together a complete package. These points often separate successful plans from unacceptable ones.

Guidelines to Remember

The following points are a collection of recommendations by experts in venture capital and new-venture development.[12] These guidelines are presented as tips for successful business plan development. Entrepreneurs need to adhere to them to understand the importance of the various segments of the business plan they create, which will be discussed in the next section.

KEEP THE PLAN RESPECTABLY SHORT

Readers of business plans are important people who refuse to waste time. Therefore, entrepreneurs should explain the venture not only carefully and clearly but also concisely. (Ideally, the plan should be no more than 25 pages long, excluding the appendix.)

ORGANIZE AND PACKAGE THE PLAN APPROPRIATELY

A table of contents, an executive summary, an appendix, exhibits, graphs, proper grammar, a logical arrangement of segments, and overall neatness are elements critical to the effective presentation of a business plan.

ORIENT THE PLAN TOWARD THE FUTURE

Entrepreneurs should attempt to create an air of excitement in the plan by developing trends and forecasts that describe what the venture *intends* to do and what the opportunities are for the use of the product or service.

AVOID EXAGGERATION

Sales potentials, revenue estimates, and the venture's potential growth should not be inflated. Many times, a best-case, worst-case, and probable-case scenario should be developed for the plan. Documentation and research are vital to the plan's credibility. (See Table 12.1 for business plan phrases.)

HIGHLIGHT CRITICAL RISKS

The critical-risks segment of the business plan is important in that it demonstrates the entrepreneur's ability to analyze potential problems and develop alternative courses of action.

GIVE EVIDENCE OF AN EFFECTIVE ENTREPRENEURIAL TEAM

The management segment of the business plan should clearly identify the skills of each key person as well as demonstrate how all such people can effectively work together as a team to manage the venture.

DO NOT OVER-DIVERSIFY

Focus the attention of the plan on one main opportunity for the venture. A new business should not attempt to create multiple markets or pursue multiple ventures until it has successfully developed one main strength.

IDENTIFY THE TARGET MARKET

Substantiate the marketability of the venture's product or service by identifying the particular customer niche being sought. This segment of the business plan is pivotal to the success of the other parts. Market research must be included to demonstrate how this market segment has been identified.

KEEP THE PLAN WRITTEN IN THE THIRD PERSON

Rather than continually stating "I," "we," or "us," the entrepreneur should phrase everything as "he," "she," "they," or "them." In other words, avoid personalizing the plan, and keep the writing objective.

CAPTURE THE READER'S INTEREST

Because of the numerous business plans submitted to investors and the small percentage of business plans funded, entrepreneurs need to capture the reader's interest right away by

Table 12.1   Common Business Plan Phrases: Statement Versus Reality

Statement	Reality
We conservatively project . . .	We read a book that said we had to be a $50 million company in five years, and we reverse-engineered the numbers.
We took our best guess and divided by 2.	We accidentally divided by 0.5.
We project a 10 percent margin.	We did not modify any of the assumptions in the business plan template that we downloaded from the Internet.
The project is 98 percent complete.	To complete the remaining 2 percent will take as long as it took to create the initial 98 percent but will cost twice as much.
Our business model is proven . . .	. . . if you take the evidence from the past week for the best of our 50 locations and extrapolate it for all the others.
We have a six-month lead.	We tried not to find out how many other people have a six-month lead.
We need only a 10 percent market share.	So do the other 50 entrants getting funded.
Customers are clamoring for our product.	We have not yet asked them to pay for it. Also, all of our current customers are relatives.
We are the low-cost producer.	We have not produced anything yet, but we are confident that we will be able to.
We have no competition.	Only IBM, Microsoft, Netscape, and Sun have announced plans to enter the business.
Our management team has a great deal of experience . . .	. . . consuming the product or service.
A select group of investors is considering the plan.	We mailed a copy of the plan to everyone in *Pratt's Guide*.
We seek a value-added investor.	We are looking for a passive, dumb-as-rocks investor.
If you invest on our terms, you will earn a 68 percent internal rate of return.	If everything that could ever conceivably go right does go right, you might get your money back.

highlighting the uniqueness of the venture. Use the title page and executive summary as key tools to capture the reader's attention and create a desire to read more.

Questions to Be Answered

A well-written business plan is like a work of art: It's visually pleasing and makes a statement without saying a word. Unfortunately, the two are also alike in that they are worth money only if they're good. Researchers Donald F. Kuratko and Jeffrey S. Hornsby recommend the following key questions to consider when writing an effective business plan.

- *Is your plan organized so key facts leap out at the reader?* Appearances do count. Your plan is a representation of yourself, so don't expect an unorganized, less than acceptable plan to be your vehicle for obtaining funds.

- *Is your product/service and business mission clear and simple?* Your mission should state very simply the value that you will provide to your customers. It shouldn't take more than a paragraph.

- *Are you focused on the right things?* Determine what phase of the business you are really in, focus on the right tasks, and use your resources appropriately.

- *Who is your customer?* Does the plan describe the business's ideal customers and how you will reach them? Is your projected share of the market identified, reasonable, and supported?

- *Why will customers buy? How much better is your product/service?* Define the need for your product and provide references and testimonial support to enhance it. Try to be detailed in explaining how the customer will benefit from buying your product.

- *Do you have a competitive advantage?* Focus on differences and any unique qualities. Proprietary processes/technology and patentable items/ideals are good things to highlight as competitive strengths.

- *Do you have a favorable cost structure?* Proper gross margins are key. Does the break-even analysis take into consideration the dynamics of price and variable costs? Identify, if possible, any economics of scale that would be advantageous to the business.

- *Can the management team build a business?* Take a second look at the management team to see whether they have relevant experience in small business and in the industry. Acknowledge the fact that the team may need to evolve with the business.

- *How much money do you need?* Financial statements—including the income statement, cash-flow statement, and balance sheet—should be provided on a monthly basis for the first year and on a quarterly basis for the following two or three years.

- *How does your investor get a cash return?* Whether it's through a buyout or an initial public offering, make sure your plan clearly outlines this important question regarding a harvest strategy.[13]

These guidelines and questions have been presented to help entrepreneurs who are preparing to write a business plan. The following section analyzes the ten major segments of a business plan.

Elements of a Business Plan

A detailed business plan usually includes eight to ten sections (depending on the industry and idea). The ideal length of a plan is 25 pages, although—depending on the need for detail—the overall plan can range from 20 to more than 35 pages if an appendix is included.[14] Table 12.2 provides an outline of a typical plan; the remainder of this section

---

Table **12.2** Complete Outline of a Business Plan

Section I: Executive Summary

Section II: Business Description

    A. General description of the business

    B. Industry background

    C. Goals and potential of the business and milestones (if any)

    D. Uniqueness of product or service

Table **12.2**   **Complete Outline of a Business Plan (*Continued*)**

Section III: Marketing

    A. Research and analysis
        1. Target market (customers) identified
        2. Market size and trends
        3. Competition
        4. Estimated market share

    B. Marketing plan
        1. Market strategy—sales and distribution
        2. Pricing
        3. Advertising and promotions

Section IV: Operations

    A. Identify location: advantages
    B. Specific operational procedures
    C. Personnel needs and uses
    D. Proximity to supplies

Section V: Management

    A. Management team—key personnel
    B. Legal structure—stock agreements, employment agreements, ownership
    C. Board of directors, advisors, consultants

Section VI: Financial

    A. Financial forecast
        1. Profit and loss
        2. Cash flow
        3. Break-even analysis
        4. Cost controls
        5. Budgeting plans

Section VII: Critical Risks

    A. Potential problems
    B. Obstacles and risks
    C. Alternative courses of action

Section VIII: Harvest Strategy

    A. Liquidity event (IPO or sale)
    B. Continuity of business strategy
    C. Identify successor

Section IX: Milestone Schedule

    A. Timing and objectives
    B. Deadlines and milestones
    C. Relationship of events

Section X: Appendix or Bibliography

Source: Donald F. Kuratko and Robert C. McDonald, *The Entrepreneurial Planning Guide* (Bloomington: Kelley School of Business, Indiana University, 2007).

describes the specific parts of the plan. A complete business plan for DropToMe.com appears in Appendix 12A at the end of this chapter.

Executive Summary

Many people who read business plans (bankers, venture capitalists, investors) like to see a summary of the plan that features its most important parts. Such a summary gives a brief overview of what is to follow, helps put all of the information into perspective, and should be no longer than two to three pages. The summary should be written only after the entire business plan has been completed. In this way, particular phrases or descriptions from each segment can be identified for inclusion in the summary. Because the summary is the first—and sometimes the only—part of a plan that is read, it must present the quality of the entire report. The summary must be a clever snapshot of the complete plan.

The statements selected for a summary segment should briefly touch on the venture itself, the market opportunities, the financial needs and projections, and any special research or technology associated with the venture. This should be done in such a way that the evaluator or investor will choose to read on. If this information is not presented in a concise, competent manner, the reader may put aside the plan or simply conclude that the project does not warrant funding.

Business Description

First, the name of the venture should be identified, along with any special significance (for example, family name, technical name). Second, the industry background should be presented in terms of current status and future trends. It is important to note any special industry developments that may affect the plan. If the company has an existing business or franchise, this is the appropriate place to discuss it. Third, the new venture should be thoroughly described, along with its proposed potential. All key terms should be defined and made comprehensible. Functional specifications or descriptions should be provided. Drawings and photographs also may be included.

Fourth, the potential advantages the new venture possesses over the competition should be discussed at length. This discussion may include patents, copyrights, and trademarks, as well as special technological or market advantages.

Marketing Segment

In the **marketing segment** of the plan, the entrepreneur must convince investors that a market exists, that sales projections *can be achieved*, and that the competition can be beaten.

This part of the plan is often one of the most difficult to prepare. It is also one of the most critical, because almost all subsequent sections of the plan depend on the sales estimates developed here. The projected sales levels—which are based on the market research and analysis—directly influence the size of the manufacturing operation, the marketing plan, and the amount of debt and equity capital required.

Most entrepreneurs have difficulty preparing and presenting market research and analyses that will convince investors the venture's sales estimates are accurate and attainable. The following are aspects of marketing that should be addressed when developing a comprehensive exposition of the market.

Market Niche and Market Share

A **market niche** is a homogeneous group with common characteristics—that is, all the people who have a need for the newly proposed product or service. When describing this niche, the writer should address the bases of customer purchase decisions: price, quality, service, personal contacts, or some combination of these factors.

Next, a list of potential customers who have expressed interest in the product or service—together with an explanation for their interest—should be included. If it is an existing business, the current principal customers should be identified and the sales trend should be discussed. It is important to describe the overall potential of the market. Sales projections should be made for at least three years, and the major factors affecting market growth (industry trends, socio-economic trends, governmental policy, and population shifts) should be discussed. A review of previous market trends should be included, and any differences between past and projected annual growth rates should be explained. The sources of all data and methods used to make projections should be indicated. Then, if any major customers are willing to make purchase commitments, they should be identified, and the extent of those commitments should be indicated. On the basis of the product or service advantages, the market size and trends, the customers, and the sales trends in prior years, the writer should estimate market share and sales in units and dollars for each of the next three years. The growth of the company's sales and its estimated market share should be related to the growth of the industry and the customer base.

COMPETITIVE ANALYSIS

The entrepreneur should make an attempt to assess the strengths and weaknesses of the competing products or services. Any sources used to evaluate the competition should be cited. This discussion should compare competing products or services on the basis of price, performance, service, warranties, and other pertinent features. It should include a short discussion of the current advantages and disadvantages of competing products and services, and why they are not meeting customer needs. Any knowledge of competitors' actions that could lead to new or improved products and an advantageous position also should be presented.

Finally, a review of competing companies should be included. Each competitor's share of the market, sales, and distribution and production capabilities should be discussed. Attention should be focused on profitability and the profit trend of each competitor. Who is the pricing leader? Who is the quality leader? Who is gaining? Who is losing? Have any companies entered or dropped out of the market in recent years?

MARKETING STRATEGY

The general marketing philosophy and approach of the company should be outlined in the **marketing strategy**. A marketing strategy should be developed from market research and evaluation data and should include a discussion of (1) the kinds of customer groups to be targeted by the initial intensive selling effort; (2) the customer groups to be targeted for later selling efforts; (3) methods of identifying and contacting potential customers in these groups; (4) the features of the product or service (quality, price, delivery, warranty, and so on) to be emphasized to generate sales; and (5) any innovative or unusual marketing concepts that will enhance customer acceptance (for example, leasing where only sales were previously attempted).

This section also should indicate whether the product or service initially will be introduced nationally or regionally. Consideration also should be given to any seasonal trends and what can be done to promote contra-seasonal sales.

PRICING POLICY

The price must be "right" to penetrate the market, maintain a market position, and produce profits. A number of pricing strategies should be examined, and then one should be convincingly presented. This pricing policy should be compared with the policies of the major competitors. The gross profit margin between manufacturing and final sales costs should be discussed, and consideration should be given to whether this margin is large enough to allow for distribution, sales, warranty, and service expenses; for amortization of development and equipment costs; and for profit. Attention also should be given to justifying any price increases over competitive items on the basis of newness, quality, warranty, or service.

ADVERTISING PLAN

For manufactured products, the preparation of product sheets and promotional literature; the plans for trade show participation, trade magazine advertisements, and direct mailings; and the use of advertising agencies should be presented. For products and services in general, a discussion of the advertising and promotional campaign contemplated to introduce the product and the kinds of sales aids to be provided to dealers should be included. Additionally, the schedule and cost of promotion and advertising should be presented; if advertising will be a significant part of the expenses, an exhibit that shows how and when these costs will be incurred should be included.

the entrepreneurial process

Common Business Planning Mistakes

Entrepreneurs endure uncertainty in most everything they do. From hiring the right employees to finding reliable suppliers, building a business requires an entrepreneur to handle significant pressure on a daily basis. Given the variability which is inherent in any new venture, a business plan is crucial for effective management. In spite of the importance of business planning, few activities are more daunting for entrepreneurs than formalizing their thoughts on paper. In order for entrepreneurs to stay driven to succeed, they have to remain optimistic, so the fear of discovering some insurmountable obstacle while planning leads some management teams to avoid the process altogether. Whether the business is a startup or a well-established corporation, a business plan, when done correctly, serves as the company's blueprint to ensure that all parties involved are in agreement regarding the business's overarching purpose. In the business plan sections listed below we present some of the common mistakes that entrepreneurs make when developing their plan:

Overall Mistakes

- Entrepreneurs are unable to clearly articulate their vision in the plan.
- Entrepreneurs fail to provide sufficient details regarding the implementation of their strategy.
- Entrepreneurs ineffectively present the goals and objectives which are most important to the business's success.
- Entrepreneurs do not convincingly present the basis for their strategy.
- Entrepreneurs do not improve their plan based on the feedback from investors.

Executive Summary

- Entrepreneurs are not precise about their needs and capabilities.
- Entrepreneurs waste words with fillers and superfluous information.

Management

- Entrepreneurs forget to include their previous successes and or failures.
- Entrepreneurs dismiss the importance investors place on an experienced management team.

Marketing

- Entrepreneurs rely heavily on secondary market research rather than soliciting the opinions of their potential customers.
- Entrepreneurs claim the percent of the market their company will own without research support.

Financials

- Entrepreneurs overlook and, in turn, underestimate their cash-flow requirements.
- Entrepreneurs inflate or understate their margins in order to arrive at their ideal profitability.

Sources: Adapted from Mark Henricks (2007, February). Build a Better Business Plan. Retrieved June 21, 2008, from Entrepreneur Magazine Website: https://www.entrepreneur.com/startingabusiness/businessplans/article174002.html; Andrew Clarke (2005, November). Top 10 Business Plan Mistakes. Retrieved June 21, 2008, from Entrepreneur Magazine Website: https://www.entrepreneur.com/startingabusiness/businessplans/article81188.html; and Andrew J. Sherman (2007) *Grow Fast, Grow Right: 12 Strategies to Achieve Breakthrough Business Growth* (pp. 20-26). Chicago: Kaplan Publishing)

These five subsets of the marketing segment are needed to detail the overall marketing plan, which should describe *what* is to be done, *how* it will be done, and *who* will do it.

Research, Design, and Development Segment

The extent of any research, design, and development in regard to cost, time, and special testing should be covered in this segment. Investors need to know the status of the project in terms of prototypes, lab tests, and scheduling delays. Note that this segment is applicable only if research and development (R&D) is involved in the business plan.

To achieve a comprehensive section, the entrepreneur should have (or seek out) technical assistance in preparing a detailed discussion. Blueprints, sketches, drawings, and models often are important.

It is equally important to identify the design or development work that still needs to be done and to discuss possible difficulties or risks that may delay or alter the project. In this regard, a developmental budget that shows the costs associated with labor, materials consulting, research, design, and the like should be constructed and presented.

Operations Segment

This segment should always begin by describing the location of the new venture. The chosen site should be appropriate in terms of labor availability, wage rate, proximity to suppliers and customers, and community support. In addition, local taxes and zoning requirements should be sorted out, and the support of area banks for new ventures should be touched on.

Specific needs should be discussed in terms of how the enterprise actually operates and the facilities required to handle the new venture (plant, warehouse storage, and offices), as well as any equipment that needs to be acquired (special tooling, machinery, computers, and vehicles).

Other factors that might be considered are the suppliers (number and proximity) and the transportation costs involved in shipping materials. The labor supply, wage rates, and needed skilled positions also should be presented.

Finally, the cost data associated with any of the operation factors should be presented. The financial information used here can be applied later to the financial projections.

Management Segment

This segment identifies the key personnel, their positions and responsibilities, and the career experiences that qualify them for those particular roles. Complete résumés should be provided for each member of the management team. In this section, the entrepreneur's role in the venture should be clearly outlined. Finally, any advisors, consultants, or members of the board should be identified and discussed.

The structure of payment and ownership (stock agreements, consulting fees, and so on) should be described clearly in this section. In summary, the discussion should be sufficient so that investors can understand each of the following critical factors that have been presented: (1) organizational structure, (2) management team and critical personnel, (3) experience and technical capabilities of the personnel, (4) ownership structure and compensation agreements, and (5) board of directors and outside consultants and advisors.

Financial Segment

The financial segment of a business plan must demonstrate the potential viability of the undertaking. Three basic financial statements must be presented in this part of the plan: the pro forma balance sheet, the income statement, and the cash-flow statement.

THE PRO FORMA BALANCE SHEET

Pro forma means "projected," as opposed to actual. The pro forma balance sheet projects what the financial condition of the venture will be at a particular point in time. Pro forma balance sheets should be prepared at start-up, semiannually for the first years, and at the end of each of the first three years. The balance sheet details the assets required to support the projected level of operations and shows how these assets are to be financed (liabilities and equity). Investors will want to look at the projected balance sheets to determine if debt/equity ratios, working capital, current ratios, inventory turnover, and so on are within the acceptable limits required to justify the future financings projected for the venture.

THE INCOME STATEMENT

The income statement illustrates the projected operating results based on profit and loss. The sales forecast, which was developed in the marketing segment, is essential to this document.

Once the sales forecast (earnings projection) is in place, production costs must be budgeted based on the level of activity needed to support the projected earnings. The materials, labor, service, and manufacturing overhead (fixed and variable) must be considered, in addition to such expenses as distribution, storage, advertising, discounts, and administrative and general expenses (salaries, legal and accounting, rent, utilities, and telephone).

THE CASH-FLOW STATEMENT

The cash-flow statement may be the most important document in new-venture creation, because it sets forth the amount and timing of expected cash inflows and outflows. This section of the business plan should be carefully constructed.

Given a level of projected sales and capital expenditures for a specific period, the cash-flow forecast will highlight the need for and the timing of additional financing and will indicate peak requirements for working capital. Management must decide how this additional financing is to be obtained, on what terms, and how it is to be repaid. The total amount of needed financing may be supplied from several sources: part by equity financing, part by bank loans, and the balance by short-term lines of credit from banks. This information becomes part of the final cash-flow forecast. A detailed cash flow, if understood properly, can direct the entrepreneur's attention to operating problems before serious cash crises arise.

In the financial segment, it is important to mention any assumptions used to prepare the figures. Nothing should be taken for granted. This segment also should include how the statements were prepared (by a professional certified public accountant or by the entrepreneur) and who will be in charge of managing the business's finances.

The final document that should be included in the financial segment is a break-even chart, which shows the level of sales (and production) needed to cover all costs. This includes costs that vary with the production level (manufacturing labor, materials, sales) and costs that do not change with production (rent, interest charges, executive salaries).

Critical-Risks Segment

In this segment, potential risks such as the following should be identified: effect of unfavorable trends in the industry, design or manufacturing costs that have gone over estimates, difficulties of long lead times encountered when purchasing parts or materials, and unplanned-for new competition.

In addition to these risks, it is wise to cover the what-ifs. For example, what if the competition cuts prices, the industry slumps, the market projections are wrong, the sales projections are not achieved, the patents do not come through, or the management team breaks up?

Finally, suggestions for alternative courses of action should be included. Certainly, delays, inaccurate projections, and industry slumps all can happen, and people reading the business plan will want to know that the entrepreneur recognizes these risks and has prepared for such critical events.

Harvest Strategy Segment

Every business plan should provide insights into the future harvest strategy. It is important for the entrepreneur to plan for a liquidity event as an exit strategy or for the orderly transition of the venture if the plan is to grow and develop it. This section needs to deal with such issues as management succession and investor exit strategies. In addition, some thought should be given to change management—that is, the orderly transfer of the company assets if ownership of the business changes; continuity of the business strategy during the transition; and designation of key individuals to run the business if the current management team changes. With foresight, entrepreneurs can keep their dreams alive, ensure the security of their investors, and usually strengthen their businesses in the process. For this reason, a harvest strategy is essential.

Milestone Schedule Segment

The **milestone schedule segment** provides investors with a timetable for the various activities to be accomplished. It is important to show that realistic time frames have been planned and that the interrelationship of events within these time boundaries is understood. Milestone scheduling

Straying from Your Business Plan?

A well-written, thoughtful business plan is an important tool for any entrepreneur; however, even the most conservative strategy can fail to address some obstacles that are encountered between the inception of a concept and the eventual harvest of the business. One example of such a hurdle is when a business encounters an economic downturn. What is the appropriate strategy when the general economy has begun to falter, leading consumers to tuck away dollars that they would have otherwise spent at your business?

The answer is that there is not one solution for dealing with an ailing economy. Despite the need for a business plan, entrepreneurs often find that strict adherence to their plan is as dangerous as not having one at all. The key is to know when to stray from your plan. Following are steps to take when your plan does not effectively address the environment in which you find your business:

Band together. Partnering with companies that offer complimentary products to your own is an effective way to share the responsibility of building the market. Not only can advertising expenses be split but you can also introduce consumer incentives that encourage crossover purchasing from customers who otherwise would not have bought from your company. A common strategy is to determine what purchases your customers are currently making at other establishments that are closely associated with their purchases at your business. For instance, if you own a coffee shop and your customers are regularly walking in with pastry purchases from a local bakery, a partnership with the bakery could be a logical fit. The key is to take advantage of the existing behavior of your customers rather than try to change it.

Talk to customers. When times are lean, your existing customers are your lifeblood, so keeping them happy becomes increasingly important. If your marketing budget will not allow for extravagant advertising, shift your focus to working closely with your current customers. Often you will find that your customers are more than willing to share their perspective on your business, which could lead to easy and cheap modifications that will build loyalty. By keeping track of prospective customers, you will be in a better position to follow-up with them when times are slow. For instance, if your business involves providing quotes to potential customers, make note of those who chose not to make a purchase. When speaking with them, you will get insight about why they went elsewhere, and your efforts might convince them to rethink doing business with you.

Be flexible. When the economy slackens, consumers become more conservative with their purchases and are more inclined to base their shopping on price alone. The problem with cutting prices during an economic downturn is that consumers will expect them to remain low when the economy improves. One way to avoid having to resort to cost-cutting measures is by offering more for the same price. For instance, extending your business's hours to better accommodate your customers' schedules or offering free in-home estimates for service-related businesses are both quick measures to take that could help set your business apart from the competition.

Build relationships. As an entrepreneur, the ability to network is an important skill, especially when your business begins to wane. One important forum for many new ventures is the local chamber of commerce. By interacting with local businesses, entrepreneurs can keep close tabs on what the local economic trends are as well as gain access to potential commercial customers. In addition, working with other businesses can help you locate resources in your community, such as local talent and sources of funding; moreover, having a group of fellow entrepreneurs can be useful for vetting ideas as well as for moral support.

This list is not meant to be exhaustive. The underlying theme is that entrepreneurs need to maintain the versatility that they had when first starting their businesses. Developing a strategy is important for entrepreneurs to effectively manage their business,

Continued

and formally documenting that strategy is important for ensuring the continuity of their business; however, entrepreneurs who depend solely on their business plan to direct their business decisions run the risk of locking themselves into a strategy that could quickly become obsolete due to a shift in the environment. Planning is crucial for your business, but knowing when to change your plan is equally important.

Source: Adapted from Rich Sloan, "Bad Economy? Time to Get Aggressive," *Fortune Small Business*, March 3, 2008, http://money.cnn.com/2008/03/03/smbusiness/startup_nation .fsb/index.htm (accessed April 2, 2008).

is a step-by-step approach to illustrating accomplishments in a piecemeal fashion. These milestones can be established within any appropriate time frame, such as quarterly, monthly, or weekly. It is important, however, to coordinate the time frame not only with such early activities as product design and development, sales projections, establishment of the management team, production and operations scheduling, and market planning, but with other activities as well:

- Incorporation of the venture
- Completion of design and development
- Completion of prototypes
- Hiring of sales representatives
- Product display at trade shows
- Signing up distributors and dealers
- Ordering production quantities of materials
- Receipt of first orders
- First sales and first deliveries (dates of maximum interest because they relate directly to the venture's credibility and need for capital)
- Payment of first accounts receivable (cash in)

These items are the types of activities that should be included in the milestone schedule segment. The more detailed the schedule, the more likely the entrepreneur will persuade potential investors that he or she has thought things out and is therefore a good risk.

Appendix and/or Bibliography Segment

The final segment is not mandatory, but it allows for additional documentation that is not appropriate in the main parts of the plan. Diagrams, blueprints, financial data, vitae of management team members, and any bibliographical information that supports the other segments of the plan are examples of material that can be included. It is up to the entrepreneur to decide which, if any, items to put into this segment. However, the material should be limited to relevant and supporting information.

Table 12.3 provides an important recap of the major segments of a business plan, using helpful hints as practical reminders for entrepreneurs. By reviewing this, entrepreneurs can gain a macro view of the planning process. Table 12.4 is a personal checklist that gives entrepreneurs the opportunity to evaluate their business plan for each segment. The step-by-step evaluation is based on coverage of the particular segment, clarity of its presentation, and completeness.

Table **12.3** **Helpful Hints for Developing the Business Plan**

I. Executive Summary
- No more than three pages. This is the most crucial part of your plan because you must capture the reader's interest.
- What, how, why, where, and so on must be summarized.
- Complete this part after you have a finished business plan.

Table **12.3** Helpful Hints for Developing the Business Plan (*Continued*)

II. Business Description Segment

- The name of your business.
- A background of the industry with history of your company (if any) should be covered here.
- The potential of the new venture should be described clearly.
- Any uniqueness or distinctive features of this venture should be described clearly.

III. Marketing Segment

- Convince investors that sales projections and competition can be met.
- Use and disclose market studies.
- Identify target market, market position, and market share.
- Evaluate all competition and specifically cover why and how you will be better than your competitors.
- Identify all market sources and assistance used for this segment.
- Demonstrate pricing strategy. Your price must penetrate and maintain a market share to produce profits; thus, the lowest price is not necessarily the best price.
- Identify your advertising plans with cost estimates to validate proposed strategy.

IV. Operations Segment

- Describe the advantages of your location (zoning, tax laws, wage rates). List the production needs in terms of facilities (plant, storage, office space) and equipment (machinery, furnishings, supplies).
- Describe the specific operations of the venture.
- Indicate proximity to your suppliers.
- Mention the need and use of personnel in the operation.
- Provide estimates of operation costs—but be careful: Too many entrepreneurs underestimate their costs.

V. Management Segment

- Supply résumés of all key people in the management of your venture.

- Carefully describe the legal structure of your venture (sole proprietorship, partnership, or corporation).
- Cover the added assistance (if any) of advisors, consultants, and directors.
- Give information on how and how much everyone is to be compensated.

VI. Financial Segment

- Give actual estimated statements.
- Describe the needed sources for your funds and the uses you intend for the money.
- Develop and present a budget.
- Create stages of financing for purposes of allowing evaluation by investors at various points.

VII. Critical-Risks Segment

- Discuss potential risks before investors point them out—for example:
  - Price cutting by competitors
  - Any potentially unfavorable industry-wide trends
  - Design or manufacturing costs in excess of estimates
  - Sales projections not achieved
  - Product development schedule not met
  - Difficulties or long lead times encountered in the procurement of parts or raw materials
  - Greater than expected innovation and development costs to stay competitive
- Provide some alternative courses of action.

VIII. Harvest Strategy Segment

- Outline a plan for a liquidity event—IPO or sale.
- Describe the plan for transition of leadership.
- Mention the preparations (insurance, trusts, and so on) needed for continuity of the business.

IX. Milestone Schedule Segment

- Develop a timetable or chart to demonstrate when each phase of the venture is to be completed. This shows the relationship of events and provides a deadline for accomplishment.

X. Appendix or Bibliography

Source: Donald F. Kuratko and Robert C. McDonald, *The Entrepreneurial Planning Guide* (Bloomington: Kelley School of Business, Indiana University, 2007).

Table **12.4**	**Business Plan Assessment: A Complete Evaluation Tool**

The Components

Presented here are ten components of a business plan. As you develop your business plan, you should assess each component. Be honest in your assessment, because the main purpose is to improve your business plan and increase your chances of success. For instance, if your goal is to obtain external financing, you will be asked to submit a complete business plan for your venture. The business plan will help a funding source to more adequately evaluate your business idea.

Assessment

Directions: The brief description of each component will help you write that section of your plan. After completing your plan, use the scale provided to assess each component.

5	4	3	2	1
Outstanding	Very Good	Good	Fair	Poor
thorough and complete in all areas	most areas covered but could use improvement in detail	some areas covered in detail but other areas missing	a few areas covered but very little detail	no written parts

The Ten Components of a Business Plan

1. **Executive Summary.** This is the most important section because it has to convince the reader that the business will succeed. In no more than three pages, you should summarize the highlights of the rest of the plan. This means that the key elements of the following components should be mentioned.

   The executive summary must be able to stand on its own. It is not simply an introduction to the rest of the business plan but rather discusses who will purchase your product or service, what makes your business unique, and how you plan to grow in the future. Because this section summarizes the plan, it is often best to write it last.

Rate this component:

5	4	3	2	1
Outstanding	Very Good	Good	Fair	Poor

2. **Description of the Business.** This section should provide background information about your industry, a history of your company, a general description of your product or service, and your specific mission that you are trying to achieve. Your product or service should be described in terms of its unique qualities and value to the customer. Specific short-term and long-term objectives must be defined. You should clearly state what sales, market share, and profitability objectives you want your business to achieve.

Key Elements	Have you covered this in the plan?	Is the answer clear? (yes or no)	Is the answer complete? (yes or no)
a. What type of business will you have?			
b. What products or services will you sell?			
c. Why does it promise to be successful?			
d. What is the growth potential?			
e. How is it unique?			

Rate this component:

5	4	3	2	1
Outstanding	Very Good	Good	Fair	Poor

Table	**12.4**	**Business Plan Assessment: A Complete Evaluation Tool (*Continued*)**

3. **Marketing.** There are two major parts to the marketing section. The first part is research and analysis. Here you should explain who buys the product or service—in other words, identify your target market. Measure your market size and trends, and estimate the market share you expect. Be sure to include support for your sales projections. For example, if your figures are based on published marketing research data, be sure to cite the source. Do your best to make realistic and credible projections. Describe your competitors in considerable detail, identifying their strengths and weaknesses. Finally, explain how you will be better than your competitors.

    The second part is your marketing plan. This critical section should include your market strategy, sales and distribution, pricing, advertising, promotion, and public awareness efforts. Demonstrate how your pricing strategy will result in a profit. Identify your advertising plans, and include cost estimates to validate your proposed strategy.

Key Elements	Have you covered this in the plan?	Is the answer clear? (yes or no)	Is the answer complete? (yes or no)
a. Who will be your customers? (*target market*)			
b. How big is the market? (*number of customers*)			
c. Who will be your competitors?			
d. How are their businesses prospering?			
e. How will you promote sales?			
f. What market share will you want?			
g. Do you have a pricing strategy?			
h. What advertising and promotional strategy will you use?			

Rate this component:

5	4	3	2	1
Outstanding	Very Good	Good	Fair	Poor

4. **Operations.** In this segment, you describe the actual operations and outline their advantages. Specific operational procedures, proximity to supplies, and personnel needs and uses should all be considered in this section.

Key Elements	Have you covered this in the plan?	Is the answer clear? (yes or no)	Is the answer complete? (yes or no)
a. Have you identified a specific location?			
b. Have you outlined the advantages of this location?			
c. Any specific operational procedures to be considered?			
d. What personnel needs are there?			
e. Will your suppliers be accessible?			

Rate this component:

5	4	3	2	1
Outstanding	Very Good	Good	Fair	Poor

Continued

5. **Management.** Start by describing the management team, their unique qualifications, and your plans to compensate them (including salaries, employment agreements, stock purchase plans, levels of ownership, and other considerations). Discuss how your organization is structured; consider including a diagram illustrating who reports to whom. Also include a discussion of the potential contribution of the board of directors, advisors, or consultants. Finally, carefully describe the legal structure of your venture (sole proprietorship, partnership, or corporation).

Key Elements	Have you covered this in the plan?	Is the answer clear? (yes or no)	Is the answer complete? (yes or no)
a. Who will manage the business?			
b. What qualifications do you have?			
c. How many employees will you have?			
d. What will they do?			
e. How much will you pay your employees and what type of benefits will you offer them?			
f. What consultants or specialists will you use?			
g. What legal form of ownership will you have?			
h. What regulations will affect your business?			

Rate this component:

5	4	3	2	1
Outstanding	Very Good	Good	Fair	Poor

6. **Financial.** Three key financial statements must be presented: a balance sheet, an income statement, and a cash-flow statement. These statements typically cover a one-year period. Be sure you state any assumptions and projections made when calculating the figures.

Determine the stages at which your business will require external financing and identify the expected financing sources (both debt and equity sources). Also, clearly show what return on investment these sources will achieve by investing in your business. The final item to include is a break-even analysis. This analysis should show what level of sales will be required to cover all costs.

If the work is done well, the financial statements should represent the actual financial achievements expected from your business plan. They also provide a standard by which to measure the actual results of operating your business. They are a very valuable tool to help you manage and control your business.

Key Elements	Have you covered this in the plan?	Is the answer clear? (yes or no)	Is the answer complete? (yes or no)
a. What is your total expected business income for the first year? Quarterly for the next two years? (*forecast*)			
b. What is your expected monthly cash flow during the first year?			

Table	**12.4**	**Business Plan Assessment: A Complete Evaluation Tool (*Continued*)**

Key Elements	Have you covered this in the plan?	Is the answer clear? (yes or no)	Is the answer complete? (yes or no)
c. Have you included a method of paying yourself?			
d. What sales volume will you need to make a profit during the three years?			
e. What will be the break-even point?			
f. What are your projected assets, liabilities, and net worth?			
g. What are your total financial needs?			
h. What are your funding sources?			

Rate this component:

```
        5           4           3           2           1
        |-----------|-----------|-----------|-----------|
   Outstanding  Very Good     Good        Fair        Poor
```

7. **Critical Risks.** Discuss potential risks before they happen. Examples include: price-cutting by competitors, potentially unfavorable industry-wide trends, design or manufacturing costs that could exceed estimates, and sales projections that are not achieved. The idea is to recognize risks and identify alternative courses of action. Your main objective is to show that you can anticipate and control (to a reasonable degree) your risks.

Key Elements	Have you covered this in the plan?	Is the answer clear? (yes or no)	Is the answer complete? (yes or no)
a. What potential problems have you identified?			
b. Have you calculated the risks?			
c. What alternative courses of action exist?			

Rate this component:

```
        5           4           3           2           1
        |-----------|-----------|-----------|-----------|
   Outstanding  Very Good     Good        Fair        Poor
```

8. **Harvest Strategy.** Establishing an exit out of a venture is hard work. A founder's protective feelings for an idea built from scratch make it tough to grapple with issues such as management succession and harvest strategies. With foresight, however, an entrepreneur can either keep the dream alive and ensure the security of his or her venture or establish a plan for a liquidity event such as an IPO or the sale of the venture. Thus, a written plan for succession of your business is essential.

Key Elements	Have you covered this in the plan?	Is the answer clear? (yes or no)	Is the answer complete? (yes or no)
a. Have you planned for the orderly transfer of the venture assets if a liquidity event is established such as an IPO or a sale?			

Continued

Key Elements	Have you covered this in the plan?	Is the answer clear? (yes or no)	Is the answer complete? (yes or no)
b. Is there a continuity of business strategy for an orderly transition if the venture is not looking for an exit?			

Rate this component:

5	4	3	2	1
Outstanding	Very Good	Good	Fair	Poor

9. **Milestone Schedule.** This section is an important segment of the business plan because it requires you to determine what tasks you need to accomplish to achieve your objectives. Milestones and deadlines should be established and monitored on an ongoing basis. Each milestone is related to all others, and together all of them provide a timely representation of how your objective is to be accomplished.

Key Elements	Have you covered this in the plan?	Is the answer clear? (yes or no)	Is the answer complete? (yes or no)
a. How have you set your objectives?			
b. Have you set deadlines for each stage of your growth?			

Rate this component:

5	4	3	2	1
Outstanding	Very Good	Good	Fair	Poor

10. **Appendix.** This section includes important background information that was not included in the other sections. It is where you would put such items as résumés of the management team, names of references and advisors, drawings, documents, licenses, agreements, and any materials that support the plan. You may also wish to add a bibliography of the sources from which you drew information.

Key Elements	Have you covered this in the plan?	Is the answer clear? (yes or no)	Is the answer complete? (yes or no)
a. Have you included any documents, drawings, agreements, or other materials needed to support the plan?			
b. Are there any names of references, advisors, or technical sources you should include?			
c. Are there any other supporting documents?			

Rate this component:

5	4	3	2	1
Outstanding	Very Good	Good	Fair	Poor

Table 12.4	Business Plan Assessment: A Complete Evaluation Tool (*Continued*)

Summary: Your Plan

Directions: For each of the business plan sections that you assessed earlier, circle the assigned points on this review sheet and then total the circled points.

Components			Points		
1. Executive summary	5	4	3	2	1
2. Description of the business	5	4	3	2	1
3. Marketing	5	4	3	2	1
4. Operations	5	4	3	2	1
5. Management	5	4	3	2	1
6. Financial	5	4	3	2	1
7. Critical risks	5	4	3	2	1
8. Harvest strategy	5	4	3	2	1
9. Milestone schedule	5	4	3	2	1
10. Appendix	5	4	3	2	1

Total Points: _____

Scoring:
50 pts. — **Outstanding!** The ideal business plan. Solid!

45–49 pts. — **Very Good.**

40–44 pts. — **Good.** The plan is sound, with a few areas that need to be polished.

35–39 pts. — **Above Average.** The plan has some good areas but needs improvement before presentation.

30–34 pts. — **Average.** Some areas are covered in detail, yet other areas show weakness.

20–29 pts. — **Below Average.** Most areas need greater detail and improvement.

Below 20 pts. — **Poor.** Plan needs to be researched and documented much better.

Source: Donald F. Kuratko and Robert C. McDonald, *The Entrepreneurial Planning Guide* (Bloomington: Kelley School of Business, Indiana University, 2007).

Updating the Business Plan

The business plan should serve as a planning tool to help guide the start-up and execution of a new venture. Once the venture is started, the business plan is still a vital tool for planning continued growth and/or profitability. There are several reasons to update the business plan, including:

- **Financial Changes.** Update your plan on at least a yearly basis to project financials and plan for fiscal needs.
- **Additional Financing.** If continued capital is needed, an updated business plan needs to reflect the current numbers and not the ones projected before the venture was started.
- **Changes in the Market.** Changes in the customer base and competition should be tracked and strategized with regard to how they might affect your venture.
- **Launch of a New Product or Service.** Updating the business plan is an essential method to assess the feasibility of any proposed new product or service and determine its viability.
- **New Management Team.** Any new members of the management team should develop their own plan to initiate strategies for growth.

- **Reflect the New Reality.** Business plans are written based on estimated numbers and projections that may not be accurate after the venture has started. Business plans should be updated to reflect the new reality that the entrepreneur experiences.[15]

A Practical Example of a Business Plan

As we have stressed in this chapter, every new venture should have a business plan; however, many entrepreneurs have no idea about the details required for a complete business plan. An example of an actual business plan prepared for funding competition is included in Appendix 12A at the end of this chapter. The plan—entitled "DropToMe.com"—was prepared for actual financial support and also was presented at two national business plan competitions. Each part of a business plan discussed earlier in the chapter is illustrated in this detailed example. By carefully reviewing this business plan, you will gain a much better perspective of the final appearance that an entrepreneur's plan must have.

Presentation of the Business Plan: The "Pitch"

Once a business plan is prepared, the next major challenge is presenting the plan to either a single financial person or, in some parts of the country, a forum at which numerous financial investors have gathered.[16] The oral presentation—commonly known as an elevator pitch (because of the analogy of riding an elevator and having only two minutes to get your story told to another person in the elevator)—provides the chance to sell the business plan to potential investors.

The presentation should be organized, well prepared, interesting, and flexible. Entrepreneurs should develop an outline of the significant highlights that will capture the audience's interest. Although the outline should be followed, they also must feel free to add or remove certain bits of information as the presentation progresses—a memorized presentation lacks excitement, energy, and interest.

An entrepreneur should use the following steps to prepare an oral presentation:

- Know the outline thoroughly.
- Use keywords in the outline that help recall examples, visual aids, or other details.
- Rehearse the presentation to get a feel for its length.
- Be familiar with any equipment to be used in the presentation—use your own laptop.
- The day before, practice the complete presentation by moving through each slide.

Suggestions for Presentation

Entrepreneurs are naturally anxious to tell (and sell) their story. However, most venture capitalists agree that the content should be focused and the delivery should be sharp. In the content of the presentation, it is important to be brief and to the point, to summarize the critical factor or unique "hook" of your venture up front, and to use no more than 12–15 PowerPoint slides. Following are some key suggestions about the actual delivery of the pitch to prospective investors:

- Focus on the pain for which your venture will be the solution. Investors want to know exactly what problem is being solved by your venture. Pinpoint the target of your solution.
- Demonstrate the reachable market. Instead of a dramatic potential market, outline the immediate reachable group of customers that will be targeted.
- Explain the business model. How this venture is designed to make money is critical to investors. Demonstrating a clear method of getting to the market for sales will indicate a successful beginning to the new venture.
- Tout the management team. Every investor wants to know the skills and ability of the venture's team to deliver and operationalize the concept. Emphasize the experienced people on your team as well as any technical advisors who are on board.

- Explain your metrics. Rather than using generic assumptions such as the famous "1% rule" (when someone claims that he or she will simply get 1% of a huge market with no research to back the claim up), highlight the metrics that were used to calculate any revenue projections.

- Motivate the audience. The entire purpose of a venture pitch is to move the audience to the next step: another meeting to discuss everything in detail. Therefore, you must remember that enthusiasm is hugely important. The investors must believe that you are excited before they can be excited.

- Why *you* and why *now*? The final point must answer the daunting questions in the minds of the investors: Why are you the right venture, and why is this the right time for it to be launched? Be confident in yourself and your team. Always demonstrate a timeline to show the speed with which your venture plans to capture a significant market.[17]

What to Expect

Entrepreneurs should realize that the audience reviewing their business plan and listening to their pitch is usually cynical and sometimes antagonistic. Venture capital sources often pressure entrepreneurs to test their venture as well as their mettle. Thus, entrepreneurs must expect and prepare for a critical (and sometimes skeptical) audience of financial sources. When you make your pitch and submit your business plan, the venture capitalist will listen and then glance at the plan briefly before beginning any initial comments. No matter how good you think your venture plan is, an investor is not going to look at it and say, "This is the greatest business plan I've ever seen!" Do not expect enthusiastic acceptance or even polite praise. It's highly likely that the remarks will be critical, and even if they aren't, they'll seem that way. Don't panic. Even if it seems like an avalanche of objections, bear in mind that some of the best venture capital deals of all time faced the same opposition. Never expect results in 20 minutes. Each pitch will be a learning experience that will build your confidence for the next one.

Entrepreneurs must be prepared to handle questions from the evaluators and to learn from their criticism. They should never feel defeated but rather should make a commitment to improving the business plan for future review. Table 12.5 outlines some of the key

Table **12.5**	**What to Do When a Venture Capitalist Turns You Down: Ten Questions**

1. *Confirm the decision:* "That means you do not wish to participate at this time?"

2. *Sell for the future:* "Can we count you in for a second round of financing, after we've completed the first?"

3. *Find out why you were rejected:* "Why do you choose not to participate in this deal?" (Timing? Fit? All filled up?)

4. *Ask for advice:* "If you were in my position, how would you proceed?"

5. *Ask for suggestions:* "Can you suggest a source who invests in this kind of deal?"

6. *Get the name:* "Whom should I speak to when I'm there?"

7. *Find out why:* "Why do you suggest this firm, and why do you think this is the best person to speak to there?"

8. *Work on an introduction:* "Who would be the best person to introduce me?"

9. *Develop a reasonable excuse:* "Can I tell him that your decision to turn us down was based on _____ ?"

10. *Know your referral:* "What will you tell him when he calls?"

Source: Joseph R. Mancuso, *How to Write a Winning Business Plan* (Englewood Cliffs, NJ: Prentice Hall, 1985), 37. Reprinted with the permission of Simon & Schuster Adult Publishing Group. Copyright © 1985 by Prentice Hall, Inc.

Getting Ahead of the Curve

The best method, albeit a difficult one, for being at the forefront of a burgeoning market is to be well positioned before the market develops. Sometimes the opportunities seem to find the entrepreneurs, but having the foresight to understand where the market is headed positions some entrepreneurs ahead of the rest. In the case of Moukhtar Dzhakishev, a 44-year-old entrepreneur from Moscow, he saw opportunity in the uranium industry when everyone else had given up on it.

Kazatomprom, Dzhakishev's mining group, controls the world's largest uranium deposit outside of Australia, which is located in Kazakhstan. He took control of the country's mining industry when the Soviets abandoned it in 1991. They left behind 600 million tons of nuclear waste, along with one of the largest uranium deposits in the world. Until Dzhakishev's arrival, Kazakhstan's mines were largely forgotten. Nuclear power had fallen out of favor after the incidents at Chernobyl and Three Mile Island, which led to the cost of mining uranium far outweighing its market price.

When Dzhakishev first reopened the mines, he could book only 3 percent of his production. He initially was forced to accept whatever terms he could get, which involved allowing the Russians to barter for their uranium with butter. Less than ten years later, Kazatomprom posted profits of $500 million. Whereas most countries that are rich in resources but lack infrastructure are forced to compromise with more developed countries, Dzhakishev has managed to build joint ventures in which his company owns approximately half of the enterprise. He provides the uranium, and his partners provide the management skill and processing technology.

The rebirth of Kazakhstan's uranium mining industry can be attributed to the shift in the perception of nuclear energy. Carbon fuels are now cited as the leading cause of global warming, which has led nuclear power to be seen as a cleaner, more efficient form of energy rather than a toxic mistake. With mounting pressure on world powers to eliminate the widespread use of coal and other carbon fuels, a nuclear renaissance has begun. Thirty-four reactors are under construction and 280 have been proposed, which leads to the next obvious question: Where will countries find the uranium needed to power the influx of new plants? Dzhakishev has the answer.

As with any opportunity that arises, luck will invariably play a part; however, those entrepreneurs savvy enough to be in the right place when the market shifts in their favor will stand the best chance of reaping the rewards.

Source: Adapted from Abrahm Lustgarten, "Nuclear Power's White-Hot Metal," *Fortune*, March 27, 2008, http://money.cnn.com/2008/03/26/news/international/uranium_kazakhstan.fortune/index.htm (accessed April 9, 2008).

questions that an entrepreneur might ask when his or her business plan is turned down. Entrepreneurs should use the answers to these questions to revise, rework, and improve their business plan. Remember that you are starting out on a journey more similar to a marathon than a sprint. The goal is not so much to succeed the *first* time as it is to *succeed*.[18]

Summary

This chapter provided a thorough definition and examination of an effective business plan. The critical factors in planning and the pitfalls to be avoided were discussed. Indicators of these pitfalls and ways to avoid them also were presented.

Next, the benefits for both entrepreneurs and financial sources were reviewed. Developing a well-conceived plan was presented from the point of view of the audience for whom the plan is written. The typical six-step reading process of a business plan was presented to help entrepreneurs better understand how to put the business plan together. Ten guidelines in developing a business plan were provided, collated from the advice of experts in venture capital and new-business development.

The next section illustrated some of the major questions that must be answered in a complete and thorough business plan. The business plan was outlined, and every major segment was addressed and explained.

The chapter then presented some helpful hints for preparing a business plan, along with a self-analysis checklist for doing a careful critique of the plan before it is presented to investors.

Finally, the chapter closed with a review of how to present a business plan to an audience of venture capital sources. Some basic presentation tips were listed, together with a discussion of what to expect from the plan evaluators.

Key Terms and Concepts

business model	management team	metrics
business plan	market niche	milestone schedule segment
elevator pitch	marketing segment	pain
five-minute reading	marketing strategy	reachable market

Review and Discussion Questions

1. What is a business plan?
2. Describe each of the five planning pitfalls entrepreneurs often encounter.
3. Identify an indicator of each pitfall named in question 2. What would you do about each?
4. Identify the benefits of a business plan (a) for an entrepreneur and (b) for financial sources.
5. What are the three major viewpoints to be considered when developing a business plan?
6. Describe the six-step process venture capitalists follow when reading a business plan.
7. What are some components to consider in the proper packaging of a plan?
8. Identify five of the ten guidelines to be used for preparing a business plan.
9. Briefly describe each of the major segments to be covered in a business plan.
10. Why is the summary segment of a business plan written last? Why not first?
11. What are five elements included in the marketing segment of a business plan?
12. What is the meaning of the term *critical risks*?
13. Describe each of the three financial statements that are mandatory for the financial segment of a business plan.
14. Why should a business plan be updated?
15. Outline some of the critical points to capture in an elevator pitch.

Experiential Exercise

PUTTING TOGETHER A BUSINESS PLAN

The ten major segments of a business plan are listed in the following left column. Identify the order in which each segment will appear in the plan by placing a *1* next to the first part, a *2* next to the second part, and so on (through *10*).

Then match each of the 20 items or descriptions on the right with the segment in which it would appear. For example, if an item would appear in the first segment, put a *1* next to this description. Two items or descriptions are listed for each segment of the report.

Answers are provided at the end of the exercise.

Segments of the Report	Contents of the Segments
_____ 1. Financial segment	_____ a. Describes the potential of the new venture
_____ 2. Marketing segment	_____ b. Discusses the advantages of location
_____ 3. Management segment	_____ c. Discusses price-cutting by the competition
_____ 4. Summary	_____ d. Provides strategy for an initial public offering
_____ 5. Operations segment	_____ e. Most crucial part of the plan
_____ 6. Business description segment	_____ f. Describes any prototypes developed
_____ 7. Critical-risks segment	_____ g. Analyzes case if any sales projections are not attained
_____ 8. Appendix	_____ h. Shows the relationship between events and deadlines for accomplishment
_____ 9. Harvest strategy segment	_____ i. Provides résumés of all key personnel
_____ 10. Milestone schedule segment	_____ j. Contains support material such as blueprints and diagrams
	_____ k. Discusses pricing strategy
	_____ l. Should be written after the business plan is completed
	_____ m. Provides a budget
	_____ n. Explains proximity to suppliers
	_____ o. Sets forth timetables for completion of major phases of the venture
	_____ p. Provides industry background
	_____ q. Explains costs involved in testing
	_____ r. Identifies target markets
	_____ s. Describes legal structure of the venture
	_____ t. Provides balance sheet and income statement

Answers: 1. 6, 2. 3, 3. 5, 4. 1, 5. 4, 6. 2, 7. 7, 8. 10, 9. 8, 10. 9, a. 2, b. 4, c. 7, d. 8, e. 1, f. 2, g. 7, h. 9, i. 5, j. 10, k. 3, l. 1, m. 6, n. 4, o. 9, p. 2, q. 4, r. 3, s. 5, t. 6

Case 12.1

IT'S JUST A MATTER OF TIME

Pedro Santini has been a computer analyst for five years. In his spare time, he has developed a word processing software program that is more comprehensive and powerful than any on the market. Because he does not have a great deal of money, Pedro believes that the first step in producing and marketing this product should be to obtain the necessary venture capital.

The software program has been written and trial-tested by Pedro and a handful of friends to whom he gave the material. Two of these friends are computer word processors who told him that the program is faster and easier to use than anything on the market. Pedro believes that these kinds of testimonials point out the profit potential of the product. However, he still needs to get financial support.

One of Pedro's friends has suggested a meeting with a venture capitalist. "These guys have all sorts of money to invest for new ventures," the friend told Pedro. "All you have to do is explain your ideas and sell them on giving you the money. They are always looking to back a profitable idea, and yours is certain to be one of the best they have seen in a long time."

Pedro agrees with his friend but believes he should not discuss the matter with a venture capitalist until he has thought through answers to the various types of questions likely to be asked. In particular, Pedro believes he should be able to provide the venture capitalist with projected sales for the first three years and be able to explain the types of expenses that would be incurred. Once he has done this, Pedro feels that he will be ready to talk to the individual. "Right now," he tells his friend, "it's just a matter of time. I think that, within seven to ten days, I'll be ready to present my ideas and discuss financial needs."

QUESTIONS

1. In addition to financial questions, what other questions is the venture capitalist likely to ask Pedro?

2. Would a business plan be of any value to Pedro? Why or why not?

3. How would you recommend Pedro get ready for his meeting with the venture capitalist? Be complete in your answer.

Case 12.2

THE INCOMPLETE PLAN

When Joan Boothe drew up her business plan, she was certain it would help her get venture capital. Joan is in the throes of putting together a monthly magazine directed toward executive women in the workplace. The objective of the periodical is to provide information that is useful to women who are pursuing careers. The first issue is scheduled to go to press in 90 days. Some of the articles included in this issue are "Managing Your Time for Fun and Profit," "What You Need to Know About Dressing for Success," and "Money Management: Do It Like the Experts." Another section, titled "Women in the News," is devoted to successful women at work. Other features include a question-and-answer section that responds to letters and inquiries from readers (the first issue's questions were submitted by a group of women executives, each of whom had been asked to help get the column started by sending in a question); a stock market section that reviews industries or companies and points out the benefits and risks associated with investing in them; and a column on the state of the economy and the developments or trends expected during the next 12 months.

Joan's business plan consists of six parts: a summary, a business description, a manufacturing segment, a management segment, a milestone schedule segment, and an appendix. When it was returned to her by a venture capital firm, the rejection letter said: "Without a marketing segment, attention to critical risks, and a financial segment, this plan is incomplete and cannot be favorably reviewed by us. If you would provide us with this additional information and submit the rewritten plan within the next 60 days, we will be happy to review the plan and give you our opinion within 10 working days."

QUESTIONS

1. What should Joan put in the marketing segment? What types of information will she need?

2. What key areas does Joan have to address for the critical-risks assessment segment? Discuss two of these.

3. What suggestions would you make to Joan regarding the kinds of information to include in the financial segment? Be as specific as possible.

Notes

1. Donald F. Kuratko and Arnold Cirtin, "Developing a Business Plan for Your Clients," *National Public Accountant* (January 1990): 24–28. For additional information on writing effective plans, see Jeffrey A. Timmons, Andrew Zacharakis, and Stephen Spinelli, *Business Plans That Work* (New York: McGraw-Hill, 2004).

2. James W. Henderson, *Obtaining Venture Financing* (Lexington, MA: Lexington Books, 1988), 13–14; see also Stephen C. Perry, "The Relationship Between Written Business Plans and the Failure of Small Businesses in the U.S.," *Journal of Small Business Management* 39, no. 3 (2001): 201–8.

3. Joseph R. Mancuso, *How to Write a Winning Business Plan* (Englewood Cliffs, NJ: Prentice Hall, 1985), 44.

4. See Donald F. Kuratko, "Demystifying the Business Plan Process: An Introductory Guide," *Small Business Forum* (Winter 1990/1991): 33–40.

5. Adapted from Henderson, *Obtaining Venture Financing*, 14–15; and Mancuso, *How to Write*, 43.

6. Henderson, *Obtaining Venture Financing*, 15.

7. Stanley R. Rich and David E. Gumpert, "How to Write a Winning Business Plan," *Harvard Business Review* (May/June 1985): 156–66; see also Colin Mason and Matthew Stark, "What Do Investors Look for in a Business Plan?" *International Small Business Journal* 22, no. 3 (2004): 227–48.

8. Gerald E. Hills, "Market Analysis in the Business Plan: Venture Capitalists' Perceptions," *Journal of Small Business Management* (January 1985): 38–46; see also Gerald E. Hills, Claes M. Hultman, and Morgan P. Miles, "The Evolution and Development of Entrepreneurial Marketing," *Journal of Small Business Management* 46, no. 1 (2008): 99–112.

9. Rich and Gumpert, "How to Write," 159.

10. Mancuso, *How to Write*, 52; see also Bruce R. Barringer, *Preparing Effective Business Plans: An Entrepreneurial Approach* (Upper Saddle River, NJ: Pearson/Prentice Hall, 2009).

11. Mancuso, *How to Write*, 65.

12. These guidelines are adapted from Jeffrey A. Timmons, "A Business Plan Is More Than a Financing Device," *Harvard Business Review* (March/April 1980): 25–35; W. Keith Schilt, "How to Write a Winning Business Plan," *Business Horizons* (September/October 1987): 13–22; William A. Sahlman, "How to Write a Great Business Plan," *Harvard Business Review* (July/August 1997): 98–108; and Donald F. Kuratko and Robert C. McDonald, *The Entrepreneurial Planning Guide* (Bloomington: Kelley School of Business, Indiana University, 2007).

13. Donald F. Kuratko and Jeffrey S. Hornsby, *New Venture Management: The Entrepreneur's Roadmap* (Upper Saddle River, NJ: Pearson/Prentice Hall, 2009).

14. See Donald F. Kuratko, "Cutting Through the Business Plan Jungle," *Executive Female* (July/August 1993): 17–27; and Donald F. Kuratko and Robert C. McDonald, *The Entrepreneurial Planning Guide* (Bloomington: Kelley School of Business, Indiana University, 2007).

15. Kuratko and Hornsby, *New Venture Management*.

16. For example, the Massachusetts Institute of Technology sponsors a business plan forum in Boston, and the Venture Club of Indiana sponsors a monthly meeting with presentations.

17. For more on venture "pitch" presentations, see Barringer, *Preparing Effective Business Plans*; and Andrew J. Sherman, *Start Fast and Start Right* (New York: Kaplan Publishing, 2007).

18. For excellent resources on business plan preparation and presentations, see Garage Technology Ventures at http://www.garage.com/resources/index.shtml.

This business plan was prepared for actual financial sources, and it was presented success-fully at two major national business plan competitions. The team leaders were Andrew Vincent, Stephen Wolff, and Justin Chafe, all MBAs from the Kelley School of Business at Indiana University–Bloomington.

Management Team:

Justin Chafe

Andrew Montgomery

George Steimer

Andrew Vincent

Stephen Wolff

Table of Contents

1. Executive Summary

Adora Interactive Corporation is proud to introduce DropToMe.com, a new online service that combines the successful trends of e-commerce with social networking to provide users with a powerful new tool for sharing, ranking, and discovering product interests.

One of the most frustrating aspects of purchasing products online is sorting through hundreds of reviews that may or may not help a user in ultimately deciding to purchase the product. For example, when shopping on Amazon.com for a new book, the user is presented with a plethora of user ratings and reviews. These reviews beg the question, does the user have the same tastes as the reviewer who gave the book five stars, or does the user have tastes more similar to the reviewer who has given the book zero stars? Matching a user's unique interests to products or services that they will like is challenging, and no one does it well currently. DropToMe.com intends to change that.

DropToMe.com uses a proprietary algorithm to identify users with similar tastes by comparing rank-ordered lists of products. A unique, tactile drag-and-drop interface makes these lists easy and fun to create, update, and share. Not only can DropToMe.com users find relevant recommendations for items that interest them, they also can easily share product and service ideas with their friends and families. DropToMe.com allows users to rank, share, and discover new products and services across many categories. Books are only one example of hundreds of product categories that DropToMe.com users will be able to add to their lists of interests.

The DropToMe.com management team has developed a plan to leverage these core features to create the next generation of social networking Web sites. As social networking sites continue to evolve, DropToMe.com will be positioned to aggressively grow its user base and create a "sticky" experience that will generate significant profits.

The Web site's initial user base will consist of Internet-savvy social networking users between the ages of 13 and 26. This segment will primarily be interested in ranking movies, Web sites, online videos, music, and television shows. Although this group will be the earliest adopters, future growth and marketing will not be limited to this segment. It is not hard to imagine baby boomers receiving wine and restaurant recommendations through DropToMe.com's proprietary algorithm.

DropToMe.com provides these services free to its users and receives revenue from four independent and scalable sources: targeted banner advertisements through Google's AdSense program, e-commerce commissions through Amazon.com's associates program, the sale of market research, and the sale of targeted sponsored advertisements.

Adora Interactive Corporation is currently seeking a total of $2,200,000 in working capital to facilitate fast user growth and future development of the DropToMe.com Web site. Agreements with Amazon and M3i Works are already in place, and the DropToMe.com algorithm has proven itself to be quite effective.

2. Business Description

DropToMe.com combines the best aspects of social networking and e-commerce Web sites to create a new online experience for users. Though the dot-com boom may have passed, the social networking boom has only just begun in the United States, and there is still significant room for growth.[1] More importantly, the potential for financial success is clear. DropToMe.com expects to achieve revenue of over $51 million by year five.

2.1 DropToMe.com Features

DropToMe.com provides a unique user experience that is not often seen on social networking Web sites. New users will be prompted to provide the Web site with information to ensure that it can remember their ranked products and better deliver its recommendations. This information will include a user's e-mail address as well as demographic data that can be used for market research in a highly confidential manner.

Every product listing throughout DropToMe.com will be a unique object that users can click and drag throughout the page, ordering lists or depositing them in particular places on the page, such as the Drop Box. This ability to drag and drop products is how users will interact with DropToMe.com, dragging items in a list to place them in rank order, or dragging items to their drop box for future ranking, or to share with their friends and family.

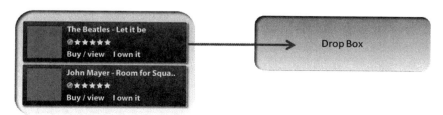

The Drop Box will be present on every page, allowing users to easily flag products in which they are interested without interrupting their surfing experience, no matter where they are on the site. Users will be able to easily find products in which they are interested in either ranking or sharing through DropToMe.com's search engine.

The My Drops page of DropToMe.com is where users will be able to rank products that have been dropped to them, either by themselves or by friends and family, creating rank-ordered lists of products. Products dropped to the user by friends and family in their network will display who has dropped the product to the user, and what the dropper's opinion of the product was.

DropToMe.com anticipates users will rank hundreds, if not thousands, of products as they use DropToMe.com. It is unrealistic to expect that users will be willing to take the time to specifically order such a long list, especially because some users may not be able or willing to accurately order a group of very similar products on such a large scale. To remove this burden from the user, the DropToMe.com ranking system consists of four very simple steps: star it, drop it, rank it, and done. The user will create and refine the correct order of his or her product list by ordering small parts of the list at a time. The more products that a user rates, the more accurate his or her overall product-ranking list will become.

2.1.1 USER-GENERATED CONTENT

The ranking and sharing of products are the main drivers behind why users will use Drop-ToMe.com. Not only do they provide constantly updated content to the Web site, they also provide the ability to create a social networking situation. People use social networking Web sites to share themselves with the world, and to see the information shared by their friends.

Users will be able to share lists of products in which they are interested on their profile page. DropToMe.com will also display lists that show the top-ranked products throughout the site as decided by its users. The user will also be able to create a profile page to display a personal picture or two, the user's top product lists, and the user's network of friends.

Finally, the lists of ranked products created by the users will be harnessed to provide accurate and personalized recommendations. DropToMe.com will provide users with two types of recommendations. The first group of recommendations will be based on the comparison of a user's rankings and the entire population of DropToMe.com. The second group of recommendations will be based on the comparison of a user's rankings to only his or her friends and family, as identified on DropToMe.com. Although the first group will provide more accurate recommendations than the second, the ability to see what a user's friends think they might like will be appealing, possibly increasing the user's level of comfort with the recommendations and increasing the likelihood that he or she will purchase items through the DropToMe.com Amazon.com associates program.

2.1.2 THE ALGORITHM

DropToMe.com has developed a proprietary algorithm that will allow the site to deliver recommendations that are much more accurate than anything currently available on the market. The algorithm works by identifying similar lists of products and recommending products present on one list but not the other.

2.2 Revenue Sources

DropToMe.com will have four distinct, scalable sources of revenue: commissions, sponsorship revenue, market research revenue, and advertising revenue. Although commissions and advertising will likely be the primary source of revenue early in the company's life, it is the sponsorship and market research revenue that will play the largest role in the company's future profits.

2.2.1 AFFILIATE PROGRAM

By signing up as a member of the Amazon.com associates program, DropToMe.com will not only gain access to its entire product database, allowing for the creation and population of the DropToMe.com database, but it will be able to collect commissions on any sales referred through DropToMe.com.

An alliance with Amazon.com is not exclusive. DropToMe.com is certainly open to exploring other alliances with other companies. For example, although not in the immediate future of DropToMe.com, the site could allow vacation spots to be ranked. DropToMe.com could then partner with travel agents, resort areas, or Orbitz.com, and users could be sent to the appropriate sites to "buy" a vacation spot while generating a referral fee for DropToMe.com.

2.2.2 ADVERTISING

DropToMe.com will use Google AdSense to populate advertising content throughout the Web site. Google ads are created dynamically based upon the content of the page in which they are embedded. Because much of the page's content will consist of particular products, these advertisements will relate specifically to said products, increasing the relevancy of the ad to the user. This should help DropToMe.com realize a greater click-through rate on its advertising, thus bypassing one of the major problems currently faced by the social networking giant Facebook.

2.2.3 FEATURED DROPS

DropToMe.com will offer companies the ability to display their item in a "Featured Drops" area throughout the Web site for a fee. This item, just like any other product listed on the Web site, will be able to be dragged and dropped into a user's drop box, thus increasing the user's involvement with the advertisement and significantly increasing the chance that the product will be added to a user's list.

2.2.4 MARKET RESEARCH

Market research firms and companies are very interested in knowing what users think of their products, and how their products compare to those of the competition. Companies go to great lengths and expenses to poll users regarding their preferences, especially in relation to other products available on the market.

Because one goal of DropToMe.com is to provide an accurate list of products in ranked order for individual users, it is placed in a unique position to gather information directly from its users and convey this information to market research firms. In order to make its data more attractive to market research firms and companies, DropToMe.com must ensure that it is able to offer a statistically significant sized sample of random, or mostly random, users and their preferences. To make this possible, DropToMe.com will collect specific data about its users as they sign up to create accounts. The identity of users and their individual data will be kept confidential.

3. Competitor Analysis

3.1 DropToMe.com Is Unique

Although DropToMe.com shares many features with popular social networking sites like MySpace and Facebook, such as a friends list, the ability to keep a miniature blog, and to leave comments on the profile pages of your friends and other DropToMe.com users, it is not designed to compete directly with these social networking giants. At the same time, while DropToMe.com does involve the evaluation of products, it is not designed to replace e-commerce sites like Amazon.com or review sites such as CNet.com. Instead, DropToMe.com is meant to complement the already well-established services and infrastructure of both social networking and e-commerce sites, thus increasing the rate of adoption of DropToMe.com by users throughout the Internet.

Online social networking has undergone many evolutions, each moving one step closer to the ideal social networking Web site. Geocities started the trend by offering free hosting services, allowing users to more easily create a personal Web site. Unfortunately, Geocities required knowledge of HTML code in order to build a good personal page.

MySpace took the trend forward another step. It provided templates and easy-to-use tools to users, making it easy for users with little or no knowledge of HTML code to create personal pages and share those pages with their friends. Unfortunately, MySpace did not provide a good way to find friends and invite them into a user's network.

Facebook was able to offer two major improvements over MySpace. First, Facebook provided a clean template around which all user profile pages would be built. No longer would pages be full of garish, blinking graphics. They would be clean and easy to read while still conveying the necessary information. Second, Facebook allowed users to find friends and family through the use of e-mail extensions. If a user had an "@indiana.edu" e-mail address, that user would be able to search for and add friends with a similar e-mail extension. This made it much easier to find friends and associates. Unfortunately, it made the assumption that if people share an e-mail address extension, they share similar interests and will want to be in each other's networks.

DropToMe.com allows users to add friends and family to their networks based on similarities between users, rather than e-mail address extensions. By comparing product interests and rankings, DropToMe.com can connect users with similar preferences, creating a true community of people who are interested in sharing their profiles, preferences, and personalities with each other, rather than people who simply share an e-mail address extension.

3.2 Amazon, Yahoo!, Netflix

Amazon, Yahoo!, and Netflix are some of the largest competitors that already offer product-ranking services. Although Amazon, Yahoo!, and Netflix have not made public the exact algorithms used to make recommendations, CIO Andrew Montgomery has been able to infer the basics about their ranking systems and is confident that DropToMe.com provides better recommendations.

4. Marketing Strategy

The DropToMe.com marketing strategy is designed to generate awareness, trial, and repeat use of the Web site. The plan uses a combination of public relations, viral marketing, and traditional event marketing over two major launch campaigns.

4.1 Initial Launch in March and April 2008

Adora Interactive will begin with a local advertising campaign to start user generation. The company will initially focus on universities and college towns throughout the state of Indiana. Any on-campus promotions will first be cleared by the appropriate campus administrators. These promotions will require printing a DropToMe.com banner, setting up tables in high-traffic areas, and handing out club card–style fliers to foot traffic. In addition, the company will have pop-up displays that illustrate the utility of the site. Adora Interactive will work to be featured appropriately in campus newspaper articles, local news reports, and local newspapers. The company is also exploring the possibility of advertising on campus shuttles and buses.

Adora Interactive can create higher awareness of DropToMe.com by partnering with local restaurants, pizza delivery services, and coffee shops, providing free advertisement on DropToMe.com in exchange for free advertisement in the form of fliers taped to pizza boxes, cards left on tables, and inserts included with carry-out meals. This strategy will lead to increased awareness of DropToMe.com throughout the targeted areas while also adding a hint of local flavor, further enticing local users to sign up and use DropToMe.com.

Furthermore, the company will encourage new users to actively invite their friends to join DropToMe.com. Part of this effort will take place on the DropToMe.com Web site, encouraging users to add friends to their networks while making it easy to send an e-mail to their friends inviting them to the Web site. DropToMe.com will also provide users with the necessary code to display their top five items of any category on their MySpace page, Facebook page, or any other space that allows users the freedom to include personal content. Viewers of these off-site lists will be provided with a link to DropToMe.com and some encouragement to share their preferences with the world. By offering this ability to share top-five lists in the social networking world, DropToMe.com acts as a supplement to the current social networking infrastructure rather than as a direct competitor. These lists will be shared with users already interested in social networking online, thus increasing the chances that they will visit DropToMe.com and sign up as a member.

4.2 National Launch, Third and Fourth Quarters, 2008

The national launch will feature two major strategies: a national public relations launch and a more targeted news release launch focused on specific market niches featured on Drop-ToMe.com, such as books, movies, music, Web sites, wine, and so forth.

The national public relations campaign will center on the benefits of the site and how it is useful to users. It will highlight the applications for existing social networks as a way to gain traction with users. Adora Interactive will need to partner with a public relations agency to properly contact national media outlets such as television, national radio, magazines, and newspapers. This PR firm will also be able to help the company generate a strong "newsworthy" story. The national launch will specifically target college campuses in the fall of 2008.

In addition to marketing toward users, Adora Interactive will need to generate substantial interest from its potential advertisers. To do this, the company will create information about both why a company should advertise on DropToMe.com and how creating a relationship with DropToMe.com is easy. This will involve brochures illustrating user growth, demographics, and impact. The first few months of operation will involve personally calling new and potential advertisers, a task that will be made easier as Adora Interactive hires its marketing and sales team.

5. Operations

5.1 Current Operations

Adora Interactive is in the process of building and launching DropToMe.com. The company has partnered with M3i Works, a premier Silicon Valley Web site designer and developer, to ensure that the launch of DropToMe.com is both timely and feature complete. The Drop-ToMe.com algorithm has been tested and is now being scaled up to properly handle expected Web site traffic.

Adora Interactive Corporation is currently seeking its second round of funding to ensure that the company will meet and exceed its user and revenue growth predictions. Adora Interactive will need funding in order to properly execute the marketing campaigns centered on its launch and expansion. The company expects that additional hardware and processing power will be required to provide real-time product recommendations as its user base grows. Adora Interactive will also need financial resources to rent and furnish office space and bring its founders on as full-time, salaried employees.

5.2 Future Operations and Features

Adora Interactive currently expects to begin the second phase of its expansion in the second half of 2008. This will involve the aggressive development and launch of new DropToMe .com features and an expanded marketing campaign that will ensure continued, healthy growth of the DropToMe.com user base.

While DropToMe.com will be fully functional at launch, Adora Interactive has identified additional features and functionality to add to the Web site post-launch. These features include picture sharing and ranking, featured product advertisements that are targeted to specific user demographics throughout the site, and the ability to attach messages to products dropped to friends within a user's network. Adora Interactive also plans to develop a mobile phone–compatible version of DropToMe.com, allowing users to access their list of recommended products and rank on the go, both through traditional cell phones and mainstream smart phones, including Apple's iPhone.

Some of these features will be developed through the continued partnership between M3i Works and Adora Interactive, but many of them, such as the mobile phone–compatible version of DropToMe.com, will be best handled by internal programmers and database managers. Adora Interactive plans to start hiring full-time employees in September 2008 to quickly develop and launch these innovations, keeping DropToMe.com fresh and worth visiting on a regular basis.

Marketing will continue to be a large priority for Adora Interactive as it develops. The company plans to hire both marketers and salespeople to spread awareness and interest in DropToMe.com, not only to consumers but also to businesses that can benefit from the site's targeted, interactive featured product advertisements and market research collections.

Adora Interactive has begun to explore long-term expansions and applications of the DropToMe.com model as well. Beyond the initial feature expansion, Adora Interaction plans to allow users to add products to their "To Rank" lists by taking pictures of product barcodes with their cell phones, expanding the DropToMe.com experience into the real world.

Marketing data gathered on DropToMe.com can also be used to better target online advertisements by tying Web site rankings on DropToMe.com with demographic data collected from DropToMe.com users. Unlike Google's AdSense program, which displays advertisements based on the content of the Web site, DropToMe.com could provide advertisements based on a Web site's demographic popularity, providing more accurate and better-targeted advertisements to companies. These long-term plans ensure that DropToMe.com will remain relevant to both its users and its clients.

6. Management

Andrew Vincent, Chief Executive Officer
avincent@adorainteractive.com
Kenyon College, BA in Economics
Indiana University Kelley School of Business MBA, Marketing and Entrepreneurship
Previous employers include FedEx and SEI Investments

- Identified new revenue opportunities (totaling $35.2 million) for FedEx and presented the findings and marketing strategy recommendations to the director of Alliance Marketing.

- Developed and presented complex sales pitches to high-level clients during his tenure at SEI Investments, resulting in the winning of $2.4 billion of new business.

- Directly supervised a team of six accountants while with SEI Investments, developing and implementing training programs and performance metrics.

Stephen Wolff, Chief Financial Officer
swolff@adorainteractive.com
University of Illinois, BA in Finance and Economics
Indiana University Kelley School of Business MBA, Finance
Previous employers include Indiana Public Employees' Retirement Fund (PERF) and Merrill Lynch Capital

- Conducted due diligence on $220 million in prospective private equity buyout and venture capital investments, and composed recommendation memos to the board and executive director while working for Indiana PERF.

- Coordinated annual budgeting process, updated monthly financial reporting, and completed various ad hoc requests at Merrill Lynch Capital while manager was on extended leave.

- CFA Level II Candidate: June 2008

Justin Chafe, Chief Marketing Officer
jchafe@adorainteractive.com
University of Utah, BS in Marketing
Indiana University Kelley School of Business MBA, Marketing
Previous employers include Boston Scientific and Echelon Biosciences, Inc.

- Planned and implemented strategic marketing changes for scientific product catalog business while with Echelon Biosciences, Inc., leading to a 30 percent sales growth in 2003, 37 percent sales growth in 2004, and 10 percent sales growth in 2005.

- Proposed and managed $10,000 annual online advertising program to Echelon Biosciences, Inc., including Google AdWords and targeted banner ads, which lead to increased Web traffic, consumer awareness, and sales.

George Steimer, Chief Technology Officer
gsteimer@adorainteractive.com
University of Illinois, BS in Management of Information Systems
TSG—Web Development Project Lead
Previous employers include Technology Services Group and Concentra Preferred Systems

- Responsible for the full Active Wizard software product development life cycle, including system planning, cost estimating, design, development, testing and implementation. Planned, managed, and implemented six releases of the Active Wizard.
- Responsible for all cost estimates and managing the project to the budget, totaling over $1.5 million worth of work.
- Directly supervised project teams ranging from one to five team members.

Andrew Montgomery, Chief Information Officer
amontgomery@adorainteractive.com
Kenyon College, BS in Mathematics
Currently employed as a Freelance Programmer

- Graduated with distinction for original research on the possibility of extending the Goldbach Conjecture to unique factorization domains other than integers.
- Perfect score on the 2002 ETS Major Field Test in Mathematics.
- Charter member, Pi Mu Epsilon, an honorary mathematics society.
- Member of Mensa.

7. Revenue Model

Monthly financials through 2009 are available upon request.

Pro Forma Revenue Model

Adora Interactive (Thousands)	2008E	2009E	2010E	2011E	2012E
Est Social Networking Industry User Base	77,024	84,752	93,227	102,550	112,805
Soc. Networking Industry Growth	10.0%	10.0%	10.0%	10.0%	10.0%
Ranked.com user % of industy	25.0%	25.0%	25.0%	25.0%	25.0%
Market Potential Capture	2.08%	6.43%	11.43%	17.85%	28.56%
# registered users	400	1,362	2,663	4,577	8,055
Growth %		241%	96%	72%	76%
Annual page views per user	2,000	2,500	2,800	3,000	3,685
Annual page views	159,333	2,302,708	7,455,896	13,730,163	29,682,782
Rev per view	0.0008354	0.0008354	0.0008354	0.0008354	0.0008354
Ad Revenue	**133**	**1,924**	**6,229**	**11,470**	**24,798**
Rev Growth %		1345%	224%	84%	116%
% members that make Amzn purchase	2.4%	5.0%	7.0%	10.0%	15.0%
# annual purchases	38	68	186	458	1,208
Avg purchase price per year	60	80	80	80	80
% referral rev	4.0%	5.0%	5.0%	5.0%	5.0%
Amazon.com Referral Revenue	**92**	**272**	**746**	**1,831**	**4,833**
Rev Growth %		195%	174%	146%	164%
Rev per 100K members	10,000	10,000	10,000	10,000	10,000
# of Firms Purchasing	1	1	10	15	20

Continued

Pro Forma Revenue Model

Adora Interactive (Thousands)	2008E	2009E	2010E	2011E	2012E
Market Data Sales	**65**	**1,105**	**2,663**	**6,865**	**16,110**
Rev Growth %		1600%	141%	158%	135%
Rev per sponsored ad	5	16.34	20.00	24.16	53.41
# of sponsored ads	5	10	50	75	100
Sponsorship Revenue	**25**	**180**	**1,000**	**1,812**	**5,341**
Rev Growth %		626%	457%	81%	195%
Total Revenue	**315**	**3,481**	**10,637**	**21,978**	**51,082**
Rev Growth %		1005%	206%	107%	132%

8. Income Statement

Pro Forma Income Statement

Adora Interactive	2007A	2008E	2009E	2010E	2011E	2012E
Registered Users	–	400,000	1,362,000	2,662,820	4,576,721	8,055,029
Ad Revenue	–	133,110	1,923,722	6,228,782	11,470,412	24,797,501
Amazon Referral Revenue	–	92,064	272,000	745,590	1,830,688	4,833,017
Market Data Sales	–	65,000	1,105,300	2,662,820	6,865,082	16,110,058
Sponsorship Revenue	–	24,750	179,685	1,000,000	1,811,824	5,341,256
Total Revenue	**–**	**314,924**	**3,480,707**	**10,637,192**	**21,978,005**	**51,081,832**
Rev Growth %			1005%	206%	107%	132%
Infrastructure	–	1,779	2,372	4,050	6,075	9,113
Other Cost of Revenue	–	113,359	693,769	2,123,388	4,389,526	10,207,254
Cost of Revenue	–	115,138	696,141	2,127,438	4,395,601	10,216,366
Gross Profit	–	199,786	2,784,565	8,509,753	17,582,404	40,865,466
Gross Margin %		80%	80%	80%	80%	80%
Technology Costs	–	143,300	380,000	2,000,000	4,000,000	6,000,000
Sales and Marketing	–	248,625	939,300	2,000,000	3,000,000	3,000,000
Salaries	–	349,167	1,404,313	2,738,463	3,681,130	4,353,976
Employees	5	11	25	35	45	51
Legal Expense	2,000	38,587	45,000	50,000	50,000	50,000
Accounting & Audit	–	5,833	10,000	25,000	25,000	25,000
Other	224	31,267	50,000	100,000	100,000	100,000
Office	–	35,000	60,000	100,000	150,000	150,000
General and administrative	2,224	459,854	1,569,313	3,013,463	4,006,130	4,678,976
Total Expenses	**2,224**	**851,779**	**2,888,612**	**7,013,463**	**11,006,130**	**13,678,976**
Operating Income	(2,224)	(651,993)	(104,047)	1,496,291	6,576,274	27,186,490
Interest income and other, net	3	820	1,200	–	–	–
Income before income taxes	(2,221)	(651,173)	(102,847)	1,496,291	6,576,274	27,186,490
Provision for income taxes	–	(190,198)	(35,996)	523,702	2,301,696	9,515,271
Tax rate	0%	35%	35%	35%	35%	35%
Net Income	**(2,221)**	**(460,976)**	**(66,851)**	**972,589**	**4,274,578**	**17,671,218**

9. Balance Sheet and Statement of Cash Flow

Pro Forma Balance Sheet

Adora Interactive	2007A	2008E	2009E	2010E	2011E	2012E
Assets						
Cash & Equivalents	7,779	1,846,804	1,779,953	2,752,542	7,027,120	24,698,339
Total Assets	**7,779**	**1,846,804**	**1,779,953**	**2,752,542**	**7,027,120**	**24,698,339**
Liabilities	–	70,000	–	–	–	–
Shareholder's Equity						
Common Stock	10,000	2,240,000	2,240,000	2,240,000	2,240,000	2,240,000
Retrained Earnings	(2,221)	(463,196)	(460,047)	512,542	4,787,120	22,458,339
Total Shareholder's Equity	**7,779**	**1,776,804**	**1,779,953**	**2,752,542**	**7,027,120**	**24,698,339**
Total Liab and SE	**7,779**	**1,846,804**	**1,779,953**	**2,752,542**	**7,027,120**	**24,698,339**
Equity Roll Forward						
BOP Equity	–	7,779	1,776,804	1,779,953	2,752,542	7,027,120
Net income	(2,221)	(460,976)	(66,851)	972,589	4,274,578	17,671,218
Dividends	–	–	–	–	–	–
Other	10,000	2,230,000	70,000	–	–	–
EOP Equity	7,779	1,776,804	1,779,953	2,752,542	7,027,120	24,698,339

Pro Forma Statement of Cash Flow

Adora Interactive	2007A	2008E	2009E	2010E	2011E	2012E
Cash Flow From Operations						
Net Income	(2,221)	(460,976)	(66,851)	972,589	4,274,578	17,671,218
Net Cash From Operations	(2,221)	(460,976)	(66,851)	972,589	4,274,578	17,671,218
Cash Flow From Investing						
Net Cash From Investing	–	–	–	–	–	–
Cash Flow From Financing						
Net Debt Issuance	–	70,000	(70,000)	–	–	–
Net Common Stock Issuance	10,000	2,230,000	70,000	–	–	–
Other						
Net Cash From Financing	10,000	2,300,000	–	–	–	–
Net Change in Cash	7,779	1,839,024	(66,851)	972,589	4,274,578	17,671,218
BOP Cash	–	7,779	1,846,804	1,779,953	2,752,542	7,027,120
EOP Cash	7,779	1,846,804	1,779,953	2,752,542	7,027,120	24,698,339

10. Harvest Strategy

10.1 Strategic Acquisition

The most likely harvest strategy is an acquisition of the business by a strategic buyer like Amazon. The DropToMe.com Web site functions as a front-end user interface that drives traffic to Amazon's products. Because Amazon has not been viably active in the social networking space, this could be a good way for the company to make users more "sticky" and increase product sales. Additionally, Amazon's product recommendations could benefit from the DropToMe.com ranking algorithm and vast user database.

Another strategic acquirer could be Google. The company has very deep pockets and has demonstrated a willingness to buy online companies that provide content sharing. For example, Google purchased YouTube for $1.7 billion in October 2006. Finally, the leading social networking sites such as Facebook and MySpace are actively seeking new ways to grow. DropToMe.com's unique drag-and-drop user interface may provide them with an easy way to add product ranking and sharing to their existing platforms.

10.2 Initial Public Offering

Alternatively, an initial public offering could provide substantial liquidity for shareholders and provide Adora Interactive Corporation the ability to increase its share of the social networking market while introducing innovative new features. Although it is difficult to estimate how much liquidity the capital markets will provide in the years to come, the current market looks very favorable for online social networking Web sites. This favorable environment has been fueled by the explosive growth of sites such as Facebook and MySpace, which have been aggressively pursued or acquired recently.

11. Timeline

- September 16, 2007: Review of the business plan and final decision to incorporate
- November 2007: Establish relationship with Amazon.com associate program
- December 2007: Contract with site-creation team and begin to build the Web site
- January 2008: Raise $70,000 from friends and family
- Mid-January 2008: Establish relationship with M3i Works to build the DropToMe.com Web site
- Early March 2008: Alpha launch of Web site for testing by company
- March 2008: Establish relationship with Google AdSense; establish relationships with companies who may be interested in advertising on DropToMe.com
- Late March 2008: Beta launch of Web site for testing by wider circle of users
- April 1, 2008: Full launch of the DropToMe.com Web site
- April 2008: Begin to raise $2.2 million of additional funding
- May 2008: Begin scouting locations in and around Chicago for a physical office
- June 2008: Begin contacting companies interested in market research to introduce them to our product, our idea, and the market research packages we will have available for purchase or subscription; start by focusing on smaller companies, slowly increasing our scope as time goes on
- Summer 2008: Continue to line up sponsored items; begin sales of our market research as user numbers become sufficient for statistically significant interpretation
- September 2008: Begin to hire full-time employees to aid the company's expansion

12. Critical Risks

12.1 User Sign-Up Is Slower Than Expected

It is possible that DropToMe.com simply will not see the anticipated number of new users signing up for its service. High user-account creation is key to the success of DropToMe.com. Many of the company's potential revenue streams require a high number of users to be successful. DropToMe.com has two options to counter low user-account creation: targeted advertising and guerrilla marketing campaigns on select college campuses.

The company expects that its initial users will be early technology adopters who are willing and anxious to try the next great service online. Users fitting this profile frequent certain Web sites, and by advertising on these sites, DropToMe.com can increase the number of visitors to its site, which should result in an increase of user-account creations. Particular Web sites of interest include ArsTechnica.com, Slashdot.com, Engadget.com, Penny-Arcade.com, and PvPOnline.com.

12.2 DropToMe.com Is Unable to Reach the Critical Mass Necessary to Make Its Data Attractive to Market Researchers

One of the largest potential DropToMe.com revenue sources is the sale of data to market researchers and other interested organizations. For this data to be attractive, subscribers to the DropToMe.com data service must be able to extract statistically significant populations for their analysis. It is therefore necessary that DropToMe.com reach a critical mass of registered users.

It is possible that DropToMe.com will not have a sufficient number of users to make this happen. If that is the case, DropToMe.com has three major options to consider: targeted advertising, forgoing market research revenue for longer than previously expected, and selling DropToMe.com data to sources that may not be as interested in statistical significance.

The sale of market research data is only one of four DropToMe.com revenue streams. Although the company expects that it will be the largest of the four sources of revenue, it may not be necessary for the immediate survival of the company. If revenue from Google AdSense, the Amazon.com associates program, and the sponsored items are large enough, DropToMe.com may be able to continue for a period of time without the market research data until its user base grows to an appropriate size.

Although DropToMe.com data may not be attractive to market research firms, there may still be organizations interested in the data collected by DropToMe.com. The company can consider selling its data to other clients, such as universities, as a reference for students. Though the data may not be statistically significant, they will still be quite extensive. These data would most strongly appeal to statistical analysis programs, marketing programs, and MBA programs.

12.3 Amazon.com Terminates Its Agreement with DropToMe.com

DropToMe.com, especially early in its life, will rely on the extensive database of products provided by Amazon.com. It is this information that will allow DropToMe.com users to rank items, create lists, and receive outstanding personalized product recommendations. DropToMe.com will be given access to this database through the Amazon.com associates program. The database will be stored on DropToMe.com servers to speed searches made by its users.

The Amazon.com associates program legal agreement makes it clear that Amazon.com can cancel an associate's agreement with DropToMe.com at any time. This includes the removal of all links to Amazon.com and all Amazon.com branding and buttons.

The legal agreement does not state that DropToMe.com has to delete the Amazon.com product database from its servers upon termination of the agreement. DropToMe.com would simply have to remove all links and references to Amazon.com. This will allow DropToMe .com to continue operations upon termination of the associate agreement.

It also means that DropToMe.com would no longer have access to Amazon.com information about new products as they are released. Fortunately, by granting DropToMe.com users the ability to add and modify certain product information to the Web site, updating the database will likely continue unencumbered.

In addition to user-provided content, DropToMe.com will make efforts to contact publishers of books, music, and movies directly. DropToMe.com can ensure that accurate and up-to-date product information is available to its users by receiving product information directly from media publishers. If DropToMe.com has enough business and support behind it, the company may be able to make inroads with music, movie, and book publishing companies.

Finally, DropToMe.com will always have the option of enrolling in the Buy.com associates program. Although its market position is not as attractive as that of Amazon.com, it would still give DropToMe.com access to a large database of product information.

12.4 A Competitor Steals the DropToMe.com Idea

The value of a social networking site lies not in its design but in its user base. News Corp. did not purchase MySpace.com because it lacked the expertise to create an equivalent of MySpace.com. News Corp. purchased MySpace.com to gain access to its user base. If a competitor copies DropToMe.com after its launch, it is unlikely that users will move to a competitor's equivalent Web site, thus providing DropToMe.com some level of security.

12.5 DropToMe.com Is Unable to Provide Safety for Young Children

A common concern regarding social networking Web sites involves the safety of children using the site. MySpace.com and Facebook.com have both come under public scrutiny regarding the posting of inappropriate comments or materials on their Web sites.

DropToMe.com hopes to avoid this problem by eliminating certain troublesome features of social networking Web sites (such as private messaging) and by limiting what biographical data users are permitted to post on their public profile. DropToMe.com will also ask that all users verify that they are at least 13 years of age when signing up for an account.

Finally, DropToMe.com will create a system that allows users to flag inappropriate content while identifying the posting user. If, upon prompt examination, that content is found to be inappropriate, that user will be banned from the DropToMe.com Web site and his or her profile will be removed.

12.6 The DropToMe.com Database Is Hacked and Personal Information Is Stolen

Data security will initially be handled by our Internet hosting provider. DropToMe.com will take all appropriate measures to ensure that its databases are secure, and that no personal information is stolen from the company.

12.7 DropToMe.com May Become Wildly Popular, to the Point Where Its Servers Cannot Handle the User Load

Although many of these critical risks discuss negative outcomes, the positive outcome of instant popularity could cause just as much trouble for DropToMe.com. Servers and service providers are only able to handle so much traffic and can become overwhelmed by large numbers of users.

DropToMe.com will seek a hosting company that includes provisions in its user agreements to dynamically increase bandwidth and processing power should usage increase unexpectedly. If the user load is incredibly large, DropToMe.com will accelerate its plans to purchase, set up, and run its own servers for use going forward.

12.8 Facebook and/or MySpace Shuts Down, Eliminating a Source of DropToMe.com "Advertising"

Facebook.com and MySpace.com are both incredibly popular, but they also are both prone to legal troubles and may not exist forever. The DropToMe.com business plan relies upon their existence for free advertising as DropToMe.com users post their top-five lists on these popular social networking sites in order to share their preferences with their friends. If Facebook.com and MySpace.com cease operations, DropToMe.com will require additional outside advertising. Fortunately, as mentioned earlier, there are other advertising options available to help DropToMe.com gain its initial user base.

It is also worth noting that, although the shutting down of both Facebook.com and MySpace.com would rob DropToMe.com of some advertising, it could also be a boon to the company, as former users of these social networking giants would be looking for a new social networking service online.

12.9 While the Ranking Technology Is Novel, Users Derive from It No Utility

Perhaps one of the most terrifying risks is that of discovering that there is no demand for the DropToMe.com differentiating factor: its ranking technology. Although our market research indicates that there will be some demand for this feature, it is possible that users will simply be unimpressed and therefore not use DropToMe.com. DropToMe.com provides additional benefits, including the sharing of products with friends and family, to make the site attractive even without its recommendations technology.

12.10 Key Personnel Decide to Leave the Company

DropToMe.com depends on knowledge specific to certain members of the founding team. Without particular members of the team, DropToMe.com would have to reevaluate its financials and bring on the appropriate talent.

13. Conclusion

Adora Interactive is poised to redefine online social networking. DropToMe.com brings together the successful trends of social networking and e-commerce while providing four clear, independent sources of revenue. The company's proprietary algorithm will deliver value not only to DropToMe.com users but also to its advertisers, allowing them to better reach their target demographics. The company is seeking a $2.2 million dollar investment to fuel its growth through 2009.

Recognizing Financial Terminology

THE ACCOUNTING EQUATION

Step A: Identify the accounting equation.

_____ = _____ + _____

Step B: Apply the accounting equation to find the missing number.

Total Assets   = $346,700
Total Liabilities =   196,300
Owner's Equity =   _____

Step C: Apply the accounting equation again to find the missing number.

Total Assets   = $_____
Total Liabilities =   110,000
Owner's Equity =   57,400

FINANCIAL TERMINOLOGY

Directions: The following is a list of financial terms. Identify each as an asset (A), liability (L), owner's equity (OE), revenue (R), or expense (E). In addition, place the correct identification letter in the appropriate statement column (balance sheet or income statement).

Terms	Balance Sheet	Income Statement
Cash in bank		
Accounts receivable		
Accounts payable		
Inventory on hand		
Payroll deductions payable		
Notes payable		
Capital stock		
Sales (credit)		
Sales (cash)		
Payroll		
Taxes		
Supplies		
Rent		
Building		
Equipment		
Purchases		
Cost of goods sold		
Gross profit		
Retained earnings		

Strategic Perspectives in Entrepreneurship

part

4

CHAPTER 13

Strategic Growth in Entrepreneurship

Entrepreneurial Thought

You often hear how companies have to "cross the threshold to professional management" once they get beyond a certain size and stage of development. The implication is usually that you do it by changing leaders—that is, by getting rid of the entrepreneurial founders and replacing them with professional managers. There are hundreds of individuals, however, who make the transition successfully on their own, and some of them have names that are familiar to us all: Gates, Walton, Ford, Hewlett and Packard, Galvin, Watson, Marriott, and so on. They all built companies in which they played critically important roles—but the companies weren't dependent on them for survival. They each made sure the business could go on without them. It had a value of its own.

— **JACK STACK** *A Stake in the Outcome*

Chapter Objectives

1 To introduce the importance of strategic planning for an entrepreneurial venture

2 To discuss some of the reasons entrepreneurs do not carry out strategic planning

3 To relate some of the benefits of strategic planning

4 To discuss the five stages of a typical venture life cycle: development, start-up, growth, stabilization, and innovation or decline

5 To explore the elements involved with an entrepreneurial firm

6 To examine the transition that occurs in the movement from an entrepreneurial style to a managerial approach

7 To identify the key factors that play a major role during the growth stage

8 To discuss the complex management of paradox and contradiction

9 To introduce the steps useful for breaking through the growth wall

10 To identify the unique managerial concerns with growth businesses

The Nature of Strategic Planning in Emerging Firms

Although most entrepreneurs do some form of planning for their ventures, it often tends to be informal and unsystematic.[1] The actual need for systematic planning will vary with the nature, size, and structure of the business. In other words, a small, two-person operation may successfully use informal planning because little complexity is involved. But an emerging venture that is rapidly expanding with constantly increasing personnel size and market operations will need to formalize its planning because a great deal of complexity exists.

An entrepreneur's planning will need to shift from an informal to a formal systematic style for other reasons. First is the degree of uncertainty with which the venture is attempting to become established and to grow. With greater levels of uncertainty, entrepreneurs have a stronger need to deal with the challenges that face their venture, and a more formal planning effort can help them to do this. Second, the strength of the competition (in both numbers and quality of competitors) will add to the importance of more systematic planning in order for a new venture to monitor its operations and objectives more closely.[2] Finally, the amount and type of experience the entrepreneur has may be a factor in deciding the extent of formal planning. A lack of adequate experience, either technological or business, may constrain the entrepreneur's understanding and thus necessitate formal planning to help determine future paths for the organization. It is only through this type of planning that entrepreneurs can manage entrepreneurial growth.

Strategic Planning

Strategic planning is the formulation of long-range plans for the effective management of environmental opportunities and threats in light of a venture's strengths and weaknesses. It includes defining the venture's mission, specifying achievable objectives, developing strategies, and setting policy guidelines. Dynamic in nature, the strategic management process (Figure 13.1) is the full set of commitments, decisions, and actions required for a firm to achieve strategic competitiveness and earn above-average returns. Relevant strategic inputs derived from analyses of the internal and external environments are necessary for effective strategy formulation and implementation. In turn, effective strategic actions are a prerequisite to achieving the desired outcomes of strategic competitiveness and above-average returns. Thus, the strategic management process is used to match the conditions of an ever-changing market and competitive structure with a firm's continuously evolving resources, capabilities, and core competencies (the sources of strategic inputs). Effective strategic actions that take place in the context of carefully integrated strategy formulation and implementation actions result in desired strategic outcomes.[3] Thus, strategic planning is the primary step in determining the future direction of a business. The "best" strategic plan will be influenced by many factors, among them the abilities of the entrepreneur, the complexity of the venture, and the nature of the industry. Yet, whatever the specific situation, five basic steps must be followed in strategic planning:

1. Examine the internal and external environments of the venture (strengths, weaknesses, opportunities, threats).

2. Formulate the venture's long-range and short-range strategies (mission, objectives, strategies, policies).

3. Implement the strategic plan (programs, budgets, procedures).

4. Evaluate the performance of the strategy.

5. Take follow-up action through continuous feedback.

Figure 13.1 illustrates these basic steps in a flow diagram.

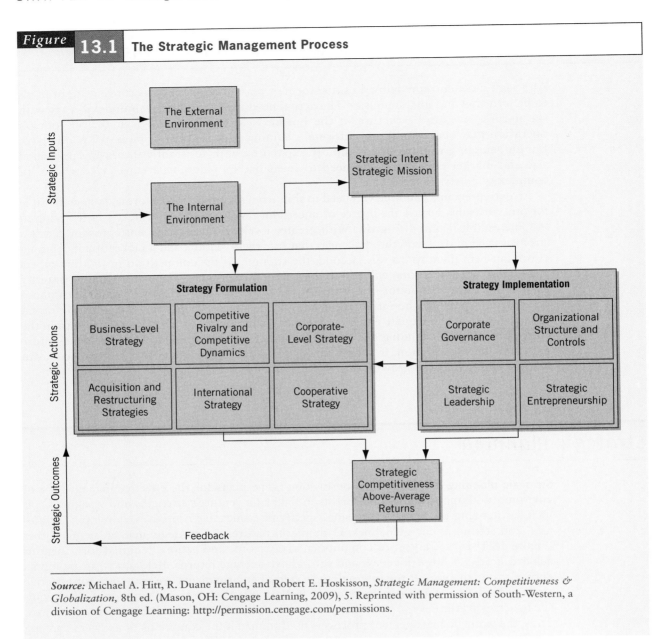

Figure **13.1** **The Strategic Management Process**

Source: Michael A. Hitt, R. Duane Ireland, and Robert E. Hoskisson, *Strategic Management: Competitiveness & Globalization*, 8th ed. (Mason, OH: Cengage Learning, 2009), 5. Reprinted with permission of South-Western, a division of Cengage Learning: http://permission.cengage.com/permissions.

The first step—examining the environment—can be one of the most critical for an emerging venture. Analyses of its external and internal environments provide a firm with the information required to develop its strategic intent and strategic mission. As shown in Figure 13.1, strategic intent and strategic mission influence strategy formulation and implementation actions. A clear review of a venture's internal and external factors is needed, and both sets of factors must be considered when performing an environmental analysis. This analysis is often called a **SWOT analysis**; SWOT is an acronym for a venture's internal *strengths* and *weaknesses* and its external *opportunities* and *threats*. The analysis should include not only the external factors most likely to occur and to have a serious impact on the company but also the internal factors most likely to affect the implementation of present and future strategic decisions. By focusing on this analysis, an emerging venture can proceed through the other steps of formulation, implementation, evaluation, and feedback.[4]

The greatest value of the strategic planning process is the "strategic thinking" it promotes among business owners. Although strategic thinking is not always articulated formally, it synthesizes the intuition and creativity of an entrepreneur into a vision for the future.[5]

The Lack of Strategic Planning

The importance of new ventures to the economy is substantial in terms of innovation, employment, and sales, and effective planning can help these new firms survive and grow. Unfortunately, research has shown a distinct lack of planning on the part of new ventures. Five reasons for the lack of strategic planning have been found:

1. **Time scarcity.** Entrepreneurs report that their time is scarce and difficult to allocate to planning in the face of day-to-day operating schedules.

2. **Lack of knowledge.** Entrepreneurs have minimal exposure to, and knowledge of, the planning process. They are uncertain of the components of the process and the sequence of those components. The entrepreneurs also are unfamiliar with many planning information sources and how they can be used.

3. **Lack of expertise/skills.** Entrepreneurs typically are generalists, and they often lack the specialized expertise necessary for the planning process.

4. **Lack of trust and openness.** Entrepreneurs are highly sensitive and guarded about their businesses and the decisions that affect them. Consequently, they are hesitant to formulate a strategic plan that requires participation by employees or outside consultants.

5. **Perception of high cost.** Entrepreneurs perceive the cost associated with planning to be very high. This fear of expensive planning causes many business owners to avoid or ignore planning as a viable process.[6]

In addition to these reasons, other factors have been reported as difficulties of the planning process. For example, both high-performing and low-performing small ventures have problems with long-range planning. Both time and expense are major obstacles. Additionally, low-performing firms report that a poor planning climate, inexperienced managers, and unfavorable economic conditions are problems. Quite obviously, strategic planning is no easy chore for new ventures. On the other hand, many benefits can be gained from such planning.

The Value of Strategic Planning

Does strategic planning pay off? Research shows it does. A number of studies have focused on the impact of planning on entrepreneurial firms.[7] These studies support the contention that strategic planning is of value to a venture. Most of the studies imply—if they do not directly state—that planning influences a venture's survival. In one study of 70,000 failed firms, lack of planning was identified as a major cause of failure,[8] and still another investigation demonstrated that firms engaged in strategic planning outperformed those that did not use such planning.[9] A study of 220 small firms further established the importance of selecting an appropriate strategy (niche strategy) for a venture to build distinctive competence and a sustainable competitive advantage.[10] Another research study examined the dynamic effects of strategies on company performance in the software industry and found that, when focus or differentiation strategies were established, performance by those firms was enhanced.[11] Finally, there was a study that examined 253 smaller firms to determine the relationship between performance and planning sophistication. The study classified companies into the following categories:

Category I: No written plan (101 firms, or 39.9 percent)

Category II: Moderately sophisticated planning, including a written plan and/or some quantified objectives, some specific plans and budgets, identification of some factors in the external environment, and procedures for anticipating or detecting differences between the plan and actual performance (89 firms, or 35.2 percent).

Category III: Sophisticated planning, including a written plan with all of the following: some quantified objectives, some specific plans and budgets, identification of some factors in the external environment, and procedures for anticipating or detecting differences between the plan and actual performance (63 firms, or 24.9 percent).

The results demonstrated that more than 88 percent of firms with Category II or Category III planning performed at or above the industry average, compared with only 40 percent of those firms with Category I planning.[12]

In summary, all of the research indicates that emerging firms that engage in strategic planning are more effective than those that do not. Most important, the studies emphasize the significance of the planning process, rather than merely the plans, as a key to successful performance.[13]

Fatal Visions in Strategic Planning

The actual execution of a strategy is almost as important as the strategy itself. Many entrepreneurs make unintentional errors when they apply a specific strategy to their own specific venture. Competitive situations differ, and the particular application of known strategies must be tailored to those unique situations.

Researcher Michael E. Porter has noted five fatal mistakes entrepreneurs continually fall prey to in their attempt to implement a strategy.[14] Outlined next are these flaws and their explanations.

- *Fatal Vision #1: Misunderstanding industry attractiveness.* Too many entrepreneurs associate attractive industries with those that are growing the fastest, appear to be glamorous, or use the fanciest technology. This is wrong, because attractive industries have high barriers to entry and the fewest substitutes. The more high-tech or high-glamour a business is, the more likely a lot of new competitors will enter and make it unprofitable.

- *Fatal Vision #2: No real competitive advantage.* Some entrepreneurs merely copy or imitate the strategy of their competitors. That may be an easy tactic, and it is certainly less risky, but it means that an entrepreneur has no competitive advantage. To succeed, new ventures must develop unique ways to compete.

- *Fatal Vision #3: Pursuing an unattainable competitive position.* Many aggressive entrepreneurs pursue a position of dominance in a fast-growing industry. However, they are so busy getting off the ground and finding people to buy their products that they forget what will happen if the venture succeeds. For example, a successful software program will be imitated quickly; therefore, the advantage it alone gives cannot be sustained. Real competitive advantage in software comes from servicing and supporting buyers, providing regular upgrades, and getting a company online with customers so their computer departments depend on the organization. That creates barriers to entry. Sometimes, small companies simply cannot sustain an advantage.

- *Fatal Vision #4: Compromising strategy for growth.* A careful balance must exist between growth and the competitive strategy that makes a new venture successful. If an entrepreneur sacrifices his or her venture's unique strategy in order to have fast growth, then the venture may grow out of business. Although fast growth can be tempting in certain industries, it is imperative that entrepreneurs also maintain and grow their strategic advantage.

- *Fatal Vision #5: Failure to explicitly communicate the venture's strategy to employees.* It is essential for every entrepreneur to clearly communicate the company's strategy to every employee. Never assume that employees already know the strategy. Always be explicit.

According to Porter, "One of the fundamental benefits of developing a strategy is that it creates unity, or consistency of action, throughout a company. Every department in the organization works toward the same objectives. But if people do not know what the objectives are, how can they work toward them? If they do not have a clear sense that low cost, say, is your ultimate aim, then all their day-to-day actions are not going to be reinforcing that goal. In any company, employees are making critical choices every minute. An explicit strategy will help them make the right ones."[15]

Entrepreneurial and Strategic Actions

Entrepreneurship and strategic management are both dynamic processes concerned with firm performance. Strategic management calls for firms to establish and exploit competitive advantages within a particular environmental context. Entrepreneurship promotes the search for competitive advantages through product, process, and market innovations. A new venture typically is created to pursue the marketplace promise from innovations.

Researchers R. Duane Ireland, Michael A. Hitt, S. Michael Camp, and Donald L. Sexton argue that entrepreneurial and strategic actions often are intended to find new market or competitive space for a firm to create wealth. Firms try to find fundamentally new ways of doing business that will disrupt an industry's existing competitive rules, leading to the development of new business models that create new competitive life forms. The degree to which a firm acts entrepreneurially in terms of innovativeness, risk-taking, and proactivity is related to dimensions of strategic management. Within these commonalties between entrepreneurship and strategic management are specific domains of innovation, networks, internationalization, organizational learning, top management teams and governance, and growth (see Figure 13.2). Understanding the critical intersections of these specific domains allow entrepreneurs to

| *Figure* | **13.2** | **The Integration of Entrepreneurial and Strategic Actions** |

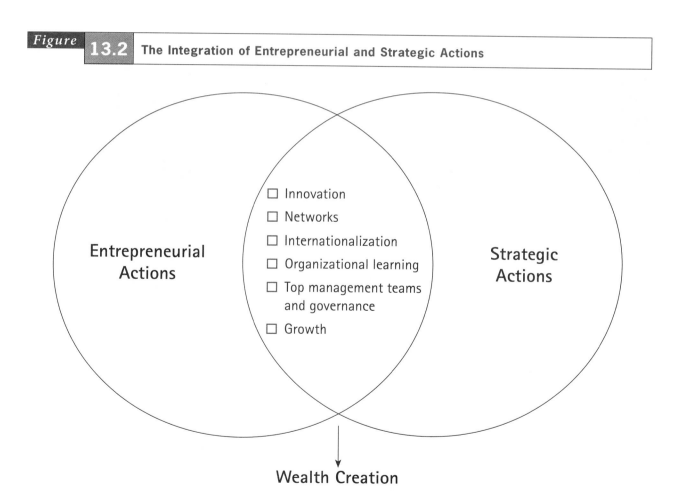

Source: R. Duane Ireland, Michael A. Hitt, S. Michael Camp, and Donald L. Sexton, "Integrating Entrepreneurship and Strategic Management Actions to Create Firm Wealth," *Academy of Management Executive* 15, no. 1 (February 2001): 51.

increase their knowledge, which in turn leads to higher quality entrepreneurial and strategic actions.[16]

Strategic Positioning: The Entrepreneurial Edge

Strategic competition can be thought of as the process of perceiving new positions that attract customers from established positions or draw new customers into the market. In principle, incumbents and entrepreneurs face the same challenges in finding new strategic positions. In practice, entrepreneurs often have the edge.

Strategic positionings often are not obvious, and finding them requires creativity and insight. Entrepreneurs frequently discover unique positions that have been available but simply overlooked by established competitors. In addition, entrepreneurial ventures can prosper by occupying a position that a competitor once held but has ceded through years of imitation and straddling.

Fundamental approaches to strategic positioning include establishing and defending a defensible position, leveraging resources to dominate a market, and pursuing opportunities to establish new markets (see Table 13.1). Entrepreneurs must understand that the pursuit of opportunities provides the best choice for capitalizing on change.

Most commonly, new positions open up because of change: New customer groups or purchase occasions arise, new needs emerge as societies evolve, new distribution channels

Table 13.1	**Strategic Approaches: Position, Leverage, and Opportunities**		
	Position	**Leverage**	**Opportunities**
Strategic logic	Establish position	Leverage resources	Pursue opportunities
Strategic steps	Identify an attractive market Locate a defensible position Fortify and defend	Establish a vision Build resources Leverage across markets	Jump into the confusion Keep moving Seize opportunities Finish strong
Strategic question	Where should we be?	What should we be?	How should we proceed?
Source of advantage	Unique, valuable position with tightly integrated activity system	Unique, valuable, inimitable resources	Key processes and unique simple rules
Works best in	Slowly changing, well-structured markets	Moderately changing, well-structured markets	Rapidly changing, ambiguous markets
Duration of advantage	Sustained	Sustained	Unpredictable
Risk	It will be too difficult to alter position as conditions change	Company will be too slow to build new resources as conditions change	Managers will be too tentative in executing on promising opportunities
Performance goal	Profitability	Long-term dominance	Growth

Source: Reprinted by permission of *Harvard Business Review* from "Strategy as Simple Rules," by Kathleen M. Eisenhardt and Donald N. Sull (January 2001): 109. Copyright © 2001 by the Harvard Business School Publishing Corporation; all rights reserved.

appear, new technologies are developed, and new machinery or information systems become available. When such changes happen, entrepreneurial ventures unencumbered by a long history in the industry can often more easily perceive the potential for a new way of competing. Unlike incumbents, these organizations can be more flexible because they face no trade-offs with their existing activities.[17]

An Entrepreneurial Strategy Matrix Model

Based on the structure of traditional strategy matrices (such as the Boston Casualty Group [BCG] matrix) that have been used for portfolio analysis, researchers Matthew C. Sonfield and Robert N. Lussier developed an entrepreneurial strategy matrix that measures risk and innovation.[18] For the purpose of this matrix, innovation is defined as the creation of something new and different. In terms of measurement, the newer and more different the proposed product or service is, the higher it would be scored on a measurement scale.

Risk is defined as the probability of major financial loss. What are the chances of the entrepreneurial venture failing? How serious would the resulting financial loss be? Whereas many ways exist to increase innovation, reducing risk largely focuses on financial factors, with a secondary consideration of self-image and ego.

The model allows even the most inexperienced entrepreneurs to characterize their new or existing venture situations and identify appropriate strategies. The model places innovation on the vertical axis and risk on the horizontal axis. It denotes the levels of these two variables by using I and R for high levels and i and r for low levels (Figure 13.3).

The value of the entrepreneurial strategy matrix is that it suggests appropriate avenues for different entrepreneurs. When the entrepreneur identifies the cell that best describes the new or existing venture being contemplated, then certain strategies are indicated as more likely to be effective (Figure 13.4).

It should be obvious that certain cells are more advantageous than others. A high-innovation/low-risk venture is certainly preferable to a low-innovation/high-risk one. Yet, for every venture found in *I-r*, large numbers of ventures can be found in *i-R*. Risk is more common than innovativeness in the business world.

Figure 13.3   The Entrepreneurial Strategy Matrix: Independent Variables

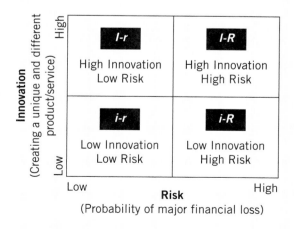

Source: Matthew C. Sonfield and Robert N. Lussier, "The Entrepreneurial Strategic Matrix: A Model for New and Ongoing Ventures." Reprinted with permission from *Business Horizons*, May/June 1997, by the trustees at Indiana University, Kelley School of Business.

Figure **13.4**   **The Entrepreneurial Strategy Matrix: Appropriate Strategies**

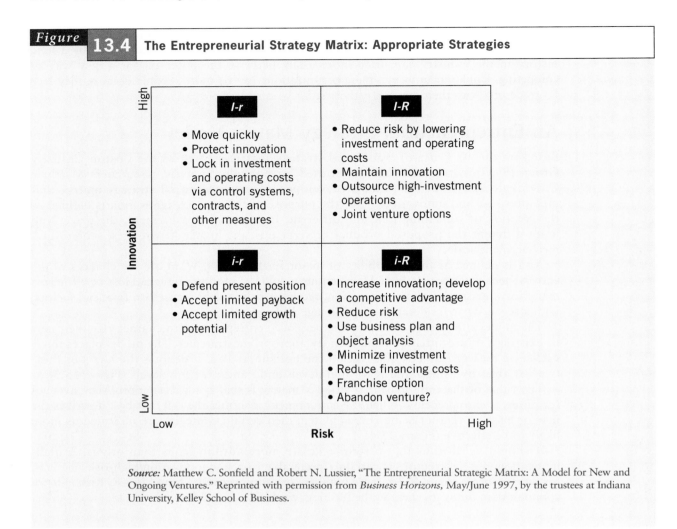

The strategic implications of the matrix are twofold. First, entrepreneurs will find certain cells preferable to others, and one set of appropriate strategies involves moving from one cell to another. Second, such movement is not always possible for an entrepreneur, so the appropriate strategies involve reducing risk and increasing innovation within a cell.

Managing Entrepreneurial Growth

Managing entrepreneurial growth may be the most critical tactic for the future success of business enterprises. After initiation of a new venture, the entrepreneur needs to develop an understanding of management change. This is a great challenge, because it often encompasses the art of balancing mobile and dynamic factors.[19]

Thus, the survival and growth of a new venture requires that the entrepreneur possess both strategic and tactical skills and abilities. Which specific skills and abilities are needed depend in part on the venture's current development; Figure 13.5 illustrates the typical venture life cycle. Managing growth can be a formidable challenge to the successful development of any venture.

| **Figure** | **13.5** | A Venture's Typical Life Cycle |

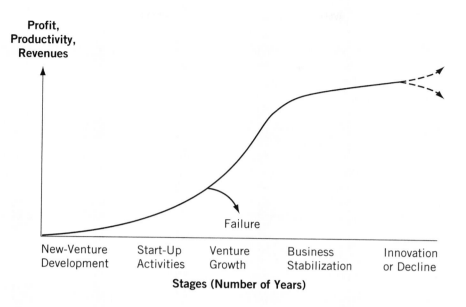

Venture Development Stages

As noted, Figure 13.5 presents the traditional life-cycle stages of an enterprise. These stages include new-venture development, start-up activities, growth, stabilization, and innovation or decline. Other authors have described these stages in different terms. For example, Alfred Chandler has presented a firm's evolution in the following stages:

1. Initial expansion and accumulation of resources

2. Rationalization of the use of resources

3. Expansion into new markets to assure the continued use of resources

4. Development of new structures to ensure continuing mobilization of resources[20]

These four phases are, in effect, the same major stages illustrated in Figure 13.5, with the exception of stabilization. In short, authors generally agree regarding a venture's life cycle. Presented next are the five major stages.

New-Venture Development

The first stage, new-venture development, consists of activities associated with the initial formulation of the venture. This initial phase is the foundation of the entrepreneurial process and requires creativity and assessment. In addition to the accumulation and expansion of resources, this is a creative, assessment, and networking stage for initial entrepreneurial strategy formulation. The enterprise's general philosophy, mission, scope, and direction are determined during this stage.

Start-Up Activities

The second stage, start-up activities, encompasses the foundation work needed to create a formal business plan, search for capital, carry out marketing activities, and develop an effective entrepreneurial team. These activities typically demand an aggressive entrepreneurial strategy with maximum efforts devoted to launching the venture. This stage is similar to Chandler's description of the rationalization of the use of resources. It is typified by strategic and operational planning steps designed to identify the firm's competitive advantage and uncover funding sources. Marketing and financial considerations tend to be paramount during this stage.[21]

Growth

The **growth stage** often requires major changes in entrepreneurial strategy. Competition and other market forces call for the reformulation of strategies. For example, some firms find themselves "growing out" of business because they are unable to cope with the growth of their ventures. Highly creative entrepreneurs sometimes are unable, or unwilling, to meet the administrative challenges that accompany this growth stage. As a result, they leave the enterprise and move on to other ventures.

This growth stage presents newer and more substantial problems than those the entrepreneur faced during the start-up stage.[22] These newer challenges force the entrepreneur into developing a different set of skills while maintaining an "entrepreneurial perspective" for the organization.[23] The growth stage is a transition from entrepreneurial one-person leadership to managerial team-oriented leadership.

Business Stabilization

The **stabilization stage** is a result of both market conditions and the entrepreneur's efforts. During this stage, a number of developments commonly occur, including increased competition, consumer indifference to the entrepreneur's good(s) or service(s), and saturation of the market with a host of "me too" look-alikes. Sales often begin to stabilize, and the entrepreneur must start to think about where the enterprise will go during the next three to five years. This stage is often a "swing" stage in that it precedes the period when the firm either swings into higher gear and greater profitability or swings toward decline and failure. During this stage, innovation is often critical to future success.

Innovation or Decline

Firms that fail to innovate will die. Financially successful enterprises often will try to acquire other innovative firms, thereby ensuring their own growth. Also, many firms will work on new product/service development to complement current offerings.

All of a venture's life-cycle stages are important strategic points, and each requires a different set of strategies. However, this chapter concentrates specifically on the growth stage because entrepreneurs often ignore it. This happens not because of incompetence but rather because of the almost hypnotic effect a successful growth stage can cause. We shall now examine the key factors that affect the ability to manage this stage.

The Entrepreneurial Company in the Twenty-First Century

The pace and magnitude of change will continue to accelerate in the new millennium; having the evolution and transformation of entrepreneurial firms match this pace will be critical. How to build dynamic capabilities that are differentiated from those of the emerging competitors is the major challenge for growing firms that seek to adapt to the changing landscape. Two ways of building dynamic capabilities are internal (utilization of the creativity and knowledge from employees) and external[24] (the search for external competencies to complement the firm's existing capabilities).[25] The trend toward globalization, the advent of new technology, and the information movement are all examples of forces in this new millennium that are causing firms to examine their cultures, structures, and systems for flexibility and adaptability. Innovation and entrepreneurial thinking are essential elements in the strategies of growing ventures.

It has been noted that entrepreneurs (1) perceive an opportunity, (2) pursue this opportunity, and (3) believe that the success of the venture is possible.[26] This belief is often due to the uniqueness of the idea, the strength of the product, or some special knowledge or skill the entrepreneur possesses. These same factors must be translated into the organization itself as the venture grows.

The Entrepreneurial Mind-Set

It is important for the venture's manager to maintain an entrepreneurial frame of mind. Figure 13.6 illustrates the danger of entrepreneurs evolving into bureaucrats who in turn stifle innovation. Table 13.2 provides a delineation of the differences between a managerial mind-set versus an entrepreneurial mind-set from the perspective of decision-making assumptions, values, beliefs, and approaches to problems.

Figure **13.6** **The Entrepreneurial Mind-Set**

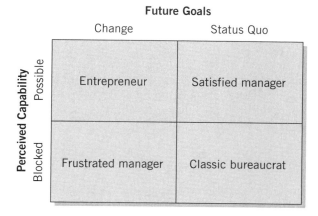

Table **13.2** **The Managerial Versus the Entrepreneurial Mind-Set**

	Managerial Mind-Set	Entrepreneurial Mind-Set
Decision-making assumptions	The past is the best predictor of the future. Most business decisions can be quantified.	A new idea or an insight from a unique experience is likely to provide the best estimate of emerging trends.
Values	The best decisions are those based on quantitative analyses. Rigorous analyses are highly valued for making critical decisions.	New insights and real-world experiences are more highly valued than results based on historical data.
Beliefs	Law of large numbers: Chaos and uncertainty can be resolved by systematically analyzing the right data.	Law of small numbers: A single incident or several isolated incidents quickly become pivotal for making decisions regarding future trends.
Approach to problems	Problems represent an unfortunate turn of events that threaten financial projections. Problems must be resolved with substantiated analyses.	Problems represent an opportunity to detect emerging changes and possibly new business opportunities.

Source: Mike Wright, Robert E. Hoskisson, and Lowell W. Busenitz, "Firm Rebirth: Buyouts as Facilitators of Strategic Growth and Entrepreneurship," *Academy of Management Executive* 15, no. 1 (2001): 114.

In some cases, success will affect an entrepreneur's willingness to change and innovate. This is particularly true when the enterprise has developed a sense of complacency and the entrepreneur likes this environment: The person does not want to change. In fact, some entrepreneurs will create a bureaucratic environment in which orders are issued from the top down and change initiated at the lower levels is not tolerated.[27] As a result, no one in the venture is willing (or encouraged) to become innovative or entrepreneurial, because the owner/founder stifles such activity.

One study found that the entrepreneur directly affects the firm's growth orientation as measured by profitability goals, product/market goals, human resource goals, and flexibility goals.[28] If the entrepreneur hopes to maintain the creative climate that helped launch the venture in the first place, specific steps or measures must be taken.

Building the Adaptive Firm

It is important for entrepreneurs to establish a business that remains flexible beyond start-up. An **adaptive firm** increases opportunity for its employees, initiates change, and instills a desire to be innovative. Entrepreneurs can build an adaptive firm in several ways.[29] The following are not inflexible rules, but they do enhance a venture's chance of remaining adaptive and innovative both through and beyond the growth stage.

Share the Entrepreneur's Vision

The entrepreneur's vision must be permeated throughout the organization for employees to understand the company's direction and share in the responsibility for its growth. The entrepreneur can communicate the vision directly to the employees through meetings, conversations, or seminars. It also can be shared through symbolic events or activities such as social gatherings, recognition events, and displays. Whatever the format, having shared vision allows the venture's personnel to catch the dream and become an integral part of creating the future.[30]

Increase the Perception of Opportunity

This can be accomplished with careful job design. The work should have defined objectives for which people will be responsible. Each level of the hierarchy should be kept informed of its role in producing the final output of the product or service. This often is known as "staying close to the customer." Another way to increase the perception of opportunity is through a careful coordination and integration of the functional areas. This allows employees in different functional areas to work together as a cohesive whole.

Institutionalize Change as the Venture's Goal

This entails a preference for innovation and change rather than preservation of the status quo. If opportunity is to be perceived, the environment of the enterprise must not only encourage it but also establish it as a goal. Within this context, a desire for opportunity can exist if resources are made available and departmental barriers are reduced.

Instill the Desire to Be Innovative

The desire of personnel to pursue opportunity must be carefully nurtured. Words alone will not create an innovative climate.[31] Specific steps, such as the following, should be taken.

A REWARD SYSTEM

Explicit forms of recognition should be given to individuals who pursue innovative opportunities. For example, bonuses, awards, salary advances, and promotions should be tied directly to the innovative attempts of personnel.

entrepreneurship **in practice**

The Difficulty of Growth at Microsoft

When a company gets as large as Microsoft, continuing to grow that company can prove difficult. Microsoft has benefited from selling the most widely used operating system and office productivity suite, which has resulted in its fortified position for the last two decades. Microsoft has been able to continue its strategy of evolutionary changes to Microsoft Windows and Microsoft Office, which primarily consisted of adding features to necessitate that its customers pay for upgrades.

This model proved effective for Microsoft until it brought its most recent operating system—called Vista—to market. For the first time in the company's history, its customers demanded that computer manufacturers such as Dell, which had begun shipping computers with Vista, return to providing XP, the preceding operation system, as an option. Clearly, Microsoft's strategy was no longer going to provide the growth that it had once enjoyed.

Microsoft will not be shutting down any time soon, given that it generated net profits of $14 billion in 2007. Yet, outside of the lackluster sales of Vista, the company is facing some significant hurdles. The first of these is Google, which is by far the largest threat to Microsoft's technical dominance. Google has slowly encroached on Microsoft's territory, but Microsoft's core products have remained insulated. As more software becomes freely available via the Internet, Microsoft has been forced to recognize that its revenue model of charging licensing fees may no longer be viable.

The difficulty for Microsoft in taking the approach that Google has taken is that it requires it to recreate its culture. When an organization has operated for more than 30 years by charging its customers for its products, restructuring the company to focus on ways in which customers can instead receive products for free by generating advertising revenue is no easy task. Microsoft's early attempts at building an online advertising business have not proven effective, which partly explains its recent $44 billion bid for Yahoo. By acquiring Yahoo, Microsoft would gain a company already familiar with building a Web-based business and generating revenue through advertising.

In 2005, Ray Ozzie—one of the creators of Lotus Notes, a popular e-mail client—was brought into Microsoft as one of three chief technology officers. His addition to Microsoft's executive team was touted as a major coup for the company and a clear indication of its commitment to being proactive as the market shifted to an open-source platform. In June 2006, Ozzie took over as Microsoft's chief software architect, a position previously held by Bill Gates. Shortly thereafter, the company announced a historic partnership with Novell that would make Microsoft's products more compatible with Novell's open-source SUSE Linux software. Ironically, Microsoft discovered that it sold more products when it allowed Windows to operate freely with Linux.

The reality is that Microsoft has not willingly transitioned to a new model. In fact, the company's top management was reported comparing open-source software to socialism; yet, with its recent strategic decisions, Microsoft has revealed that it has decided to embrace rather than fight what the market has been indicating for several years, which is that its old business model will no longer be effective. Ozzie has been given the daunting task of "Webifying" everything Microsoft has to offer, from its business and consumer software to its Xbox gaming systems.

The company appears to be further plagued by the departure of its long-time CEO Bill Gates, who plans to transition to part-time chairman of the board. When Microsoft recently announced that it was promoting greater interoperability, Gates did not participate. Some analysts would point to Gates's departure as a sure sign of more trouble ahead for Microsoft; however, others have argued that Gates is ill equipped to take the company where it needs to go, which is an important consideration for all entrepreneurs. No matter how successful a company becomes, it has to be willing to change to continue to grow. If current management cannot make the transition, they have to be willing to allow those who can to take over.

Source: Adapted from David Kirkpatrick, "Microsoft Is Finally Growing Up," *Fortune*, February 22, 2008, http://money.cnn.com/2008/02/22/technology/kirkpatrick_microsoft.fortune/index.htm (accessed April 15, 2008).

AN ENVIRONMENT THAT ALLOWS FOR FAILURE

The fear of failure must be minimized by the general recognition that often many attempts are needed before a success is achieved. This does not imply that failure is sought or desired. However, learning from failure, as opposed to expecting punishment for it, is promoted. When this type of environment exists, people become willing to accept the challenge of change and innovation.

FLEXIBLE OPERATIONS

Flexibility creates the possibility of change taking place and having a positive effect. If a venture remains too rigidly tied to plans or strategies, it will not be responsive to new technologies, customer changes, or environmental shifts. Innovation will not take place because it will not "fit in."

THE DEVELOPMENT OF VENTURE TEAMS

In order for the environment to foster innovation, venture teams and team performance goals need to be established. These must not be just work groups but visionary, committed teams that have the authority to create new directions, set new standards, and challenge the status quo.[32]

The Transition from an Entrepreneurial Style to a Managerial Approach

The transitions between stages of a venture are complemented (or in some cases retarded) by the entrepreneur's ability to make a transition in style. A key transition occurs during the growth stage of a venture when the entrepreneur shifts into a managerial style. This is not easy to do. As researchers Charles W. Hofer and Ram Charan have noted, "Among the different transitions that are possible, probably the most difficult to achieve and also perhaps the most important for organizational development is that of moving from a one-person, entrepreneurially managed firm to one run by a functionally organized, professional management team."[33]

A number of problems can occur during this transition, especially if the enterprise is characterized by factors such as (1) a highly centralized decision-making system, (2) an overdependence on one or two key individuals, (3) an inadequate repertoire of managerial skills and training, and (4) a paternalistic atmosphere.[34] Although these characteristics often are effective for the new venture's start-up and initial survival, they pose a threat to the firm's development during the growth stage. Quite often, these characteristics inhibit development by detracting from the entrepreneur's ability to manage the growth stage successfully.

Balancing the Focus—Entrepreneurial Versus Managerial

When managing the growth stage, entrepreneurs must remember two important points. First, an adaptive firm needs to retain certain entrepreneurial characteristics to encourage innovation and creativity. Second, the entrepreneur needs to translate this spirit of innovation and creativity to his or her personnel while personally making a transition toward a more managerial style.[35] This critical entrepreneur/manager balance is extremely difficult to achieve. Although every firm wants to be as innovative, flexible, and creative as Apple, Google, and Facebook, there are thousands of new restaurants, internet businesses, retail stores, and high tech ventures that presumably have tried to be innovative and grow but have failed.

Remaining entrepreneurial while making the transition to some of the more administrative traits is vital to the successful growth of a venture. Table 13.3 provides a framework for

Table **13.3**	The Entrepreneurial Culture Versus the Administrative Culture

	Entrepreneurial Focus		Administrative Focus	
	Characteristics	Pressures	Characteristics	Pressures
Strategic Orientation	Driven by perception of opportunity	Diminishing opportunities Rapidly changing technology, consumer economics, social values, and political rules	Driven by controlled resources	Social contracts Performance measurement criteria Planning systems and cycles
Commitment to Seize Opportunities	Revolutionary, with short duration	Action orientation Narrow decision windows Acceptance of reasonable risks Few decision constituencies	Evolutionary, with long duration	Acknowledgement of multiple constituencies Negotiation about strategic course Risk reduction Coordination with existing resource base
Commitment of Resources	Many stages, with minimal exposure at each stage	Lack of predictable resource needs Lack of control over the environment Social demands for appropriate use of resources Foreign competition Demands for more efficient use	A single stage, with complete commitment out of decision	Need to reduce risk Incentive compensation Turnover in managers Capital budgeting systems Formal planning systems
Control of Resources	Episodic use or rent of required resources	Increased resource specialization Long resource life compared with need Risk of obsolescence Risk inherent in the identified opportunity Inflexibility of permanent commitment to resources	Ownership or employment of required resources	Power, status, and financial rewards Coordination of activity Efficiency measures Inertia and cost of change Industry structures
Management Structure	Flat, with multiple informal networks	Coordination of key non-controlled resources Challenge to hierarchy Employees' desire for independence	Hierarchy	Need for clearly defined authority and responsibility Organizational culture Reward systems Management theory

comparing the entrepreneurial and administrative characteristics and pressures relative to five major factors: strategic orientation, commitment to seize opportunities, commitment of resources, control of resources, and management structure. Each of these five areas is critical to the balance needed to manage entrepreneurially. At the two ends of the continuum (from entrepreneurial focus to administrative focus) are specific points of view. One study characterized these using a question format.

The Entrepreneur's Point of View

- Where is the opportunity?
- How do I capitalize on it?
- What resources do I need?
- How do I gain control over them?
- What structure is best?

The Administrative Point of View

- What resources do I control?
- What structure determines our organization's relationship to its market?
- How can I minimize the impact of others on my ability to perform?
- What opportunity is appropriate?[36]

The logic behind the variance in the direction of these questions can be presented in a number of different ways. For example, the commitment of resources in the entrepreneurial frame of mind responds to changing environmental needs, whereas the managerial point of view is focused on the reduction of risk. In the control of resources, entrepreneurs will avoid ownership because of the risk of obsolescence and the need for more flexibility, whereas managers will view ownership as a means to accomplish efficiency and stability. In terms of structure, the entrepreneurial emphasis is placed on a need for flexibility and independence, whereas the administrative focus is placed on ensuring integration with a complexity of tasks, a desire for order, and controlled reward systems.

These examples of differences in focus help establish the important issues involved at both ends of the managerial spectrum. Each point of view—entrepreneurial and administrative—has important considerations that need to be balanced if effective growth is going to take place.

Understanding the Growth Stage

The growth stage often signals the beginning of a metamorphosis from a personal venture to a group-structured operation. Domination by the lead entrepreneur gives way to a team approach based heavily on coordination and flexibility.

Key Factors During the Growth Stage

Entrepreneurs must understand four key factors about the specific managerial actions that are necessary during the growth stage. These factors are control, responsibility, tolerance of failure, and change.

CONTROL

Growth creates problems in command and control. When dealing with these problems, entrepreneurs need to answer three critical questions: (1) Does the control system imply trust? (2) Does the resource allocation system imply trust? (3) Is it easier to ask permission than to ask forgiveness? These questions reveal a great deal about the control of a venture. If they are answered with "yes," the venture is moving toward a good blend of control and participation. If they are answered with "no," the reasons for each negative response should be closely examined.

RESPONSIBILITY

As the company grows, the distinction between authority and responsibility becomes more apparent. This is because authority can always be delegated, but it is most important to create a sense of responsibility. This action establishes flexibility, innovation, and a supportive environment. People tend to look beyond the job alone if a sense of responsibility is developed, so the growth stage is better served by the innovative activity and shared responsibility of all of the firm's members.

TOLERANCE OF FAILURE

Even if a venture has avoided the initial start-up pitfalls and has expanded to the growth stage, it is still important to maintain a tolerance of failure. The level of failure the entrepreneur experienced and learned from at the start of the venture should be the same level expected, tolerated, and learned from in the growth stage. Although no firm should seek failure, to continually innovate and grow it should tolerate a certain degree of failure as opposed to punishing it.

Three distinct forms of failure should be distinguished:

- **Moral failure.** This form of failure is a violation of internal trust. Because the firm is based on mutual expectations and trust, this violation is a serious failure that can result in negative consequences.

- **Personal failure.** This form of failure is brought about by a lack of skill or application. Usually, responsibility for this form of failure is shared by the firm and the individual. Normally, therefore, an attempt is made to remedy the situation in a mutually beneficial way.

- **Uncontrollable failure.** This form of failure is caused by external factors and is the most difficult to prepare for or deal with. Resource limitations, strategic direction, and market changes are examples of forces outside the control of employees. Top management must carefully analyze the context of this form of failure and work to prevent its recurrence.

CHANGE

Planning, operations, and implementation are all subject to continual changes as the venture moves through the growth stage and beyond. Retaining an innovative and opportunistic posture during growth requires a sense of change and variation from the norm. Entrepreneurs must realize, however, that change holds many implications for the enterprise in terms of resources, people, and structure. It is therefore important during growth that the flexibility regarding change be preserved. This allows for faster managerial response to environmental conditions.

Managing Paradox and Contradiction

When a venture experiences surges in growth, a number of structural factors begin to present multiple challenges. Entrepreneurs constantly struggle over whether to organize these factors—such as cultural elements, staffing and development of personnel, and appraisal and rewards—in a rigid, bureaucratic design or a flexible, organic design.

Research has shown that new-venture managers experiencing growth, particularly in emerging industries, need to adopt flexible, organic structures.[37] Rigid, bureaucratic structures are best suited for mature, stabilized companies. Thus, the cultural elements need to follow a flexible design of autonomy, risk taking, and entrepreneurship. This type of culture is a renewal of the entrepreneur's original force that created the venture. Although the entrepreneur's focus makes a transition toward a more administrative style, as mentioned earlier, the culture of the organization must be permeated with a constant renewal of the virtues of innovation and entrepreneurship.

When entrepreneurs design a flexible structure for high growth, they must realize that a number of contradictory forces are at work in certain other structural factors. Consider the following.

BUREAUCRATIZATION VERSUS DECENTRALIZATION

Increased hiring stimulates bureaucracy: Firms formalize procedures as staffing doubles and triples. Employee participation and autonomy decline, and internal labor markets develop. Tied to growth, however, is also an increased diversity in product offering that favors less formalized decision processes, greater decentralization, and the recognition that the firm's existing human resources lack the necessary skills to manage the broadening portfolio.

ENVIRONMENT VERSUS STRATEGY

High environmental turbulence and competitive conditions favor company cultures that support risk taking, autonomy, and employee participation in decision making. Firms confront competitors, however, through strategies whose implementation depends on the design of formal systems that inhibit risk taking and autonomy.

STRATEGIC EMPHASES: QUALITY VERSUS COST VERSUS INNOVATION

Rapidly growing firms strive to simultaneously control costs, enhance product quality, and improve product offerings. Minimizing costs and undercutting competitors' product prices, however, are best achieved by traditional hierarchical systems of decision making and evaluations. Yet these strategies conflict with the kinds of autonomous processes most likely to encourage the pursuit of product quality and innovation.[38]

These factors emphasize the importance of managing paradox and contradiction. Growth involves the multiple challenges of (1) the stresses and strains induced by attempts to control costs while simultaneously enhancing quality and creating new products to maintain competitive parity, and (2) centralizing to retain control while simultaneously decentralizing to encourage the contributions of autonomous, self-managed professionals to the embryonic corporate culture. Rapidly growing firms are challenged to strike a balance among these multiple pulls when designing their managerial systems.

Confronting the Growth Wall

In attempting to develop a managerial ability to deal with venture growth, many entrepreneurial owners confront a growth wall that seems too gigantic to overcome. Thus, they are unable to begin the process of handling the challenges that growth brings about.

Researchers have identified a number of fundamental changes that confront rapid-growth firms, including instant size increases, a sense of infallibility, internal turmoil, and extraordinary resource needs. In addressing these changes that can build a growth wall, successful growth-oriented firms have exhibited a few consistent themes:

- The entrepreneur is able to envision and anticipate the firm as a larger entity.
- The team needed for tomorrow is hired and developed today.
- The original core vision of the firm is constantly and zealously reinforced.
- New "big-company" processes are introduced gradually as supplements to, rather than replacements for, existing approaches.
- Hierarchy is minimized.
- Employees hold a financial stake in the firm.[39]

These themes are important for entrepreneurs to keep in mind as they develop their abilities to manage growth.

the entrepreneurial process

From Entrepreneur to Manager

For many entrepreneurs, one of the most difficult tasks is to make the successful transition from a creative, task-juggling entrepreneur to a business-skill-applying manager. A number of top entrepreneurial experts were asked their advice on making this transition successfully. Their answers were consolidated into the following list of key management strategies to help entrepreneurs grow their companies and boost their bottom line.

- **Don't be the company handyperson.** When starting a new business, the entrepreneur must be able to do every job in the company. But as the company grows, the entrepreneur must learn to delegate. If he or she continues to do every little task, the business will certainly suffer. Jay Conrad Levinson, coauthor of *Guerrilla Marketing Online Weapons*, has some advice on how to escape from the do-it-yourself trap. He suggests that the owner keep a log of all the things he or she does. "You'll see there are things you must do and things you don't have to do. Never do anything you can delegate," Levinson says. By delegating, the entrepreneur will have more time to concentrate on essential leadership functions, such as setting long-term strategic goals.

- **Hire to your shortcomings.** Oftentimes, the strong entrepreneurial characteristics of a new venture owner—such as the willingness to take risks—can become a hazard to an established business, according to Ned Herrmann, author of *The Whole Brain Business Book*. "Many business owners keep entrepreneuring when they should be focusing on the quality of product, competition, receivables, the kind of stuff that's boring," Herrmann says. The best remedy is to hire managers that complement the owner by filling in knowledge gaps. Herrmann explains that "Entrepreneurs tend to hire in their own image, so you get people who all think alike. But if you hire people who are different, it will lead to more innovative ideas."

- **Don't overhire.** Today's labor market offers numerous staffing alternatives—such as temps, part-timers, and contract workers—that enable entrepreneurial firms to keep taxes and insurance costs low. These alternatives also give businesses the flexibility to match their labor costs to the demand of their services, according to the late Irving Grousbeck, who was a consulting professor of management at the Stanford Business School and cofounder of Continental Cablevision. "In addition," he stated, "if one of your key people is sick or out for some other reason, you can bring in a trained person on an as-needed basis."

- **Call out the "SWOT" team.** David H. Bangs, Jr., author of *The Business Planning Guide*, suggests that a SWOT meeting should be held at least once a year to keep an ongoing business on track. The meeting would evaluate the company's strengths, weaknesses, opportunities, and threats (SWOT) in order to set goals and objectives for the company. SWOT meetings should encourage frank, open discussions to be most productive. In addition, all employees should be required to attend, and the meeting should be facilitated by someone who is not involved in the company's day-to-day operations.

- **Give employees a stake in the company's success.** In a small, lean business, it is important to keep core employees motivated and loyal. "If you only have a small number of people working for you, obviously you count on these people for the success of the company," Joanna T. Lau, president of Lau Technologies in Acton, Massachusetts, says. Lau, also Ernst & Young's 1995 Turnaround Entrepreneur of the Year award winner, adds, "You might want to provide some of those people with the opportunity for equity in the business to create better loyalty."

- **Hold down expenses.** The math is simple. Regardless of how much business is done, if a company's costs are outweighing its revenues, hard times are sure to follow. William F. Williams, president and CEO of Glory Foods Inc. in Columbus, Ohio, which was *Black Enterprise* magazine's Emerging Company of

Continued

the Year for 1996, makes a conscious effort to keep his costs down by consistently pressing for better deals from suppliers and service providers. "The most important thing is to negotiate the best possible cost reductions you can at the outset of every business relationship," Williams claims. Cost-cutting opportunities are everywhere, such as bargaining rent space and shopping for interest rates.

- **Go global.** "If you have an established business and you're not pursuing the international market, you're probably missing out on potential sales," says Tammy L. Flor, president and CEO of Laurel Engineering Inc. in Chula Vista, California, and the Small Business Administration's 1995 Exporter of the Year. Although many small businesses may be intimidated by the thought of global competition, real opportunities do exist in these markets for even the smallest of companies.

- **Scratch the customer's itch.** All types of business—regardless of what they sell—should adopt a cradle-to-grave approach toward their customers. Tom Hopkins, author of *Selling for Dummies*, describes this as a commitment to a follow-up system that starts by figuring out the "itch cycle" for the company's customers and product. The itch cycle is Hopkins's term for the period of time after a purchase from a company during which the customer is particularly receptive to making another commitment to that company. Hopkins's suggestion for benefiting from this cycle is to contact customers with handwritten letters expressing the company's hope that they are happy with their recent purchase. An example of this type of approach is a car salesperson who knows which customers usually buy a new car about every 30 months. "After about 28 months, the salesperson gets the latest model, drives it over to where the customer works, and invites him to drive it for a few days," Hopkins says. "And 85 percent of those cars are sold."

- **Adapt to change.** "If customers want us to do things differently, we'll try to accommodate them. In fact, we ask them for suggestions," says Peter Mendoza, Jr., president of MBE Electric, a contracting business in Riverside, California. Peter

and his vice-president brother, Brian, agree that one of their biggest challenges in customer relations is staying abreast of changes. In 1994, when the earthquake destroyed the Santa Monica Freeway, the Mendozas were asked to design a new electrical system—promptly. Although changes were made in the original contract twice and the scope of the work tripled, the job was completed in 66 days. Adapting to change has paid off for the Mendoza brothers. MBE Electric has grown from $2.6 million in sales to $5.5 million in three years, and the Mendozas were named the Small Business Administration's Young Entrepreneurs of the Year in 1996.

- **Seek customer advice.** According to Susan RoAne, author of *How to Work a Room* and *The Secrets of Savvy Networking*, "Entrepreneurs fail when they have no relationship with the people who buy their products." She suggests calling or sending personal notes (via regular mail or e-mail) to key customers at least once every three months to gather their advice. Another suggestion is to ask customers to fill out a customer survey. According to RoAne, the survey should be no longer than one page, it should offer a discount on customers' next purchase if it is completed, and it should ask customers to tell what the company does or does not do well, in addition to providing space to include specific examples.

- **Sniff out the silver linings.** Fred Lager—the former president of Ben & Jerry's Ice Cream and author of *Ben & Jerry's: The Inside Scoop*—says, "If I had one piece of advice, it would be to look for opportunities in the face of adversity." In his book, Lager describes the 1984 incident in which Pillsbury Company, owners of Häagen-Dazs, attempted to stop independent ice-cream dealers from offering Ben & Jerry's ice cream. "We were able to turn it to our advantage by asking 'What's the doughboy afraid of?' We got a lot of publicity. The result was that we got tremendous brand recognition—way beyond what we could have afforded with paid advertising," Lager recalls.

Source: Stephen J. Simurda, "Instant MBA," *Small Business Computing* (February 1997): 60–63.

One researcher found that internal constraints such as lack of growth capital, limited spans of control, and loss of entrepreneurial vitality occur in growth firms that struggle to survive versus those that successfully achieve high growth. In addition, fundamental differences exist in the firms' approach to environmental changes and trends.[40] Thus, a few key steps are recommended for breaking through the inability to handle environmental changes or trends. These include: *creating a growth task force* to organize and interpret the environmental data, to identify the venture's strengths and weaknesses, to brainstorm new ideas that leverage the firm's strengths, and to recommend key ideas that should be developed further; *planning for growth* with strategies to resolve the stagnation, a set of potential results, and identification of the necessary resources; *maintaining a growth culture* that encourages and rewards a growth-oriented attitude; and *developing an outside board of advisors* to become an integral part of the venture's growth. This board should help determine, design, and implement an organizational structure to enhance the desire for growth.[41]

Unique Managerial Concerns of Growing Ventures

Emerging businesses differ in many ways from larger, more structured businesses. Several unique managerial concerns involve growing businesses in particular. These concerns may seem insignificant to the operation of a large business, but often they become important to emerging entrepreneurs.

The Distinctiveness of Size

The distinction of smallness gives emerging businesses certain disadvantages. The limited market, for example, restricts a small firm. Because a small size limits a company's ability to geographically extend throughout a region or state, the firm must recognize and service its available market. Another disadvantage is the higher ordering costs that burden many small firms. Because they do not order large lots of inventory from suppliers, small businesses usually do not receive quantity discounts and must pay higher prices. Finally, a smaller staff forces small firms to accept less specialization of labor. Thus, employees and managers are expected to perform numerous functions.

However, the distinction of small size is not all bad, and the advantages to smallness should be recognized and capitalized on. One advantage is greater flexibility. In smaller ventures, decisions can be made and implemented immediately, without the input of committees and the delay of bureaucratic layers. Production, marketing, and service are all areas that can be adjusted quickly for a competitive advantage over larger businesses in the same field. A second advantage is constant communication with the community.[42] An entrepreneur lives in the community and is personally involved in its affairs. The special insight of this involvement allows the entrepreneur to adjust products or services to suit the specific needs or desires of the particular community. This leads to the third and probably most important advantage of closeness to the customer: the ability to offer personal service. The personal service that an entrepreneur can provide is one of the key elements of success today. Major corporations work feverishly to duplicate or imitate the idea of personal service. Because the opportunity to provide personal service is an advantage that emerging firms possess by nature of their size, it *must* be capitalized on.

The One-Person-Band Syndrome

Most entrepreneurs start their businesses alone or with a few family members or close associates. In effect, the business *is* the entrepreneur and the entrepreneur is the business.[43] However, a danger arises if the entrepreneur refuses to relinquish any authority as the emerging business grows. The one-person-band syndrome exists when an entrepreneur fails to delegate responsibility to employees, thereby retaining *all* decision-making authority. One study revealed that most planning in entrepreneurial firms is done by the owner alone, as are other operational activities.[44] This syndrome often is derived from the same pattern of independence that helped start the business in the first place. However, the owner who continues to perform as a one-person band can restrict the growth of the firm, because the owner's ability is limited. How can proper planning for the business be accomplished if the owner is immersed in daily operations? Thus, the entrepreneur must recognize the importance of delegation. If the owner can break away from the natural tendency to do *everything*, then the business will benefit from a wider array of that person's abilities.

Time Management

Effective time management is not exclusively a challenge to entrepreneurs. However, limited size and staff force the entrepreneur to face this challenge most diligently. It has been said a person never will *find* time to do anything but must, in fact, *make* time. In other words, entrepreneurs should learn to use time as a resource and not allow time to use them.[45] To perform daily managerial activities in the most time-efficient manner, owner/managers should follow four critical steps:

1. *Assessment.* The business owner should analyze his or her daily activities and rank them in order of importance. (A written list on a notepad is recommended.)

2. *Prioritization.* The owner should divide and categorize the day's activities based on his or her ability to devote the necessary time to the task that day. In other words, the owner should avoid a procrastination of duties.

3. *Creation of procedures.* Repetitive daily activities can be handled easily by an employee if instructions are provided. This organizing of tasks can be a major time-saver for the owner that would allow the fourth and last step to be put into effect.

4. *Delegation.* Delegation can be accomplished after the owner creates procedures for various jobs. As mentioned in the description of the one-person-band syndrome, delegation is a critical skill entrepreneurs need to develop.

All of these steps in effective time management require self-discipline on the part of entrepreneurs.

Community Pressures

Proximity to the community was mentioned earlier as a size advantage for small emerging ventures. However, unlike major corporations with public relations departments, the entrepreneur is involved with community activities directly. The community presents unique pressure to emerging entrepreneurs in three ways: participation, leadership, and donations.

Each of these expectations from the community requires entrepreneurs to plan and budget carefully. Many community members believe that the entrepreneur has "excess" time because he or she owns the business. They also believe that the owner has leadership abilities needed for various community activities. Although the latter may be true, the owner usually does not have excess time. Therefore, entrepreneurs need to plan carefully the activities they believe would be most beneficial. One consideration is the amount of advertising or recognition the business will receive for the owner's participation. When the owner can justify his or her community involvement, both the business and the community benefit.

Financial donations also require careful analysis and budgeting. Again, because consumers have access to the entrepreneur (as opposed to the chief executive officer of a major corporation), he or she may be inundated with requests for donations to charitable and community organizations. Although each organization may have a worthy cause, the entrepreneur cannot support every one and remain financially healthy. Thus, the owner needs to decide which of the organizations to assist and to budget a predetermined amount of money for annual donations. Any other solicitations for money must be placed in writing and submitted to the entrepreneur for consideration. This is the only way entrepreneurs can avoid giving constant cash donations without careful budget consideration.

The critical fact to remember is that time and money are extremely valuable resources for an entrepreneur. They should be budgeted in a meaningful way. Therefore, entrepreneurs need to analyze their community involvement and to continuously reassess the costs versus the benefits.[46]

Continuous Learning

A final unique concern for the entrepreneur is continuous learning. All of the previously mentioned concerns leave very little time for owners to maintain or improve their managerial and entrepreneurial knowledge. However, the environment of the twenty-first century has produced dramatic changes that can affect the procedures, processes, programs, philosophy, or even the product of a growing business. The ancient Greek philosopher Epictetus once said, "It is impossible for a man to learn what he thinks he already knows." This quote illustrates the need for entrepreneurs to dedicate time to learning new techniques and principles for their businesses. Trade associations, seminars, conferences, publications, and college courses all provide opportunities for entrepreneurs to continue their entrepreneurial education. Staying abreast of industry changes is another that entrepreneurs can maintain a competitive edge.

The International Environment: Global Opportunities

The twenty-first century has introduced global entrepreneurs—entrepreneurs who rely on global networks for resources, design, and distribution. This trend has escalated the global economy, allowing it to reach new heights. By all accounts, the pace and magnitude of this global economy are likely to continue to accelerate. The new breed of global entrepreneurs—who are adept at recognizing opportunities—understand that success in the new marketplace requires agility, certainty, and ingenuity with a global perspective. These entrepreneurs are the true vanguards in the new millennium.[47]

Therefore, one of the most exciting and promising avenues for entrepreneurs to expand their businesses is by participating in the global market. Each year, thousands of entrepreneurial enterprises are actively engaged in the international arena. Two of the primary reasons for this emerging opportunity are the decline in trade barriers—especially among major trading nations—and the emergence of major trading blocs brought about by the North American Free Trade Agreement and the European Union. In addition, the Far East (e.g. China, India, and Korea) has become a hotbed of entrepreneurial opportunity.

"Global thinking" is important because today's consumers can select products, ideas, and services from many nations and cultures. Entrepreneurs who expand into foreign markets must be global thinkers in order to design and adopt strategies for different countries.

Entrepreneurship has developed across the globe. Research conducted by Babson College and the London Business School—entitled the *Global Entrepreneurship Monitor*—examined 42 countries representing approximately 2.5 billion people. Random samples of at least 2,000 adults from each participating country were surveyed to ascertain several measures of entrepreneurial activity.

The overall level of entrepreneurial activity for each country is presented in Figure 13.7. The percentage of the population between the ages of 18 and 64 that are engaged in setting up or running their own business is a way of gauging a country's overall entrepreneurial activity. The vertical bars represent the share of that population involved as nascent entrepreneurs, owners of new businesses, or owners of established businesses within high-income countries, Europe and Asia, and Latin America.[48] The major point is that, in all 42 countries, entrepreneurial activity is prospering. The world has truly become entrepreneurial.

Doing business globally is rapidly becoming a profitable and popular strategy for many entrepreneurial ventures.[49] The myth that international business is the province of giant multinational enterprises has long since been disproved by capable and opportunistic entrepreneurs.

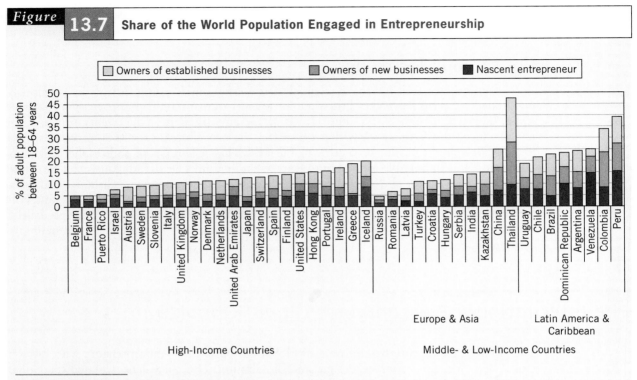

Figure **13.7** **Share of the World Population Engaged in Entrepreneurship**

□ Owners of established businesses ■ Owners of new businesses ■ Nascent entrepreneur

Source: Niels Bosma, Kent Jones, Erkko Autio, and Jonathan Levie, *Global Entrepreneurship Monitor* (Babson College, Babson Park, MA, and London Business School, London, 2007).

the global perspective

How Outsourcing Can Lead to Increased Competition

Companies in developed countries, such as those in the United States and Europe, have grown comfortable with the fact that firms in other less-developed countries, specifically those in China and India, have developed a niche for low-cost, high-quality manufacturing. Despite the contention surrounding the correlation between outsourcing work overseas and the loss of domestic jobs, the relationship between U.S. and European companies developing intellectual property and Chinese and Indian companies handling the manufacturing process has become generally accepted. The issue is that countries that have been in a position to profit from the manufacturing inefficiencies prevalent in foreign countries are beginning to realize that there is much more profit to be made in controlling the entire life cycle of a product, from inception to commercialization.

In particular, the Chinese government has declared that it will make an economic shift in the country toward becoming an innovative society by 2015. As part of this initiative, the government has begun offering incentives, R&D grants, and favorable bank credit to emerging privately operated Chinese companies. Additionally, Chinese universities are training their students in the art and business of design so that they will be well versed in the creation and ownership of intellectual property. The Chinese manufacturers are aware that they are losing a significant portion of the profits to be made on commercial products. If they no longer had to pay licensing fees, the bulk of the profits would be theirs.

The reality is that Chinese companies are no longer willing to serve as subsidiaries for U.S. companies, which is reflected in a $7.2 billion drop in related-party imports from China between 2004 and 2006. This figure measures imports to U.S. companies from Chinese subsidiaries and indicates that Chinese companies are in the process of becoming direct sellers. Competition presented by these firms will impact entrepreneurs on the domestic front. IntelliTouch, a technology company with 22 employees and annual sales of $11 million, is already feeling the impact of the "China direct" trend. The company had to abandon selling telephones due

to the erosion of margins caused by Chinese firms underselling it.

Some analysts argue that China has significant hurdles to overcome, including the development of international brands and the implementation of customer support; however, the wheels are in motion, and China shows no sign of slowing down. Even if Chinese companies are not effective at dominating their respective markets, the added pressure that they will introduce to domestic entrepreneurs is one more environmental factor that entrepreneurs will have to maneuver around to ensure that their companies can not only survive, but continue to grow.

Source: Adapted from Chris Penttila, "Can You Compete?" *Entrepreneur*, January 2008, http://www.entrepreneur.com/magazine/entrepreneur/2008/january/187616.html (accessed April 2, 2008).

Achieving Entrepreneurial Leadership in the New Millennium

Entrepreneurial leadership may be the most critical element in the management of high growth ventures. Terms such as *visionary* and *strategic* have been used when describing different types of leaders. Table 13.4 provides a comprehensive description of strategic leaders, visionary leaders, and managerial leaders. Research has demonstrated that the concept behind strategic leadership is the most effective in growing organizations.[50] Researchers R. Duane Ireland and Michael A. Hitt identified some of the most important concepts in effective strategic leadership.[51] This type of leadership can be classified as **entrepreneurial leadership**, which arises when an entrepreneur attempts to manage a fast-paced, growth-oriented company.[52]

Entrepreneurial leadership can be defined as the entrepreneur's ability to anticipate, envision, maintain flexibility, think strategically, and work with others to initiate changes that will create a viable future for the organization. If these leadership processes are difficult for competitors to understand—and, hence, to imitate—the firm will create a competitive advantage.

Today's fast-paced economy has created a new competitive landscape—one in which events change constantly and unpredictably. These changes are revolutionary in nature—that is, they happen swiftly and are relentless in their frequency, affecting virtually all parts of an organization simultaneously. The ambiguity that results from revolutionary changes challenges firms and their strategic abilities to increase the speed of the decision-making processes through which strategies are formulated and implemented.[53]

Growth-oriented firms need to adopt a new competitive mind-set—one in which flexibility, speed, innovation, and strategic leadership are valued highly. With this mind-set, firms can identify and completely exploit opportunities that emerge in the new competitive landscape. These opportunities surface primarily because of the disequilibrium that is created by continuous changes (especially technological changes). More specifically, although uncertainty and disequilibrium often result in seemingly hostile and intensely rivalrous conditions, these conditions may simultaneously yield significant product-driven growth opportunities. Through effective entrepreneurial leadership, growth firms can adapt their behaviors and exploit such opportunities.[54]

Table 13.4 Strategic, Visionary, and Managerial Leadership

Strategic Leaders

- √ synergistic combination of managerial and visionary leadership
- √ emphasis on ethical behavior and value-based decisions
- √ oversee operating (day-to-day) and strategic (long-term) responsibilities
- √ formulate and implement strategies for immediate impact and preservation of long-term goals to enhance organizational survival, growth, and long-term viability
- √ have strong, positive expectations for the performance they expect from their superiors, peers, subordinates, and themselves
- √ use strategic controls and financial controls, with emphasis on strategic controls
- √ use, and interchange, tacit and explicit knowledge on individual and organizational levels
- √ use linear and nonlinear thinking patterns
- √ believe in strategic choice, that is, their choices make a difference in their organizations and environment

Visionary Leaders

- √ are proactive, shape ideas, change the way people think about what is desirable, possible, and necessary
- √ work to develop choices and fresh approaches to long-standing problems; work from high-risk positions
- √ are concerned with ideas; relate to people in intuitive and empathetic ways
- √ feel separate from their environment; work in, but do not belong to, organizations; sense of who they are does not depend on work
- √ influence attitudes and opinions of others within the organization
- √ concerned with insuring future of organization, especially through development and management of people
- √ more embedded in complexity, ambiguity, and information overload; engage in multifunctional, integrative tasks
- √ know less than their functional area experts
- √ more likely to make decisions based on values
- √ more willing to invest in innovation, human capital, and creating and maintaining an effective culture to ensure long-term viability
- √ focus on tacit knowledge and develop strategies as communal forms of tacit knowledge that promote enactment of a vision
- √ utilize nonlinear thinking
- √ believe in strategic choice, that is, their choices make a difference in their organizations and environment

Managerial Leaders

- √ are reactive; adopt passive attitudes toward goals; goals arise out of necessities, not desires and dreams; goals based on past
- √ view work as an enabling process involving some combination of ideas and people interacting to establish strategies
- √ relate to people according to their roles in the decision-making process
- √ see themselves as conservators and regulators of existing order; sense of who they are depends on their role in organization
- √ influence actions and decisions of those with whom they work
- √ involved in situations and contexts characteristic of day-to-day activities
- √ concerned with, and more comfortable in, functional areas of responsibilities
- √ expert in their functional area
- √ less likely to make value-based decisions
- √ engage in, and support, short-term, least-cost behavior to enhance financial performance figures
- √ focus on managing the exchange and combination of explicit knowledge and ensuring compliance to standard operating procedures
- √ utilize linear thinking
- √ believe in determinism, that is, the choices they make are determined by their internal and external environments

Source: W. Glenn Rowe, "Creating Wealth in Organizations: The Role of Strategic Leadership," *Academy of Management Executive* 15, no. 1 (2001): 82.

Summary

Although many ways of strategically planning a venture exist, all have one common element: Each is an extension of the entrepreneur's vision—each takes the owner's concept of the business and puts it into action. Entrepreneurs may not use strategic planning for many reasons, among them scarcity of time, lack of knowledge about how to plan, lack of expertise in the planning process, and lack of trust in others.

A number of benefits to strategic planning exist. In particular, studies have shown that small firms that use this process tend to have better financial performance than those that do not. Other benefits include more efficient resource allocation, improved competitive position, higher employee morale, and more rapid decision making.

A typical life cycle of a venture has five stages: development, start-up, growth, stabilization, and innovation or decline. This chapter focused on ways to maintain an entrepreneurial frame of mind while making the necessary adjustments to deal with the growth phase.

When building the desired adaptive firm, entrepreneurs need to be concerned with three important responsibilities: (1) increasing the perception of opportunity, (2) institutionalizing change as the venture's goals, and (3) instilling the desire to be innovative.

The balance of entrepreneurial and managerial approaches was reviewed in this chapter. This balance was demonstrated by considering five major factors: strategic orientation, commitment to seize opportunities, commitment of resources, control of resources, and management structure. This differentiation of major factors is important for analyzing aspects of the venture that need either more administrative or more entrepreneurial emphasis.

The chapter then examined the importance of a venture's growth stage. Underscoring the metamorphosis a venture goes through, four factors were discussed: control, responsibility, tolerance of failure, and change. In addition, the challenge of managing paradox and contradiction was presented, and the unique managerial concerns of growing ventures were outlined. Doing business globally has rapidly developed into one of the most profitable and popular strategies for many entrepreneurial ventures. Finally, the concept of entrepreneurial leadership was introduced as a way for entrepreneurs to anticipate, envision, maintain flexibility, think strategically, and work with others to initiate changes that will create a viable future for the growth-oriented venture.

Key Terms and Concepts

adaptive firm	lack of knowledge	stabilization stage
entrepreneurial leadership	lack of trust and openness	start-up activities
entrepreneurial strategy matrix	life-cycle stages	strategic planning
global entrepreneurs	moral failure	strategic positionings
growth stage	new-venture development	SWOT analysis
growth wall	one-person-band syndrome	time scarcity
innovation	perception of high cost	uncontrollable failure
lack of expertise/skills	personal failure	

Review and Discussion Questions

1. In what way does an entrepreneur's vision affect the company's strategic plan?
2. How is the strategic plan of an engineer/scientist entrepreneur likely to be different from that of an entrepreneur whose primary strength is in the manufacturing area? Be complete in your answer.
3. Give three reasons why many entrepreneurs do not like to formulate strategic plans.
4. Does strategic planning really pay off for entrepreneurial ventures?
5. Describe the entrepreneurial strategy matrix and explain why it is effective for entrepreneurs.

6. Briefly identify and describe the stages of development for a new venture.
7. Firms that fail to innovate will die. What does this statement mean in the context of new ventures?
8. How can entrepreneurs build an adaptive firm? Be complete in your answer.
9. Successful ventures balance entrepreneurial characteristics with managerial style. What does this statement mean?
10. Comparing the entrepreneurial focus with the administrative focus involves five major areas of consideration. What are these areas?

11. Identify and describe the four key factors that need to be considered during the growth stage.
12. What is meant by managing paradox and contradiction?
13. Identify five unique managerial concerns of growing businesses.
14. Define the one-person-band syndrome.
15. Explain the concept of entrepreneurial leadership.

Experiential Exercise

THE VENTURE LIFE CYCLE

Following are the five basic phases or stages of the typical life cycle of a venture, labeled A through E. Rank these from *1* to *5*, beginning with the first phase and continuing to the last. Then examine the list of activities (a through j) and place a *1* next to those that happen during the first phase of the venture, and continue numbering until you place a *5* next to those that occur during the last phase. Answers are provided at the end of the exercise.

A. _____ Growth

B. _____ Innovation or decline

C. _____ Start-up

D. _____ Stabilization

E. _____ New-venture development

a. _____ Transition from one-person leadership to team management leadership

b. _____ New-product development

c. _____ Search for capital

d. _____ Increased competition

e. _____ Venture assessment

f. _____ Attempts to acquire other firms

g. _____ Consumer indifference to the entrepreneur's goods or services

h. _____ Accumulation of resources

i. _____ Major changes in entrepreneurial strategy

j. _____ Development of an effective entrepreneurial team

Answers: A. 3, B. 5, C. 2, D. 4, E. 1, a. 3, b. 5, c. 2, d. 4, e. 1, f. 5, g. 4, h. 1, i. 3, j. 2

Case 13.1

HENDRICK'S WAY

When Hendrick Harding started his consumer products firm, he was convinced he had a winning product. His small, compact industrial drill was easier to use than any other on the market and cost 30 percent less than any of the competitors' drills. The orders began to pour in, and within six months, Hendrick's sales surpassed his first year's estimate. At the end of the first 12 months of operation, his firm was grossing more than $50,000 a month, and he had a six-week backlog in filling orders.

The rapid growth of the firm continued for two years. Beginning about four months ago, however, Hendrick began to notice a dip in sales. The major reason appeared to be a competitive product that cost 10 percent less than Hendrick's drill and offered all the same benefits and features. Hendrick believes that, with a couple of minor adjustments, he can improve his product and continue to dominate the market.

On the other hand, Hendrick is somewhat disturbed by the comments of one of his salespeople, George Simonds. George spends most of his time on the road and gets to talk to a great many customers. Here is what he had to say to Hendrick: "Your industrial drill has really set the market on its ear. And we should be able to sell a modified version of it for at least another 36 months before making any additional changes. However, you need to start thinking about adding other products to the line. Let's face it; we are a one-product company. That's not good. We have to expand our product line if we are to grow. Otherwise, I can't see much future for us."

The problem with this advice is that Hendrick does not want to grow larger. He is happy selling just the industrial drill. He believes that, if he continues to modify and change the drill, he can maintain a large market share and the company will continue to be profitable. As he explained to George, "I see the future as more of the past. I really don't think there will be a great many changes in this product. There will be modifications, sure, but nothing other than that. I think this firm can live off the industrial drill for at least the next 25 years. We've got a great thing going. I don't see any reason for change. And I certainly don't want to come out with a second product. There's no need for it."

QUESTIONS

1. What is the danger in Hendrick's thinking? Explain in detail.

2. Could the concept of understanding the managerial versus entrepreneurial mind-set as described in the chapter be of any value to Hendrick? Why or why not?

3. Using Table 13.3 as your point of reference, how would you describe Hendrick's focus? Based on your evaluation, what recommendations would you make to him?

Case 13.2

KEEPING THINGS GOING

The Clayton Company has grown 115 percent in the past year and 600-plus percent in the past three years. A large portion of this growth is attributable to Jan Clayton's philosophy of hiring the best possible computer systems people and giving them the freedom they need to do their jobs.

Most of Jan's personnel operate as part of work teams that analyze, design, and implement computer systems for clients. The process works as follows: First, the company will get a call from a potential client indicating that it needs to have a computer system installed or special software written for its operations. Jan will send over one of her people to talk to the client and analyze the situation. If it turns out that the Clayton Company has the expertise and personnel to handle the job, the client will be quoted a price. If this price is acceptable, a Clayton group will be assigned the project.

An example of a typical project is the client who called three weeks ago and wanted to purchase five personal computers for the firm's engineering staff. The company wanted these machines hooked up to the main computer. Additionally, the firm wanted its computer-aided design software to be modified so the engineers could see their computer-generated drawings in a variety of colors, not just in monochrome. The Clayton group installed the entire system and modified the software in ten working days.

Jan realizes that the growth of her enterprise will be determined by two factors. One is the creativity and ingenuity of her workforce. The other is the ability to attract talented personnel. "This business is heavily labor intensive," she explained. "If someone wants a computer system installation, that may take 100 labor hours. If I don't have the people to handle the project, I have to turn it down. My expansion is heavily dependent on hiring and training talented people. Additionally, I need more than just hard workers. I need creative people who can figure out new approaches to handling complex problems. If I can do these two things, I can stay a jump ahead of the competition. Otherwise, I won't be able to survive."

To try to achieve these key factors for success, Jan has initiated three changes. First, she has instituted a bonus system tied to sales; these bonuses are shared by all of the personnel. Second, she gives quarterly salary increases, with the greatest percentages going to employees who are most active in developing new programs and procedures for handling client problems. Third, she has retreats every six months in which the entire staff goes for a long weekend to a mountain area, where they spend three days discussing current work-related problems and ways to deal with them. Time is also devoted to social events and to working on developing an esprit de corps among the personnel.

QUESTIONS

1. In what phase of the venture life cycle is Jan's firm currently operating? Defend your answer.

2. How are Jan's actions helping to build an adaptive firm? Give three specific examples.

3. If Jan's firm continues to grow, what recommendations would you make for future action? What else should Jan be thinking about doing to keep things moving smoothly? Be specific in your answer.

Notes

1. Amar Bhide, "How Entrepreneurs Craft Strategies That Work," *Harvard Business Review* (March/April 1994): 150–61; and Marc Gruber, "Uncovering the Value of Planning in New Venture Creation: A Process and Contingency Perspective," *Journal of Business Venturing* 22, no. 6 (2007): 782–807.

2. Scott Shane and Frédéric Delmar, "Planning for the Market: Business Planning before Marketing and the Continuation of Organizing Efforts," *Journal of Business Venturing* 19, no. 6 (November 2004): 767–85.

3. Michael A. Hitt, R. Duane Ireland, and Robert E. Hoskisson, *Strategic Management: Competitiveness and Globalization,* 8th ed. (Mason, OH: Cengage Learning, 2009).

4. See James R. Lang, Roger J. Calantone, and Donald Gudmundson, "Small Firm Information Seeking as a Response to Environmental Threats and Opportunities," *Journal of Small Business Management* 35, no.1 (1997): 11–23; and Reginald M. Beal, "Competing Effectively: Environmental Scanning, Competitive Strategy, and Organizational Performance in Small Manufacturing Firms," *Journal of Small Business Management* 38, no. 1 (2000): 27–47.

5. Henry Mintzberg, "The Fall and Rise of Strategic Planning," *Harvard Business Review* (January/February 1994): 107–14.

6. Charles H. Matthews and Susanne G. Scott, "Uncertainty and Planning in Small and Entrepreneurial Firms: An Empirical Assessment," *Journal of Small Business Management* 33, no. 4 (1995): 34–52; and Sigal Haber and Arie Reichel,

"The Cumulative Nature of the Entrepreneurial Process: The Contribution of Human Capital, Planning, and Environmental Resources to Small Venture Performance," *Journal of Business Venturing* 22, no. 1 (2007): 119–45.

7. John W. Mullins and David Forlani, "Missing the Boat or Sinking the Boat: A Study of New Venture Decision Making," *Journal of Business Venturing* 20, no. 1 (January 2005): 47–69; and Michael D. Ensly, Craig L. Pearce, and Keith M. Hmieleski, "The Moderating Effect of Environmental Dynamism on the Relationship between Entrepreneur Leadership Behavior and New Venture Performance," *Journal of Business Venturing* 21, no. 2 (2006): 243–63.

8. "The Business Failure Record," *Dun & Bradstreet,* 1995.

9. Richard B. Robinson, "The Importance of Outsiders in Small Firm Strategic Planning," *Academy of Management Journal* 25, no. 2 (March 1982): 80–93.

10. A. Bakr Ibrahim, "Strategy Types and Small Firm's Performance: An Empirical Investigation," *Journal of Small Business Strategy* (Spring 1993): 13–22.

11. Elaine Mosakowski, "A Resource-Based Perspective on the Dynamic Strategy–Performance Relationship: An Empirical Examination of the Focus and Differentiation Strategies in Entrepreneurial Firms," *Journal of Management* 19, no. 4 (1993): 819–39.

12. Leslie W. Rue and Nabil A. Ibrahim, "The Relationship Between Planning Sophistication and Performance in Small Business," *Journal of Small Business Management* 36, no. 4 (1998): 24–32.

13. Charles R. Schwenk and Charles B. Shrader, "Effects of Formal Strategic Planning on Financial Performance in Small Firms: A Meta Analysis," *Entrepreneurship Theory and Practice* 17, no. 3 (Spring 1993): 53–64; see also Philip D. Olson and Donald W. Bokor, "Strategy Process–Content Interaction: Effects on Growth Performance in Small, Startup Firms," *Journal of Small Business Management* 33, no. 1 (1995): 34–44.

14. Michael E. Porter, "Knowing Your Place–How to Assess the Attractiveness of Your Industry and Your Company's Position in It," *Inc.* (September 1991): 90–94.

15. Ibid., 93.

16. R. Duane Ireland, Michael A. Hitt, S. Michael Camp, and Donald L. Sexton, "Integrating Entrepreneurship and Strategic Management Actions to Create Firm Wealth," *Academy of Management Executive* 15, no. 1 (February 2001): 49–63.

17. Michael E. Porter, "What Is Strategy?" *Harvard Business Review* (November/December 1996): 61–78.

18. Matthew C. Sonfield and Robert N. Lussier, "The Entrepreneurial Strategy Matrix: A Model for New and Ongoing Ventures," *Business Horizons* (May/June 1997): 73–77.

19. Jeanie Daniel Duck, "Managing Change: The Art of Balancing," *Harvard Business Review* (November/December 1993): 109–18; Yolande E. Chan, Niraj Bhargava, and Christopher T. Street, "Having Arrived: The Homogeneity of High Growth Small Firms," *Journal of Small Business Management* 44, no. 3 (2006): 426–40; and Hyung Rok Yim, "Quality Shock vs. Market Shock: Lessons from Recently Established Rapidly Growing U.S. Startups," *Journal of Business Venturing* 23, no. 2 (2008): 141–64.

20. Alfred Chandler, *Strategy and Structure* (Cambridge, MA: MIT Press, 1962); see also Enno Masurel and Kees van Montfort, "Life Cycle Characteristics of Small Professional Service Firms," *Journal of Small Business Management* 44, no. 3 (2006): 461–73.

21. Jeffrey G. Covin, Dennis P. Slevin, and Michael B. Heeley, "Pioneers and Followers: Competitive Tactics, Environment, and Firm Growth," *Journal of Business Venturing* 15, no. 2 (2000): 175–210.

22. David E. Terpstra and Philip D. Olson, "Entrepreneurial Start-up and Growth: A Classification of Problems," *Entrepreneurship Theory and Practice* 17, no. 3 (Spring 1993): 5–20; and Bret Golan, "Achieving Growth and Responsiveness: Process Management and Market Orientation in Small Firms," *Journal of Small Business Management* 44, no. 3 (2006): 369–85.

23. See Jacqueline N. Hood and John E. Young, "Entrepreneurship's Requisite Areas of Development: A Survey of Top Executives in Successful Entrepreneurial Firms," *Journal of Business Venturing* 8, no. 2 (March 1993): 115–35; and Michael H. Morris, Nola N. Miyasaki, Craig R. Watters, and Susan M. Coombes, "The Dilemma of Growth: Understanding Venture Size Choices of Women Entrepreneurs," *Journal of Small Business Management* 44, no. 2 (2006): 221–44.

24. Morten T. Hansen, Nitin Nohria, and Thomas Tierney, "What's Your Strategy for Managing Knowledge?" *Harvard Business Review* 77, no. 2 (1999): 106–16.

25. Shaker A. Zahra, "The Changing Rules of Global Competitiveness in the 21st Century," *Academy of Management Executive* 13, no. 1 (1999): 36–42.

26. Howard H. Stevenson and Jose Carlos Jarillo-Mossi, "Preserving Entrepreneurship as Companies Grow," *Journal of Business Strategy* (Summer 1986): 10.

27. Jill Kickul and Lisa K. Gundry, "Prospecting for Strategic Advantage: The Proactive Entrepreneurial Personality and Small Firm Innovation," *Journal of Small Business Management* 40, no. 2 (2002): 85–97.

28. Vesa Routamaa and Jukka Vesalainen, "Types of Entrepreneurs and Strategic Level Goal Setting," *International Small Business Journal* (Spring 1987): 19–29; see also Lanny Herron and Richard B. Robinson, Jr., "A Structural Model of the Effects of Entrepreneurial Characteristics on Venture Performance," *Journal of Business Venturing* 8, no. 3 (May 1993): 281–94.

29. Donald F. Kuratko, Jeffrey S. Hornsby, and Laura M. Corso, "Building an Adaptive Firm," *Small Business Forum* (Spring 1996): 41–48.

30. Steven H. Hanks and L. R. McCarrey, "Beyond Survival: Reshaping Entrepreneurial Vision in Successful Growing Ventures," *Journal of Small Business Strategy* (Spring 1993): 1–12.

31. See Sanjay Prasad Thakur, "Size of Investment, Opportunity Choice and Human Resources in New Venture Growth: Some Typologies," *Journal of Business Venturing* 14, no. 3 (May 1999): 283–309.

32. Jon R. Katzenbach and Douglas K. Smith, "The Discipline of Teams," *Harvard Business Review* (March/April 1993): 111–20; Alexander L. M. Dingee, Brian Haslett, and Leonard E. Smollen, "Characteristics of a Successful Entrepreneurial Management Team," in *Annual Editions 00/01* (Guilford, CT: Dushkin/McGraw-Hill, 2000/2001), 71–75; and G. Page West III, "Collective Cognitions: When Entrepreneurial Teams, Not Individuals, Make Decisions," *Entrepreneurship Theory and Practice* 31, no. 1 (2007): 77–102.

33. Charles W. Hofer and Ram Charan, "The Transition to Professional Management: Mission Impossible?" *American Journal of Small Business* (Summer 1984): 3; see also William Lowell, "An Entrepreneur's Journey to the Next Level," *Small Business Forum* (Spring 1996): 68–74.

34. Hofer and Charan, 4.

35. John B. Miner, "Entrepreneurs, High Growth Entrepreneurs, and Managers: Contrasting and Overlapping Motivational Patterns," *Journal of Business Venturing* (July 1990): 221–34; and Michael J. Roberts, "Managing Growth," in *New Business Ventures and the Entrepreneur* (New York: Irwin/McGraw-Hill, 1999), 460–64.

36. Howard H. Stevenson and David E. Gumpert, "The Heart of Entrepreneurship," *Harvard Business Review* (March/April 1985): 86–87.

37. Jeffrey G. Covin and Dennis P. Slevin, "New Venture Strategic Posture, Structure, and Performance: An Industry Life Cycle Analysis," *Journal of Business Venturing* 5, no. 4 (March 1990): 123–33; see also Jeffrey G. Covin, Kimberly M. Green, and Dennis P. Slevin, "Strategic Process Effects on the Entrepreneurial Orientation-Sales Growth Rate Relationships," *Entrepreneurship Theory and Practice* 30, no. 1 (2006): 57–82.

38. Charles J. Fombrun and Stefan Wally, "Structuring Small Firms for Rapid Growth," *Journal of Business Venturing* 4, no. 2 (March 1989): 107–22; Donna J. Kelley and Mark P. Rice, "Advantage Beyond Founding: The Strategic Use of Technologies," *Journal of Business Venturing* 17, no. 1 (2002): 41–58; see also Andrew J. Sherman, *Grow Fast Grow Right* (Chicago: Kaplan, 2007).

39. Donald C. Hambrick and Lynn M. Crozier, "Stumblers and Stars in the Management of Rapid Growth," *Journal of Business Venturing* 1, no. 1 (January 1985): 31–45.

40. Richard L. Osborne, "Second Phase Entrepreneurship: Breaking Through the Growth Wall," *Business Horizons* (January/February 1994): 80–86.

41. Ibid., 82–85.

42. See Jerry R. Cornwell, "The Entrepreneur as a Building Block for Community," *Journal of Developmental Entrepreneurship* (Fall/Winter 1998): 141–48.

43. David E. Gumpert and David P. Boyd, "The Loneliness of the Small Business Owner," *Harvard Business Review* (November/December 1984): 19–24.

44. Douglas W. Naffziger and Donald F. Kuratko, "An Investigation into the Prevalence of Planning in Small Business," *Journal of Business and Entrepreneurship* 3, no. 2 (October 1991): 99–110.

45. Charles R. Hobbs, "Time Power," *Small Business Reports* (January 1990): 46–55; and Jack Falvey, "New and Improved Time Management," *Small Business Reports* (July 1990): 14–17.

46. Terry L. Besser, "Community Involvement and the Perception of Success Among Small Business Operators in Small Towns," *Journal of Small Business Management* 37, no. 4 (October 1999): 16–29; and Rhonda Walker Mack, "Event Sponsorship: An Exploratory Study of Small Business Objectives, Practices, and Perceptions," *Journal of Small Business Management* 37, no. 3 (July 1999): 25–30.

47. Shaker A. Zahra, "The Changing Rules of Global Competitiveness in the 21st Century," *Academy of Management Executive* 13, no. 1 (1999): 36–42; Rosebeth Moss Kanter, "Managing the Extended Enterprise in a Globally Connected World," *Organizational Dynamics* (Summer 1999): 7–23; Mike W. Peng, "How Entrepreneurs Create Wealth in Transition Economies," *Academy of Management Executive* 15, no. 1 (2001): 95–110; and Stephanie A. Fernhaber, Patricia P. McDougall, and Benjamin M. Oviatt, "Exploring the Role of Industry Structure in New Venture Internationalization," *Entrepreneurship Theory and Practice* 31, no. 4 (2007): 517–42.

48. Niels Bosma, Kent Jones, Erkko Autio, and Jonathan Levie, *Global Entrepreneurship Monitor* (Babson College, Babson Park, MA, and London Business School, London, 2007).

49. Shaker Zahra, James Hayton, Jeremy Marcel, and Hugh O'Neill, "Fostering Entrepreneurship During International Expansion: Managing Key Challenges," *European Management Journal* 19, no. 4 (2001): 359–69; Peggy A. Cloninger and Benjamin M. Oviatt, "Service Content and the Internationalization of Young Ventures: An Empirical Test," *Entrepreneurship Theory and Practice* 31, no. 2 (2007): 233–56; and Shaker A. Zahra and James A. Clayton, "The Effect of International Venturing on Firm Performance: The Moderating Influence of Absorptive Capacity," *Journal of Business Venturing* 23, no. 2 (2008): 195–220.

50. W. Glenn Rowe, "Creating Wealth in Organizations: The Role of Strategic Leadership," *Academy of Management Executive* 15, no. 1 (2001): 81–94.

51. R. Duane Ireland and Michael A. Hitt, "Achieving and Maintaining Strategic Competitiveness in the 21st Century: The Role of Strategic Leadership," *Academy of Management Executive* 13, no. 1 (1999): 43–57.

52. Michael A. Hitt, R. Duane Ireland, S. Michael Camp, and Donald L. Sexton, "Strategic Entrepreneurship: Entrepreneurial Strategies for Wealth Creation," special issue, *Strategic Management Journal* 22, no. 6 (2001): 479–92; see also John L. Thompson, "A Strategic Perspective of Entrepreneurship," *International Journal of Entrepreneurial Behavior & Research* 5, no. 6 (1999): 279–96; and Sharon A. Alvarez, R. Duane Ireland, and Jeffrey J. Reuer, "Entrepreneurship and Strategic Alliances," *Journal of Business Venturing* 21, no. 4 (2006): 401–4.

53. E. H. Kessler and A. K. Chakrabarti, "Innovation Speed: A Conceptual Model of Context, Antecedents, and Outcomes," *Academy of Management Review* 21, no. 4 (1996): 1143–91.

54. Donald F. Kuratko, R. Duane Ireland, and Jeffrey S. Hornsby, "Improving Firm Performance Through Entrepreneurial Actions: Acordia's Corporate Entrepreneurship Strategy," *Academy of Management Executive* 15, no. 4 (2001): 60–71.

CHAPTER 14

The Valuation Challenge in Entrepreneurship

Entrepreneurial Thought

Market transactions are often not observable for assets such as privately held businesses. Thus, fair market value must be estimated. An estimate of fair market value is usually subjective due to the circumstances of place, time, the existence of comparable precedents, and the evaluation principles of each involved person. Opinions on value are always based upon subjective interpretation of available information at the time of assessment.

— WIKIPEDIA.COM

Chapter Objectives

1 To explain the importance of valuation

2 To describe the basic elements of due diligence

3 To examine the underlying issues involved in the acquisition process

4 To outline the various aspects of analyzing a business

5 To present the major points to consider when establishing a firm's value

6 To highlight the available methods of valuing a venture

7 To examine the three principal methods currently used in business valuations

8 To consider additional factors that affect a venture's valuation

The Importance of Business Valuation

Every entrepreneur should be able to calculate the value of his or her business and also should be able to determine the value of a competitor's operation. Such **business valuation** is essential in the following situations:

- Buying or selling a business, division, or major asset
- Establishing an employee stock option plan (ESOP) or profit-sharing plan for employees
- Raising growth capital through stock warrants or convertible loans
- Determining inheritance tax liability (potential estate tax liability)
- Giving a gift of stock to family members
- Structuring a buy/sell agreement with stockholders
- Attempting to buy out a partner
- Going public with the company or privately placing the stock

Equally important is the entrepreneur's desire to know the real value of the venture. This valuation can provide a scorecard for periodically tracking the increases or decreases in the business's value.[1]

Underlying Issues When Acquiring a Venture

As we demonstrated in Chapter 6, acquisition of a venture is one pathway to entering the entrepreneurial arena. Because one of the main reasons a valuation would take place with a venture is that it is being sold, we will examine a few more points concerning acquisition of a venture. Three issues underlie the proper valuation of a venture set to be acquired: (1) the differing goals of a buyer and seller, (2) the emotional bias of the seller, and (3) the reasons for the acquisition.

Goals of the Buyer and Seller

It is important to remember one's reasons for valuing an enterprise. Both major parties to the transaction, buyer and seller, will assign different values to the enterprise because of their basic objectives. The seller will attempt to establish the highest possible value for the business and will not heed the realistic considerations of the market, the environment, or the economy. To the seller, the enterprise may represent a lifetime investment—or at the very least one that took a lot of effort. The buyer, on the other hand, will try to determine the lowest possible price to be paid. The enterprise is regarded as an investment for the buyer, and he or she must assess the profit potential. As a result, a pessimistic view often is taken. An understanding of both positions in the valuation process is important.

Emotional Bias

The second issue in valuing a business is the **emotional bias** of the seller. Whenever someone starts a venture, nurtures it through early growth, and makes it a profitable business, the person tends to believe that the enterprise is worth a great deal more than outsiders believe it is worth. Entrepreneurs therefore must try to be as objective as possible in determining a fair value for the enterprise (realizing that this fair amount will be negotiable).

Reasons for the Acquisition

The third issue in valuing a business is the reason an entrepreneur's business is being acquired. The following are some of the most common reasons for acquisition:

- Developing more growth-phase products by acquiring a firm that has developed new products in the company's industry

entrepreneurship **in practice**

The "Rollup Frenzy": An Acquisition Nightmare

Big industry players such as AutoNation and the now defunct NationsRent characterized the acquisition spree of the late 1990s. These "rollups" of mom-and-pop businesses into national chains were geared to provide a standardized and efficient system by trimming office costs and boosting purchasing power. Unfortunately, many former owners are now suffering big losses as the former moms and pops are buying back their businesses for sometimes less than half of what they were acquired for.

Brad Daniel built up his florist business into five stores throughout south Florida before he decided to sell out for $130 million to an industry rollup. The rollup quickly overinflated and filed for Chapter 11 bankruptcy protection; Daniel gained back his business for less than half of the acquisition price. However, many small-business owners were not as lucky. Entrepreneurs who sold their businesses often got burned by plunging share prices and were left to deal with unpaid workers and deteriorating services.

The rollups' cost savings never materialized, because of conflicting office systems and people's reluctance to work together. In general, these rollups grew too fast and used too much debt during expansion. It is estimated that investors put $30 billion into rollups through stock offerings and private investments through the late 1990s. Since 1996 alone, rollups that had initial public offerings raised approximately $3.6 billion in equity while taking on $10 billion in debt.

Across the nation, the smartest entrepreneurs are digging through assets of failed rollups and finding treasures. The founders of Webshots, an online photo-sharing service, sold their company and 13 million registered users to Excite@Home, which made them instant millionaires. When the high-speed Internet provider liquidated in 2001, Webshots was returned to the hands of its founders at a bargain price.

These rollups may have had the purchasing power and recognition to raise capital for further expansion, but they lost touch of what became their liabilities—service and experience.

Source: Charles Haddad and Brian Grow, "Snapping Up the Spoils of Ruptured Rollups," *BusinessWeek Online,* March 5, 2002, http://www.businessweek.com/smallbiz/content/mar2002/sb2002035_3812.htm (accessed April 17, 2008).

- Increasing the number of customers by acquiring a firm whose current customers will broaden substantially the company's customer base
- Increasing market share by acquiring a firm in the company's industry
- Improving or changing distribution channels by acquiring a firm with recognized superiority in the company's current distribution channel
- Expanding the product line by acquiring a firm whose products complement and complete the company's product line
- Developing or improving customer service operations by acquiring a firm with an established service operation, as well as a customer service network that includes the company's products
- Reducing operating leverage and increasing absorption of fixed costs by acquiring a firm that has a lower degree of operating leverage and that can absorb the company's fixed costs
- Using idle or excess plant capacity by acquiring a firm that can operate in the company's current plant facilities
- Integrating vertically, either backward or forward, by acquiring a firm that is a supplier or distributor

- Reducing inventory levels by acquiring a firm that is a customer (but not an end user) and adjusting the company's inventory levels to match the acquired firm's orders
- Reducing indirect operating costs by acquiring a firm that will allow for elimination of duplicate operating costs (for example, warehousing and distribution)
- Reducing fixed costs by acquiring a firm that will permit the elimination of duplicate fixed costs (for example, corporate and staff functional groups)[2]

In summary, it is important that the entrepreneur and all other parties involved objectively view the firm's operations and potential. An evaluation of the following points can assist in this process:

- A firm's potential to pay for itself during a reasonable period of time
- The difficulties the new owners face during the transition period
- The amount of security or risk involved in the transaction; changes in interest rates
- The effect on the company's value if a turnaround is required
- The number of potential buyers
- Current managers' intentions to remain with the firm
- The taxes associated with the purchase or sale of an enterprise[3]

Due Diligence

When considering the acquisition of a venture, an entrepreneur should perform a complete **due diligence**, which means a thorough analysis of every facet of the existing business. Table 14.1 provides a due diligence outline that is used to assess the viability of a firm's business plan. Notice how each major segment is analyzed by applying specific questions to that part.

Table 14.1 **Due Diligence Evaluation**

Executive Summary

A. Company name. *Does the management team have what it takes to implement the plan?*
B. Product/Service Offering. *Is the idea viable?*
C. Key considerations uncovered by external research. *Are there conditions in the industry, competitive environment, market, or other areas not addressed in the plan?*
D. Key considerations discovered through analysis of the plan. *Is there something the plan does not uncover or that needs to be put into the plan?*
E. Financial summary
  1. Funding request. *Is it appropriate for success?*
  2. Valuation (pre-money). *What is their starting point?*
  3. Burn rate. *Is it sufficient or excessive? Does their request take this into account?*
  4. Evaluation of the viability of the stated rate of return/investment potential. *When operations are adjusted by your analysis, is the stated return still there?*

Narrative Analysis

I. Introduction *(May be presented in bullets)*
  A. Date
  B. Review team members

Table **14.1**   **Due Diligence Evaluation (*Continued*)**

    C. Name of company
    D. Name of CEO
    E. Date founded
    F. Location
    G. Funding goal
    H. Founders investment
    I. Prior venture funding
       1. When?
       2. How much?
       3. From whom?

II. The Industry (broad focus)
    A. General industry information
       1. What are the chief characteristics of the industry (economic, technological, political, social, change)?
       2. How does the plan address these? How is the proposed venture impacted by these?
       3. How attractive is the industry in terms of its prospects for above average profitability?
       4. What has the industry growth rate been for the past five years, and what is it projected to be for the next five? Give specific support or justification for these projections.
       5. Have there been any recent transactions in the industry, such as IPOs, LBOs, private placements, mergers, or acquisitions? Describe the transactions and provide a brief explanation of the financial arrangements of each transaction.
    B. Competitive environment
       1. What competitive forces (entry barriers, substitutes, power of buyers and suppliers—rivalry is addressed in next section) are at work in the industry, and how strong are they?
       2. Has the plan identified the competitive environment and how the company will fit into that environment?
       3. Calculate total market available in dollars.
       4. Calculate degree of market saturation.
    C. Primary Competitor Analysis—*In-depth*
       1. Compare and contrast *major* competitors (from the plan and your own research) along core competitive dimensions, including but not limited to:

Product/Service	1st Mover
Pricing	Market Share
Distribution	Technology
Marketing	Financial Backing
Operations	Financial Performance
Strategic Partnerships	P/E (if publicly traded) or revenue multiplier

       2. Calculate market share available for this firm not already captured by competitors (dollars and users). Is this enough market share to achieve the financial projections in the plan?
       3. Which companies are in the strongest/weakest competitive position?
       4. Who will likely make what competitive moves next?
       5. What key factors will determine competitive success or failure?

III. Target Market/Customer Base (narrow focus)
    A. Describe the target market: size, scope, growth, growth potential, growth/demand drivers, price sensitivity, sales cycle.
    B. What is the need or want that the company is satisfying?

Continued

Table **14.1**	**Due Diligence Evaluation (*Continued*)**

    C.   What are the barriers that will keep competitors from copying this venture's product or service? What market inefficiencies exist?

    D.   How strong are competitive forces (rivalry, substitutes) within this target market?

    E.   What has the growth rate of the target market been for the past five years, and what is it projected to be for the next five? Provide support/justification for these projections.

IV. The Company *(This section asks you to evaluate the plan in terms of the industry and target market characteristics discussed.)*

    A.   Value proposition: What does the company do, and how does it provide value to its customers and investors?

    B.   Management team
        1.   Does this team have what it takes to make this venture a success?
        2.   Is success dependent on one key person? If so, is this recognized and dealt with in the plan (succession, key man replacement, etc.)?
        3.   HR gaps? Plans to address gaps?

    C.   Business model
        1.   How does the company make money?
        2.   How and when does it plan to be profitable?
        3.   Does the plan follow a demonstrated success formula? Support with 1 to 2 examples. For example, briefly discuss similar companies in terms of size (revenues/employees), operations, revenue model, and/or business model. These companies could be direct competitors or similar firms that are not in the same market, but instead just a similar type of company/model.

    D.   Strategy
        1.   How does the company plan on achieving success in its business model?
        2.   What other strategic approaches might work well in this situation? Give examples.

    E.   Marketing plan
        1.   How will the company convert prospects into customers?
        2.   Who makes the customer's purchase decisions? When and how are the decisions made? What dimensions are critical to the customer in making the decisions? Is the plan specific in defining their strategy in this area?
        3.   Does the company have a base of current customers? Does their plan address customer retention?

    F.   Operations
        1.   Does the company's operating plan make sense in terms of supporting its strategy and business model?

V. Company Situation Analysis

    A.   What are the company's strengths, weaknesses, opportunities, and threats?

    B.   Look at your competitor analysis; is the company competitive on cost? Is it differentiated compared to competitors? How?

    C.   How strong is the company's competitive position? Are there entry barriers that protect the company? What key strategic factors support this proposition? Which ones are counter to its success?

    D.   What strategic issues does the company face?

VI. Financial Analysis *(Select the ones that apply to this plan. Provide the analysis if it is appropriate and especially note if it is not included in the plan.)*

    A.   Ratio analysis: liquidity, solvency, profitability, viability.

    B.   Compare projected growth rates versus historical industry growth rates. State why this company will be able to sustain the projected rate above that of its industry. If it is determined that the projections are too optimistic, what can be expected?

   C. Valuation
1. Calculate pre-money valuation. What supports this valuation (number of shares × price per share, current audited balance sheet/accepted revenue multiples, etc.)?
2. Triangulate this valuation by (1) comparing the P/E ratios or revenue multiples of similar companies and (2) discounting the company's cash flow projections.

   D. Other financial considerations:
1. Start-up cash spent or needed
2. Current burn rate
3. Cash needed for years one to five
4. Five-year revenues
5. Five-year profits
6. Break even:
   a. Revenues
   b. When

   E. Comments regarding financial statements, such as:
1. Accuracy
2. Abnormalities. Is the budget in line or out of hand? Is the accounting correct?
3. Needed assumptions
4. Other

VII. Additional Comments and Concerns
   A. Is the plan well written? Is it concise and to the point?
   B. Can the "layperson" understand it?
   C. Is the idea viable?
   D. Is this appropriate for venture investing? Can we expect enough growth? What is the risk/reward relationship?
   E. Other

Appendices
   I. Resources/Bibliography
  II. Other detailed support organized by section in order of reference

Source: Bethesda, MD: Beacon Venture Capital, 2008.

The entrepreneur also may apply a more general approach to better assess the viability of the potential purchase; however, one critical area that always needs to be addressed is *the future trends of the business*, which require an overall look at the particular industry trends and how this business will fit into them. In addition, the financial health of the business needs to be projected, and *how much capital is needed to buy the venture* must be determined; this step requires understanding that the final purchase price is not the only factor that needs to be taken into consideration. Repairs, new inventory, opening expenses, and working capital are just a few of the additional costs that should be considered. Figure 14.1 illustrates how to calculate the total amount needed to buy a business venture.[4]

Figure 14.1 Total Amount Needed to Buy a Business

Family Living Expenses	From last paycheck to takeover day	$ _____
	Moving expense	_____
	For three months after takeover day	_____
Purchase Price	Total amount (or down payment plus three monthly installments)	_____
Sales Tax	On purchased furniture and equipment	_____
Professional Services	Escrow, accounting, legal	_____
Deposits, Prepayments, Licenses	Last month's rent (first month's rent in Operating Expense below)	_____
	Utility deposits	_____
	Sales tax deposit	_____
	Business licenses	_____
	Insurance premiums	_____
Takeover Announcements	Newspaper advertising	_____
	Mail announcements	_____
	Exterior sign changes	_____
	New stationery and forms	_____
New Inventory		_____
New Fixtures and Equipment		_____
Remodeling and Redecorating		_____
Three Months' Operating Expense	Including loan repayments	_____
Reserve to Carry Customer Accounts		_____
Cash	Petty cash, change, etc.	_____
	Total $	_____

NOTE: Money for living and business expenses for at least three months should be set aside in a bank savings account and not used for any other purpose. This is a cushion to help get through the start-up period with a minimum of worry. If expense money for a longer period can be provided, it will add to peace of mind and help the buyer concentrate on building the business.

Analyzing the Business

When analyzing small, closely held businesses, entrepreneurs should not make comparisons with larger corporations. Many factors distinguish these types of corporations, and valuation factors that have no effect on large firms may be significantly important to smaller enterprises. For example, many closely held ventures have the following shortcomings:

- *Lack of management depth.* The degrees of skills, versatility, and competence are limited.
- **Undercapitalization**. The amount of equity investment is usually low (often indicating a high level of debt).
- *Insufficient controls.* Because of the lack of available management and extra capital, measures in place for monitoring and controlling operations are usually limited.
- **Divergent goals**. The entrepreneur often has a vision for the venture that differs from the investors' goals or stockholders' desires, thus causing internal conflicts in the firm.

These weaknesses indicate the need for careful analysis of the small business.

The checklist in Table 14.2, which is patterned after the information required for an effective business plan (see Chapter 12), provides a concise method for examining the various factors that differentiate one firm from another.

Table 14.2   Checklist for Analyzing a Business

History of the Business

The original name of business and any subsequent name changes

Date company was founded

Names of all subsidiaries and divisions; when they were formed and their function

States where company is incorporated

States where company is licensed to do business as a foreign corporation

Review of corporate charter, bylaws, and minutes

Company's original line of business and any subsequent changes

Market and Competition

Company's major business and market

Description of major projects

Sales literature on products

Growth potential of major markets in which company operates

Name, size, and market position of principal competitors

How does company's product differ from that of the competition?

Company's market niche

Information on brand, trade, and product names

Sales pattern of product lines—that is, are sales seasonal or cyclical?

Review of any statistical information available on the market—for example, trade associations, government reports, and Wall Street reports

Comparative product pricing

Gross profit margin on each product line (analyze sales growth and profit changes for three years)

Concentration of government business

Research and development expenditures—historical and projected

Sales and Distribution

How does company sell—own sales force or through manufacturer representatives?

Compensation of sales force

Details on advertising methods and expenditures

Details on branch sales offices, if any

Details on standard sales terms, discounts offered, and return and allowance policies

Are any sales made on consignment?

Does company warehouse its inventory?

If company uses distributors, how are they paid, and what are their responsibilities? (For example, do they provide warranty services?)

Are company's products distributed nationwide or in a certain geographic area?

Continued

Table **14.2** **Checklist for Analyzing a Business (*Continued*)**

Names and addresses of company's principal customers

Sales volume of principal customers by product line for last few years

How long have customers been buying from company?

Credit rating of principal customers

Historical bad-debt experience of company

Details on private-label business, if any

Do sales terms involve any maintenance agreements?

Do sales terms offer any express or implied warranties?

Has company experienced any product liability problems?

Does company lease, as well as sell, any of its products?

What is the percentage of foreign business? How is this business sold, financed, and delivered?

Have any new products come on the market that would make company's products obsolete or less competitive?

Have any big customers been lost? If so, why?

Size and nature of market—fragmented or controlled by large companies?

Manufacturing

Full list of all manufacturing facilities

Are facilities owned or leased?

Does company manufacture from basic raw materials, or is it an assembly-type operation?

Types and availability of materials required to manufacture the product

Time length of production cycle

Does company make a standard shelf-type product, manufacture to specification, or both?

How is quality control handled in the factory?

What is the accounting system for work in process?

Are any licenses needed to manufacture product?

What is the present sales capacity based on current manufacturing equipment?

Does company have a proprietary manufacturing process?

What is company's safety record in its factory operations?

Do any problems with OSHA or federal or state environmental regulations exist?

What is stability of company's supplier relationships?

Employees

Total number of employees by function

Does a union exist? If not, what is the probability of unionization? If a union exists, what have been its historical relations with company?

Any strikes or work stoppages?

Details on local labor market

Details on company's wage and personnel policies

Is employee level fixed, or can workforce be varied easily in terms of business volume?

What is company's historical labor turnover, especially in key management?

Analysis of working conditions

Table **14.2**	Checklist for Analyzing a Business (*Continued*)

Analysis of general employee morale

Has the company ever been cited for a federal violation—for example, OSHA, Pregnancy Discrimination Act, Fair Labor Practices?

What are fringe benefits, vacation time, sick leave, and so on?

Physical Facilities

List of all company-used facilities, giving location, square footage, and cost

Which facilities are owned? Which leased?

What is present condition of all facilities, including machinery and equipment?

If any facilities are leased, what are the details of expiration term, cost, renewal options, and so forth?

Are current facilities adequate for current and projected needs?

Will any major problems occur if expansion is needed?

Is adequate insurance maintained?

Are facilities adequately protected against casualty loss, such as fire damage, through sprinkler systems, burglar alarms, or other measures?

Are facilities modern and functional for work process and employees?

Are facilities air conditioned and do they have adequate electric, heat, gas, water, and sanitary service?

Are facilities easily accessible to required transportation?

What is cost, net book value, and replacement value for company-owned buildings and equipment?

Ownership

List of all current owners of the company's common and preferred stock, by class if applicable

List of all individuals and the number of their shares exercisable under stock option and warrant agreements with prices and expiration dates

Breakdown of ownership by shares and percentage: actual and pro forma (assuming warrants and stock options exercised)

Does common stock have preemptive rights or liquidation or dividend preference?

Do the shares carry an investment letter?

Do restrictions on the transferability of the shares or on their use as collateral exist?

Do any buy/sell agreements exist?

Does an employee stock ownership plan or stock bonus plan exist?

Are the shares fully paid for?

Are any shareholders' agreements outstanding?

Has any stock been sold below par or stated value?

Does cumulative voting exist?

With respect to the principal owner's stock, have any shares been gifted or placed in a trust?

How many shares does the principal stockholder own directly and beneficially (including family)?

If all stock options and warrants are exercised, will the principal stockholder still control 51 percent of the company?

If a business is being bought or sold, what percentage of the total outstanding shares is needed for approval?

Continued

Table **14.2**	**Checklist for Analyzing a Business (*Continued*)**

Financial

Three years of financial statements

- Current ratio and net quick ratio
- Net working capital and net quick assets
- Total debt as a percentage of stockholder's equity
- Source and application of funds schedules

Analysis of the company's basic liquidity and turnover ratios

- Cash as a percent of current liabilities
- Accounts receivable and inventory turnovers
- Age of accounts payable
- Sales to net working capital

If company has subsidiaries (or divisions), consolidating statements of profit and loss

Verification of the cash balance and maximum and minimum cash balances needed throughout year

If company owns marketable securities, what is their degree of liquidity (salability) and current market values?

Age of all accounts and notes receivable, any customer concentration, and the adequacy of bad debt reserve

Cost basis for recording inventories and any inventory reserves; age of inventory and relation to cost of sales (turnover)

Details on all fixed assets, including date of purchase, original cost, accumulated depreciation, and replacement value

Current market appraisals on all fixed assets, real estate, and machinery and equipment

Analysis of any prepaid expenses or deferred charges as to nature and as to amortization in or advance to affiliates; comparison of true value to book value; financial statements

Personal financial statements of principal stockholders

If company carries any goodwill or intangible items, such as patents or trademarks, what is their true value (to extent possible)? Does company have any intangible assets of value not carried on books (such as mailing lists in a publishing operation)?

Analysis of all current liabilities, including age of accounts payable and details of all bank debt and lines of credit, including interest rate, term, and collateral; loan agreements

Details on all long-term debt by creditor, including loan agreement covenants that may affect future operations

Do any contingent liabilities or other outstanding commitments, such as long-term supplier agreements exist?

Details on franchise, lease, and royalty agreements

Income statement accounts for at least three years and analysis of any significant percentage variances, that is, cost of sales as percent of sales

Company's tax returns—do they differ from its financial statements? Which years still may be open for audit?

Three-year projection of income and cash flow for reasonableness of future sales and profits and to establish financing needs

Pension, profit-sharing, and stock bonus plans for contractual commitments and unfunded past-service liability costs

Table	**14.2**	**Checklist for Analyzing a Business (*Continued*)**

Management

Details on all officers and directors—length of service, age, business background, compensation, and fringe benefits

Ownership positions: number of shares, stock options, and warrants

Similar details on other nonofficer/nondirector key management

Organizational chart

What compensation-type fringe benefits are offered to key management: bonuses, retirement-plan stock bonuses, company-paid insurance, deferred compensation?

What is management's reputation in its industry?

Does management have any personal interests in any other businesses? Does it have any other conflicts of interest?

Does key management devote 100 percent of its time to the business?

Any employment contracts—amount of salary, length of time, other terms

Has key management agreed to a noncompete clause and agreed not to divulge privileged information obtained while employed with company?

Establishing a Firm's Value

After using the checklist in Table 14.2, the entrepreneur can begin to examine the various methods used to valuate a business. The establishment of an actual value is more of an art than a science—estimations, assumptions, and projections are all part of the process. The quantified figures are calculated based, in part, on such hidden values and costs as goodwill, personal expenses, family members on the payroll, planned losses, and the like.[5]

Several traditional valuation methods are presented here, each using a particular approach that covers these hidden values and costs. Employing these methods will provide the entrepreneur with a general understanding of how the financial analysis of a firm works. Remember, also, that many of these methods are used concurrently and that the *final* value determination will be the actual price agreed on by the buyer and seller.

Valuation Methods

Table 14.3 lists the various methods that may be used for business valuation. Each method is described and key points about them are presented. In this section, specific attention will be concentrated on the three methods that are considered the principal measures used in current business valuations: (1) adjusted tangible assets (balance sheet values), (2) price/earnings (multiple earnings value), and (3) discounted future earnings.

ADJUSTED TANGIBLE BOOK VALUE

A common method of valuing a business is to compute its net worth as the difference between total assets and total liabilities. However, it is important to adjust for certain assets in order to assess true economic worth, because inflation and depreciation affect the value of some assets.

In the computation of the **adjusted tangible book value**, goodwill, patents, deferred financing costs, and other intangible assets are considered with the other assets and deducted from or added to net worth. This upward or downward adjustment reflects the excess of the fair

Table **14.3**	Methods for Venture Valuation

Method	Description/Explanation	Notes/Key Points
Fixed price	Two or more owners set initial value Based on what owners "think" business is worth Uses figures from any one or a combination of methods Common for buy/sell agreements	Inaccuracies exist due to personal estimates Should allow periodic update
Book value (known as balance sheet method) 1. Tangible 2. Adjusted tangible	1. *Tangible book value:* Set by the business's balance sheet Reflects net worth of the firm Total assets less total liabilities (adjusted for intangible assets) 2. *Adjusted tangible book value:* Uses book value approach Reflects fair market value for certain assets Upward/downward adjustments in plant and equipment, inventory, and bad debt reserves	Some assets also appreciate or depreciate substantially; thus, not an accurate valuation Adjustments in assets eliminate some of the inaccuracies and reflect a fair market value of each asset
Multiple of earnings	Net income capitalized using a price/earnings ratio (net income multiplied by P/E number) 15% capitalization rate often used (equivalent to a P/E multiple of 6.7, which is 1 divided by 0.15) High-growth businesses use lower capitalization rate (e.g., 5%, which is a multiple of 20) Stable businesses use higher capitalization rate (e.g., 10%, which is a multiple of 10) Derived value divided by number of outstanding shares to obtain per-share value	Capitalization rates vary as to firm's growth; thus, estimates or P/E used must be taken from similar publicly traded corporation
Price/earnings ratio (P/E)	Similar to a return-on-investment approach Determined by price of common stock divided by after-tax earnings Closely held firms must multiply net income by an appropriate multiple, usually derived from similar publicly traded corporations Sensitive to market conditions (prices of stocks)	More common with public corporations Market conditions (stock prices) affect this ratio
Discounted future earnings (discounted cash flow)	Attempts to establish future earning power in current dollars Projects future earnings (five years), calculates present value using a then discounted rate Based on projected "timing" of future income	Based on premise that cash flow is most important factor Effective method if (1) business being valued needs to generate a return greater than investment and (2) only cash receipts can provide the money for reinvesting in growth

Table
14.3   **Methods for Venture Valuation (*Continued*)**

Method	Description/Explanation	Notes/Key Points
Return on investment (ROI)	Net profit divided by investment Provides an earnings ratio Need to calculate probabilities of future earnings Combination of return ratio, present value tables, and weighted probabilities	Will *not* establish a value for the business Does not provide projected future earnings
Replacement value	Based on value of each asset if it had to be *replaced* at current cost Firm's worth calculated as if building from "scratch" Inflation and annual depreciation of assets are considered in raising the value above reported book value Does *not* reflect earning power or intangible assets	Useful for selling a company that's seeking to break into a new line of business Fails to consider earnings potential Does not include intangible assets (goodwill, patents, and so on)
Liquidation value	Assumes business ceases operation Sells assets and pays off liabilities Net amount after payment of all liabilities is distributed to shareholders Reflects "bottom value" of a firm Indicates amount of money that could be borrowed on a secured basis Tends to favor seller since all assets are valued as if converted to cash	Assumes each division of assets sold separately at auction Effective in giving absolute bottom value below which a firm should liquidate rather than sell
Excess earnings	Developed by the U.S. Treasury to determine a firm's intangible assets (for income tax purposes) Intent is for use only when no better method available Internal Revenue Service refers to this method as a last resort Method does not include intangibles with estimated useful lives (i.e., patents, copyrights)	Method of last resort (if no other method available) Very seldom used
Market value	Needs a "known" price paid for a similar business Difficult to find recent comparisons Methods of sale may differ—installment versus cash Should be used only as a reference point	Valuable only as a reference point Difficult to find recent, similar firms that have been sold

market value of each asset above or below the value reported on the balance sheet. Following is an example:

	Book Value	Fair Market Value
Inventory	$100,000	$125,000
Plant and equipment	400,000	600,000
Other intangibles		(50,000)
	—	—
	$500,000	$675,000

Excess = $175,000

Remember that, in industry comparisons of adjusted values, only assets used in the actual operation of the business are included.

Other significant balance sheet and income statement adjustments include (1) bad debt reserves; (2) low-interest, long-term debt securities; (3) investments in affiliates; and (4) loans and advances to officers, employees, or other companies. Additionally, earnings should be adjusted. Only true earnings derived from the operations of the business should be considered. One-time items (from the sale of a company division or asset, for example) should be excluded. Also, if the company has been using a net operational loss carry forward, so its pretax income has not been fully taxed, this also should be considered.

Upward (or downward) income and balance sheet adjustments should be made for any unusually large bad-debt or inventory write-off, and for certain accounting practices, such as accelerated versus straight-line depreciation.

PRICE/EARNINGS RATIO (MULTIPLE OF EARNINGS) METHOD

The **price/earnings ratio (P/E)** is a common method used for valuing publicly held corporations. The valuation is determined by dividing the market price of the common stock by the earnings per share. A company with 100,000 shares of common stock and a net income of $100,000 would have earnings per share of $1. If the stock price rose to $5 per share, the P/E would be 5 ($5 divided by $1). Additionally, since the company has 100,000 shares of common stock, the valuation of the enterprise now would be $500,000 (100,000 shares × $5).

The primary advantage of a price/earnings approach is its simplicity. However, this advantage applies only to publicly traded corporations. Closely held companies do not have prices in the open market for their stock and thus must rely on the use of a multiple derived by comparing the firm to similar public corporations. This approach has four major drawbacks:[6]

1. The stock of a private company is not publicly traded. It is illiquid and may actually be restricted from sale (that is, not registered with the Securities and Exchange Commission). Thus, any P/E multiple usually must, by definition, be subjective and lower than the multiple commanded by comparable publicly traded stocks.

2. The stated net income of a private company may not truly reflect its actual earning power. To avoid or defer paying taxes, most business owners prefer to keep pretax income down. In addition, the closely held business may be "overspending" on fringe benefits instituted primarily for the owner's benefit.

3. Common stock that is bought and sold in the public market normally reflects only a small portion of the business's total ownership. The sale of a large controlling block of stock (typical of closely held businesses) demands a premium.

4. It is very difficult to find a truly comparable publicly held company, even in the same industry. Growth rates, competition, dividend payments, and financial profiles (liquidity and leverage) rarely will be the same.

entrepreneurship in practice

Dusting Off Shelved Opportunities

The successful entrepreneur is always on the lookout for the next opportunity to seize. Some opportunities are more evident than others. For instance, when social networking became all the rage with the growing popularity of MySpace and Facebook, companies began to sprout up to offer various add-ons for both systems. Another example is the proliferation of accessory providers that followed the success of Apple's iPods, iPhone, and iTouch. Although Apple manufactures its own accessories, many off-brand substitutes also have flooded the market.

Mobile device accessories and social networking applications are markets that developed as part of a growing social trend, both of which were movements that were fairly obvious to the casual observer. Not all opportunities are so easy to spot. Human nature is to ignore paths that have been previously dismissed, but with various economic forces constantly impacting the environment, disregarding opportunities simply because they were previously considered is shortsighted.

The oil industry presents a recent example of a market that has been opened to opportunities that were long forgotten, offering challenges and, in turn, significant potential for both established companies and start-ups. The two areas that have recently become popular are tar sands and oil shale. The first requires significant cost due to the state in which the oil is recovered, as a thick slurry of tar and sand; the second also requires an expensive process to recover the oil as result of it being trapped in rock. The required capital for both processes is what led companies to dismiss the reserves; however, as a result of the rise in the price of oil, they have become financially viable to pursue.

The tar sands are now being heavily sourced, but companies have been slower to pursue oil shale due to the energy required to heat the rock and extract the oil. The Green River Formation is a 17,000 square mile stretch of a prehistoric riverbed that holds approximately 800 billion barrels of recoverable oil, which is triple the amount of Saudi Arabia's reserves. This unconventional reserve, arguably the largest on the planet, presents a significant prize for the company able to develop an operationally efficient method to recover the oil. Royal Dutch Shell believes that it has cracked the code.

One of Shell's scientists has engineered a technology that will profitably extract the oil from the shale as long as the price of oil stays at $30 a barrel or higher. By 2020, the company is estimating it can produce 2 million barrels a day. The United States currently consumes 21 million barrels daily, so the reserve would not lead to the country becoming self-sufficient in respect to its fuel needs; however, the reserve would alleviate some of the risk and reduce the premium currently charged for oil domestically due to international instability.

Shell has filed more than 200 patents for recovering the oil shale and has begun the process of winning public approval for starting the process of diversifying the country's oil supply through oil shale. Unlike other oil reserves, such as those found in Alaska, the company projects that oil shale could support consistent production for hundreds of years. Shell's technology, known as the In Situ Conversion Process (ICP), requires the company to drill 1,800-foot wells, insert heating rods, and raise the temperature of the shale to 650 degrees Fahrenheit. The company has spent 28 years and $200 million exploring the potential for oil shale, despite its competitors abandoning similar efforts and the market for oil, until recently, being unable to support the costs incurred.

Where other companies have failed, Shell has found an environmentally friendly, financially feasible method for producing high-grade oil from oil shale. The climbing price of oil was necessary for Shell's investment to pay off; yet, its commitment has led other companies to revisit an opportunity they abandoned decades before. Shell's foresight—along with a favorable market—has positioned the company as the leader in a venture that could generate $2.2 billion in annual pretax profits at 300,000 barrels a day and as much as $22 billion at 3 million barrels a day. Oil shale's revenue potential, proven through Shell's efforts, has forced companies to rethink their strategic positions in order to remain competitive.

Source: Adapted from Jon Birger, "Oil Shale May Finally Have Its Moment," *Fortune,* November 1, 2007, http://money.cnn.com/2007/10/30/magazines/fortune/Oil_from_stone.fortune/index.htm (accessed April 9, 2008).

When applied to a closely held firm, the following is an example of how the multiple-of-earnings method could be used:

Shares of common stock	=	100,000
2010 net income	=	$100,000
15% capitalization rate assumed	=	6.7 price/earnings multiple (derived by dividing 1 by 15 and multiplying the result by 100)
Price per share	=	$6.70
Value of company	=	100,000 × $6.70 = $670,000

DISCOUNTED EARNINGS METHOD

Most analysts agree that the real value of any venture is its potential earning power. The **discounted earnings method**, more than any other, determines the firm's true value. One example of a pricing formula that uses earning power as well as adjusted tangible book value is illustrated in Figure 14.2.

The idea behind discounting the firm's cash flows is that dollars earned in the future (based on projections) are worth less than dollars earned today (due to the loss of purchasing power). With this in mind, the "timing" of projected income or cash flows is a critical factor.

"Entrepreneurial Process: What Is This Venture Worth?" provides a step-by-step example of the process of discounting cash flows. Basically, the method uses a four-step process:

1. Expected cash flow is estimated. For long-established firms, historical data are effective indicators, although adjustments should be made when available data indicate that future cash flows will change.

2. An appropriate discount rate is determined. The buyer's viewpoint has to be considered in the calculation of this rate. The buyer and seller often disagree, because each requires a particular rate of return and will view the risks differently. Another point the seller often overlooks is that the buyer will have other investment opportunities to consider. The appropriate rate, therefore, must be weighed against these factors.

3. A reasonable life expectancy of the business must be determined. All firms have a life cycle that depends on factors such as whether the business is a one product/one market or multiproduct/multimarket.

4. The firm's value is then determined by discounting the estimated cash flow by the appropriate discount rate over the expected life of the business.[7]

Term Sheets in Venture Valuation

Whenever investors are examining a venture for potential infusion of capital, the value of the venture comes into play. This always involves what is called the **term sheet**. This document outlines the material terms and conditions of a venture agreement. After a *term sheet* has been executed, it guides legal counsel in the preparation of a proposed final agreement. It then guides, but is not necessarily binding, the final terms of the agreement.

Term sheets are very similar to **letters of intent (LOI)** in that they are both preliminary, mostly nonbinding documents meant to record two or more parties' intentions to enter into a future agreement based on specified (but incomplete or preliminary) terms. Many LOIs, however, contain provisions that are binding, such as nondisclosure agreements, a covenant to negotiate in good faith, or a "stand-still" provision that promises exclusive rights to negotiate.

Figure **14.2**	**A Traditional Pricing Model**

The following step-by-step process outlines the traditional pricing formula used when calcuating the value of a business:

Step 1. Determine the adjusted tangible net worth of the business. (The total market value of all current and long-term assets less liabilities.)

Step 2. Estimate how much the buyer could earn annually with an amount equal to the value of the tangible net worth invested elsewhere.

Step 3. Add to this a salary normal for an owner-operator of the business. This combined figure provides a reasonable estimate of the income the buyer can earn elsewhere with the investment and effort involved in working in the business.

Step 4. Determine the average annual net earnings of the business (net profit before subtracting owner's salary) over the past few years.

This is before income taxes, to make it comparable with earnings from other sources or by individuals in different tax brackets. (The tax implications of alternative investments should be carefully considered.)

This trend of earnings is a key factor. Have they been rising steadily, falling steadily, remaining constant, or fluctuating widely? The earnings figure should be adjusted to reflect these trends.

Step 5. Subtract the total of earning power (2) and reasonable salary (3) from this average net earnings figure (4). This gives the extra earning power of the business.

Step 6. Use this extra earnings figure to estimate the value of the intangibles. This is done by multiplying the extra earnings by what is termed the "years-of-profit" figure.

This "years-of-profit" multiplier pivots on these points. How unique are the intangibles offered by the firm? How long would it take to set up a similar business and bring it to this stage of development? What expenses and risks would be involved? What is the price of goodwill in similar firms? Will the seller be signing an agreement with a covenant not to compete?

If the business is well-established, a factor of five or more might be used, especially if the firm has a valuable name, patent, or location. A multiplier of three might be reasonable for a moderately seasoned firm. A younger but profitable firm might merely have a one-year profit figure.

Step 7. Final price equals adjusted tangible net worth plus value of intangibles (extra earnings times "years of profit").

Example

	Enterprise X	Enterprise Y
1. Adjusted value of tangible net worth (assets less liabilities)	2,000,000	2,000,000
2. Earning power at 8%[a] of an amount equal to the adjusted tangible net worth, if invested in a comparable risk business	160,000	160,000
3. Reasonable salary for owner-operator in the business	50,000	50,000
4. Net earnings of the business over recent years (net profit before subtracting owner's salary)	255,000	209,000
5. Extra earning power of the business (line 4 minus lines 2 and 3)	45,000	(1,000)
6. Value of intangibles—using three-year profit figure for moderately well-established firm (3 times line 5)	135,000	0
7. Final price (lines 1 and 6)	2,135,000	2,000,000 (or less)

With *Entreprise X*, the seller receives a value for goodwill because the business is moderately well established and earning more than the buyer could earn elsewhere with similar risks and effort.

With *Enterprise Y*, the seller receives no value for goodwill because the business, even though it may have existed for a considerable time, is not earning as much as the buyer could through outside investment and effort. In fact, the buyer may feel that even an investment of $2,000,000—the current appraised value of net assets—is too much because it cannot earn sufficient return.

[a]This is an arbitrary figure, used for illustration. A reasonable figure depends on the stability and relative risks of the business and the investment picture generally. The rate of return should be similar to that which could be earned elsewhere with the same approximate risk.

the entrepreneurial process

What Is This Venture Worth?

When looking at a venture you wish to acquire, you will do the following:

1. Present the *net* cash-flow projections for this business for five years (2010 through 2014).

2. Change the format for presenting the data (you may find it easier to use).

3. Use a present value rate of 24 percent.

Assume you have an opportunity to buy a small division of a large company. Because you know the business intimately, you can accurately forecast the company's growth. Right now it's not profitable, but with your expertise and plans, you expect that it can generate $380,000 net cash flow over five years and have a value (net worth) of $400,000 at the end of year five. (The $380,000 net cash flow is *after* all cash outlays.)

Question

Because you want to earn a minimum annual return of 24 percent on your investment (that is, the purchase price), how much should you pay for the division?

Here are the facts: Assume that the acquisition will occur on December 31, 2010, and the projected annual net cash flow (the excess of all cash inflow over all cash outflow) looks like this:

	2010	2011	2012	2013	2014
Net cash flow (thousands)	$0	$40	$80	$110	$150

Answer

Because you want an annual return of 24 percent on your money, simply compute the present value of the projected net cash-flow stream. You also must compute the value of the $400,000 net worth position (projected assets less liabilities) at the end of year five.

Referring to present value tables in financial handbooks (or using a calculator), you can obtain the following data:

Year	Present Value Factor For 24% Rate of Return
Today	1.000
1	0.806
2	0.650
3	0.524
4	0.423
5	0.341

All that is needed now is to prepare a table showing the net cash flows for the five-year period. You then multiply the present value factor (for a 24 percent return) by the net cash flow for each year.

Year	Net Cash Flow	Present Value Factor	Today's Value
2010	$0	0.806	$0
2011	40,000	0.650	26,000
2012	80,000	0.524	41,920
2013	110,000	0.423	46,530
2014	550,000[a]	0.341	187,550[a]
Totals	$780,000		$302,000

As computed, the total value of the projected net cash-flow stream is $302,000 today—and this includes the projected $400,000 net worth at the end of year five.

In other words, if the division were purchased *today* for its net cash-flow value of $302,000, and if the projected cash flows for the five years were generated (including the projected net worth value of $400,000), you would realize a 24 percent annual rate of return on your $302,000 investment over the five-year period.

[a]Includes $150,000 net cash flow and $400,000 net worth of division at end of fifth year.

Source: Thomas J. Martin, *Valuation Reference Manual* (Hicksville, NY: Thomar Publications, 1987), 68. Figures updated, 2008.

The purposes of an LOI may be:

*   To clarify the key points of a complex transaction for the convenience of the parties
*   To declare officially that the parties are currently negotiating
*   To provide safeguards in case a deal collapses during negotiation

The difference between a term sheet and an LOI is slight and mostly a matter of style: An LOI is typically written in letter form and focuses on the intentions; a term sheet skips most of the formalities and lists deal terms in bullet-point format. To help clarify the concepts of term sheets in the valuation process, we present the following terminology that is common in these documents.

Price/Valuation The value of a company is what drives the price investors will pay for a piece of the action. The information used to determine valuation comes out of the due diligence process and has to do with the strength of the management team, market potential, the sustainable advantage of the product/service, and potential financial returns. Another way to look at valuation is how much money it will take to make the company a success. In the end, the value of a company is the price at which a willing buyer and seller can complete a transaction.

Fully Diluted Ownership and valuation is typically calculated on a fully diluted basis. This means that all securities (including preferred stock, options, and warrants) that can result in additional common shares are counted in determining the total amount of shares outstanding for the purposes of determining ownership or valuation.

Type of Security Investors typically receive convertible preferred stock in exchange for making the investment in a new venture. This type of stock has priority over common stock if the company is acquired or liquidated and assets are distributed. The higher priority of the preferred stock justifies a higher price, compared to the price paid by founders for common stock. *Convertible* means that the shares may be exchanged for a fixed number of common shares.

Liquidation Preference When the company is sold or liquidated, the preferred stockholders will receive a certain fixed amount before any assets are distributed to the common stockholders; this is known as liquidation preference. A *participating preferred* stockholder not only will receive the fixed amount but will also share in any additional amounts distributed to common stock.

Dividend Preference Dividends are paid first to preferred stock and then to common stock. This dividend may be cumulative, so that it accrues from year to year until paid in full—or noncumulative and discretionary.

Redemption Preferred stock may be redeemed or retired, either at the option of the company or the investors, or on a mandatory basis—frequently at some premium over the initial purchase price of the stock. One reason why venture firms want this right is due to the finite life of each investment partnership managed by the firm.

Conversion Rights Preferred stock may be converted into common stock at a certain conversion price, generally whenever the stockholder chooses. Conversion may also happen automatically in response to certain events, such as when the company goes public.

Antidilution Protection The conversion price of the preferred stock is subject to adjustment for certain diluting events, such as stock splits or stock dividends; this is known as antidilution protection. The conversion price is typically subject to *price protection,* which is an adjustment based on future sales of stock at prices below the conversion price. Price protection can take many forms. One form is called *ratchet* protection, which lowers the conversion price to the price at which any new stock is sold no matter the number of shares. Another form is broad-based *weighted average* protection, which adjusts the conversion price according to a formula that incorporates the number of new shares being issued and their price. In many cases, a certain number of shares are exempted from this protection to cover anticipated assurances to key employees, consultants, and directors.

Voting Rights Preferred stock has a number of votes equal to the number of shares of common stock into which it is convertible. Preferred stock usually has special voting rights, such as the right to elect one or more of the company's directors, or to approve certain types of corporate actions, such as amending the articles of incorporation or creating a new series of preferred stock.

Right of First Refusal Holders of preferred stock typically have the right to purchase additional shares when issued by the company, up to their current aggregate ownership percentage.

Co-Sale Right Founders will often enter into a co-sale agreement with investors. A co-sale right gives investors some protection against founders selling their interest to a third party by giving investors the right to sell some of their stock as part of such a sale.

Registration Rights Registration rights are generally given to preferred investors as part of their investment. These rights provide investors liquidity by allowing them to require the company to register their shares for sale to the public—either as part of an offering already planned by the company (called piggyback rights), or in a separate offering initiated at the investors' request (called demand rights).

Vesting on Founders' Stock A percentage of founders' stock, which decreases over time, can be purchased by the company at cost if a founder leaves the company. This protects investors against founders leaving the company after it gets funded.[8]

Additional Factors in the Valuation Process

After reviewing these valuation methods, the entrepreneur needs to remember that additional factors intervene in the valuation process and should be given consideration. Presented next are three factors that may influence the final valuation of the venture.

Avoiding Start-Up Costs

Some buyers are willing to pay more for a business than what the valuation methods illustrate its worth to be. This is because buyers often are trying to avoid the costs associated with start-up and are willing to pay a little more for an existing firm. The higher price they pay will be still less than actual start-up costs and also avoids the problems associated with working to establish a clientele. Thus, for some buyers a known commodity may command a higher price.

Accuracy of Projections

The sales and earnings of a venture are always projected on the basis of historical financial and economic data. Short histories, fluctuating markets, and uncertain environments are all reasons for buyers to keep projections in perspective. It is critical that they examine the trends, fluctuations, or patterns involved in projections for sales revenues (higher prices or more customers?), market potential (optimistic or realistic assumptions?), and earnings potential (accurate cost/revenue/market data?), because each area has specific factors that need to be either understood or measured for the accuracy of the projection.

Control Factor

The degree of control, or **control factor**, an owner legally has over the firm can affect its valuation. If the owner's interest is 100 percent or such that the complete operation of the firm is under his or her influence, then that value is equal to the enterprise's value. If the owner does not possess such control, then the value is less. For example, buying out a 49 percent shareholder will not be effective in controlling a 51 percent shareholder. Also, two 49 percent shareholders are equal until a 2 percent "swing vote" shareholder makes a move. Obviously, minority interests also must be discounted due to lack of liquidity—a minority interest in a privately held corporation is difficult to sell. Overall, it is important to look at the control factor as another facet in the purchase of any interest in a firm.

If Dubai Can Do It . . .

One of the biggest things happening in the Middle East in the new millennium is the development of Dubai, a small city-state that saved itself by building an international airport as well as high-priced, high-class hotels and entertainment venues after it had run out of oil. The novel strategy that Dubai embraced allowed it not only to salvage its economy but to simultaneously become an expert on architecture and urban development. This makeover has led to its developers being recruited to provide services to other countries, all of which are aspiring to build the next Dubai. First world companies planning buildings on a similar scale to the ones recently constructed in Dubai have also solicited the assistance of its developers.

The success of Dubai is made more spectacular by the innovative approach it has taken to garner international attention. While its petroleum-rich neighbors—including Saudi Arabia, Abu Dhabi, and Kuwait—have continued to make conservative investments in *Fortune* 500 companies, Dubai has abandoned the traditional strategy altogether by promising developing areas around the world the same kind of economic success that it has experienced. When the Burj Al Arab, the world's tallest freestanding hotel, was completed in 1999, it ushered in a new period for the region. More investments followed the completion of the hotel, with each project being equally if not more extravagant. Countries including Algeria, Vietnam, Indonesia, and Senegal have hired Dubai's developers to engineer strategies that will revitalize their economies.

The key to Dubai's success is its ruler, Sheikh Mohammed bin Rashid Al Maktoum. Despite the successful turnaround that he has managed to produce in Dubai, he realized that the only way for the emirate to continue to grow was for his largest development companies—namely, Dubai Holding, Dubai World, and Emaar Properties—to diversify their clientele by offering their services to the world. He understood that expanding the businesses outside of Dubai not only would ensure that they would be able to hedge against the inevitable slowdown in Dubai's massive development efforts, but also would guarantee that the world continued to view Dubai as a model to emulate. The companies are selling nothing less than the Dubai-ification of the globe, which involves applying a simple formula: Run a country's port, establish free-trade zones to encourage commerce, and build luxury hotels with residential properties nearby to establish a stable economy.

Dubai is a testament to the ability of an organization—in this case, a region—to reinvent itself. Change is rarely easy, especially when it involves completely restructuring an establishment; however, management bears the burden of knowing when the existing strategy must be abandoned in order for the company to survive and prosper.

Source: Adapted from Barney Gimbel, "Searching for the Next Dubai," *Fortune,* February 22, 2008, http://money.cnn .com/2008/02/20/news/international/Dubai_djibouti.fortune/ index.htm (accessed April 9, 2008).

Summary

Entrepreneurs need to understand how to valuate a business for either purchase or sale. Many would like to know the value of their businesses. Sometimes this is strictly for informational purposes, and other times it is for selling the operation. In either case, a number of ways of valuing an enterprise exist.

The first step is to analyze the business's overall operations, with a view to acquiring a comprehensive understanding of the firm's strong and weak points. Table 14.2 provided a checklist for this purpose. The second step is to establish a value for the firm. Table 14.3 set forth ten methods for the valuation of a venture. Three of the most commonly used are (1) adjusted tangible assets, (2) price/earnings ratio (multiple of earnings), and (3) discounted future earnings.

The adjusted tangible book value method computes the value of the business by revaluing the assets and then subtracting the liabilities. This is a fairly simple, straightforward process.

The price/earnings ratio method divides the market price of the common stock by the earnings per share and then multiplies by the number of shares issued. For example, a company with a price/earnings multiple of 10 and 100,000 shares of stock would be valued at $1 million.

The discounted earnings method takes the estimated cash flows for a predetermined number of years and discounts these sums back to the present using an appropriate discount rate. This is one of the most popular methods of valuing a business. Other factors to consider for valuing a business include start-up costs, accuracy of projections, and the control factor.

Key Terms and Concepts

adjusted tangible book value	divergent goals	liquidation preference
antidilution protection	due diligence	price/earnings ratio (P/E)
business valuation	emotional bias	term sheet
control factor	fully diluted	undercapitalization
discounted earnings method	letter of intent (LOI)	

Review and Discussion Questions

1. Identify and discuss the three underlying issues in the evaluation of a business.
2. Define the term *due diligence*. How is it applied to the acquisition of an existing venture?
3. To analyze a business, what types of questions or concerns should the entrepreneur address in the following areas: history of the business, market and competition, sales and distribution, management, and finances?
4. One of the most popular methods of business valuation is the adjusted tangible book value. Describe how this method works.

5. Explain how the price/earnings ratio method of valuation works. Give an example.
6. What are the steps involved in using the discounted earnings method? Give an example.
7. How do the following methods of valuing a venture work: fixed price, multiple of earnings, return on investment, replacement value, liquidation value, excess earnings, and market value? In each case, give an example.
8. Explain why the following are important factors to consider when valuing a business: start-up costs, accuracy of projections, degree of control.

Experiential Exercise

WHAT WOULD YOU RECOMMEND?

Jane Winfield would like to buy Ted Garner's company. She has conducted a detailed financial analysis of Ted's firm and has determined the following:

1. Book value of the inventory: $250,000

2. Discount rate on future earnings: 24 percent

3. Book value of the plant and equipment: $150,000

4. Fair market value of the inventory: $400,000

5. Fair market value of other intangibles: $60,000

6. Number of shares of common stock: 100,000

7. Fair market value of the plant and equipment: $400,000

8. Price/earnings multiple: 9

9. Book market value of other intangibles: $30,000

10. Estimated earnings over the next five years:

Year 1	$200,000
Year 2	300,000
Year 3	400,000
Year 4	500,000
Year 5	600,000

Based on this information, how much should Jane valuate the business according to each of the following methods: adjusted tangible assets, price/earnings ratio, and discounted future earnings? Based on your findings, recommend the valuation method she should use. Finally, given all of your calculations, estimate what the final price will be. Give reasons for this estimate. Enter your answers here.

a) Adjusted tangible assets valuation: _____

b) Price/earnings valuation: _____

c) Discounted future earnings valuation: _____

d) Final sales price: _____

Case 14.1

A VALUATION MATTER

Charles Jackson has always been interested in determining the value of his small business. He started the operation five years ago with $1,500 of savings, and since then it has grown into a firm that has 15 employees and annual sales of $1.88 million.

Charles has talked to his accountant regarding methods that can be used in valuing his business. His accountant has briefly explained two of these to Charles: adjusted tangible book value and discounted earnings. Charles has decided to use both methods in arriving at a valuation. Following is the information he has gathered to help him use both methods:

Adjusted Assets and Total Liabilities		Estimated Earnings Over Next Five Years	
Total liabilities	$700,000	Year 1	$100,000
After revaluation		Year 2	125,000
Inventory	600,000	Year 3	150,000
Plant and equipment	400,000	Year 4	200,000
Other assets	100,000	Year 5	250,000

Charles also believes that it is best to use a conservative discount rate. He has settled on 24 percent.

QUESTIONS

1. Using the adjusted tangible book value method, what is Charles's business worth? Show your calculations.

2. Using the discounted earnings method, what is Charles's business worth? Show your calculations.

3. Which of the two methods is more accurate? Why?

Case 14.2

WHICH WILL IT BE?

Georgia Isaacson and her son Rubin have been thinking about buying a business. After talking to seven entrepreneurs, all of whom have expressed an interest in selling their operations, the Isaacsons have decided to make an offer for a retail clothing store. The store is very well located, and its earnings over the past five years have been excellent. The current owner has told the Isaacsons he will sell for $500,000. The owner arrived at this value by projecting the earnings of the operation for the next seven years and then using a discount factor of 15 percent.

The Isaacsons are not sure the retail store is worth $500,000, but they do understand the method the owner used for arriving at this figure. Georgia feels that since the owner has been in business for only seven years, it is unrealistic to discount seven years of future earnings. A five-year estimate would be more realistic, in her opinion. Rubin feels that the discount factor is too low. He believes that 20 to 22 percent would be more realistic.

In addition to these concerns, the Isaacsons feel they would like to make an evaluation of the business using other methods. In particular, they would like to see what the value of the company would be when the adjusted tangible book value method is employed. They also would like to look at the replacement value and liquidation value methods.

"We know what the owner feels his business is worth," Georgia noted to her son. "However, we have to decide for ourselves what we think the operation is worth. From there, we can negotiate a final price. For the moment, I think we have to look at this valuation process from a number of different angles."

QUESTIONS

1. If the owner reduces the earnings estimates from seven to five years, what effect will this have on the final valuation? If he increases the discount factor from 15 percent to 20 to 22 percent, what effect will this have on the final valuation?

2. How do the replacement value and liquidation value methods work? Why would the Isaacsons want to examine these methods?

3. If the Isaacsons conclude that the business is worth $410,000, what will be the final selling price, assuming a sale is made? Defend your answer.

Notes

1. See, for example, W. G. Sanders and S. Bovie, "Sorting Things Out: Valuation of New Firms in Uncertain Markets," *Strategic Management Journal* 25, no. 2 (February 2004): 167–86; and Saikat Chaudhuri and Behnam Tabrizi, "Capturing the Real Value in High-Tech Acquisitions," *Harvard Business Review* (September/October 1999): 123–30.

2. "Acquisition Strategies—Part 1," *Small Business Reports* (January 1987): 34. Reprinted with permission from *Small Business Reports;* see also Laurence Capron, "The Long-Term Performance of Horizontal Acquisitions," *Strategic Management Journal* (November 1999): 987–1018.

3. "Valuing a Closely Held Business," *The Small Business Report* (November 1986): 30–31; see also Hal B. Heaton, "Valuing Small Businesses: The Cost of Capital," *The Appraisal Journal* (January 1998): 11–16; and Alan Mitchell, "How Much Is Your Company Really Worth?" *Management Today* (January 1999): 68–70.

4. For additional insights, see Ted S. Front, "How to Be a Smart Buyer," *D & B Reports* (March/April 1990): 56–58; and Alfred Rappaport and Mark L. Sirower, "Stock or Cash? The Trade-Offs for Buyers and Sellers in Mergers and Acquisitions," *Harvard Business Review* (November/December 1999): 147–58.

5. Gary R. Trugman, *Understanding Business Valuation: A Practical Guide to Valuing Small to Medium-Sized Businesses* (New York: American Institute of Certified Public Accountants, 1998); and Robert W. Pricer and Alec C. Johnson, "The Accuracy of Valuation Methods in Predicting the Selling Price of Small Firms," *Journal of Small Business Management* 35, no. 4 (October 1997): 24–35; see also Wayne Lonergan, *The Valuation of Businesses, Shares and Other Equity* (Australia: Allen & Unwin, 2003).

6. Adapted from Albert N. Link and Michael B. Boger, *The Art and Science of Business Valuation* (Westport, CT: Quorum Books, 1999).

7. "Valuing a Closely Held Business," 34.

8. Justin J. Camp, *Venture Capital Due Diligence* (New York: Wiley & Sons, 2002); see also John B. Vinturella and Suzanne M. Erickson, *Raising Entrepreneurial Capital* (Burlington, MA: Elsevier, 2004).

APPENDIX 14A: *Term Sheet*

This sample document is the work product of a coalition of attorneys who specialize in venture capital financings, working under the auspices of the NVCA. See the NVCA website for a list of the Working Group members. This document is intended to serve as a starting point only, and should be tailored to meet your specific requirements. This document should not be construed as legal advice for any particular facts or circumstances. Note that this sample presents an array of (often mutually exclusive) options with respect to particular deal provisions.

TERM SHEET
FOR SERIES A PREFERRED STOCK FINANCING OF
[*Insert Company Name*], INC.

[_____ __, 200_]

This Term Sheet summarizes the principal terms of the Series A Preferred Stock Financing of [_____], Inc., a [Delaware] corporation (the "**Company**"). In consideration of the time and expense devoted and to be devoted by the Investors with respect to this investment, the No Shop/Confidentiality and Counsel and Expenses provisions of this Term Sheet shall be binding obligations of the Company whether or not the financing is consummated. No other legally binding obligations will be created until definitive agreements are executed and delivered by all parties. This Term Sheet is not a commitment to invest, and is conditioned on the completion of due diligence, legal review and documentation that is satisfactory to the Investors. This Term Sheet shall be governed in all respects by the laws of the [State of Delaware].

Offering Terms

Closing Date:	As soon as practicable following the Company's acceptance of this Term Sheet and satisfaction of the Conditions to Closing (the "**Closing**"). [*provide for multiple closings if applicable*]
Investors:	Investor No. 1: [_____] shares ([__]%), $[_____] Investor No. 2: [_____] shares ([__]%), $[_____] [as well other investors mutually agreed upon by Investors and the Company]
Amount Raised:	$[_____], [including $[_____] from the conversion of principal [and interest] on bridge notes].[1]
Price Per Share:	$[_____] per share (based on the capitalization of the Company set forth below) (the "**Original Purchase Price**").
Pre-Money Valuation:	The Original Purchase Price is based upon a fully-diluted pre-money valuation of $[_____] and a fully diluted post-money valuation of $[_____] (including an employee pool representing [__]% of the fully diluted post-money capitalization).
Capitalization:	The Company's capital structure before and after the Closing is set forth below:

	Pre-Financing		Post-Financing	
Security	# of Shares	%	# of Shares	%
Common — Founders				
Common — Employee Stock Pool				
Issued				
Unissued				
[Common — Warrants]				
Series A Preferred				
Total				

---

[1]Modify this provision to account for staged investments or investments dependent on the achievement of milestones by the Company.

Charter[2]

Dividends:	[*Alternative 1:* Dividends will be paid on the Series A Preferred on an as-converted basis when, as, and if paid on the Common Stock] [*Alternative 2:* Non-cumulative dividends will be paid on the Series A Preferred in an amount equal to $[_____] per share of Series A Preferred when and if declared by the Board.] [*Alternative 3:* The Series A Preferred will carry an annual [__]% cumulative dividend [compounded annually], payable upon a liquidation or redemption. For any other dividends or distributions, participation with Common Stock on an as-converted basis.][3]
Liquidation Preference:	In the event of any liquidation, dissolution, or winding up of the Company, the proceeds shall be paid as follows: [*Alternative 1 (non-participating Preferred Stock):* First pay [one] times the Original Purchase Price [plus accrued dividends] [plus declared and unpaid dividends] on each share of Series A Preferred. The balance of any proceeds shall be distributed to holders of Common Stock.] [*Alternative 2 (full participating Preferred Stock):* First pay [one] times the Original Purchase Price [plus accrued dividends] [plus declared and unpaid dividends] on each share of Series A Preferred. Thereafter, the Series A Preferred participates with the Common Stock on an as-converted basis.] [*Alternative 3 (cap on Preferred Stock participation rights):* First pay [one] times the Original Purchase Price [plus accrued dividends] [plus declared and unpaid dividends] on each share of Series A Preferred. Thereafter, Series A Preferred participates with Common Stock on an as-converted basis until the holders of Series A Preferred receive an aggregate of [_____] times the Original Purchase Price.] A merger or consolidation (other than one in which stockholders of the Company own a majority by voting power of the outstanding shares of the surviving or acquiring corporation) and a sale, lease, transfer, or other disposition of all or substantially all of the assets of the Company will be treated as a liquidation event (a **"Deemed Liquidation Event"**), thereby triggering payment of the liquidation preferences described above [unless the holders of [_____]% of the Series A Preferred elect otherwise].
Voting Rights:	The Series A Preferred Stock shall vote together with the Common Stock on an as-converted basis, and not as a separate class, except (i) the Series A Preferred as a class shall be entitled to elect [_____] [(__)] members of the Board (the **"Series A Directors"**), (ii) as provided under "Protective Provisions" below or (iii) as required by law. The Company's Certificate of Incorporation will provide that the number of authorized shares of Common Stock may be increased or decreased with the approval of a majority of the Preferred and Common Stock, voting together as a single class, and without a separate class vote by the Common Stock.[4]
Protective Provisions:	So long as [*insert fixed number, or %, or "any"*] shares of Series A Preferred are outstanding, the Company will not, without the written consent of the holders of at least [__]% of the Company's Series A Preferred, either directly or by amendment, merger, consolidation, or otherwise: (i) liquidate, dissolve, or wind up the affairs of the Company, or effect any Deemed Liquidation Event; (ii) amend, alter, or repeal any provision of the Certificate of Incorporation or Bylaws [in a manner adverse to the Series A Preferred];[5] (iii) create or authorize the creation of or issue any other security convertible into or exercisable for any equity security, having rights, preferences, or privileges senior to or on parity with the Series A Preferred, or increase the authorized number of shares of Series A Preferred; (iv) purchase or redeem or pay any dividend on any capital stock prior to the Series A

(continued)

---

[2]The Charter is a public document, filed with the [Delaware] Secretary of State, that establishes all of the rights, preferences, privileges, and restrictions of the Preferred Stock. Note that if the Preferred Stock does not have rights, preferences, and privileges materially superior to the Common Stock, then (after Closing) the Company cannot defensibly grant Common Stock options priced at a discount to the Preferred Stock.

[3]In some cases, accrued and unpaid dividends are payable on conversion as well as upon a liquidation event. Most typically, however, dividends are not paid if the preferred is converted. Another alternative is to give the Company the option to pay accrued and unpaid dividends in cash or in common shares valued at fair market value. The latter are referred to as "PIK" (payment-in-kind) dividends.

[4]For California corporations, one cannot "opt out" of the statutory requirement of a separate class vote by Common Stockholders to authorize shares of Common Stock.

[5]Note that, as a matter of background law, Section 242(b)(2) of the Delaware General Corporation Law provides that if any proposed charter amendment would adversely alter the rights, preferences, and powers of one series of Preferred Stock, but not similarly adversely alter the entire class of all Preferred Stock, then the holders of that series are entitled to a separate series vote on the amendment.

Preferred [other than stock repurchased from former employees or consultants in connection with the cessation of their employment/services, at the lower of fair market value or cost;] [other than as approved by the Board, including the approval of [_____] Series A Director(s)]; or (v) create or authorize the creation of any debt security [if the Company's aggregate indebtedness would exceed $[____]][other than equipment leases or bank lines of credit][other than debt with no equity feature][unless such debt security has received the prior approval of the Board of Directors, including the approval of [_____] Series A Director(s)]; (vi) increase or decrease the size of the Board of Directors.

Optional Conversion: The Series A Preferred initially converts 1:1 to Common Stock at any time at option of holder, subject to adjustments for stock dividends, splits, combinations, and similar events and as described below under "Anti-dilution Provisions."

Anti-dilution Provisions: In the event that the Company issues additional securities at a purchase price less than the current Series A Preferred conversion price, such conversion price shall be adjusted in accordance with the following formula:
[*Alternative 1:* "Typical" weighted average:]

$CP_2 = CP_1 * (A + B)/(A + C)$

CP_2 = New Series A Conversion Price

CP_1 = Series A Conversion Price in effect immediately prior to new issue

A = Number of shares of Common Stock deemed to be outstanding immediately prior to new issue (includes all shares of outstanding common stock, all shares of outstanding preferred stock on an as-converted basis, and all outstanding options on an as-exercised basis; and does not include any convertible securities converting into this round of financing)

B = Aggregate consideration received by the Corporation with respect to the new issue divided by CP_1

C = Number of shares of stock issued in the subject transaction]

[*Alternative 2:* Full-ratchet — the conversion price will be reduced to the price at which the new shares are issued.]
[*Alternative 3*: No price-based anti-dilution protection.]
The following issuances shall not trigger anti-dilution adjustment:[6]
(i) securities issuable upon conversion of any of the Series A Preferred, or as a dividend or distribution on the Series A Preferred; (ii) securities issued upon the conversion of any debenture, warrant, option, or other convertible security; (iii) Common Stock issuable upon a stock split, stock dividend, or any subdivision of shares of Common Stock; and (iv) shares of Common Stock (or options to purchase such shares of Common Stock) issued or issuable to employees or directors of, or consultants to, the Company pursuant to any plan approved by the Company's Board of Directors [including at least [_____] Series A Director(s)] [(v) shares of Common Stock issued or issuable to banks, equipment lessors pursuant to a debt financing, equipment leasing, or real property leasing transaction approved by the Board of Directors of the Corporation [including at least [_____] Series A Director(s)].

Mandatory Conversion: Each share of Series A Preferred will automatically be converted into Common Stock at the then applicable conversion rate in the event of the closing of a [firm commitment] underwritten public offering with a price of [____] times the Original Purchase Price (subject to adjustments for stock dividends, splits, combinations, and similar events) and [net/gross] proceeds to the Company of not less than $[_____] (a "**QPO**"), or (ii) upon the written consent of the holders of [__]% of the Series A Preferred.[7]

---

[6]Note that additional exclusions are frequently negotiated, such as issuances in connection with equipment leasing and commercial borrowing.

[7]The per-share test ensures that the investor achieves a significant return on investment before the Company can go public. Also consider allowing a non-QPO to become a QPO if an adjustment is made to the Conversion Price for the benefit of the investor, so that the investor does not have the power to block a public offering.

Pay-to-Play:	[Unless the holders of [___]% of the Series A elect otherwise,] on any subsequent down round all [Major] Investors are required to participate to the full extent of their participation rights (as described below under "Investor Rights Agreement – Right to Participate Pro Rata in Future Rounds"), unless the participation requirement is waived for all [Major] Investors by the Board [(including vote of [a majority of] the Series A Director[s])]. All shares of Series A Preferred[8] of any [Major] Investor failing to do so will automatically [lose anti-dilution rights] [lose right to participate in future rounds] [convert to Common Stock and lose the right to a Board seat if applicable].[9]
Redemption Rights:[10]	The Series A Preferred shall be redeemable from funds legally available for distribution at the option of holders of at least [___]% of the Series A Preferred commencing any time after the fifth anniversary of the Closing at a price equal to the Original Purchase Price [plus all accrued but unpaid dividends]. Redemption shall occur in three equal annual portions. Upon a redemption request from the holders of the required percentage of the Series A Preferred, all Series A Preferred shares shall be redeemed [[except for any Series A holders who affirmatively opt-out]].[11]

Stock Purchase Agreement

Representations and Warranties:	Standard representations and warranties by the Company. [Representations and warranties by Founders regarding [technology ownership, etc.].[12]
Conditions to Closing:	Standard conditions to Closing, which shall include, among other things, satisfactory completion of financial and legal due diligence, qualification of the shares under applicable Blue Sky laws, the filing of a Certificate of Incorporation establishing the rights and preferences of the Series A Preferred, and an opinion of counsel to the Company.
Counsel and Expenses:	[Investor/Company] counsel to draft closing documents. Company to pay all legal and administrative costs of the financing [at Closing], including reasonable fees (not to exceed $[_____]) and expenses of Investor counsel [unless the transaction is not completed because the Investors withdraw their commitment without cause].[13]

Company Counsel: [_____

_____

_____]

Investor Counsel: [_____

_____

_____]

(continued)

---

[8]Alternatively, this provision could apply on a proportionate basis (e.g., if Investor plays for ½ of pro rata share, receives ½ of antidilution adjustment).

[9]If the punishment for failure to participate is losing some but not all rights of the Preferred (e.g., anything other than a forced conversion to common), the Charter will need to have so-called "blank check preferred" provisions at least to the extent necessary to enable the Board to issue a "shadow" class of preferred with diminished rights in the event an investor fails to participate. Note that, as a drafting matter, it is far easier to simply have (some or all of) the preferred convert to common.

[10]Redemption rights allow Investors to force the Company to redeem their shares at cost [plus a small guaranteed rate of return (e.g., dividends)]. In practice, redemption rights are not often used; however, they do provide a form of exit and some possible leverage over the Company. While it is possible that the right to receive dividends on redemption could give rise to a Code Section 305 "deemed dividend" problem, many tax practitioners take the view that if the liquidation preference provisions in the Charter are drafted to provide that, on conversion, the holder receives the greater of its liquidation preference or its as-converted amount (as provided in the NVCA model Certificate of Incorporation), then there is no Section 305 issue.

[11]Due to statutory restrictions, it is unlikely that the Company will be legally permitted to redeem in the very circumstances where investors most want it (the so-called "sideways situation"), investors will sometimes request that certain penalty provisions take effect where redemption has been requested but the Company's available cash flow does not permit such redemption—e.g., the redemption amount shall be paid in the form of a one-year note to each unredeemed holder of Series A Preferred, and the holders of a majority of the Series A Preferred shall be entitled to elect a majority of the Company's Board of Directors until such amounts are paid in full.

[12]Note that, while it is not at all uncommon in East Coast deals to require the Founders to personally rep and warrant (at least as to certain key matters, and usually only in the Series A round), such Founders reps are rarely found in West Coast deals.

[13]The bracketed text should be deleted if this section is not designated in the introductory paragraph as one of the sections that is binding upon the Company regardless of whether the financing is consummated.

Investor Rights Agreement

Registration Rights:

Registrable Securities: All shares of Common Stock issuable upon conversion of the Series A Preferred and [any other Common Stock held by the Investors] will be deemed **"Registrable Securities."**[14]

Demand Registration: Upon earliest of (i) [three–five] years after the Closing; or (ii) [six] months following an initial public offering (**"IPO"**), persons holding [___]% of the Registrable Securities may request [one][two] (consummated) registrations by the Company of their shares. The aggregate offering price for such registration may not be less than $[5–10] million. A registration will count for this purpose only if (i) all Registrable Securities requested to be registered are registered and (ii) it is closed, or withdrawn at the request of the Investors (other than as a result of a material adverse change to the Company).

Registration on Form S-3: The holders of [10–30]% of the Registrable Securities will have the right to require the Company to register on Form S-3, if available for use by the Company, Registrable Securities for an aggregate offering price of at least $[1–5 million]. There will be no limit on the aggregate number of such Form S-3 registrations, provided that there are no more than [two] per year.

Piggyback Registration: The holders of Registrable Securities will be entitled to "piggyback" registration rights on all registration statements of the Company, subject to the right, however, of the Company and its underwriters to reduce the number of shares proposed to be registered to a minimum of [30]% on a pro rata basis and to complete reduction on an IPO at the underwriter's discretion. In all events, the shares to be registered by holders of Registrable Securities will be reduced only after all other stockholders' shares are reduced.

Expenses: The registration expenses (exclusive of stock transfer taxes, underwriting discounts, and commissions) will be borne by the Company. The Company will also pay the reasonable fees and expenses [not to exceed $_____] of one special counsel to represent all the participating stockholders.

Lock-up: Investors shall agree in connection with the IPO, if requested by the managing underwriter, not to sell or transfer any shares of Common Stock of the Company [(excluding shares acquired in or following the IPO)] for a period of up to 180 days following the IPO (provided all directors and officers of the Company and [1–5]% stockholders agree to the same lockup). Such lockup agreement shall provide that any discretionary waiver or termination of the restrictions of such agreements by the Company or representatives of the underwriters shall apply to [Major] Investors, pro rata, based on the number of shares held. A **"Major Investor"** means any Investor who purchases at least $[_____] of Series A Preferred.

Termination: Earlier of [5] years after IPO, upon a Deemed Liquidation Event, or when all shares of an Investor are eligible to be sold without restriction under Rule 144(k) within any 90-day period.
No future registration rights may be granted without consent of the holders of a [majority] of the Registrable Securities unless subordinate to the Investor's rights.

Management and Information Rights: A Management Rights letter from the Company, in a form reasonably acceptable to the Investors, will be delivered prior to Closing to each Investor that requests one.[15]
Any Major Investor [(who is not a competitor)] will be granted access to Company facilities and personnel during normal business hours and with reasonable advance notification. The Company will deliver to such Major Investor (i) annual, quarterly, [and monthly] financial statements, and other information as determined by the Board; (ii) 30 days prior to the end of each fiscal year, a comprehensive operating budget forecasting the Company's revenues, expenses, and cash position on a month-to-month basis for the upcoming fiscal year; and (iii) promptly following the end of each quarter an up-to-date capitalization table, certified by the CFO.

Right to Participate Pro Rata in Future Rounds: All [Major] Investors shall have a pro rata right, based on their percentage equity ownership in the Company (assuming the conversion of all outstanding Preferred Stock into Common Stock and the exercise of all options outstanding under the Company's stock plans), to participate in subsequent issuances of equity securities of the Company (excluding those issuances listed at the end of the

---

[14]Note that Founders/management sometimes also seek registration rights.

[15]See commentary in introduction to NVCA model Managements Rights Letter, explaining purpose of such letter.

"Anti-dilution Provisions" section of this Term Sheet and issuances in connection with acquisitions by the Company). In addition, should any [Major] Investor choose not to purchase its full pro rata share, the remaining [Major] Investors shall have the right to purchase the remaining pro rata shares.

Matters Requiring Investor Director Approval:

[So long as [__]% of the originally issued Series A Preferred remains outstanding] the Company will not, without Board approval, which approval must include the affirmative vote of [_____] of the Series A Director(s):

(i) make any loan or advance to, or own any stock or other securities of, any subsidiary or other corporation, partnership, or other entity unless it is wholly owned by the Company; (ii) make any loan or advance to any person, including any employee or director, except advances and similar expenditures in the ordinary course of business or under the terms of a employee stock or option plan approved by the Board of Directors; (iii) guarantee any indebtedness except for trade accounts of the Company or any subsidiary arising in the ordinary course of business; (iv) make any investment other than investments in prime commercial paper, money market funds, certificates of deposit in any United States bank having a net worth in excess of $100,000,000, or obligations issued or guaranteed by the United States of America, in each case having a maturity not in excess of [two years]; (v) incur any aggregate indebtedness in excess of $[_____] that is not already included in a Board-approved budget, other than trade credit incurred in the ordinary course of business; (vi) enter into or be a party to any transaction with any director, officer, or employee of the Company or any "associate" (as defined in Rule 12b-2 promulgated under the Exchange Act) of any such person [except transactions resulting in payments to or by the Company in an amount less than $[60,000] per year], [or transactions made in the ordinary course of business and pursuant to reasonable requirements of the Company's business and upon fair and reasonable terms that are approved by a majority of the Board of Directors];[16] (vii) hire, fire, or change the compensation of the executive officers, including approving any option plans; (viii) change the principal business of the Company, enter new lines of business, or exit the current line of business; or (ix) sell, transfer, license, pledge, or encumber technology or intellectual property, other than licenses granted in the ordinary course of business.

Noncompetition and Non-Solicitation and Agreements:[17]

Each Founder and key employee will enter into a [one] year noncompetition and non-solicitation agreement in a form reasonably acceptable to the Investors.

Nondisclosure and Developments Agreement:

Each current and former Founder, employee, and consultant with access to Company confidential information/trade secrets will enter into a nondisclosure and proprietary rights assignment agreement in a form reasonably acceptable to the Investors.

Board Matters:

Each Board Committee shall include at least one Series A Director.
The Board of Directors shall meet at least [monthly][quarterly], unless otherwise agreed by a vote of the majority of Directors.
The Company will bind D&O insurance with a carrier and in an amount satisfactory to the Board of Directors. In the event the Company merges with another entity and is not the surviving corporation, or transfers all of its assets, proper provisions shall be made so that successors of the Company assume Company's obligations with respect to indemnification of Directors.

Employee Stock Options:

All employee options to vest as follows: [25% after one year, with remaining vesting monthly over next 36 months].
[Immediately prior to the Series A Preferred Stock investment, [_____] shares will be added to the option pool creating an unallocated option pool of [_____] shares.]

(continued)

---

[16]Note that Section 402 of the Sarbanes-Oxley Act of 2003 would require repayment of any loans in full prior to the Company filing a registration statement for an IPO.

[17]Note that noncompete restrictions (other than in connection with the sale of a business) are prohibited in California, and may not be enforceable in other jurisdictions, as well. In addition, some investors do not require such agreements for fear that employees will request additional consideration in exchange for signing a Noncompete/Non-Solicit (and indeed the agreement may arguably be invalid absent such additional consideration—although having an employee sign a noncompete contemporaneous with hiring constitutes adequate consideration). Others take the view that it should be up to the Board on a case-by-case basis to determine whether any particular key employee is required to sign such an agreement. Noncompetes typically have a one-year duration, although state law may permit up to two years.

Key Person Insurance:	Company to acquire life insurance on Founders [*name each Founder*] in an amount satisfactory to the Board. Proceeds payable to the Company.
[IPO Directed Shares:[18]	To the extent permitted by applicable law and SEC policy, upon an IPO consummated one year after Closing, Company to use reasonable best efforts to cause underwriters to designate [10]% of the offering as directed shares, 50% of which shall be allocated by Major Investors.]
[QSB Stock:	Company shall use reasonable best efforts to cause its capital stock to constitute Qualified Small Business Stock unless the Board determines that such qualification is inconsistent with the best interests of the Company.]
Termination:	All rights under the Investor Rights Agreement, other than registration rights, shall terminate upon the earlier of an IPO, a Deemed Liquidation Event, or a transfer of more than 50% of Company's voting power.

Right of First Refusal/Co-Sale Agreement and Voting Agreement

Right of First Refusal/ Right of Co-Sale (Take-Me-Along):	Company first and Investors second (to the extent assigned by the Board of Directors) have a right of first refusal with respect to any shares of capital stock of the Company proposed to be sold by Founders [and employees holding greater than [1]% of Company Common Stock (assuming conversion of Preferred Stock)], with a right of oversubscription for Investors of shares unsubscribed by the other Investors. Before any such person may sell Common Stock, he will give the Investors an opportunity to participate in such sale on a basis proportionate to the amount of securities held by the seller and those held by the participating Investors.[19]
Board of Directors:	At the initial Closing, the Board shall consist of [_____] members comprised of (i) [*Name*] as [the representative designated by [____], as the lead Investor, (ii) [*Name*] as the representative designated by the remaining Investors, (iii) [*Name*] as the representative designated by the Founders, (iv) the person then serving as the Chief Executive Officer of the Company, and (v) [____] person(s) who are not employed by the Company and who are mutually acceptable [to the Founders and Investors][to the other directors].
Drag Along:	Holders of Preferred Stock and the Founders [and all current and future holders of greater than [1]% of Common Stock (assuming conversion of Preferred Stock and whether then held or subject to the exercise of options)] shall be required to enter into an agreement with the Investors that provides that such stockholders will vote their shares in favor of a Deemed Liquidation Event or transaction in which 50% or more of the voting power of the Company is transferred, approved by [the Board of Directors] [and the holders of a [majority][super majority] of the outstanding shares of Preferred Stock, on an as-converted basis].
Termination:	All rights under the Right of First Refusal/Co-Sale and Voting Agreements shall terminate upon an IPO, a Deemed Liquidation Event, or a transfer of more than 50% of Company's voting power.

Other Matters

Founders' Stock:	All Founders to own stock outright subject to Company right to buyback at cost. Buyback right for [___]% for first [12 months] after Closing; thereafter, right lapses in equal [monthly] increments over following [__] months.
[Existing Preferred Stock:[20]	The terms set forth below for the Series [_] Stock are subject to a review of the rights, preferences and restrictions for the existing Preferred Stock. Any changes necessary to conform the existing Preferred Stock to this term sheet will be made at the Closing.]

---

[18]SEC Staff examiners have taken position that, if contractual right to friends and family shares was granted less than 12 months prior to filing of registration statement, this will be considered an "offer" made prematurely before filing of IPO prospectus. So, investors need to agree to drop shares from offering if that would hold up the IPO. While some documents provide for alternative parallel private placement where the IPO does occur within 12 months, such a parallel private placement could raise integration issues and negatively impact the IPO. Hence, such an alternative is not provided for here.

[19]Certain exceptions are typically negotiated, e.g., estate planning or *de minimis* transfers.

[20]Necessary only if this is a later round of financing, and not the initial Series A round.

No Shop/Confidentiality: The Company agrees to work in good faith expeditiously toward a closing. The Company and the Founders agree that they will not, for a period of [six] weeks from the date these terms are accepted, take any action to solicit, initiate, encourage, or assist the submission of any proposal, negotiation, or offer from any person or entity other than the Investors relating to the sale or issuance, of any of the capital stock of the Company [or the acquisition, sale, lease, license, or other disposition of the Company or any material part of the stock or assets of the Company] and shall notify the Investors promptly of any inquiries by any third parties in regards to the foregoing. [In the event that the Company breaches this no-shop obligation and, prior to [_____], closes any of the above-referenced transactions [without providing the Investors the opportunity to invest on the same terms as the other parties to such transaction], then the Company shall pay to the Investors $[_____] upon the closing of any such transaction as liquidated damages.][21] The Company will not disclose the terms of this Term Sheet to any person other than officers, members of the Board of Directors, and the Company's accountants and attorneys and other potential Investors acceptable to [_____], as lead Investor, without the written consent of the Investors.

Expiration: This Term Sheet expires on [_____ __, 200_] if not accepted by the Company by that date.

EXECUTED THIS [__] DAY OF [_____], 200[_].

[SIGNATURE BLOCKS]

---

[21]It is unusual to provide for such "breakup" fees in connection with a venture capital financing, but might be something to consider where there is a substantial possibility the Company may be sold prior to consummation of the financing (e.g., a later-stage deal).

15

The Final Harvest of a New Venture

Entrepreneurial Thought

Entrepreneurs tend to be control addicts. In a sense they have to be. They started their companies to be their own bosses, and at the start, they are usually in charge of everything. But as the company grows, being in charge of everything becomes increasingly impossible to manage. . . . Company building is a marathon, not a sprint. To avoid the loneliness of the long-distance runner, an entrepreneur needs to tap the support and experience of others. The entrepreneurial course is not only easier to traverse but also more enjoyable to run with others cheering one along!

— **RAY SMILOR** *Daring Visionaries*

Chapter Objectives

1 To present the concept of "harvest" as a plan for the future

2 To examine the key factors in the management succession of a venture

3 To identify and describe some of the most important sources of succession

4 To discuss the potential impact of recent legislation on family business succession

5 To relate the ways to develop a succession strategy

6 To examine the specifics of an IPO as a potential harvest strategy

7 To present "selling out" as a final alternative in the harvest strategy

Harvesting the Venture: A Focus on the Future

Entrepreneurs must realize that the eventual success of their venture will lead them to a decision concerning the future operation and management of the business. A *harvest plan* defines how and when the owners and investors will realize an actual cash return on their investment. Note that "harvest" does not mean that the challenges and responsibility of the entrepreneur are over. There are challenging decisions to be made. It may be a decision regarding managerial control and succession for successful continued operations as a privately held firm.[1] It may be a desire to initiate a liquidity event, through which the venture is able to generate a significant amount of cash for the investors. It may be that the venture has grown to a stage at which the possibility of an initial public offering (IPO), which we discussed in Chapter 8, is a reality. Or it may be that the most realistic opportunity is for the sale of the business. In any of these situations, the entrepreneur is confronted with a myriad of choices and possibilities. Although it is impossible for this chapter to answer all of the questions that an entrepreneur faces at this point, because each venture presents a unique set of circumstances, it is the goal of this final chapter to review some of the more common challenges that confront entrepreneurs during this stage. Thus, we examine the challenge of a management succession strategy and the two most notable harvest strategies for ventures: the initial public offering and the sale of the venture.

The Management Succession Strategy

Research shows that many privately held firms go out of existence after ten years; only three of ten survive into a second generation. More significantly, only 16 percent of all privately held enterprises make it to a third generation.[2] The average life expectancy for a privately held business is 24 years, which is also the average tenure for the founders of a business.[3] One of the major problems most privately held businesses face is the lack of preparation for passing managerial control to the next generation. The cruel fact is that one generation succeeds the other with biological inevitability, yet most privately held firms never formulate succession plans.

Management succession, which involves the transition of managerial decision making in a firm, is one of the greatest challenges confronting owners and entrepreneurs in privately held businesses. At first glance, succession would not seem to be a major problem. All an owner has to do is designate which heir will inherit the operation or, better yet, train one (or more) of them to take over the business during the founder's lifetime. Unfortunately, this is easier said than done—a number of problems exist. One of the major ones is the owner. To a large degree, the owner is the business; the individual's personality and talents make the operation what it is. If this person were to be removed from the picture, the company might be unable to continue. Additionally, this individual may not want to be removed. So, if the owner/manager begins to have health problems or is unable to manage effectively, he or she may still hang on. The owner often views any outside attempt to get him or her to step aside as greedy efforts to plunder the operation for personal gain. What's more, the owner and family members may feel anxiety about death, because discussing the topic of death conjures up a negative image in everyone's mind.

Other barriers to succession include sibling rivalry, family members' fear of losing status, or a complete aversion to death for fear of loss or abandonment.[4] Table 15.1 provides a list of barriers to succession attributed to the owner and to the family.

The basic rule for privately held businesses is this: The owner should develop a succession plan. Because many people want to keep the business in their families, decisions have to be made regarding heirs. This is often psychologically difficult. Choosing an heir can be like buying a cemetery plot—it is an admission of one's mortality. Owners who refuse to face the succession issue, however, place an unnecessary burden on those whom they leave behind. Successor problems are not insurmountable. For our consideration of these problems, the best place to begin is with an identification of the key factors in succession.

Table **15.1**	Barriers to Succession Planning in Privately Held Businesses

Founder/Owner	Family
Death anxiety	Death as taboo
Company as symbol	• Discussion is a hostile act
• Loss of identity	• Fear of loss/abandonment
• Concern about legacy	Fear of sibling rivalry
Dilemma of choice	Change of spouse's position
• Fiction of equality	
Generational envy	
• Loss of power	

Source: Manfred F. R. Kets de Vries, "The Dynamics of Family-Controlled Firms: The Good News and the Bad News," *Organizational Dynamics* (winter 1993): 68.

Key Factors in Succession

It has been said that the concept of "smooth succession" in a privately held business is a contradiction of terms. This contradiction is because succession is a highly charged emotional issue that requires not only structural changes but cultural changes as well.[5] Family succession includes the transfer of ethics, values, and traditions, along with the actual business itself. The "family business" and the "business family" are two distinct components that must be dealt with and disentangled if progress toward succession is to be made.[6]

A number of considerations affect the succession issue.[7] One way to examine them is in terms of pressures and interests inside the firm and outside the firm. Another way is to examine forcing events. A third way is to examine the sources of succession. Finally, we will discuss the legal restrictions that may affect succession decisions.

Pressures and Interests Inside the Firm

Two types of succession pressures originate within the privately held business (see Figure 15.1). One comes from the family members; the other comes from nonfamily employees.[8]

FAMILY MEMBERS

When members of the family are also employees, a number of succession-type problems can arise. One is that the family members may want to keep the business in existence so that they and their families will be able to manage it. Sometimes this results in the members wanting to get, or increase, control over operations. Another common development is pressure on the owner/manager to designate an heir. A third possible development is rivalry among the various branches of the family. For example, each of the owner's children may feel that the owner should put him or her (or one of his or her children) in charge of the operation. Given that only one of the family branches can win this fight, the rivalry can lead to the sale or bankruptcy of the business.[9]

NONFAMILY EMPLOYEES

Nonfamily employees sometimes put pressure on the owner/manager in an effort to protect their personal interests. For example, long-term employees often think that the owner should give them an opportunity to buy a stake in the company, or they believe that they should be

Figure 15.1   Pressures and Interests in a Family Business

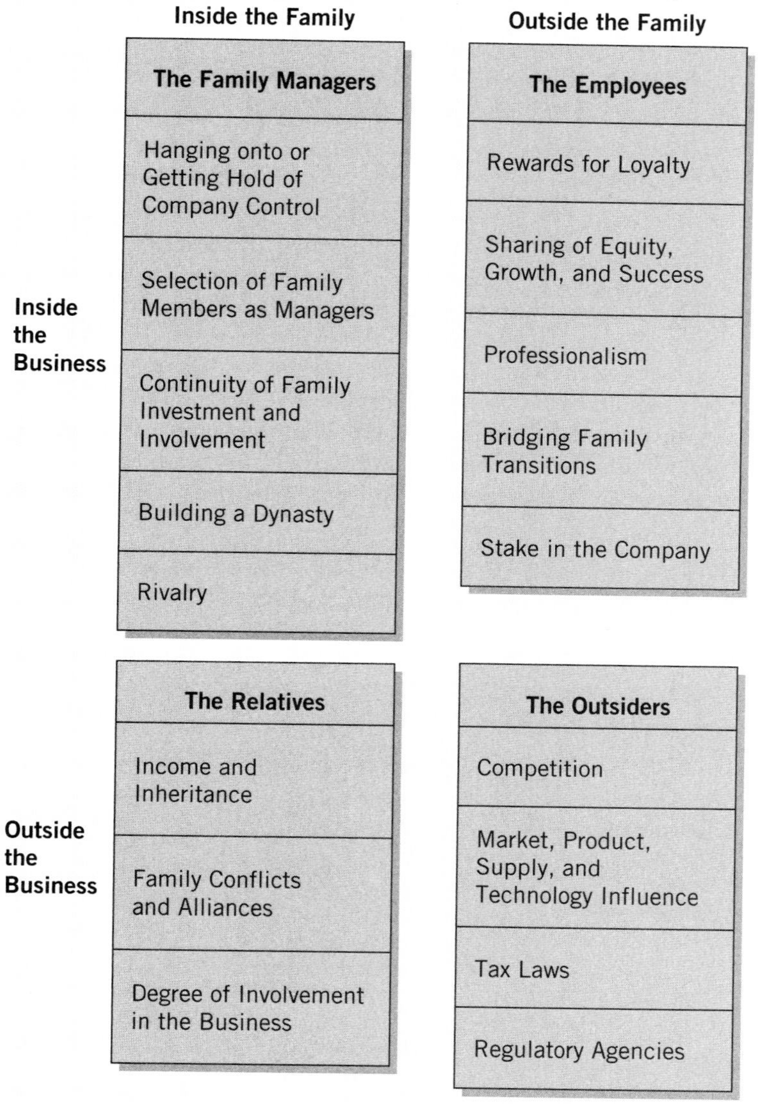

Inside the Family

Inside the Business

The Family Managers
Hanging onto or Getting Hold of Company Control
Selection of Family Members as Managers
Continuity of Family Investment and Involvement
Building a Dynasty
Rivalry

Outside the Family

The Employees
Rewards for Loyalty
Sharing of Equity, Growth, and Success
Professionalism
Bridging Family Transitions
Stake in the Company

Outside the Business

The Relatives
Income and Inheritance
Family Conflicts and Alliances
Degree of Involvement in the Business

The Outsiders
Competition
Market, Product, Supply, and Technology Influence
Tax Laws
Regulatory Agencies

Source: Adapted and reprinted by permission of the *Harvard Business Review*. An Exhibit from "Transferring Power in the Family Business," by Louis B. Barnes and Simon A. Hershon (July/August 1976): 106. Copyright © 1976 by the President and Fellows of Harvard College; all rights reserved.

given a percentage of the business in the owner's will. Such hopes and expectations are often conveyed to the owner and can result in pressure for some form of succession plan. Moreover, to the extent that the nonfamily employees are critical to the enterprise's success, these demands cannot be ignored. The owner must reach some accommodation with these people if the business is to survive.

Pressures and Interests Outside the Firm

Outside the firm, both family members and nonfamily elements exert pressure on and hold interest in the firm's succession.

FAMILY MEMBERS

Even when family members do not play an active role in the business, they can apply pressure. Quite often these individuals are interested in ensuring that they inherit part of the operation, and they will put pressure on the owner/manager toward achieving that end. In some cases, they pressure to get involved in the business. Some family members will pressure the owner/manager to hire them. Quite often these appeals are resisted on the grounds of the firm not needing additional personnel or needing someone with specific expertise (sales ability or technical skills), and thus the owner sidesteps the request.

NONFAMILY ELEMENTS

Another major source of pressure comes from external environmental factors. One of these is competitors who continually change strategy and force the owner/manager to adjust to new market considerations. Other factors include customers, technology, and new-product development. These forces continually change, and the entrepreneur must respond to them. Tax laws, regulatory agencies, and trends in management practices constitute still other elements with which the owner/manager must contend.[10] Depending on the situation, any of these sources of pressure can prove troublesome.

Figure 15.2 illustrates the distinction of family and business issues in a systems model. At the interface of the family and business systems, both the family and the business respond to disruptions in their regular transaction patterns. These disruptions may come from outside

| Figure 15.2 | Sustainable Family Business Model |

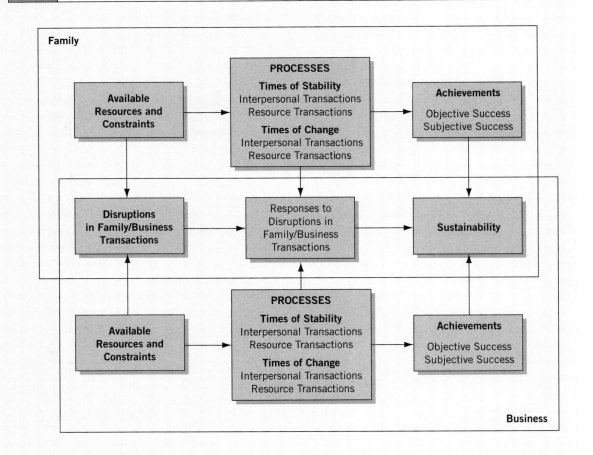

Source: Kathryn Stafford, Karen A. Duncan, Sharon Dane, and Mary Winter, "A Research Model of Sustainable Family Business," *Family Business Review* (September 1999): 197–208.

the family and business or from within them. Outside sources of disruption include public policy changes, economic upheavals, and technological innovation. Inside sources of disruption include marriage, birth, death, and divorce of family members. These disruptions may be either good or bad. In either case, they require a response from both the family and the business.

The extent of overlap between the family and business systems will vary from family business to family business. In privately held businesses, where the prevailing orientation is to keep the family and the business separate, there is little overlap—diagrammatically, this case is illustrated by a small area of interface between the two systems. Conversely, in privately held businesses characterized by great overlap, the area of interface between the family and business systems is considerable.

Sustainability results from the confluence of family success, business success, and appropriate responses to disruptions. In other words, sustainability requires consideration of the family as well as the business. It also requires consideration of the ability of the family and business to cooperate in responding to disruptions in a way that does not impede the success of either.[11]

Forcing Events

Forcing events are those happenings that cause the replacement of the owner/manager. These events require the entrepreneur to step aside and let someone else direct the operation. The following are typical examples:

- Death, resulting in the heirs immediately having to find a successor to run the operation
- Illness or some other form of nonterminal physical incapacitation
- Mental or psychological breakdown, resulting in the individual having to withdraw from the business
- Abrupt departure, such as when an entrepreneur decides, with no advance warning, to retire immediately
- Legal problems, such as incarceration for violation of the law (if this period of confinement is for more than a few weeks, succession usually becomes necessary, if in name only)
- Severe business decline, resulting in the owner/manager deciding to leave the helm
- Financial difficulties, resulting in lenders demanding the removal of the owner/manager before lending the necessary funds to the enterprise

These types of events often are unforeseen, and the family seldom has a contingency plan for dealing with them. As a result, when they occur they often create a major problem for the business.

These considerations influence the environment within which the successor will operate. Unless that individual and the environment fit well, the successor will be less than maximally effective.

Sources of Succession

An **entrepreneurial successor** is someone who is high in ingenuity, creativity, and drive. This person often provides the critical ideas for new-product development and future ventures. The **managerial successor** is someone who is interested in efficiency, internal control, and the effective use of resources. This individual often provides the stability and day-to-day direction needed to keep the enterprise going.

When looking for an inside successor, the entrepreneur usually focuses on a son, daughter, nephew, or niece, with the intent of gradually giving the person operational responsibilities followed by strategic power and ownership. An important factor in the venture's success is whether the founder and the heir can get along. The entrepreneur must be able to turn from being a leader to being a coach, from being a doer to being an advisor. The heir must respect the founder's attachment to the venture and be sensitive to this person's possessive feelings. At the same time, the heir must be able to use his or her entrepreneurial flair to initiate necessary changes.[12]

When looking ahead toward choosing a successor from inside the organization, the founder often trains a team of executive managers that consists of both family and nonfamily members. This enables the individual to build an experienced management team capable of producing a successor. The founder assumes that, in time, a natural leader will emerge from the group.[13]

Two key strategies center on the entry of the inside younger generation and when the "power" actually changes hands. Table 15.2 illustrates the advantages and disadvantages of the early entry strategy versus the delayed entry strategy. The main question is the ability of the successor to gain credibility with the firm's employees. The actual transfer of power is a critical issue in the implementation of any succession plan.[14]

If the founder looks for a family member outside the firm, he or she usually prefers to have the heir first work for someone else. The hope is that the individual will make his or her initial mistakes early on, before assuming the family business reins.

Sometimes the founder will look for a nonfamily outsider to be the successor, perhaps only temporarily. The entrepreneur may not see an immediate successor inside the firm and may decide to hire a professional manager, at least on an interim basis, while waiting for an heir to mature and take over.

Another form of nonfamily outsider is the specialist who is experienced in getting ventures out of financial difficulty. The founder usually gives the specialist total control, and this person later hands the rejuvenated venture to another leader.

Still another nonfamily approach is for the founder to find a person with the right talents and to bring this individual into the venture as an assistant, with the understanding that he or she will eventually become president and owner of the venture. No heirs may exist, or perhaps no eligible family member is interested.

Table 15.2 Comparison of Entry Strategies for Succession in Privately Held Businesses

	Advantages	Disadvantages
Early Entry Strategy	Intimate familiarity with the nature of the business and employees is acquired. Skills specifically required by the business are developed. Exposure to others in the business facilitates acceptance and the achievement of credibility. Strong relationships with constituents are readily established.	Conflict results when the owner has difficulty with teaching or relinquishing control to the successor. Normal mistakes tend to be viewed as incompetence in the successor. Knowledge of the environment is limited, and risks of inbreeding are incurred.
Delayed Entry Strategy	The successor's skills are judged with greater objectivity. The development of self-confidence and growth independent of familial influence are achieved. Outside success establishes credibility and serves as a basis for accepting the successor as a competent executive. Perspective of the business environment is broadened.	Specific expertise and understanding of the organization's key success factors and culture may be lacking. Set patterns of outside activity may conflict with those prevailing in the family firm. Resentment may result when successors are advanced ahead of long-term employees.

Source: Jeffrey A. Barach, Joseph Ganitsky, James A. Carson, and Benjamin A. Doochin, "Entry of the Next Generation: Strategic Challenge for Family Firms," *Journal of Small Business Management* (April 1988): 53.

the entrepreneurial process

Harvesting a Business Online

Selling a business, also known as harvesting a business, is normally a time-consuming, stressful experience for entrepreneurs. Between the due diligence performed by the buyer and the emotional distress felt by the entrepreneur as a result of leaving the business, the sales process is far more involved than selling a car or even a house. Employees have to be considered, financial statements have to be organized and analyzed, and the entrepreneur has to figure out what to do after the business has sold.

Purchasing a business is a complex procedure, which is difficult to simplify; however, companies looking to facilitate the buying and selling of businesses are gaining in popularity. These companies are offering online services designed to match entrepreneurs with potential buyers. The objective is to provide greater visibility for businesses to eliminate much of the anxiety felt by entrepreneurs, which results from completing the most difficult part of the process: locating an interested party.

Business brokers have been around for decades. Most, if not all, brokers now have Web sites with directories of businesses currently for sale, not unlike those provided by realtors. These brokers usually keep their lists private and limit their scope to a given region. The new services are planning to differentiate themselves by providing global listings to maximize exposure for entrepreneurs and to entice buyers to frequent their sites. In addition, these sites will offer the added functionality of broadcasting their listings to popular search services such as Craigslist and Google.

BizTrader.com, one such company, is positioning itself to become an all-inclusive provider for anyone looking to buy, sell, or value a small business. The company has received positive feedback from existing brokerage agencies, a fact that it attributes to hiring a chief operating officer with experience running operations for online real estate services. Many similarities exist between the tasks of brokering businesses and selling real estate—a fact that BizTrader.com has successfully exploited. CEO Colby Sambrotto believes that his company will modernize the industry with its novel approach.

Another similar site is BizBuySell.com, which has been in business since 1996. The company boasts that it has 50,000 companies listed at any given time. Its first-mover advantage has positioned it as the industry leader. Although the site does not offer the same global exposure that BizTrader.com is promoting, the company's general manager, Mike Handelsman, argues that the size of BizBuySell.com and its significant head start allow it to provide greater value than any new service could.

Both BizTrader.com and BizBuySell.com provide valuable functionality for entrepreneurs. The services are subscription based, with BizBuySell.com's service starting at $60 per month for membership and BizTrader.com charging $40. In addition to their primary service of listing businesses, both sites offer ancillary services, which include helping entrepreneurs find financing opportunities and assisting them with valuing their business. As online advertising becomes increasingly important to businesses, newspaper classified ads are waning in popularity. The success of the Internet as a forum to promote businesses is largely attributed to the opportunity it provides for entrepreneurs to more effectively promote their businesses at a reduced cost.

Although some experts strongly encourage entrepreneurs to focus their resources on Internet postings, entrepreneurs who have sold their businesses tend to utilize all available channels. The notion that more is better certainly applies when selling a business, and online services such as BizBuySell.com and BizTrader.com serve to increase the resources at entrepreneurs' disposal.

Source: Adapted from Konstantin Shishkin, "Selling Your Business? Click Here," *Fortune Small Business*, April 14, 2008, http://money.cnn.com/2008/04/14/smbusiness/biztrader.fsb/index.htm (accessed April 17, 2008).

Legal Restrictions

The first source for succession often is family and in-house personnel prospects. However, such traditions of succession practices in privately held businesses were challenged in the Oakland Scavenger Company case.

This suit was brought in 1984 by a group of black and Hispanic workers in the California-based **Oakland Scavenger Company** (a garbage collection firm), who complained of employment discrimination because of their race. The U.S. District Court of Northern California dismissed the suit on the basis that it had no relation to antidiscrimination laws. However, the U.S. Court of Appeals for the Ninth Circuit reviewed the decision and held that "nepotistic concerns cannot supersede the nation's paramount goal of equal economic opportunity for all."[15]

According to Oakland Scavenger's legal brief, the question focused on the Fifth Amendment versus Title VII of the 1964 Civil Rights Act: If discrimination overrides the protection of life, liberty, and property from unreasonable interference from the state, then the rights of parents to leave their property and business to anyone can be abolished. This decision can have a major effect on the management succession plans of privately held businesses.

The case was appealed to the Supreme Court. However, before the Court could make a ruling, the Oakland Scavenger Company was purchased by the Waste Management Corporation, and an out-of-court, $8 million settlement was reached. The settlement allocated sums of at least $50,000 to 16 black and Hispanic plaintiffs, depending on their length of service, and also provided for payments to a class of more than 400 black and Hispanic workers Oakland Scavenger employed after January 10, 1972.[16]

As K. Peter Stalland, legal representative for the National Family Business Council, has stated, "The effect this case can have on small business is tremendous. It means, conceivably, that almost any small business can be sued by an employee of a different ethnic origin than the owner, based upon not being accorded the same treatment as a son or daughter. The precedent is dangerous."[17] Thus, **nepotism** is something that now must be considered seriously in light of the legal ramifications.

The Oakland Scavenger case has started a movement that is sure to result in more guidelines and limitations for family employment, and privately held businesses will have to be aware of this challenge when preparing succession plans. (See "Entrepreneurship in Practice: Legal Concerns Regarding Nepotism" for more on this topic.)

Developing a Succession Strategy

Developing a succession strategy involves several important steps: (1) understanding the contextual aspects, (2) identifying successor qualities, and (3) developing a written succession plan.[18]

Understanding the Contextual Aspects

The five key aspects that must be considered for an effective succession follow.

TIME

The earlier the entrepreneur begins to plan for a successor, the better the chances of finding the right person. The biggest problem the owner faces is the prospect of events that force immediate action and result in inadequate time to find the best replacement.

TYPE OF VENTURE

Some entrepreneurs are easy to replace; some cannot be replaced. To a large degree, this is determined by the type of venture. An entrepreneur who is the idea person in a high-tech operation is going to be difficult to replace. The same is true for an entrepreneur whose personal business contacts throughout the industry are the key factors for the venture's success. On the other hand, a person running an operation that requires a minimum of knowledge or expertise usually can be replaced without too much trouble.

CAPABILITIES OF MANAGERS

The skills, desires, and abilities of the replacement will dictate the future potential and direction of the enterprise. As the industry matures, the demands made on the entrepreneur also may change. Industries where high tech is the name of the game often go through a change in which marketing becomes increasingly important. A technologically skilled entrepreneur with an understanding of marketing, or with the ability to develop an orientation in this direction, will be more valuable to the enterprise than will a technologically skilled entrepreneur with no marketing interest or background.

ENTREPRENEUR'S VISION

Most entrepreneurs have expectations, hopes, and desires for their organization. A successor—it is hoped—will share this vision, except, of course, in cases where the entrepreneur's plans have gotten the organization in trouble and a new vision is needed. Examples are plentiful today because of the huge increase in life sciences ventures, high-technology ventures, and other emerging technologies in which the founding entrepreneur possesses the initial vision to launch the company but lacks the managerial experience to grow the venture. Outside executive experience is sought because the board of directors may feel that a more managerial, day-to-day entrepreneurial manager is needed to replace the highly conceptual, analytical entrepreneur who founded the company.

ENVIRONMENTAL FACTORS

Sometimes a successor is needed because the business environment changes and a parallel change is needed at the top. An example is Edwin Land of Polaroid. Although his technological creativity had made the venture successful, Land eventually had to step aside for someone with more marketing skills. In some cases, owners have had to allow financial types to assume control of the venture because internal efficiency was more critical to short-run survival than was market effectiveness.

Identifying Successor Qualities

Successors should possess many qualities or characteristics. Depending on the situation, some will be more important than others. In most cases, however, all will have some degree of importance. Some of the most common of these successor qualities are: sufficient knowledge of the business or a good position (especially marketing or finance) from which to acquire this knowledge within an acceptable time frame; fundamental honesty and capability; good health; energy, alertness, and perception; enthusiasm about the enterprise; personality compatible with the business; high degree of perseverance; stability and maturity; reasonable amount of aggressiveness; thoroughness and a proper respect for detail; problem-solving ability; resourcefulness; ability to plan and organize; talent to develop people; personality of a starter and a finisher; and appropriate agreement with the owner's philosophy about the business.[19]

A Written Succession Strategy

These elements prepare the entrepreneur to develop a management continuity strategy and policy. A written policy can be established using one of the following strategies.

1. The owner controls the *management continuity strategy* entirely. This is very common, yet legal advice is still needed and recommended.

2. The owner consults with selected family members. Here, the legal advisor helps to establish a *liaison* between family and owner in constructing the succession mechanism.

entrepreneurship **in practice**

Legal Concerns Regarding Nepotism

In certain cases, entrepreneurs may be in violation of the law if they employ too many family members. The law considers nepotism a neutral policy—that is, it's not discriminatory by itself. Such a policy is lawful unless it has an "adverse impact" on women or minority groups (as in the Oakland Scavenger Company case). In another case, the Supreme Court increased the burden of proving adverse impact to plaintiffs and, at the same time, made it easier for employers to defend such lawsuits. It is expected, however, that Congress will eventually enact a civil rights bill—with or without the president's signature—that will require employers to provide a strong business justification for a policy that results in racial or gender imbalance.

Nepotism is more vulnerable to attack for "disparate impact" by racial minorities than by women. As the U.S. Court of Appeals noted in *Platner v. Cash & Thomas:* "It is difficult to see how nepotism could mask systematic gender discrimination. While a person's relatives will usually be of the same race, men and women will presumably be equally represented both within and without the family."

The smallest companies—those with 15 or fewer employees—are specifically excluded from the provisions of the Civil Rights Law of 1964 that deal with employment discrimination, but many states have similar statutes with broader coverage. The following guidelines may help growing ventures avoid any charge of employment discrimination:

- Find out as much as you can about the racial and gender composition of the labor pool in your area, and try to bring your own shop in line with it.

- The argument that most hiring in your business is through industry connections or word of mouth is a weak defense, because these traditional sources often perpetuate an in-group.

- Avoid stereotyping in job assignments or communications. Jokes or epithets aimed at women or minority-group members will be taken in court as evidence of a "hostile environment" for these groups.

- When hiring or promoting a family member, explain the decision in job-related terms. If a disappointed applicant asks why he or she was passed over, emphasize the qualifications for the job, commitment to the long-term success of the company, and firsthand knowledge or skills—for whoever was selected.

- Never make or explain a hiring decision or promotion by reasoning that "our customers won't like it if we send them a black salesman or a woman." Customer preference is not a defense in a lawsuit based on a discrimination claim.

Source: Howard Muson, "Dangerous Liaisons," *Family Business* (January/February 1991): 22–27.

3. The owner works with professional advisors. This is an actual board of advisors from various professional disciplines and industries that works with the owner to establish the mechanism for succession (sometimes referred to as a "quasi-board").[20]

4. The owner works with family involvement. This alternative allows the core family (blood members and spouses) to actively participate in and influence the decisions regarding succession.

   If the owner is still reasonably healthy and the firm is in a viable condition, the following additional actions should be considered.

5. The owner formulates **buy/sell agreements** at the very outset of the company, or soon thereafter, and whenever a major change occurs. This is also the time to consider an

appropriate insurance policy on key individuals that would provide the cash needed to acquire the equity of the deceased.

6. The owner considers **employee stock ownership plans** (ESOPs). If the owner has no immediate successor in mind and respects the loyalty and competence of his or her employees, then an appropriate ESOP might be the best solution for passing control of the enterprise. After the owner's death, the employees could decide on the management hierarchy.

7. The owner sells or liquidates the business when losing enthusiasm for it but is still physically able to go on. This could provide the capital to launch another business. Whatever the owner's plans, the firm would be sold before it fails due to disinterest.

8. The owner sells or liquidates after discovering a terminal illness but still has time for the orderly transfer of management or ownership.[21]

Legal advice is beneficial for all of these strategies, but of greater benefit is having advisors (legal or otherwise) who understand the succession issues and are able to recommend a course of action.

Entrepreneurial founders of privately held businesses often reject thoughts of succession. However, neither ignorance nor denial will change the inevitable. It is therefore crucial for entrepreneurs to design a plan for succession very carefully. Such plans prevent today's flourishing privately held businesses from becoming a statistic of diminishing family dynasties.

CONSIDER OUTSIDE HELP

Promotion from within is a morale-building philosophy. Sometimes, however, it is a mistake. When the top person does a poor job, does promoting the next individual in line solve the problem? The latter may be the owner/manager's clone. Conversely, consider family-owned businesses that start to outgrow the managerial ability of the top person. Does anyone in the firm *really* have the requisite skills to manage the operation? The questions that must be answered are: How can the business be effectively run, and who has the ability to do it? Sometimes answering these questions calls for an outside person. Privately held businesses also face the ever-present ego factor. Does the owner/manager have the wisdom to step aside and the courage to let someone else make strategic decisions? Or is the desire for control so great that the owner prefers to run the risks associated with personally managing the operation? The lesson is clear to the dispassionate observer; unfortunately, it is one that many owners have had to learn the hard way.[22]

The Exit Strategy: Liquidity Events

It is true that most entrepreneurs are focused on launching and growing their ventures rather than the plan for exiting the venture in the years to come. However, an exit strategy is always of prime importance to outside investors. Investors' commitment to capital will always reside on the confidence that they will recover their initial investment with a healthy profit. Entrepreneurs need to be aware that an exit strategy *for* the venture may mean the entrepreneur's exit *from* the venture as well.

An **exit strategy** is defined as that component of the business plan where an entrepreneur describes a method by which investors can realize a tangible return on their investment. The questions of "how much," "when," and "how" need to be addressed. Investors always want to convert their share of the investment into a more "liquid" form, known as a **liquidity event**, which refers to the positioning of the venture for the realization of a cash return for the owners and the investors. This "event" is most often achieved through an initial public offering or complete sale of the venture. In either scenario, the entrepreneur must seek professional advice and legal counsel due to the significant regulations and legal parameters involved. For our purposes, we delve into the basic concepts involved with each of these liquidity events.

entrepreneurship in practice

Buy/Sell Agreements

Many entrepreneurs owe their continued success to the combined skills of two or more owners. But did any owner, at the inception of the venture, contemplate involuntarily continuing the business with a co-owner's children? With a co-owner's ex-spouse? With a co-owner's creditors? Probably not. But smart entrepreneurs plan ahead, in order to deal with issues of control that may unpredictably arise by virtue of one of the "Four *D*s": Disability, Death, Dissolution, and Debtorship. Should a co-owner become disabled, die, be involved in a marital dissolution, or have assets seized by his or her creditors, ownership of his or her interest in the business may be in jeopardy of transfer to one or more third parties. Fortunately, it is possible (and imperative) that the parties take the steps necessary to assure that the transfer of any ownership interest in the business is carried out in a way that protects the future of the business, the ownership interests of remaining shareholders, and the financial security of the departing owner's family. A buy/sell agreement can provide just such protection. It ensures that, in the event of one of these "triggering events," interest in a closely held business is transferred in a manner that is advantageous to all involved parties. This type of agreement can be designed to make certain the following:

1. The remaining shareholder(s) has the first right to retain the ownership interest.

2. The departing owner (or beneficiaries) receives a fair market price for the ownership interest.

3. Lawsuits and disputes that could threaten the company's existence are avoided.

4. Funds are available to purchase the ownership interest.

Legal counsel is necessary to ensure that a buy/sell agreement addresses all of the unique circumstances of a particular company.

The two basic types of agreements are the cross-purchase agreement, in which the shareholders are obligated to purchase the departing owner's stock, and the redemption agreement, in which the company is obligated to purchase the departing owner's stock. Each case has certain advantages, disadvantages, and tax implications that need to be considered, and some agreements include "blended" options and obligations for such purchases. Thus, both a lawyer and a tax accountant should be consulted.

Source: Thomas Owens, "Buy-Sell Agreements," *Small Business Reports* (January 1991): 57–61; and Mark E. Need, Elmore Entrepreneurship Law Clinic Director, Indiana University-Bloomington, 2008.

The Initial Public Offering (IPO)

As we covered in Chapter 8, many entrepreneurs have sought capital through the public markets. Just to reiterate, the term **initial public offering (IPO)** is used to represent the registered public offering of a company's securities for the first time. In 2007, there were 275 IPOs that raised $65.7 billion. These figures reflect the tremendous volatility that exists within the stock market; however, entrepreneurs should be aware of the concerns that confront them when they pursue the IPO market. Many entrepreneurs already have begun to recognize some of the complex requirements involved with going public.[23] Table 15.3 provides a complete illustration of the steps involved with an IPO.

The Securities and Exchange Commission (SEC) requires the filing of a registration statement that includes a complete prospectus on the company. The SEC then reviews the registration, ensuring that full disclosure is made before giving permission to proceed. (See Table 15.4 for a presentation of the registration process.)

| *Table* | **15.3** | **The IPO Process** |

The entire initial public offering process is at once fast-moving and highly structured, governed by an interlocking set of federal and state laws and regulations and self-regulatory organization rules. Each member of the IPO team has specific responsibilities to fulfill; however, the company ultimately calls the plays for the team.

The following steps in the IPO process apply to both U.S. and non-U.S. companies.

Present proposal to the board. The IPO process begins with management making a presentation to the company's board of directors, complete with business plan and financial projections, proposing their company enter the public market. The board should consider the proposal carefully.

Restate financial statements and refocus the company *(applies only to companies not in compliance with U.S. GAAP).* If the board approves the proposal to go public, the company's books and records should be reviewed for the past two to three years. Financial statements should be restated to adhere to GAAP in order for them to be certified. Any intracompany transactions, compensation arrangements, and relationships involving management or the board that are customary to a private enterprise—*but improper for a public company*—must be eliminated and the statements appropriately restated. Also, companies should consider whether any outside affiliations (operations tangential to the company's core business) will be perceived negatively by the market.

Find an underwriter and execute a "letter of intent." At this point, a company should select an underwriter, if it has not already engaged one. A company's relationship with an underwriter should then be formalized through a mutual "letter of intent," outlining fees, ranges for stock price and number of shares, and certain other conditions.

Draft prospectus. After a letter of intent is executed, the IPO attorneys can begin work on the prospectus.

Respond to due diligence. The next step is to ask your investment banker and accountant to begin an elaborate investigation of your company (the due diligence process). Your underwriter will examine your company's management, operations, financial conditions, performance, competitive position, and business plan. Other factors open to scrutiny are your labor force, suppliers, customers, creditors, and any other parties that have a bearing on the viability of the company as a public entity and could affect the proper, truthful, adequate disclosure of its condition in the prospectus. The accounting firm will examine financial information and such specific documents as contracts, billings, and receipts to ensure the accuracy and adequacy of financial statements.

Select a financial printer. Your company should select an experienced financial printer—one that is familiar with SEC regulations governing the graphic presentation of a prospectus and has the facilities to print sufficient quantities under severe time constraints.

Assemble the syndicate. After the preliminary prospectus has been filed with the SEC and is available for circulation among potential investors, your underwriter should assemble the "syndicate," consisting of additional investment bankers who will place portions of the offering to achieve the desired distribution. Your underwriter should also accumulate "indications of interest"—solicited through its efforts as well as those of the syndicate—from institutions and brokers that have approached their clients. These indications give assurance that the IPO is viable and help to determine the final number of shares to be offered and the allocations to investors.

Perform the road show. Next, your company and your investment banker should design and perform the "road show," a series of meetings held with potential investors and analysts in key cities across the country and, if appropriate, overseas. The road show has become increasingly important not only to communicate key information to investors but also to display the managerial talent and expertise that will be leading the company.

Prepare, revise, and print the prospectus. In the meantime, the preliminary prospectus should have been prepared and revised according to SEC and NASDR (National Association of Securities Dealers Regulations) comments. Upon completion of these revisions, the company can expect NASDR to issue a letter stating that it has no objections to the underwriting compensation, terms, and arrangements,

Continued

| Table | 15.3 | The IPO Process (*Continued*) |

and the SEC to indicate its intent to declare their registration effective. The preliminary prospectus should be circulated to potential investors at least two days before the effective date, then the final version of the prospectus can be printed.

Price the offering. Just before the underwriting agreement is signed, on the day before the registration becomes effective and sales begin, the offering is priced. The investment banker should recommend a price per share for management's approval, taking into account the company's financial performance and competitive prospects, the stock price of comparable companies, general stock market conditions, and the success of the road show and ensuing expressions of interest. While the company will want to price the offering as high as possible, an offering that does not sell or sell completely will not be in its best interest or in the interest of the investors who find the share price declining in the market immediately after their initial purchase. In fact, investors look for at least a modest increase in the market price to reassure them about their investment decision.

Determine the offering size. The investment banking team should also consult with management regarding the offering size, taking into consideration how much capital the company needs to raise, the desired degree of corporate control, and investor demand. Often, the more shares outstanding, the greater the liquidity of the stock, which will increase institutional interest.

Source: Adapted from *Going Public* (New York: The NASDAQ Stock Market, Inc., 2005), 5–9. http://www.nasdaq.com/about/GP2005_cover_toc.pdf Accessed: April, 2008.

| Table | 15.4 | The Registration Process |

Event	Participants	Agenda	Timetable
Preliminary meeting to discuss issue	President, VP Finance, independent accountants, underwriters, counsel	Discuss financial needs; introduce and select type of issue to meet needs	1 July (Begin)
Form selection	Management, counsel	Select appropriate form for use in registration statement	3 July (3 days)
Initial meeting of working group	President, VP Finance, independent accountants, underwriter, counsel for underwriter, company counsel	Assign specific duties to each person in the working group; discuss underwriting problems with this issue; discuss accounting problems with the issue	8 July (8 days)
Second meeting of working group	Same as for initial meeting	Review work assignments; prepare presentation to board of directors	22 July (22 days)
Meeting of board of directors	Board of directors, members of working group	Approve proposed issue and increase of debt or equity; authorize preparation of materials	26 July (26 days)
Meeting of company counsel with underwriters	Company counsel, counsel for underwriters, underwriters	Discuss underwriting terms and blue-sky problems	30 July (30 days)

Table **15.4**   **The Registration Process (_Continued_)**

Event	Participants	Agenda	Timetable
Meeting of working group	Members of working group	Review collected material and examine discrepancies	6 August (37 days)
Prefiling conference with SEC staff	Working group members, SEC staff, other experts as needed	Review proposed registration and associated problems: legal, financial, operative	9 August (40 days)
Additional meetings of working group	Members of working group	Prepare final registration statement and prospectuses	12–30 August (61 days)
Meeting with board of directors	Board of directors, members of working group	Approve registration statement and prospectuses; discuss related topics and problems	6 September (68 days)
Meeting of working group	Members of working group	Draft final corrected registration statement	10 September (72 days)
Filing registration statement with SEC	Company counsel or representative and SEC staff	File registration statement and pay fee	12 September (74 days)
Distribution of "red herring" prospectus	Underwriters	Publicize offering	16 September (78 days)
Receipt of letter of comments	Members of working group	Relate deficiencies in registration statement	15 October (107 days)
Meeting of working group	Members of working group	Correct deficiencies and submit amendments	21 October (113 days)
Due diligence meeting	Management representatives, independent accountants, company counsel, underwriter's counsel, underwriters, other professionals as needed	Exchange final information and discuss pertinent problems relating to underwriting and issue	24 October (116 days)
Pricing amendment	Management, underwriters	Add the amounts for the actual price, underwriter's discount or commission, and net proceeds to company to the amended registration statement	25 October (117 days)
Notice of acceptance	SEC staff	Report from SEC staff on acceptance status of price-amended registration statement	28 October (120 days)
Statement becomes effective			30 October (122 days)

Source: From _An Introduction to the SEC_, 5th ed. by K. Fred Skousen. Copyright © 1991. Reprinted by permission of South-Western, a division of Cengage Learning.

The prospectus must disclose fully all pertinent information about a company and must present a fair representation of the firm's true prospects. All negative information must be clearly highlighted and explained. Some of the specific, detailed information that must be presented follows:

- History and nature of the company
- Capital structure
- Description of any material contracts
- Description of securities being registered
- Salaries and security holdings of major officers and directors and the price they paid for holdings
- Underwriting arrangements
- Estimate and use of net proceeds
- Audited financial statements
- Information about the competition with an estimation of the chances of the company's survival

Some of the more important disclosure requirements for annual reports follow.

- Audited financial statements that include the balance sheets for the past two years and income and funds statements for the past three years
- Five years of selected financial data
- Management's discussion and analysis of financial conditions and results of operations
- A brief description of the business
- Line-of-business disclosures for the past three fiscal years
- Identification of directors and executive officers, with the principal occupation and employer of each
- Identification of the principal market in which the firm's securities are traded
- Range of market prices and dividends for each quarter of the two most recent fiscal years
- An offer to provide a free copy of the 10-K report to shareholders on written request unless the annual report complies with Form 10-K disclosure requirements[24]

Some of the forms the SEC requires follow:

- Form S-1 (information contained in the prospectus and other additional financial data)
- Form 10-Q (quarterly financial statements and a summary of all important events that took place during the three-month period)
- Form 8-K (a report of unscheduled material events or corporate changes deemed important to the shareholder and filed with the SEC within 15 days of the end of a month in which a significant material event transpired)
- Proxy statements (information given in connection with proxy solicitation)[25]

Entrepreneurs who pursue the public securities route should be prepared for these reporting requirements, disclosure statements, and the shared control and ownership with outside shareholders.

Complete Sale of the Venture

After considering the various succession ideas presented in this chapter, as well as the potential for an initial public offering, many privately held business entrepreneurs choose a **harvest strategy** that involves complete sale of the venture. If this becomes the proper choice for an entrepreneur (keep in mind that it may be the best decision for an entrepreneur who has no interested family members or key employees), then the owner needs to review some important considerations. The idea of "selling out" actually should be viewed in the positive sense of "harvesting the investment."

Entrepreneurs consider selling their venture for numerous reasons. Based on 1,000 business owners surveyed, some of the motivations are (1) boredom and burnout, (2) lack of operating and growth capital, (3) no heirs to leave the business to, (4) desire for liquidity, (5) aging and health problems, and (6) desire to pursue other interests.[26]

Whether it is due to a career shift, poor health, a desire to start another venture, or retirement, many entrepreneurs face the sellout option during their entrepreneurial lifetime. This harvesting strategy needs to be carefully prepared in order to obtain the adequate financial rewards.[27]

Steps for Selling a Business

There are generally eight recommended steps for the proper preparation, development, and realization of the sale of a venture, as follows.[28]

STEP 1: PREPARE A FINANCIAL ANALYSIS

The purpose of such an analysis is to define priorities and forecast the next few years of the business. These fundamental questions must be answered:

- What will executive and other workforce requirements be, and how will we pay for them?
- If the market potential is so limited that goals cannot be attained, should we plan an acquisition or develop new products to meet targets for sales and profits?
- Must we raise outside capital for continued growth? How much and when?

STEP 2: SEGREGATE ASSETS

Tax accountants and lawyers may suggest the following steps to reduce taxes:

- Place real estate in a separate corporation, owned individually or by members of the family.
- Establish a leasing subsidiary with title to machinery and rolling stock. You can then lease this property to the operating company.
- Give some or all of the owner's shares to heirs when values are low, but have the owner retain voting rights. Thus, when a sale is made, part or all of the proceeds can go directly to another generation without double taxation.
- Hold management's salaries and fringe benefits at reasonable levels to maximize profits.

STEP 3: VALUE THE BUSINESS

The various methods used to valuate a venture were discussed in Chapter 14. Obviously, establishing the valuation of a company constitutes a most important step in its sale.

STEP 4: IDENTIFY THE APPROPRIATE TIMING

Knowing when to offer a business for sale is a critical factor. Timing can be everything. A few suggestions follow:

- Sell when business profits show a strong upward trend.
- Sell when the management team is complete and experienced.
- Sell when the business cycle is on the upswing, with potential buyers in the right mood and holding excess capital or credit for acquisitions.
- Sell when you are convinced that your company's future will be bright.

STEP 5: PUBLICIZE THE OFFER TO SELL

A short prospectus on the company that provides enough information to interest potential investors should be prepared. This prospectus should be circulated through the proper professional channels: bankers, accountants, lawyers, consultants, and business brokers.

STEP 6: FINALIZE THE PROSPECTIVE BUYERS

Inquiries need to be made in the trade concerning the prospective buyers. Characters and managerial reputation should be assessed to find the best buyer.

STEP 7: REMAIN INVOLVED THROUGH THE CLOSING

Meeting with the final potential buyers helps to eliminate areas of misunderstanding and to negotiate the major requirements more effectively. Also, the involvement of professionals such as attorneys and accountants usually precludes any major problems arising at the closing.

STEP 8: COMMUNICATE AFTER THE SALE

Problems between the new owner and the remaining management team need to be resolved to build a solid transition. Communication between the seller and the buyer and between the buyer and the current management personnel is a key step.

the global perspective

Acquiring a Venture:
Through the Eyes of the Beholder

When entrepreneurs sell, they need to remember that the buyer's perspective is not necessarily consistent with their own. The fact that they no longer have a need for what they are attempting to sell—whether their business, intellectual property, or assets—should not anchor their expectations for finding a buyer. Recently, Ford Motor Company verified this point when it sold its Jaguar and Land Rover companies, based in the United Kingdom, for $2.3 billion to the Tata Group, one of India's two largest conglomerates.

At first glance, the prospect of purchasing two of the most popular brands in the world seems like a logical business decision; yet, the long and tumultuous history of the two brands has led analysts to question whether the Indian company can profitably manufacture cars under the brands, a feat that has eluded previous owners. Forty years ago, the British government offloaded languishing car brands—including Austin, Rover, Jaguar, Riley, and Morris—in an attempt to rebuild the country's automobile industry. Many attempts have been made to resuscitate the brands, but any success has been short lived.

Some analysts argue that Ratan Tata, Tata Group's manager, will be integral to the acquisition's success. He is seen as a hands-on leader, which many observers believe will win him the support of the British employees, making the transition that much smoother. Another advantage that the company has is access to India's inexpensive IT and design capabilities, not to mention that the connection of the brands to India will help boost sales throughout Asia. Tata is convinced that synergies will evolve between the existing manufacturing operations of the two brands and the engineering expertise available through the Tata Group's existing resources in India.

There are no guarantees that the Tata Group will be able to accomplish what it has planned; however, the fact that its strategy makes use of two brands that had been dismissed by other companies is a lesson for entrepreneurs looking to sell. Buyers might be willing to pay significantly more for a business than the entrepreneur would think to request. The key is for the entrepreneur to not limit her valuation based on her plans for the business but rather to value the business based on the buyer's perspective. By taking this approach, the entrepreneur might be surprised to find that the business is worth much more than she would have ever guessed.

Source: Adapted from John Elliott, "Tata Buys into 40 Years of Trouble," *Fortune*, March 25, 2008, http://ridingtheelephant .blogs.fortune.cnn.com/2008/03/25/tata-buys-into-trouble/ (accessed April 17, 2008).

In addition to these eight steps, an entrepreneur must be aware of the tax implications that arise from the sale of a business. For professional advice, a tax accountant specializing in business valuations and sales should be consulted.

The eight steps outlined here, combined with the information on valuation in Chapter 14, will help entrepreneurs harvest their ventures. The steps provide a clear framework within which entrepreneurs can structure a fair negotiation leading to a sale. If the purpose of a valuation is to sell the business, then the entrepreneur must plan ahead and follow through with each step.

Summary

This chapter focused on the harvesting of the venture. Beginning with the issue of management succession as one of the greatest challenges for entrepreneurs, a number of considerations that affect succession were discussed. Using privately held firms as the focal point in this chapter, key issues such as family and nonfamily members—both within and outside the firm—were identified to show the unique pressures on the entrepreneur. Some family members will want to be put in charge of the operation; others simply want a stake in the enterprise.

Two types of successors exist: An entrepreneurial successor provides innovative ideas for new-product development, whereas a managerial successor provides stability for day-to-day operations. An entrepreneur may search inside or outside the family as well as inside or outside the business. The actual transfer of power is a critical issue, and the timing of entry for a successor can be strategic.

The Oakland Scavenger Company case revealed how legal concerns now exist about the hiring of only family members. Nepotism has been challenged in the courts on the basis of discrimination.

Developing a succession plan involves understanding these important contextual aspects: time, type of venture, capabilities of managers, the entrepreneur's vision, and environmental factors. Also, forcing events may require the implementation of a succession plan, regardless of whether or not the firm is ready to implement one. This is why it is so important to identify successor qualities and carry out the succession plan.

The chapter closed with a discussion of the entrepreneur's decision to sell out. The process was viewed as a method to "harvest" the investment, and eight specific steps were presented for entrepreneurs to follow.

Key Terms and Concepts

buy/sell agreements	entrepreneurial successor	liquidity event
delayed entry strategy	exit strategy	management succession
early entry strategy	forcing events	managerial successor
employee stock ownership plans (ESOPs)	harvest strategy	nepotism
	initial public offering (IPO)	Oakland Scavenger Company

Review and Discussion Questions

1. What are the potential choices for an entrepreneur to examine as the venture matures?

2. A number of barriers to succession in privately held businesses exist. Using Table 15.1, identify some of the key barriers.

3. What pressures do entrepreneurs sometimes face from inside the family? (Use Figure 15.1 in your answer.)

4. What pressures do entrepreneurs sometimes face from outside the family? (Use Figure 15.1 in your answer.)

5. An entrepreneur can make a number of choices regarding a successor. Using Table 15.2 as a guide, discuss each of these choices.

6. How might the Oakland Scavenger case affect succession decisions in small businesses?

7. What are three of the contextual aspects that must be considered in an effective succession plan?

8. In what way can forcing events cause the replacement of an owner/manager? Cite three examples.

9. What are five qualities or characteristics successors should possess?

10. Why do entrepreneurs look forward to the day when they can take their company public?

11. What eight steps should be followed to harvest a business? Discuss each of these steps.

Experiential Exercise

PASSING IT ON

Management succession and continuity are two critical concerns of most entrepreneurs. In your library or on the Internet (if accessible), look through the past-year issues of these magazines: *Business Week, U.S. News & World Report, Inc., Fortune Small Business, Entrepreneur,* and *Fast Company*. Focus on articles related to the management succession and continuity of specific firms. Then choose the two you find to be most interesting and informative and answer the following questions:

Firm 1

1. What business is this company in? _____

2. What difficulties did the owner have formulating a strategy regarding his or her succession?

_____

_____

_____

_____

3. What was the entrepreneur's final decision on how to handle the succession?

_____

_____

_____

4. What lessons can be learned from this individual's experience? _____

_____

_____

_____

Firm 2

1. What business is this company in?_____

_____

2. What difficulties did the owner have formulating a strategy regarding his or her succession?

_____

_____

_____

3. What was the entrepreneur's final decision on how to handle the succession?

_____

_____

_____

4. What lessons can be learned from this individual's experience? _____

_____

_____

_____

In Conclusion

Based on what you have learned from these two cases, what recommendations would you give to an entrepreneur who is in the process of developing a succession plan? Be as helpful as possible.

Case 15.1

JUST AS GOOD AS EVER

When Pablo Rodriguez was found in the storage area, no one knew for sure how long he had been unconscious. Within 30 minutes he was in the emergency room of Mercy Hospital, and by early evening the doctors had determined that Pablo had suffered a mild heart attack.

During the first few days he was in the hospital, Pablo's family was more concerned with his health than anything else. However, as it became clear that Pablo would be released within a week and allowed back at work within two weeks, family members talked about his stepping aside as president of the operation and allowing someone else to take over the reins.

Pablo is president of a successful auto-parts supply house. Gross sales last year were $3.7 million. Working with him in the business are his son, daughter, and two nephews. Pablo started the business 22 years ago, when he was 33. After working for one of the large oil firms for ten years as a sales representative to auto-parts supply houses, Pablo broke away and started his own company. At first, he hired outside help. During the past five years, however, he has been slowly bringing his family on board. It was Pablo's hope that his son would one day take over the business, but he did not see this happening for at least another 10 to 15 years.

Pablo's wife, Rebecca, believes that although he should continue to work, he should begin to train his son to run the business. On the day before he left the hospital, she broached this idea with Pablo and asked him to think about it. He replied: "What is there to think about? I'm too young to retire, and José does not know the business well enough to take over. It will take at least five more years before he is ready to run the operation. Besides, all I have to do is slow down a bit. I don't have to retire. What's the hurry to run me out of the company? I'm as good as ever."

Rebecca and José believe that, during the next couple of months, they must continue working on Pablo to slow down and to start training José to take over the reins.

QUESTIONS

1. Why is Pablo reluctant to turn over the reins to José? Include a discussion of Figure 15.1 in your answer.

2. Cite and discuss two reasons Pablo should begin thinking about succession planning.

3. What would you recommend Rebecca and José do to convince Pablo that they are right? Offer at least three operative recommendations.

Case 15.2

NEEDING SOME HELP ON THIS ONE

In the past, most people who wanted to get their foreign sports cars fixed had to turn to the dealer from which they had purchased the car. In recent years, however, auto repair shops that specialize in foreign sports cars have become popular in some areas of the country. When Jack Schultz started his company ten years ago, he was lucky if he had two cars a day to work on. Today, Jack has 15 people working for him, and he usually has a backlog of about five days' work. Some of this work is repairs caused by auto accidents; a lot of it is a result of improper maintenance by the owners.

Jack is 64 years old and feels he will work for about six more years before retiring. The business is very profitable, and Jack and his wife do not need to worry about retirement income—they have saved more than enough. However, Jack is concerned about what to do with the business. He has two children who work with him, Bob (31 years old) and Tim (29 years old). Jack has not asked either of them if they would want to take over the operation. He assumes they will. He also has a nephew, Richard (35 years old), working for him. All three of these relatives have been with Jack for nine years.

Jack believes that any one of the three could successfully head the venture. But he is concerned about in-fighting should he favor one over the others. On the other hand, if he turns the business over to all three of them collectively, will they be able to get along with one another? Jack has no reason to believe that the three cannot work things out amicably, but he is unsure.

Jack has decided that he cannot wait much longer to groom an heir. The major stumbling block is identifying who that person will be. Additionally, Jack really does not know anything about picking a successor. What characteristics should the individual possess? What types of training should the person be given? What other steps should be followed? Jack feels that he needs to answer these questions as soon as possible. "I know how to plan business operations," he told his wife last week, "but I don't know how to go about planning for the succession of business operations. It's a whole different idea. I need some help on this one."

QUESTIONS

1. Identify and briefly describe four characteristics you would expect to find in a successful manager of this type of venture.

2. What steps does Jack need to follow to successfully identify and groom a successor? Be complete in your answer.

3. If you were going to advise Jack, what would you recommend he do first? How should he get started with his succession plan? What should he do next? Offer him some general guidance on how to handle this problem.

Notes

1. Tammi S. Feltham, Glenn Feltham, and James J. Barnett, "The Dependence of Family Businesses on a Single Decision-Maker," *Journal of Small Business Management* 43, no. 1 (January 2005): 1–15; see also Timothy Bates, "Analysis of Young, Small Firms that Have Closed: Delineating Successful from Unsuccessful Closures," *Journal of Business Venturing* 20, no. 3 (May 2005): 343–58.

2. John L. Ward, *Keeping the Family Business Healthy* (San Francisco: Jossey-Bass, 1987), 1–2.

3. Richard Beckhard and W. Gibb Dyer, Jr., "Managing Continuity in the Family-Owned Business," *Organizational Dynamics* (Summer 1983): 7–8.

4. Manfred F. R. Kets de Vries, "The Dynamics of Family-Controlled Firms: The Good News and the Bad News," *Organizational Dynamics* (Winter 1993): 59–71; and Richard A. Cosier and Michael Harvey, "The Hidden Strengths in Family Business: Functional Conflict," *Family Business Review* (March 1998): 75–79.

5. Peter Davis, "Realizing the Potential of the Family Business," *Organizational Dynamics* (Summer 1983): 53–54; and Thomas Hubler, "Ten Most Prevalent Obstacles to Family Business Succession Planning," *Family Business Review* (June 1999): 117–22.

6. Phyllis G. Holland and William R. Boulton, "Balancing the 'Family' and the 'Business' in the

Family Business," *Business Horizons* (March/April 1984): 19; Michael D. Ensley and Allison W. Pearson, "An Exploratory Comparison of the Behavioral Dynamics of Top Management Teams in Family and Non-Family New Ventures: Cohesion, Conflict, Potency, and Consensus," *Entrepreneurship Theory & Practice* 29, no. 3 (May 2005): 267–84; and Paul Westhead and Carole Howorth, "Ownership and Management Issues Associated with Family Firm Performance and Company Objectives," *Family Business Review* 19 (2006): 301–16.

7. See Donald F. Kuratko, "Understanding the Succession Challenge in Family Business," *Entrepreneurship, Innovation, and Change* (September 1995): 185–91; see also Heather A. Haveman and Mukti V. Khaire, "Survival Beyond Succession? The Contingent Impact of Founder Succession on Organizational Failure," *Journal of Business Venturing* 19, no. 3 (May 2004): 437–63.

8. See Neil C. Churchill and Kenneth J. Hatten, "Non-Market-Based Transfers of Wealth and Power: A Research Framework for Family Business," *American Journal of Small Business* (Fall 1987): 53–66; and Timothy P. Blumentritt, Andrew D. Keyt, and Joseph H. Astrachan, "Creating an Environment for Successful Nonfamily CEOs: An Exploratory Study of Good Principals," *Family Business Review* 20 (2007): 321–36.

9. Peter S. Davis and Paula D. Harveston, "The Influence of Family on the Family Business Succession Process: A Multi-Generational Perspective," *Entrepreneurship Theory and Practice* 22, no. 3 (Spring 1998): 31–54; Eleni T. Stavrou, "Succession in Family Business: Exploring the Effects of Demographic Factors on Offspring Intentions to Join and Take Over the Business," *Journal of Small Business Management* 37, no. 3 (1999): 43–61; and Sue Birley, "Attitudes of Owner-Managers' Children Toward Family and Business Issues," *Entrepreneurship Theory and Practice* 26, no. 3 (2002): 5–19.

10. See Donald F. Kuratko, Helga B. Foss, and Lucinda L. VanAlst, "IRS Estate Freeze Rules: Implications for Family Business Succession Planning," *Family Business Review* (Spring 1994): 61–72; and Joseph H. Astrachan and Roger Tutterow, "The Effect of Estate Taxes on Family Business: Survey Results," *Family Business Review* (Fall 1996): 303–14.

11. Shaker A. Zahra, James C. Hayton, and Carlo Salvato, "Entrepreneurship in Family vs. Non-Family Firms: A Resource-Based Analysis of the Effect of Organizational Culture," *Entrepreneurship Theory and Practice* 28, no. 4 (Summer 2004): 363–82; and Matthew W. Rutherford, Lori A. Muse, and Sharon L. Oswald, "A New Perspective on the Developmental Model for Family Business," *Family Business Review* 19 (2007): 317–33.

12. For an interesting perspective, see Kathryn Stafford, Karen A. Duncan, Sharon Dane, and Mary Winter, "A Research Model of Sustainable Family Business," *Family Business Review* (September 1999): 197–208; see also Lucia Naldi, Mattias Nordqvist, Karin Sjöberg, and Johan Wiklund, "Entrepreneurial

13. Orientation, Risk Taking, and Performance in Family Firms," *Family Business Review* 20 (2007): 33–48.

13. See Kevin C. Seymour, "Intergenerational Relationships in the Family Firm: The Effect on Leadership Succession," *Family Business Review* (Fall 1993): 263–82; Eleni T. Stavrou and Paul Michael Swiercz, "Securing the Future of Family Enterprise: A Model of Offspring Intentions to Join the Business," *Entrepreneurship Theory and Practice* 22, no. 2 (Winter 1998): 19–40; and James P. Marshall, Ritch Sorenson, Keith Brigham, Elizabeth Wieling, Alan Reifman, and Richard S. Wampler, "The Paradox for the Family Firm CEO: Owner Age Relationship to Succession-Related Processes and Plans," *Journal of Business Venturing* 21, no. 3 (2006): 348–68.

14. Jeffrey A. Barach, Joseph Ganitsky, James A. Carson, and Benjamin A. Doochin, "Entry of the Next Generation: Strategic Challenge for Family Firms," *Journal of Small Business Management* 26, no. 2 (1988): 49–56; see also Matthew W. Rutherford, Donald F. Kuratko, and Daniel T. Holt, "Examining the Link between Familiness and Performance: Can the F-PEC Untangle the Family Business Theory Jungle?" *Entrepreneurship Theory and Practice* (forthcoming, 2008)

15. "Nepotism on Trial," *Inc.*, July 1984, 29.

16. David Graulich, "You Can't Always Pay What You Want," *Family Business* (February 1990): 16–19.

17. "Feuding Families," *Inc.*, January 1985, 38.

18. Donald F. Kuratko and Richard M. Hodgetts, "Succession Strategies for Family Businesses," *Management Advisor* (Spring 1989): 22–30; see also Mark Fischetti, *The Family Business Succession Handbook* (Philadelphia: Family Business, 1997).

19. James J. Chrisman, Jess H. Chua, and Pramodita Sharma, "Important Attributes of Successors in Family Business: An Exploratory Study," *Family Business Review* (March 1998): 19–34; and Franz W. Kellermanns, Kimberly A. Eddleston, Tim Barnett, and Allison Pearson, "An Exploratory Study of Family Member Characteristics and Involvement: Effects on Entrepreneurial Behavior in the Family Firm," *Family Business Review* 21 (2008): 1–14.

20. Adapted from Harold W. Fox, "Quasi-Boards: Useful Small Business Confidants," *Harvard Business Review* (January/February 1982): 64–72.

21. Glenn R. Ayres, "Rough Family Justice: Equity in Family Business Succession Planning," *Family Business Review* (Spring 1990): 3–22; Ronald E. Berenbeim, "How Business Families Manage the Transition from Owner to Professional Management," *Family Business Review* (Spring 1990): 69–110; and Michael H. Morris, Roy O. Williams, Jeffrey A. Allen, and Ramon A. Avila, "Correlates of Success in Family Business Transitions," *Journal of Business Venturing* 12, no. 5 (1997): 385–402.

22. Johannes H. M. Welsch, "The Impact of Family Ownership and Involvement on the Process of Management Succession," *Family Business Review* (Spring 1993): 31–54.

23. See *Going Public* (New York: The NASDAQ Stock Market, Inc., 2005), 5–9, see also Richard C. Dorf and Thomas H. Beyers, *Technology Ventures: From Idea to Enterprise,* 2nd ed. (New York: McGraw-Hill, 2008).

24. K. Fred Skousen, *An Introduction to the SEC,* 5th ed. (Mason, OH: South-Western/Cengage Learning), 157; see also Catherine M. Daily, S. Travis Certo, and Dan R. Dalton, "Investment Bankers and IPO Pricing: Does Prospectus Information Matter?" *Journal of Business Venturing* 20, no. 1 (January 2005): 93–111.

25. For a complete listing, see Skousen, *An Introduction to the SEC,* 60; see also Andrew J. Sherman, *Raising Capital* (New York: AMACOM, 2005).

26. James Fox and Steven Elek, "Selling Your Company," *Small Business Reports* (May 1992): 49–58; see also John B. Vinturella and Suzanne M. Erickson, *Raising Entrepreneurial Capital* (Burlington, MA: Elsevier, 2004).

27. See Donald Reinardy and Catherine Stover, "I Want to Sell My Business. Where Do I Begin?" *Small Business Forum* (Fall 1991): 1–24; see also J. William Petty, "Harvesting Firm Value: Process and Results," *Entrepreneurship 2000* (Chicago: Upstart, 1997), 71–94; and Carolin Decker and Thomas Mellewigt, "Thirty Years after Michael E. Porter: What Do We Know About Business Exit?" *Academy of Management Perspectives* 21, no. 2 (2007): 41–55.

28. From the *Harvard Business Review,* "Packaging Your Business for Sale," by Charles O'Conor, March/April 1985, 52–58. Copyright ©1985 by the President and Fellows of Harvard College; all rights reserved; see also Michael S. Long, *Valuing the Closely Held Firm* (Oxford: Oxford University Press, 2008).

The TOWS Matrix

DIRECTIONS:

Using the concept of the SWOT Analysis presented in Chapter 13, the TOWS Matrix allows an analysis of a new venture based on its combined Strengths, Weaknesses, Opportunities, and Threats.

Find a new start-up venture and work with the CEO to establish the combinations of the following: Strengths, in light of Opportunities; Strengths, in light of Threats; Weaknesses, in light of Opportunities; and Weaknesses, in light of Threats. This combination of the SWOT Matrix will help you to understand the tactics a firm should develop based on its own recognized strengths and weaknesses within the framework of the external environment.

TOWS Matrix		
	Strengths—S	Weaknesses—W
Opportunities—O	SO Strategies	WO Strategies
Threats—T	ST Strategies	WT Strategies

entrepreneurial

CASE ANALYSIS

Homeboy Industries: An Incubator of Hope and Businesses

entrepreneurial CASE ANALYSIS

Homeboy Industries: An Incubator of Hope and Businesses

The cool, pleasant morning was rapidly turning into a typically steamy summer day in Los Angeles. Michael Baca, a retired firefighter and—since 2003—the operations director for Homeboy Industries drove along First Street toward the organization's headquarters, where a staff meeting soon would begin. He had pondered all morning what to do about Homeboy Industry's merchandising division, whether to make the investment of capital and effort to expand the division's business or to leave it the way it was. Several people in the organization had become excited about the market potential of Homeboy Merchandise over the years, and now in 2004 they were eager to take the next steps. They wanted to propose an expansion plan for the division to Father Boyle, the founder and executive director of Homeboy Industries, and they wanted Michael's support. Others in the organization thought that the merchandising division was a poor fit with Homeboy Industries. Father Boyle and still others worried that its merchandise might become gang wear—the last thing that the organization wanted to have happen. Michael knew that all the staff members wanted his opinion. As he pulled into Homeboy's parking lot and entered the building, he knew he had only a few minutes to make a decision one way or the other.

BOYLE HEIGHTS

To a middle-class visitor driving down First Street, the Boyle Heights neighborhood of East Los Angeles felt like a different world, both familiar and strange. A local market sold milk, and children were walking to school. A group of heavily tattooed young men in baggy pants and Los Angeles Raiders football jerseys also walked along the street, their eyes seeming to show both fear and anger. Beyond a police station, a building adorned with graffiti came into view: Homeboy Industries. Across the street from the police station, children milled around their school yard. Farther down the block, a pushcart vendor sold fruit to two older women.

Boyle Heights, named in 1875 for Andrew Boyle of the Boyle-Workman family, was notorious for having one of the worst gang problems in all of Los Angeles. Within its 16 square miles, 60 different gangs claimed 10,000 members among an official population of 90,000.[1] Their presence ensured violence and plenty of action for the Los Angeles Police Department (LAPD).

The neighborhood's intense gang activity had historical roots in the rapid migration of illegal immigrants to Los Angeles, where the poorest of them concentrated in East Los Angeles. Once the center of Jewish and Japanese-American life in the early twentieth century, Boyle Heights was now 94–95% Hispanic or Latino. Two large housing projects, Pico Gardens and Aliso Village, made up much of the neighborhood; most kids lived in one or the other.

Attempts to slow the growth of the gangs had proved futile. Community Resources Against Street Hoodlums (CRASH), the LAPD's special gang unit, constantly patrolled Boyle Heights. Even so, gang violence continued to wreak havoc.[2] Something else needed to be done. Needless to say, Boyle Heights—like much of East Los Angeles—offered its children few opportunities. Instead of jobs, kids found themselves looking for membership in the local gangs. They saw their brothers and sisters, sometimes their only role models, running with gangs. For some, gangs were all they knew and the only way to get what they wanted in this neighborhood.

Homeboy Industries

Inside the Homeboy Industries building unfolded a study of contrasts and juxtaposition. The fashionably decorated, air-conditioned lobby displayed a hub of personal computers, no different from a customer service center at a larger corporation. The receptionist was a polite young Latino, professional in dress and appearance. A closer look revealed multiple tattoos on his fingers and face, all related to the gang life he formerly called his own. Young men and one woman sat at the computers, answering phones and working busily. They wore baggy shorts and either black shirts bearing the Homeboy Industries logo or Raiders jerseys. A tattooed "LA" showed through the stubble of one recently shaved head. Another employee had horns tattooed on his forehead. The art displayed on the office walls included pictorial collages of life in the rough housing projects of Boyle Heights. They served as a reminder to Homeboy's employees that they had good reasons to stay out of the gang life.

Father Greg Boyle founded Jobs for a Future (JFF), a nonprofit employment referral center, in 1988 (see Exhibit 1). He believed that, to eliminate gang violence, it was necessary to root out its cause: the lack of hope arising from a lack of opportunities. He was confident that gang violence in Boyle Heights would disappear if its young people had the opportunity to "plan their futures not their funerals." JFF's slogan expressed its

Source: David Choi and W. Fred Kiesner, "Homeboy Industries: An Incubator of Hope and Businesses," *Entrepreneurship Theory and Practice* 31, no. 5 (September 2007): 769–90.

Exhibit   **1**   **Jobs For a Future: Homeboy Industries**

objective: "Nothing stops a bullet like a job." Here, former gang members could receive counseling, job placement assistance, and coaching in interview skills, all in an attempt to provide a new future.

Many of JFF's clients had been ordered to receive individual or family counseling as a condition of probation. JFF employed two professional therapists on-site to provide these services to the probationers and to anyone in the community who needed the extra support that counseling could not provide. Both JFF employees and volunteers acted as "navigators" for JFF's clients. Navigators helped juveniles released from detention facilities to enroll in school, register for any required classes, check in with probation officers, obtain driver's licenses, and attend job interviews. One of the more interesting and unusual services provided by JFF was free tattoo removal. Ya 'Stuvo[3] Tattoo Removal offered gang members a way to erase a link to their past and start clean. The program was available to anyone who wanted it done, although priority was given to facial tattoos. Because of its popularity, there was a nine-month wait for this service.

JFF annually placed more than 350 clients in jobs—only a small fraction of the more than 1,000 gang members who passed through the office in a typical month. Demand far exceeded supply! The organization desperately wanted to have a greater impact. Many clients continued to struggle against obstacles to their employment, such as felony records, visible gang tattoos, and lack of work experience.

It was for these most challenged individuals that Father Boyle created Homeboy Industries in 1992, following the Los Angeles riots. Homeboy shared the building used by JFF. Homeboy developed several business enterprises, each of which hired the "homies" who attended JFF's training programs. Homeboy Industries started with the purchase of a bakery that became Homeboy Bakery. It grew to include Homeboy Silkscreen, Homeboy Merchandise, and Homeboy Graffiti Removal and Maintenance. These businesses and the Homeboy headquarters employed more than 70 homies at any one time. Employees learned to clock in on time, to build lasting work habits and skills, and to work side by side with former members of enemy gangs.

A visitor to the Homeboy Industries office in 2004 likely would notice its playful mood. The teenagers laughed and told stories. The receptionist spoke with evident pride about everything Homeboy Industries had done to help him and the community. He pointed to the Homeboy brochure, which quoted an employee:

entrepreneurial CASE ANALYSIS

"Because Homeboy Industries decided to believe in me, I decided to believe in myself. And the best way I can think of paying them back is by changing my life, and that's exactly what I've decided to do."

"FATHER G"

For more than 20 years, Father Greg Boyle (see Exhibit 2), known throughout the neighborhood as "Father G," "G," or even "G Dog," had embraced the boys and girls others shunned. While visiting them in hospitals and prisons, he had prodded hundreds of gang members to trade their lives of violent crime for honest work. He had become a legendary figure in the barrio, where widespread stories told of Father Boyle driving his car or riding his bike into the middle of a gunfight in an attempt to part feuding gangs. Father Boyle was known to be willing to give up his life to keep the kids from killing one another. Even so, Father Boyle had been forced to bury more than 120 young people from the neighborhood, a somber reminder of the challenges that remained.

Father Boyle, who was a Los Angeles native and was ordained a priest in 1984, became a pastor of the Dolores Mission church in Boyle Heights in 1986. There, he saw firsthand one of the worst gang problems in the United States. Believing that someone must help the young people escape from the horrible cycle that had engulfed them, Father Boyle developed a vision: Get these kids jobs, get them off the street, give them marketable skills, and remove them from the gangs that surround them. "Jobs not jails" and "Nothing stops a bullet like a job"

| Exhibit | 2 | Father Greg Boyle |

became mottos that expressed his vision. As he put it, "At Homeboy Industries what we try to do always is be a manufacturer of hope in a community with a fatal lack of it."

Father Boyle regularly was asked to speak at functions and tell stories about Homeboy Industries. Those speeches both informed and inspired his audiences:

> [The homies] think they're the bad son. I keep telling them over and over, "You are the son that any parents would be proud to claim as their own." That's the truth. That's not some fantasy. As soon as they know that they're exactly what God had in mind when God made them, then they become that. Then they like who they are. Once they can do that—love themselves—they're not inclined to shoot somebody or hurt somebody or be out there gang-banging.[4]

Father Boyle may have seemed a legend to many in the neighborhood, but his mortality was revealed in March 2003, when he was diagnosed with leukemia. He was deluged with visits, calls, and letters from a wide variety of people, ranging from the LAPD chief to homies in prison. Homies he hadn't seen in a decade turned up, tears streaming down their faces, to offer their organs and blood. Other admirers brought juices, vitamins, and offers of Mexican healers and folk remedies. Actor Martin Sheen urged Father Boyle to take an all-expense-paid trip to Lourdes, France, where healing miracles were said to occur. "Death and life-threatening illnesses are not even on my top 10 list of things I dread," Father Boyle said, shrugging off the bad news. "How are we going to pay our bills on Friday? That's real-life dread." Despite chemotherapy, Father Boyle looked fit and energetic. He claimed his cancer was in remission. No one at Homeboy Industries was sure about his true health. When people asked him about it, his typical response was, "Sometimes I run out of gas, but so do cars."

THE HOMIES

Each employee of Homeboy Industries had his own stories to tell, one story of violence and the second an inspirational story of a life being transformed. The following two examples are representative of others as well.

Carlos Nieto's résumé at age 24 included an armed robbery conviction, several stints in state prison for parole violations, and a 12-year membership in the notorious Toonerville street gang, where his moniker had been "Sneaky." His job skills, acquired in prison, included the abilities to make tattoo ink by melting down chess pieces and to fashion a spear from a rolled newspaper and syrup. Tattoos of demonic horns seemingly sprouted from both sides of his shaved head; murals of jailhouse ink ran the lengths of his arms. But in two months at Homeboy Industries, Carlos had begun to acquire skills that could far better serve him outside

prison. He learned to show up daily at 9:00 a.m.—clean, sober, and ready to work. Talking on the phone without using vernaculars was another lesson, as was suppressing the urge to react belligerently to a coworker.

Carlos said he planned to use what he was learning at Homeboy Industries to launch a new life, which he hoped would include college and a career as a counselor to troubled teens. A recent conversation with Father Boyle had convinced Carlos that he would stay out of prison for good. "He looked at me the other day and said, 'I want you to know that I'm very proud of you,'" Nieto recalled. "He said, 'Now I know that when my day comes I can rest in peace knowing that my son is doing something with himself.'"

Felipe Antonio also had turned his life around thanks to Homeboy Industries. A young man with a gentle demeanor, he recalled his childhood as follows: "I didn't have parents. My sister raised me from the time I was eight. Nobody was checking on me—I was free. I was in a gang. We went to parties, got into fights. We did graffiti." In 1997, as Felipe climbed from his car one evening, he was shot in the spine. He was only 17. "I just passed away a little bit," he recounted, "and when I woke up I couldn't feel my legs no more." Now he was in a wheelchair, paralyzed from the chest down. Nevertheless, Felipe was hopeful about his future and planned to attend California State University–Los Angeles for a degree in social services.

A Series of Commercial Enterprises

Since its founding in 1992, Homeboy Industries had launched a series of business ventures. By 2004, Homeboy's commercial ventures comprised four units.

HOMEBOY BAKERY: THE FIRST VENTURE

Following the riots in 1992, Fr. Boyle raised enough money to buy an old bakery in Boyle Heights. In Homeboy Bakery, Father Boyle saw his vision become a reality. His homies turned the bakery into a fully operational, successful business. It put troubled teens to work, gave them hands-on job experience, and generated profits to fund other Homeboy ventures—until a fire destroyed the bakery in 1999. Since then, Fr. Boyle had been on a mission to start another bakery. In 2003, an opportunity presented itself for Homeboy Industries to acquire a profitable bakery with monthly revenue of $700,000 and an impressive customer list that included Trader Joe's.[5] All of the bakery's 75 employees eventually could be replaced by homies. Father Boyle thought that the bakery could earn up to $800,000 annually, which would support all of Homeboy's operations without future fund-raising.

Father Boyle and the board of Homeboy Industries decided to pursue the acquisition. The business, including

entrepreneurial CASE ANALYSIS

its land and building, was priced at $4.8 million. Father Boyle and the board engaged in an aggressive capital campaign to purchase the bakery. They planned to raise the purchase price plus enough for needed renovations and contingencies. With the help of private foundations, the federal government, and private donors, Homeboy had raised more than $3.6 million by early 2004.

HOMEBOY SILKSCREEN

The idea for Homeboy Silkscreen came from Ruben Rodriguez, who believed that he owed his changed life to Father Boyle. Ruben, struggling with drinking and holding down a job, had looked to Father Boyle for direction. Just a few meetings with Father Boyle changed Ruben's life forever. Father Boyle got him to stop drinking and helped him land a steady job with the city.

Ruben wanted to repay this kindness, and he saw an opportunity to utilize his wife's silk-screening skills. In the spring of 1996, he presented Father Boyle with the idea of starting a business that would offer custom silk-screen and embroidery services for T-shirts, sweatshirts, hats, bags, and several other products. Most important, it would employ some of the kids from the neighborhood. Father Boyle loved the idea, because it would provide even more jobs for young people in Boyle Heights.

Ruben spent hours searching for great deals on used, high-quality silk-screen equipment. When he showed Father Boyle his budget based on what he had found, Boyle was concerned by the numbers. He told Ruben that he need not find the cheapest equipment; in fact, he said, a new business should have all-new, top-of-the-line machines. Father Boyle did not want to cut costs at the outset, for fear of dooming the venture from the beginning. Although new equipment meant significantly higher investment, Father Boyle thought that skimping on equipment could be extremely costly in the long run. Ruben revised his figures to reflect the new equipment, and Father Boyle approved the new budget.

Finding a location for Homeboy Silkscreen proved to be difficult. Landlords feared that the ex-gang members would break into other tenants' or customers' cars. Another challenge was that several of the possible sites lay inside the territory of one gang or another. Members (or former members) of rival gangs would have to risk their lives just to get to work. Eventually, Ruben found the perfect place outside the gang territories but still close enough so the kids could get there.

Homeboy Silkscreen received a boost in its early months when Power 106 FM, a favorite radio station of teenagers throughout Los Angeles, ordered 10,000 T-shirts for $45,000 and began running free commercials for the business. Every time a commercial aired, 20 callers would ask Homeboy Silkscreen about its services. Over the years, Power 106 remained one of Homeboy Silkscreen's biggest clients. Through the radio station's connections, several record labels also became silk-screening customers.

Ruben and his employees were proud of the quality of their work. Homeboy Silkscreen employed 11 to 15 workers at any time and had employed a total of 350 homies over the life of the business. Homeboy Silkscreen usually kept employees for 90 days—to ensure proper job training and adjustment to the working world—before they were deemed ready for other employment by Michael or Father Boyle and referred back to JFF.

HOMEBOY GRAFFITI REMOVAL SERVICES AND HOMEBOY MAINTENANCE SERVICES

Homeboy Graffiti Removal Services removed graffiti in an effort to beautify Boyle Heights and reduce the violence that gang graffiti provoked. The service, available to anyone in the neighborhood, proved very popular; Homeboy received several requests a day.

Newer to Homeboy Industries was its maintenance program, a separate but related business. Homeboy Maintenance acted as a general service to "keep the neighborhood clean." It collected and hauled refrigerators, furniture, and other large items to its reclamation center. Homeboy Maintenance also sponsored neighborhood cleanups and trash collection for the residents of Boyle Heights.

Both Graffiti Removal Services and Maintenance Services proved very powerful because they not only put the teens to work, they also helped to make the neighborhood a better place to live. Both services were paid for by the city of Los Angeles.

HOMEBOY MERCHANDISE

Homeboy Merchandise started soon after Homeboy Silkscreen began production in 1996. No one was sure who should be credited for starting Homeboy Merchandise or who created the initial design for the merchandise. Homeboy Industries had begun printing T-shirts with the Homeboy logo that many employees wore proudly (see Exhibit 3). Even Father Boyle often sported a denim shirt with the logo embroidered on the right pocket. The uniforms proved to be popular; soon, friends of Homeboy were asking where they could get a Homeboy T-shirt. In response, Homeboy Industries began printing a wide range of Homeboy-themed products.

Exhibit

Exhibit	3	Sample Homeboy Merchandise

Homeboy's new catalog contained all of its current merchandise. The catalog was professionally done, with sharp pictures of merchandise surrounded by social messages in the foreground. Its approximately 40 items included T-shirts with the Homeboy or Homegirl logo, children's and baby clothes, bags, mouse pads, wallets, hats, and coffee mugs. Prices ranged from $15 for basic T-shirts to $25 for the Homeboy attaché bag. All of the items came in a range of colors, and some had different types of artwork on them. The T-shirts displayed various catchy phrases associated with Homeboy Industries. Customers could mail or fax orders, and they paid by credit card, check, or money order.

Homeboy Merchandise was in charge of the design, marketing, and distribution, and it outsourced the production of its clothing to Homeboy Silkscreen. In reality, most ideas for new products appeared to come from the silk-screen operation. However, some Homeboy employees felt that the Homeboy logo and the design of the merchandise offered by Homeboy Merchandise needed a makeover.

Homeboy Merchandise struggled to find retail outlets for its products (its online catalog was a passive Web

site that did not make transactions). Its biggest sales occurred at religious conferences at which Father Boyle spoke. The Religious Education Congress was Homeboy Industries' biggest sales event each year. At one such event, Homeboy would sell $6,000–$7,000 worth of its merchandise. In fact, Father Boyle was the company's top salesperson.

Michael Baca

Michael Baca, a good friend of Father Boyle's, was similarly dedicated to the cause of helping homies. Having grown up in the projects himself, he was very familiar with the gangs and the devastation they caused to families. In fact, Michael's three brothers had been gang members, and one was still serving a 26-year prison sentence. Even as a child, Michael was never interested in joining the gangs. Instead, he wanted to make a life for himself; at the age of 20, he became a firefighter and a certified emergency medical technician. Unfortunately, six years later (in 2000), his career ended abruptly when he fell from a roof and injured his back.

entrepreneurial CASE ANALYSIS

Rather than feel sorry for himself while he was hospitalized, Michael began giving back to his community. He realized that the best opportunity to intervene in the life of a gang member was at a crucial moment—for him, it was when he was being received at the hospital for a gunshot wound, had just been connected to an IV, and was crying "Don't let me die!" As a result, Michael started the first hospital-based gang intervention program. It offered extensive counseling, GED planning, tattoo removal, and job mentoring—many of the services that Father Boyle offered. Thus, when the operations director of Homeboy Industries resigned in late 2002, Father Boyle asked Michael to accept the position. Although Michael was not an experienced corporate manager, Father Boyle was confident that he had many talents critical to Homeboy Industries.

Michael projected a vastly different personality than Father Boyle. He was less philosophical and more serious, intense, and hands-on. Although Michael shared Father Boyle's vision, he was more focused on day-to-day operations and achieving measurable results. Michael mentioned to the case writer that most of the pressures and stress he felt on the job were self-imposed. He felt a sense of urgency that the organization should be doing even better and accomplishing more. The more successful Homeboy Industries was, the more homies it could help.

The Homeboy Organization and Processes

Although many observers were impressed with Homeboy Industries' ability to create new businesses, Father Boyle did not view Homeboy Industries as an incubator—at least not in the same sense most businesspeople would. Homeboy Industries remained a division of a 501(c)(3) nonprofit organization, with a community-based board of directors overseeing the operation. Its stated mission was "to assist at-risk and former gang-involved youth to become contributing members of our community" and mentioned nothing about businesses. Furthermore, Father Boyle did not consider himself to be an entrepreneur or businessman.

Homeboy Industries' standard for success was vastly different from those of most business incubators. Actually, Father Boyle hesitated to speak in terms of success or failure. "I feel called to be faithful, not successful," he expressed in a Catholic family magazine.[6] "I feel called to be faithful to an approach and to a certain wisdom about who these kids are. I believe that if they are given a chance, then they'll thrive and they'll begin to imagine a future for themselves."

Michael thought that one quantitative measure of success was the number of Homeboy Industries' past and current clientele. But he agreed with Father Boyle that there were other important standards of success. "We also measure success in terms of how much an individual changes," Michael explained. "Also, when two enemy gang members all of a sudden get along, that is success." However, Homeboy Industries as an organization was not systematically tracking the number of "successes" or "failures" of any kind. Michael agreed that there were still a wide range of financial and operational objectives that could be defined and measured. "We cannot depend on divine intervention alone," Michael explained. "We must do a much better job and be more effective operationally. To be more effective, we need to define our goals and measure our progress."

Certainly, everyone at Homeboy Industries regarded it as a success when an ex-gang member who learned good work habits and skills "graduated" from Homeboy and landed a respectable job. Some of the homies were ready for the workforce in 90 days, whereas others would take six months or even years to change their ways. About half dropped out of Homeboy's programs rather than graduate. While they worked for Homeboy Industries, most homies were paid close to $9 an hour.

Father Boyle's approach to his ventures was quite different from that of Brother James Holub of Milwaukee, Wisconsin, who borrowed the concept and started Homeboy Enterprises, his own version of Homeboy Industries. Brother Holub's Homeboy Enterprises included Homeboy Printing and Homeboyz Graphics. Unlike Father Boyle, Brother Holub saw himself as a businessman and focused on making his ventures self-sufficient. Although Homeboy Enterprises' main purpose remained getting gang members off the streets, its businesses were believed to be profitable. On the contrary, most of Father Boyle's ventures were struggling (see Exhibits 4A, 4B, and 4C).

Homeboy Industries operated with an annual capital budget that was reviewed and approved by its board of directors each year. The business operations were far from profitable and had to be supplemented by three major fund-raising activities: a yearly dinner, a direct-mail campaign, and Father Boyle's speaking engagements.

Homeboy Industries employed several professional staff members in the office who headed up the programs or divisions within Homeboy Industries and Jobs for a Future (see Exhibit 5). Some business units did not have full-time general managers. Michael often found himself rushing between businesses and projects—in effect continuing his career as a firefighter but now with figurative, business "fires" to put out. Turnover among the staff members and homies, although not documented,

Exhibit 4A	Homeboy Industries Statement of Activities 2003

PUBLIC SUPPORT	Total
Contributions	$879,609
Foundation Grants	635,080
Government Grants and Subcontracts	1,499,136
TOTAL PUBLIC SUPPORT	3,013,825
REVENUE	
Silkscreen Sales	693,104
Merchandise Income	12,410
Other Income	6,369
TOTAL REVENUE	711,883
TOTAL PUBLIC SUPPORT AND REVENUE	3,725,708
EXPENSES	
Program Services	3,201,321
Management and General	435,070
Fundraising	234,913
TOTAL EXPENSES	3,871,304
CHANGE IN NET ASSETS	(145,596)
NET ASSETS, BEGINNING OF YEAR	1,825,576
NET ASSETS, END OF YEAR	$1,679,980

was thought to be low compared to most businesses or nonprofit organizations.

Father Boyle had not implemented formal structures or consistent processes for making important decisions for Homeboy Industries. He queried and consulted with Michael or the board of directors on some issues, and, other times, he made decisions all by himself. Despite Father Boyle's imperfections as a manager, the board was usually sympathetic with him. Father Boyle was, after all, a beloved figure, and the directors did not want to challenge what were certainly admirable methods and achievements. Nevertheless, there were talks among board members about setting up finance and human resources committees that would create more formal structure and processes at Homeboy Industries.

The Merchandising Opportunity

Many people at Homeboy Industries, including Michael, had often thought that Homeboy Merchandise could be a much bigger business and raise the brand recognition of the entire organization. Merchandising offered a chance to tell the "story" of Homeboy Industries, which could have a broad commercial appeal.

In the past, Homeboy Industries had attempted to sell its merchandise to various retailers in the Los Angeles area. This was a challenge from the beginning: Many of the homies who worked as sales reps reacted badly to rejections, taking them personally and reacting with anger or dejection. Michael Baca thought that selling was a difficult task for most homies, considering that they had faced rejection all their lives.

In the mid-1990s, Homeboy Industries placed its merchandise in a handful of stores in shopping malls, but was unable to maintain stable relationships with the merchants, which caused most of the arrangements to disintegrate. For a time, Homeboy Merchandise sold its items via a kiosk in the Santa Monica Shopping Center, a hub for shoppers and tourists. Unfortunately, it could not sell enough volume to pay for the lease and operation of the kiosk, so it had to cancel the project and forfeit all of the investments that had been made. Furthermore, there were rumors that other merchants complained that Homeboy's presence detracted from the mall's atmosphere.

Homeboy Merchandise had never attempted direct marketing. Unfortunately, Homeboy Industries had not kept a good database of its past supporters or customers. Nonetheless, a direct-mail campaign for donations

entrepreneurial CASE ANALYSIS

Exhibit	4B	Homeboy Industries Schedule of Revenues and Expenditures 2003

REVENUE

Management and General	$280,989
Fundraising	312,175
Drop Off Center	645,558
Bakery	208,538
Grafiiti	462,731
Jobs for A Future	824,057
Merchandise	14,702
Silkscreen	695,470
Release Program	218,888
Project WIN	62,600
TOTAL REVENUES	3,725,708

EXPENSES

Salary and Wages	1,234,572
Payroll Taxes	110,687
Health Insurance	68,048
Worker's Compensation	88,775
SUBTOTAL	1,502,082
Accounting	20,631
Advertising	130
Bad Debt Expense	12,760
Bank Charges	2,365
Depreciation	100,698
Equipment Expense	3,567
Fundraising	135,867
Insurance	72,142
Maintenance & Repairs	25,539
Miscellaneous	17,138
New Development Expense	118,292
New Image Clothing	16,801
Office Supplies	20,826
Paint and Graffiti Supplies	98,443
Permits/License/Taxes	15,765
Postage and Delivery	7,916
Printing and Reproduction	23,496
Professional Fees	64,580
Program Activities	132,006
Program Activities - Vouchers	489,878
Rentals/Leases	46,568
Security	888
Stipends	441,978
Subscription/Seminars/Internet	1,634
Telephone Expense	78,108
Travel, Meals, and Entertainment	38,853
Utilities	13,726
Vehicle Expenses	51,600
Cost of Goods Sold	306,107
Embroidery Machine Supplies	1,896
Silkscreening Supplies	9,124
TOTAL EXPENSES	$3,871,304
NET INCREASE	$(145,596)

| Exhibit | 4C | Homeboy Merchandise Schedule of Revenues and Expenditures 2003 |

TOTAL REVENUES	$14,702
EXPENSES	
Salary and Wages	13,629
Payroll Taxes	1,272
Health Insurance	-
Worker's Compensation	1,140
SUBTOTAL	16,041
Accounting	-
Advertising	-
Bad Debt Expense	-
Bank Charges	-
Depreciation	-
Equipment Expense	-
Fundraising	-
Insurance	-
Maintenance & Repairs	-
Miscellaneous	-
New Development Expense	-
New Image Clothing	-
Office Supplies	418
Paint and Graffiti Supplies	-
Permits/License/Taxes	946
Postage and Delivery	658
Printing and Reproduction	-
Professional Fees	-
Program Activities	475
Program Activities - Vouchers	-
Rentals/Leases	-
Security	-
Stipends	-
Subscription/Seminars/Internet	-
Telephone Expense	-
Travel, Meals, and Entertainment	-
Utilities	-
Vehicle Expenses	-
Cost of Goods Sold	6,882
Embroidery Machine Supplies	-
Silkscreening Supplies	-
TOTAL EXPENSES	$ 25,420
NET INCREASE	$(10,718)

at the end of 2003 yielded a 12-percent response and raised $180,000. To Michael, the campaign's success indicated the level of support Homeboy Industries received from the community. He thought that direct marketing by Homeboy Merchandise could garner a similar response.

Homeboy's financial statement showed that the merchandising business had sales of about $14,000 in 2003 (Exhibit 4C). However, the figures did not account for the free merchandise that Father Boyle gave liberally to donors, visitors, and friends. There was a storage room inside the office for merchandise, but until recently no one had kept track of the inventory.

Another reason for Michael's optimism about the merchandising business was that many celebrities had expressed interest in helping Homeboy Industries. The producer of ABC's television show *8 Simple Rules for Dating My Teenage Daughter*, whom Father Boyle had taught in high school, placed a large merchandise order and was interested in having his cast's teenage girls wear Homegirl T-shirts. Actor Martin Sheen was a longtime supporter and personal friend of Father Boyle. Angelica Huston was an

entrepreneurial CASE ANALYSIS

Exhibit	5	Homeboy Industries Organization Chart

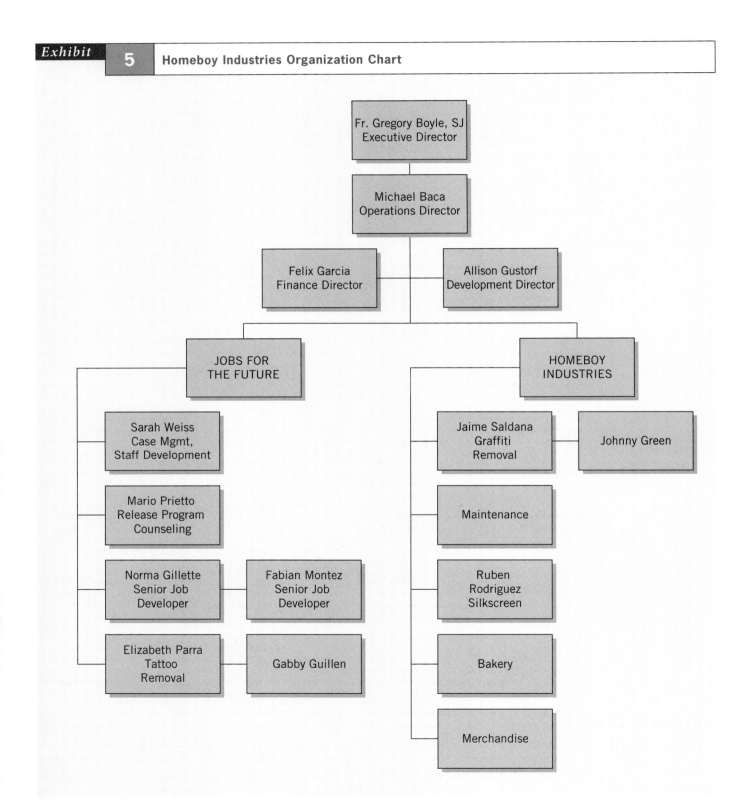

associate board member of Homeboy Industries, and Kirk Douglas had donated quite a bit of money.

Nevertheless, Michael was perplexed about Homeboy's target market. Speaking broadly, the teen market was the largest target. However, he was aware that not all teens would want to own Homeboy clothing. Homeboy Industry was seen as an "eastside" organization, and teens elsewhere might not want merchandise tied to East Los Angeles. On the other hand, he thought, the gang culture had become so popular that a "white boy" from Pacific Palisades might want to buy Homeboy gear.

Michael could foresee targeting the "hip-hop" culture that had been so lucrative in the past few years. Two related growth areas in the apparel market were the "urban youth" and the "antiestablishment" segments. One leading urban youth brand was Phat Farm, owned by record mogul Russell Simmons. Fubu was another firm that was popular with the urban youth. Fubu (which stood for "For Us, By Us") began as a clothing firm that targeted young African Americans but successfully crossed over to other segments, reaching annual revenues of $1 billion. The antiestablishment segment also appeared to have exploded in high schools across the United States. The trend had been around for years, and now retailers like Hot Topic were able to cash in on it. Hot Topic specialized in punk fashion by selling T-shirts that featured bands, skulls and crossbones, and anarchist symbols, as well as chains and body piercings.

Homeboy Industries projected an image vastly different from the usual hip-hop or antiestablishment brands. Its brand stood for positive messages, such as "a second chance" or "a place of hope." Still, Michael suspected, some parents (mostly in middle-class Los Angeles suburbs) could worry that their kids might be labeled as gang members if they wore Homeboy clothing.

Michael also wondered about licensing, a lucrative business in recent years even for organizations that were not part of the fashion industry. Examples included National Geographic's codeveloped outerwear for multiple climates, Mountain Dew's branded apparel, and the SNL brand that started *Saturday Night Live's* fashion licensing. Success in licensed fashion had become a promotional catalyst for the core businesses of these organizations.

Michael, who devoted about 10–20 percent of his time to Homeboy Merchandise, was the closest thing to a general manager for the division. He oversaw most of the business and did most of the ordering from Homeboy Silkscreen. One of the homies, Juan Carlos, was in charge of filling mail orders, which eased Michael's burden.

The New Venturing Decision

Father Boyle, Michael, and the staff were constantly looking for new opportunities. The more jobs Homeboy Industries' businesses offered, the better the chance that someone who walked into the office could find something he or she would pursue. However, starting a new business inside Homeboy Industries was complicated and depended on a wide range of financial and nonfinancial factors.

Pointing to the picture of a proposed "Homegirl Cleaners" on his office wall, Father Boyle recalled how someone came in with the idea for that business. However, Father Boyle turned down many business ideas. Some were rejected not because they were bad ideas, but because Father Boyle questioned the intentions of the people proposing them. Inevitably there were people who seemed to be trying to take advantage of Father Boyle's generous nature. It was up to him, the staff, and the board of directors to sort out the genuine ideas. Some business ventures did not fit well within Homeboy Industries, whereas other ideas fit nicely but lacked the right personnel to run them. Homeboy Industries already lacked a champion or manager for several of its existing businesses.

A few years earlier, two brothers from the neighborhood had wanted to start a plumbing business. Father Boyle welcomed the idea and bought a truck and equipment for them. However, Homeboy's board of directors, which consisted of attorneys, businessmen, and community leaders, were concerned about the venture. They worried about its viability and the costs involved, especially because the management of Homeboy Industries was already spread thin. The board ordered it closed after only a couple of months in operation, due to the concern that it was a poor fit.

Another new business idea was the Homeboy Café. In 2001, Homeboy Industries had bought an empty lot in downtown Los Angeles, near Little Tokyo, with the idea of building a new bakery. In 2004, with the pending acquisition of an existing bakery, it seemed the land could be used for a café instead. However, Father Boyle and his staff were so focused on planning for the new bakery that they had not given it much thought.

Few of Homeboy Industries' staff worried about the start-up funding for the café or other business ventures. They relied on Father Boyle, a prolific fund-raiser. Although money was scarce, it appeared that whatever Homeboy Industries needed, Father Boyle would generate somehow. As long as he had an idea and a plan, he found a way to raise the necessary funds.

Father Boyle was at times successful in recruiting highly skilled volunteers to help with Homeboy's and JFF's services and businesses. Dr. Luis Moreno of

entrepreneurial CASE ANALYSIS

Ya'Stuvo Tattoo Removal Clinic had graduated from Harvard Medical School and was finishing his residency at the University of California–Los Angeles. Luis was making hospital rounds when Father Boyle walked in and asked him to work for Homeboy. After eight or nine months, Homeboy Industries officially added Luis to its staff. He came in twice a week while still working in the emergency rooms at three hospitals.

With regard to Homeboy Merchandise, Father Boyle and Michael were not sure whether they should try to turn it into a serious business or maintain it as a sort of "gift shop" for visitors and donors of Homeboy Industries. Some of the volunteers had told Father Boyle and Michael that the Homeboy brand was a gold-mine. With the right mix of design, sales, and support, Michael agreed, the business could be hugely successful. Furthermore, Homeboy Merchandise's success could enhance the silk-screen business. Michael imagined many positive messages and slogans that the merchandise could display, such as "Be part of the story" or "Work for a better tomorrow." Not all products had to mention Homeboy Industries, he noted. The opportunity might even be larger if the business could make items with positive social messages that didn't include any reference to Homeboy.

Volunteers often came up with ideas to expand the merchandising business. One idea was to sell to the Chicano stores and colleges in East Los Angeles, so that the residents could have access to the positive messages. Another interesting idea came from Jesuit-in-training Phil Cooke, a summer volunteer. He thought that a great target market would be the 28 Jesuit colleges and universities in the United States. These schools would be willing to do business with them, because many of them would be aware of Father Boyle and Homeboy Industries. Jesuit universities in the United States included Georgetown, Santa Clara University, Loyola University of Chicago, and Loyola Marymount University (see Exhibit 6 for a complete list of Jesuit institutions in the United States). Phil thought that this initial customer base, though small, could be a great starting point while Homeboy Merchandise established its credibility and fine-tuned its business operations. The next target could be additional hundreds of Catholic and Christian colleges, followed by other universities nationwide. Phil could imagine a section of each college bookstore carrying Homeboy goods next to a life-size image of Father Boyle promoting the merchandise.

Phil also believed that Homeboy Industries could more aggressively pursue direct mailing. The response rate that Homeboy experienced over Christmas was too impressive to ignore. Phil believed that, with some

investment in mailing addresses and online ordering capability, the business could grow substantially.

However, Michael was not sure whether merchandising was the right business for Homeboy Industries. The venture appeared to be a misfit with the skills and temperaments of the youths Homeboy served. The venture also required marketing and sales expertise that Homeboy did not possess. Michael pondered: "It takes weeks to train our guys to show up to work on time. They are so far away from developing marketing skills. Selling is probably the worst type of job for our homies. What if our kids took those rejections personally?" However, Michael also knew that some of the necessary resources and expertise could be hired, and in some cases borrowed. For example, as a volunteer had suggested, Homeboy Merchandise could engage one of the well-known fashion colleges in Los Angeles to develop a new design concept.

The biggest concerns were expressed by Father Boyle and Ruben of Homeboy Silkscreen, who were against promoting Homeboy gear. Ruben was concerned that, if everything worked out well, Homeboy clothing would be hip enough to become gang wear. "The last thing I want to do," said Ruben, "is to see some kid committing crime in the clothing we make." Both Father Boyle and Ruben wanted to make sure that the Homeboy name was used only in a positive light. Michael understood Ruben's concern. Without knowing for sure how big or successful Homeboy Merchandise could become, it was difficult to muster a strong argument for investment in the business. At times, Michael thought that it would just be easier to keep the merchandising business at the current level.

Homeboy Café was another option that Michael could pursue immediately. The location appeared to be viable—though part of Boyle Heights, it was near Little Tokyo, a much nicer part of town. Daytime foot traffic included professionals who worked nearby in downtown Los Angeles. A Starbucks and similar shops were close by, and many shopping malls, restaurants, and retail stores were within walking distance. The café could train homies quickly and provide job opportunities for dozens of them. However, Michael realized that the decision was much more complicated:

Everyone seems to love the Homeboy Café idea, but they don't know the challenges associated with running a coffee shop or restaurant day in and day out. Poor service could destroy the business. The local professional clientele wouldn't have any patience with any kind of misbehavior, especially with all those other coffee shops like Starbucks

Exhibit 6   Jesuit Colleges and Universities in the United States

Institution	Location	Enrollment
Boston College	Chestnut Hill, MA	14,528
Canisius College	Buffalo, NY	5,095
College of the Holy Cross	Worcester, MA	2,773
Creighton University	Omaha, NE	6,226
Fairfield University	Fairfield, CT	5,060
Fordham University	Bronx, NY	15,814
Georgetown University	Washington, DC	13,164
Gonzaga University	Spokane, WA	6,100
John Carroll University	Cleveland, OH	4,350
Le Moyne College	Syracuse, NY	2,900
Loyola College in Maryland	Baltimore, MD	6,111
Loyola Marymount University	Los Angeles, CA	7,500
Loyola University Chicago	Chicago, IL	12,605
Loyola University New Orleans	New Orleans, LA	5,279
Marquette University	Milwaukee, WI	10,892
Regis University	Denver, CO	9,129
Rockhurst University	Kansas City, MO	2,727
Saint Joseph's University	Philadelphia, PA	6,961
Saint Louis University	St. Louis, MO	13,847
Saint Peter's College	Jersey City, NJ	3,282
Santa Clara University	Santa Clara, CA	7,356
Seattle University	Seattle, WA	5,852
Spring Hill College	Mobile, AL	1,484
University of Detroit Mercy	Detroit, MI	6,023
University of San Francisco	San Francisco, CA	7,917
University of Scranton	Scranton, PA	4,615
Wheeling Jesuit University	Wheeling, WV	1,515
Xavier University	Cincinnati, OH	6,523

within a couple of blocks. And what if there is a drive-by-shooting? The business would go under in a minute. Plus, does serving coffee really train our kids for better jobs in the future? At least in Homeboy Merchandise, we could provide training for skills that could be really useful for their future careers.

Michael was still pondering the options as he pushed open the door to the meeting room. Several of the volunteers and employees of Homeboy Industries were already

inside, discussing the future strategies for Homeboy Merchandise. All heads turned to Michael as he shut the door behind him. They were eager to hear what Michael had to say.

Questions

1. What are the goals and objectives of Homeboy Industries? What are Father Boyle's motivations? Is it just about jobs? How important is profit? What kind of jobs should it offer?

entrepreneurial CASE ANALYSIS

2. How would you rate the current performance of Homeboy Industries as a social enterprise or a business? What measures are you using to evaluate its performance?

3. What is your assessment of the market opportunity for Homeboy Merchandising? Could Homeboy expand the business, given the lack of management and financial resources? Is this business a good fit with the homeboys?

4. What should Michael do about Homeboy Merchandising? What do you recommend they do about Homeboy Café? Which business should they start first? Why?

REFERENCES

1. United States Census 2000, United States Census Bureau, http://www.census.gov/.

2. See, for example, Earl Ofari Hutchinson "L.A. Has to Gang Up on Violence," *Los Angeles Times,* November 24, 2002, M5, which discusses how years of anti-gang campaigns have been unsuccessful despite the CRASH program.

3. Translates to "That's enough, I'm done with that."

4. Carol Ann Morrow, "Jesuit Greg Boyle, Gang Priest," *St. Anthony Messenger,* August 1999, http://www.americancatholic.org/Messenger/Aug1999/feature1.asp.

5. Trader Joe's is a popular specialty retail grocery store with about 200 stores in Arizona, California, Connecticut, Delaware, Illinois, Indiana, Maryland, Massachusetts, Michigan, Missouri, Nevada, New Jersey, New Mexico, New York, Ohio, Oregon, Pennsylvania, Virginia, and Washington. It is widely know for its unique grocery items and for having the highest revenue per square footage in the industry.

6. Morrow, "Jesuit Greg Boyle, Gang Priest."

entrepreneurial

CASE ANALYSIS

Dealer Trade Group: High-Tech Venturing in a Low-Tech Industry

entrepreneurial CASE ANALYSIS

Early Morning Thoughts

Early one morning in August 2001, Carter Crockett groaned as he pulled his rickety Honda Accord into the parking lot at 6:53 A.M. Todd Greenway's new, oversized bright red truck was already there. Crockett was president of Dealer Trade Group (DTG), and Greenway was vice president of sales. Arriving before anyone else gave Crockett time to get ahead of the daily rush of activity; it used to be the best part of his day. But Greenway had started arriving earlier just so he could say he worked the longest hours. This early-bird competition used to be fun but was becoming antagonistic. Greenway had an office next to the main entrance, and Crockett had begun to resent the gloating of his unavoidable morning greetings.

Despite a series of "bumps in the road," Crockett, other senior managers, and investors believed that DTG was faring better than many online business-to-business (B2B) ventures. They knew the road would not be smooth. Indeed, it had not been: DTG offered a revolutionary, high-tech way of doing business to dealers who were mostly comfortable with traditional, low-tech automobile wholesaling. Yet sales were growing, and DTG was beginning to establish credibility despite its online marketplace business model. Although DTG was still burning more cash than it was making, profitability seemed just a few months away.

Crockett, who once worked at Microsoft, felt a growing sense of unease. Friction was rising between him and Greenway, who was an auto industry veteran. It had begun to undermine his authority with employees and his relationships with DTG's investors and board. Privately, Crockett assumed much of the blame. He wondered if it was possible for him to earn Greenway's respect and the board's trust. He knew both were necessary to run DTG effectively.

Crockett had headed DTG for two years. He knew other entrepreneurs who hurt their ventures by refusing to "let go of the wheel" when they should have. Was he taking this venture down a similar road? The original plan called for him to run DTG until they hired an industry veteran. When he suggested the idea of resigning to the board, however, they interpreted his concerns as common venture growing pains and expressed no interest in finding an expensive CEO. Still, Crockett was uneasy. Would an industry veteran lead DTG more effectively? Was it time to get out?

Designing a Race Car

Dealer Trade Group was established in 2000 as a B2B venture serving automobile dealers in the northwestern United States. The company's strategy combined wireless and online technologies with relationship-based sales to offer dealers an efficient vehicle inventory management service. By 2002, DTG employed almost 70 people and served more than 250 dealers throughout the Pacific Northwest and Alaska. The company outgrew its Seattle headquarters for a second time and established facilities in Kent, Washington, with satellite offices in Spokane, Washington; Salt Lake City, Utah; and Juneau, Alaska. Clientele included auto wholesalers, independent and franchised dealers, and large dealer groups (e.g., AutoNation and Lithia Group). In September alone, DTG completed 792 vehicle transactions and generated more than $250,000 in revenue.

THE DRIVER: CARTER CROCKETT, ENTREPRENEUR

Crockett's professional career began in 1992 as a consultant in the financial services industry. He had earned a bachelor's degree in business and economics and had a talent for communicating with people and establishing relationships. Ambitious and hard working, he soon became marketing manager at the Los Angeles offices of BDO Seidman, a global accounting and consulting firm. During this time, Crockett also married his college sweetheart. By 1994, he resigned from BDO Seidman, hoping to find a more central role in a more dynamic industry. After moving to Seattle, he found such an opportunity in software publishing. For two years, he worked with various new business ventures (NBVs) that were developing children's educational products. He loved the entrepreneurial sector, where it seemed anything could happen. Finances were tight, however, and Crockett supplemented his income as a valet parking attendant and by performing other odd jobs. By 1995, venture capital investors closed the NBV where Crockett worked as product marketing manager. With some help from his friends, he landed a job at Microsoft providing marketing expertise for new-product development teams.

The thought of working in a large, stable company was initially a welcome change for Crockett, whose family now had the addition of a new daughter. As a product planner at Microsoft, he was responsible for interpreting

Source: Patrick J. Murphy and Carter Crockett, "Dealer Trade Group: High-Tech Venturing in a Low-Tech Industry," *Entrepreneurship Theory and Practice* 31, no. 4 (July 2007): 643–66.

industry trends and consumer demands to determine product features and develop market entry strategies, often years before product launch. Crockett supported various Microsoft products (e.g., Picture It!, Works Suite, Publisher, and Windows 2000) for three years. Although Microsoft was known as an innovative company, he eventually grew uncomfortable in a large corporate setting and began to miss the excitement of the entrepreneurial sector. The routines and bureaucracy seemed to restrict Crockett from the professional objective he had listed on his résumé: "To excel in the strategic marketing of inspiring consumer products." After coordinating the retail marketing plans for the launch of Windows 2000 in February 2000, Crockett felt overdue for a change and began searching for entrepreneurial opportunities.

THE SPONSOR: BILL HAYWORTH, ANGEL INVESTOR

An opportunity for change presented itself unexpectedly to Crockett during an informal meeting with a college friend who was working for Bill Hayworth, a Seattle venture capitalist. Hayworth had invested recently in a used auto dealership in Houston, Texas. Each week, the dealer attended regional auto auctions and competed with other dealers to buy and sell inventory. Crockett's friend explained that Hayworth wondered whether an online B2B market model might be applicable to automobile wholesaling but did not know how to evaluate the opportunity or create a company to take advantage of it. Crockett was familiar with such business models and had a knack for identifying opportunities. Although he was uncertain of the applicability of such a model to an industry he did not know, the prospect of an entrepre-

neurial venture was compelling, and he agreed to meet Hayworth to discuss the idea.

Hayworth had many investment opportunities but worked only with people he felt he could trust. He took comfort because he and Crockett attended the same church, and one of his employees was Crockett's longtime acquaintance. It became clear during their first meeting that they did not have the industry experience to answer a number of simple market research questions. Because Hayworth did not want to pay for a detailed feasibility analysis, Crockett proposed evaluating the idea as a one-month consulting project in which he would present results by the end of May 2000 with rationale and a recommendation either to pursue the opportunity or to invest elsewhere. When Hayworth accepted, Crockett left his job at Microsoft.

TIME TRIALS: MARKET RESEARCH

Right away, Hayworth sent Crockett to Houston to learn the used car business from J. R. Fontana, owner of the Houston dealership in which Hayworth had invested. Fontana operated his business from two locations: a converted mobile home and a garage/warehouse on a dirt lot. Crockett shadowed him for one week (noting extreme dissimilarities from Microsoft's culture) and, with Fontana's help, conducted dealer focus groups to glean information about auto wholesaling.

Dealers explained the difficulties facing their businesses and offered ideas for what it would take to resolve them. Crockett learned that their biggest problem was an urgent need to move inventory, because vehicles on the lot used space that could be filled by newer inventory. As shown in Exhibit 1 (from Crockett's notes), the urgency

| *Exhibit* | **1** | **Declining Profits for an Average Vehicle Over Time** |

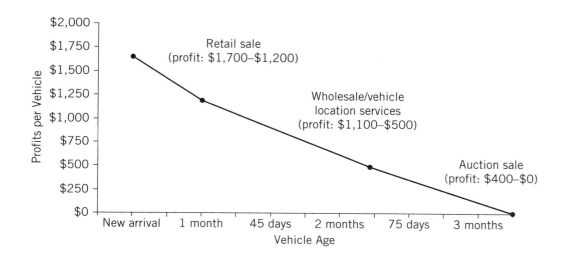

entrepreneurial CASE ANALYSIS

intensified daily as vehicle value (published in monthly valuation books) and potential profits diminished over time. Crockett immediately saw the need for a more efficient way to move inventory that dealers had been unable to sell at retail. Dealers like Fontana were desperate for an alternative to move inventory faster but that would be equally fair to large and small dealers. In their opinion, the physical auctions favored large, institutional sellers such as banks and manufacturers who could provide large volumes of vehicles for wholesale. The need for an alternative was reinforced by the fact that auctions were institutionalized as an industry norm: They were the default destination point for vehicles not purchased by retail customers.

Auctions were so entrenched they could dictate their own terms, and dealers had no alternative to consider. Crockett saw that, over the years, their monopoly position and inertia had made them inefficient as a solution. When he returned to Seattle, he pondered the nature of the inefficiency, the niche it created, and how an entrepreneurial venture might respond to the opportunity. Exhibit 2 lists additional market facts obtained through his research.

Further results of his research supported the applicability of an online market. For example, wholesale vehicles varied by make and model (e.g., Ford versus Honda), target customers (e.g., luxury versus economy), and regional demographics (e.g., California versus Washington). Buyers and sellers frequently had trouble finding others with complementary needs, and those involved with wholesaling had trouble finding others whom they felt they could trust. Because idiosyncrasy was standard in the industry, regional wholesalers like Fontana liked to call themselves "market makers for incongruent inventory." Crockett saw the promise of facilitating timely and trustworthy transactions—similar to eBay's model—between buyers and sellers who otherwise would not have found each other.

As part of due diligence, Crockett also assessed the competition, as the opportunity seemed too obvious to have eluded others. Indeed, there were new entrants, many rooted deeply in high-technology backgrounds, but none seemed sufficiently on target. Most ignored the wholesale business, choosing instead to target individual buyers. Crockett thought an online market model fit wholesaling much better than retailing. For one, wholesalers already were buying and selling vehicles without seeing or test-driving them. They also returned frequently to buy or sell more vehicles, whereas satisfied retail customers might take years to return. Additionally, wholesaling performance derives from sales volume and velocity, whereas profit margin is paramount in the retail segment. Crockett imagined how the model could mimic a physical auction with a fixed profit margin and nominal fees to parties on each side of every transaction. He discovered that there

---

Exhibit **2**	**U.S. Market Information Gathered by Crockett in 2000**

1 Used auto retail sales generated $361 billion in 1999, and were expected to generate $408 billion by 2004.[1]

2 The used auto industry is enduring: in a thriving economy, consumers buy higher value vehicles and trade frequently. During economic downturns consumers are still likely to buy (although used instead of new).

3 Approximately 85,000 franchised and independent dealers make up the wholesale auto industry.

4 Industry analysts estimate the used vehicle wholesale market to be $170 billion per year.[2]

   a Physical wholesale auctions generate $93 billion in transactions.[3]

   b Many of the more desirable (i.e., newest, nicest) vehicles are traded directly between dealers that know and trust one another.

   c The most desirable vehicles account for approximately $105 billion of the annual wholesale market.

   d The used auto industry is one of the most fragmented and vertically segmented industries.

---

[1] CNW Marketing/Research 1999 Report (www.cnwmr.com).
[2] Manheim Auctions (acquirer of ADT Automotive Holdings in October 2000) Annual Report (www.manheimauctions.com).
[3] ADT 2000 Used Car Market Report.

were nearly 300 used vehicle auctions in the United States, each employing about 260 people and maintaining more than 70 acres of vehicle inventory, facilities, and equipment.[1] The most established auctions (e.g., Manheim and Adesa) publicized their intentions to employ online models but had not yet made substantial efforts in that direction.

Crockett drew on information from the focus groups in Houston and additional online market data to develop the idea. He then refined it with the help of Fontana and industry veterans. Exhibit 3 presents Crockett's breakdown of costs to buyers and sellers, comparing an online market to the physical auctions. An online market would bring dealers possible savings of more than 60 percent.

Proceed with Caution

When his one-month contract ended, Crockett presented this recommendation to Hayworth: Proceed with caution. Based on his research, Crockett gave the opportunity a 70 percent chance of proving viable. He found no reason (other than the usual risks) not to pursue it. Crockett found himself surprisingly energized by the idea and volunteered to lead the NBV until the risks were mitigated and an industry veteran could be hired. Hayworth extended his contract indefinitely.

Crockett completed a business plan in April 2000, just as the dot-com bubble burst. Virtually overnight,

the investment community regretted the billions of dollars already poured into online ventures like the one Crockett wanted to launch. However, Crockett and Hayworth were skeptics of "get big fast" strategies. They remained optimistic. They believed increased wariness in the investment community would force them to build a solid business. However, finding major investors would now be much more difficult. Hayworth, the sole investor up to this point, quipped, "If we can survive this, we can survive anything."

"Gentlemen, Start Your Engines"

For the next six months, Crockett worked in a corner of a conference room in Hayworth's offices. As Hayworth evaluated other investment opportunities, Crockett saw hundreds of business plans and dozens of entrepreneurs come through the door, each instance an opportunity for him to learn. The groundwork for launching the NBV was laid during this time. Health insurance, legal counsel, and banking and accounting services were established through professional service partners. The company was initially called Dealers Lane (after the industry term used to describe the "lane" or line of vehicles at auctions). It was later changed to Dealer Trade Group to avoid potential legal hassles with an even newer Canadian venture called Dealer Lanes.

Exhibit 3 Potential Savings Through an Online Market

	Estimated wholesale expenses per vehicle	
	Physical auctions	Online market
Presale reconditioning	$75	$0
Transportation to auction	105	0
Sale fee	350	150
Buy fee	100	150
No-sale fee	20	0
Auction certification	50	0
Transportation from auction	125	0
Warranty	75	75
Post-sale reconditioning	25	25
Personnel travel costs	200	0
Total	$1,125	$400

NOTE: Physical auction expenses also include an opportunity cost based on personnel being away from the dealership and not conducting retail business transactions. The same expense does not apply to online markets. Crockett did not factor these costs into the estimations.

entrepreneurial CASE ANALYSIS

Besides, Dealer Trade Group sounded more established and credible. One of Crockett's friends, a corporate branding professional, created a logo to evoke the feel of a classic automobile brand (Exhibit 4). He even did it "off the clock," without charging the exorbitant fees of his employer.

Crockett began to form an advisory board. To off-set his low industry experience, he sought to surround himself with experts from various segments of the auto industry. They included owners of dealerships, wholesale industry veterans, and retired senior sales personnel. Crockett's vision of transforming the industry usually was sufficient to procure informal offers of guidance or assistance from such experts. He would extend an invitation to join the advisory board or contribute in other ways when he sensed interest and felt he could trust that person. By June 2000, the advisory board included Fontana and six other industry veterans with expertise in auto transportation, industry research and analysis, dealer ownership, dealer management, dealer software/sales, auto wholesaling, and vehicle financing. Martin Billings, an automobile industry software entrepreneur, was invited to be chairman of the board and interim vice president of business development. Billings promised to generate investment capital. Even though Billings had impressive industry experience, contacts, and "grey hair," Crockett and Hayworth knew it would be very difficult to obtain venture capital—financiers had lost their taste for online business ventures.

Strategic partnerships were sought with others connected to the industry (e.g., sellers of auto warranties and publishers of wholesale price guides). Crockett began

sending monthly updates on DTG's progress to investors, board members, top management, and even family and friends. Through all of this activity, the initial DTG vision was tempered by input from industry experts and dealers, guiding its design into a model that exploited the perceived inefficiencies of auto wholesaling (Exhibit 5).

Despite their dislike for bureaucracy and titles, Hayworth and Crockett were cofounders of DTG for administrative and legal purposes. Sometimes Crockett found it difficult to establish credibility with industry figures and financiers when he was viewed as "someone who used to work at Microsoft." Thus, both Crockett and Hayworth used the title of CEO when the occasion warranted.

In early 2000, Crockett learned that DealerSwap, a competitor based in Spokane, was experiencing friction between investors and its founder, Todd Greenway. DealerSwap was started a year before DTG and had 23 employees and significant financing. Depending on what issues were causing the conflict, Crockett saw a potential opportunity: Greenway was from the auto industry, and Crockett had been struggling to find people who understood both auto wholesaling *and* the huge promise of online markets. He suspected that Greenway might be such a person. Although Crockett was wary of making contact, he invited Greenway and DealerSwap's board chairman to Seattle. They accepted. DTG initially contemplated acquiring DealerSwap, but it soon became clear that the venture had more legal problems than DTG cared to assume—lawyers were already active on both sides of the conflict between Greenway and his investors. But Crockett remained interested in what

---

Exhibit **4** **Original Logos for Dealers Lane and Dealer Trade Group**

Source: DTG promotional material.

Greenway's expertise might offer DTG. He arranged to meet privately with Greenway so they could get to know each other, compare business models, and assess strategic compatibility.

Checking Map and Compass: Formulating Competitive Strategy

The potential for collaboration became evident as the two conversed. Multiple NBVs and established companies were fumbling in the same niche for the right business model, but the mix of Crockett's and Greenway's diverse backgrounds and unified vision seemed to hold the key. They agreed on the strategic aspects of Crockett's vision for DTG (Exhibit 6), with few exceptions. Greenway argued, for example, that the reporting of the vehicle condition was too central a component to outsource. Crockett deferred to Greenway's firsthand experience in this area.

Crockett and Greenway discussed DTG's competitive environment. As shown in Exhibit 7, competitors could be categorized broadly in terms of inventory source (dealer versus institutional) and target market (consumers versus dealers). Within the categorization, venture strategies fell generally into three categories,

---

Exhibit **5** **DTG Comparative Advantage over Traditional Wholesaling**

1   Traditional auto wholesaling takes too much time:
Considerable depreciation occurs while waiting for physical auction opportunities.

    DTG allows dealers to participate in online auctions anytime, using telephone or Internet, resulting in less time spent traveling or balancing inventory.

2   Buyer confidence is an issue in traditional wholesaling:
Sellers are able to disguise damaged inventory and accountability is low.

    DTG is an independent and treats dealers equally regardless of size or type. Every vehicle undergoes inspection, includes a detailed condition report, and comes with an extensive third-party warranty.

3   Traditional auto wholesaling costs too much:
Dealers incur exorbitant wholesale auction fees and travel expenses.

    DTG saves dealers up to 60% of wholesaling fees. Dealers are less likely to miss retail opportunities and can balance inventory without incurring hefty expenses.

Source: DTG promotional material.

Exhibit **6** **The Strategic Aspects of DTG's Vision**

1   Target market: Dealers as buyers *and* sellers connected by relationship with DTG

2   Market bias: Neutral, favor buyers and sellers equally

3   Primary revenue: Transaction-based service fees

4   Inventory focus: Quality used vehicles, guaranteed and in dealer possession

5   Service standard: High quality and personal; both face-to-face and online

6   Third-party condition reporting: Standardized vehicle inspections provided by qualified vehicle inspectors

Source: DTG internal document.

entrepreneurial CASE ANALYSIS

Exhibit	7	Target Markets and Sources of Vehicles

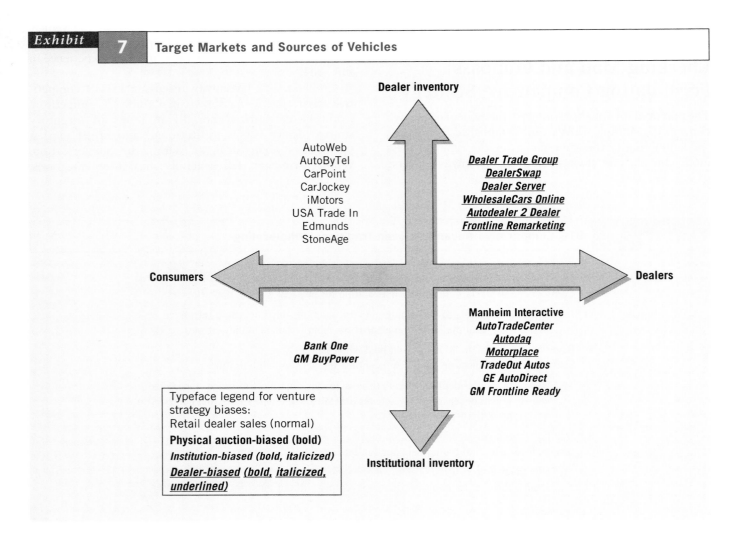

described as follows. (1) *Physical auction-biased* competitors (e.g., Manheim Interactive) had an intrinsic tie to conducting business in a traditional physical setting. Dealers had been meeting at these auctions at the same time every week for years; thus, physical auctions embodied social norms that could not be duplicated easily. DTG would likely be seen as a threat to these companies, because they had the most to lose. They had already taken a defensive stance toward new entrants like DTG, but fear of cannibalizing existing business discouraged direct competition with new entrants. (2) *Institution-biased* competitors (e.g., GM, BuyPower, GE Auto Direct) were linked to sellers such as banks or manufacturers. These companies were run independently or by the sellers themselves. Generally, these ventures preferred to work directly with a few physical auctions rather than thousands of individual dealers, and dealers who wanted a variety of makes and types

of vehicles could not depend solely on the inventory provided by just one of these sellers. (3) *Dealer-biased* competitors (e.g., Autodaq, Motorplace) sought to treat dealers as buyers *and* sellers, which involved transacting business between small, disparate parties. At the time (2000), these kinds of B2B transactions relied especially on trust and reliability. DTG intended to target this sector without being seen as an unreliable dot-com—how Greenway and others described the short-lived ventures in this sector led by people with technology or investment (not auto industry) experience.

Greenway was a third-generation car dealer; Crockett had a high-tech background. Yet they had arrived at similar strategies for resolving the same inefficiencies in the wholesaling industry. As their synergy became more evident and DealerSwap's problems intensified, DTG hired Greenway to serve as its vice president of sales. Greeting Greenway at the airport in Seattle, Crockett said, "You know, I couldn't do this without you." Greenway replied, "I couldn't do it without you either." Crockett was pleased because Greenway's experience was valuable: Although DealerSwap was essentially defunct, it had traversed some hazards DTG had yet to face.

FUELING UP: PROCURING FINANCIAL CAPITAL

In November 2000, DTG faced its first crisis. Preparations for venture launch had nearly depleted Hayworth's initial funding of $750,000. Billings, Crockett, and Greenway had not succeeded in closing the next round of funding, despite concerted effort and dozens of pitches to investor groups. Crockett decided to present Hayworth with the following options:

1. Stay the course and hope for large investors: Continue to finance DTG operating expenses at current levels until funding is secured.

2. Batten down the hatches: Provide $275,000 to sustain DTG on a shoestring budget for four months while continuing to seek funding.

3. Abandon ship: Write off losses and dissolve DTG.

Hayworth chose the second option and committed to securing the next round of funding—with his own money, if necessary—so management could concentrate on developing the venture. Similar ventures were floundering from funding shortages. In fact, Crockett and Greenway knew of no venture with such short-term funding, so Hayworth's commitment provided a rare feeling of security. Crockett decided part of the "shoestring budget" called for Billings to resign, as he had not secured any venture capital. He asked Hayworth to serve as chairman of the board. Hayworth's age, experience, and commitment to DTG signaled credibility.

Crockett and Greenway worked intensely to prepare DTG for launch. They began to establish strategic partnerships with vehicle warranty, market data, and physical auction companies. Believing that he and the board still needed an experienced external advisor they could trust, Crockett sought the services of Donald Jenkins, a manager and investor who had been a catalyst for multiple online B2B ventures. He became DTG's only paid advisor. Regular coaching and discussions with Jenkins were useful as Crockett and Greenway drafted contracts and templates, collected industry intelligence, and began looking for employees.

Thanks to five angel investors whom Hayworth knew, DTG closed a $1.2 million round of financing in January 2001. It was a timely move: Crockett and Greenway knew the venture would not have lasted another month.

DTG Gets a Green Light

The influx of funding brought cascading changes as DTG began to establish itself. Industry figures and competitors started to take notice. Within a month, eight new employees were hired. Each brought a unique network of relationships, usually gained from previous dealership experience. Crockett saw this as a critical time for shaping the new venture's culture. He tried to mold DTG on sound principles and developed three guiding values that were disseminated to all new employees (Exhibit 8).

By early 2001, it was clear that Hayworth's conference room could no longer contain all of the activity at DTG. Hayworth preferred that DTG share space with his venture capital firm in an upscale office complex, which necessitated an inflexible three-year lease and high monthly expenses. Crockett agreed that sharing space was

---

Exhibit 8   DTG's Three Guiding Values

1 Value **Relationships**

    No transaction is worth jeopardizing relationships with employees, dealers, investors, partners, or vendors

2 Maintain a **Positive Attitude**

    Be fun and flexible; support a cohesive team; request empowerment where needed to make a difference; be responsible; turn problems into opportunities

3 Don't just speak: **Deliver**

    Stand by your word; under-promise/over-provide, go above and beyond, keep it simple; exceed personal and DTG $$$ goals; support the local community where possible

Source: Crockett's notes.

entrepreneurial CASE ANALYSIS

convenient but thought it hindered the development of DTG's own culture. He preferred a location in the Rainier Valley, the somewhat rundown but revitalizing central Seattle neighborhood where he lived. It was convenient and would cost two-thirds less than Hayworth's location, and it could be leased flexibly for one year. Crockett wanted to avoid friction, especially during this early and uncertain stage, but the issue became their first significant disagreement. DTG wanted the image of a traditional company (not a dot-com), and Crockett saw the location, appearance, and size of DTG headquarters as a way to establish such an image. Hayworth disagreed. He secured a long-term lease at market rates in the suburban office complex shared with his venture capital firm. To Crockett's dismay, although he was doing most of the work and carrying a considerable risk to his livelihood, it seemed Hayworth could take control whenever he wanted.

BUILDING THE RACING TEAM: HUMAN RESOURCE DEVELOPMENT

The company's first transaction, a 1999 BMW Z3 Coupe, occurred in May 2001. It was basically a traditional wholesale trade, because DTG's technology played a minimal role. When Crockett took the car for a drive prior to the sale, he gained a new appreciation for the excitement and emotion associated with vehicle sales. These transactions were complicated, however, and a number of logistical problems immediately presented themselves. Each DTG transaction involved transferring ownership from one dealer to another via a third party, a process nearly as complex as buying a home.

Crockett and Greenway were not interested—or qualified—in the details of wholesaling vehicles, so they hired Pat Atkins, the number-two executive at a local physical auto auction, to handle financial and administrative matters. She completed the top management team (Exhibit 9) with complementary skills and proficiency. Atkins immediately played a critical role, using her industry experience to develop operational policies and

transaction logistics that were analogous to what dealers found at physical auctions. Crockett hoped DTG's initial transactions would fine-tune the online marketplace before eventual high sales volumes put DTG's model to the true test. As shown in Exhibit 10, the plan was to implement increasingly DTG's Web-based technology in a way that would mirror traditional auctions without their week-long sales cycle.

DTG's plan also relied on experienced salespeople to close sales until Web-based technology could take over—the only questions were how many to hire and how long to rely on them as the venture developed. Crockett and Greenway knew sales transactions were the engine that would propel the company forward, so Greenway hired several seasoned salespeople. Personal reputation in the industry was more important than education or technological skill. Most salespeople came from dealerships or physical auctions and were attracted to DTG's vision. Within a few months, DTG had a 15-member sales team that represented more than 150 years of industry experience. The average salesperson was at least 40 years old (some were over 60) and did not know how to type or use computers; few had any college education. For example, Eddie Barnhard joined DTG with 22 years of industry experience. He was 60 years old and had managed used car departments and wholesale purchasing operations for several dealerships. He knew most dealers in the region personally. They knew him, too, and vouched for his character when his references were checked. Notwithstanding Barnhard's impressive experience and enthusiasm for DTG, however, the learning curve was steep. He had never even used a computer before Crockett issued him a laptop, pager, wireless personal digital assistant (PDA), and mobile telephone.

Crockett was also learning a lot at this point. The communication style he had used in the high-tech industry and at Microsoft did not work in the auto industry. The language used in magazines and journals to describe emerging B2B models like DTG's was

Exhibit	9	DTG's Senior Management Team in March 2001

Name	Position	Responsibilities
Carter Crockett	President	Strategy, marketing, technology
Todd Greenway	Vice President, Sales	Dealer relations, sales management
Pat Atkins	Business Manager	Administration, accounting, finance

Exhibit **10**   **DTG's Business Model**

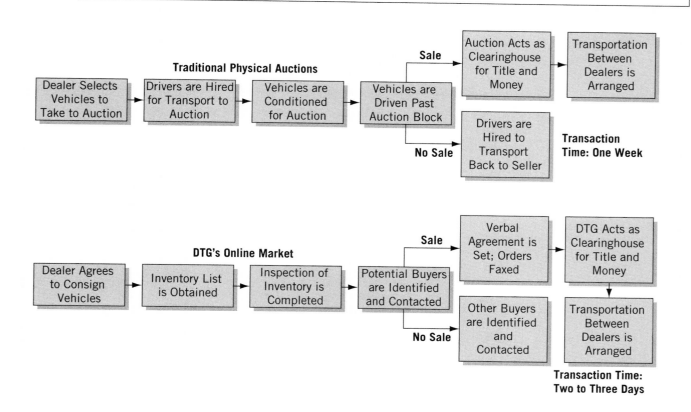

even less applicable. With frequent consultation from Greenway and other industry veterans, Crockett wrote and designed the first DTG brochure. When he showed it to his wife one night, she noted what seemed to be a lot of industry jargon and awkward phrasing (e.g. "If the vehicle isn't what we say it is, you don't need to own it!"). "Who wrote this?" she asked. Crockett responded that it was his own attempt to employ auto industry vernacular.

TUNING UP: TECHNOLOGICAL DEVELOPMENT

One Seattle-based consulting firm and systems integrator offered to develop DTG's Web site for $2.1 million, but an Ohio firm with automotive e-commerce experience got the contract by promising better work on the same schedule for just $120,000. Although elements of the Web site were functional in April 2001 (Exhibit 11), the finished product was not delivered until much later.

The same Ohio vender was contracted to develop DTG's Remote Inventory Acquisition Device (RIAD) software. The RIAD (Exhibit 12), a handheld PDA-based program, recorded detailed vehicle information on-site and transmitted inspection reports wirelessly into the

online inventory catalog. Although it was designed to facilitate transactions, it sometimes made life difficult for employees like Barnhard. Yet, it eventually proved effective for capturing and utilizing vehicle data. The industry standard paper-based inspection reports required transcription of identical data (e.g., vehicle inspection numbers) as many as 12 times when processing a vehicle transaction. The RIAD reduced transcription and other user errors by recording these data only once for subsequent use in a variety of standardized procedures and forms.

RULES OF THE ROAD: IMPLEMENTING STRATEGY

Amid the hectic day-to-day operations, Crockett's mantra could be heard frequently throughout the DTG offices: "Without trust, we're toast!" The message underscored a unifying purpose for all employees—build loyal relationships with customers. Virtually everything DTG did was related to building trust and presenting itself as industry savvy: meeting potential customers in person, providing detailed inspections and guarantees for every vehicle, hiring and training expert vehicle inspectors, minimizing technical difficulties, and offering an honest

entrepreneurial CASE ANALYSIS

Source: DTG promotional material.

service that exceeded expectations and industry standards. For Crockett, it was the only way DTG could hope to fulfill its mission statement: "To be the dealer's most efficient wholesale inventory solution." Some dealers were so pleased with DTG they immediately became loyal to the new venture. These devoted customers were attracted by DTG's experienced, reputable salespeople at least as much as its novel business model. Greenway explained, "It's still about shaking hands and looking someone in the eye." Without DTG's salespeople, dealers might have ignored DTG as an alternative solution. As one dealer explained to Crockett regarding a DTG salesperson, "I've known Roger for 20 years. You may be a new company, but I know I can trust Roger to do what he says. You've got a real gem right there." To support DTG's image as accommodating industry norms rather than as a brash dot-com, Crockett expunged "revolutionary" from all DTG business plans, marketing literature, Web site content, and other materials. Dealers and industry partners shunned such language, Crockett reasoned, and were more likely to trust companies that

respected existing ways without offering revolutionary solutions. He would let them decide for themselves if DTG was revolutionary. Crockett had developed ten strategic principles for DTG (Exhibit 13) to complement the original guiding values (Exhibit 8) and mission statement. These were reinforced through communication to DTG's employees.

Greenway would persistently inform the sales force, "The day we *require* dealers to use our Web site is the day this company will die!" At the same time, Crockett relentlessly pushed technical development to make transactions more efficient. In this way, they acknowledged that "behavior changes slowly" and, by their reasoning, engaged the seemingly paradoxical strategic objective of introducing a revolutionary business model that accommodated traditional wholesaling practices. Role modeling was also used to instill the principles. For example, DTG top management frequently visited dealers. Greenway reported that the sales force appreciated Crockett and Atkins being out there shaking hands with potential customers, too.

Exhibit

Exhibit **12** **The RIAD Vehicle Inspection Tool**

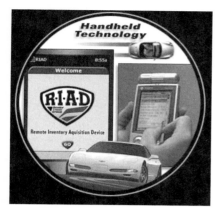

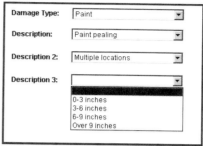

Item			
Front left fender (drivers side)	○ Yes	○ No	
Front Bumper	○ Yes	○ No	
Grill	○ Yes	○ No	
Hood	○ Yes	○ No	
Engine compartment	○ Yes	○ No	
Right front fender (passengers side)	○ Yes	○ No	
Passengers door	○ Yes	○ No	
Rear passengers door	○ Yes	○ No	
Passenger Rocker panel	○ Yes	○ No	
Right rear quarter panel / bed side (truck)	○ Yes	○ No	
Trunk / tail gate (truck)	○ Yes	○ No	
Bed (truck) or inside trunk	○ Yes	○ No	
Rear Bumper	○ Yes	○ No	
Left rear quarter panel / bed side (truck)	○ Yes	○ No	
Driver rocker panel	○ Yes	○ No	
Rear driver door	● Yes	○ No	
Driver door	○ Yes	○ No	
Glass	○ Yes	○ No	
Roof	○ Yes	○ No	
Tires Passenger	○ Yes	○ No	
Wheels Passenger	○ Yes	○ No	
Tires Driver	○ Yes	○ No	
Wheels Driver	○ Yes	○ No	

Source: DTG promotional material.

Exhibit **13** **DTG's Ten Strategic Principles**

1 Don't kick the gorilla: Physical auctions dominate the industry; partner rather than complete

2 Behavior changes slowly: Let dealers participate as they are accustomed (i.e., off-line at first)

3 Handshakes build more loyalty than features: People matter more than processes

4 Relationships outrun transactions: Lose a deal — save a relationship

5 Business is intimate: In-person visits are customary and essential

6 Avoid imports: Develop native solutions that adapt to existing behavior

7 Saving time + money + hassle = maximum success: Create win-win-win solutions

8 Slow and steady wins: Quality companies cannot grow overnight

9 Don't push for maximum margin: Transaction volume makes the model fly

10 Knowledge is power: We benefit when dealers have good data to make good decisions

entrepreneurial CASE ANALYSIS

CRUISING AT THE SPEED OF ENTREPRENEURSHIP

Frantic negotiation, hard-driving salesmanship, and the exuberant celebration of closed deals were standard at DTG—especially in the "bullpen." Originally a conference room, the bullpen had become a negotiation "war room" packed with loud salespeople working deals between buyers and sellers. The salespeople were able to communicate effectively with DTG's customers because they were similar to them. It was not atypical to see a salesperson eating lunch and negotiating with a buyer over a telephone on one ear while conversing with the seller over a mobile phone on the other ear. A whiteboard showed the status of each deal, which salesperson closed it, and a tally proclaiming the best performer of the day. Sometimes the whiteboard displayed the results of sales competitions so that everyone would know who performed well (or poorly). In a nearby room, the administrative staff handled finances and logistics with silent precision while trying to ignore the loud salespeople. Just next door, the technology developers' room was a dimly lit domain full of pagers, PDAs, laptops, and other technical devices. Posters featuring alternative music bands covered the walls. The reclusive developers arrived late each morning, closed their door, and worked late into the night to the trendy sounds of techno music.

By June 2001, DTG served 180 dealers in Washington and surrounding states. Despite complications, sales climbed to 89 vehicles that month, generating more than $1 million in vehicle transactions and $28,000 in revenues. An income statement summarizing DTG's actual revenues and expenses for 2000 and financial projections for 2001–2003 appears in Exhibit 14.

Speed Bumps

The technology meant to streamline processes often just slowed things down, and by mid-2001 some technological aspects of the business model came into question. For example, the Web site facilitated transactions by making employees more efficient, but it was still not ready for customers to access. When a deal was made, it was DTG's salesperson—not the dealer—who filled in the appropriate fields on the Web site. Nonetheless, sales growth continued. Greenway and Crockett began to wonder if dealers would *ever* need to access the Web site. DTG's efficiency behind the scenes was encouraging though, and the approach still permitted dealers to conduct business through their preferred methods: face to face or by telephone. Every employee was working long hours under stressful and uncertain conditions. Every day seemed to bring news of a new competitor or another failed start-up. To raise spirits, Crockett decided

---

Exhibit 14 DTG Income Statement for Fiscal Years 2000 and Projections for 2001–2003

Year ending September 30		2000	2001	2002	2003
Income					
Sales-based revenues		$0	$1,321,988	$9,297,662	$13,191,787
Selling expenses		0	201,659	1,549,610	2,378,847
	Gross margin	0	1,120,329	7,748,052	10,812,940
Expenses					
Operating		205,749	1,301,833	3,834,752	4,810,164
Advertising and marketing		52,000	130,183	348,614	400,847
Research and development (wireless, Web site)		312,500	1,171,650	2,788,910	2,805,929
	Operating expenses	570,249	2,603,666	6,972,276	8,016,940
	Net earnings	(570,249)	(1,483,337)	775,776	2,796,000

Source: DTG internal documents.

to organize a holiday event for employees and their families; however, Hayworth and DTG's board poured cold water on the idea. They thought it would send the wrong message and distract employees from making DTG profitable. Crockett thought the party would help establish a culture, nurture commitment, and strengthen relationships, which might speed DTG toward profitability. He was even prepared to pay for the event himself. As he explained his plan to one board member over the telephone, the investor interrupted him: "There'll be plenty of time for parties after the company makes a profit."

Crockett tabled his plan, feeling that he had more important battles to fight. Hayworth was still sharing office space with DTG. Although he was removed from day-to-day issues and operations, his presence was difficult to ignore. For example, frequently he would bellow to everyone in the office: "How many cars have we sold today?!" When DTG moved to its suburban location, Greenway grabbed the office next to Hayworth's and left Crockett an office at the opposite end of the hall. Crockett thought little of it until Greenway began slipping into Hayworth's office at regular intervals. Shortly thereafter, Greenway began to disagree openly with Crockett in meetings; he would complain about Crockett's decisions with a nod toward Hayworth. He would sometimes be heard instructing employees: "No, you see, this is what Hayworth really wants. . . ." Eventually, Greenway began to schedule and preside over company-wide meetings to which everyone except Crockett was invited. Challenged by Crockett on the oversight, Greenway replied, "You can come to any of these, but I don't know why you would want to."

Friction with Greenway was beginning to compromise Crockett's otherwise healthy relationship with Hayworth, and Crockett felt powerless to change the situation. Greenway seemed to exacerbate any minor disagreements between Crockett and Hayworth over how to lead DTG. From Crockett's perspective, he did not think he had the industry experience to gain Greenway's respect or enough support from the board to address Greenway's behavior directly. He knew it would be difficult to take disciplinary action, because DTG's current sales success was largely attributable to Greenway and his team. In fact, it seemed that Greenway had become more essential to DTG's future growth than he was. Crockett waited a bit longer before meeting with Hayworth about the issue.

Once Hayworth and Crockett compared notes, it was clear that Greenway had been playing them against each other for his own advantage. They agreed that, even if Greenway felt capable of leading DTG, he was not the right person for the job—the more they worked with Greenway, the less they trusted him. Furthermore, he did not have the polish required to present DTG to potential investors.

Meanwhile, the Ohio technology developer continued to miss important deadlines. Crockett wondered out loud if they would ever deliver: "Perhaps *this* is why they were so much more affordable than the others!" Demands

for results escalated until the vendor actually threatened to terminate DTG's Web site. Feeling a sudden need to protect the investment, Crockett launched an internal development effort. Two new developers were hired and given responsibility for smoothing relations with the vendor, transferring development in-house, and providing DTG's technical support. Just eight months after closing its initial round of investment, DTG's employee ranks had expanded to 32. Most of these employees were salespeople, but the number also included eight administrative staff and five vehicle inspectors. The leased office space had been filled, and small satellite offices were established in Spokane, Salt Lake City, and Juneau, Alaska.

Some aspects of DTG did not accommodate the technology developers very well. Unlike the experienced salespeople and administrative staff, the developers were young, tech savvy, and formally educated. Their only experience with auto dealers was as retail customers, yet they were responsible for translating the traditional auto wholesaling process into meaningful Web-based features that could expedite transactions. They did not speak the same language as the industry veterans. For example, Greenway would tell the developers, "A dealer's pager needs to go off whenever over-aged inventory in our catalog matches the standing order placed in our vehicle locater service." Typical first responses from the developers included, "What's an 'over-aged' inventory?" "What's a 'standing order,' and who placed it?" and "Does that guy think we're miracle workers?" Greenway would deliver his messages in a tone that implied any child should be able to understand him. It could take hours to clear up the confusion, and the developers' initial attempts to deliver such features were inevitably and significantly flawed.

DTG made about 200 vehicle transactions in August 2001. Management projected a breakeven transaction volume of 600 vehicles per month, which seemed attainable by the end of the year, but no one was sure whether the approaching winter season would affect the current sales growth. They all knew that the online market was important to generating the sales volume required to reach profitability, but there was debate about the nature of its role. Crockett and Greenway agreed that it was not possible for DTG to fulfill its mission and prove the new business model until the online market reached dealers directly. Any company could increase sales by hiring more salespeople, but the DTG model required online technology to drive growth.

Achieving technology-based growth became Crockett's chief objective by June 2001. DTG's Web site was being reworked constantly. Trial versions were launched and relaunched, but dealers were not yet invited to participate directly. Few dealers expressed an interest in accessing the Web site anyway. As the sales force continued closing deals, DTG continued to grow by adding salespeople. Before Crockett knew it, his orientation had shifted away from the entrepreneurial activity he loved

entrepreneurial CASE ANALYSIS

Exhibit	15	Re-creation of an Excerpt from Crockett's Journal in August 2001

Who?	What's missing?
Hayworth/Investors	Trust
Greenway	Respect

and toward the operations side of the venture—away from the vision and into the details.

Warning Signs

Crockett began to feel forced by his DTG experience to be someone he was not. In August 2001, he tried to put in writing what was troubling him. His personal journal showed divergences between what he desired and what existed. Personal and relational matters seemed to be at the heart of his predicament (Exhibit 15). It was not lost on Crockett that "trust" and "respect" must be earned.

If he were not capable of earning trust and respect, Crockett felt it was perhaps the right time to find a leader who could. Crockett felt like a misfit in the auto industry anyway, where you were either "one of the guys" or you were not. Most DTG employees were industry veterans— "car guys" who were older than Crockett and drove much nicer cars. With sales commissions, Greenway and others made more money than Crockett. They understood industry nuances with which he still struggled. Communication continued to be a source of frustration. Crockett found the original contract he had signed with Hayworth, and was reminded in black and white that the original intent was to pass leadership to an industry veteran once the high risk of the start-up phase had been mitigated.

Unexpectedly, that month the National Outdoor Leadership School approached Crockett. The social venture was raising money for charity by leading a three-day expedition nearly 11,000 feet to the summit of Mt. Baker. Participants were each asked to contribute $2,000. Crockett saw a unique opportunity to ponder career options, or even a nice parting gesture and exit mechanism if DTG would sponsor him. He discussed resigning with Hayworth, but it was clear that the board was not interested in hiring an expensive industry veteran to lead DTG. Hayworth told him, "We don't want you to leave, and we'll sponsor the mountain climb." But it did little to change Crockett's perception

of things. If he wanted to resign, he was going to have to force the issue.

A couple of weeks later, Crockett was on the side of a mountain with 12 other climbers in tandem. The team plodded carefully around dizzying glacial chasms. He was told his ice ax was the best hope if he began to fall or slide. As the final ascent began and his helmet lamp shone through the 3:00 a.m. darkness, Crockett felt like he was in another world. He saw parallels between this adventure and DTG: Hayworth funded both, and Crockett worked hard. Moreover, both had begun to entail risks to life or livelihood along with the exhilaration of reaching new heights. After three freezing days, as the expedition neared Mt. Baker's summit, Crockett had gained a new perspective on many issues. He asked himself again: Would DTG be led more effectively by an industry veteran? Was it time to get out?

Questions

1. What would you have done about Greenway's behaviors if you were in Crockett's position? Were the eventual problems detectable in the beginning?
2. What types of people fit better in large organizations versus entrepreneurial ventures? Does Crockett exemplify such characteristics or not? What about Greenway? How trainable are such characteristics?
3. What kinds of people should occupy leadership positions in entrepreneurial ventures? Based on what is known about Greenway, was he such a person? What about Crockett?
4. What challenges and issues emerged as DTG became a more established entrepreneurial venture? What are some alternative ways they could have been handled?

Notes

1. Manheim Auction, 2003 Used Car Market Report (www.manheimauctions.com).

entrepreneurial

CASE ANALYSIS

Community Web.com: An Internet Firm's Effort to Survive

entrepreneurial CASE ANALYSIS

Introduction

Dan Pale, a 30-year-old CEO of an Internet start-up company, CommunityWeb.com, was faced with the most important decision of his business career. After more than a year of operation that was funded with approximately $1.6 million in start-up capital, his company was experiencing difficult times. Pale and cofounder, Jim Mack, were faced with some tough decisions. A lack of cash flow to the business coupled with rapidly increasing debt were causing mounting financial pressures. Potential legal problems were also on the horizon. Sitting at his desk on June 8, 2001, Pale now ponders a decision to sign a funding agreement with Wall Street Venture Capital.

Formation of the Initial Business Concept: CommunityWeb.com

Dan Pale had talked about and researched the idea of a localized Internet portal for many months. In the fall of 1999, Pale—determined that the idea seemed technologically feasible—visited Jim Mack, owner of a financial planning firm in Seymour, Indiana. After three meetings, Mack agreed to join the venture. They contacted the Information and Communication Sciences' Applied Research Institute at Ball State University to conduct further research on the concept. In March 2000, CommunityWeb, Inc., was officially established. Jim Mack served as the CEO and chairman of the board of directors while Dan Pale served as the president/COO.

The basic idea behind the business concept was to localize the Internet. This would be done through a Web site that would allow users to narrow information found on the Web to a localized and specific geographic area. In turn, the Web site would then generate advertisements specific to the geographic area from which the user had originated his or her visit. The idea was to contain these capabilities within one national Web site. This site would also give users the ability to interact by posting stories about local sporting and news events.

Building the Organization and Its Product

Dan Pale recruited and hired a talented, young team at CommunityWeb. For several months, employees mined and categorized an extensive database of URLs and built a model for taking CommunityWeb.com to market. The firm used in-house software to locate, capture, and categorize these Web site addresses. Pale and Mack planned to take their concept of localized Internet utilization to market via franchising. Franchisees would buy the rights to sell CommunityWeb.com advertising (banner ads, e-mail marketing, pop-up ads) to specific territories. Each franchise would sell for $35,000 and would cover a geographic region populated by approximately 100,000 people. Pale and Mack expected to use the franchise fees to fund CommunityWeb's further growth. The company planned on retaining ownership of the 50 largest metropolitan markets in the United States.

Jim Mack and Dan Pale initially estimated that the company would need $2 million in start-up equity. Raising this amount of money as an Internet start-up, especially in a small, midwestern city, was not an easy task. Jim Mack tapped his extensive base of financial planning clients and raised nearly all of the company's angel capital. However, the fund-raising efforts proved to be quite costly. A great deal of money was spent promoting CommunityWeb to potential investors. The amount contributed by each investor averaged between $25,000 and $50,000. By mid-January 2001, the company had raised $1.6 million of its original $2 million target but had sold only two franchises. Pale and Mack developed the company's business plan for the sole purpose of attracting investors (see Appendix). CommunityWeb's business model and the projected financial forecasts seemed to change on a near-weekly basis, making it difficult to constantly update the business plan. Very few changes were ever made to the firm's original business plan. As the business model began to change, financial projections were hastily adapted, and the business plan was never adjusted accordingly. The firm's first set of pro forma financial statements estimated that revenues would exceed $1 billion within two years. After consulting venture capital firms and other dot-com businesses that had already been in operation, CommunityWeb reduced its estimations to a more conservative figure. The projected third-year revenues would be just over $160 million. The company's June 2001 projected financial statements business plan addendum shows the earnings estimates also had been scaled back even further (see Table 1).

Because the firm's historical financial statements had not been audited, communication with potential institutional investors and venture capitalists was difficult.

Source: This case was prepared by Donald F. Kuratko of Indiana University and Robert D. Mathews of Ball State University, as a basis for class discussion rather than to illustrate effective or ineffective handling of an administrative situation. All rights reserved to the author.

Table **1**	Financial Projections CommunityWeb, Inc.

Projected Profit and Loss 2002–2004

Income Statement	2002	2003	2004
Sales	$1,761,201.00	$7,508,323.00	$26,240,359.00
Direct Cost of Sales	$1,190,785.00	$5,508,538.00	$ 8,817,481.00
Other	—	—	—
Total Cost of Sales	$1,190,785.00	$5,508,538.00	$ 8,817,481.00
Gross Margin	$ 570,416.00	$1,999,785.00	$17,422,878.00
Gross Margin %	32.39%	26.63%	66.40%
Operating Expenses			
Accountant Fees	$ 2,400.00	$ 2,700.00	$ 3,000.00
Attorney Fees	12,000.00	12,300.00	12,600.00
Commissions or Referrals	111,322.80	386,265.00	597,412.50
Equipment Leases	67,608.00	67,608.00	67,608.00
Insurance—General Liability, WC, etc.	1,344.00	1,644.00	1,944.00
Insurance—Auto	2,208.00	2,508.00	2,808.00
Internet Connection	4,254.00	4,554.00	4,854.00
Web Hosting and Security	24,000.00	24,300.00	24,600.00
Advertising/Marketing	18,250.00	75,083.00	93,854.04
Miscellaneous	6,000.00	6,300.00	6,600.00
Office Supplies	6,000.00	6,300.00	6,600.00
Professional Dev./Subscription/ Membership Fees	2,400.00	2,700.00	3,000.00
Payroll	568,795.02	812,557.50	934,441.13
Payroll Burden	170,069.71	243,767.25	280,332.34
Rent	22,200.00	22,200.00	22,200.00
Telephone	21,600.00	22,680.00	23,760.00
Trade Shows	6,000.00	6,300.00	6,600.00
Travel	4,250.00	4,550.00	4,850.00
Utilities	6,000.00	6,300.00	6,600.00
Total Overhead	$1,056,701.53	$ 1,710,616.75	$ 2,103,664.01
Total Operating Expense	$2,247,486.53	$7,219,154.75	$ 10,921,145.01
Profit Before Interest and Taxes	$ (486,285.53)	$ 289,168.25	$ 15,319,213.99
Interest Expense (Short-term)	—	—	—
Interest Expense (Long-term)	—	—	—
Taxes Incurred	0	0	4,940,000.00
Net Profit	$ (486,286.00)	$ 289,168.00	$ 10,379,213.99

There was also the issue that Jim Mack never registered the distribution of equities for private placement with the Securities and Exchange Commission (SEC). Therefore, the legality of these securities could be in question. (The SEC provides Regulation D for selling stock to private parties. Rules 504a, 504, 505, and 506 cover the specific requirements.)

entrepreneurial CASE ANALYSIS

The Founders and the Management Team

Dan Pale's business career began at age 23 when he founded a clothing store that quickly grew to more than $1.2 million in annual sales. Pale was also co-owner of his family's business, a True Value hardware store and Just Ask Rental Center. In 1998, he repositioned himself in telecommunications and took over management of WKBY-AM talk radio in Seymour, Indiana. In less than two years, he increased the station's revenue by 600 percent. He also helped position WKBY as the largest talk-format station in southern Indiana. He served in a management role in Indiana Regional Radio Partners, Inc., through April 2000.

Jim Mack was a certified financial planner and registered financial consultant. He had 13 years experience in the financial services industry. He was cofounder and president of the Financial Investors Group based in Seymour, Indiana, and had clients in 17 states. Mack hosted a weekly radio program at WKBY and was a contributor to *The Roaring 2000's Investor's Guide,* one of the *New York Times* business best sellers. He also served on the advisory board of the H. S. Dent Foundation and was a noted speaker in areas of business development and fundamental economic trends.

The rest of the management team was very young and energetic. Most of the team members were recent college graduates. The following were the original management team at CommunityWeb and their credentials as of spring 2001:[1]

JEFFREY LEHM

Director of Database Development and Technology

Lehm left his position as computer information systems regional program chair for Ivy Tech State College in Seymour, Indiana, to join CommunityWeb.

MICHAEL HUNT

Chief Information Officer

Hunt completed his master's degree in information and communication sciences from Ball State University in December 2000.

JONATHAN LESTER

Director of Communications

Lester earned degrees in both advertising and marketing from Ball State University and is currently completing a master's degree in public relations.

TONY BAKER

Director of Franchise Sales and Business Development

Baker was the director of marketing for the largest franchise of BD's Mongolian Barbecue restaurants.

JIM McDUFFY

Director of Special Markets

McDuffy had more than ten years of management experience in various business environments, ranging from the entertainment industry to Web development.

JOHN TAYLOR

Director of Wireless Strategies/Research and Development

Taylor received his bachelor of arts in marketing from Ball State University with a double minor in Japanese and Asian studies. He was also pursuing a master's degree in information and communication sciences.

TROY SIMON

Director of Indianapolis Operations

Simon completed his master's degree in information and communication sciences from Ball State University in 1998. Simon then served as a business development representative at Intelliseek, a leading provider in personalized Internet services.

Business, Industry, and Economic Conditions

The Internet had a significant impact on the global business climate between 1999 and 2001. By 2001, there were more than 160 million Internet users worldwide, and they were beginning to spend a significant amount of time online—averaging more than 18 hours connected monthly. Internet retailing had also become a dominant business force in the American economy, as monthly Internet spending was approaching $4 billion, an average of $270 per consumer.[2]

The economic conditions during 2001 made it difficult for growing businesses, especially Internet-based, to obtain funding. The Internet boom of 1999 and 2000, during which Internet companies received equity investment at alarming rates, was definitely a thing of the past. Many venture capitalists had gone back to basic business fundamentals and only considered firms with sound business models and solid business plans. In addition, private investors were becoming more cautious because of the recent plunge ("tech wreck") of the NASDAQ stock market (see Figure 1).

Figure **1**   NASDAQ Composite

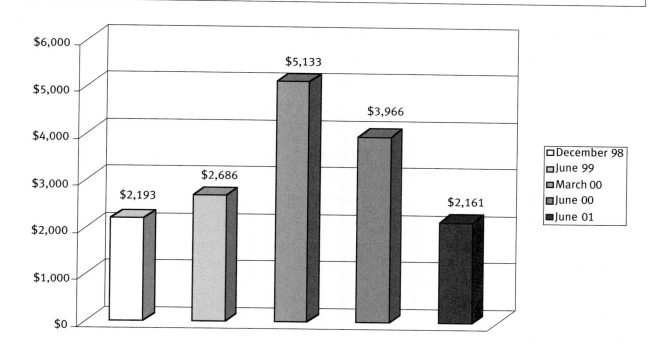

Figure 1   NASDAQ Composite

The NASDAQ composite peaked at a value of $5,133 in March 2000. Since that point, the NASDAQ composite value had declined to its June 2001 level of $2,161.[3] According to emarketer.com, more than 555 Internet businesses worldwide closed in the first half of 2001.

Internet firms such as Citysearch.com, localbusiness.com, and cityworks.com, among others, began to make major cutbacks or ceased operations. Double Click, the largest online ad broker, continued to lose more than $100 million per quarter. In addition, most companies, including dot-coms, were cutting their advertising budgets across the board. Competitive Media Reporting estimated that 2001 advertising spending across all media would fall more than $102.4 billion from 2000 levels.[4] Although there still seemed to be interest in specialized and localized Internet ads, many industry factors were causing negative pressures on ad revenue–based business models. According to John Groth, CEO of BeaconVentureCapital (Bethesda, Maryland), the capital markets were not looking favorably on firms with the majority of revenues coming from Internet advertising sales.

The Competitive Landscape

By June 2001, CommunityWeb faced competition from firms such as DigitalCity.com, OneMain.com, MyCity.com, Yahoo! Get Local, Visionvibes.com, Wowtown.com, URL-Surfer.com, Citysearch.com, megago.com, move.com, busyreceptionist.com, usaonline.com, switchboard.com, relocationcentral.com, MyWay.com, and numerous yellow pages Web sites, among others. CommunityWeb believed, however, that none of these sites truly provided local information across the nation. They contended that these sites were geared toward larger cities or were restricted to very small regions. Thus, CommunityWeb never viewed any of these competitors as major threats to the success of its business model. DigitalCity.com and Citysearch.com, however, were engaged in significant national advertising campaigns and had developed the greatest name recognition among localized Internet sites. CommunityWeb considered its main competitors to be local newspapers and radio stations. The firm saw these traditional media forms as its greatest rivals.

CommunityWeb.com in Operation

The CommunityWeb.com Web site was officially launched on January 28, 2001. Visitors to the site could read and post local news and sports stories, check the local weather forecast, and search for Uniform Resource Locators (URLs, or Web site addresses) tailored to specific locales and business categories. The URL searches used CommunityWeb's tool and its database, which by April 2001 included more than 200,000 URLs.

During the first few months of 2001, CommunityWeb was able to establish partnerships and alliances with several strong companies such as AT&T, Infospace.com,

entrepreneurial CASE ANALYSIS

and Hargiss Communication. CommunityWeb, however, soon realized that many of these partners did not fit into its vision and broke all ties with most of these partners to pursue other partnerships with companies like LocaLine and valupage.com.

CommunityWeb continued to struggle to get its business concept off the ground. Tony Baker, the person hired as director of franchise sales, had managed to sell just two franchises, leaving Dan Pale and Jim Mack to contemplate their next move. They were faced with the immediate need to generate positive cash flow within the next two to three months.

CommunityWeb's workforce had peaked to approximately 175 employees in March 2001, causing the company to incur over $200,000 of payroll expenses. Pale and Mack had expected to sign more than 100 franchisees in the first year, but their efforts produced only failed prospects. Running short of funds in April 2001, they imposed major cutbacks, leaving only 15 key employees and a monthly expenditure of about $75,000 (Table 2). Pale and Mack saw these cuts as a necessary

move to keep their firm alive. With no incoming revenue, mounting debt, and a failing business model, they began to panic and felt that cutbacks across the board were their only option.

At this point, CommunityWeb had abandoned its original business plan and now focused on selling its Web site tools to Internet service providers (ISPs). They believed that CommunityWeb's tools could be used by the ISPs in their default browsers and portals (gateways). CommunityWeb would become their provider of local information and their "face" to users. However, the firm was forced to drop its URL database from its set of tools offered to ISPs, due to significant technical errors that reduced both the effectiveness and size (reduced to under 40,000 URLs) of the database. This was a major setback to CommunityWeb, but the company just did not have the financial resources needed to fix the database errors (see Table 3 for a timeline of critical events). To generate additional revenues, CommunityWeb also introduced a Web development division to its business. In addition, the company attempted to market itself as an ISP.

Table 2	Summary Financial Information as Provided by Management

	March 2001	April 2001
Professional and consulting fees	$ 9,500	$ 2,000
Equipment lease and depreciation	19,000	3,000
Software/Connectivity/Hosting	35,000	–
Employee/Payroll expenses:		
CEO—Mack	10,000	6,250
President—Pale	10,000	5,000
Staff—Other	142,500	25,850
Contract labor—Mining	20,000	–
Taxes	14,300	3,265
Training	10,000	–
Other	2,600	2,500
Employee/Payroll expenses—total	209,400	42,865
Marketing expenses	20,050	5,000
Rent/Utilities	3,655	2,100
Web site maintenance/design	14,000	13,000
Office supplies	4,000	3,100
Interest/Other	5,400	4,400
Total expenses	$ 320,005	$75,465

Table	3	Timeline of Critical Events

- January–February 2000—Dan Pale researches the possibility of localizing the Internet.
- February 2000—Pale meets with Jim Mack of the Financial Investors Group to discuss the possibility of building a localized Internet portal.
- March 2000—Mack and Pale agree to start the business, which they name CommunityWeb. They incorporate as a C corporation and begin staffing the company.
- April 2000–January 2001—The large staff of "miners" collect and capture a comprehensive database of URLs.
- January 28, 2001—The Web site, http://www.CommunityWeb.com, is officially launched.
- February–May 2001—CommunityWeb management works on developing business relationships that will strengthen its position in the marketplace. The firm also works on raising equity and selling franchises.
- April 2001—Due to mounting financial pressures, Mack is forced to make major cutbacks in workforce and expenditures.
- May 2001—CommunityWeb changes its business model to sell its Web site tools to ISPs. The firm discontinues the use of its URL database. Mack steps down as CEO and chairman of the board, and Pale takes over as CEO. Mack remains on the board of directors.
- June 2001—CommunityWeb considers entering a deal with Wall Street Venture Capital of New York.

Mounting Financial Pressure and Internal Conflict

Jim Mack and Dan Pale recognized their financial crisis. They believed that CommunityWeb had only a few months to establish a positive cash flow. Mack planned to continue raising funds through his client base and personal network while Pale and his staff feverishly marketed their new business model to ISPs. Capital markets had become tighter and Mack seemingly had exhausted his personal resources. By the end of April 2001, Mack and Pale resorted to "bootstrapping" for short-term financing, pushing several of their own credit cards to their limits, delaying payments to most of the company's creditors, and falling more than $200,000 behind in remitting payroll taxes and employee withholdings to the Internal Revenue Service (IRS). The company had also accrued other debts in excess of $1 million (Table 4). Pale and Mack's personal debt had grown to more than $300,000. Employees also started to feel the pinch of the firm's cash flow problems as the issuance of paychecks was often delayed by as much as three to four weeks.

Amid the financial pressures, personal conflicts arose between Mack and the employees. Mack was often criticized for being too controlling. Key management personnel had questioned his desire to make all of the company's strategic decisions. Because of Mack's constant changing of the business model, employees rarely knew the "latest" direction of the company. Conflict between Mack and Pale also began to surface. Mack and Pale often did not see "eye to eye" on strategic or financial issues. Pale felt as though Mack, the CEO, was taking control over the daily activities, which Pale considered his job as president and COO. In May 2001, due to the mounting conflicts and Mack's apparent mismanagement of the company, the board of directors removed Jim Mack as CEO and chairman of the board and appointed Pale as his replacement. Mack would remain on the board of directors but would relinquish all day-to-day operations of the company to Dan Pale. Mack maintained his role in raising capital for the company.

The Wall Street Venture Capital Deal

During the past several months of funding efforts, Mack and Pale had been working on developing a relationship with a relatively unknown firm named Wall Street Venture Capital from New York City. In June 2001, Pale and Mack capitalized on an invitation to present their business model to this venture capital firm. After seeing their presentation, Wall Street Venture Capital agreed to raise funding for CommunityWeb through a partnership. If CommunityWeb accepted the agreement, Wall Street Venture Capital would acquire 30 percent equity of the company, and CommunityWeb would be charged a $20,000 commitment fee. CommunityWeb would then

entrepreneurial CASE ANALYSIS

Table 4	Balance Sheet—Fiscal Year Ending February 2002

Assets

Current Assets		
Checking Account	$41.09	
Expense Account	237.11	
Client Fees Receivable	904.94	
Investments	50,000.00	
Total Current Assets		$51,183.14
Property and Equipment		
Furniture and Fixtures	$21,804.26	
Computer Equipment	257,960.30	
Leasehold Improvements	19,275.25	
Accum. Depreciation—Furniture	(7,014.80)	
Accum. Depreciation—Computer Equipment	(112,411.33)	
Accum. Depreciation—Leasehold	(6,203.74)	
Total Property and Equipment		$173,409.94
Total Assets		$224,593.08

Liabilities and Capital

Current Liabilities		
Accounts Payable	$355,748.64	
Deductions Payable	785.71	
Federal Payroll Taxes Payable	266,406.50	
FUTA Tax Payable	4,450.64	
State Payroll Taxes Payable	32,715.16	
SUTA Payable	8,907.29	
Local Payroll Taxes Payable	7,630.73	
Employee Benefits Payable	18,705.47	
Total Current Liabilities		$695,350.14
Long-Term Liabilities		
Loan from Shareholder—Dan Pale	$304,929.20	
Loan from Shareholder—Jim Mack	68,500.00	
Long-Term Liabilities		$373,429.20
Total Liabilities		$1,068,779.34
Capital		
Treasury Stock	$(7,545.00)	
Paid-In Capital	1,892,008.68	
Retained Earnings	(1,017,263.51)	
Net Income	(1,711,386.43)	
Total Capital		$(844,186.26)
Total Liabilities and Capital		$224,593.08

be limited to raising an additional $500,000 outside of Wall Street Venture Capital during the next six months to fund current operations. Wall Street Venture Capital would agree to raise $5 million for CommunityWeb within six months, as well as position the firm for a buyout. CommunityWeb would also be able to use its relationship with Wall Street Venture Capital as leverage in meeting financial obligations to current investors and for forming new partnerships.

For almost two months, Jim Mack and Dan Pale attempted to investigate the viability of this New York–based venture capital firm. However, as of June 2001, Mack and Pale had been unable to establish whether or not Wall Street Venture Capital had a proven track record with multimillion-dollar start-up investing. Any information on the firm was hard to obtain. As an example, its Web site was not functional and the New York Chamber of Commerce did not have any information on the firm. When Mack and Pale asked the president of Wall Street Venture Capital, Joseph McElroys, to give documentation of the firm's successfully funded projects, the response was that most of Wall Street's deals were international and documentation was not readily available.

The Dilemma

Dan Pale now faces his toughest decision as CEO of CommunityWeb. He has the mounting pressures of sinking deeper and deeper into debt, risking more and more invested capital, and facing the legal issues associated with the debt to the IRS and the improper sale of securities. Pale is seriously considering entering the agreement with Wall Street Venture Capital. The following issues plague Pale as he considers his next move.

- *Federal Tax Liability*—The company owes the IRS an amount in excess of $200,000. The company has filed the IRS form 656 "Offer in Compromise" to settle this debt. There is no assurance that the IRS will accept this offer in compromise. The IRS may counteroffer or reject the offer completely. In this case, CommunityWeb may not have sufficient funds to pay the delinquent taxes, interest, and any penalties. Furthermore, the IRS can even foreclose on the company's assets if it chooses.

- *Indiana State Tax Liability*—The company owes the state of Indiana an amount in excess of $20,000. The company has entered into a payment agreement with the State of Indiana on this debt. If the company fails to make the required payments to the State of Indiana, the Indiana Department of Revenue could foreclose on the company's assets.

- *Securities Violations*—The company has previously sold investments in the company in excess of $1.6 million. The sale of these securities may not have been in compliance with all federal and state securities laws. They face the probability that a rescission offer would be made to all purchasers and that an action could be filed by the securities regulatory agencies. In addition, the company's officers could possibly face criminal charges for these SEC violations.

- *Failure to Make a Profit*—Since its inception in 2000, the company has been primarily involved in the research and development of its Internet technology and has had no chance to develop revenues. Currently, the company has not made a profit—and there is no future assurance it ever will. The company is operating with a "burn rate" (a popular term used to denote expenditures without sufficient revenue to at least approach a break-even point) and has yet to establish a working business model that can successfully show a profit. Much of the initial $1.6 million of raised capital was spent on developing the URL database, marketing franchises to potential buyers, and attracting potential investors.

Dan Pale needs to make a move to save his company. Taking into account all of these issues, the agreement with Wall Street Venture Capital may be the best choice—or is it?

Notes

1. See Appendix for more detailed management biographies.
2. http://www.clickz.com/stats/.
3. http://www.nasdaq.com.
4. http://www.emarketer.com.

entrepreneurial CASE ANALYSIS

APPENDIX: BUSINESS PLAN

Executive Summary

CommunityWeb, Inc. is the Internet with local flavor and a personal touch. With CommunityWeb's unique search technology and full range of connectivity and other Web-related solutions, it enables businesses, nonprofit organizations, and individuals to interact in a specific geographic locale via the Internet. People who use the CommunityWeb portal to search CommunityWeb's Web site database find content that is most relevant to them, from news and sports scores to classified ads and even a community calendar. The free, simple search process is based on the individual needs of each end user, which allows him or her to search for information, goods, and services in his or her hometown or almost any specific area without wading through the useless links that traditional search engines yield as results.

While optimizing localized Web searches for private citizens, CommunityWeb provides area businesses the same luxury for specific geographic areas. A business knows with reasonable certainty that someone who searches a specific location either lives in that community or plans to visit it. CommunityWeb enables businesses of all sizes to participate in Internet advertising. CommunityWeb's dynamic one-to-one marketing enables businesses to market toward specific geographic areas as well as to specific age groups, income ranges, and interests. To motivate end users to register, CommunityWeb offers them the free Local Rewards program. Registered members earn points for visiting local advertisers' sites. They can then redeem accumulated points for services and merchandise, or donate them to a local charity. Becoming a member is simple and free; in less than one minute, a user can join by providing basic geographic, demographic, and psychographic information. For example, a user may like music but have no interest in apparel. Businesses spend more than $2 billion per quarter on marketing on the World Wide Web, but they collect little to no information about end users. Local Rewards addresses that issue. CommunityWeb's Local Rewards program demonstrates yet another way that CommunityWeb provides a win-win scenario for businesses and residents of the communities it services.

CommunityWeb provides a human approach to the Internet. Through its franchise model, CommunityWeb will place community coordinators around the country in communities of all sizes. This provides a name and a face for people to call upon when things get confusing and technology changes, as it always does.

CommunityWeb brings the Internet together for the individual and the community. CommunityWeb provides a customized browser that carries its name, Internet services from dial-up to high-speed connectivity solutions (through an alliance with AT&T), and Web design, hosting, and other related services (from alliances with various Web-design firms).

Many companies have attempted to enter local communities from an Internet perspective. More than 20 companies have succeeded in tier-one cities that are defined as *metropolitan statistical areas* (MSAs); MSAs contain more than 1 million residents each and represent more than one-third of the American population in 42 distinct areas. Companies that venture into tier-two and tier-three markets have failed from a global perspective. Individual community sites exist in these markets, but without continuity, they do nothing for commerce or community development in their respective areas. CommunityWeb is the platform that combines these communities, serving as the cord that provides individuality while binding communities together to provide true business relevance. CommunityWeb plans to corporately maintain these MSA market operations but will focus on initially proving its product through fully operational corporately owned test markets. CommunityWeb has partially funded the Indianapolis MSA as a test market and is seeking funding to start one corporately owned mid-market franchise each month, which started in April 2001.

CommunityWeb's success depends on a loyal number of users and massive name-brand recognition. CommunityWeb will employ three immediate strategies to gather these members and create product awareness. All three of these models provide built-in loyalty of membership as well as the opportunity for quick-start franchises. CommunityWeb will also allow select entrepreneurs to acquire franchise rights.

CommunityWeb will continue to franchise the business model in small-to-midsize markets nationwide. Franchisees can come from four different business backgrounds: (1) companies currently providing Internet service on a more local and/or regional basis; (2) traditional media outlets with built-in membership loyalty that provides a profitable alliance for both the company and CommunityWeb; (3) companies currently involved in Web site design; and (4) existing "specific community" Web sites with an identifiable user base.

CommunityWeb's main attack toward the franchise marketplace is through regional ISPs. CommunityWeb has found in its preliminary research that there are more than 600 regional ISPs in the Midwest that have less than 50,000 subscribers. CommunityWeb has also found that this will add very little to its current cost structure. These ISPs generally have somewhere around 5,000 subscribers, but they typically only generate approximately $2 per month toward their bottom line per customer. CommunityWeb's offer to these ISPs is simple: CommunityWeb will provide them with a CommunityWeb franchise in exchange for their conversion to the CommunityWeb system. This includes automatically registering their subscribers with CommunityWeb.com memberships, converting their subscribers' accounts to the CommunityWeb/AT&T virtual ISP, and selling CommunityWeb.com advertising in their markets. CommunityWeb has contacted more than 50 of these ISPs in Indiana alone and has gotten appointments with nearly all of them.

CommunityWeb is designed to be profitable by August 2001 and remain that way. The company uses Internet technology but is truly an interactive communications company focusing on dynamic one-to-one marketing.

Based on current Internet standards for usage and advertising, CommunityWeb can generate $15.60 per month per member. The business model and current plan calls for $2 million of initial investment with a positive cash flow of over $17 million in the second year of operations.

CommunityWeb has also recently seen the value of its unique URL database come to fruition. The database is proving to be highly marketable to thousands of Web sites at a monthly licensing fee of anywhere from $500 to $5,000.

CommunityWeb has more than 35 potential franchisees and has raised over $1,400,000. CommunityWeb is currently seeking an additional $600,000 in first-round funding and another $2 million in bridge financing. CommunityWeb is currently offering shares at $4 per share with the minimum investment of $25,000. That investment represents 6,250 voting-class shares controlling 1/8th percent (.00125) of the company.

The CommunityWeb Business Model

The CommunityWeb business model revolves around four main areas: members, community coordinators, content, and advertising. These four areas are simple in nature, but they drive the success of CommunityWeb.

MEMBERS

The most important aspect of CommunityWeb.com is membership. CommunityWeb has put a great deal of emphasis on the development of a dedicated user base. Member interaction through viewing advertisements, submitting content, and using the exclusive *CommunityWeb Directory*[1] drives the success of CommunityWeb. Members are encouraged to submit local content of interest to them.

COMMUNITY COORDINATORS

Community coordinators, which exist both as franchisees and as MSA coordinators, provide a local "heartbeat" to the Internet for each community. These community coordinators and their sales force will have established relationships with community businesses, not-for-profits, and the general population, which allows for fast membership growth and accelerated advertising sales.

CONTENT

Content—such as calendar events, local sports stories, local news stories, local press releases, and the *CommunityWeb Directory*—is what makes CommunityWeb.com an attractive, useful, informative, and successful Web site. CommunityWeb will provide the *CommunityWeb Directory* as well as localized content through news and sports stories, calendar events, and press releases, but members are encouraged to submit the bulk of this local content and represent their community on the Internet.

ADVERTISING

Localized advertising is the main revenue engine of CommunityWeb.com. Very specifically targeted and localized advertising is what makes CommunityWeb's advertising system unique to the Internet. Local advertising will be utilized in the community section through promotional windows, CommunityWeb's *CommunityWeb Directory*, targeted e-mail marketing, and follow-up e-mail.

STRATEGIC ALLIANCES

CommunityWeb has developed several key technological and business relationships to better position itself in the marketplace.

AT&T: CommunityWeb has formed a strategic alliance with global communications giant AT&T in several areas. AT&T expects to better reach local markets through CommunityWeb, and CommunityWeb will utilize AT&T's resources to host the CommunityWeb.com Web site and provide private-labeled Internet connectivity services through a virtual ISP (VISP) system. This alliance will enable CommunityWeb to act as an ISP without having the initial capital expenses usually associated with launching local Internet services. Income from this alliance will come from every home or business that signs up for Internet access service. CommunityWeb's wholesale cost for dial-up accounts will be $13.95 per month. CommunityWeb plans to resell this service at a very competitive rate of $18.95 per month. This alliance should prove to be very powerful, given AT&T's

entrepreneurial CASE ANALYSIS

position in the ISP market. AT&T is the world's largest and highest rated ISP.[2]

Hargiss Communication/Quad Entertainment: The proprietary Set Top Box that Hargiss Communication has developed is a hardware and software solution that provides "Movies On Demand," Internet access, games, digital cable TV, and a local guide to the surrounding area (through CommunityWeb) to hotel or resort amenities, hospitals, and homes. CommunityWeb has entered into a strategic partnership with Hargiss Communication to provide a local guide portal for their interface using the CommunityWeb index of local URLs and its local content. CommunityWeb currently has a 15 percent ownership in a new subsidiary company formed with Hargiss Communication, called Quad Entertainment, and will be an integral part of developing the Set Top Box business model. In addition, Jed Delke of CommunityWeb will serve as CEO of Quad Entertainment and CommunityWeb will occupy three of the six board of directors spots on the company.

InfoSpace.com: CommunityWeb has partnered with InfoSpace.com to increase the options and content that CommunityWeb can provide to members. InfoSpace is one of the largest information sources on the Web, thus providing a very powerful resource to CommunityWeb members. The information resources that InfoSpace provides enhance CommunityWeb's content, allowing CommunityWeb to concentrate on its core business. InfoSpace will provide these resources on contract through a co-branded system. CommunityWeb members will see the CommunityWeb Web site, color scheme, and structure when navigating the InfoSpace content through CommunityWeb.com. This partnership also provides CommunityWeb with a revenue source through the advertising revenue sharing model.

LEGAL, PROFESSIONAL, ACCOUNTING, AND TECHNICAL PARTNERS AND ASSOCIATES

Thomas Reardon, partner of James, Austin, Cooper, and Burr Law Offices, located in Seymour, Indiana, heads the legal counsel. Reardon's role is to help determine any specialized counsel that CommunityWeb will need along the business development process. In addition, CommunityWeb has partnered with franchise attorney Mark Jacoby of Indianapolis.

CommunityWeb will work with the Commercial Services Group of Crowe Chizek LLP for assistance with SEC and accounting issues. As a leading accounting and consulting organization, Crowe Chizek offers specialized services with a client-focused relationship

culture. Crowe is the leading member firm of Howarth International, an international network of independent accounting and consulting firms, with more than 100 members and 400 offices in 372 cities throughout the world. Crowe Chizek's clients include IBM, Microsoft, Oracle, and Onyx Software. Specifically, Crowe Chizek will provide CommunityWeb assistance in finding an appropriate enterprise accounting package. They will also provide independent audits of CommunityWeb's financial statements. Crowe Chizek will be able to provide consulting expertise should the need arise in the future. Four different individuals handle the accounting department. Donald Hager is chief advisor. He has contributed to acquisition planning and stock distribution. Jim Mack is serving in the capacity of controller. Gregory Borst, CPA, will handle current payroll and day-to-day taxation issues.

TECHNOLOGY EXPERTISE—INTERNAL AND EXTERNAL

CommunityWeb has a team of highly educated and experienced database developers, programmers, and system architects. In addition, CommunityWeb has partnered with several higher-education institutions in the area. CommunityWeb has developed a dynamic site, which requires expertise from several different technology sectors. A commercially viable product was released on January 28, 2001, and is continuing to be built and improved. CommunityWeb has accomplished this mission by using its own talented employees and by contracting for services from Joseph A. Graves and Associates (JGA). Michael Hunt has led this team through the development phases and will continue to lead this team through continuous improvement phases. JGA has provided project management and programming expertise on different components of the site. Jeff Lehm has provided the database expertise.

COMMUNITYWEB ASSOCIATES

CommunityWeb has assembled a very talented, energetic, and enthusiastic group of entrepreneurial, business, and creative minds to drive this venture. Associate education backgrounds include marketing, entrepreneurship, political science, communication, journalism, and information sciences at both the undergraduate and graduate levels. Experiences include financial planning, retail management, franchise development, business development, education, and mass media management.

Officers, Board of Directors, Principals, and Significant Associates

JAMES A. MACK, CFP, RFC

Chairman, Board of Directors and CEO

Jim Mack is a certified financial planner and registered financial consultant. Mack serves as president and cofounder of the Financial Investors Group, based in Seymour, Indiana, with clients in 17 states. He has spent 13 years in the financial services industry creating and evaluating business and succession plans. He hosted a weekly radio show for five years and helped contribute to *The Roaring 2000s Investor: Strategies for the Life You Want*. Mack sits on the advisory board to the H. S. Dent Foundation and speaks nationally to thousands on business development concepts that focus on fundamental trends that drive the U.S. economy.

DANIEL E. PALE

President

Dan Pale has more than ten years of experience in retail business operations. At the age of 23, he started a retail clothing business that quickly grew to generate more than $1.2 million in sales per year. Pale also co-owns a True Value hardware store and a Just Ask Rental Center. In 1998, he entered the broadcast industry, taking over the management of WKBY Talk Radio in Seymour, Indiana. In less than two years, he increased station revenue by 600 percent and increased listenership, making the station the number one talk radio format in southern Indiana. He is also a member of the adjunct faculty at a local university's telecommunications program and—through April 2000—maintained a management role with Indiana Regional Radio Partners, Inc.

GREG DENT

Board of Directors

Greg Dent is currently president and CEO of Healthx .com. Dent has more than 20 years of experience in the health care and technology industries. In 1987, Greg founded First Benefit Corp., a Midwest-based third-party administrator (TPA) that appeared in *Inc.* magazine's top 500 growth companies in 1991, 1992, and 1993. He also founded Qubic, a nationwide organization that comprises 12 independently owned TPAs. In 1993, First Benefit Corp. was acquired by CoreSource. In 1995, Dent founded a new company, Intermark, and began development of what is now the Healthx .com product. In 1998, the company officially became Healthx.com.

DOMINIC MANCINO

Board of Directors

A native of Southern California and a resident of Indiana for the past eight years, Dominic Mancino has been with AT&T for several years and works as a sales director for business services in Indiana. He comes with a wealth of industry knowledge, having worked within telecommunications for 20 years for companies like Western Electric and Pacific Bell. His responsibilities have taken him from sales and engineering to his current position as sales director. Mancino has consulted with companies all around the United States to define Internet strategies and the practical application of IP-based solutions for business development. Mancino is a graduate of Ricks College, which is now known as Brigham Young University of Idaho.

DR. NATHAN WALKER

Board of Directors

Nathan Walker was recently with the National Association of Broadcasters in Washington, DC, where he was vice president of television operations. He currently teaches courses in technology, business aspects, and regulatory issues at the Center for Information and Communication Sciences at Ball State University, along with serving as codirector of the Applied Research Institute. His work includes the development of the network, interactive kiosk system. Dr. Walker regularly consults with AT&T Bell Labs, U.S. West Advanced Technologies, Ameritech, McDonald's Corporation, and GTE Labs.

SHERI WATERS

Board of Directors

Sheri Waters is a motivational speaker, trainer, and coach. She is the president/owner of the Waters Connection, Inc., a Midwest-based national consulting firm that specializes in improving organizational performance through leadership development, sales and customer services coaching/training, team building, and organizational development. Waters developed her expertise through years of service at Ameritech Corporation. Her responsibilities included training, developing, coaching, and supporting more than 3,000 senior managers and 4,000 associates in the Consumer Market Unit, which includes 17 Customer Care Centers across the states of Indiana, Illinois, Michigan, Wisconsin, and Ohio. Her most recent clients include Ameritech Consumer Services, Ameritech New Media, Cheap Tickets, Inc., and 21st Century Telecom, among others. Waters is a "Gold" member of the Indianapolis Chamber of Commerce.

entrepreneurial CASE ANALYSIS

MICHAEL A. MARELL

Board of Directors

Mike Marell is the owner of Michael A. Marell & Associates, a consulting firm established to assist businesses in continuous improvement strategies using statistical methods. The firm uses many improvement methods, including the methods of Dr. W. Edwards Deming, Dr. Donald Wheeler, Dr. Genichi Taguchi, and William Conway. The firm's objective for its clients is to train and support them to make their business processes and customer services more effective. Marell was employed at Delco Remy Division of General Motors and Delphi Automotive Systems for more than 31 years in engineering, quality, and statistical assignments. For 18 years, Marell trained employees from all areas of the company to make improvements and to assist in the application of statistical process control, machine qualification, supplier development, design of experiments, and robust engineering. Marell is a licensed professional engineer and certified quality engineer.

WILLIAM VACARRO, MD

Board of Directors

William Vacarro has served the public through the practice of family medicine since 1973. Dr. Vacarro currently serves as the president and CEO of Community Hospital in Seymour, Indiana. Dr. Vacarro is on the board of directors for the Anderson Chamber of Commerce and the Corporation for Economic Development. Dr. Vacarro serves on the Executive Committee, Health Status Committee, and the Facilities and Technology Committee for the Madison Health Partners.

DR. MICHAEL FOSTER

Board of Directors

Michael Foster received his bachelor's degree in accounting from the University of Wisconsin–Whitewater and his master's degree in guidance and counseling, also from Wisconsin–Whitewater. Dr. Foster went on to earn his doctoral degree in higher education from Indiana University in 1984. Since that time, Dr. Foster has consulted for several organizations, both for-profit and nonprofit in nature. Dr. Foster has also served since 1982 as a professor of management in Seymour University's School of Business. Dr. Foster served as the president and CEO of Marcon, Inc., in Seymour, Indiana, from 1995 to 1997.

DR. STEPHAN REECE

Principal

Stephan Reece is the codirector of the Applied Research Institute at Ball State University and an associate professor at the Center for Information and Communication Sciences, also at Ball State University. He was the owner of Communications and Digital Services, Inc., for ten years and engineered all system installations, data networks, and peripheral equipment (T-1, E&M, DID, voice processing, call sequencers, call accounting systems, CLID, ACDs, Centrex, ISDN services and products).

JEFFREY LEHM

Director of Database Development and Technology

Jeff Lehm, as owner of Valcour Computer Group, Inc., constructed data management systems for government agencies and entities such as the Indiana Department of Workforce Development, and associations such as the National Free Flight Association. He is the Computer Information Systems regional program chair for Ivy Tech State College in Seymour, Indiana, and has extensive knowledge in database research and technology as it applies to the Internet. Lehm played an instrumental role in the development of the E-commerce Certification Program at Ivy Tech State College.

MICHAEL HUNT

Chief Information Officer

Michael Hunt is a 1995 graduate of Ball State University's Entrepreneurship and Small Business Management program. In addition, Hunt recently completed his master's degree in information and communication sciences at the Center for Information and Communication Sciences at Ball State University. Hunt contributed to the Network Integration Center (NIC), the Ball-Foster Unified Messaging Team, and the VPN Forum project. From 1995 to 1997, Hunt wrote the business plan and helped start Escapades, Inc., a family entertainment center in Marion, Indiana. After leaving Escapades in 1997, he worked at Knapp Supply Co., Inc., as the network administrator and purchasing agent.

JONATHAN LESTER

Director of Communications

Jon Lester earned degrees in both advertising and marketing from Ball State University and is currently finishing a master's degree in public relations. As owner and operator of a successful advertising agency, JL Unlimited, Lester built a reputation within the small-to-midsize business market, winning several Addy Awards and Citations of Excellence. Clients include Alltrista; Community Hospitals, Indianapolis; and Community Hospital, Seymour, among others. Realizing the impact that the Internet is having on the advertising industry, Lester established webaxis, LLC—a high-end e-solutions provider—to coexist with his agency. Under his direction, webaxis has achieved several large strides in just under a year—a user window for controlling their e-environment (Executive Dashboard Systems), Web leasing financing, Perpetual Marketing Systems, and more.

TONY BAKER

Director of Franchise Sales and Business Development

Tony Baker was the director of marketing for the largest franchise of BD's Mongolian Barbeque restaurants, one of the fastest growing casual dining concepts in America. Baker strengthened and advanced the growth of BD's Mongolian Barbeque while spending less than 2 percent of its marketing budget on conventional advertising mediums. His local, or neighborhood, marketing techniques have brought franchises as much as 20 percent growth in sales in an industry that marvels at anything above 5 percent. Baker has designed and executed five record openings for franchisees. He has overseen marketing and operations for this $10 million franchise for three years.

JIM McDUFFY

Director of Special Markets

McDuffy has more than ten years of management experience in various business environments, ranging from the entertainment industry to Web development. He has served as lead developer and consultant for many Web-based projects, including the Web strategy of Connecticut Electric, one of the world's largest suppliers of replacement circuit breakers. McDuffy's leadership enabled the Degerberg Academy in Chicago to grow to a 600 percent student increase during a four-year period, resulting in a national award from the United States Martial Arts Association in 1993. He studied theatre and filmmaking at Indiana University and worked in several production venues in Chicago between 1987 and 1997. McDuffy has also served as a radio personality, hosting a weekly computer talk show called "Computer Digest."

JOHN TAYLOR

Director of Wireless Strategies/Research and Development

John Taylor received his bachelor of arts degree in marketing from Ball State University with a double minor in Japanese and Asian studies. He has demonstrated success in international relationship building, developing promotional material, marketing media, and project management. Taylor also recently completed his graduate degree at the Ball State University Center for Information and Communication Sciences. His project experience includes work with a leading wireless manufacturer and network hardware manufacturers and Web development for industry, nonprofit, and research organizations. His Web development portfolio includes the Applied Research Institute, the Virtual Private Network Forum, the Ohana Foundation, and the Institute for Wireless Innovation, among others.

TROY SIMON

Director of Indianapolis Operations

Troy Simon is a 1997 graduate of Ball State University, where he earned a degree in corporate management and financial institutions as a scholar athlete. In December 1998, he completed his master's of science degree in information and communication sciences at the Center for Information and Communication Sciences, also at Ball State University. Simon then served as a business development representative at Intelliseek, a leading provider in personalized Internet services. He implemented more than 40 partnerships and created an estimated user count of 6 million. He brings knowledge of search technologies and experience in working with start-up companies to CommunityWeb.

Stock Distribution

The following chart details the stockholders in CommunityWeb and their ownership percentage. Five million shares have been authorized, and another 2.3 million shares are being held for future authorizations, issued as follows:

Owner	Number of Shares
Investors	2,300,000
Dan Pale	850,000
Jim Mack	850,000
Associates	600,000
Board of Directors	200,000
Stephan Reece	100,000
Nathan Walker	100,000

Of the 2.3 million investor shares, 1.8 million are being held for future placements and 500,000 are dedicated to the current placement.

It will be the practice of CommunityWeb to allow all employees to participate in stock ownership. Each of the directors has the opportunity to earn 50,000 options each year. The board of directors will determine the execution price on a year-by-year basis. For the year

entrepreneurial CASE ANALYSIS

August 1, 2000 through July 31, 2001, the price will be $10 per share.

Each new full-time employee will receive 1,000 options at the same price provided to the directors.

Each board of directors member will receive 5,000 shares per year of participation.

Partners

BALL STATE UNIVERSITY—CENTER FOR INFORMATION AND COMMUNICATION SCIENCES

Ball State University has contributed extensively to this project. More than 150 students at Ball State University have tested and developed concepts to further the scopes of the CommunityWeb Web site. Ball State also has elected to use CommunityWeb in a senior-level public relations curriculum. Six students initially were assigned to CommunityWeb to help in micro and macro development of the company. Their emphasis was in creating partnerships with local nonprofit and government organizations, as well as national firms. CommunityWeb has access to more than 150 undergraduate and graduate students from the Applied Research Institute Laboratory at Ball State University's Center for Information and Communication Sciences for research, testing, and employee recruitment. Present clients of the center include Ameritech, Cisco, Ericsson, First Consulting Group, Lucent, McDonald's, and Nortel.

IVY TECH STATE COLLEGE—COMPUTER SCIENCE LABORATORY

Ivy Tech State College has created an entire curriculum for a two-year degree to help provide assistance in development as well as provide CommunityWeb with a long-term employee pool. Ivy Tech students, under the direction of professors and CommunityWeb staff, provide developmental solutions to assure that CommunityWeb is the most technologically advanced local Web portal.

CommunityWeb.com Exclusive Features

GEOGRAPHICALLY AND CATEGORICALLY SEARCHABLE COMMUNITYWEB DIRECTORY

CommunityWeb's valuable directory of locally based Web sites is searchable by state, city, category, and subcategory. Searches by zip code and county are also planned for future search tool revisions. According to research conducted at the Center for Information and Communication Sciences at Ball State University, *no search index of this kind currently exists on the Internet.* Research has shown that the major local search engines today catalog only half of the URLs in existence. This would help to explain why just 6.86 percent of global Web site referrals are through traditional search engines.[3] A poll recently taken by Roper Starch found that 71 percent of all users view their search engine experiences as being very frustrating.[4] CommunityWeb gathers URLs in a unique manner that enables CommunityWeb to gather and catalog more URLs than any other search engine site. This "data-mining" method of gathering URLs also enables CommunityWeb to screen the contents of the Web sites to *avoid any adult-oriented or other objectionable material.* The directory offers unique Web marketing opportunities for the future development of business-to-business and business-to-consumer sales.

LOCAL REWARDS PROGRAM

CommunityWeb has created a unique free membership program to businesses, nonprofit organizations, and individuals that accepts press releases, sports scores, editorials, birth announcements, calendar events, and more. The membership program will allow members to be rewarded with "Local Rewards" points for visiting advertisers' Web sites, interacting with promotions geared at driving traffic to a retailer's Web site and physical storefront location, and submitting content to CommunityWeb. Local Rewards points can then be redeemed in the CommunityWeb Online Prize Catalog to win products, services, merchandise, and more. The technology that powers this membership program will allow for advertising by specific geographic locations and demographic/psychographic groupings with the delivery of targeted banner advertising to a viewer's interest. *This membership program has demonstrated click-through rates of more than 5,000 times the national average.*[5]

COMMUNITYWEB.COM UNIQUE FEATURES

- An events community calendar for the display of event times, locations, and other information specific by location and category classification. End users can customize the calendar to display only those events that they have identified as important to them.

- A News and Sports section featuring national, state, and local content.

- Weather forecasts dynamically generated by CommunityWeb from data supplied by the National Weather Service. Forecasts can be viewed by geographic location and can be delivered daily via e-mail to the end user. The ABC affiliate weatherman for Indianapolis,

Paul Poteet, will provide a human face to the site as the national forecaster on CommunityWeb.com.

- Direct links to local media sites with local radio and TV broadcast listings.

- A Web directory of community-based Web sites searchable by geographic location and keywords. The Web directory consists of the Web site name, categorization and subcategory listing, site description, and a direct link to the site.

Industry Background

Without a doubt, the world has been turned upside down since the Internet became commercialized in the early 1990s. An estimated 57 million people used the Internet in 1997, according to CyberAtlas. Internet usage grew to 200 million in 1999 and is expected to reach more than 300 million by the year 2005, which is approximately 5 percent of the world's population. Internet usage patterns are reported by CyberAtlas every month on their Web site.

A typical Internet user:

- Uses the Internet 19 times per month
- Views 671 pages per month
- Visits 11 unique sites per session
- Views an average of 36 pages per session

According to the Census Bureau, 80 percent of the people who use the Internet use it for e-mail or to find government, business, health, or education information. The next most sought-after information is news, weather, and sports. People access the Internet primarily through analog phone lines. The U.S. market for Internet service providers generated $32.5 billion in revenue in 2000, a 37 percent increase over 1999. Twelve million homes accessed the Internet through high-speed services in 2000. High-speed Internet access is expected to surpass dial-up services by the year 2005.[6]

Online Advertising Market

This newer medium has created another avenue for businesses to reach customers. Advertising on the Internet started with simple Web sites and links to a company's site from other Web sites. Online advertisements have become the way to reach customers on the Internet. Contrary to popular myth, online advertising is still growing at a significant rate. Internet advertising increased over 63 percent in the third quarter of 2000 compared to the third quarter of 1999.[7] In addition, online advertising revenues grew more than 53 percent in 2000. Those revenues from online advertisements exceeded $8 billion in 2000 and are expected to reach $32 billion by 2005.[8]

Market Analysis

TARGET MARKET

CommunityWeb is targeting its product to the baby boomer market, aged 35 to 54. This target group provides the best base to grow CommunityWeb into a profitable business. Demographics of this age group include:

- 83% Caucasian, 12% African American
- 50% male/female
- 70% married
- 30% attended or graduated from college
- 34% have an income above $75,000
- 76% work full-time
- more than 30% are in professional and/or managerial positions

Internet usage:

- 66% have Internet access at home and/or work
- 15% use the Internet on a daily basis
- 9% use the Internet three to six times per week
- 52% prefer products that offer the latest technology

"Older" Internet users now constitute the fastest growing demographic group in the Internet market. Approximately 20 percent of U.S. Internet users are aged 45 to 64. This same group is on the Internet more often, stays on longer, and visits more sites than their younger counterparts. Baby boomers typically use the Internet to communicate with friends and family as well as to search for health- and lifestyle-related information.

CommunityWeb will reach this target market through key community influences. These influencing individuals include nonprofit organization leaders and constituents, public opinion leaders, and community coordinators (franchisees). CommunityWeb has developed an aggressive grassroots marketing plan that will drive membership through localized community influences. CommunityWeb's presence in each community will show these community leaders how their organizations and communities can benefit from CommunityWeb.com.[9]

MARKET POSITION

According to Media Metrix, baby boomers and seniors are the fastest growing section of the online population. Last year, this demographic grew by 18.4 percent and outpaced the 18- to 24-year-old demographic, which had a 17.5 percent growth rate. The report by Media Metrix also shows that this group stays online longer and views more pages. On average, they access the Internet 6.3 more days per month and stay logged on 235.7 minutes longer. Lifestyle- and health-related sites are the most popular among the baby boomers. CommunityWeb will capture

entrepreneurial CASE ANALYSIS

this market by catering to this demographic group's desire for localized lifestyle information. CommunityWeb is pursuing a franchise model for market penetration. This grassroots effort will help establish the heartbeat in a local community that has been lacking from most Internet Web sites.

COMPETITION

CommunityWeb is positioning itself to be the premier local content provider and largest local search index in the world. Current attempts to localize content and services on the Web are being made by Internet service providers, search engines, media sites, local government, and others.

- Current attempts at providing this content and service have primarily been limited to only major market cities with populations above one million. America Online's Digital City, Yahoo!, Citysearch.com, and many others have maintained a narrow focus with limited community information and no content for small- to medium-size cities and towns.

- The competition for providing Internet services and e-commerce solutions is intense. *CommunityWeb's niche is the "human factor," putting real people in their own communities as a franchise owner.* Whereas most companies depend heavily on costly national advertising and direct mail campaigns, CommunityWeb will launch a grassroots effort that will provide the highest level of customer service available today.

The chart below details the competitive strengths and weaknesses of CommunityWeb's competition.

MARKETING PLAN

- Goal 1—To establish CommunityWeb as the leading supplier of local content and Internet-related services on the Web.

- Goal 2—To maintain and continually grow the world's deepest and most comprehensible index of local, regional, national, and global URLs in existence.

- Goal 3—To create the most extensive database of individuals classified geographically, demographically, and psychographically available on the Web.

BRAND EVALUATION

CommunityWeb is the first company on the Internet to compile all of the necessary tools that enable users to stay in touch with their local environment in such an in-depth manner. CommunityWeb makes all of these tools available in an easy-to-understand Web portal specifically designed to provide local content and services to individual communities.

BRAND AWARENESS

CommunityWeb strives to be the decisive winner in providing a public forum and information source for specific communities and/or geographic regions. The Web site strives to relate reliable data and provide a place for community interaction on issues that are most important to individual families. "Community for You" will instantly be associated with family-friendly content and user-friendly navigation. "The community portal on the Web" is the branding stance CommunityWeb will take. The company is a step ahead of its competition because of the focus on depth of information in conjunction with breadth of local information, interaction, and community services. Whereas others try to do a little of everything, CommunityWeb focuses on providing the most comprehensive source of content that is user perpetuated.

	CommunityWeb	OneMain	MyCity	DigitalCity	Yahoo!
Local Calendar	√				
Local News	√	√		√	
Local Sports	√			√	
Movie Times	√	√	√	√	√
Dining	√	√	√		
Maps	√	√	√	√	√
Local Advertisement	√			√	
Reward System	√	√			
Personalization	√	√	√	√	√

CUSTOMER PROMISE

"We strive to be your one stop comprehensive resource for providing insight into your local environment and in doing so, never creating a disappointing experience."

CONSUMER MARKET

In terms of target markets, CommunityWeb will focus its efforts on those markets it believes not only will benefit greatly from its technology but also will be the most receptive to its products and services, notably:

- Educational sector
- Corporate sector
- Small business sector
- Nonprofit sector
- Government

CommunityWeb market share will be achieved through:

- Grassroots efforts with the local franchisees
- Volunteers within each community helping the grassroots effort to take hold
- Direct competition in the marketplace
- Affiliations with other companies with dominant positions in their fields
- High-profile, local, regional, and national marketing and advertising campaigns

Technology Plan

CommunityWeb has developed and continues to further develop a dynamic site, which requires expertise from several different technology sectors. CommunityWeb has accomplished this mission by using its own talented employees and by contracting for services from Joseph A. Graves and Associates (JGA). Michael Hunt has led this team through the development phases and will continue to lead this team through continuous improvement phases. JGA has provided project management and programming expertise on different components of the Web site. Jeff Lehm has provided the databases expertise. A commercially viable product was released on January 28, 2001. This product is continuing to be built and improved.

- CommunityWeb will populate the directory database with more than one million URLs representing a broad range of community-based Web sites across the nation by April 1, 2001. This index will be the most comprehensive of its kind when compared to the Open Directory Project (approximately 300,000 URLs as of January 31, 2001) at www.dmoz.org. To accomplish this, CommunityWeb hired more than 100 full-time employees to harvest this data. A custom application was written to aid these data miners to ensure the quality and quantity of the information collected.

- The 100 full-time employees will be responsible for maintaining and adding new URLs after the initial population of the database has occurred. They will also be responsible for screening content that is submitted to our community pages.

The design, testing, and implementation of this Web site took place in approximately 12 weeks, starting October 17, 2000.

Financial Segment

ONLINE ADVERTISING—PER USER REVENUE

A typical Internet user accesses the Internet an average of 19 times per month, visits 17 unique sites per month, and views an average of 36 pages per session.[10] CommunityWeb has projected that a user of the site will visit it 15 times per month and view 6 pages on each of the 11 community sections (2 on the *CommunityWeb Directory*) per month. CommunityWeb has designed a Web site that has the capability to show a user five online advertisements per page. Each ad "impression" will result in an average of 3 cents of revenue. The result, coupled with one page of national advertising, is $15.60 in revenue from each member from online advertising. CommunityWeb has the ability to dynamically display advertising by geographic regions and in targeted categories of information. This will allow advertising customers to target not only a specific demographic but also a specific geographic region as small as a zip code. CommunityWeb has used these numbers to generate all of its monthly revenue projections.

AT&T INTERNET SERVICES

Dial-up access will continue to be the main method of accessing the Internet during the next few years. High-speed access subscription is increasing and is expected to take over the dial-up access market by the year 2005.[11] CommunityWeb is currently developing a high-speed Internet access program with AT&T. The alliance with AT&T will provide CommunityWeb with the ability to offer both dial-up access (short-term) and high-speed connectivity solutions (long-term) to the Internet. Franchisees will be able to sell dial-up access to users at $18.95 per month, which costs CommunityWeb $13.95 per month. CommunityWeb will have the luxury of a constant one-month cash float from revenues of this service through AT&T. CommunityWeb has projected that 5 percent of its members, in addition to an undetermined amount of non-members, will use CommunityWeb for Internet access.

INFOSPACE.COM ADVERTISING REVENUES

Although CommunityWeb will outsource the InfoSpace content for a $5,000 monthly fee, CommunityWeb expects to recover and exceed this cost with advertising

entrepreneurial CASE ANALYSIS

revenue gains once a member navigates the InfoSpace content through CommunityWeb.com. CommunityWeb will receive 35 percent of the banner advertising revenues on the co-branded pages once a unique visitor per day threshold of 10,000 is met.

FRANCHISE SALES AND FEES

Revenue from franchising is generated in two ways: (1) through a one-time fee for the sale of franchises, and (2) through a continuous revenue stream from fees charged to the franchise owner on a monthly basis. The average starting sale price for a franchise will be $35,000 per 100,000 capita. This price will increase as membership numbers are established in given areas. In other words, a market with an established membership will result in a larger investment for a potential franchisee. This is because CommunityWeb has already increased the value and potential of the market by providing an established membership, thus providing revenue existing streams to the franchisee. The sale of franchises will provide a great deal of revenue during the infancy and growth stage of the company. Each franchisee will also pay 12.5 percent of revenues as a royalty fee to CommunityWeb.

QUAD ENTERTAINMENT

Everyone who stays in a hotel or resort that is Hi-5 Set Top Box equipped will receive a free membership to CommunityWeb.com. Of the free memberships provided, CommunityWeb expects that 5 percent will continue to use CommunityWeb's Web site when they return home. The hotel and resort industry experiences a 67.5 percent utilization of the rooms available, and the average stay is 2.75 days. Given that there will be 40,000 rooms available, 27,000 will be occupied during a one-month period. Each of those rooms will accommodate 11 distinct visitors (30 days/2.75), resulting in 297,000 visitors and free memberships.[12] Five percent of those visitors, or 14,850, will continue to use CommunityWeb.com upon their return home. Revenue models for Internet access, the membership program, and normal Web site usage will apply to these end users as well. Revenue projections for the first month (starting in August 2001) are as follows:

Internet Access = $3,712 ($5.00 × 14,850 × 5%)

Online Advertising = $220,522 ($14.85 × 14,850)

Memberships will increase exponentially after the first month. Quad will continue to add boxes each month, and each box in place will provide CommunityWeb with two additional members per month.

LICENSING OF THE COMMUNITYWEB DIRECTORY

Another revenue opportunity has recently surfaced for CommunityWeb: CommunityWeb has taken offers to lease its database of categorized URLs. Through research and its contact with the CEO of MyCoupons.com, Randy Conrad, CommunityWeb has learned that there are more than 7,500 Web sites that would be willing to pay an average of more than $500 per month to lease the *CommunityWeb Directory* (as it exists today) in a co-branded environment. The directory is currently populated with more than 400,000 URLs—this number and the marketable value of the directory stand to increase drastically due to relationships that CommunityWeb has developed with NUOS and ListGuy. CommunityWeb is in the process of partnering with the two to further develop and market its database of URLs. ListGuy specializes in business mailing lists, has a database with more than 4 million URLs, and wishes to be the marketing and brokering arm of the *CommunityWeb Directory*. NUOS was started by two Harvard professors and has been very involved in the creation and maintenance of Dunn and Bradstreet's online database. They have more than 6 million URLs, which can be loaded into CommunityWeb's database. NUOS and ListGuy see value in merging the databases while utilizing CommunityWeb's expertise and search tool. Commission levels are still in negotiation, but CommunityWeb expects to retain 60 percent of the profits from this venture. (See the financial projection highlights that follows.)

Financial Projection Highlights (Corporate)

$ Millions	Year 1	Year 2	Year 3
Revenues	2.22	30.83	182.15
Net Income	(.41)	19.08	148.64
Cash Flow	2.87	19.08	148.64

NOTE: Net Income and Cash totals merely represent earning potential, as the majority of the positive cash flow and net profit earned will be utilized to further market the CommunityWeb name and product. Year 1 cash flow of $2.87 million includes $3.38 million in investment capital.

MILESTONE SCHEDULE

Goal: 10 MSAs, 100 Franchises

CommunityWeb believes that the Midwest is the best market to penetrate using our "warm marketing" approach. We will use marketing dollars and the loyalty of the Midwest to attack the west and east coasts.

Franchises Rollout—Year 1:

- Phase 1: 12 franchises by March 31, 2001
- Phase 2: 28 franchises by June 31, 2001

- Phase 3: 30 franchises by September 31, 2001
- Phase 4: 30 franchises by December 31, 2001

First-Year Franchise Rollout by Region:

- 40 franchises in Indiana, Illinois, and Michigan (Midwest)
- 20 franchises in California
- 20 franchises on East Coast

MSA Phase 1:

- Indianapolis—currently in operation
- Detroit—currently in operation
- Cleveland—currently in operation
- Louisville—April 1, 2001

CommunityWeb knows that a large part of the online community in the United States is located in the state of California. CommunityWeb's plan is to develop the three largest MSAs in California to capture this market early in our development. Silicon Valley is the cradle of many technology companies. This region's ability to duplicate CommunityWeb's concept and develop its own version is the primary reason California is in the second phase of the rollout. California also has 10 percent of the total population of the United States within its borders. CommunityWeb's marketing plans will reach more users more cost-effectively in this highly populated state. CommunityWeb will focus its marketing efforts on the MSAs. The marketing mediums in these MSAs are expected to bleed into the rest of the state.

MSA Phase 2:

- Los Angeles—April 1, 2001
- San Diego—March 1, 2001
- San Francisco—May 1, 2001

MSA Phase 3:

- New York—June 1, 2001
- Washington—July 1, 2001
- Philadelphia—August 1, 2001
- Boston—September 1, 2001

MSA Phase 4:

- Dallas—November 1, 2001
- Houston—December 1, 2001
- San Antonio—January 1, 2002

Questions

1. Should CommunityWeb utilize Wall Street Venture Capital as its primary funding source? If not, why, and what should the firm's next step be?
2. Assess the company's burn rate (cash expenditure without any notable cash inflow) and financial outlook.
3. What are some critical mistakes made by CommunityWeb?
4. Are there any ethical and/or legal concerns in this case?
5. What were some of the major reasons that CommunityWeb was having problems taking its business model to market?
6. What were some of the reasons that CommunityWeb was having trouble obtaining financing?
7. Evaluate the CommunityWeb business plan as an effective tool for raising capital.

Notes

1. See the "CommunityWeb.com Exclusive Features" section.
2. AT&T promotional literature.
3. "Banners Effective Even When People Don't Click," *Media* (January 2001): 7.
4. http://www.nua.com/surveys/.
5. Based on Media Rewards, LLC, and CommunityWeb research and beta testing.
6. http://www.clickz.com/stats/.
7. "Search Engines Refer Just 7% of Traffic," *Media* (January 2001): 6.
8. www.clickz.com/stats/.
9. EchoPoint Media Research—MRI Data.
10. http://www.clickz.com/stats/.
11. http://www.clickz.com/stats/.
12. Hargiss Communication Business Plan.

entrepreneurial
CASE ANALYSIS

ElectroChem, Inc.: Energy for a Clean Planet

Introduction

In January 2002, Radha Jalan sat in her office in Woburn, Massachusetts, reflecting on the latest news about global oil prices. She shivered slightly as she looked up from her newspaper to gaze out the window at snow-filled streets and ice-covered trees and utility lines. That winter, the northeastern United States was hit hard with record-breaking snowfalls. After shortages of oil and natural gas through the fall, energy prices escalated further, with crude oil approaching $30 per barrel. Moreover, OPEC announced its plans to *reduce* petroleum production. Normally taciturn Yankees complained out loud about high oil prices at church suppers and high school basketball games. Across the country, California was nearly in a state of emergency as its power grid proved to be woefully inadequate for the energy demand, and sporadic blackouts created economic losses in the billions.

Since taking over the helm of ElectroChem, Inc. in 1992, after her husband's abrupt and tragic death, Radha felt that the prospects for fuel cell development and commercial use had become increasingly bright. Indeed, news headlines about escalating energy costs provided opportunities for producers of alternative energy sources such as fuel cells, photovoltaic, solar, and wind. In spite of that, however, the last ten years had not been easy. Although ElectroChem had revenues of $400,000 in 1991, the company had not yet achieved profitability. Radha's leadership after the death of her husband led to a turnaround that positioned ElectroChem as a small but important player in fuel cell research and manufacturing—one that generated a profit for four consecutive years, from 1996 to 1999, and achieved more than $2 million in revenues by the year 2001.

Nevertheless, both 2000 and 2001 proved to be difficult years, resulting in losses once again. Cash flow continued to be a problem, and Radha struggled to find sources of capital that would allow her to fund ongoing operations as well as further growth. What would the first decade of the twenty-first century bring as fuel cell technology became more widely understood and, hopefully, more commercially viable? If the past was any indication of the future, ElectroChem might survive—the question for Radha at this point was "how?"

THE FUEL CELL INDUSTRY

In 1839, a Welsh physicist named Sir William Grove (later considered to be the "Father of the Fuel Cell") developed fuel cell technology while experimenting with electrolysis (the process by which water is divided into hydrogen and oxygen by an electric current). The term *fuel cell* was adopted by Ludwig Mond and Charles Langer, who tried to build the first prototype in 1889. However, it was not until 1959 that British scientist Francis Thomas Bacon and his colleagues produced a five-kilowatt system that powered a welding machine. Shortly thereafter, Harry Karl Shrig of Allis-Chalmers Manufacturing demonstrated a 20-horsepower fuel cell-powered tractor.[1] The U.S. National Aeronautics and Space Administration (NASA) became interested and provided research grants to develop a compact generator for space flights. Since then, fuel cell technology has been used as a reliable source of electric power and water for Apollo and other space shuttle missions.

Unlike a battery, a fuel cell never needs to be recharged. Using hydrogen and oxygen or hydrogen and air, an electrolyte sandwiched between two electrodes causes an electrochemical reaction that produces electricity, water, and heat (see Exhibit 1). A fuel cell generates electricity when hydrogen enters the negatively charged electrode (anode) where a catalyst separates the gas into H+ ions (individual protons) and electrons. The protons are drawn through a membrane into the positively charged electrode (cathode). At the same time, the electrons pass through a wire on the anode to the device that the fuel cell is being used to power and back to the cathode to complete the circuit. When the electrons and protons reach the cathode, they bond back together—along with oxygen (O_2) gas—to create water. A major advantage of fuel cells is that they use no hazardous materials and represent a renewable and nonpolluting energy source. Fuel cells generate electricity without burning fuel. Furthermore, because they operate on pure hydrogen, they do not generate any oxides of nitrogen or sulfur, major causes of acid rain. The only byproduct of fuel cell operation is water, which can be returned to the ground or atmosphere.

Five major types of fuel cells were distinguished by the type of electrolyte used.[2] These were polymer electrolyte (PEFC) or proton exchange membrane (PEMFC), phosphoric acid (PAFC), molten carbonate (MCFC), solid oxide (SOFC), and alkaline (AFC). The characteristics of each are described in Exhibit 2. PEMFCs were more suitable for portable, small stationary, and automotive applications. Buses and stationary applications were most appropriate for PAFC. MCFC technology was suitable for large-scale stationary applications and was used to power buildings. SOFCs were used for stationary power and automotive applications. AFCs were among the first fuel cells to be developed and

Source: This case was prepared by Frances M. Amatucci at Slippery Rock University and Susan Coleman at the University of Hartford. The case was prepared solely to provide material for discussion and is not intended to illustrate either effective or ineffective handling of managerial situations.

entrepreneurial CASE ANALYSIS

Exhibit	**1**	**How a PEM Fuel Cell Works**

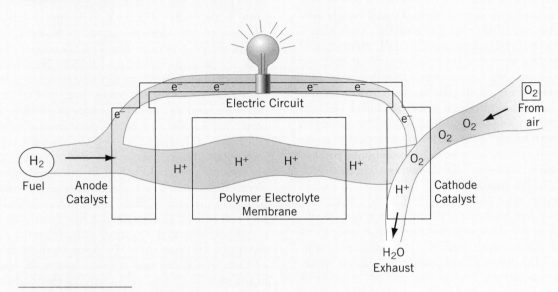

Source: Fuel Cells 2000, http://www.fuelcells.org.

Exhibit	**2**	**Types of Fuel Cells**

Type	Operating Temp.	Present or Potential Applications
Alkaline (AFC)	50–100°C	Used by NASA on space missions; achieve up to 70% efficiency. Costly for commercial applications. Possible uses in land vehicles and submarines.
Proton Exchange Membrane (PEMFC)	50–100°C	Relatively low temperatures with high power density. Great potential for light duty vehicles (such as automobiles), for buildings, and for smaller applications.
Phosphoric Acid (PAFC)	200°C	Medium-scale systems. 200 kW units. Commercially available in hospitals, nursing homes, hotels, office buildings, schools, and utility power plants. Generate electricity at more than 40% efficiency.
Molten	600°C	Medium- to large-scale systems; 1–2 MW. Promise high fuel to electricity Carbonate (MCFC) efficiencies. Stationary applications successful in Japan and Italy.
Solid oxide (SOFC)	500–1,000°C	All sizes of systems, 2 kW to multi MW. Least developed technology. Fuel cell efficiency 50–60%. Potential for stationary power or automotive.

Source: Fuel Cells 2000, http://www.fuelcells.org, and U.S. Fuel Cell Council, http://www.usfcc.com.

were used onboard the Apollo space vehicles. Technological innovation was continuous and newer types of fuel cells were introduced, such as the direct methanol fuel cell (DMFC), regenerative fuel cell (RFC), zinc air fuel cell (ZAFC), and protonic ceramic fuel cell (PCFC).

Global demand for fuel cells was projected to be $46 billion by 2011 and could reach $2.6 trillion by 2021. The most important applications for generated electricity through hydrogen and fuel cell technology included: residential, industrial applications, transportation, portable power, and wastewater treatment plants. The stationary market was projected to be $17.9 billion; the portable market was estimated to be $17.6 billion; and the transportation applications market was estimated to be $10.3 billion.[3] Comments supporting this exponential industry growth are as follows:

> Fuel cells are not just the wave of the future; *they are the tsunami of the future* [emphasis added] (Gregory Dolan, former executive director, U.S. Fuel Cell Council).[4]

> I believe fuel cell vehicles will finally end the hundred-year reign of the internal combustion engine as the dominant source of power for personal transportation. It's going to be a winning situation all the way around—consumers will get an efficient power source, communities will get zero emissions, and automakers will get another major business opportunity—a growth opportunity (William C. Ford, Jr., chairman of Ford, International Auto Show, January 2000).[5]

> Fuel cells allow us to disconnect motor vehicle travel from pollution, which is an incredible feat—something that has been 100 years in the making. It allows us to transform transportation for the 21st century. When you consider that the world's automobile population is doubling every 25 years, a fuel cell technology that is clean and efficient is exactly the sort of technology that is required for the 21st century (Jason Mark, Union of Concerned Scientists).[6]

Although forecasts for industry growth remained optimistic, industry incumbents had difficulty generating profits. Fuel cell technology was still in its early stages and was not widely used for commercial purposes. As a result, fuel cells were not produced in sufficient quantity to generate economies of scale. The per-kilowatt cost for fuel cell power plants ranged from $3,000 to $4,500. To be commercially viable, that cost needed to decline to around $1,500 per kilowatt. Most industry participants in the United States survived thanks to grants and contracts from government agencies such as the Department of Defense, the Department of Energy, the Department of Transportation, and NASA.

Although several large companies existed, as shown in Exhibit 3, the industry was fragmented in terms of the numbers of suppliers of components, hydrogen infrastructure, and related services. Moreover, major global initiatives were being developed in Canada, the European Union, Australia, China, and Japan. Competitors in North America included Ballard Power Systems, Fuel Cell Energy, H Power, Plug Power, and ElectroChem, Inc.

Major Competitors

Ballard Power Systems (BPS), headquartered in Vancouver, British Columbia, was among the largest competitors in the fuel cell industry, with a market capitalization of $5.77 billion in 2001. The company was founded in 1979 to develop and commercialize proton exchange membrane (PEM) fuel cells and fuel cell systems. Through strategic alliances, BPS was developing products to be used in transportation, automobiles, and portable markets.[7]

Fuel Cell Energy (FCE), headquartered in Danbury, Connecticut, had a market capitalization of $1.19 billion in 2001. FCE was a developer of molten carbonate fuel cell-based power plants. It had been developing this technology since 1977, with numerous contracts from government agencies such as the Department of Defense, the Defense Advanced Research Projects Agency, and NASA. Department of Energy funding provided 87 percent, 97 percent, and 92 percent of revenues in 1997, 1998, and 1999, respectively.[8]

Plug Power, headquartered in Latham, New York, designed and developed power generation systems using PEM fuel cells for residential applications. The firm—which had a $1.1 billion market capitalization—planned to launch its first product in 2001, with expansion to other market segments by 2003. The company was formed in 1997 as a joint venture between Mechanical Technology, Inc. and Edison Development Corporation. It was involved in a joint venture with GE MicroGen, Inc. to provide 485 systems with local market distribution partners.[9]

H Power was headquartered in Clifton, New Jersey, and had a market capitalization of $377 million in 2001. Its products consisted of PEM fuel cell systems for stationary, portable, and mobile power. H Power intended to be among the first to mass-market both military and commercial applications.[10]

ITC Fuel Cells in South Windsor, Connecticut, was a global leader in fuel cell production and development for commercial, transportation, residential, and space applications. It was a unit of United Technologies Corporation, a *Fortune* 30 company with $25 billion revenues. Toshiba Corporation of Tokyo, Japan, had been an equity owner of ITC since 1985. Because ITC was a subsidiary of United Technologies, Inc., separate data on its performance could not be obtained.[11]

entrepreneurial CASE ANALYSIS

Exhibit	3	Fuel Cell Companies

Acumentrics

Adaptive Materials Inc.

Angstrom Power, Inc.

Ansaldo Fuel Cells SPA (Italy)

Anuvu Fuel Cell Products, Inc.

Aperion Energy Systems

Apollo Energy Systems

Asia Pacific Fuel Cell Technologies, Ltd. (Taiwan)

Astris Energi Inc. (Canada)

Axane Fuel Cell Systems

Ball Aerospace

Ballard Power Systems (Canada)

Ceramic Fuel Cells, Ltd. (Australia)

Cellex Power Products, Inc. (Canada)

CellTech Power

CeresPower (UK)

Clean Fuel Generation

CMR Fuel Cells (UK)

Dais-Analytic (ChevronTexaco)

DAVID Fuel Cell Components (Spain)

Delphi

Distributed Energy Systems

Direct Methanol Fuel Cell Corp.

DTI Energy, Inc.

Dupont

Eco Soul

Ectro-Chem-Technic

ElectroChem, Inc.

ENECO, Ltd.

Ener1

Energy Conversion Devices

Energy Partners, L.C.

Energy Visions, Inc.

Fideris, Inc.

Fuel Cell Energy, Inc.

Fuel Cell Control, Ltd.

Fuel Cell Technologies, Ltd.

GE Power Systems

GEFC

GenCell

General Motors

Giner Electrochemical Systems, LLC

Global Thermoelectric (Canada)

H2 ECOnomy

H2Japan (Japan)

H Power (acquired by Plug Power)

Heliocentris (Germany, Canada)

Hoku Scientific

Honeywell

Hydrogenics

IdaTech

Independent Power Technologies (Russia)

Intelligent Energy (UK)

Ishikawajima-Harima (Japan)

ITM Power, Ltd. (UK)

Johnson Matthey Fuel Cells (UK)

Kainos Energy

Lynntech Industries, Ltd.

Manhattan Scientifics

Masterflex

McDermott Technology, Inc.

MTI MicroFuel Cells, Inc.

Medis Technologies, Inc.

Millennium Cell

Mitsubishi

Morgan Fuel Cell

Motorola

Neah Power Systems, Inc.

Nedstack

Novars GmbH

Nu Element, Inc.

NuVant Systems

Nuvera Fuel Cells

P21 GmbH

Palcan Fuell Cells Ltd.

Plug Power

PolyFuel

Porvair Fuel Cell (UK)

PowerZyme

Proton Energy Systems, Inc.

Quantum Technologies, Inc.

ReliOn

Renew Power

Rolls-Royce Plc

Schatz Energy Research Center

Siemens AG (Germany)

Smart Fuel Cell GmbH (Germany)

Sulzer Hexis Ltd. (Switzerland)

TechSys, Inc.

Tekion Solutions, Inc. (Canada)

Teledyne Energy Systems

Third Orbit Power Systems

T/J Technologies

Toshiba

Umicor

UTC Fuel Cells

Voller Energy

XCELLSIS

Ztek Corporation

Source: Hydrogen and Fuel Cell Investor, http://www.h2fc.com.

ElectroChem, Inc. in Woburn, Massachusetts, started in 1986 as a research and development firm. With sales of more than $2 million in 2001, ElectroChem was a worldwide supplier of fuel cell power systems, fuel cell test equipment, and fuel cell research supplies, and it was a market leader in the fuel cell test station business.[12] Its flagship product, ECcell™, was being developed to provide up to 10 kW of clean energy for portable, remote, and backup applications. (See Exhibit 4 for financial details of the major fuel cell competitors.)

The Role of Government

As noted earlier, government agencies—both domestic and worldwide—have played an important role in the development and commercialization of fuel cell technology.[13] Throughout the 1970s and early 1980s, the U.S. Department of Energy (DOE) ran a program to develop phosphoric acid fuel cell systems. Thanks to these efforts, United Technologies Fuel Cells was able to manufacture and sell PAFCs around the world. By the

---

Exhibit 4   Financial Performance of Major Fuel Cell Companies

	1997	1998	1999	2000	2001
Ballard Power Systems, Inc. (BLDP NASDAQ)					
Net Sales	24.2	25.1	48.9	25.8	36.2
Cost of Goods Sold	22.8	20.4	29.8	34.6	33.4
Gross Profit	1.4	4.7	19.1	(8.8)	2.8
SG and A Expenses	8.5	11	15	10.2	17.8
R&D Expenditures	1.81	36.3	62	50.5	77.2
Total Operating Expenses	27.9	51	80.7	68.2	106.2
Net Income	2	0.8	(74.2)	(53.8)	(92.2)
Fuelcell Energy, Inc. (FCEL NASDAQ)					
Net Sales	24.8	24.3	20	20.7	26.2
Cost of Goods Sold	15.6	14.6	1	17.5	35.2
Gross Profit	9.2	9.7	18.9	3.2	(9.1)
SG and A Expenses	6.1	7	6.6	8.1	9.1
R&D Expenditures	1.3	2.3	13.2	1.9	3.1
Total Operating Expenses	9.5	11	21.4	8.0	12.3
Net Income	0.4	−0.4	−1	(4.5)	(15.4)
H Power Corp[1] (HPOW NASDAQ)					
Net Sales	1	1	3.7	3.6	n/a
Cost of Goods Sold	1.4	1.1	3.5	5.5	n/a
Gross Profit	−0.4	−0.1	0.2	−1.8	n/a
SG and A Expenses	4	3.8	12.6	11.8	n/a
R&D Expenditures	2.5	3.1	5.3	13.5	n/a
Total Operating Expenses	6.5	6.9	18	25.3	n/a
Net Income	−6.2	−6.8	−17	−22.2	n/a
Plug Power Inc. (PLUG NASDAQ)					
Net Sales	1.2	6.5	11	8.4	5.7
Cost of Goods Sold	1.2	8.9	15.5	13.1	11.3
Gross Profit	0	−2.3	−4.5	−4.7	(5.5)
SG and A Expenses	0.6	2.8	9.9	16.2	7.5
R&D Expenditures	5.3	4.6	20.5	70.9	59.3
Total Operating Expenses	6	7.4	30.6	87.4	67.1
Net Income	−5.9	−9.6	−33.5	−86.2	(73.1)

Source: http://www.cbs.marketwatch.com.

[1]Acquired by Plug Power in 2002.

entrepreneurial CASE ANALYSIS

late 1980s, this same program had shifted its emphasis to molten carbonate and solid oxide fuel cell systems.

In 1996, the Department of Defense (DOD) launched a Climate Change Fuel Cell Program that provided grants of $1,000/kilowatt to purchasers of fuel cell power plants. This "buy down" program awarded more than $18.8 million toward the purchase of 94 fuel cell units. The DOD also developed a residential fuel cell demonstration program that involved more than 21 units at 12 different military locations. The Department of Transportation maintained a fuel cell research program for buses, and the Environmental Protection Agency had a program to facilitate the use of fuel cells at landfills and wastewater treatment plants.

In 2000, the U.S. Department of Energy committed $135 million in research funding for projects involving the development of fuel cell, hydrogen, and gasoline engines. During that same year, the DOE formed the Solid State Energy Conversion Alliance (SECA), which comprised commercial developers, universities, national laboratories, and government agencies to develop low-cost, high power density, solid-state fuel cells for a broad range of applications. More recently, in January 2002, the DOE established "FreedomCAR," a cooperative research partnership between the U.S. Council for Automotive Research and the "Big Three" automakers (Ford, General Motors, and Daimler Chrysler), with the goal of advancing the development of fuel cells in vehicles.[14]

Governments around the world were active in promoting fuel cell research and commercialization. In 2002, Iceland declared that it would be the first country to eliminate oil in its economy by 2030 and replace it with hydrogen-fueled vehicles.[15] In Canada, early fuel cell research was conducted by the University of Toronto, the Defense Research Establishment, and the National Research Council. Canadian firms, with government support, had achieved world leadership in the development and commercialization of fuel cell technology.[16] In Japan, the Fuel Cell Commercialization Initiative enabled the Japanese government to increase investment in fuel cell technology by 40 percent, to $280 million in 2003. As a part of that initiative, NEC Corporation developed a fuel cell-powered laptop, which could operate for 40 hours with one refill. The Dalian Institute of Chemical Physics and the Chinese Academy of Sciences (CAS) announced a $12 million program to develop proton exchange membrane (PEM) fuel cell technology. Transportation was considered to be the largest and most important market in China.[17] Finally, the European Commission has supported the development and commercialization of fuel cell technology for more than 30 years. Investment has increased from 8 million euros in the early 1990s to 130 million euros in the Fifth Framework Programme (1999–2002).

Radha Jalan's Background

Radha Jalan was born in Calcutta, India. At the end of World War II, Calcutta was an intellectually driven city on the east coast of India with a very strong industrial base that included the manufacture of jute, chemicals, and textiles. Radha's family was from the Marwari community. Marwari values include being practical, good in business, and thrifty on a daily basis, with occasional lavish celebrations. Marwaris also believed that to work for someone else was undignified. Radha's father was a businessman who had a small, family-owned textile business.

Through a traditional arranged marriage when she was 19, Radha married a 21-year-old chemical engineer named Vinod Jalan. After the marriage, she continued her education and received her master's degree in Hindi Literature from Calcutta University in 1966. In June 1968, she emigrated from India to the United States, where her husband had begun graduate studies at the University of Florida. To pass the time and satisfy her intellectual yearnings, Radha took courses of interest without enrolling in a degree program. After she had completed a number of courses in the education department, the department chair convinced Radha to enroll in a graduate program, which eventually led to a master's degree in education.

The Jalans' first daughter was born in 1972. During that same year, Radha accepted an offer of university funding, in return for a research assistantship, and began her doctoral studies in education. By 1973, she had completed all of the requirements for her doctorate except for the thesis. At that time, Vinod Jalan accepted a position at United Technologies in Connecticut, and the couple relocated again. While working on her thesis in Connecticut, Radha became pregnant with their second child. She returned to Florida to complete her dissertation, and, with the help of her faculty advisor, finished the doctoral program in 1976. Her PhD thesis examined the educational work of Rabindranath Tagore, a Nobel laureate in literature (poetry) whose philosophies were very similar to those of American philosopher and educator John Dewey. In the same year, the Jalans' second daughter was born. Although Radha was a stay-at-home mom for most of the time, she did some consulting for universities in Connecticut and developed a course on global multicultural education. She believed that she would eventually pursue an academic career when her children were older.

In 1979, the couple moved to Massachusetts, where Vinod Jalan took a position with a small technology firm. As time passed, Vinod became well known in the field and was the inventor of several patents. Several years later, in 1986, he founded his own company, ElectroChem, Inc., to provide leading-edge research and development in fuel cell technology. By this time, after several moves to further her husband's career, Radha had given up on having a career of her own and decided to become involved in community activities. Vinod was increasingly preoccupied with the new firm, and she felt that she needed to develop friendships beyond the home, as well as an outlet for her intellectual curiosity and energy. She already had developed friendships in the local Indian community. At the same time, Radha joined organizations involved with education, the fine arts, and human rights. She assumed leadership positions as president of the local chapter of the American Association for University Women and of the Concord-Carlisle Human Rights Council. She occasionally gave seminars and presentations on multicultural education and participated in activities promoting U.S./Indian cultural exchange.

When Vinod Jalan was diagnosed with a heart condition in 1989, the couple decided that, to relieve some of his stress, Radha would become more involved with ElectroChem's operations. Although the Jalans had been having marital difficulties for some time, Radha was deeply concerned about Vinod's condition and wanted to support him in every way possible. Unfortunately, the number and intensity of their conflicts increased as Radha began spending more time in the office. Stresses associated with the business and with the marriage took a toll on both of the Jalans until one morning in February 1992, when Vinod suffered a fatal heart attack.

RADHA AS PRESIDENT OF ELECTROCHEM, INC.

While she was away at a one-day, out-of-state conference, Radha learned of her husband's death. She went home immediately to attend to the funeral preparations. The following day, she went to ElectroChem and met individually with each employee to discuss the company's future. At that time, ElectroChem employed a secretary, three full-time engineers, and several part-time contract engineers, as well as a few consultants on contract. Because it was payday, Radha arranged for all employees to receive their regular paychecks. During a telephone conversation before Vinod's funeral, the company's accountant presented two options: sell ElectroChem to another fuel cell company, or close it. When Radha realized that the buyer he had in mind was another client, she became suspicious. Obviously, he had not presented a third option: that she take over leadership of the firm. She remembered that the accountant had commented to her once, "A person is worth only what he makes." Thus, she believed that—even though she had a PhD—as a nonworking mother she had little credibility with him.

Of course, there were good reasons to doubt that Radha could lead ElectroChem to profitability. She knew little about the technical aspects of the business, had no business or financial training, and the financial condition of the company was precarious at best. Like most firms in the industry, ElectroChem was heavily dependent on government contracts and grants, and several of those were coming to an end. Beyond that, Vinod had used a home equity loan and credit card debt as sources of financing and had run up high balances. Radha also discovered three months' unpaid bills from suppliers. Despite the odds, Radha decided to become president of ElectroChem. She was intrigued by the possibility of participating in the early stages of a growth industry, and she looked forward to the intellectual stimulation and challenge. She also thought that ElectroChem would serve as a good outlet for her high energy and drive to achieve. She told herself, "I'll give it two years and see what happens."

The Turnaround Years

In 1992, immediately after she assumed leadership of ElectroChem, the most pressing problems Radha faced were cash-flow deficits and short-term debt obligations. Although sales in 1991 were more than $400,000, the firm was not profitable. She used the proceeds of her husband's life insurance to fund the payroll for the next two weeks. She wrote letters to ElectroChem's vendors explaining her husband's death and requesting extensions on their payment deadlines. Shortly thereafter, two of ElectroChem's primary engineers resigned. One left because the Phase II Small Business Innovation Research (SBIR) government grant on which he was supposed to be working was not funded following the death of Vinod, the principal investigator. The second engineer joined a recycling technology firm that subsequently filed for Chapter 11. Although Radha regretted losing two valuable employees, their departures reduced overhead and enabled her to pay down supplier credit to a more reasonable level.

As ElectroChem's existing grants expired, however, Radha became increasingly concerned about generating further revenues. ElectroChem had been largely supported by government grants—in particular, from the SBIR Program, which funded high-risk projects in early developmental stages before companies could attract venture capital.[18] A round of SBIR proposals was due in the summer of 1992, and Radha and the remaining ElectroChem staff wrote as many as possible. Radha believed that, if they could get just one grant based on their existing capabilities, the company would gain some financial relief and credibility. Strategically, Radha wanted to shift the company's focus from research and development toward commercial fuel cell applications, believing that it would be more difficult to obtain funding for basic research. Just when the situation looked its worst,

entrepreneurial CASE ANALYSIS

ElectroChem received a six-month government research grant with the possibility of continuation for two years, and Radha was able to hire an engineering graduate student from the Massachusetts Institute of Technology.

Prior to his death, Vinod Jalan had been discussing ElectroChem's portable fuel-cell-in-a-suitcase with the DOE. In March, three weeks after the funeral, Radha requested a meeting with NASA to discuss her plans regarding the future of the company. She knew little about the company's research, so she recorded the titles of different projects on a piece of paper. She was honest in admitting that she didn't know what the titles meant, but perhaps NASA would! If she was trying to build credibility, Radha figured she had to be honest—there was no point in pretending that she knew more than she did. She invited three representatives from NASA to meet with her technical team. Marvin Warshay, head of the fuel cell program at NASA's Glenn Research Center, was planning to travel to New England for a wedding the following week and agreed to stop by the office. He spent two to three hours with ElectroChem's three technical people. When he left, he told Radha that although he was impressed with the company's products and patented technologies, he did not have any funding possibilities at the moment. She informed him that she planned to keep the company going, and any assistance he could provide in terms of putting in a good word would be important to ElectroChem's survival.

Shortly afterward, Radha received an order from the DOE for the suitcase fuel cell unit. ElectroChem wanted the order so badly that it based the price of the unit on material cost only and underpriced it at $15,000. Nevertheless, it was a sale to an influential government agency! In November 1992, Radha took the suitcase unit to the national fuel cell meeting, along with flyers and notification of the award from the DOE. Although fuel cell research had existed for years, this was the first time representatives from the DOE had seen an operational portable fuel cell in a small suitcase, and the sale represented a significant marketing success for ElectroChem. The DOE planned to use the small fuel cell unit to market fuel cell technology to Congressional leaders. Radha never knew whether Warshay was involved in the DOE order, but several years later ElectroChem also sold this fuel cell directly to NASA.

Acquiring Capital

By early 1993, ElectroChem was still desperately in need of cash to fund operations, and Radha was having a difficult time covering her family's basic living expenses. The life insurance policy was insufficient to cover finan-

cial obligations such as her home mortgage and auto loans. Beyond that, she had one daughter in college and a second still at home. She described the debt position and the company's growth as follows:

> We were a typical '80s family. The company started in 1986 and in 1987 it started to take off. We borrowed and, to some extent, there was a lack of organization. You know when a small business grows suddenly and the structure is not ready, it can collapse. Then he was diagnosed with his heart problems. So we were stretched to the limits. When I look back, I see that he was borrowing on a very large scale. But, you know, when you are upbeat, those are the risks you take.

Radha was faced with the decision of whether to invest more in the firm, sell it, or close it. Then she remembered that she had promised herself to give it two years. Soon after, ElectroChem received another government contract. Even though the contract would not start for three months, it brought renewed hope, and Radha was able to hire a new full-time technician.

At a luncheon in 1993, a friend introduced Radha to Bill West, a PhD with a background in electronics. West was a serial entrepreneur who had become independently wealthy from previous business investments. He took an interest in ElectroChem and offered assistance without compensation. West believed that he could improve ElectroChem's fuel cell test station business by making it more technically advanced. A fuel cell test station measures and controls key variables, such as reactant flow, water management, and temperature, to accurately gauge fuel cell performance. West's proposal was particularly appealing because test stations were one of the commercial applications in ElectroChem's product portfolio and a potential source of future revenue growth. He convinced Radha that—as a woman in a high-tech industry—the odds were against her if she tried to go it alone, and that he could help further the goals of the company. In the ensuing months, West worked diligently on ElectroChem's behalf and adopted the company as if it were his own.

By 1994, ElectroChem's financial situation had improved, and revenues rose to $588,000. However, West was concerned about the firm's continued dependence on government funding and encouraged Radha to think about obtaining an infusion of cash from the private equity market. When he spoke to his friends about potential investment, they expressed reluctance due to Radha's lack of managerial and technological experience. However, they were willing to invest in ElectroChem if Radha hired a manager with more business and industry experience. Radha reflected about this choice:

I trusted Bill and his judgment. I had read about equity investing for cash infusion and it seemed we were growing at a pace where we needed to do something. Also, I wasn't totally confident about my abilities. I read that this was the right thing to do. In hindsight, I've learned that textbooks are not always correct.

West set out to find such a person and eventually recommended Peter Clinton. Clinton was hired to develop a business plan to raise $500,000 from the informal private equity market, or business angel investors. In his mid-forties, Clinton had an impressive resume and was an easygoing—but savvy—dealmaker with an opportunistic sense of financial gain. Clinton had known West since childhood, and he had a large network of acquaintances developed on the golf course or during long lunches.

The funds were earmarked for developing ElectroChem's fuel cell test station business. Research laboratories were the primary target market for this product, but there were also potential commercial opportunities in the alternative energy market. Although ElectroChem was very small in comparison to other industry competitors, it had an advantage in its leadership in the development of fuel cell test stations. Clinton had started several of his own companies in the past and was brought on as chief operating officer (COO). He requested a $150,000 salary and a generous benefits package. Although Radha objected to the large sum, West convinced her to let Clinton write the business plan and to allow potential investors to review both the plan and his proposed compensation. Radha acceded to this request, and in August 1994, Clinton started working at ElectroChem on contract at $5,000 per month until funding could be secured to hire him full-time with a complete compensation package.

As the months passed, Radha thought Clinton was taking too long to develop the business plan. Moreover, he presented drafts to her that seemed incomplete and grammatically incorrect. She sensed that he really didn't care about her comments, because he thought he knew more about the business than she did. Even though she was having problems with Clinton, West supported him and called him a "business genius." The business plan was completed in January 1995, but it raised only $200,000. The four angel investors were friends of West who were willing to participate primarily because of Clinton's involvement. The deal was negotiated at $50,000 each, of which $30,000 would go toward debt and $20,000 toward equity. A vesting agreement stated that Clinton would receive stock, beginning with 4,103 shares on July 1, 1995. One year later, he would receive another 4,100 shares, and every six months he would receive additional stock. The last stock issue of 2,730 shares on July 1, 1997, would give him ownership of more than 10 percent of the company—an amount nearly equal to that of Bill West. Despite warnings from Radha's lawyer about the downside risks of the term sheet, she knew that ElectroChem needed the capital and trusted West enough to proceed with the deal.

The Struggle for Control

In the weeks following the completion of the business plan, problems between Radha and Clinton increased. In addition to the business plan, Clinton was responsible for creating a brand image for ElectroChem's products. Therefore, Radha requested that he develop a product catalog for distribution at a trade show in Japan that she planned to attend. Clinton never completed this project, and she had to create the catalog the evening before her departure. In March 1995, Radha wrote a memo to both Clinton and West expressing her disappointment with Clinton's performance. At the same time, Clinton was pushing to accelerate his vesting schedule and reduce the one-year period to six months. Radha was increasingly concerned about the test station business, because a great deal of investment was being made without any progress. She imposed a deadline and stated that she wanted the product ready by the end of the year.

As COO, Clinton also was charged with developing a new financial accounting system for the company. Although ElectroChem had received $200,000 in response to the business plan, the financial accounting system still was not in place. Moreover, Clinton kept two sets of financial statements with different numbers, and it was difficult to determine exactly how financial resources were being utilized. Radha began to doubt the financial information that Clinton provided in response to her requests. As her concerns increased, she realized that she had several options: 1) retain Clinton and try to make the best of it, 2) spin off the test station business, 3) buy out the investors and fire Clinton, or 4) declare bankruptcy. In early May, she proposed that the test station business become a separate division to improve accountability for both revenues and costs. She quickly saw a change in Clinton's behavior, in that he assumed he would take control of the spin-off. He requested the customer list and seemed to become aggressive toward her. It was obvious that the investors wanted the test station business and that her control and equity would be negligible at best. With the impending vesting date approaching, Radha decided that this arrangement was not going to work and spoke to West about dismissing Clinton.

West cautioned Radha that she could not dismiss Clinton, as he was the basis for investor confidence in ElectroChem. Radha scheduled a meeting with Howard Weatherhead, the lead investor of the angel alliance. The meeting was a disaster. Radha later said that no one had ever made her feel so humiliated or inferior. Weatherhead gave her an ultimatum:

You know $50,000 is nothing for me—I don't care about that amount of money, but I can put you

entrepreneurial CASE ANALYSIS

out in the streets! Either you split the company and give us the test station business or, since we make the majority, we will force you to declare bankruptcy. That's your option.

When a friend heard of Radha's dilemma, he stated, "They are all wolves around you! So *you* need wolves! Who are the people you know?" With his help, Radha developed a cadre of supporters through her connections with the Massachusetts Technology Development Corporation,[19] the Babson College Entrepreneurial Management Program, and the Small Business Association of New England (SBANE). During this difficult time, Radha also was encouraged by friends in the Indian community who rallied to support her and her daughters, who regarded Radha as a role model. They urged her to fight back and not to allow the company to be lost after so much hard work.

Radha demanded Clinton's resignation in June 1995. He left ElectroChem, and West resigned immediately afterward. Radha filled the two vacant board seats, promptly created a new board of directors, and scheduled an emergency meeting. ElectroChem's new board tried unsuccessfully to negotiate a settlement with the investors. In August 1995, the investors sued the company and Radha for $200,000, claiming that she had knowingly, willfully, and intentionally misrepresented facts about the company to induce their investment.

Radha Takes Control

At the end of 1995, ElectroChem was negotiating with a utility company for a large contract that involved developing a fuel cell. This time, Radha was much smarter about contract negotiation and made sure that ElectroChem was protected in case the utility changed its mind about the structure of the relationship. ElectroChem was awarded $1 million over a two-year period in a licensing and technology development agreement. The contract was a milestone, and in 1996 ElectroChem generated its first annual profit. A year later, ElectroChem won a very competitive grant from the DOE to develop low-cost plates for fuel cells. Although the two-year contract called for 25 percent cost sharing and would not be profitable, it put ElectroChem in a league with firms like 3M and Allied Signal that also received such contracts. In 1997, ElectroChem's net income nearly doubled to $147,000 on $1.3 million in revenues. The DOE was so impressed with ElectroChem's performance that the agency extended the contract for a second term.

The investors' suit was finally resolved in June 1996. Per the terms of the agreement, ElectroChem and Radha paid the plaintiffs $200,000, plus an additional $30,000 to Bill West, a third-party defendant in the suit. Repayment also included accrued interest over seven years, through 2002.[20] Radha negotiated a prepayment discount whereby the plaintiffs would settle for only the debt (i.e., $30,000 of the $50,000 for each investor) if the payment was received within seven years. Although it was a considerable challenge, by the end of 1998 Radha had prepaid the four angel investors the debt portion of their investment.

Bill West retained his shares until 1999, when he angrily requested a buyout at a stockholders' meeting. In determining the value of his stock, he calculated the equity portion of his friends' investment, which was not paid due to the prepayment discount *plus* accrued interest to 1999. He requested five separate checks to be issued to the investors and stated that his terms were nonnegotiable. Although Radha's accountant reminded her that these funds could be used more effectively by reinvesting them in the company, she felt betrayed by West, whom she had trusted so much in the beginning. She also felt paranoid, thinking—if she did not meet these demands—"What would they ask for next?" Thus, rather than objecting to West's demands or arranging a payoff that extended over a long period of time, Radha paid another $103,000 to settle the matter.

Despite the company's recent successes, by 1999 Radha was worried about future revenue growth because there were no more government contracts in ElectroChem's pipeline. Moreover, she wanted to decrease dependence on government research and development grants to establish ElectroChem more firmly in the commercial market. Cash flow was always problematic and, although Radha had applied for a line of credit at several banks, applications were consistently rejected despite ElectroChem's profitability and revenue growth. Given the unclear explanations she received, over time she began to suspect that there was more to these denials, and that being a female minority business owner in a high-tech field was hurting her ability to obtain critical financial resources. Still, Radha never downplayed her ethnicity and frequently wore her sari, a traditional garment of Hindu women, to business meetings and venture capital presentations. When she shared her concerns with a banker she met at a networking event, he confirmed, "They're just not giving you the whole story!" Given her persistence and drive, Radha continued to apply for a line of credit to ease her cash-flow worries, while also considering other alternatives for acquiring resources.

Although ElectroChem experienced a setback in the fuel cell test station business due to the business angel debacle, it was still committed to that market. In fact, an alliance with another test station company that also created the system-related software assisted ElectroChem in resolving many of its software problems. In 1998, ElectroChem's largest competitor in the test station business was Texas-based Global Technologies, Inc. The chairman and founder, George Landau, was a world-renowned electrochemist who had been a professional colleague of Vinod Jalan. Learning that Landau was ready to retire and would consider selling the company, Radha initiated discussions about a possible merger. Global Technologies was somewhat larger than ElectroChem and, more importantly, had a number of commercial customers. Its product line overlapped with ElectroChem's, so a merger would enable Radha to eliminate a rival and increase market share in some key portions of the test station market.

Landau was well established and respected in the industry and, by extension, so was his company. Landau liked and admired Radha, and had mentored her through some of ElectroChem's difficult periods. He felt that Radha's courage and persistence in the face of seemingly insurmountable odds would help her to be one of the survivors in the emerging fuel cell industry. One morning over breakfast—when Landau and his wife were guests at Radha's home—the merger deal was negotiated and finalized. It was a noncash deal, and Landau's company would remain intact; however, he would receive 10 percent on future test station sales until the selling price was reached. The merger surprised the industry and signaled ElectroChem's commitment to establishing a strong market presence. One rival commented to Radha, "It's very interesting that you acquired Global Technologies. I would have thought that it would be the other way around."

In 1999, Radha began to organize ElectroChem to be a serious competitor in the commercial market and, once again, started working on a business plan. Moving away from government contract work, ElectroChem's product line included PEMFCs and PAFCs as well as fuel cell systems, models, test stations, and fuel cell supplies and components. She hired a chief technology officer, sales manager, and someone to oversee business development. The management team, including the board of directors, showed decades of experience in fuel cell technology by the end of 2001 (see Exhibit 5).

Into the New Millennium

In anticipation of competing more vigorously in the commercial market, Radha was concerned about ElectroChem's image and low profile. It would be very difficult for her to compete with her larger rivals in terms of marketing dollars spent. As an alternative, building the organization and getting recognition for its technological strengths and potential was a priority. She strongly believed that, despite fuel cell technology's long-term prospects in the automotive industry, there were more immediate commercial applications—especially in the small stationary market—that also were appropriate for PEM fuel cells. Toward this end, ElectroChem began working on the commercialization of the ECcell, a first-to-market fuel cell unit designed for energy storage and backup power for the average household.

Because the emerging digital economy needed a dependable supply of power, Radha resolved to develop strategic alliances with customers, distributors, and vendors competing in electronic commerce, computing, and communications.[21] Sensing that potential partners might be reluctant to give credibility to a small, woman-owned company, Radha decided to install a few of ElectroChem's better fuel cell units at these companies' sites as a way to raise the firm's profile. Based upon these preliminary relationships, she would then be in a better position to create formal strategic alliances.

In addition to providing commercial products and services for the digital economy, Radha wanted to establish ElectroChem in the long term as a supplier of power that would contribute to "sustainable development" of the world economy. With sustainable development, natural resources are not depleted as an economy grows. ElectroChem could provide fuel cells that would be environmentally safe and capable of generating electricity for business, education, and infrastructure demands in developing countries. As a step in this direction, Radha had discussions to establish an ElectroChem subsidiary in India. Several managers from China's largest battery firm also visited ElectroChem to discuss an international joint venture arrangement. However, India and China, with the largest populations in the world, were only two of the many global markets offering opportunities for the commercial application of fuel cells.

Radha continued to develop and use a network of relationships, both to improve the image and reputation of ElectroChem and for support as a female minority CEO in a high-tech industry. She served on various nonprofit boards in education and business, including the Small Business Association of New England and the Mass Energy Consumers Alliance. In 1997, she received the Entrepreneurial Achiever of the Year award from Asian Women in Business (AWIB).[22] She was an executive member of the Emerson Umbrella Community Arts Center, a trustee of Nashoba Brooks School, and a counselor at Saheli: Women to Women. She benefited greatly from the relationships developed through the Commonwealth Institute, an organization that provided peer support for women entrepreneurs, CEOs, and senior corporate executives whose companies were in critical growth stages.

Although 2000 and 2001 were very difficult years and cash flow continued to be a major concern, ElectroChem won a highly competitive $3.5 million contract from NASA in addition to two separate orders for fuel cell test stations. Major customers included NASA and other

entrepreneurial CASE ANALYSIS

CASE ANALYSIS

Exhibit	5	ElectroChem, Inc. Board of Directors and Management Team, 2002

Radha Jalan, PhD, President and Chief Executive Officer. Dr. Jalan was instrumental in the strategic planning that made ElectroChem a significant player in the fuel cell market. Along with her work at ElectroChem, she was chair and trustee of a number of nonprofit community and educational organizations. She held a PhD and master's degree in education from the University of Florida and BA and MA degrees in Hindi literature from Calcutta University.

Alfred B. Campbell, PhD, Vice President, Chief Technology Officer. Dr. Campbell had more than 13 years of experience in fuel cell technology research. He received a PhD in chemical engineering from Texas A&M and was the author of more than 30 technical publications.

Patrick D. Francis, PE, Vice President of Operations. Mr. Francis had more than 20 years of professional experience in energy and planning. He had a bachelor's of science in engineering, a master's of science in industrial engineering, and an MS in administration and policy from Purdue University.

Lester Pine, PhD, Lead Engineer and Research Scientist. He joined ElectroChem's R&D team in 1994 and helped establish quality control in the PEM manufacturing process. He received his PhD in chemical engineering from the University of Akron and was a co-inventor of three patent applications in PEM technologies.

Bruce Marcus, PhD, Senior Scientist and Market Development Specialist. Dr. Marcus had been involved in PEM fuel cell stack assembly, internal humidification, and sealing. He held a PhD in chemistry from Princeton University.

Charles I. Clough, Jr., Member of the Board (2000).[1] Mr. Clough was the chief executive officer of Clough Capital Partners LP, a private investment firm in Boston, Massachusetts. He held a BS in economics from Boston College and an MBA from the University of Chicago.

J. Marvin Reynolds, Member of the Board (1999). Mr. Reynolds was the vice president and cofounder of Congruent International. He had 25 years of experience in international business. He held a BS in engineering physics from Virginia Technical Institute and an MBA from the University of Hartford.

Marvin Warshay, PhD, Member of the Board (2001). Dr. Warshay had a 36-year career at NASA and played an international role in fuel cell and battery power system development. He held a MS and a doctorate in chemical engineering from Illinois Institute of Technology.

S. Srinivasan, PhD, Member of the Board (2000). Dr. Srinivasan was internationally renowned for his contributions to fuel cell, hydrogen energy, and electrochemical research. He had more than 25 years of experience and published more than 150 articles and publications. He held a PhD in physical chemistry from the University of Pennsylvania.

Calvin L. Bushnell, Board of Advisors. For 32 years, Mr. Bushnell managed the fuel cell laboratory at International Fuel Cells and held more than 15 patents in fuel cell technology. He held a MS in mechanical engineering from Rensselaer Polytechnic Institute.

---

[1] The year he joined the board.

governmental agencies, a number of research universities, and U.S. and global companies such as Allied-Signal, DuPont, Exxon, General Motors, and Tokyo Gas. ElectroChem had more than 500 customers around the world, with a revenue base that included more than 50 percent from the commercial market.

In 2002, Radha celebrated her tenth anniversary as president of ElectroChem. In that time, she had decreased the company's large debt, freed herself from the failed angel investor relationship, and once again become the company's sole owner. Both of her daughters had graduated with university degrees. ElectroChem had been profitable for four consecutive years—from 1996 to 1999—and achieved revenues of more than $2 million in 2001. (A ten-year financial summary is provided in Exhibits 6 and 7.) As she took a rare quiet

Exhibit 6 — ElectroChem, Inc. Balance Sheet Summary, 1991–2001

	1991	1992	1993	1994	1995	1996	1997	1998	1999	2000	2001
Current Assets											
Cash	(18,963)	7,594	602	636	30,312	50,121	54,189	15,293	40,288	21,216	22,602
Accounts Receivable	104,523	52,193	21,693	89,360	93,472	111,061	196,427	139,458	182,971	162,605	430,107
Unbilled Costs – Contracts	78,720	123,851	55,114	31,768					31,628		
Inventory	18,056	8,933	14,298	68,991	120,675	129,369	90,321	89,190	98,045	91,603	91,603
Prepaid Expenses				3,565	3,565	3,565	3,565	3,072	1,502	1,495	1,503
Due from Stockholders										131,482	
Total Current Assets	182,335	192,571	91,707	194,321	248,024	294,116	344,502	247,012	354,434	408,401	545,816
Fixed Assets	133,552	133,552	134,145	134,145	187,858	194,323	225,052	225,909	225,908	219,000	225,920
Depreciation	(107,607)	(116,676)	(123,842)	(130,102)	(138,880)	(150,524)	(168,454)	(190,207)	(208,258)	(196,970)	(211,924)
Other Assets	12,077	7,095	7,095	7,095	11,143	11,143	10,121	10,121	68,452	73,601	36,005
Total Assets	220,356	216,541	109,105	205,459	308,145	349,058	411,221	292,835	440,536	504,032	595,817
Current Liabilities											
Accounts Payable – Trade	12,160	27,773	34,077	74,514	114,050	125,422	82,132	150,518	185,328	222,665	310,916
Notes Payable – Bank	102,066	100,196	101,208	100,322	100,322				7,591	88,557	88,557
Notes Payable – Officers			81,633	207,258	217,243	146,704				158,138	316,275
Accrued Liabilities	63,230	88,594	89,052	148,348	124,373	181,878	40,878	13,822	38,624	87,298	100,732
Current Portion LTD					8,288	18,226	32,593	11,486	2,564	14,585	4,213
Deferred Revenue						103,548	38,147				18,200
Due to Former Owner of GT									71,558	50,361	89,367
Total Current Liabilities	177,456	216,562	305,969	530,443	564,276	575,779	193,749	175,826	305,665	621,604	928,260
Deferred Expenses							193,123	197,265			76,232
Due to Stockholder							133,521	94,416	292,801	295,836	235,531
Capital Lease Obligation										4,217	
Long-Term Debt					197,530	138,188	108,864	2,564			
Total Debt	177,456	216,562	305,969	530,443	761,807	713,967	629,257	470,071	598,466	921,657	1,240,023
Common Stock	1,265	1,265	1,265	1,265	1,265	1,265	1,265	1,265	1,565	1,631	1,631
Paid-In Capital	88,557	88,557	88,557	88,557	88,557	88,557	88,557	88,557	88,384	94,837	94,837
Stock Subscrip. Rec.									(127)	(127)	
Accumulated Deficit	(46,921)	(89,844)	(286,687)	(414,806)	(543,483)	(454,731)	(307,858)	(267,058)	(247,752)	(513,966)	(740,674)
Shareholders Equity	42,901	(22)	(196,865)	(324,984)	(453,661)	(364,909)	(218,036)	(177,235)	(157,930)	(417,625)	(644,207)
Total Liabilities and Shareholders Equity	220,356	216,541	109,105	205,459	308,145	349,058	411,221	292,835	440,536	504,032	595,817

entrepreneurial CASE ANALYSIS

Exhibit 7　ElectroChem, Inc. Income Statement Summary, 1991–2001

	1991	1992	1993	1994	1995	1996	1997	1998	1999	2000	2001
Revenues	422,345	427,988	219,295	587,896	688,843	909,835	1,308,788	935,677	1,116,138	1,537,635	2,062,164
Cost of Sales	198,564	199,425	106,740	292,859	254,006	312,481	525,381	462,603	532,419	865,320	934,765
Gross Profit	223,781	228,563	112,555	295,037	434,838	597,354	783,407	471,282	583,720	672,316	1,127,399
Operating Expenses	342,896	283,732	301,196	357,984	630,822	495,551	605,383	414,997	553,119	894,326	1,313,059
Operating Profit/Loss	(119,115)	(55,168)	(188,642)	(62,948)	(195,984)	101,803	178,024	56,285	30,600	(222,010)	(185,660)
Interest Expense	9,811	71	7,626	10,058	25,900	31,774	35,051	19,122	11,603	46,040	42,525
Other Income	-	118	-	-	4,651	18,723	3,900	1,846	309	1,836	1,476
Earnings Before Taxes	(128,926)	(55,122)	(196,268)	(73,005)	(217,234)	88,752	146,873	39,009	19,305	(266,214)	(226,708)
Income Taxes	(50,227)	(12,201)	577	-	-	-	-	-	-	-	-
Net Income/Loss	(78,699)	(42,921)	(196,844)	(73,005)	(217,234)	88,752	146,873	40,801	19,305	(266,214)	(226,708)

moment to reflect on the past and future, Radha realized that ElectroChem's continued financial success would depend on her ability to continue to secure government and research contracts while simultaneously building the firm's reputation among a growing number of commercial customers.

Questions

1. Why did Jalan take over the management of Electro-Chem? What challenges did she face?
2. What does a SWOT analysis reveal about Electro-Chem's position within the fuel cell industry?
3. What steps did Jalan take to turn around Electro-Chem? How has Jalan positioned ElectroChem strategically in the market for fuel cell technology so far?
4. How could Jalan have avoided the incident with Bill West and Peter Clinton? What lessons can be learned for future interaction with equity investors? What other sources of external funding could Jalan have considered?
5. Evaluate Jalan's performance during the ten years she has led ElectroChem. Develop a set of recommendations for her to strategically position ElectroChem for the future.

Notes

1. "What Is a Fuel Cell?" Fact Sheet, Fuel Cell Commercialization Group (FCCG), Washington, DC, 1999.
2. "The Fuel Cell Story," Fuel Cells 2000, http://www.fuelcells.org, and the U.S. Fuel Cell Council, http://www.usfcc.com.
3. "Fuel Cells: The Opportunity for Canada," PricewaterhouseCoopers, June 2002.
4. U. S. Fuel Cell Council, http://www.usfcc.com.
5. Fuel Cell Basics Quotes, http://www.fuelcells.org/basics/quotes.html.
6. Ibid.
7. See http://ballard.com and http://www.business.com.
8. See http://www.fce.com and http://www.business.com.
9. See http://www.plugpower.com and http://www.business.com.
10. See http://www.hpower.com and http://www.business.com.
11. See http://www.internationalfuelcells.com.
12. See http://www.fuelcell.com.
13. "Fuel Cell Report to Congress," submitted by the U.S. Department of Energy, February 2003.
14. See the U.S. Council for Automotive Research at www.uscar.org.
15. Alanna Mitchell, "A World Without Oil," *Globe and Mail*, December 7, 2002.
16. See Fuel Cells Canada at www.fuelcellscanada.ca.
17. J. Qian, B. Finamore, and T. Clegg, "Fuel Cell Vehicle Development in China," *National Resource Defense Council*, http://www.nrdc.org.
18. SBIR Phase 1 contracts last for six months, with a maximum funding of $70,000. SBIR Phase 2 contracts last for 24 months, with a maximum funding of $600,000.
19. Venture capital firm for start-up and early-stage technology companies in Massachusetts.
20. In the business plan, payback period for the investors was five years. In the settlement, they gave her two extra years.
21. "Daring to be Different Fuels Radha Jalan," Women to Watch 2002, *Boston Women's Business*, January 2002.
22. "Radha Jalan: Clean Energy," *Business India*, January/February 2001, 94.

Glossary

The following are key terms and concepts that have been used in this book. In some cases, the description or definition has been expanded to provide information in addition to that presented in the text.

Abandonment Nonuse of a trademark for two consecutive years without justification or a statement regarding abandonment of the trademark.

Accounts payable Liabilities incurred by a business when goods or supplies are purchased on credit.

Accounts receivable Claims of a business against its customers for unpaid balances from the sale of merchandise or the performance of services.

Accounts receivable financing Short-term financing that involves either the pledge of receivables as collateral for a loan or the outright sale of receivables. (See also **Factoring**.)

Accredited purchaser A category used in Regulation D that includes institutional investors; any person who buys at least $150,000 of the offered security and whose net worth is in excess of $1 million; a person whose individual income was greater than $200,000 in each of the last two years; directors, partners, or executive officers selling securities; and certain tax-exempt organizations with more than $500,000 in assets.

Accumulated depreciation of building The amount of the building that has been written off the books due to wear and tear.

Adaptive firm A venture that remains adaptive and innovative both through and beyond the growth stage.

Adjusted tangible book value A common method of valuing a business by computing its net worth as the difference between total assets and total liabilities.

Adjustment of debts Under Chapter 13 of the Bankruptcy Act, individuals are allowed to avoid a declaration of bankruptcy, have the opportunity to pay their debts in installments, and are protected by the federal court. (See also **Bankruptcy Act**.)

Administrative culture A culture typified by the presence of such characteristics as a hierarchical management structure, ownership of enterprise resources, a competitive commitment of resources, and a long-run time perspective. (See also **Entrepreneurial culture**.)

Administrative expenses Operating expenses not directly related to selling or borrowing.

Advisory board A board of professionals established to enhance a venture's growth.

Affiliation The specific interests that a business represents.

Allowance for uncollectible accounts Accounts receivable judged to be uncollectible.

Amoral management Management is neither moral nor immoral, but decisions lie outside the sphere to which moral judgments apply.

Angel capital Investments in new ventures that come from wealthy individuals referred to as "business angels."

Angel investor Wealthy people who invest capital in public and private placements but are not considered professional venture capitalists (also known as Informal Risk Investor).

Antidilution protection The conversion price of the preferred stock is subject to adjustment for certain diluting events, such as stock splits or stock dividends. The conversion price is typically subject to "price protection," which is an adjustment based on future sales of stock at prices below the conversion price.

Appositional relationship A relationship among things and people existing in the world in relation to other things and other people.

Assets Anything of value that is owned by you or your business.

Background or knowledge accumulation The first step in the creative thinking process, which involves investigation and information gathering related to the matter under analysis.

Balance sheet A financial statement that reports the assets, liabilities, and owners' equity in the venture at a particular point in time.

Balance sheet equation A basic accounting equation that states that assets equal liabilities plus owners' equity.

Bank loan A long-term liability due to a loan from a lending institution.

Bankruptcy A legal process for insolvent debtors who are unable to pay debts as they become due. For business, this includes Chapters 7, 11, and 13 of the federal bankruptcy code.

Bankruptcy Act Federal law that provides for specific procedures in handling insolvent debtors.

Barriers to entry Elements restricting an emerging industry, such as proprietary technology, access to distribution channels, access to raw materials and other inputs, cost disadvantages due to lack of experience, and risk.

Better widget strategy Innovation that encompasses new or existing markets.

Book value The value of a business determined by subtracting total liabilities (adjusted for intangible assets) from total assets.

Bootlegging Secretly working on new ideas on company time as well as on personal time.

Break-even analysis A technique commonly used to assess expected product profitability, which helps to determine how many units must be sold to break even at a particular selling price.

Break-even point The point at which the company neither makes nor loses money on a particular project. The formula for computing this point (in units) is Fixed Cost/Selling Price per Unit minus Variable Cost per Unit.

Budget A statement of estimated income and expenses over a specified period of time.

Business angel (informal risk capitalist) Wealthy people in the United States looking for investment opportunities.

Business assets The tangible (physical) and intangible (e.g., reputed) assets of the business.

Business broker A professional individual or company that specializes in the valuations and sales of businesses.

Business description segment That segment of a business plan that provides a general description of the venture, industry background, company history or background, goals, potential of the venture, and uniqueness of the product or service.

Business environment The local environment for business that should be analyzed to establish the potential of the venture in its present location.

Business incubator A facility with adaptable space that small businesses can lease on flexible terms and at reduced rent.

Business model How a venture is designed to make money, demonstrating a clear method of getting to the market for sales.

Business plan The written document that details a proposed venture. It must illustrate current status, expected needs, and projected results of the new business.

Business valuation The calculated value of the business, used to track its increases or decreases.

Buy/sell agreements Agreements designed to handle situations in which one (or more) of the entrepreneurs wants to sell her interest in the venture.

Calculated risk taking Occurs when successful entrepreneurs carefully think out a venture and do everything possible to turn the odds in their favor.

Cancellation proceedings A third party's challenge to the trademark's distinctiveness within five years of its issuance.

Capital budgeting A budgeting process used to determine investment decisions. It relies heavily on an evaluation of cash inflows.

Career risk Whether an entrepreneur will be able to find a job or go back to an old job if his or her venture fails.

Cash Coins, currency, and checks on hand. It also includes money the business has in its checking and savings accounts.

Cash-flow budget A budget that provides an overview of inflows and outflows of cash during a specified period of time.

Cash-flow leveraged buyout (LBO) Type of buyout that relies heavily on the target company's cash receipts with indicators of that positive cash flow continuing.

Cash-flow statement A financial statement that sets forth the amount and timing of actual and/or expected cash inflows and outflows.

Champion Within the context of corporate entrepreneurship, this is a person with an innovative vision and the ability to share it.

Claims A series of short paragraphs, each of which identifies a particular feature or combination of features, protected by a patent.

Cleaning-out procedure The failure of a trademark owner to file an affidavit stating that it is in use or justifying its lack of use within six years of registration.

Close corporation A corporation in which all shares of stock are held by one person or a small group of people and in which purchase of the stock is not available to the general public.

Code of conduct A statement of ethical practices or guidelines to which an enterprise adheres.

Collective entrepreneurship Individual skills integrated into a group wherein the collective capacity to innovate becomes something greater than the sum of its parts.

Common stock The most basic form of ownership, usually carrying the right to vote for the board of directors.

Community demographics The composition or makeup of consumers who live within a community.

Company profitability The amount of net profit a company produces after expenses.

Competitive analysis An analysis of both the quality and quantity of the competition, which needs to be carefully scrutinized by the entrepreneur.

Comprehensive feasibility approach A systematic analysis incorporating external factors.

Consumer-driven philosophy A marketing philosophy that relies on research to discover consumer preferences, desires, and needs before production actually begins. (See also **Production-driven philosophy** and **Sales-driven philosophy**.)

Consumer pricing Combining penetration and competitive pricing to gain market share; depends on consumer's perceived value of product.

Contribution margin approach A common approach to break-even analysis, determined by calculating the difference between the selling price and the variable cost per unit.

Control factor The degree of control an owner legally has over the firm can affect its valuation.

Convenience goods Goods that consumers want but are not willing to spend time shopping for.

Convertible debentures Unsecured loans that can be converted into stock.

Copyright A legal protection that provides exclusive rights to creative

individuals for the protection of their literary or artistic productions.

Corporate entrepreneurship A new "corporate revolution" taking place due to the infusion of entrepreneurial thinking into bureaucratic structures.

Corporate Entrepreneurship Assessment Instrument (CEAI) A questionnaire designed to measure the key entrepreneurial climate factors.

Corporate venturing The adding of new businesses (or portions of new businesses via equity investments) to the corporation. This can be accomplished through three implementation modes: internal corporate venturing, cooperative corporate venturing, and external corporate venturing.

Corporation An entity legally separate from the individuals who own it, created by the authority of state laws, and usually formed when a transfer of money or property by prospective shareholders takes place in exchange for capital stock in the corporation.

Corridor principle States that with every venture launched, new and unintended opportunities arise.

Creative process The four phases of creative development: background or knowledge accumulation, incubation process, idea experience, and evaluation or implementation.

Creativity The generation of ideas that results in an improvement in the efficiency or effectiveness of a system.

Critical factors Important new-venture assessments.

Critical risks segment The segment of the business plan that discusses potential problems, obstacles and risks, and alternative courses of action.

Customer availability Having customers available before a venture starts.

Dark side of entrepreneurship A destructive side that exists within the energetic drive of successful entrepreneurs.

Debt financing Borrowing money for short- or long-term periods for working capital or for purchasing property and equipment.

Debtor-in-possession When a debtor involved in a Chapter 11 proceeding continues to operate the business.

Delayed entry strategy A succession strategy that encourages the younger generation to enter the business at a later age to gain experience outside the family held firm.

Delegating Having trained people complete tasks for entrepreneurs to help them save time.

Demand-oriented pricing A flexible strategy that bases pricing decisions on the demand level for the product.

Design patent Gives the owner exclusive rights to hold, transfer, and/or license the production and sale of the product or process for 14 years.

Discounted earnings method A method that determines the true value of the firm with a pricing formula that includes earning power as well as adjusted tangible book value.

Discounting the future cash flows The cost of capital is the rate used to adjust future cash flows to determine their value in present period terms.

Displacement school of thought A school of entrepreneurial thought that focuses on group phenomena such as the political, cultural, and economic environments.

Divergent goals When the entrepreneur has a vision for the venture that differs from the investors' goals or stockholders' desires, thus causing internal conflicts in the firm.

Diversified marketing A marketing stage during which the organization focuses on decentralizing operations by examining individual product life cycles and developing portfolio management approaches to product lines.

Domain name The last part of a URL that includes the organization's unique name followed by a top-level domain name designating the type of organization, such as .com for "commercial" or .edu for "educational."

Domestic corporation A corporation doing business in the state in which it has been incorporated.

Drive to achieve A strong desire to compete, to excel against self-imposed standards, and to pursue and attain challenging goals.

Due diligence A thorough analysis of every facet of the existing business.

Duplication A basic type of innovation that involves the replication of an already existing product, service, or process.

Early entry strategy A succession strategy that encourages the younger generation to enter the business at an early age to gain experience.

Economic base The base that includes the nature of employment (which influences the size and distribution of income) and the purchasing trends of consumers in the area.

Ecovision Leadership style for innovative organizations. Encourages open and flexible structures that encompass the employees, the organization, and the environment, with attention to evolving social demands.

Effective delegation Assignment of specific duties, granting authority to carry out these duties, and creating the obligation of responsibility for necessary action.

Elevator pitch The brief oral presentation for selling a business plan to potential investors (named for the analogy of riding an elevator and having only two minutes to get your story told to another person in the elevator).

Emotional bias The tendency to believe an enterprise is worth a great deal more than outsiders believe it is worth.

Employee stock ownership plans (ESOPs) Passing control of the enterprise to the employees if the owner has no immediate successor in mind.

Entrepreneur An innovator or developer who recognizes and seizes opportunities; converts these opportunities into workable/marketable ideas; adds value through time, effort, money, or skills; assumes the risks of the competitive marketplace to implement these ideas; and realizes the rewards from these efforts.

Entrepreneurial assessment approach Stresses making assessments qualitatively, quantitatively, strategically, and ethically in regard to the entrepreneur, the venture, and the environment.

Entrepreneurial behavior An entrepreneur's decision to initiate the new-venture formation process.

Entrepreneurial culture A culture typified by the presence of characteristics such as a flat management structure with multiple informal networks, episodic use or rent of required resources, a long-run time perspective, and a strategic orientation driven by perception of opportunity. (See also **Administrative culture.**)

Entrepreneurial economy A new emphasis on entrepreneurial thinking that developed in the 1980s and 1990s and is prevalent now in the twenty-first century.

Entrepreneurial leadership An entrepreneur's ability to anticipate,

envision, maintain flexibility, think strategically, and work with others to initiate changes that will create a viable future for the organization.

Entrepreneurial leveraged buyout (E-LBO) Having at least two-thirds of the purchase price generated from borrowed funds, more than 50 percent of the stock after acquisition owned by a single individual or his or her family, and the majority investor devoted to the active management of the company after acquisition.

Entrepreneurial management The theme or discipline that suggests entrepreneurship is based on the same principles, whether the entrepreneur is an existing large institution or an individual starting his or her new venture single-handedly.

Entrepreneurial marketing A marketing stage in which the enterprise attempts to develop credibility in the marketplace by establishing a market niche.

Entrepreneurial mind-set All the characteristics and elements that compose the entrepreneurial potential in every individual.

Entrepreneurial motivation The willingness of an entrepreneur to sustain his or her entrepreneurial behavior.

Entrepreneurial Revolution The tremendous increase in entrepreneurial business and entrepreneurial thinking that has developed during the last 20 years. This revolution will be as powerful to the twenty-first century as the Industrial Revolution was to the twentieth century (if not more!).

Entrepreneurial strategy matrix Measures risk and innovation.

Entrepreneurial stress A function of discrepancies between one's expectations and one's ability to meet those demands.

Entrepreneurial successor A successor to a venture who is highly gifted with ingenuity, creativity, and drive.

Entrepreneurial trait school of thought A school of entrepreneurial thought that focuses on identifying traits that appear common to successful entrepreneurs.

Entrepreneurship A dynamic process of vision, change, and creation. It requires an application of energy and passion toward the creation and implementation of new ideas and creative solutions. Essential ingredients include the willingness to take calculated risks—in terms of time, equity, or career; the ability to formulate an effective venture team; the creative skill to marshal needed resources; the fundamental skill of building a solid business plan; and, finally, the vision to recognize opportunity where others see chaos, contradiction, and confusion.

Environmental analysis Entails evaluating the general economic environment, the government-regulating environment, and the industry.

Environmental awareness A reawakening of the need to preserve and protect our natural resources.

Environmental school of thought A school of entrepreneurial thought that focuses on the external factors and forces—values, mores, and institutions—that surround a potential entrepreneur's lifestyle.

Equity financing The sale of some ownership in a venture in order to gain capital for start-up.

Ethics A set of principles prescribing a behavioral code that explains what is good and right or bad and wrong.

Evaluation and implementation The fourth step in the creative thinking process, during which the individual makes adjustments in the approach so that it more closely approximates the necessary solution.

Excess earnings A method of determining a firm's intangible assets. It is a method of last resort that does not include intangibles with estimated useful lives, such as patents and copyrights.

Exit strategy That component of the business plan where an entrepreneur describes a method by which investors can realize a tangible return on their investment.

Expenses An expired cost; any item or class of cost of (or loss from) carrying on an activity; a present or past expenditure defraying a present operating cost or representing an irrecoverable cost or loss; an item of capital expenditures written down or off; or a term often used with some qualifying expression denoting function, organization, or time, such as a selling expense, factory expense, or monthly expense.

Experimentation A form of research that concentrates on investigating cause-and-effect relationships.

Extension A basic type of innovation that involves extending the life of a product, service, or process already in existence.

External locus of control A point of view in which external processes are sometimes beyond the control of the individual entrepreneur.

External optimism Ceaseless optimism emanating from entrepreneurs as a key factor in the drive toward success.

External problems Related to customer contact, market knowledge, marketing planning, location, pricing, product considerations, competitors, and expansion.

External resources Resources outside the venture.

Factoring The sale of accounts receivable.

Failure prediction model Based on financial data from newly founded ventures; assumes the financial failure process is characterized by too much initial indebtedness and too little revenue financing.

Fair use doctrine An exception to copyright protection that allows limited use of copyrighted materials.

Family and social risk Starting a new venture uses much of the entrepreneur's energy and time. Entrepreneurs who are married, and especially those with children, expose their families to the risks of an incomplete family experience and the possibility of permanent emotional scars. In addition, old friends may vanish slowly because of missed get-togethers.

Feasibility criteria approach A criteria selection list from which entrepreneurs can gain insights into the viability of their venture.

Finance companies Asset-based lenders that lend money against assets such as receivables, inventory, and equipment.

Financial/capital school of thought A school of entrepreneurial thought that focuses on the ways entrepreneurs seek seed capital and growth funds.

Financial expense The interest expense on long-term loans. Many companies also include their interest expense on short-term obligations as part of their financial expense.

Financial risk The money or resources at stake for a new venture.

Financial segment The segment of the business plan that discusses the financial forecast, the sources and uses of funds, budgeting plans, and stages of financing.

Five-minute reading A six-step process that venture capitalists use when they are reviewing a business plan for potential investment.

Fixed assets Land, building, equipment, and other assets expected to remain with the firm for an extended period.

Fixed cost A cost that does not change in response to changes in activity for a given period of time.

Forcing events Happenings that cause the replacement of the owner/manager.

Foreign corporation A corporation doing business in a state other than the one in which it is incorporated.

Franchise Any arrangement in which the owner of a trademark, trade name, or copyright has licensed others to use it to sell goods or services.

Franchisee An individual who purchases and operates a franchise.

Franchise fee The initial amount of money needed to purchase a franchise.

Franchisor An individual (or company) who offers to sell or license his operation in the form of a franchise.

Franchisor control The overriding control that a franchisor exhibits in regard to the major operations of a franchise system.

Free Trade Agreement (FTA) Global economic development that has provided new potential environments within which entrepreneurs could prosper.

Fully diluted All securities—including preferred stock, options, and warrants—that can result in additional common shares are counted in determining the total amount of shares outstanding for the purposes of determining ownership or valuation.

Functional perspective Viewing things and people in terms of how they can be used to satisfy one's needs and to help complete a project.

Gazelle A business establishment with at least 20 percent sales growth every year, starting with a base of at least $100,000.

General Agreement on Tariffs and Trade (GATT) A major trade liberalization organization whose objectives are to create a basic set of rules under which trade negotiations take place.

General partner A person who is active in the business, is known to be a partner, and has unlimited liability.

Generic meaning Allowance of a trademark to represent a general grouping of products or services (for example, Kleenex has come to represent tissue).

Global entrepreneur An entrepreneur who relies on global (international) networks for resources, design, and distribution.

Goodwill The amount of value created by an owner of a business in terms of his or her time, effort, and public image with the business itself.

Great chef strategies The skills or special talents of one or more individuals around whom a venture is built.

Green capitalism A new force in examining the manner in which business is conducted in relation to the environment. It refers to a concept of *ecologically* sustainable development being transformed into *economically* sustainable development.

Growth of sales The growth pattern anticipated for new-venture sales and profits.

Growth stage The third stage of a new-venture life cycle, typically involving activities related to reformulating strategy in the light of competition.

Growth wall A psychological wall against change that prevents entrepreneurs from developing a managerial ability to deal with venture growth.

Harvest strategy A strategy of how and when the owners and investors will realize an actual cash return on their investment in a venture.

High-growth venture When sales and profit growth are expected to be significant enough to attract venture capital money and funds raised through public or private placements.

Horizontal analysis Looks at financial statements and ratios over time.

Idea experience The third step in the creative thinking process, during which the individual discovers the answers he or she has been pursuing.

Immersion in business When the successful entrepreneur devotes all of his or her time to the business rather than taking some time for leisure activities.

Immoral management Management decisions that imply a positive and active opposition to what is ethical.

Income statement A financial document that reports the sales, expenses, and profits of the enterprise over a specified period (usually one year).

Incongruities Whenever a gap or difference exists between expectations and reality.

Incremental innovation The systematic evolution of a product or service into newer or larger markets.

Incubation process The second step in the creative thinking process, during which one's subconscious is allowed to mull over the information gathered during the preparation phase.

Incubator A building designed to provide low cost space and shared business services to fledgling new ventures.

Informal risk investors Wealthy people who invest capital in public and private placements but are not considered professional venture capitalists (also known as "Angel Investors").

Infringement budget A realistic budget for prosecuting violations of the patent.

Initial public offering (IPO) A corporation's raising of capital through the sale of securities on the public markets.

Innovation The process by which entrepreneurs convert opportunities into marketable ideas.

Innovation team (I-team) An internal corporate team formulated for the purpose of creating new innovations for the organization.

Insolvent debtors Those who are unable to pay debts as they become due.

Intellectual property right Provides protection such as patents, trademarks, or copyrights against infringement by others.

Interactive learning Learning ideas within an innovative environment that cut across traditional, functional lines in the organization.

Internal locus of control The viewpoint in which the potential entrepreneur has the ability or control to direct or adjust the outcome of each major influence.

Internal problems Involve adequate capital, cash flow, facilities/equipment, inventory control, human resources, leadership, organizational structure, and accounting systems.

Internal rate of return (IRR) method A capital-budgeting technique that involves discounting future cash flows to the present at a rate that makes the net present value of the project equal to zero.

Internet A worldwide, publicly accessible interconnected computer network that transmits data. It is a "network of networks" that consists of millions of smaller domestic, academic, business, and government networks, which together carry various information and services, such as electronic mail and the interlinked Web pages of the World Wide Web.

Internet marketing Allows the firm to increase its presence and brand equity in the marketplace; allows the company to cultivate new customers, allows Web site visitors to match their needs with the offerings of the company; and can improve customer service by allowing customers to serve themselves when and where they choose.

Intracapital Special capital set aside for the corporate entrepreneur to use whenever investment money is needed for further research ideas.

Intrapreneurship Entrepreneurial activities that receive organizational sanction and resource commitments for the purpose of innovative results within an established corporation (see also **Corporate entrepreneurship**).

Invention A basic type of innovation that involves the creation of a new product, service, or process that is often novel or untried.

Inventory Merchandise held by the company for resale to customers.

Investing activities Cash-flow effects from long-term investing activities, such as purchase or sale of plant and equipment.

Joint venture An organization owned by more than one company—a popular approach to doing business overseas.

Lack of expertise/skills When small-business managers lack the specialized expertise/skills necessary for the planning process.

Lack of knowledge Small-firm owners/managers' uncertainty about the components of the planning process and their sequence due to minimal exposure to, and knowledge of, the process itself.

Lack of trust and openness When small-firm owners/managers are highly sensitive and guarded about their businesses and the decisions that affect them.

Learning curve concept The time needed for new methods or procedures to be learned and mastered.

Left brain The part of the brain that helps an individual analyze, verbalize, and use rational approaches to problem solving. (See also **Right brain.**)

Legal restraint of trade A legal document signed by the seller of a business that restricts him or her from operating in the same business for a reasonable amount of time and within a reasonable geographic jurisdiction.

Letter of intent (LOI) Nonbinding document meant to record two or more parties' intentions to enter into a future agreement based on specified (but incomplete or preliminary) terms. Many LOIs contain provisions that are binding, such as nondisclosure agreements, a covenant to negotiate in good faith, or a "stand-still" provision promising exclusive rights to negotiate.

Leveraged buyout (LBO) Allows the entrepreneur to finance the transaction by borrowing on the target company's assets.

Liabilities The debts of a business, incurred either through normal operations or through the process of obtaining funds to finance operations. (See also **Short-term liabilities** and **Long-term liabilities.**)

Licensing A business arrangement in which the manufacturer of a product (or a firm with proprietary rights over technology or trademarks) grants permission to a group or an individual to manufacture that product in return for specified royalties or other payments.

Life-cycle stages The typical life cycle through which a venture progresses, including venture development, start-up, growth, stabilization, and innovation or decline.

Lifestyle venture A small venture in which the primary driving forces include independence, autonomy, and control.

Limited liability A restriction on the amount of financial responsibility assumed by a partner or stockholder. (See also **Unlimited liability.**)

Limited liability company (LLC) A hybrid form of business enterprise that offers the limited liability of a corporation but the tax advantages of a partnership.

Limited liability limited partnership (LLLP) A relatively new variant of the limited partnership. An LLLP has elected limited liability status for all of its partners, including general partners. Except for this liability status of general partners, limited partnerships and LLLPs are identical.

Limited liability partnership (LLP) A relatively new form of partnership that allows professionals the tax benefits of a partnership while avoiding personal liability for the malpractice of other partners.

Limited partnership Organizational arrangement that allows investors to put money into a partnership without assuming liability for any losses beyond this initial investment.

Liquidation See **Bankruptcy.**

Liquidation preference When the company is sold or liquidated, the preferred stockholders will receive a certain fixed amount before any assets are distributed to the common stockholders.

Liquidation value A method of valuing a business in which the value of all assets is determined on the basis of their current sale value.

Liquidity event The positioning of the venture for the realization of a cash return for the owners and the investors. This "event" is most often achieved through an initial public offering or complete sale of the venture.

Loan payable The current installment on a long-term debt that must be paid this year.

Loan with warrants A loan that provides the investor (lender) with the right to buy stock at a fixed price at some future date.

Loneliness Isolation from persons with whom entrepreneurs can confide because of their long hours at work.

Long-term liabilities Business debts that are not due and payable within the next 12 months.

Loss leader pricing Pricing the product below cost in an attempt to attract customers to other products.

Macro view of entrepreneurship A broad array of factors that relate to success or failure in contemporary entrepreneurial ventures.

Management segment The segment of a business plan that discusses the management team, legal structure, board of directors, advisers, and consultants.

Management succession The transition of managerial decision making in a firm, one of the greatest challenges that confronts owners and entrepreneurs in family businesses.

Management team The founders of a new venture who plan on managing the company, as well as any advisors, consultants, or members of the board.

Managerial successor A successor to a venture who is interested in efficiency, internal control, and the effective use of resources.

Manufacturing segment The segment of a business plan that discusses location analysis, production needs, suppliers, transportation, labor supply, and manufacturing cost data.

Market A group of consumers (potential customers) who have purchasing power and unsatisfied needs. (See also **Market niche** and **Niche.**)

Market niche A homogeneous group of consumers with common characteristics.

Market planning The process of determining a clear, comprehensive approach to the creation of a consumer.

Market segmentation The process of identifying a specific set of characteristics that differentiates one group of consumers from the rest.

Market strategy A general marketing philosophy and strategy of the company developed from market research and evaluation data.

Market value A method of valuing a business that involves an estimation based on prices recently paid for similar enterprises as well as on the methods of sale.

Marketability Assembling and analyzing relevant information about a new venture to judge its potential success.

Marketing information system A system that compiles and organizes data relating to cost, revenues, and profit from the customer base.

Marketing research A gathering of information about a particular market, followed by an analysis of that information.

Marketing segment The segment of a business plan that describes aspects of the market such as the target market, the market size and trends, the competition, estimated market share, market strategy, pricing, and advertising and promotion.

Marketing strategy The general marketing philosophy of the company should be outlined to include the kinds of customer groups to be targeted by the initial intensive selling effort; the customer groups to be targeted for later selling efforts; methods of identifying and contracting potential customers in these groups; the features of the product or service (quality, price, delivery, warranty) to be emphasized to generate sales; and innovative or unusual marketing concepts that will enhance customer acceptance.

Metrics Assumptions and calculations used for any revenue projections.

Micro view of entrepreneurship Examines the factors specific to entrepreneurship and part of the internal locus of control.

Milestone planning approach A planning approach based on the use of incremental goal attainment that takes a new venture from start-up through strategy reformulation.

Milestone schedule segment The section of a business plan that provides investors with timetables for the accomplishment of various activities such as completion of prototypes, hiring of sales representatives, receipt of first orders, initial deliveries, and receipt of first accounts receivable payments.

Minority-owned business Business owned and operated by a minority, which may include blacks, Asians, Native Americans, and Hispanics.

Mixed costs A blend of fixed and variable costs.

Moral failure This form of failure is a violation of internal trust.

Moral management Management activity that conforms to a standard of ethical behavior.

Mountain gap strategies Identifying major market segments as well as interstice (in-between) markets that arise from larger markets.

Muddling mind-sets When creative thinking is blocked or impeded.

Multidimensional approach Viewing entrepreneurship as a complex, multidimensional framework that emphasizes the individual, the environment, the organization, and the venture process.

Multiple of earnings A method of valuing a venture that consists of multiplying earnings by a predetermined multiple to arrive at a final value.

Multistage contingency approach Strategic analysis that includes the individual, the venture, and the environment in relation to a venture's stages as well as to the entrepreneur's career perspective.

National Federation of Independent Business (NFIB) The largest advocacy group representing small and independent businesses in Washington, DC, and all 50 state capitals; has a membership of more than 600,000 business owners.

Need for control The strong desire entrepreneurs have to control both their ventures and their destinies.

Nepotism The hiring of relatives in preference to other, more qualified candidates.

Net income The excess of revenue over expenses during a particular period.

Net present value (NPV) method A capital-budgeting technique used to evaluate an investment that involves a determination of future cash flows and a discounting of these flows to arrive at a present value of these future dollars.

Networking Meeting key people in a particular field of business for purposes of gaining connections in the industry; also valuable for sharing experiences with other business owners as a way to relieve loneliness.

New-new approach A start up approach to business in which the concept is a brand new idea to the marketplace.

New-old approach A start up approach to business in which the concept provides a new angle to something that already exists in the marketplace.

New-venture development The first stage of a venture's life cycle that involves activities such as creativity and venture assessment.

Niche A homogeneous group with common characteristics, such as people who all have a need for a newly proposed good or service.

Non-compete clause An agreement stating that when purchasing an existing venture the previous owner will refrain from conducting the same business within a reasonable distance for a reasonable period of time. Also known as *legal restraint of trade* or an agreement not to compete.

Nonprofit corporation A corporation whose main objective is not profit, such as a religious, charitable, or educational institution.

Nonprofit-sponsored incubator An incubator organized and managed through industrial development associations of private industry, chambers of commerce, or community-based organizations and whose primary objective is area development.

Nonrole Refers to unethical instances in which a person is acting outside of his or her role as manager yet committing acts against a firm.

Notes payable Promissory notes given as tangible recognition of a supplier's claim or notes given in connection with an acquisition of funds, such as for a bank loan.

Oakland Scavenger Company A garbage collection firm based in California that was involved in a legal dispute over nepotism in a family business.

Observational methods Methods of collecting primary data that do not involve any direct contact with the respondents. (See also **Questioning methods**.)

One-person-band syndrome Exists when an entrepreneur fails to delegate responsibility to employees, thereby retaining all decision-making authority.

Operating budget A budget that sets forth the projected sales forecast and expenses for an upcoming period.

Operating cash flows Cash generated from or used in the course of business operations of the firm.

Operating expenses The major expenses, exclusive of costs of goods sold, in generating revenue.

Operational planning Short-range or functional planning consisting of specific practices established to carry out the objective set forth in the strategic plan.

Opportunistic marketing A marketing stage in a growing venture in which the organization attempts to develop high sales volume through market penetration.

Opportunity identification The ability to recognize a viable business opportunity within a variety of good ideas.

Opportunity orientation A pattern among successful, growth-minded entrepreneurs to focus on opportunity rather than on resources, structure, or strategy.

Owners' equity What remains after the firm's liabilities are subtracted from its assets.

Pain The nickname that venture capitalists use for exactly what problem is being solved by your venture.

Partnership An association of two or more persons acting as co-owners of a business for profit.

Patent An intellectual property right granted to an inventor, giving him or her the exclusive right to make, use, or sell an invention for a limited time period (usually 20 years).

Patent and Trademark Office An office of the federal government through which all patent and trademark applications are filed.

Payback method A capital-budgeting technique used to determine the length of time required to pay back an original investment.

Penetration Setting prices at such a low level that products are able to gain market share.

Perception of high cost When small-business owners perceive the cost associated with planning to be very high.

Personal failure A form of failure brought about by a lack of skill or application.

Planning The process of transforming entrepreneurial vision and ideas into action, involving three steps: (1) commitment to an open planning process, (2) accountability to a corporate conscience, and (3) establishment of a pattern of subordinate participation in the development of the strategic plan.

Policies Fundamental guides for the venture as a whole.

Preferred stock Equity that gives investors a preferred place among the creditors in case the venture is dissolved.

Prepaid expenses Expenses the firm already has paid but that have not yet been used.

Price/earnings ratio (P/E) A method of valuing a business that divides the price of the common stock in the market by the earnings per share and multiplies the result by the number of shares of stock issued.

Primary data New data that are often collected using observational or questioning methods.

Private corporation A corporation created either wholly or in part for private benefits; another name for a close corporation or family corporation, in which the rights of shareholders are restricted regarding transfer of shares.

Private offering The raising of capital through the private placement of securities to groups such as friends, employees, customers, relatives, and local professionals. (See also **Public offerings.**)

Private placement A method of raising capital through securities; often used by small ventures.

Pro forma financial statement A financial statement that projects the results of future business operations, such as a pro forma balance sheet, an income statement, or a cash-flow statement.

Pro forma statement Projection of a firm's financial position during a future period (pro forma income statement) or on a future date (pro forma balance sheet).

Probability thinking Relying on probability to make decisions in the struggle to achieve security.

Product availability The availability of a salable good or service at the time the venture opens its doors.

Production-driven philosophy A market philosophy based on the principle of producing efficiently and letting sales take care of themselves. (See also **Consumer-driven philosophy** and **Sales-driven philosophy.**)

Professional corporation A corporation made up of practicing professionals such as lawyers, accountants, or doctors.

Profits, sales, and operating ratios Used to estimate a business's potential earning power, which is a key factor in evaluating the attractiveness of the venture and in later determining a reasonable buying price.

Profit trend A venture's ability to generate a profit over a sustained period.

Psychic risk The great psychological impact on and the well-being of the entrepreneur who creates a new venture.

Public corporation A corporation the government forms to meet a political or governmental purpose.

Public offerings The raising of capital through the sale of securities on public markets. (See also **Private offerings.**)

Publicly sponsored incubators An incubator set up by a public entity—such as a municipal economic development department, an urban renewal authority, or a regional planning and development department—with the main objective of job creation.

Questioning methods Methods of collecting primary data directly from the respondents, such as surveys and telephone interviews. (See also **Observational methods.**)

R&D limited partnership A popular tool for funding research and development expenses in entrepreneurial ventures; it is a limited partnership in many ways.

Radical innovation The inaugural breakthroughs launched from experimentation and determined vision that are not necessarily managed but must be recognized and nurtured.

Ratio Designed to show relationships among financial statement accounts.

Rationalizations What managers use to justify questionable conduct.

Reachable market The immediate reachable group of customers that will be targeted by a new venture.

Regulation D Regulation and exemption for reports and statements required for selling stock to private parties based on the amount of money being raised.

Reorganization A common form of bankruptcy in which the debtor attempts to formulate a plan to pay a portion of the debts, have the remaining sum discharged, and continue to stay in operation.

Replacement value A method of valuing a business in which the cost of replacing each asset is determined at current cost.

Research, design, and development segment The part of a business plan that discusses the development and design plan, technical research results, research assistance needs, and cost structure.

Responsive marketing A marketing stage during which the organization attempts to develop high customer satisfaction through product market development.

Retained earnings The accumulated net income over the life of the corporation to date.

Return on investment Net profit divided by investment.

Revenues The gross sales made by a business during a particular period under review.

Revised Uniform Limited Partnership Act (RULPA) A section of the Uniform Commercial

Code (specifically within the Uniform Partnership Act) that deals primarily with the legal restrictions and guidelines surrounding limited partnerships.

Right brain The part of the brain that helps an individual understand analogies, imagine things, and synthesize information. (See also **Left brain**.)

Risk Involves uncertain outcomes or events. The higher the rewards, the greater the risk entrepreneurs usually face.

Risk vs. reward Within the financial capital domain, it is the trade-off between the amount of risk taken weighed against the potential reward to be gained.

Role assertion Unethical acts involving managers/entrepreneurs who represent the firm and who rationalize that they are in a position to help the firm's long-run interests.

Role distortion Unethical acts committed on the basis that they are "for the firm" even though they are not, and involving managers/entrepreneurs who commit individual acts and rationalize that they are in the firm's long-run interests.

Role failure Unethical acts against the firm involving a person failing to perform his or her managerial role, including superficial performance appraisals (not being totally honest) and not confronting someone who is cheating on expense accounts.

S corporation A corporation that retains some of the benefits of the corporate form while being taxed similarly to a partnership.

Sales-driven philosophy A marketing philosophy that focuses on personal selling and advertising to persuade customers to buy the company's output. (See also **Consumer-driven philosophy** and **Product-driven philosophy**.)

Sales forecast The process of projecting future sales by applying statistical techniques to historical sales figures.

Selling expenses Result from activities such as displaying, selling, delivering, and installing a product or performing a service.

Secondary data Data that have already been compiled. Examples are periodicals, articles, trade association information, governmental publications, and company records.

Shopping goods Goods that consumers will take time to examine carefully and compare for quality and price.

Short-term liabilities Business debts that must be paid during the coming 12 months (also called *current liabilities*).

Simple linear regression A technique in which a linear equation states the relationship among three variables used to estimate the sales forecast.

Skimming Deliberately setting a high price to maximize short-term profits.

Skunk Works A highly innovative enterprise that uses groups functioning outside traditional lines of authority.

Small Business Administration A governmental agency that aids small business by providing financial, consulting, and managerial assistance.

Small profitable venture A venture in which the entrepreneur does not want venture sales to become so large that he or she must relinquish equity or ownership position and thus give up control over cash flows and profits, which it is hoped will be substantial.

Social entrepreneurship A new form of entrepreneurship that exhibits characteristics of nonprofits, government, and businesses; it applies traditional (private-sector) entrepreneurship's focus on innovation, risk taking, and large-scale transformation to social problem solving.

Social obligation Reacting to social issues through obedience to the laws.

Social responsibility Reacting to social issues by accepting responsibility for various programs.

Social responsiveness Being proactive on social issues by being associated with various activities for the social good.

Sole proprietorship A business owned and operated by one person.

Sophisticated investors Wealthy individuals who invest more or less regularly in new and early- and late-stage ventures. They are knowledgeable about the technical and commercial opportunities and risks of the businesses in which they invest.

Specialty goods Products or services that consumers make a special effort to find and purchase.

Specification The text of a patent; it may include any accompanying illustrations.

Stabilization stage The fourth stage of a new-venture life cycle, typified by increased competition, consumer indifference to the entrepreneur's good(s) or service(s), and saturation

of the market with a host of "me too" look-alikes. During this stage, the entrepreneur begins planning the venture's direction for the next three to five years.

Start-up activities The second stage of a new-venture life cycle, encompassing the foundation work needed to create a formal business plan, search for capital, carry out marketing activities, and develop an effective entrepreneurial team.

Start-up problems A perceived problem area in the start-up phase of a new venture, such as lack of business training, difficulty obtaining lines of credit, and inexperience in financial planning.

Stereotyping Refers to averages that people fabricate and then, ironically, base decisions on as if they were entities existing in the real world.

Straight bankruptcy A bankruptcy arrangement in which the debtor is required to surrender all property to a court-appointed trustee who sells the assets and turns the proceeds over to the creditors; sometimes known as *liquidation*.

Strategic entrepreneurship The exhibition of large-scale or otherwise highly consequential innovations that are adopted in the firm's pursuit of competitive advantage. Using strategic entrepreneurship approaches, innovation can be in any of five areas: the firm's strategy, product offerings, served markets, internal organization (i.e., structure, processes, and capabilities), or business model.

Strategic formulation school of thought A school of entrepreneurial thought that focuses on the planning process used in successful venture formulation.

Strategic planning The primary step in determining the future direction of a business influenced by the abilities of the entrepreneur, the complexity of the venture, and the nature of the industry.

Strategic positioning The process of perceiving new positions that attract customers from established positions or draw new customers into the market.

Stress A function of discrepancies between a person's expectations and ability to meet demands, as well as discrepancies between the individual's expectations and personality. If a person is unable to fulfill role demands, then stress occurs.

Surveys Methods of collecting primary data, such as a mail, telephone, or personal interview.

Sustainable competitive advantage When a venture has implemented a strategy that other companies cannot duplicate or find it too costly to compete with a particular element. Every sustainable competitive advantage can only be maintained for a certain amount of time. depending on the speed with which competitors are able to duplicate or substitute.

SWOT analysis A strategic analysis that refers to strengths, weaknesses, opportunities, and threats.

Synthesis A basic type of innovation that involves combining existing concepts and factors into a new formulation.

Taxes payable Liabilities owed to the government—federal, state, and local.

Technical feasibility Producing a product or service that will satisfy the expectations of potential customers.

Telemarketing The use of telephone communications to directly contact and sell merchandise to consumers.

Term sheet Document that outlines the material terms and conditions of a venture agreement and lists deal terms in bullet-point format.

Time scarcity Lack of time and the difficulty of allocating time for planning in the face of continual day-to-day operating problems.

Tolerance for ambiguity Ability of the entrepreneur to thrive on uncertainty and constant changes that introduce ambiguity and stress into every aspect of the enterprise.

Tolerance for failure The iterative, trial-and-error nature of a successful entrepreneur due to serious setbacks and disappointments that are an integral part of the entrepreneur's learning experience.

Top management support When upper-level managers in a corporation can concentrate on helping individuals within the system develop more entrepreneurial behavior.

Trade credit Credit given by a supplier who sells goods on account. A common arrangement calls for the bill to be settled within 30 to 90 days.

Trademark A distinctive name, mark, symbol, or motto identified with a company's product(s).

Trade secrets Customer lists, plans, research and development, pricing information, marketing techniques, and production techniques. Generally, anything that makes an individual company unique and has value to a competitor could be a trade secret.

Uncontrollable failure Form of failure caused by external factors that are outside the control of employees, such as resource limitations, strategic direction, and market changes.

Undercapitalization The amount of equity investment is usually low (often indicating a high level of debt).

Uniform Franchise Offering Circular (UFOC) A disclosure form the Federal Trade Commission requires of all potential franchisors.

Uniform Limited Partnership Act (ULPA) This act contains 11 articles and 64 sections of guidelines. If a limited partnership appears to be the desired legal form of organization, the prospective partners must examine these ULPA guidelines.

Uniform Partnership Act Generally followed by most states as the guide for legal requirements of forming a partnership.

Uniqueness Special characteristics and/or design concepts that draw the customer to the venture and should provide performance or service superior to competitive offerings.

University-related incubators An incubator that is a spin-off of an academic research project, with the major goal to transfer the findings of basic research and development to a new product or technology.

Unlimited liability A condition existing in sole proprietorships and partnerships wherein someone is responsible for all of the enterprise's debts.

Unscrupulous practices Business practices that are devoid of ethics and seek personal gain at any cost.

Unsought goods Goods that consumers neither currently need nor seek, such as encyclopedias and cemetery plots.

Upside gain and downside loss Within the financial capital domain, this is the best possible gain weighed against the worst loss possible. (See also **Risk vs. reward.**)

Value added A basic form of contribution analysis in which sales minus raw materials costs equals the value added.

Variable cost A cost that changes in the same direction as, and in direct proportion to, changes in operating activity.

Venture capitalists Individuals who provide a full range of financial services for new or growing ventures, such as capital for start-ups and expansions, marketing research, management consulting, assistance with negotiating technical agreements, and assistance with employee recruitment and development of employee agreements.

Venture opportunity school of thought A school of entrepreneurial thought that focuses on the search for idea sources, on concept development, and on implementation of venture opportunities.

Venture team A small group of people that operates as a semiautonomous unit to create and develop a new idea.

Vertical analysis The application of ratio analysis to one set of financial statements.

Vision A concept of what the entrepreneur's idea can become.

Water well strategies The ability to gather or harness special resources (land, labor, capital, raw materials) over the long term.

Web site A site (location) on the World Wide Web. Each Web site contains a home page, which is the first document users see when they enter the site. A site might also contain additional documents and files. Each site is owned and managed by an individual, company, or organization.

Women-owned businesses Businesses that women own—the fastest-growing segment of small business in the nation.

Name Index

Subject Index